Lewis and Clark Road Trips
Exploring the Trail Across America

www.lewisandclarkroadtrips.com

Oregon Coast near Saltworks

by Kira Gale

Publisher's Cataloging-In-Publication Data
(Prepared by The Donohue Group, Inc.)

Gale, Kira.
Lewis and Clark road trips: exploring the trail across America / by Kira Gale ; maps by River Junction Press ; topo maps by GCS-Research ; campsite data by Bob Bergantino.

p. : ill. , maps ; cm. -- (Great American road trips)

ISBN-13: 978-0-9649315-2-7
ISBN-10: 0-9649315-2-4
Includes bibliographical references and index.
Further information available at: http: \\www.lewisandclarkroadtrips.com

1. Lewis and Clark National Historic Trail--Guidebooks. 2. Lewis and Clark National Historic Trail--Maps. 3. Lewis and Clark Expedition (1804-1806) 4. Campsites, facilities, etc.--United States--Directories. 5. Automobile travel--United States--Guidebooks. 6. United States--Tours. I. River Junction Press. II. GCS-Research. III. Bergantino, R. N. IV. Title.

E158 .G35 2006
917.304/93 2006901711

Library of Congress Control Number: 2006901711
ISBN-13: 978-0-9649315-2-7
ISBN-10: 0-9649315-2-4

Maps by River Junction Press
Topo maps by GCS-Research
Campsite data by Bob Bergantino

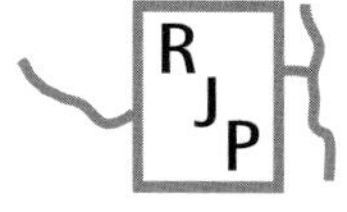
River Junction Press LLC
Omaha, Nebraska

Distributed by Independent Publishers Group
814 N Franklin St, Chicago IL 60610
(312) 337-6912 www.ipgbook.com

Printed in Beauceville, Quebec, Canada
by Transcontinental Interglobe
10 9 8 7 6 5 4 3 2 1

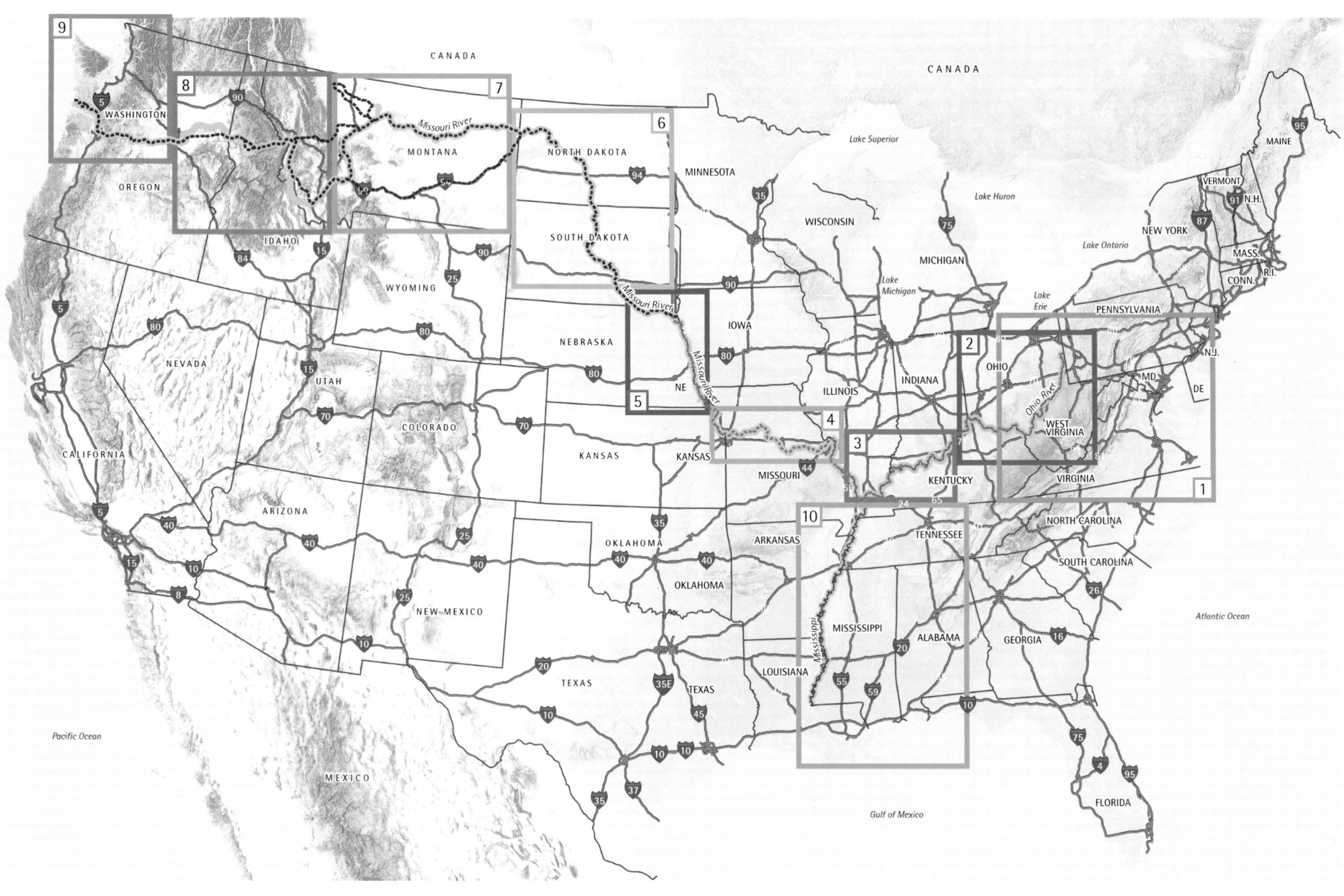

CANADA
CANADA
Pacific Ocean
Atlantic Ocean
Gulf of Mexico
MEXICO
Lake Superior
Lake Huron
Lake Michigan
Lake Ontario
Lake Erie
Missouri River
Ohio River
Mississippi
WASHINGTON
OREGON
CALIFORNIA
NEVADA
IDAHO
MONTANA
WYOMING
UTAH
ARIZONA
COLORADO
NEW MEXICO
NORTH DAKOTA
SOUTH DAKOTA
NEBRASKA
NE
KANSAS
OKLAHOMA
TEXAS
MINNESOTA
IOWA
MISSOURI
ARKANSAS
LOUISIANA
WISCONSIN
ILLINOIS
MICHIGAN
INDIANA
KENTUCKY
TENNESSEE
MISSISSIPPI
ALABAMA
GEORGIA
FLORIDA
OHIO
WEST VIRGINIA
VIRGINIA
NORTH CAROLINA
SOUTH CAROLINA
PENNSYLVANIA
NEW YORK
MD
DE
N.J.
CONN.
R.I.
MASS.
VERMONT
N.H.
MAINE
1
2
3
4
5
6
7
8
9
10

Table of Contents

Preface

In 1996 I was standing around my local independent bookstore in Omaha, Nebraska, when they asked me to help make arrangements for an author who was coming to town promoting his latest book, *Undaunted Courage*. They knew I liked history and bought history books. That is how I met Stephen Ambrose, wound up going to dinner with him, and getting a signed first edition copy of his very famous book. I remember telling him I would like to do a guidebook for the Lewis and Clark Trail, and his urging me to do it. Almost ten years later, here it is.

Back then I was researching and writing a guidebook to the early history of Omaha and its neighbor, Council Bluffs, Iowa; the time period of 1800-1854, when west of the Missouri River was "Indian Country." I liked the era of the early explorers, soldiers, missionaries, fur traders, artists and writers; and the Indians who dealt with them. Omaha's Joslyn Art Museum, has a world class collection of the art of the Early American West, featuring paintings by Karl Bodmer, Alfred Jacob Miller, and George Catlin. All of these people knew William Clark, who lived in St Louis after the expedition and authorized their travels into "Indian Country" as Superintendent of Indian Affairs. I decided to learn more, and prepare to do a Lewis and Clark book. In 2001 I started a Lewis and Clark Study Group at the Western Historic Trails Center in Council Bluffs. Darrel Draper, who performs as a historical "edu-tainer" agreed to join me in co-leading the group as he wanted to prepare an impersonation of George Drouillard, the hunter-interpreter who went with the expedition. We both needed to read the six primary Lewis and Clark Journals. Study Group was an immediate success; 15-20 people came every week on Tuesday morning to read the journals. After five years, and three complete read-throughs, Study Group is still going strong, doing special topics this year.

Study Group started a chapter of the Lewis and Clark Trail Heritage Foundation, Mouth of the Platte, Inc, and I became its founding president. Darrel continued to be my co-captain. It is thanks to this remarkable group of people that I have gained so much knowledge about activities on the Trail. We have had monthly dinner programs for five years. MOP Members also volunteer at the National Park Service's headquarters for the National Historic Lewis and Clark Trail located on Omaha's riverfront. And most anytime of the year someone is out traveling the trail. My husband Henry and I went on the Trail in 2002; traveling over 8,000 miles, coast to coast, in two road trips. This was the final motivation to do a guidebook. We figured out we were lost about 20% of the time! So we sat down and dreamed up how a travel book might be organized, with maps and information on facing pages, readable type, phone numbers, hours, prices, websites, and grouped destinations.

Since then, for the last three years I have been working full time on *Lewis and Clark Road Trips*. I had just enough skills when I started to think I could do maps; and as a historian, I was determined to do them. "Geography is destiny" is an old saying of historians and geographers. It became our family's destiny, as first our daughter and then Henry took over the making of maps, and I went on to other aspects of the project.

I look forward to the launching of the website, www.lewisandclarkroadtrips.com. If you have corrections to suggest, or comments, please contact me through the website. It will be a work in progress, and I am interested in the contributions we will all make to it.

Acknowledgments

First I would like to acknowledge my husband Henry, who got me into this; and then helped me do it, and then finish it. It's been a great journey together. Beth Schmitz, our daughter, made beautiful maps for the first year of the project and showed how they could be done. Our son and his wife, Bill and Xue Gale, software engineers in the mapping industry, encouraged and advised us.

Professor Bob Bergantino of the University of Montana's Montana Tech in Butte was generous enough to let us use his historic campsite data, his work of over twenty years, in the campsite spreadsheet tables. Henry did the cross references to the journals, and created the modern location references based on Bergantino's unpublished latitude and longitude data. Alex Philp of GCS-Research, a premier map making company in the Lewis and Clark world, supplied the topo maps.

I would like to acknowledge the experts in the field of Lewis and Clark who patiently answered my questions, starting with the late Dr. Strode Hinds of Sioux City, who didn't laugh when I asked, where did they put the horses on the keelboat? The late Mildred Goosman of of Joslyn Art Museum first instructed me on Lewis and Clark sites. Butch Bouvier, the keelboat builder, has shared his expertise. Authors and scholars Gary Moulton, Jim Holmberg, and Bob Moore have always been helpful. I consult Joe Mussulman's website of hyperlinked history, www.lewis-clark.org, regularly.

Both the Trail Heritage Foundation, and the National Park Service have been an inspiration in their dedication as "Keepers of the Story and Stewards of the Trail." I feel fortunate to have known Gerard Baker, Superintendent of the Trail, and Dick Williams, Trail Manager, during the bicentennial commemoration years.

Mike McElhatton, the photographer who created the cover photo, met a critical early deadline for the book. Many photographers have generously contributed photos: Betty Kluesner, Lyn Topinka, Gene Burch, Janet Sproull, Don Peterson, Lee Myers, Kathy Getsinger, Tom Danisi Ev Orr and Bob Pawloski. Their photos bring the trail to life. There are over 450 photos in the book. The uncredited ones are my own.

I also want to thank the state tourism, historical society and museum people across the country who have come to my aid by sending photos and materials and answering countless questions.

Another special group of people are those who shared their knowledge of local areas and took me on tours: Mark Kelly, Carol Kuhn and Jim Auld of the History Caravan days in Missouri, Kansas, and Illinois; Scott Sproull of Rocky Mountain Discovery Tours in Missoula; Don Peterson on the Portage Route in Great Falls; Dark Rain and Jim Thom on Indian Mounds in Central Ohio; Dana Olson on Prince Madoc at the Falls of the Ohio; and Jane Lewis Henley on Meriwether Lewis in Charlottesville.

Anthony Blue, Colin Casper, Bob Pawloski and Cory Pawloski all worked on the book doing web research. Adobe technical support has made this book possible. Emily Brackett of Visible Logic created the cover design. Our distributor, Independent Publishers Group (IPG) has been consistently helpful.

I thank you all.

This book is dedicated to our grandchildren:
Cassie, Christy, Dan, Ethan, Karissa, Kristen, Savannah and Tim.

REGION ONE
EAST OF THE ALLEGHENIES

- Southwestern Virginia
- Charlottesville
- Central Virginia
- Harpers Ferry and the Shenandoah Valley
- Washington D. C.
- Philadelphia
- Old Roads to Pittsburgh

1. Fincastle Museum, Fincastle VA 2. Blue Ridge Mountains, VA 3. William Clark Birthplace Marker, Chilesburg, VA 4. William Clark Portrait, Philadelphia PA 5. White House, Washington DC 6. Meriwether Lewis Portrait, Philadelphia 7. Iron Boat, Harpers Ferry WV 8. American Philosophical Society, Philadelphia PA 10. *The Artist in His Museum* Philadelphia PA

Credits: (4) (6) William Clark and Meriwether Lewis portraits by Charles Willson Peale, Independence Historical National Park; (5) The White House, The White House Collection, White House Historical Association; (7) *The Experiment* by Marsha Starkey, Harpers Ferry National Historical Park; (9) *The Artist in His Museum* by Charles Willson Peale ,1822, oil on canvas, Pennsylvania Academy of Fine Arts, gift of Mrs. Sarah Harrison, the Joseph Harrison Jr. Collection.

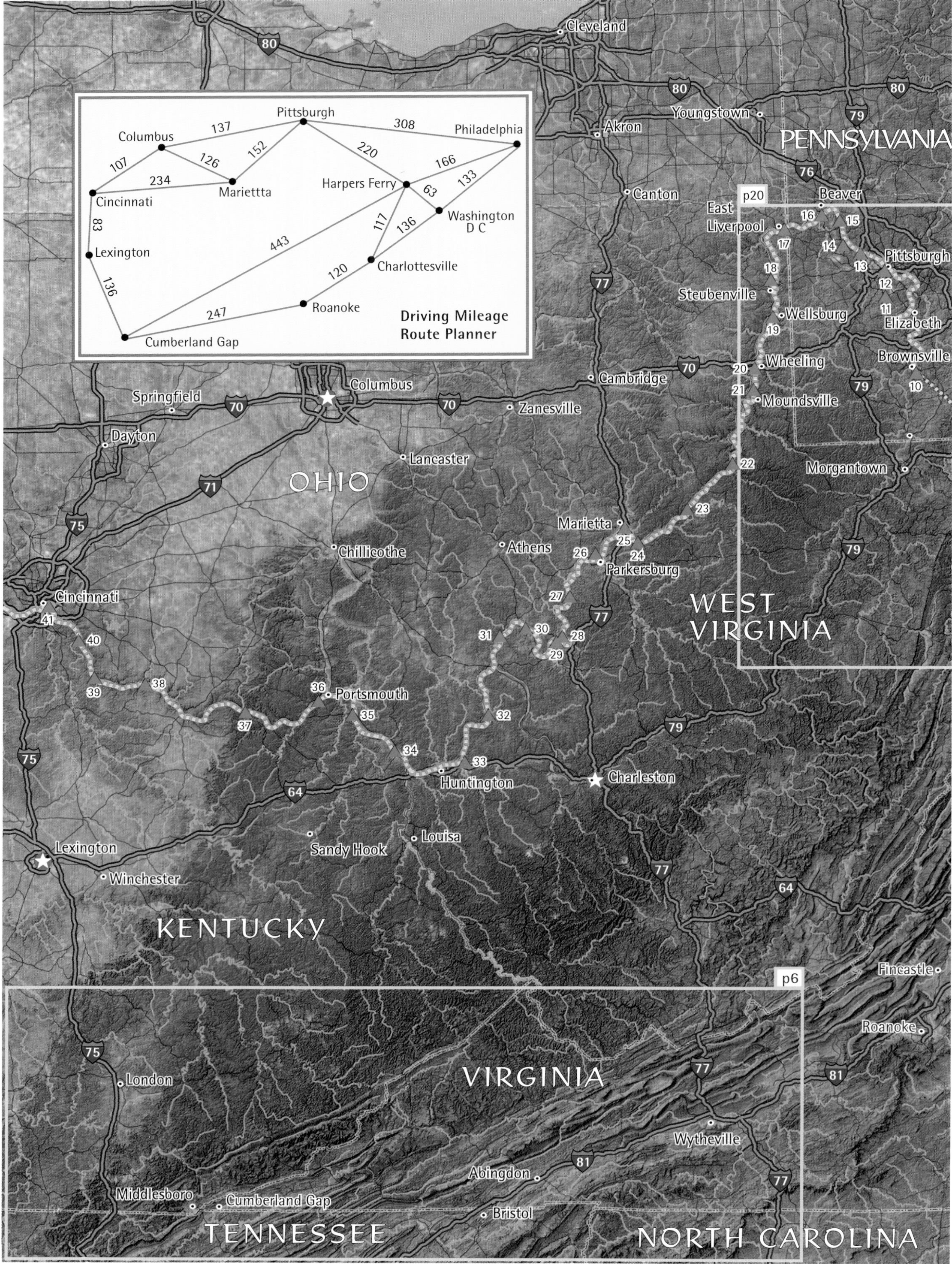

Driving Mileage
Route Planner
Pittsburgh
Columbus
Philadelphia
Cincinnati
Mariettta
Harpers Ferry
Washington D C
Lexington
Charlottesville
Roanoke
Cumberland Gap
137
308
107
126
152
220
166
234
63
133
83
117
136
443
120
136
247
Cleveland
Youngstown
Akron
Canton
PENNSYLVANIA
Beaver
East Liverpool
Pittsburgh
Steubenville
Wellsburg
Elizabeth
Brownsville
Wheeling
Moundsville
Cambridge
Columbus
Springfield
Zanesville
Dayton
Lancaster
OHIO
Morgantown
Marietta
Chillicothe
Athens
Parkersburg
Cincinnati
WEST VIRGINIA
Portsmouth
Huntington
Charleston
Sandy Hook
Louisa
Lexington
Winchester
KENTUCKY
Fincastle
Roanoke
London
VIRGINIA
Wytheville
Abingdon
Middlesboro
Cumberland Gap
Bristol
TENNESSEE
NORTH CAROLINA
p20
p6

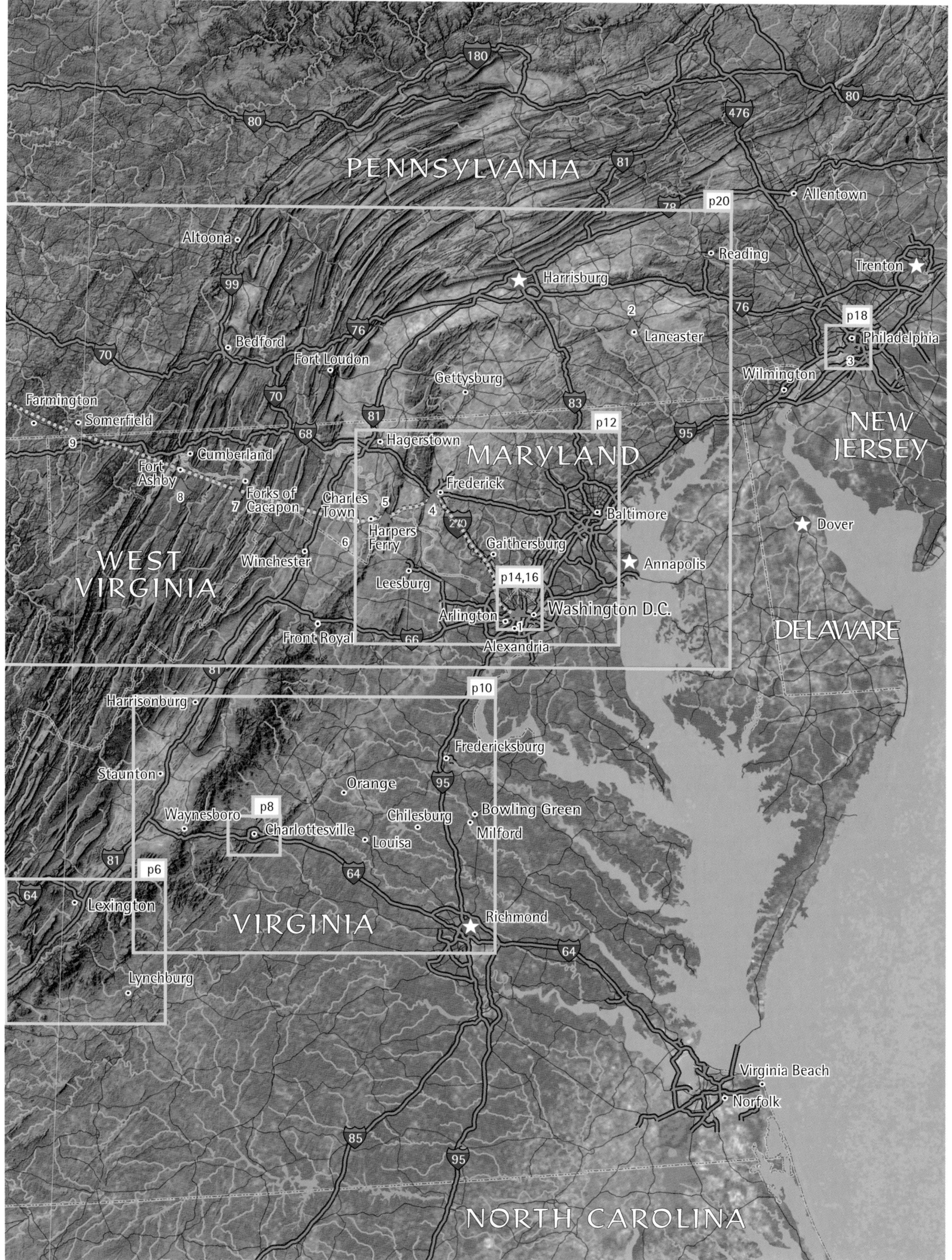

PENNSYLVANIA
MARYLAND
NEW JERSEY
DELAWARE
WEST VIRGINIA
VIRGINIA
NORTH CAROLINA
180
80
476
81
78
99
76
70
68
83
95
270
66
64
85
Allentown
Altoona
Reading
Trenton
Harrisburg
Bedford
Lancaster
Philadelphia
Fort Loudon
Wilmington
Gettysburg
Farmington
Somerfield
Hagerstown
Cumberland
Fort Ashby
Forks of Cacapon
Charles Town
Frederick
Baltimore
Dover
Harpers Ferry
Gaithersburg
Winchester
Annapolis
Leesburg
Washington D.C.
Arlington
Front Royal
Alexandria
Harrisonburg
Fredericksburg
Staunton
Orange
Bowling Green
Waynesboro
Chilesburg
Charlottesville
Milford
Louisa
Lexington
Richmond
Lynchburg
Virginia Beach
Norfolk
p20
p18
p12
p14,16
p10
p8
p6
1
2
3
4
5
6
7
8
9

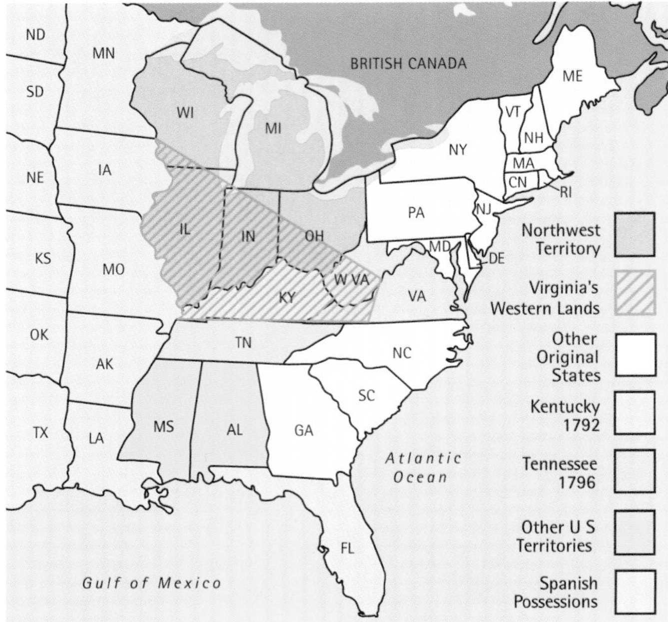

America 200 Years Ago

After the Revolutionary War, Virginia and other states surrendered their western land claims to the federal government in payment of war debts. Old Northwest Territory was created from these lands in 1787. The area remained in dispute between the United States and Britain until the end of the War of 1812. The conflict between the United States and Britain went on for forty years.

Fincastle Museum in Botetourt County, "the Mother of all Counties"

Virginia and Its Western Lands

Virginia: Birthplace of Lewis and Clark

Virginia was the leader of the original thirteen British colonies: it was the oldest, and had the largest population. It was also the birthplace of Meriwether Lewis and William Clark, and four of the first five Presidents of the United States. Colonial Virginia claimed land west to the Mississippi River. Tobacco farming exhausted the land, and Virginia farmers always needed new land. They led the westward movement into the Ohio Valley. However, the Allegheny Mountains formed a natural barrier between Virginians and the Indians of the Ohio Valley, who were determined to keep settlers out of their homelands.

The Cumberland Gap at the tip of southwestern Virginia was the only practical route through the mountains. An estimated 200,000 to 300,000 settlers traveled through the Gap in 1775-1810. To reach the Gap they traveled on the Great Valley Wagon Road, the route of today's Interstate 81 and US Highway 11. The Great Valley is bordered by the Alleghenies on the west and the Blue Ridge Mountains on the east. The Wagon Road joined the Wilderness Roads at Bristol on the Virginia-Tennessee border.

Charlottesville on the Old Frontier

Charlottesville lies east of the Blue Ridge Mountains in Albemarle County on the edge of Virginia's early frontier. The Jefferson, Lewis, and Clark families all lived in Charlottesville. Thomas Jefferson was a generation older than Meriwether Lewis and William Clark, but he knew Meriwether Lewis and his family.

The city has two World Heritage sites: Jefferson's home, Monticello, and the University of Virginia, which Jefferson founded. The birthplace home of Meriwether Lewis remains a private residence. The Clark family lived in Charlottesville before William Clark was born; they left Albemarle County when they inherited property and moved back east. William Clark was born near Fredericksburg, Virginia in Caroline County. However, his famous older brother, General George Rogers Clark, was born in Charlottesville.

Fincastle and Botetourt County

Fincastle, the home of Clark's sweetheart, was once the headquarters for Virginia's western empire. The town has been the county seat of Botetourt County since 1770. (Bot' e tot is pronounced somewhat like "bottle-top.") It is called "the mother of all counties" as it formerly contained all of Kentucky, and parts of West Virginia, Ohio, Indiana, Illinois, and Wisconsin (Virginia's Western Lands on the map).

A year after his return from the expedition, William Clark married Julia (Judith) Hancock. They often returned to the Fincastle area for extended stays. After Julia's death in 1821, leaving Clark a widower with five young children, he married her cousin, the widow Harriet Kennerly Radford of Fincastle. William Clark named the Judith River in Montana for his first wife.

Kentucky, the New Frontier

George Rogers Clark, William Clark's older brother, is called the "Saviour of Kentucky." His campaigns as a Virginia Militia leader on Virginia's western frontier during the Revolutionary War won the Old Northwest Territory from the British, nearly doubling the size of the United States. He is considered second only to George Washington as a military leader. There are many memorials to George Rogers Clark throughout the region.

Virginia ceded its western lands to the federal government in 1784—Kentucky became a state in 1792; Ohio in 1803, and Indiana in 1816. Louisville, Kentucky and Clarksville, Indiana across the river from Louisville, were both founded by George Rogers Clark. After the end of the war, in 1784, the Clark family moved to Louisville. Young Billy Clark was 13 years old, ninth in a family of ten children. All of his five older brothers had served in the Revolutionary Army; two were Generals.

Meriwether Lewis
Independence National Historical Park

Thomas Jefferson
Thomas Jefferson Foundation

Monticello: Though Thomas Jefferson never travelled west of the Allegheny Mountains, his home at Charlottesville contained the finest library on the West in all of America. Thomas Jefferson Foundation, Inc.

George Rogers Clark
Filson Historical Society

Three famous native sons of Albemarle County, Virginia

The Discovery Virginia keelboat was built by children and adult volunteers at the Lewis and Clark Exploratory Center on the Rivanna River in Charlottesville near the George Rogers Clark birthplace. Spieden, Lewis and Clark Exploratory Center

Lewis and Clark Meet in Ohio

William began his military career in 1789, at the age of 19. The Ohio Valley remained in conflict. The British continued to arm the Indians, and refused to relinquish their forts until 1796. He participated in the Ohio campaigns of General "Mad" Anthony Wayne, including the Battle of Fallen Timbers in 1794, which ended the Indian Wars in Ohio.

Captain Clark was the commander of an elite rifle unit which Meriwether Lewis joined in 1796. The two young officers served together for only a few months, but it was the start of a lasting friendship and a great epic story in American history. Clark resigned from the army in 1796 with the intention of going into business and straightening out the tangled legal affairs of his older brother George Rogers.

Meriwether Lewis was promoted to Captain in 1800. He retained his army commission when he became private secretary to the newly elected President Thomas Jefferson in 1801 and took up residence in the White House.

Lewis at the White House

Jefferson and Lewis began planning to send Lewis with a small military expedition to find the "Northwest Passage" The quest for an all water route across the continent which could be easily navigated had been their dream for years.

Jefferson had made three previous attempts to sponsor such an expedition—in 1783, 1786, and 1794. He asked George Rogers Clark in 1783, at the close of the War for Independence. Meriwether Lewis had volunteered for the job in 1794, when he was 18 years old. None of these plans had worked out. Now they were in a position to make it happen.

In 1801 Jefferson learned that Spain had made a secret deal with France in which France reaquired Louisiana from Spain. He wrote "the day France takes possession of New Orleans....we must marry ourselves to the British fleet and nation." Louisiana was part of the North American Empire that France had lost in her war with Great Britain in 1754-63. New Orleans was the key port for commerce for the western United States.

In 1802 Jefferson sent a delegation to Paris to negotiate the purchase of New Orleans and West Florida from France. Napoleon, however, made a surprise offer to sell all of Louisiana for fifteen million dollars. He needed the money to pursue war in Europe and against Great Britain. The delegates accepted, acquiring over 800,000 square miles of land, which nearly doubled the size of the United States. The Louisiana Purchase stretched from the Mississippi River to the Rocky Mountains, and from New Orleans to Canada.

Philadelphia and Harpers Ferry

Jefferson was not only President of the United States, he was President of the American Philosophical Society in Philadelphia. Lewis went to Philadelphia and Lancaster PA, in May, 1803 to be tutored by members of the society; he received training in botany, mathematics, paleontology, medicine, and celestial navigation. He also filled the expedition's shopping list, obtaining 3500 pounds of equipment, medicine, Indian trade goods, and an air gun.

At Harpers Ferry, West Virginia, site of the national arsenal, Lewis ordered fifteen rifles and other supplies. He spent a precious month supervising the building of an iron boat called The Experiment.

The purchase of Louisiana was announced in the nation's newspapers on July 4, 1803, the 27th anniversary of America's Declaration of Independence from Great Britain. Lewis set out from the White House the next day to go to Pittsburgh, where the keelboat was being built. En route, he stopped at Harpers Ferry to arrange for a wagon to deliver the rifles and his custom boat frame.

Lewis traveled on some of America's most historic roads from Washington to Pittsburgh, a route which can still be followed today; part of which includes US Highway 40, America's first National Road.

1

PEAKS OF OTTER

The mountains of the Blue ridge, and of these, the Peaks of Otter, are thought to be of greater height, measured from their base, than any other in our country, and perhaps in North America.

—Thomas Jefferson
Notes on the State of Virginia (1785)

The Peaks of Otter:
Sharp Top (3,865 ft)
Flat Top (4001 ft)
Harkening Hill (3,375 ft)

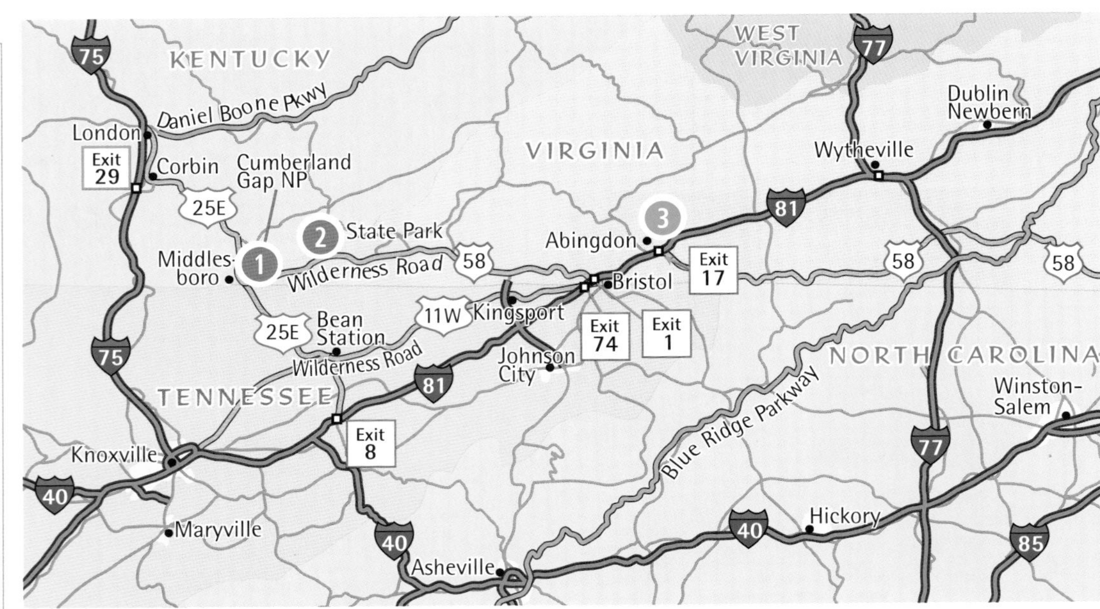

Cumberland Gap

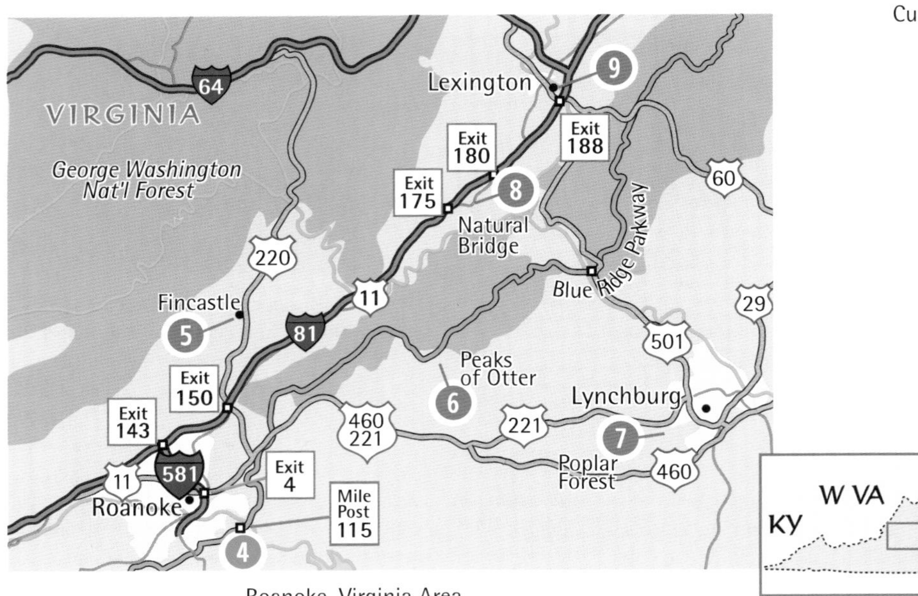

Roanoke, Virginia Area

1 CUMBERLAND GAP NAT'L HISTORICAL PARK

The Visitor Center is located east of Middlesboro KY at the intersection of U S Hwys 25 and 58. There were two Wilderness Road routes to the Gap from the border cities of Bristol, Virginia and Bristol, Tennessee. After exiting the Gap, the road continued north in Kentucky to forks leading to either to Fort Harrod and Louisville, or to Fort Boonesboro and Lexington. Both replica forts are Kentucky State Park attractions.
From I-81 Exit 8 (Morristown), go 50 miles northwest on US 25E.
From I-75 Exit 29 (Corbin) go 50 miles southeast on US 25E.

WILDERNESS ROADS

About 100 miles to the Cumberland Gap on either route of the old Wilderness Roads from Bristol.
From I-81 Exit 1 (Bristol VA), go west on US 58 to the Gap.
From I-81 Exit 74 (Bristol TN) go west on US-11W. At Bean Station, go north on US-25E to the Gap.

2 WILDERNESS ROAD STATE PARK

Intersection of US-58 and SR-923. Five miles west of Ewing, Virginia. Six miles east of Cumberland Gap National Historic Park.

3 ABINGDON TAVERN

222 East Main Street.
From I-81 Exit 17 go east on Main St (US 11).

4 VIRGINIA'S EXPLORE PARK

From I-81 Exit 143 (Roanoke) go south on I-581/US-220 through Roanoke to Blue Ridge Parkway. Go north on Blue Ridge Parkway to Milepost 115. Turn right onto Roanoke River Parkway.

5 FINCASTLE MUSEUM

From I-81 Exit 150 go north on US 220 for nine miles. The museum is on Courthouse Square.

6 PEAKS OF OTTER AND BLUE RIDGE PARKWAY

45 miles per hour speed limit. Allow plenty of time; call ahead for weather alerts. Directions are from Roanoke, the region's largest city, north to US-501 near Lexington. Reverse as needed.

From I-81 Exit 143 (Roanoke) take I-581 through Roanoke to Exit 4 for U S 220A. Parkway is 8.4 miles northeast on US 220A/221.
From I-81 Exit 150 (Roanoke) take Alt. US 220 South to US 221. Take US-221 northeast to Parkway. Allow $1^{3}/_{4}$ hours drive time for the 60 mile drive on the Parkway to US-501. The Peaks of Otter are midway at milepost 85.6 (30 miles from Roanoke). Exiting at US-501, Natural Bridge is 15 miles north; Poplar Forest is 20 miles south.

7 POPLAR FOREST

From Blue Ridge Parkway go south on US-501 (Lee Jackson Hwy) 14.5 miles. At Lynchburg take Peace St. to U S-221 (Lakeside Drive), Go west 3.2 miles. Turn at Bateman Bridge Road. Follow the Poplar Forest signs.

From I-581 (Roanoke) take I-581 Exit 4 to U S-221. Go 45 miles east on US-221 to Bateman Bridge Road. Follow signs.
From I-81 Exit 188 (Lexington) take US 60 south 4 miles to US 501. Follow directions as given for Blue Ridge Parkway.

8 NATURAL BRIDGE

From Blue Ridge Parkway go nine miles north on US 501, then 6.3 miles west on State Route 130.
South from I-81 Exit 175 or 180. Less than 5 minutes from the interstate. Follow signs.

9 VMI MUSEUM—LEXINGTON

Museum is in Jackson Hall next to Barracks on VMI campus. Take first exit on I-64 (Exit 55). Go south one mile on Lee Highway to campus.

Abingdon Tavern

Fincastle Museum

Blue Ridge Mountains

Southwestern Virginia

1 CUMBERLAND GAP NATIONAL HISTORICAL PARK

Daniel Boone blazed the famous Cumberland Gap Wilderness Trail from Virginia to Kentucky in 1774. Pinnacle Overlook in the national park, reached by car and a short trail, provides a view of Virginia, Tennessee, and Kentucky. There is a 1½ mile hiking trail recreating the Wilderness Trail; a Wilderness Road Campground and Backcountry Campsites. The Visitor Center has Appalachian crafts, bookstore, exhibits, film showings. Located east of Middlesboro KY.

■ Open daily 8-6 Memorial Day-Labor Day; and from 8-5 Labor Day-Memorial Day. Closed Christmas. Free admission.
(606) 248-2817 www.nps.gov/cuga

1 WILDERNESS ROAD STATE PARK

Lewis and Clark surely stopped at Captain Joseph Martin's Way Station on their travels, now a replica fort at this state park. Also the scene of George Rogers Clark's dramatic adventures in 1776 during the Revolutionary War.

■ (276) 445-3065 www.martinsstation.com

3 ABINGDON TAVERN

Did Lewis and Clark stay at the 1779 Tavern? Abingdon is one of the oldest English speaking settlements west of the Blue Ridge Mountains. Reservations recommended.

■ Open for dinner Mon-Sat 5-10 p.m.
www.abingdontavern.com (276) 628-1118

■ Virginia's State Theatre, the Historic Barter Theatre; and Martha Washington Inn are also on Main St. Visitors Bureau (800) 435-3440
www.abingdon.com

4 VIRGINIA'S EXPLORE PARK—ROANOKE

During the season, travel footpaths through hardwood forests to 3 historic areas: a 1600's Totero Indian Village, a 1700's frontier fort and settler's cabin, and an 1800's valley community. Reenactors portray life as it once was in early Roanoke. The 1,000 acre Explore Park is open year round for hiking and mountain bikes; fishing, canoeing and kayaking on Roanoke River.

POPLAR FOREST: Thomas Jefferson designed Poplar Forest as an octagon, an eight-sided shape which "squares the circle." Monticello was his first octagon design.
(Corporation for Jefferson's Poplar Forest)

■ Historic Explore Park open April-Oct, Weds-Sat 10-5 and Sundays from noon-5. Admission: $8 adults; $6 seniors; $4.50 ages 3-11
(540) 427-1880 (800) 842-9163
www.explorepark.org

■ Blue Ridge Parkway Visitor Center interprets 469 mile Parkway. Open 9-5 during season.

■ Did Lewis and Clark ever visit Historic Brugh Tavern? The German style tavern circa 1800, was originally from Botetourt County; open for dining during the season at Explore Park.
(540) 427-2440 www.explorepark.org

5 FINCASTLE MUSEUM

Fincastle was the home of Julia (Judith) Hancock, William Clark's sweetheart; and after their marriage, their eastern home. Botetourt County Historical Museum is located in Courthouse Square. Historic Fincastle walking tours.

■ Open daily Mon-Sat, 10-2; and Sun, 2-4.
(540) 473-8394 (museum); (540) 473-2706 (Historic Fincastle tours) www.hisfin.org

6 BLUE RIDGE PARKWAY SCENIC ROUTE—PEAKS OF OTTER

The 469 mile mountain roadway is the National Park Service's most popular attraction. The Peaks of Otter has a visitor center, campground, lodge and restaurant, hiking trails, living history, and parkway's only gas station in Virginia.

■ (828) 350-3939 for weather info.
For Peaks info call (540) 586-1081
www.nps.gov/blri/peaks
www.blueridgeparkway.org

7 POPLAR FOREST—LYNCHBURG

This National Historic Landmark near Lynchburg was Thomas Jefferson's personal retreat, where he could "enjoy the solitude of a hermit."

■ Open daily 10-4, from April to November
Last tour at 4 PM.
Admission: $7 adult; $6 senior; $1 (6-16).
(434) 525-1806 www.poplarforest.org

8 NATURAL BRIDGE

Jefferson purchased the Natural Bridge in 1774, calling it "the most sublime of Nature's works." This National Historic Landmark, over 215 feet tall, is one of "the seven natural wonders of the world." Hotel and conference center on the site. Visitors may buy tickets to see the rock bridge, and various other tourist attractions: museums, caverns, living history at a Monacan Indian Village, and an evening pageant.

■ Open daily 8 AM to dark. Admission: adult combination ticket $22.50-$14; single ticket $10-$8. Child combo tickets $11.25-$7; single $5. (800) 533-1410, or (540) 291-2121
www.naturalbridgeva.com

9 VA MILITARY INSTITUTE MUSEUM

The Lewis and Clark airgun made by Isaiah Lukens of Philadelphia is on display at the museum. The museum's Henry M Stewart Antique Firearms Collection with over 800 pieces is one of the world's great collections.

■ Open 9 -5 daily. (540) 464-7334
www4.vmi.edu/museum/HMS.html
www.beemans.net

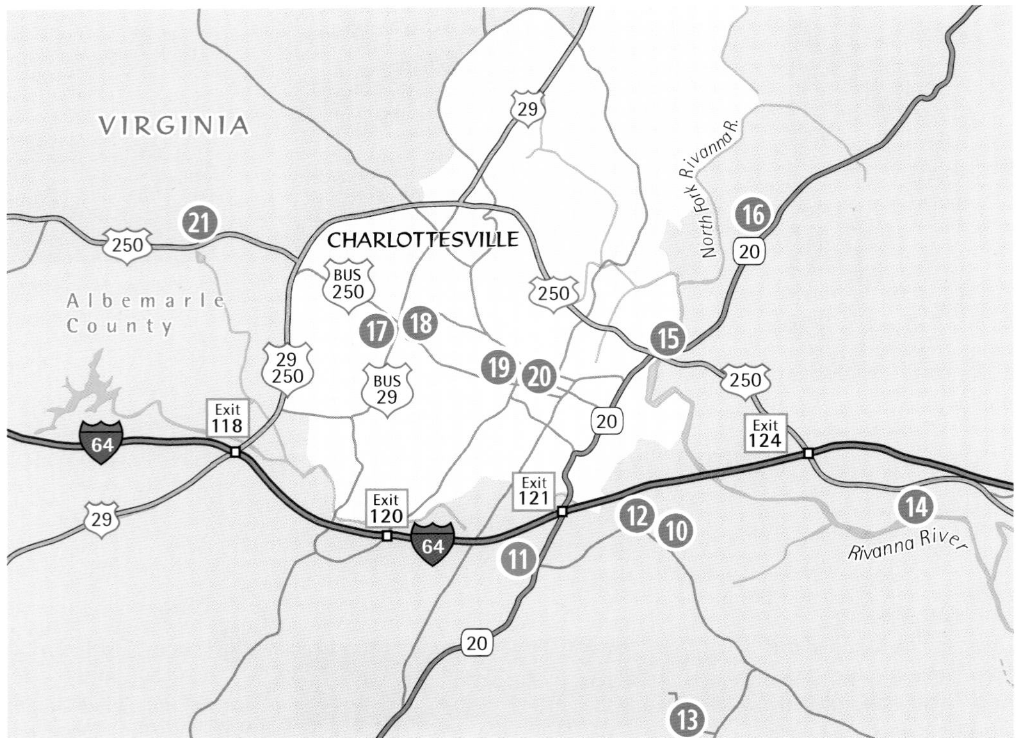

10 MONTICELLO
From I-64 Exit 121 take SR 20 South (Scottsville Rd) 1/2 mile to SR 53 (Thomas Jefferson Parkway). Turn left, go 1.7 miles to Monticello Road. Go north 1/2 mile to parking lot.

11 MONTICELLO VISITOR CTR
From I-64 Exit 121 take SR 20 South (Scottsville Road) 0.6 mile. Turn right at first stoplight.

12 MICHIE TAVERN
From I-64 Exit 121 take SR 20 South (Scottsville Rd) 1/2 mile to SR 53 (Jefferson Pkwy). Turn left, go one mile to Tavern.

13 JAMES MONROE HOME ASHLAWN-HIGHLAND
From I-64 Exit 121 take SR 20 South (Scottsville Road) 1/2 mile to SR 53 (Thomas Jefferson Parkway). Turn left, go 3.1 miles on Jefferson Parkway to SR 795 (James Monroe Pkwy). Turn right, go south one mile to Ashlawn-Highland home.

14 THOMAS JEFFERSON BIRTHPLACE MARKER
From I-64 Exit 124 take US 250 South (Richmond Rd) southeast for 0.9 mile. Marker is on south side of highway.

15 LEWIS AND CLARK EXPLORATORY CENTER
From I-64 Exit124 take US 250 North (Richmond Rd) 1.7 mile to SR 20 (Stony Point Road). Turn right, go 1/2 mile to Elk Drive. Turn left, go 1/4 mi. south to Darden Towe Park on the Rivanna River. Look for boathouse beyond parking lot.

16 GEORGE ROGERS CLARK BIRTHPLACE MARKER
From I-64 Exit 124 take US 250, Richmond Road, northwest 1.7 miles to SR 20 North (Stony Point Road). Turn right, go northwest 1.4 miles. A cabin on the west side of Stony Point Road, just north of Elk Drive, commemorates the birthplace. Marker is at driveway entrance.

17 UVA ROTUNDA
From I-64 Exit 118B take US 29/250 Bypass north 2.5 miles to Business 250E Exit. Turn right off the exit ramp and go east on Ivy Road. At third traffic light turn right on Emmet St (Bus-29) for UVA parking garage (hourly fees). The Rotunda is two blocks east, near Ivy Road and Rugby St. (Ivy Rd becomes West Main St. east of UVA campus).

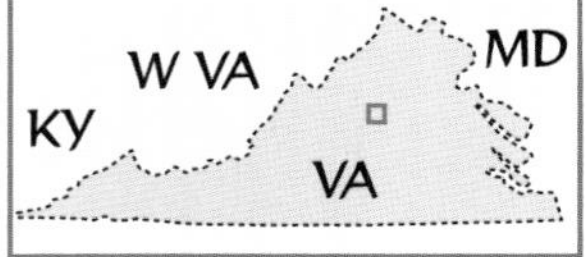

18 GEORGE ROGERS CLARK MEMORIAL
Memorial is at intersection of West Main St and Jefferson Park Ave just east of the UVA campus.

19 LEWIS AND CLARK AND SACAGAWEA MEMORIAL
The Memorial is at the intersection of West Main St (US 250 Bus), Ridge St (SR 631) and McIntire Road (US 250 Bus and SR 631).

20 YORK PLACE
112 West Main Street.
York Place shopping mall is at the intersection of West Main St and First Sreet North. (Two blocks east of Memorial at Ridge and Main Streets).

21 LOCUST HILL: MERIWETHER LEWIS BIRTHPLACE MARKER
From I-64 Exit 118B take US 29/250 Bypass north to US 250 Exit (Ivy Road). Go left, west, on Ivy Road 4.3 miles to SR 678 (Owensville Rd). Go north on Owensville Rd 0.4 mile to marker.

West Main Street (US-250 Business Route)

From I-64 Exit 120 to West Main Street Go north on SR-631, or Fifth St SW, which divides and becomes one-way north at Ridge St. Go north on Ridge St two blocks to West Main St.

From I-64 Exit 121 to West Main St Monticello Ave (SR-20) goes northwest into Charlottesville. It joins Ridge St two blocks south of West Main St.

From West Main Street to US-250 West (Ivy Road)
West Main Street becomes Ivy Road (US-250) going west past campus towards Locust Hill.

From West Main Street to US-250 East via SR-20
West Main St splits and divides at Ridge Street. Go east on Water St to 9th St NE. Turn left on 9th St and go north 3 blocks to East High St (SR-20). Turn right on East High St. Go about 1.5 miles to US-250 at the Rivanna River. East High St becomes Stony Point Road after crossing US-250.

Indian Hall at Monticello
Thomas Jefferson Foundation, Inc.

University of Virginia Rotunda
University of Virginia

Jefferson's Epitaph
(in his own words)

Here was buried
THOMAS JEFFERSON

Author of the
Declaration
of
American Independence

of the
Statute of Virginia
for Religious Freedom

and Father of the
University of Virginia

Charlottesville

10 MONTICELLO NATIONAL HISTORIC LANDMARK THOMAS JEFFERSON HOME

This National Historic Landmark, home of Thomas Jefferson, third President of the United States (1800-1809), is the only American residence on the United Nations World Heritage list. Monticello was a 5,000 acre estate with extensive gardens and four working farms employing up to 135 slaves. Jefferson's gravesite is located here.

■ All tours are guided, on a first-come, first-served basis. Arrive early. Allow at least three hours for a visit. Free parking at ticket office. Shuttle bus service to Monticello.

House Tours every 30 minutes.

Garden and Grounds Tours (Apr 1–Oct 31): 45 minute tours at 15 minutes past the hour start at West Lawn.

Plantation Community Tours 45 minute tours on the hour from 10–3 start at museum shop. Open daily except Christmas. Mar 1-Oct 31: 8–5. Nov 1–Feb 28: 9–4:30 Admission: adults $13; children, 6–11 $6. (434) 984-9822 www.monticello.org/jefferson/lewisandclark

11 MONTICELLO VISITORS CENTER

Over 400 Jefferson objects are on permanent display at the Visitor Center. The Charlottesville-Albemarle County Convention and Visitors Bueau is located here. Monticello Museum shop.

■ Mar 1–Oct 31: 9–5:30, Nov 1–Feb 28: 9–5. Award winning film at 11 and 2, daily. (434) 977-1783 or toll free (877) 386-1162 wwwcharlottesvilletourism.org

■ *Presidents Pass Combination Ticket,* $24 for admission to Monticello, Michie Tavern and Ashlawn. Available at all locations.

12 MICHIE ('MICKEY") TAVERN-MUSEUM

The tavern has welcomed guests since 1784. Tours of tavern, general store, gift shop, grist mill. Living history/activities for young people.

■ Open daily. Colonial southern style luncheon buffet $13.50. April–Oct buffet 11:15–3:30 Nov–March buffet 11:30–3

Tours 9–5 Tour admission $6 with meal price or $8 adult; $7 senior and AAA; $6 children (434) 977-1234 www.michietavern.com

13 JAMES MONROE HOME ASHLAWN-HIGHLAND

A friend and neighbor of Thomas Jefferson, James Monroe became the fifth President of the United States (1817–1825). Jefferson sent Monroe to France to negotiate the Louisiana Purchase. The Monroes lived here from 1799–1823. The James Monroe Museum is located in Fredericksburg VA.

■ Open daily Nov–March 10–5; Apr–Oct. 9–6. Admission: adults $9; seniors $8; 6–11 $7.50 (434)293-9539 www.avenue.org/ashlawn

14 THOMAS JEFFERSON BIRTHPLACE

Thomas Jefferson was born on April 13, 1743 at Shadwell. When Shadwell was destroyed by fire in 1770 he moved to Monticello, which he was in the process of building. He spent forty years building Monticello. He wrote about his hobby: "Architecture is my delight. and putting up and pulling down, one of my favorite amuseuments."

■ www.americanpresidents.org/places www.monticello.org

15 LEWIS AND CLARK EXPLORATORY CENTER OF VIRGINIA

The Lewis and Clark Exploratory Center is located just north of Darden Towe Park on the Rivanna River. Keelboat builder Butch Bouvier assisted in the construction of a 55 foot keelboat replica, built by about 75 children and adult volunteers. The Center continues to provide activities for young people. Visitor Center and trails to the nearby Clark Cabin.

■ (434) 979-2425 www.lewisandclarkeast.org

16 GEORGE ROGERS CLARK BIRTHPLACE

William Clark's older brother, George Rogers Clark, was born near here on Nov. 19, 1752. The cabin dates from the time period but is not the original Clark family cabin.

■ Not open to visitors, currently on private property. www.lewisandclarkeast.org

17 UNIV OF VIRGINIA ROTUNDA (NHL)

The Rotunda and other buildings were designed by Jefferson as his "academical village." His design is also a World Heritage Site. There are ten Pavilion buildings with covered walkways and 18th century gardens. Modern Alderman Library has historic maps and Lewis and Clark materials.

■ Free guided tours of Rotunda and Lawn year round (except a 3 week period in Dec–Jan and May graduation). Tours at 10, 11, 2, 3, and 4 meet at Rotunda entrance facing the Lawn. For tours: (434) 924-7969 www.virginia.edu For info: www.vcdh.virginia.edu/lewisandclark

18 GEORGE ROGERS CLARK MEMORIAL

The "Conqueror of the Northwest" Memorial is a monumental statue group. Erected in 1921.

19 LEWIS AND CLARK AND SACAGAWEA MEMORIAL

One of the oldest statues erected to the memory of the expedition, dating to 1919.

20 YORK PLACE

A downtown shopping mall featuring noted western artist John Clymer's painting of York.

■ www.yorkplaceonline.com

21 LOCUST HILL MERIWETHER LEWIS BIRTHPLACE

Meriwether Lewis was born on August 18, 1774 at Locust Hill in Albemarle County, approximately ten miles west of Monticello. At age 18, he inherited the 2,000 acre plantation. After the death of his stepfather, he brought his mother and siblings back from Georgia to live at Locust Hill. The house and family graveyard remain in private ownership. The marker is located on Owensville Road.

■ Not open to visitors. (434) 979-2425 www.lewisandclarkeast.org

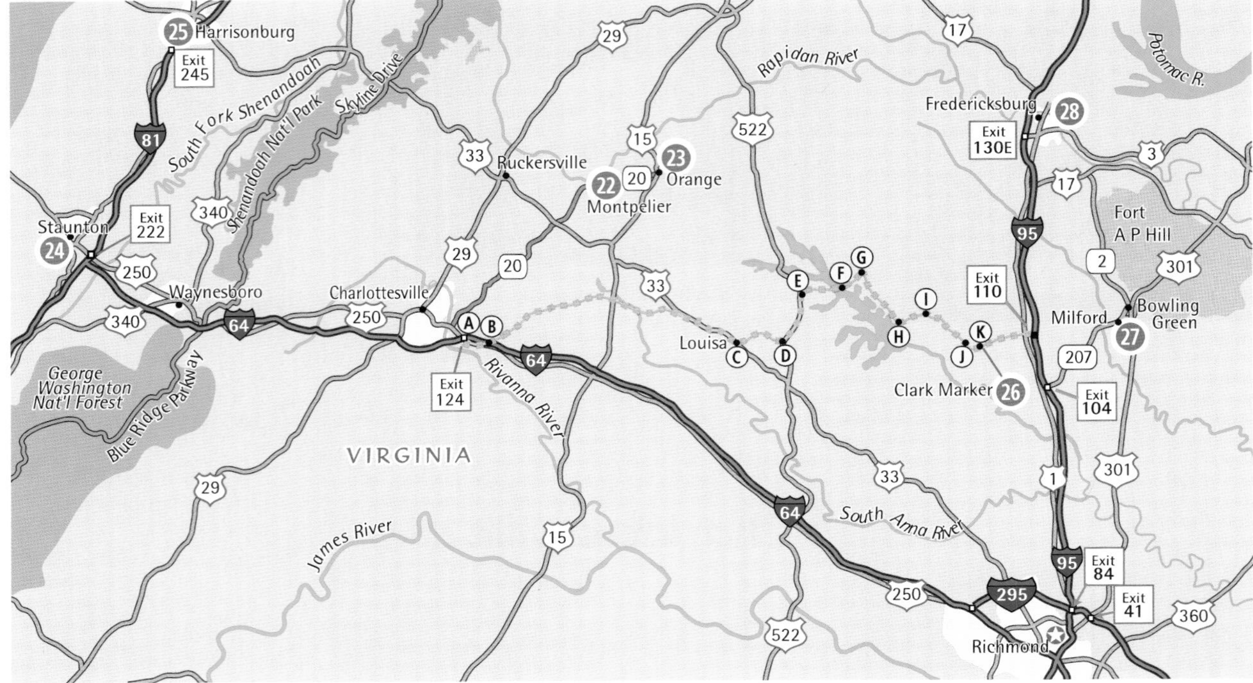

Central Virginia

22 MONTPELIER

From I-64 Exit 124 (Charlottesville) take US 250 (Richmond Rd) 1.8 miles to SR 20 North (Stony Point Road). Take Stony Point Rd north 15 miles to Barboursville. (SR 20 becomes Constitution Hwy near Barboursville). Take Constitution Hwy (SR 20) 8.2 mi. to Montpelier Visitor Center (left side of road).

23 JAMES MADISON MUSEUM ORANGE VA

129 Caroline St.

Go 3 miles north of Montpelier (destination 22 above) on US 15 to the intersection with SR 20 in the town of Orange.

24 FRONTIER CULTURE MUSEUM – STAUNTON VA

From I-81 Exit 222 go 1/2 mile west on US 250 to the Museum.

25 JAMES MADISON CENTER HARRISONSBURG VA

From Montpelier (destination 25 above) go 8.2 miles south on SR 20. Go west 43 miles on US 33 to I-81. Take I-81 two miles south to Exit 245. From Exit 245 go one block west. Turn right for James Madison University. Go north on Bluestone Drive past stop sign, 2 traffic lights, and stop sign. Take right fork in road to parking lot for Maury and Wilson Halls. The Center is in Wilson Hall R. 205.

26 WILLIAM CLARK BIRTHPLACE MARKER

From Charlottesville to the marker via interstate highways is 109 miles. For the adventuresome, the back roads route is 60 miles. Both routes are about equal in travel time.

■ I-64, I-295, I-95 ROUTE

From Charlottesville I-64 Exit 121 go 61 miles southeast to I-295 at Richmond. Go east on I-295 14 miles to I-95 North. Go 28 mi. north on I-95 to Exit 110. Go west 5 miles on Ladysmith Road (SR 639) past US 1 (Jefferson Davis Highway) to the intersection of Ladysmith Road with SR 603, or Countyline Church Road. Countyline Church Road joins Ladysmith on the right, or north side of the road. The marker is across from the church.

■ BACK ROADS ROUTE

Ⓐ From I-64 Exit 124 take Richmond Road southeast for 2 miles (past Jefferson's birthplace at Shadwell) to Louisa Rd (SR 22).

Ⓑ Take Louisa Road 19 mi. northeast to Trevilians where Louisa Road joins US 33. Continue southeast 4.6 miles on US 33/SR 22 to the town of Louisa.

Ⓒ From Louisa take Jefferson Davis Highway (SR-208) 5 miles east to Mineral.

Ⓓ At Mineral take Zachary Taylor Hwy (US 522/SR 208) north 5.5 miles to New Bridge Road (SR 208).

Ⓔ Turn right (east) on New Bridge Rd (SR 208) and go 2 miles to the bridge across Lake Anna.

Ⓕ From the bridge go 3.3 miles on SR 208 (which becomes Courthouse Rd) to Lewiston Rd (SR 601).

Ⓖ Lewiston Rd (SR 601) comes into SR 308 from the right, and goes southeast. Take Lewiston Rd 6.9 miles to Fairview Rd (SR 622).

Ⓗ Go east on Fairview Rd (SR 622) 2.9 miles to its junction with SR 738 (Partlow Road).

Ⓘ Turn right onto Partlow Road (SR 738) go southeast 5.3 miles to Chilesburg.

Ⓙ Turn left at Chilesburg onto Ladysmith Road (SR 639).

Ⓚ Go 1/2 mile east on Ladysmith Road to Countyline Church Road. The marker is on the north side of Ladysmith Road across from the church.

27 CLARK AND YORK MARKER

The marker is located 3 miles south of Bowling Green Bypass on US-301 (southbound lane) in front of the Caroline County Community Services Center at 17202 Richmond Turnpike Road.

From I-295 Exit 41 (Richmond) take US 301 (Richmond Turnpike) north 27 miles.

From Fredericksburg take US 17 Bus./SR 2 south (Fredericksburg Turnpike) 20 mi.

From I-95 Exit 104 take SR 207 east 10 miles to Bowling Green Bypass. Take US 301 south.

28 JAMES MONROE MUSEUM FREDERICKSBURG

■ James Monroe Museum

908 Charles St.

From I-95 Exit 103 go 2.1 miles east on William St (SR 3). Turn right on Charles St. Go one block to the Museum

The museum is two blocks north and two blocks west of the Visitor Center.

■ Fredericksburg Visitor Center

706 Caroline St.

From I-95 Exit 103 take SR 3E east 6 traffic lights to William St (Bus 3E). Follow William St into Historic District. Turn right onto one-way Princess Anne St (Bus US 1 and Bus US 17). Go three blocks south to Charlotte St. Turn left. Go one block. The Visitor Center is at Charlotte and Caroline Streets, one block from the Rappahannock River.

Montpelier, the home of James Madison (duPont years)
Philip Beaurline

William Clark
Independence Nat'l Historical Park

Clark birthplace marker

Central Virginia: Back Roads Adventure

22 MONTPELIER NATIONAL HISTORIC LANDMARK JAMES MADISON HOME–ORANGE

Built in 1760, Montpelier was the family estate of James Madison, who lived here most of his life. Madison created the U. S. Constitution in the library of Montpelier. The house was enlarged in 1797 when he brought his bride Dolly to live here. Then in 1809, when Madison succeeded Jefferson and became the fourth President of the United States (1809–1817), two wings were added. President Madison died in 1836. Dolly continued to run the plantation until 1844 when the property was sold. James Madison was Secretary of State during both terms of Jefferson's administration (1801–1809). When Lewis and Clark reached the Three Forks headwaters of the Missouri River in Montana, they named the middle fork the Madison River.

William duPont Sr purchased Montpelier in 1901. During the duPont years (1901–83) the house was nearly doubled in size, and two race tracks were added. In 2003 the Montpelier Foundation began a four year project to restore the house to the size and structure it was during the Madison era of the 1820's.

■ Allow 1–2 hours for a visit to Montpelier; orientation film, gift shop, and an audio tour. Guided tours from mid March – October.
Behind the Scenes Restoration Tour Daily, mid-March through Oct 31st, every half hour, 10:30 to 4:00. Nov through mid-March, tours every hour from 10–4
Enslaved Community Tour 11 AM Sat
duPont Estate Tour 2 PM Sat
Walking Tour of Grounds 2 PM Sun
Admission: $11 adults , $10 seniors and AAA, $6 children 6–14
(540) 672-2728 www/montpelier.org

23 JAMES MADISON MUSEUM – ORANGE

A small museum in nearby Orange honors James Madison. Personal items of Madison include his favorite chair. Antique farm tools.

■ Open Mon-Fri 9-5, year round. On weekends 10-5 Sat, and 1-5 Sun from Mar-Dec. Admission: $4 adults, $3 seniors, $1 ages 6-16.
(540) 672-1776 www.jamesmadisonmus.org

24 FRONTIER CULTURE MUSEUM STAUNTON

Shenandoah Valley heritage at this open-air museum near Staunton (pronounced "Stanton"). Living history at four historic farms: German (early 1700's), Scotch-Irish (early 1700's), English (late 1600's), and American (mid-1800's). Visitors center, exhibits, gift shop.

■ Open daily 9–5 (Call ahead in bad weather.) Winter hours, 10–4, Dec.1–mid March. Closed Christmas, Thanksgiving, New Year's. Admission: adult $10; srs $9.50; ages 6–12, $6
(540) 332-7850 www.frontiermuseum.org

25 JAMES MADISON CENTER HARRISONBURG

The Center at James Madison University has a website with links to 400 internet sources; newsletter, workshops, conferences, lesson plans, essay contests, and fellowships for future teachers, emphasizing James Madison's role in writing the Constitution, the Federalist Papers and the Bill of Rights. Harrisonburg is the birthplace of expedition member John Shields.

■ To arrange a visit, call (540) 568-2549 or use e-mail at www.jmu.edu/madison/center

26 WILLIAM CLARK BIRTHPLACE MARKER

John and Ann Clark moved back to Caroline County from Albemarle in 1757 when they inherited property. The ninth of their ten children, William Clark was born here on August 1, 1770. The family moved to Louisville, Kentucky at the end of the War for Independence in 1784. Ann Clark's brother-in-law, Donald Robertson, was the teacher of both George Rogers Clark, the "Hannibal of the West" and James Madison, "Framer of the Constitution." Madison later said of Robertson: "All that I have been in life I owe to that man."

The birthplace marker is located in Chilesburg, Virginia; 5 miles west of I-95, and 30 miles south of Fredericksburg near County Line Baptist Church, established in 1784. Back roads travelling on the old roads from Monticello will bring you into contact with the world of Lewis and Clark as they experienced it.

27 CLARK AND YORK MARKER–MILFORD

In 2003, an oak tree was planted in Milford honoring William Clark and York as "Native Sons of Caroline County." The county seat of Bowling Green must have been familiar to the two men as youngsters. Did they attend George Washington's party for Lafayette celebrating the surrender of Cornwallis in 1781? It was held on the lawn of Bowling Green's "Old Mansion," Virginia's third oldest building (c.1669).

■ Self-guided Bowling Green tour information at town hall or on website. (804) 633-4074
www.town.bowling-green.va.us
www.foundersofamerica.org

28 JAMES MONROE MUSEUM AND MEMORIAL LIBRARY–FREDERICKSBURG

Fredericksburg, at the falls of the Rappahannock River, has been called "America's most historic city." The James Monroe Museum, in the heart of the city's 40 square block historic district, displays hundreds of family heirlooms, including Louis XVI furniture the family purchased in Paris. James Monroe, the fifth President of the United States (1817–1825), was the last President of the Revolutionary War generation to serve in office. A war hero, Monroe was wounded in the Battle of Trenton and spent the winter at Valley Forge with George Washington. His home in Charlottesville is located near Jefferson's Monticello estate.

■ The Monroe Museum is open Mar–Nov 10–5 Mon–Sat, and 1–5 on Sunday. Dec–Feb 10–4 on Mon-Sat and 1–4 on Sunday. Closed Thanksgiving, Dec. 24, 25, 31 and Jan.1. A guided tour takes about 30 minutes. Admission: $5 adult, $1 student (540) 654-1043
www.mwc.edu/jmmu/www/visit

■ *Pass to Historic Fredericksburg*
Sold at the Fredericksburg Visitor Center. It provides access to 9 historic sites including Kenmore Plantation, Chatham Mansion, Rising Sun Tavern (NHL), Hugh Mercer Apothecary Shop, and the Fredericksburg and Spotsylvania National Military Park. Pass (40% discount): $24 adults, $8 ages 6–18, free under 5.
(800) 678-4748 or (540) 373-1776
www.fredericksburgvirginia.net

Washington D. C. to Harpers Ferry, West Virginia

29 HARPERS FERRY NAT'L HISTORICAL PARK

■ It is 52 miles from Washington to Harpers Ferry, West Virginia. From I-495/I-270 (Washington DC) take I-495 Washington Beltway Loop to I-270 at Bethesda, Maryland. Then take I-270 (Dwight Eisenhower Hwy) north for 32 miles before joining I-70/US 40 at Frederick. At Frederick take I-70 North (for Hagerstown). Go one mile to US 340 (Jefferson Pike). Take I-70 Exit 52 (Charles Town/Leesburg) to US 340/US 15. Go south for 19 miles to Harpers Ferry. Go 1/2 mile to Harpers Ferry NPS Visitor Center.

■ From I-81 Exit 315 Winchester VA

It is 28 miles from Winchester to Harpers Ferry. Take SR 7 (Berryville Pike and Harry Byrd Hwy) for 8.8 miles to US 340. Take US 340 (Jefferson Pike) north for 18 miles to Harpers Ferry. Go 1/2 mile to Visitor Center.

■ From Skyline Drive (Front Royal VA) via US-340

It is about 43 miles to Harpers Ferry from Front Royal. US 340 is located one mile from the Skyline Drive Entrance/Exit Station at Front Royal. From Skyline Drive station, go north on Belair Ave to 6th St. Turn left on 6th St. Take 6th to Commerce St. (US 522). Turn right (north) on Commerce St. Turn right (north) again when Commerce joins Royal Ave (US 340). It is about one hour's drive time to Harpers Ferry.

30 FREDERICK, MARYLAND HISTORIC DISTRICT

■ It is 32 miles from Washington to Frederick via I-270. This is the route that Meriwether Lewis took when he left the White House. I-270 connects the I-495 beltway of Washington to I-70/US-40 at Frederick. (I-70/US-40 is the route of the Historic National Road Trail, which starts in Baltimore.) I-270 ends at Frederick when it joins I-70. Take I-70 east to the first exit, Exit 54 (North Market St.) for the Historic District, which is located one mile north of I-70. Take North Market St. 1.3 miles to Church St. (one block north of Patrick St). Turn right for Visitor Center.

■ From Frederick to Philadelphia

It is about 165 miles to Philadelphia from Frederick. Take I-70 east 41.5 miles to the Baltimore Beltway Loop, I-695. Take I-695 around the north end of the beltway loop for 21 miles to I-95, the John F. Kennedy Memorial Hwy. (I-95 becomes a toll road.) It is about 100 miles to Philadelphia on I-95.

■ From Frederick to Charlottesville

It is 129 miles from Frederick to Charlottesville via US 15. This route also goes past Harpers Ferry and James Madison's Montpelier home en route to Charlottesville.

31 SKYLINE DRIVE SCENIC ROUTE–SHENANDOAH NATIONAL PARK

Skyline Drive is a continuation of the Blue Ridge Parkway. It is a limited access two lane mountain roadway winding for 105 miles through Shenandoah National Park. Allow 3-4 hours travel time; 35 miles per hour speed limit.

■ The south entrance to Skyline Drive is from I-64 Exit 99 (Waynesboro; see *Central Virginia map*, **p. 10)** **through the** Rockfish Gap Entrance Station. This entrance is near Afton, and 9 miles east of the junction of I-64 and I-81 at Staunton. Charlottesville is about 20 miles east on I-64.

■ The north entrance for Skyline Drive is from I-66 Exit 6 through the Front Royal Entrance Station. This entrance is 6 miles east of the junction of I-66 and I-81 (near Middletown). Winchester is 19 miles northwest via US 340 (Stonewall Jackson Hwy) and US 522 (Front Royal Pike).

32 GEORGE WASHINGTON OFFICE MUSEUM—WINCHESTER

The George Washington Office Museum is located at Braddock and Cork Streets in downtown Winchester. From I-81 exit 313 take Millwood Ave (US 17) west to Braddock Street (US 11). Go right on Braddock Street seven blocks north to Cork Street.

THE IRON BOAT
The Experiment

Meriwether Lewis arrived at Harpers Ferry on March 16, 1803. He ordered 15 rifles and powder horns; 15 spare interchangeable rifle locks; tomahawks, knives, other supplies. and gunsmith repair tools. (This order of 15 rifles indicates he originally planned on a much smaller expedition.)

One week's stay stretched to a month as he worked with army mechanics to design an iron boat, custom made to his own design. The iron frame could be bolted together into several different sizes, up to 36 feet in length. The framework, weighing 196 pounds, would be transported by boat to the Rocky Mountains where it would be put together and covered with animal skins. It was called *The Experiment.*

From there, the plan was to carry the iron boat over (the supposed) single ridge of mountains, and use it to transport their heavy goods to the Pacific Ocean. It was a good plan, but he didn't include one crucial item. (See the Great Falls, Montana section in Region Seven.)

On April 18th, Lewis went back east, where he spent the next 11 weeks making final preparations. On July 7th he returned to Harpers Ferry and tested the weapons. The next day he started for Pittsburgh. Two wagons carrying over 3500 pounds of goods went by a separate route.

> VIEW FROM JEFFERSON'S ROCK
>
> The passage of the Patowmac through the Blue Ridge is perhaps one of the most stupendous scenes in nature....This scene is worth a voyage across the Atlantic.
>
> –Thomas Jefferson, *Notes on the State of Virginia* (1785)

Stone steps leading to Jefferson's Rock

"The Experiment" Reconstructed Iron Boat

Marsha Starkey
Harpers Ferry NHP

View from the Cavalier Heights Visitor Center near Harpers Ferry

Harpers Ferry and the Shenandoah Valley

29 HARPERS FERRY NATIONAL HISTORICAL PARK

George Washington established the United States Armory and Arsenal in 1796 at Harpers Ferry, located at the confluence of the Shenandoah and Potomac Rivers. The Shenandoah is a tributary of the Potomac. The strategically important Potomac River originates in the mountains of West Virginia and flows past Washington D C through Chesapeake Bay to the Atlantic Ocean.

Harpers Ferry National Historical Park covers over 2000 acres in West Virginia, Virginia, and Maryland. The town of Harpers Ferry, West Virginia has many historic buildings owned and operated by the National Park Service. Exhibits interpret six historical themes: the armory and other industry, railroads and canal building, the Civil War, John Brown's Raid, Natural Heritage, and African-American History.

Two locations in Harpers Ferry date to the time of Meriwether Lewis: Jefferson's Rock and Harper House, both are located on the hill above Lower Town. Thomas Jefferson, George Washington and Meriwether Lewis all visited Harper House. The stone steps leading to Jefferson's Rock were built sometime during the early 1800's.

■ The Lewis and Clark Exhibit is at the corner of Hog Alley and Potomac Street. There is a self-guided Meriwether Lewis Walking Tour.

■ Cavalier Heights Visitors Center is open daily from 8 to 5. Shuttle buses take visitors back and forth to the old town of Harpers Ferry, which has limited parking and narrow streets. One entrance fee of $6 per vehicle to enter and park at Cavalier Heights. Exhibits and shuttle are included in admission.
(304) 535-6298 www.nps.gov/hafe

■ Harpers Ferry Historical Association operates the Park Bookshop on Shenandoah St in Lower Town. Proceeds from the bookstore support programs and activities. Open daily, 9-5.
(800) 821-5206 www.harpersferryhistory.org

■ The Appalachian Trail Conference manages over 2,000 miles of trails in the Appalachian Mountains covering fourteen states from Maine to Georgia. The voluteer association's office and store is at 799 Washington St.
(304) 535-6331 www.appalachiantrail.org

30 FREDERICK, MARYLAND HISTORIC DISTRICT

The Frederick Historic District contains 50 blocks of preserved 18th and 19th century buildings.Frederick is also on the Civil War Trail, and the Historic National Road Trail. Frederick is a natural "hub city" for the history tourist. On July 5th, 1803 Meriwether Lewis spent the first night of his journey to the Pacific Ocean in "Fredericktown." He solved his first transportation problem, finding a replacement wagon driver to haul his goods from Harpers Ferry to Pittsburgh.

■ The Frederick Visitor Center is open daily 9-5 at 19 East Church St in the historic district. Guided walking tours depart from the Center on Saturdays and Sundays, 1:30 P M, April–Nov. Price: $5.50 adult, $4.50 seniors, $2.50 under 12. (800) 999-3613.
www.fredericktourism.org

■ Solve your own transportation problem by commuting to Washington D C (45 miles from Frederick) via car and the Metrorail Red Line at Shady Grove Station in Rockville MD (27 miles). Take I-270-S to Exit 9A for I-370 East. Get off at I-370 Exit 3B for Shady Grove. Parking is $3.25 per day. Arrive early, the Red Line is the Metro's busiest. See p. 17 for details.
(202) 637-7000 www.metroopensdoors.com

31 SKYLINE DRIVE SCENIC ROUTE SHENANDOAH NATIONAL PARK

Shenandoah National Park is a favorite Virginia get-away. The park has more than 500 miles of hiking trails, including 101 of the most beautiful miles of the Appalachian Trail. The Skyline Drive mountain roadway through the park has 75 overlook stopping points.

■ Shenandoah National Park has 3 Visitor Centers, ranger programs, Herbert Hoover's retreat, seasonal lodging and campgrounds.

■ Skyline Drive is a limited access roadway. Entrance fee: $10 vehicle fee, good for 1–7 days; or use $10 Golden Age Pass
(540) 999-3500 www.nps.gov/shen
(800) 778-2851 www.visitshenandoah.com

32 GEORGE WASHINGTON'S OFFICE MUSEUM—WINCHESTER, VIRGINIA

Winchester is the oldest established town west of the Blue Ridge Mountains. George Washington began his career as a 16 year old surveyor in Winchester, spending much of his early life here. Winchester was an important crossroads town linking the Pioneer Road from Alexandria to the Great Valley Road. Tour historic mansions, some of the grandest gardens in the Shenandoah Valley, and many Civil War sites. There is a 45 mile driving tour in the local countryside, "Follow the Apple Trail" with audio tape and brochure; and self-guided walking tours around town.

■ Washington's Office Museum is open from April 1–Oct 31, Mon–Sat 10–4, Sunday 12–4.
(540)662-4412 www.fortedwards.org

■ Winchester-Frederick County Visitor Center open daily in Abram's Delight House and Museum (the oldest home in Winchester, built in 1754).
(800) 662-1360 www.visitwinchesterva.com

The National Mall, Washington D. C.

GETTING TO THE NATIONAL MALL FROM I-395 and I-295

The National Mall may be accessed from all directions, but I-395 is the interstate road closest to the Mall. In the vicinity of the Mall, I-395 goes east and west. However, the eastbound lanes are called I-395 North, and the westbound lanes are called I-395 South. (Also see the interstate "beltway" map on page 17.)

I-395 North
Coming from Virginia (west side of the Potomac River) on I-395:
After passing Exit 11, keep left onto US-1. The road changes its name to 14th St. You are now in local traffic.

I-395 South
Coming from I-295, which feeds into I-395:
Take the off-ramp to 12th Street SW. You are now in local traffic.

Washington D. C. The Nation's Capital

National Museum of the American Indian
Jeff Tinsley, Smithsonian Institution

33 THE WHITE HOUSE VISITORS CENTER AND WHITE HOUSE TOURS

The White House is the only official residence of a head of state in the whole world which is open to visitors on a regular basis. Apply in advance and follow current guidelines.

■ The Visitors Center is located at 15th and E Streets, near the White House on Pennsylvania Ave. It features six permanent exhibits and a museum shop. Open daily, from 7:30–4. www.nps.gov/whho (202) 208-1631

■ White House Tours are available for groups of ten or more people. Contact your Member of Congress from one to six months in advance for free tickets.Tours:Tues–Sat. 7:30–11:30 AM (202) 456-7041 www.whitehouse.gov

34 NATIONAL ARCHIVES

The Nation's Recordkeeper has almost a million visitors a year. The "Charters of Freedom" are on permanent exhibit on the Rotunda—the Declaration of Independence, the Constitution, and the Bill of Rights. The Louisiana Purchase is also on exhibit. Other attractions: a documentary film theater, public vaults, and exhibition gallery.

■ 700 Pennsylvania Ave NW (Rotunda entrance is on Constitution Ave.) Rotunda hours: Spring: 10–7, Summer: 10–9, Fall:10–5:30. Geneaology and history researchers should check website. (202) 501-5400 www.archives.gov

35 WASHINGTON MONUMENT

The 555 feet tall obelisk provides a great view of the capital city.

■ Obtain free timed-tickets from the kiosk at 15th St. on the National Mall. Timed-tickets are available at 8 AM, and generally run out by noon. Reservations may be made in advance for a small fee. Hours: 9–5. (800) 967-2283 reservations www.nps.gov/wamo

36 THOMAS JEFFERSON MEMORIAL

The Jefferson Memorial is one of Washington's most famous memorials. A 19-foot bronze statue of Thomas Jefferson is displayed in the rotunda of this classical building, modeled after the Roman Pantheon. Museum exhibits and a bookstore are located in the basement.

■ Open 8 AM-11:45 PM daily. Bookstore hours are 9 AM-7PM.
(202) 426-6841 www.nps.gov/thje

37 "THE CASTLE" SMITHSONIAN INFORMATION CENTER

Begin visits to the Smithsonian's 14 museums and National Zoo at the Castle on the National Mall. The Smithsonian is the world's largest museum and research complex. All museums and zoo are free. Explore the Smithsonian website in planning your trip.

■ 1000 Jefferson Drive, SW. Open daily from 9:00-5:30. Fine dining daily from 11-2 at The Commons Restaurant. Full buffet.
(202) 633-1000 www.si.edu

38 NAT'L MUSEUM OF AMERICAN INDIAN

This new Smithsonian museum, which opened in 2004, explores the past, present and future through the eyes of Native Americans. Three permanent exhibits: "Our Universes," "Our Peoples," and"Our Lives," and annual exhibits.

■ 4th St. and Independence Ave, SW. Open daily 10–5:30. Museum shops and Mitsitam ("Let's eat") Native Foods Cafe.
(202) 633-1000 www.americanindian.si.edu

39 NAT'L MUSEUM OF AMERICAN HISTORY

Called the "Nation's Attic,"featuring U S cultural, scientific and technological heritage. William Clark's expedition compass is on display.

■ 14th St and Constitution Ave, NW. Open daily 10-5:30. Free admission. Main St Cafe, Coffee Bar, Cafe and Ice Cream Parlor.
(202) 357-2700 www.americanhistory.si.edu

40 NAT'L MUSEUM OF NATURAL HISTORY

The most visited natural history museum in the world. See "Lewis and Clark as Naturalists" at www.mnh.si.edu/lewisandclark.

■ 10th St and Constitution Ave, NW. Free admission. Open daily, 10-5:30 P M. May 23-Sept 1, 10:30–7 PM. Free tours: Mon–Thurs 10:30 and 1:30; Friday at 1:30. (No tours July and August.) Atrium Cafe and Fossil Cafe. Free jazz music at Jazz Cafe, Fridays, 5:30–10 PM.
(202) 357-2700 www.mnh.si.edu

41 SEWALL-BELMONT HOUSE MUSEUM

This National Historic Landmark was once the home of Albert Gallatin, Secretary of the Treasury from 1802–1813. Gallatin drafted the Louisiana Purchase in this house. He lived here from 1801–1813. In 1929 it became the home of sufferagette Alice Paul, author of the Equal Rights Amendment and founder of the National Woman's Party, which still owns and operates the house. Built in 1799 on Capitol Hill, the Sewall-Belmont House is one of the oldest buildings in Washington.

■ 144 Constitution Ave, NE. Open Tues–Fri 11–3; Sat, 12–4. Donation $3. Tours hourly.
(202) 546-1210 www.sewallbelmont.org

42 U S BOTANIC GARDEN CONSERVATORY

The oldest continually operating botanical garden in the United States, established in 1820. The Victorian era Conservatory is located on the grounds of the U S Capitol.

■ Maryland Ave and First St SW. Open daily, 10–5. (202) 226-4083 www.usbg.gov

43 RENWICK GALLERY

The crafts gallery is part of the Smithsonian American Art Museum. The Renwick has George Catlin's Indian Gallery; featuring 287 paintings of Indians in the 1830's. William Clark arranged for Catlin's travels in Indian Country.

■ Pennsylvania Ave at 17th St. NW. Open 10-5:30 daily. Free admission. (202) 633-1000
www.americanart.si.edu/renwick
www.catlinclassroom.si.edu

44 UNITED STATES CAPITOL

The symbol of our representative democracy. Sacagawea's statue is displayed at the Capitol.

■ Guided tours only: 9-4:30 Mon-Sat. Free timed-tickets daily starting at 9 AM at kiosk near First St and Independence SW.
(202) 225-6827 www.aoc.gov

45 LIBRARY OF CONGRESS

The Visitors' Center is located at the First St entrance of the Thomas Jefferson Building, between Independence Ave and East Capitol St.

■ Open10-5:30 PM Mon-Sat. Free tours at 10:30, 11:30, 1:30, 2:30 and 3:30 Monday-Friday. Saturday at 10:30, 11:30, 1:30 and 2:30.
(202) 707-8000 www.loc.gov

46 NATIONAL ZOO

The zoo has a North American exhibit area. Visit the zoo website to plan your visit.

■ 3001 Connecticut Ave NW at Rock Creek Park. Open daily. Free admission. April 6-Oct. 25, 10 AM-6 PM
Oct. 26-April 4, 10 AM-4:30 PM

■ Take the Metro, or arrive by 9:30 during summer months for parking. $5 for 3 hours; $2 each additional hour, $11 per day.
(202) 357-2700 www.natzoo.si.edu

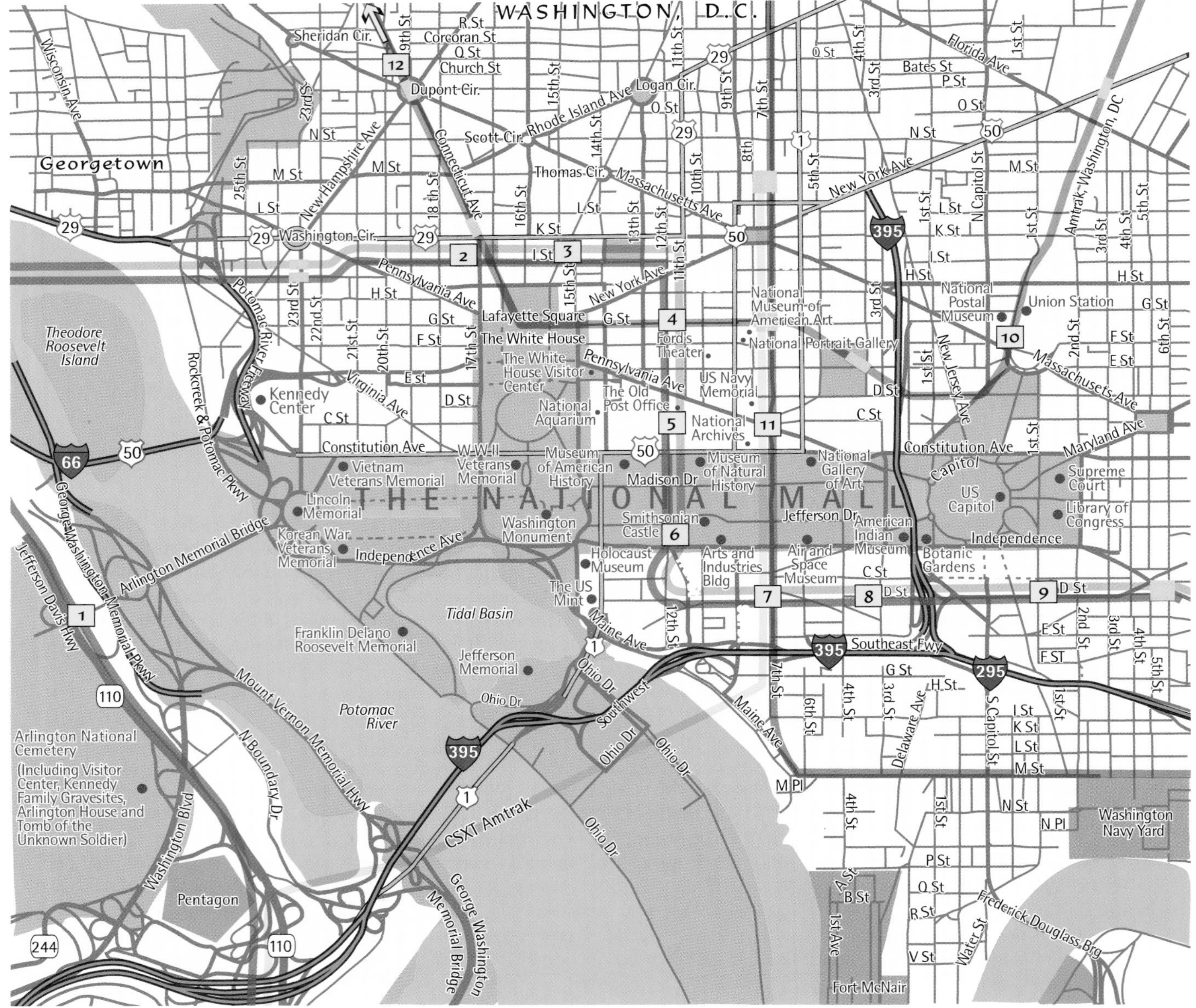

Washington D. C. Metro Area Transportation

Tourmobile buses are the only sightseeing buses authorized by the National Park Service. They provide daily narrated shuttle tours with free reboarding, making continuous round trips between Arlington National Cemetery and the National Mall area. It is an economical and informative way to visit the capital.

■ One day tickets: adults $20, ages 3-11, $10. Two day tickets: $30 and $15. Daily except Christmas and New Year's. Hours of operation: 9:30-4:30. Final reboarding one hour before closing. Tickets may be purchased from bus drivers or at ticket booths at Arlington Cemetery, Union Station, or in season at Washington Monument. 1-800-551-SEAT, or (202) 432-SEAT. www.tourmobile.com

TOURMOBILE BUS SIGHTSEEING ROUTE

- Arlington Cemetery
- Kennedy Family Grave Sites
- Tomb of the Unknown Soldier
- Arlington House
- Kennedy Center
- Lincoln Memorial/Korean War Veteran's Memorial/ Vietnam Veteran's Memorial
- World War II Veteran's Memorial
- Washington Monument
- Arts and Industries/ Smithsonian Castle
- Air and Space Museum
- U S Botanic Gardens/ National Museum of the American Indian
- United States Capitol/ Library of Congress/ Supreme Court
- National Gallery of Art
- National Museum of Natural History
- National Museum of American History
- Bureau of Engraving and Printing/National Holocaust Museum
- Jefferson Memorial
- Frankin Delano Roosevelt Memorial

Note: Tours and Routes are subject to change.

PARKING/METRO ACCESS

■ Parking at Arlington National Cemetery, $1.25 hour, first 3 hours, $2 thereafter. (703) 979-0690

■ Parking at Union Station, $7 for first 3 hours, $15 maximum for 24 hours. (202) 898-1221

■ Free all day parking at West Potomac Park on Ohio Drive SW, south of Lincoln Memorial, and East Potomac Park south of Jefferson Memorial.

■ 15 minute drop-off and pick-up at certain stops on Mall.

■ Blue Line Metro subway goes to Arlington Cemetery; Red Line goes to Union Station. The Yellow/ Green Line and the Blue/Orange Line make stops within 1-3 blocks of the Mall.

Metro Subway Lines

- RED LINE
  Glenmont to Shady Grove
- ORANGE LINE
  New Carrollton to Vienna/Fair GMU
- BLUE LINE
  Franconia-Springfield to Largo Town Center
- GREEN LINE
  Branch Avenue to Greenbelt
- YELLOW LINE
  Huntington to Mt. Vernon Square/
  7th St. Convention Center

METRO OPENS DOORS WEBSITE
www.metroopensdoors.com

The Washington Metropolitan Area Transit Authority website has a Ride Guide trip planning service. Enter start and finish information, and your ride will be planned, including travel time and walking directions.

Call (202) 637-7000 to talk with a customer service representative.

USING THE METRORAIL SUBWAY

Metrorail subway station entrances are marked by large brown columns with the letter "M," and colored stripes identifying the lines served by the station. Follow directional signs to decide which platform to use.

■ Station wall maps show fare rates and travel times. Free maps are available at station manager's booth. Some visitors may have trouble reading the small type. Be prepared with your own travel information.

■ Passengers needs a farecard to enter and exit. Farecard machines are in every station. Bring small bills, as machines only provide up to $5 in change (all in coins). Some machines accept credit and debit cards. Buy roundtrip farecards to avoid lines. Fares are deducted at exit gates. You may add value to your farecard, if you have run out. Fares range from $1.10 to $3.25. Two children, 4 and under, may ride free with any paying customer.

■ A bargain One Day Metrorail Pass may be purchased for $5; good for all day travel after 9:30 AM on weekdays; and all day on weekends and federal holidays.

■ The Metro subway and bus system is crowded. Avoid the weekday rush hours from 4-6 PM. During the height of tourist season, avoid the Smithsonian Mall station.

■ Hours of operation: Opens 5:30 AM on weekdays and 8 AM on weekends and holidays. Closes Sun-Thurs at midnight; Fri-Sat at 2 AM.

Metro Stations (Selected List)

1 ARLINGTON CEMETERY
Memorial Drive
ARLINGTON NATIONAL CEMETERY

2 FARRAGUT WEST
NW corner 18th and I Sts NW
SE corner 17th and I Sts NW
RENWICK GALLERY, WHITE HOUSE

3 MCPHERSON SQUARE
SW corner 14th and I Sts NW
SW corner Vermont Ave and I St
WHITE HOUSE

4 METRO CENTER
SE corner 11th and G Sts NW
SW corner 12th and F Sts
SE corner 13th and G Sts
NE corner 12th and G Sts
TRANSFER STATION

5 FEDERAL TRIANGLE
West side of 12th St. between Pennsylvania and Constitution Aves. NW
WHITE HOUSE VISITORS CENTER
NAT'L MUSEUM OF NATURAL HISTORY
NAT'L MUSEUM OF AMERICAN HISTORY
NATIONAL ARCHIVES

6 SMITHSONIAN
12th St at Jefferson Dr SW (The Mall)
SW corner, 12th St; NW corner Independence Av
SMITHSONIAN CASTLE
WASHINGTON MONUMENT
NAT'L MUSEUM OF NATURAL HISTORY
NAT'L MUSEUM OF AMERICAN HISTORY
JEFFERSON MEMORIAL

7 L'ENFANT PLAZA
SE corner Maryland Ave and 7th St SW
SW corner and DOT Courtyard,
D St between 6th and 7th Sts
L'Enfant Plaza Mall Concourse, 9th and D Sts
NAT'L MUSEUM OF AMERICAN INDIAN
TRANSFER STATION

8 FEDERAL CENTER SOUTHWEST
SW corner of 3rd and D Sts SW
U S BOTANIC GARDEN
NAT'L MUSEUM OF AMERICAN INDIAN

9 CAPITOL SOUTH
First St. between C and D Sts. SE
U S CAPITOL BUILDING, LIBRARY OF CONGRESS

10 UNION STATION
Entrance to Amtrak Terminal, east side of 1st St
North of Massachusetts Ave NE (west side Union Station)
U S CAPITOL, SEWALL–BELMONT HOUSE

11 ARCHIVES–NAVY MEMORIAL
North of Pennsylvania Ave, west of 7th St NW
NATIONAL ARCHIVES

12 WOODLEY PARK–ZOO/ ADAMS–MORGAN
SW corner Connecticut Ave and 24th St NW
SW corner Connecticut Ave and Woodley Rd
NATIONAL ZOO

Washington, D. C.

The famous Washington "Beltway" is a system of interstates surrounding the capital city. Washington was designed by Major Pierre L'Enfant, a French architect and an officer in the Revolutionary Army. The city's broad and spacious vistas are preserved by a law limiting the height of buildings to 160 feet.

Surveyors Andrew Ellicott and Benjamin Banneker laid out the District of Columbia in a ten mile diamond square in 1791-92. (In 1846 the land west of the Potomac was ceded to Arlington, Virginia.) Banneker, a free black, was a self-taught astronomer and mathematician. Ellicott taught Meriwether Lewis celestial navigation. Two Ellicott house-museums are included in this travel guide: one in Lancaster, Pennsylvania; the other in Natchez, Mississippi.

USING THE METROBUS REGIONAL SYSTEM

Metrobus stops are marked by red, white and blue signs. You will need exact change, or a smart card, to use the bus, as drivers do not carry cash. Buses connect with other bus and rail systems in Maryland, Virginia, and the District of Columbia. Check the METRO OPENS DOORS website for further information.

■ Transfers: When transferring from the Metro- rail subway to a Metrobus, get the bus transfer when you enter the station. Transfers are 35 cents, or $1.65 for express bus routes. Transfers are free between buses, if used within 2 hours.

■ A bargain One Day Regional Bus Pass may be purchased from bus drivers for $2.50; good for all day travel after 9:30 AM on weekdays; and all day on weekends and federal holidays. There is a 90 cents additional charge for express buses.

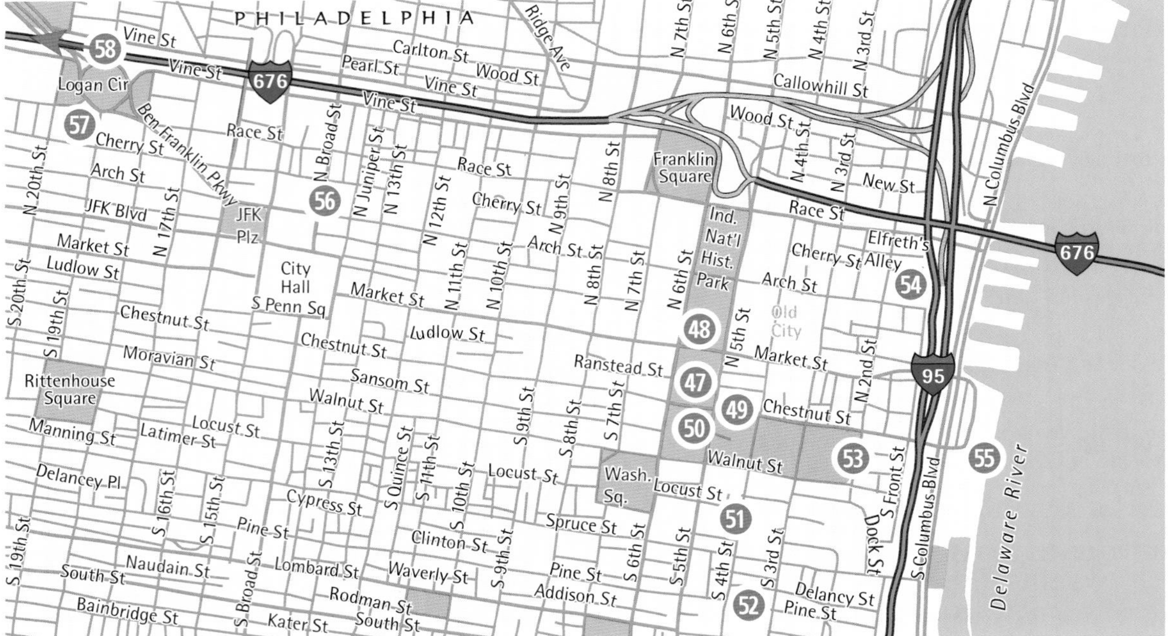

Philadelphia, Pennsylvania

PHILADELPHIA

Philadelphia was the capital of the United States from 1790-1800; it was also the intellectual and cultural center of the new nation. President Jefferson—who was President of the American Philosophical Society from 1797 to 1815—asked his colleagues to help Lewis. Lewis spent more than a month in Philadelphia being tutored by leading scientists and buying supplies.

Artist and museum proprietor Charles Willson Peale painted the famous portraits of Lewis and Clark. His museum, located on the second floor of Independence Hall, displayed the plants, skins, skeletons, Indian materials and other items collected on the expedition. Even a live magpie and a "burrowing squirrel of the prairies" came to live in Independence Hall.

The Lewis and Clark journals, edited by Nicholas Biddle, were published here in 1814. The original journals and plant specimens remain in Philadelphia in the collections of the American Philosophical Society and the Academy of Natural Sciences.

47 INDEPENDENCE HALL

48 VISITOR CENTER

The parking facility is located directly beneath the Visitor Center building on 6th St. between Arch and Market Streets. (Market is the dividing line between North and South Streets.)

From the South on I-95 N
At Exit 22 follow signs for Phila/ Independence Hall/Callowhill St. Keep right at fork in the ramp. Stay straight to go to Callowhill St. Turn left onto No 6th St. Go 3 blocks.

From the North on I-295S or New Jersey Turnpike and I-295 S
At NJ Turnpike Exit 4 take SR-73 one mi. to I-295 S. Take 1-295 S 11 mi. to I-76 W. Take I-76W 3 mi. to I-676 N. Go north 7 mi. on I-676, then cross the Delaware River on the Ben Franklin toll bridge. Take Exit 4 (North 5th St). Go north 2 blocks to Wood St, turn left, go one block to 6th St. Turn left, go south 3 blocks.

From the West on PA Turnpike
Take I-76 (PA Turnpike) to Valley Forge Exit (Exit 326). Follow signs to Philadelphia I-76 East. Go about 25 mi. to the Central Philadelphia Exit (Exit 344). Stay on I-676 E (Vine St. Expwy) to 8th St. Exit. Make a right onto 8th St. Then left onto Race St. and then a right onto 6th St.

Coming from the East
Take the Atlantic City Expressway to SR 42 North. Follow SR 42 to the Ben Franklin toll bridge. Follow signs for 5th and 6th Sts. Stay in right hand lane. Go past 5th St. Exit. Follow signs for Independence Hall and 6th St. Make a right at first light onto Franklin St. Go around a bend; merge onto 6th St. South. Stay towards your left.

49 SECOND BANK OF THE U S PORTRAIT GALLERY

420 Chestnut St between South 4th and South 5th Sts; one block south of Market St.

50 AMER PHIL SOCIETY

104 South 5th St. Around the corner from Independence Hall.

51 CASPAR WISTAR MARKER

SW corner of 4th and Locust, about 2 blocks south of Independence Hall on 4th St., en route to St. Peter's.

52 ST PETER'S CHURCH

3/4 mile from Visitor Center to the church. Go south 3 blocks from Market St. to Pine St. The church is at 313 Pine, between 3rd and 4th Sts.

53 CITY TAVERN

138 South Second St. Two blocks south of Market, between Chestnut and Walnut Sts, on Second St.

54 ELFRETH'S ALLEY

Four blocks north of Market Street between Front and Second Streets, and Arch and Race Streets.

55 PENN'S LANDING/THE DUCKS

The landing on the waterfront is two blocks east of Independence Park. The Ducks Tour departs from 6th and Chestnut Sts, south of the Independence Hall Visitor Center.

56 PA ACADEMY OF FINE ARTS

118 North Broad St.
Located between Arch and Cherry Sts. (Broad St is about eight blocks west of the Visitor Center.)

57 ACADEMY OF NATURAL SCIENCES

1900 Ben Franklin Parkway.
Between Race and Cherry Sts. at 19th St. facing Logan Circle, one of Philadelphia's most beautiful areas.

58 BARTRAM'S GARDENS

54th St and Lindbergh Blvd.
Historic Bartram's Gardens is about six miles from the Independence Hall Visitor Center. Located at So 54th St and Lindbergh Blvd on the west bank of the Schuykill River.

Take I-676 (Vine St Expwy) west to I-76 (Schuykill Expwy) Go south on Schuykill Expwy to Exit 346B, (South 34th St Exit). Go left on 34th St (also called University Bridge Ave) across the Schuykill River to Grays Ferry Avenue. Turn right onto Grays Ferry Ave and go across the river again. Bear left onto Paschall Ave. Go 4 blocks on Paschall Ave to 49th St. After crossing the railroad tracks, turn right onto Grays Avenue. Grays Ave becomes Lindbergh Blvd. Turn left at 54th St. Follow signs.

1

American Philosophical Society

Park Interpreter Independence Hall

Elfreth's Alley

City Tavern

Philadelphia

Charles Willson Peale lifts the curtain on the Peale Museum, America's first "Lewis and Clark Interpretive Center." The museum was located on the second floor of Independence Hall.
Pennsylvania Academy of Fine Arts

47 INDEPENDENCE NAT'L HISTORICAL PARK AND INDEPENDENCE HALL

The "Birthplace of Our Nation" features the Liberty Bell Center, Independence Hall, and another dozen buildings open to the public, with no admission charge. Independence Hall is a World Heritage Site where the Declaration of Independence and U S Constitution were created, and Lewis and Clark artifacts were once displayed.

■ Security Check Point
There is one security check point for all visitors to Independence Hall at the Liberty Bell Center. The screening process takes about 45 minutes or less. The fewer personal belongings (camera bags, totes) you bring, the faster the line moves. Open daily 9-5. www.nps.gov/inde

48 INDEPENDENCE VISITOR CENTER

Plan your visit here; pick up a visitor's guide and timed-tickets; make reservations; buy event tickets; sign up for tours. Video theater, gift and book shop, and coffee bar.

■ The Center is open daily from 8:30-5. Located at 6th and Market Sts, with underground parking facilities. Parking rate: $13 for up to 10 hours. www.independencevisitorcenter.com (800) 537-7676 or (215) 965-7676

■ Independence Hall Tour Timed-Tickets
Tickets are available free on the day of your visit at the National Park Service desk in the Visitor Center (or you may reserve tickets up to one year in advance for a $1.50). Be sure to allow 45 minutes to one hour for the screening process when arriving for your timed-ticket tour. The tour itself last 40 minutes. Allow more time if you want to see the Liberty Bell exhibits before exiting the building.

■ *AudioWalk Tour of Historic Philadelphia*
The Independence Hall Association has an excellent website. They also have a 72 minute CD with a guide map. Rent an *AudioWalk* CD player at the Visitor Center. Rental fees: $10/1 person; $14/2; $16/3; $20/4. Or buy the CD in advance and listen to it before you arrive: Send a check for $18.45 to "Audio Walk Tour." 2026 Waverly St, Philadelphia PA, 19146. To order by phone: (215) 272-5886 www.ushistory.org

49 SECOND BANK OF THE UNITED STATES PORTRAIT GALLERY NATIONAL HISTORIC LANDMARK

The Lewis and Clark portraits and other famous portraits are on display in this Greek revival style building. Nicholas Biddle, editor of the journals, was President of the Second Bank.

■ Free admission.11-5, Weds through Sunday. www.nps.gov/inde/second-bank

50 AMERICAN PHILOSOPHICAL SOCIETY NATIONAL HISTORIC LANDMARK

America's oldest learned institution has 18 small notebooks of Lewis and Clark journals in their collection. Each year some are displayed during July-August at Library Hall, across the street from the APS building.

■ Library Hall exhibits: Mon-Fri, 9-5. Check with APS for their exhibition schedule. (215) 440-3400 www.amphilsoc.org

51 CASPAR WISTAR HOME MARKER

Dr. Wistar tutored Meriwether Lewis in medicine and paleontology here. He wrote the first American textbook on anatomy.

■ www.lewisandclarkphila.org
www.amphilsoc.org/library/mole/w/wista

52 ST. PETER'S EPISCOPAL CHURCH NATIONAL HISTORIC LANDMARK

Osage orange trees grown from seeds sent back by Lewis and Clark grow in the churchyard of this 1761 Church. Charles Willson Peale and Nicholas Biddle are buried here. George Washington worshipped here.

■ Guided tours 11-3 P M on Saturday. Church open Mon-Fri 8:30-4 Saturday 8-3; churchyard open til dusk daily. Sunday services 9 and 11. (215)925-5988 www.stpetersphila.org

53 CITY TAVERN

A reconstruction of a 1773 tavern often visited by our founding fathers.

■ Reservations recommended. 138 S. 2nd St (215) 413-1443 www.citytavern.com

54 ELFRETH'S ALLEY AND MUSEUM NATIONAL HISTORIC LANDMARK

The Nation's oldest residential street has existed since 1702. House Museum and tours.

■ Admission: $2 adults, $1 (6-12)
March-Oct: Mon-Sat. 10-5 , Sun 12-5
Nov-Feb: Thurs-Sat, 10-5, Sun 12-5
May-August special programs, living history
(215) 574-0560 www.elfrethsalley.org

55 PENN'S LANDING ON THE RIVERFRONT AND "RIDE THE DUCKS" TOUR

Penn's Landing on the Delaware riverfront, and an 80 minute sightseeing tour on a land and water vessel called "The Ducks" are both fun.

■ "The Ducks" departs from 6th and Chestnut, near the Visitor Center where tickets are sold: $23 adults, $22 seniors/military, $13 (3-12). (215) 227-DUCK www.phillyducks.com

56 PA ACADEMY OF THE FINE ARTS

In 1805 Charles Willson Peale was one of the founders of the Academy, the nation's oldest art museum and school.

■ Open Tues-Sat 10-5, Sun 11-5. Closed Mondays and legal holidays. Tours at 11:30 and 12:30 weekdays, 12 and 1:00 on weekends. Admission: $7 adults, $6 seniors, $5 (5-18) 215) 972-7600 www.pafa.org

57 ACADEMY OF NATURAL SCIENCES

Home for over 200 Lewis and Clark plant specimens. The oldest natural sciences institution in the western hemisphere, founded in 1812.

■ Open Mon-Fri 10-4:30, Sat-Sun and holidays,10-5. Admission: $9 adult, $8.25 senior, $8 (3-12). (215) 299-1000 www.acnatsci.org

58 HISTORIC BARTRAM'S GARDEN NATIONAL HISTORIC LANDMARK

National Historic Landmark home of John Bartram, naturalist, botanist and explorer. One of America's oldest botanical gardens.

■ House Museum and gift shop open 12-4, March to 2nd week of Dec. Guided tours offered Tues-Sun, ten past the hour.
Grounds open 10-5.
Admission: $8 adult, $7 senior and student
(215) 729-5281 www.bartramsgarden.org

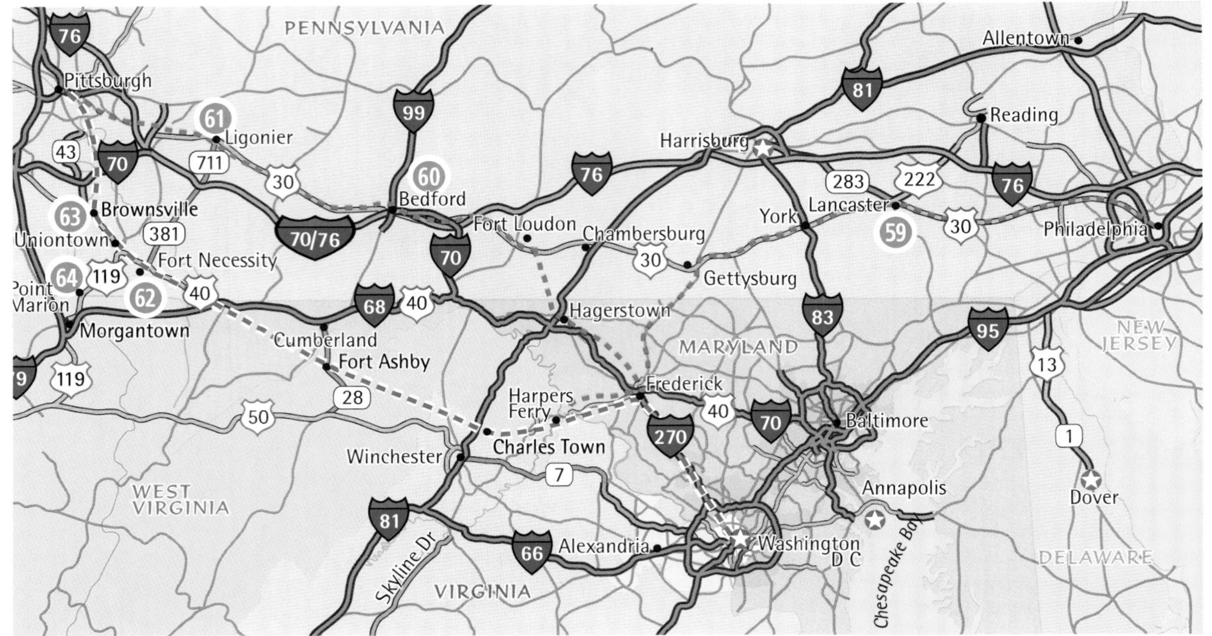

Old Roads to Pittsburgh

PHILADELPHIA TO PITTSBURGH PENNSYLVANIA TURNPIKE

306 miles (about 5 hours) via I-76 and I-70, the PA Turnpike toll road. Current toll fees are $17.25 for cars.

59 ELLICOTT HOUSE LANCASTER PA

80 mi. from Philadelphia on the PA Turnpike. Take Exit 286 for Lancaster (US 222 South). Go south 15 miles. US 222 temporarily joins US-30 for about one mile. Get off at the exit for SR 272/US 222. Bear left onto US 222. Go 1.1 mile, turn right (west) onto East McGovern Ave (US 222). Go 0.3 mi. on McGovern. Turn left at Prince St (US 222). Go about 1 mile to 123 North Prince St.

60 OLD BEDFORD VILLAGE FORT BEDFORD MUSEUM

203 miles from Philadelphia. Take Exit 146 PA Turnpike. Go less than one mile south on North Richard St. (US 220 Bus) to Sawblade Road for Old Bedford Village. Fort Bedford Museum is located 1.5 miles further south on N Richard St (US 220 Bus) near its intersection with the Lincoln Highway (West Pitt Street).

61 FORT LIGONIER

50 miles east of Pittsburgh on Route 30 and SR 711 in Ligonier PA. Via the PA Turnpike/I-70, take Exit 91 go 13 miles north on SR 711.

HARPERS FERRY TO PITTSBURGH: TWO ROUTES

- OLD ROADS (Lewis's Route)
238 miles (about 6 hours) via roads near Lewis's Route through the Allegheny Mountains, including the Old National Road.
- INTERSTATES
220 miles (3.5 hours) via US-340, I-70, and PA Turnpike

62 FORT NECESSITY FARMINGTON PA

One mile northeast of Farmington on US-40. About 30 miles south of either I-70 or the PA Turnpike. From I-70 Exit 36: Take the Mon-Fayette Expressway to US-40. From PA Turnpike Exit 91 (Donegal) SR 711 south to US-381 to US 40.

63 NEMACOLIN CASTLE BROWNSVILLE PA

From I-70 Exit 36: Take Mon-Fayette Expressway six miles to Brownsville. Cross the river turn right at 4th Ave, turn right again onto Front St.

64 GALLATIN'S FRIENDSHIP HILL POINT MARION PA

From Brownsville, take SR 166 28 miles to Friendship Hill. From Uniontown go 16 miles on US 119 to Point Marion, then go right (north) on SR 166 three miles to Gallatin's estate.

LEWIS' 1803 ROUTE TO PITTSBURGH

"I shall set out myself in the course of an hour, taking the route of Charlestown, Frankfort, Uniontown and Redstone old fort to Pittsburgh, at which place I shall most probably arrive on the 15th."

—at Harpers Ferry, Meriwether Lewis to President Thomas Jefferson, July 8, 1803
Letters of the Lewis and Clark Expedition

FOLLOWING LEWIS' ROUTE TODAY ON OLD ROADS

- TO CHARLESTOWN WV

From Harpers Ferry take US 340 7 miles southwest to Charles Town.

- TO FRANKFORT (FT ASHBY WV)

Continue south on US 340 12 miles to SR-7 (Harry Byrd Hwy) at Berryville. Go west on SR 7 for 11 miles to Winchester. At Braddock St go 2 blocks south to US 50. Go 42 miles on US 50 (Northwestern Pike) to SR 28 (North High St) in the town of Romney. Go 14 miles north on SR 28 to Fort Ashby WV (old Frankfort).

- TO UNIONTOWN PA

From Fort Ashby, continue north 13 miles on SR 28 and CR 12 to Cumberland Maryland. Cumberland is a historic old town with 27 sites listed on the National Register. It was the original start of the National Road, now called US-40. The path of the old National Road, US-40 Alternate, runs parallel to I-68/US 40 from Cumberland at I-68 Exit 43 west to I-68 Exit 14. Highway historians may want to drive the US 40 Alternate route, the beginning of the first interstate highway in the US.

At Exit 14, US 40 leaves the interstate and heads north through the beautiful Laurel Highlands. Fort Necessity is 21 miles north at Farmington PA. It is 11 miles from Fort Necessity to Uniontown. Uniontown, the county seat of Fayette County, was founded on July 4,1776.

- TO REDSTONE OLD FORT (BROWNSVILLE PA)

13 miles southeast of Uniontown on US 40.

- TO PITTSBURGH

Cross the Monongahela River at Brownsville and take Mon-Fayette Expressway, 22 miles to SR 51 (the Pittsburgh Road). Take SR 51 north 13 miles to I-279, the beltway around downtown Pittsburgh. Go right (north) 3 miles on I-279 across the river to Point State Park, where the Monongahela joins the Alleghany River to form the beginning of the Ohio River.

Old Roads to Pittsburgh

Conestoga Wagons were painted blue with red wheels. Pulled by 6-8 Conestoga horses, they averaged 15 miles a day and carried up to 6000 pounds.

HISTORIC HIGHWAYS

There were two roads to Pittsburgh in 1803. Lewis went by horseback on Braddock's Road, (also called the Cumberland Road because it went through Cumberland, MD). His two wagon drivers either took this road or the wagon road known as Forbes Road. One wagon load of goods came from Philadelphia via the Lancaster Turnpike. The 62 mile turnpike, paved with stone and gravel from Philadelphia to Lancaster, was the only paved road in the entire United States. When the driver arrived at Harpers Ferry he didn't have enough room to carry the additional supplies. Lewis hired a second wagon and driver from nearby Frederick MD.

Braddock's Road (US-40) and Forbes Road (US-30) both started as military roads during the French and Indian War (1754-63). They are among the most historic highways in the United States. Modern travelers can scarcely imagine how difficult and dangerous travel was in the old days.

Braddock's Road, US-40

In 1753 Braddock's Road was laid out by 21 year old George Washington. He was following a path from Cumberland to the Forks of the Ohio River marked out by the Delaware Indian Chief Nemacolin. Washington, who was a military aide to the British governor of Virginia, delivered a warning to the French military commander to get out of the Ohio Valley.

In 1754, as a young lieutenant colonel, Washington commanded two companies of soldiers building Braddock's Road. When they killed the leader of a French military expedition, Jumonville, it was the start of the war between Britain and France and their Indian allies for control of the North American continent.

Washington built Fort Necessity, planning to attack the French Fort Duquesne at the Forks on the Ohio (today's Pittsburgh). However, he was forced to surrender the fort after it was attacked by the French. It was the only surrender in Washington's military career. General Edward Braddock, Commander of British forces in North America continued work on Washington's Road. Braddock, who was killed in a major battle defeat in 1755, is buried at Fort Necessity.

Forbes Road, US-30

In 1758, General John Forbes built a new military road from Bedford, Pennsylvania to the Forks of the Ohio. Forbes Road became the main wagon road to the West, carrying freight and settlers to the Ohio River. Today, US-30 and parts of I-76, follow the same route as the old Pennsylvania wagon road.

The National Road, US-40

Albert Gallatin promoted the idea of a national road, the first interstate highway, for the purpose of western expansion and economic development. He was Secretary of the Treasury under Presidents Jefferson and Madison. Gallatin was a Swiss emigrant who became a congressman from western Pennsylvania.

Financed by the sale of western lands, the National Road ran parallel to Braddock's Road from Cumberland, Maryland to Uniontown, Pennsylvania. From there it headed west to Wheeling, West Virginia, rather than north to Pittsburgh. It was a natural shortcut to the Ohio River, used by many pioneers who traveled by flatboat down the river. Built between 1811-1838, the National Road eventually connected Baltimore, Maryland to Vandalia, Illinois. It later became part of the transcontinental US Highway 40 and Interstate 68. The National Road Zane Grey Museum is located in Zanesville, Ohio.

■ Roads and Highways:
www.route40.net
www.pahighways.com
www.nps.gov.fone./natlroad.htm
www.ohiohistory.org/places/natlroad
www.nationalroadpa.org
www.historicnationalroad.org

■ Lewis's Route:
www.nps.gov/hafe/lewis/ travel-route
www.lewisandclark.net/horseride/lewis.html

59 ELLICOTT HOUSE—LANCASTER PA

Meriwether Lewis studied celestial navigation with Andrew Ellicott here. Another Ellicott house museum is located in Natchez, Mississippi.

■ Open 9-3, Mon-Fri. Home of the Historic Preservation Trust of Lancaster Co, 123 N Prince St. (717) 291-5861 www.lancasterpa.net

60 OLD BEDFORD VILLAGE AND FORT BEDFORD MUSEUM—BEDFORD PA

Over 30 original and reconstructed log homes and shops. Colonial crafts and living history. The Museum is a blockhouse structure on Forbes Road (now Pitt Street).

■ Village open daily 9-5 (except Weds)from Memorial Day to Labor Day. Open Sept and Oct, Thurs–Sun, 9–5. Admission $8 adults, $7 seniors, $4 students, under 6 free.
(800) 238-4347 www.oldbedfordvillage.com

■ Museum is open daily June–August 10–5; May, Sept and Oct 1–5 (closed Tuesday). Admission $4
(814) 623-8891 www.bedfordcounty.net

61 FORT LIGONIER—LIGONIER PA

Reconstructed French and Indian War fort (1758-66), the finest of its kind.

■ Open daily May 1-Oct.31, Mon-Sat, 10-4:30 Admission: $6.75 adult, $3.75 (6-14)
www.fortligonier.org (724) 238-9701

62 FORT NECESSITY BATTLEFIELD NATIONAL HISTORIC SITE FARMINGTON PA

Visitor center, reconstructed fort, Mount Washington Tavern, General Braddock's grave, and Jumonville Glen. 11 miles southeast of Uniontown, featuring the French and Indian War and the National Road.

■ Open daily 9-5. Closed federal holidays. Grounds open sunrise-sunset. Admission $3; under 16, free. (724) 329-5805
www.nps.gov/fone

63 NEMACOLIN CASTLE—BROWNSVILLE PA

22-room house museum (1789–1852) on Front St overlooking the Monongahela River; built on the site of a trading post visited by Lewis on his way to Pittsburgh. Redstone Old Fort was named for an old Indian Mound fortress. The Clark family stayed here in the winter of 1784-85, while en route to their new home in Louisville KY.

■ June, July, Aug: open daily (except Mon.) 11-5.Easter–mid Oct: weekends 11-5.
(724) 785-6882 www.nemacolincastle.org

64 GALLATIN'S FRIENDSHIP HILL ESTATE NATIONAL HISTORIC LANDMARK POINT MARION PA

Exhibits highlight the life and many accomplishments of Albert Gallatin, Secretary of the Treasury from 1801-1814. (See also Sewall-Belmont house in Washington D C)

■ Open daily 9–5. Closed federal holidays. Free. Bookstore, self-guided audio house tour.
(724) 725-9190 www.nps.gov/frhi

Region One: References

LEWIS AND CLARK

CONTRIBUTIONS OF PHILADELPHIA TO LEWIS AND CLARK HISTORY (with map) by Paul Russell Cartwright. Annotated map by Frank Muhly. Philadelphia Chapter, Lewis and Clark Trail Heritage Foundation, 6010 Cannon Hill Rd. Suite 202, Fort Washington PA 19034-1802

DEAR BROTHER: LETTERS OF WILLIAM CLARK TO JONATHAN CLARK Edited and with an Introduction by James Holmberg. Foreward by James Ronda. Filson Historical Society and Yale Univ Press (2002)

EXPLORATIONS INTO THE WORLD OF LEWIS AND CLARK: ESSAYS FROM THE PAGES OF WE PROCEEDED ON, THE QUARTERLY JOURNAL OF THE LEWIS AND CLARK TRAIL HERITAGE FOUNDATION (Volume 1) edited by Robert A. Saindon. Digital Scanning Inc. (2003) www.digitalscanning.com

FROM SEA TO SHINING SEA by James Alexander Thom. Random House (mass market, 1986). Story of the Clark family.

GEORGE ROGERS CLARK AND THE WAR IN THE WEST by Lowell Harrison. Univ Press of KY (1976)

A HISTORY OF THE LEWIS AND CLARK JOURNALS by Paul Russell Cartwright. Univ of OK Press (1976)

IN SEARCH OF YORK: THE SLAVE WHO WENT TO THE PACIFIC WITH LEWIS AND CLARK by Robert B. Betts. James J. Holmberg (epilogue) University Press of Colorado (2000)

LETTERS OF THE LEWIS AND CLARK EXPEDITION WITH RELATED DOCUMENTS 1783-1854 by Donald Jackson. Univ of IL, 2 vol (2nd ed, 1979)

MERIWETHER LEWIS: A BIOGRAPHY by Richard Dillon. Great Westerm Books (2nd ed, 2003).

UNDAUNTED COURAGE: MERIWETHER LEWIS, THOMAS JEFFERSON AND THE OPENING OF THE AMERICAN WEST by Stephen A. Ambrose. Touchstone Edition/Simon and Schuster (1997).

THE VISITS OF LEWIS AND CLARK TO FINCASTLE, VIRGINIA: WHY WAS A MONTANA RIVER NAMED FOR A FINCASTLE GIRL? by Gene Crotty. The History Museum and Historical Society of Western Virginia. P O Box 1904, Roanoke VA 24011 (2003) www.history-museum.org (540) 342-5770

WILDERNESS JOURNEY: THE LIFE OF WILLIAM CLARK by William Foley. Univ of MO Press (2004)

WILLIAM CLARK AND THE SHAPING OF THE WEST by Landon Jones. Farrar, Strauss and Giroux (2004)

HISTORY AND BIOGRAPHY

AMERICAN SPHINX: THE CHARACTER OF THOMAS JEFFERSON by Joseph Ellis. Vintage Books (1998)

BOUND AWAY: VIRGINIA AND THE WESTWARD MOVEMENT by David Hackett Fischer and James Kelly. Univ Press of VA (2000)

FACING EAST FROM INDIAN COUNTRY: A NATIVE HISTORY OF EARLY AMERICA by Daniel Richter. Harvard Univ Press (2001)

FOLLOW THE RIVER by James Alexander Thom. An American classic. Ballantine Book (1981; mass market, 1983)

FOUNDING BROTHERS: THE REVOLUTIONARY GENERATION by Joseph Ellis, Vintage Books (2002)

FRENCH AND INDIAN WAR 1754-1763: THE IMPERIAL STRUGGLE FOR NORTH AMERICA by Seymour L. Schwartz. Castle Books (1994)

JAMES MADISON: THE FOUNDING FATHER by Robert Rutland, Univ of MO Press (reprint, 1997)

JAMES MONROE: THE QUEST FOR NATIONAL IDENTITY by Harry Ammon. Univ Press of VA (reprint, 2001)

JEFFERSON AND MONTICELLO: THE BIOGRAPHY OF A BUILDER by Jack McLaughlin. Henry Holt and Co (1988)

MANY THOUSANDS GONE: THE FIRST TWO CENTURIES OF SLAVERY IN NORTH AMERICA by Ira Berlin. The Belknap Press of Harvard University Press (1998)

MR. JEFFERSON'S LOST CAUSE: LAND, FARMERS, SLAVERY AND THE LOUISIANA PURCHASE by Roger G. Kennedy. Oxford Univ Press (2003)

NOTES ON THE STATE OF VIRGINIA by Thomas Jefferson. First published in France 1785. Penguin Classics (1999)

A WILDERNESS SO IMMENSE: LOUISIANA PURCHASE AND THE DESTINY OF AMERICA by John Kukla. Alfred A. Knopf (2003)

A YEAR AT MONTICELLO-1795 by Donald Jackson. Fulcrum, Inc., 16100 Table Mountain Parkway, Golden CO 80403 (1989)

ROADS, TRAILS AND MAPS

GATEWAY: DR. THOMAS WALKER AND THE OPENING OF KENTUCKY by David M. Burns. Photographs by Adam Jones. Introduction by Thomas D. Clark. Bell County Historical Society, P O Box 1344, Middlesboro KY 40965 (2000) Story of Cumberland Gap.

THE GREAT WAGON ROAD: FROM PHILADELPHIA TO THE SOUTH. HOW SCOTCH-IRISH AND GERMANICS SETTLED THE UPLANDS by Park Rouse, Jr., The Dietz Press, 1004 N Thompson St, Richmond VA 23230 (reprint, 2001)

LEWIS AND CLARK: THE MAPS OF EXPLORATION 1507-1814 UNIVERSITY OF VIRGINIA LIBRARY. Foreword by John Logan Allen. Howell Press (2002)

MAP GUIDE TO AMERICAN MIGRATION ROUTES, 1735 -1815 by William Dollarhide. Heritage Quest, P O Box 329, Bountiful UT 84011 (1999)

TRAVELING THE NATIONAL ROAD: ACROSS THE CENTURIES ON AMERICA'S FIRST HIGHWAY by Merritt Herley. Overlook Press, Lewis Hollow Rd, Woodstock NY 12498 (1990)

THE WILDERNESS ROAD by Robert L. Kincaid. Lincoln Memorial University, Harrogate TN 37752 (7th edition,1999)

MISCELLANEOUS

LIBRARY OF CONGRESS: AMERICAN MEMORY, HISTORICAL COLLECTIONS FOR THE NATIONAL DIGITAL LIBRARY.
www.loc.gov Search History, *American Notes:* Travels in America, 1750-1920; History, *Jefferson, Thomas: Papers, 1606-1827. Travels in America* contains the rare *Early Western Travels* series edited by Reuben Gold Thwaites and the 1814 *Lewis and Clark Journals*, plus many more treasures.

LEWIS AND CLARK TRAIL HERITAGE FOUNDATION
www.lewisandclark.org
P O Box 3434, Great Falls MT 59403.
(888) 701-3434

PHILADELPHIA CHAPTER, LCTHF
www.lewisandclarkphila.org

HOMEFRONT CHAPTER, LCTHF (CHARLOTTESVILLE, VA)
www.lewisandclarkeast.org

REGION TWO
PITTSBURGH TO CINCINNATI

2

■ Pittsburgh ■ Around the Bend to Wellsburg

■ Wheeling and Moundsville ■ Marietta and Parkersburg

■ Alternate Routes Across Ohio ■ River Roads to Cincinnati

■ Lexington & Frankfort ■ Old Wilderness Roads

1. Triple Towers, Frankfort KY 2. Duquesne Incline, Pittsburgh PA 3. Broken Peace Pipe, Tecumseh Outdoor Drama, Chillicothe OH 4. Moonrise, Octagon Earthworks, Newark OH 5. Campus Martius Museum, Marietta OH 6. Big Bone Lick, Covington KY 7. Blennerhassett Mansion, Parkersburg WV 8. Ohio River, Marietta OH

Credits: (1) Gene Burch; (2) Pittsburgh Convention and Visitors Bureau (3) Joe E Murray
(4) Center for the Electronic Reconstruction of Historical and Archaeological Sites
(7) West Virginia Tourism

2

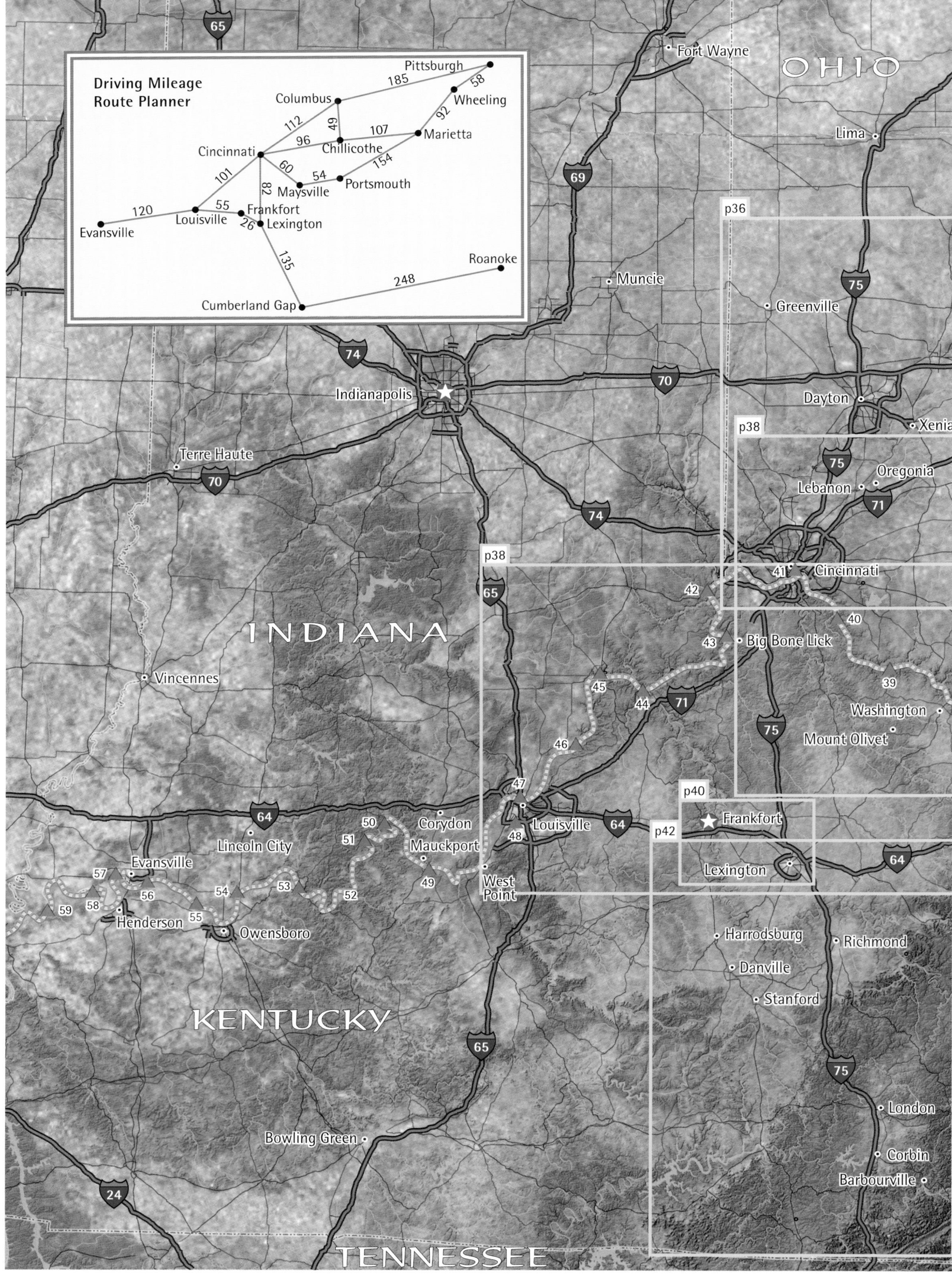
Driving Mileage
Route Planner
Pittsburgh
185
58
Columbus
Wheeling
112
49
92
107
96
Marietta
Cincinnati
Chillicothe
154
60
54
101
Portsmouth
82
Maysville
120
55
Frankfort
Louisville
26
Lexington
Evansville
135
Roanoke
248
Cumberland Gap
Fort Wayne
OHIO
Lima
Muncie
Greenville
Indianapolis
Dayton
Xenia
Terre Haute
Oregonia
Lebanon
Cincinnati
INDIANA
Big Bone Lick
Vincennes
Washington
Mount Olivet
Frankfort
Louisville
Corydon
Lincoln City
Mauckport
Evansville
Lexington
West Point
Henderson
Owensboro
Harrodsburg
Richmond
Danville
Stanford
KENTUCKY
London
Corbin
Bowling Green
Barbourville
TENNESSEE
p36
p38
p40
p42

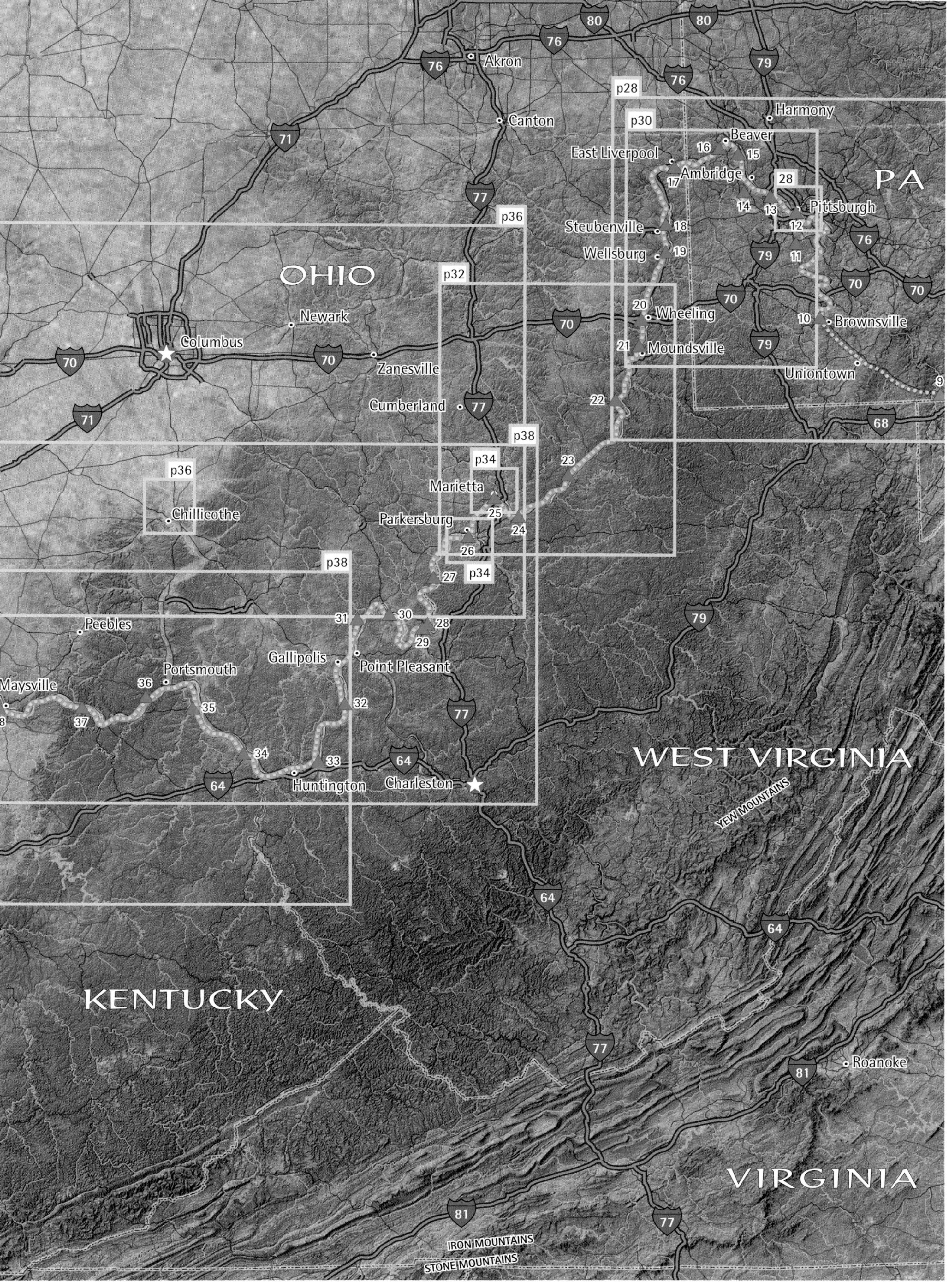
OHIO
PA
WEST VIRGINIA
KENTUCKY
VIRGINIA
Akron
Canton
Harmony
Beaver
East Liverpool
Ambridge
Pittsburgh
Steubenville
Wellsburg
Wheeling
Moundsville
Brownsville
Uniontown
Columbus
Newark
Zanesville
Cumberland
Chillicothe
Marietta
Parkersburg
Peebles
Gallipolis
Point Pleasant
Portsmouth
Maysville
Huntington
Charleston
Roanoke
YEW MOUNTAINS
IRON MOUNTAINS
STONE MOUNTAINS
p28
p30
p28
p36
p32
p38
p34
p36
p34
p38

2

"View of Pittsburg in 1796 from General Collot's Voyage in North America in 1796" from *The Ohio River, A Course of Empire* by Archer B. Hulbert (1906)

"Fort Duquesne from an old print" from *The Ohio River, A Course of Empire* by Archer B. Hulbert (1906). The French Fort (1754-59) was apparently built on a mound. It was replaced by the British Fort Pitt (1769-1772). Both were located at "The Point" in Pittsburgh. Fort Pitt remained in service as an American fort until it was demolished in 1792.

History and Mystery On the Beautiful Ohio

Pittsburgh

Meriwether Lewis spent six frustrating weeks in Pittsburgh waiting for the keelboat to be built in the summer of 1803. The only bright spot was that he acquired his faithful companion, Seaman, the Newfoundland dog who went to the Pacific Ocean and back with him.

The small town on the western frontier was familiar territory to him. He had come there as a 20 year old volunteer in the Virginia militia in 1794. The militia was called up to put down the taxpayer's revolt known as the "Whiskey Rebellion." Westerners were protesting a 25% tax on the manufacture of distilled spirits which was being levied to pay off the national war debt. Turning corn into whiskey was the most efficient way to send produce back East across the Allegheny Mountains.

Lewis joined the Legion of the United States Army in 1795, serving under General Anthony Wayne. He then became an army paymaster in the newly established regular army, traveling throughout the region. He first met William Clark at the Treaty of Greenville in 1795, which ended the Ohio Valley Indian Wars.

Now Lewis was on his way to meet Clark at the Falls of the Ohio. He had invited his friend to serve as co-captain on the expedition to the Pacific Ocean. Clark's letter accepting his invitation arrived on July18th. Clark wrote, "I will chearfully join you in an "official Charrector" as mentioned your letter....This is an undertak ing fraited with many difeculties, but My friend I do assure you that no man lives whith whome I would perfor to undertake Such a Trip etc. as yourself." Clark was living with his brother George Rogers Clark at Clarksville, Indiana at the Falls of the Ohio. He would look for good men to recruit for the Discovery Corps, while waiting for Lewis.

Lewis had arrived in Pittsburgh on July 15th, expecting the boat would be ready on July 20th. The boat was not finished until August 31st. In the meanwhile the Ohio River was low and getting lower. He wrote to Clark that the boat builders were a "set of most incorrigible drunkards" that he could not influence by either threats or entreaties.

On the Ohio

By the time he set out on August 31st with a crew of 11 men, the river was so low that old timers said it couldn't be done. They had lightened the load by sending as much as possible by wagon to Wheeling, West Virginia and by purchasing a second boat, a pirogue.

At times they had to lift and drag the two boats over bars of small stones and driftwood called "riffles," in water that was not more than six inches deep. When it was too much for the men, he hired horse and ox teams. Lewis wrote to Jefferson that he found horses and oxen "the most efficient sailors in the present state of navigation, altho' they may be considered somewhat clumsey." They encountered as many as five riffles in a single day. Lewis added that "The river is lower than it has ever been known by the oldest settler in the country."

The Three Boats

They reached Wheeling on September 8th, "much fatigued." Many travelers on the river started at Wheeling, as the river was deep enough for travel in all seasons of the year from this point on. Lewis purchased another pirogue. The two pirogues have gone down in history as the white pirogue and the red pirogue ("peerow"). It is not known which one was purchased at Wheeling. The goods sent down from Pittsburgh were transferred to the new boat and another hand was hired.

Pirogues were oversized rowboats, with masts for sails. The white pirogue rowed with six oars, and the red with seven. The keelboat was 55 feet long and 8 feet wide with a cabin in the rear for the captains. It rowed with 22 oars, and had a 32 foot sailing mast.

The boats were mostly rowed, but they were also pulled by a cordelle rope, and poled. If the wind was right, they were sailed. The long cordelle rope was attached to the mast and threaded through a ring on the bow ("bauw"), or front of the boat. The men walked along the water's edge pulling, or "cordelling," the boats. The keelboat was poled with 20 foot poles, with the men working in unison. They would walk towards the stern, or back of the boat, pushing against the river bottom with the poles, using shoulder pads, propelling it forward.

HARMAN AND MARGARET BLENNERHASSETT: These aristocratic adventurers lived in a mansion on Blennerhassett Island near Parkersburg WV

Blennerhassett Mansion
Steve Shaluta, WV Tourism

AARON BURR: Burr was Vice President of the United States during the time Meriwether Lewis was Jefferson's private secretary, or assistant.

Portraits from *The Ohio River, A Course of Empire* by Archer B Hulbert (1906)

2

Ancient Mysteries: Moundsville WV

Lewis stopped at Moundsville, West Virginia on September 10th to investigate Grave Creek Mound. The Ohio River Valley was filled with ancient mounds and complex earthwork patterns—over ten thousand of them across the landscape. What happened to the builders is a mystery. Many still remain, including the "Sacra Via" avenues and mounds at Marietta; the Hopewell and Serpent Mounds in central Ohio; and the Great Circle and Octagon Earthworks at Newark, Ohio.

They were so commonplace, that unless there was something special about them, they weren't mentioned by early travelers. Most were destroyed. Many cities have been built where mounds and earthworks were once located. They were used as burial places, ceremonial sites, astronomical alignment centers, and road networks. Modern scientists have learned that they were precisely engineered.

Political Intrigue

On September 15th, Lewis passed a palatial mansion on an island in the Ohio River without any comment in his journal. It was the grandest home in the Ohio River Valley, the home of Harman Blennerhassett, an eccentric Irish aristocrat and his young wife, Margaret. Three years later, in December, 1806, as Lewis and Clark returned to Washington, the Burr-Wilkinson conspiracy would come to an end on Blennerhassett Island.

Aaron Burr, the Vice President of the United States during Jefferson's first term in office, was at the center of intrigue and scandal during the years that Lewis and Clark were on their expedition. On July 11,1804, Burr killed the Treasurer of the United States, Alexander Hamilton, in a duel. Duels were common (though illegal), and Burr never faced prosecution. His political career, however, was ended.

Conspiracy on Blennerhassett Island

Burr then entered into a conspiracy in 1805 with the Commanding General of the United States Army, James Wilkinson, who was also serving as the first Governor of Louisiana Territory in New Orleans. The two men plotted to invade Texas (then controlled by Spain), and perhaps to conquer the silver mines of Mexico and set up an independent government in the American West. It was publicly charged by Wilkinson's enemies at the time that he was in the secret pay of Spain. (This was conclusively proven over a hundred years later when historians examined Spanish records.) They recruited young men from good families to go on this "filibustering" expedition. The Blennerhassetts supplied funds to build flatboats at Marietta.

Rumors of the impending expedition circulated throughout the nation. True to form, Wilkinson betrayed Burr to Jefferson, and members of the expedition were arrested on Blennerhassett Island. In 1807, Lewis attended Burr's trial for treason in Richmond, Virginia as an observer for President Jefferson. Burr was acquitted, and Wilkinson was never charged. Lewis then went on to assume his office as Governor of Louisiana Territory in St. Louis, where one of his duties was to remove suspected "Burrites" from positions of influence. Wilkinson, while continuing to serve his country, survived one court martial, two congressional investigations, and many attacks on his reputation.

Big Bone Lick—Covington KY

Lewis's journal stops on September 18th at Letart's Falls, near the bend where the Ohio River takes a westward course. He resumed writing again on November 11th at Fort Massac. He spent almost a week in the Cincinnati area, where he visited Big Bone Lick to collect fossils to send back to President Jefferson. The fossil bed was an old salt lick, where animals had come to find salt for over ten thousand years, and Indians had come to hunt them.

Giant mastodon and mammoth bones were found here. Big Bone Lick was internationally famous, and the ancient elephants were a matter of national pride. Charles Willson Peale had a mastodon skeleton on exhibit in his museum. George Rogers Clark had a mastodon bone bench on his front porch overlooking the Falls of the Ohio. Jefferson even hoped that Lewis might find elephants still living out west. In later years travelers on the Oregon Trail would still claim they were "going to see the elephant" when they went out west.

2

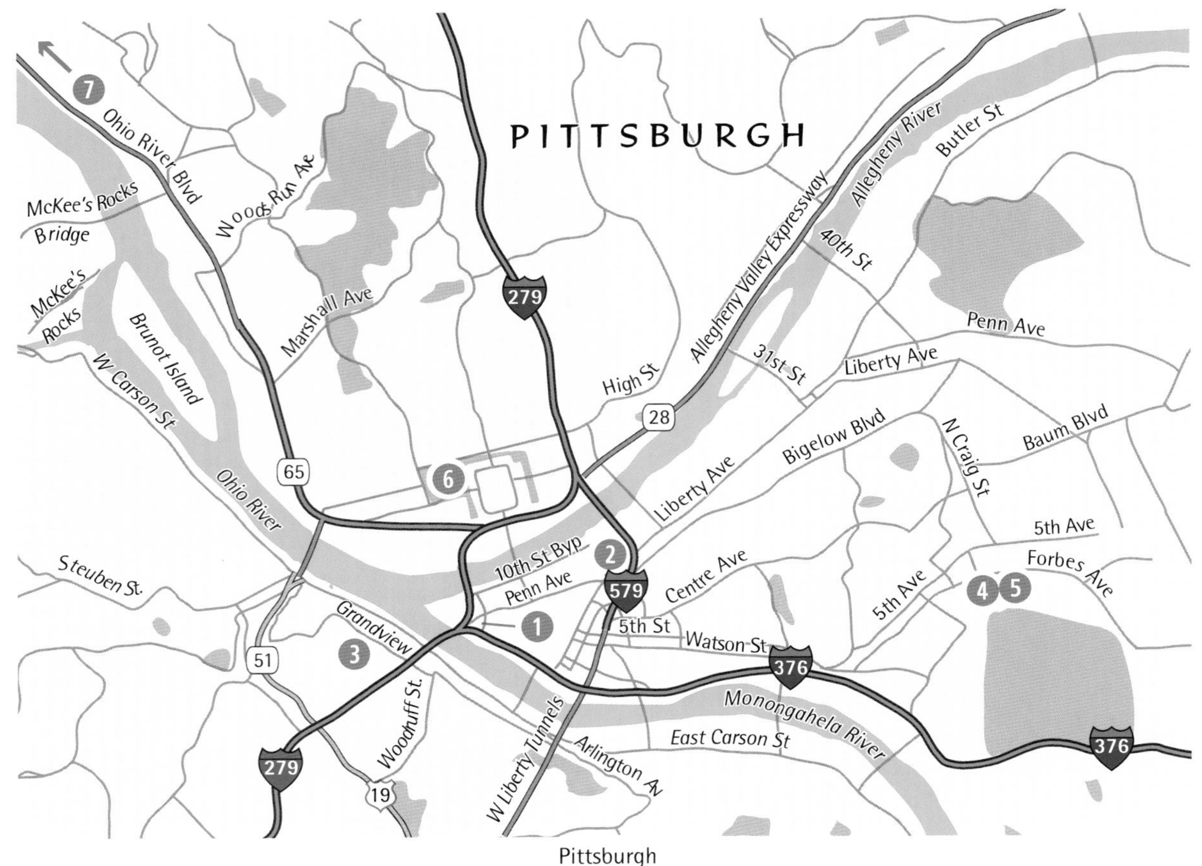

Pittsburgh

> Dear Sir,
> It was not untill 7 O'Clock on the morning of the 31st Ultmo. that my boat was completed, she was instantly loaded, and at 10. A.M. on the same day I left Pittsburgh, where I had been most shamefully detained by the unpardonable negligence of my boat-builder.
>
> —Lewis to President Jefferson from Wheeling WV Sept. 8, 1803 *Letters of the Lewis and Clark Expedition*

Pittsburgh Area

1 FORT PITT MUSEUM
Located in Point State Park at 100 Commonwealth Place
From the *EAST* take I-376 W to the Stanwix St Exit. From the *SOUTH* or *WEST* take I-279 N to the Boulevard of the Allies Exit. From the *NORTH* take I-279 S to I-376 E then take the Stanwix St Exit.

2 HEINZ CENTER
1212 Smallman Street
From the *EAST* take I-376 to the Grant St Exit. Take Grant St to 11th St. Turn left, go two blocks to Smallman St. Turn right. From the *NORTH* take I-279 South to I-376 West then follow the *EAST* directions. From the *SOUTH* take I-279 North to I-376 W. Then follow the *east* directions.

3 DUQUESNE INCLINE
1197 West Carson Street
From *DOWNTOWN PITTSBURGH* take I-279 South acoss the Fort Pitt Bridge; immediately after crossing the river take the West End Exit onto West Carson St. The Incline is less than a block west of the off-ramp. Free parking is nearby.

4 5 CARNEGIE MUSEUMS OF ART AND NATURAL HISTORY
4400 Forbes Avenue
From the *WEST* or *EAST* take I-376 to Forbes Ave Exit. Follow Forbes Av east to the museums. From the *NORTH* take I-279 S to the Monroeville Exit. Then take Boulevard of the Allies to Forbes Av. Follow Forbes Av east to the museums. From the *SOUTH* take I-279 N to I-376; then follow *NORTH* directions.

6 NATIONAL AVIARY.
Arch St and North Avenue
From the *WEST* take I-376 to I-279 N. Take the North Shore Exit. Turn right onto Allegheny Ave. Go to Western Ave, turn right Go to Arch St, turn left. From the *EAST* take I-376 to I-279 N. Then follow the *WEST* directions. From the *NORTH* take I-279 S. Take the East St Exit and turn right onto North Ave. Go west to Arch St and turn left. From the *SOUTH* take I-279 N to the North Shore Exit. Turn right onto Allegheny Ave. Go to Western Ave, turn right. Go to Arch St, turn left.

7 CARNEGIE SCIENCE CENTER
One Allegheny Avenue
From the *NORTH* take I-279 S to the North Shore Exit. Take North Shore Drive to Allegheny Avenue. Turn left. From the *SOUTH* take I-279 N to the North Shore Exit. Take North Shore Drive to Allegheny Avenue. Turn left. From the *EAST* take I-376 W to I-279 N to the North Shore Exit. Take North Shore Drive to Allegheny Avenue. Turn left. From the *NORTH* take I-279 N to the North Shore Exit. Take North Shore Drive to Allegheny Avenue. Turn left.

The fountain identifies Point State Park at the Pittsburgh Triangle, where the Allegheny (on the left) and the Monongahela (on the right) unite to form the beginning of the Ohio River. The 1877 Duquesne Incline cable car is seen on Mount Washington. Pittsburgh Convention and Visitors Bureau

Keelboat and re-enactors from St. Charles MO at Pierre SD

2

Pittsburgh

1 FORT PITT MUSEUM IN POINT STATE PARK

Fort Pitt Museum is located at the junction of the three rivers, inside the recreated Monongahela Bastion. Many dramatic events for control of the North American continent took place at this strategic location. Dioramas and exhibits tell the story of the French and Indian War, the American Revolution and early Pittsburgh during the years Meriwether Lewis was here. The Fort was dismantled in 1792, but the historic Point symbolizes and commemorates the expedition's departure in1803.

■ Open Weds-Sun, 9-5. Admission: $5 adults, $4 seniors, $2 ages 6-17.
(412) 281-9284 www.fortpittmuseum.com

2 HEINZ REGIONAL HISTORY CENTER

The Senator John Heinz Regional History Center is Pennsylvania's largest history museum, and operates in conjunction with the Smithsonian. A five story addition opened in 2004 featuring the Western Pennsylvania Sports Museum, traveling exhibits and more. The museum has a 1790's log cabin, and many other exhibits telling the story of more than 250 years of western Pennsylvania life.

■ Open daily 10-5. Admission $7.50 adults, $6 seniors,$5 with student i d,$3.50 ages 6-18.
(412) 454-6000 www.pghhistory.org

3 DUQUESNE INCLINE

The Duquesne Incline has provided safe and reliable public transportation since 1877. Utilizing two 1877 cable cars, the Incline is a *working museum* which serves the Duquesne Heights and Mount Washington neighborhoods of Pittsburgh. The funicular railway works on the principle of balance: one cable car is going up the mountain, while the other is going down. *USA Weekend* Magazine rates the view from the observation deck, as the second most beautiful view in America. The Upper Station has exhibits on the history of the Incline and other funicular railways around the world.

■ Open Mon-Sat, 5:30 AM—12:45 AM; Sundays and holidays, 7 AM—12:45 AM. Admission: $1.75 adults, 85 cents ages 6-11. Seniors are free except 7-8 AM and 4:30-5:30 PM.
(412) 381-1665 www.incline.cc

4 5 CARNEGIE MUSEUMS OF ART AND NATURAL HISTORY

Two museums—located right next to each for the price of one—showcase the collections of Pittsburgh steel magnate Andrew Carnegie, one of the world's great collectors and philanthropists. The Carnegie Museum of Art has a Hall of Architecture and Hall of Sculpture replicating the Parthenon. Its art collection includes film and video; late 19th century American Art; French Impressionist and Post Impressionist art; and decorative arts. The Carnegie Museum of Natural History's famous collection of dinosaurs has been newly remounted in Dinosaur Hall. There are many hands on displays the whole family can enjoy.

■ Open Tues-Sat, 10-5; Sunday 12-5. Closed Monday. Admission $10 adults, $7 seniors, $6 with student i d, and ages 3-18.
(412) 622-3131 for both museums
www.cmoa.org www.carnegiemnh.org

6 NATIONAL AVIARY

The nation's only National Aviary has interactive wetlands and tropical rain forest walk through exhibits. Visitors may get up close to the birds, talk to a parrot, and walk with a penguin. Over 600 exotic and endangered birds in their natural habitats. Daily tropical rain storm at 12:30 PM. Feeding time at 1:30.

■ Open daily 9-5. except Christmas. Admission: $6 adults, $5 seniors, $4.50 ages 2-12.
(412) 323-7235 www.aviary.org

7 CARNEGIE SCIENCE CENTER

Take the time to explore one of America's top science museums, with Omnimax Theaters and Laser Light music shows. The Sports Works Center is the world's largest science of sport exhibition. Bring your running shoes and camera. The MovieMaking exhibit highlights movie making and the careers associated with it. The Henry Buhl Planetarium and Observatory is one of the world's most sophisticated interactive planetariums. The Exploration Station and Miniature Railroad and Village are fun for all ages.

■ Open Sun-Fri, 10-5. Saturday, 10-7. Admission: $14 adults, $10 seniors, and ages 3-12. Additional charge for Omnimax and laser shows.
(412) 237-3400 www.carnegiesciencecenter.org

FIRST DAY ADVENTURES

Lewis left Pittsburgh on August 31, 1803 with "a party of 11 hands 7 of which are soldiers, a pilot and three young men on trial they having proposed to go with me throughout the voyage." It is thought that one of these young men was George Shannon, age 18, who became the youngest member of the permanent party. The keelboat was accompanied by a pirogue, or small boat, which Lewis purchased to share the load.

Brunot's Island Airgun

When the boats arrived at Brunot's Island Lewis stopped to say goodbye to friends. After demonstrating his new airgun, Lewis loaned it to someone who accidentally shot a woman bystander—"we were all in the greatest consternation supposed she was dead [but] in a minute she revived to our enespressable satisfaction."

McKee's Rock Riffle

The next adventure was at McKee's Rocks where they encountered their first riffle; and had to carry the 55 foot wooden keelboat and the pirogue 30 yards over the riffle. It was too late in the year to be traveling on the Ohio. They passed two more riffles the first day. Lewis wrote in his journal "the river is extreemly low; said to be more so than it has been known for four years."

(See map opposite for Brunot's Island and McKee's Rocks)

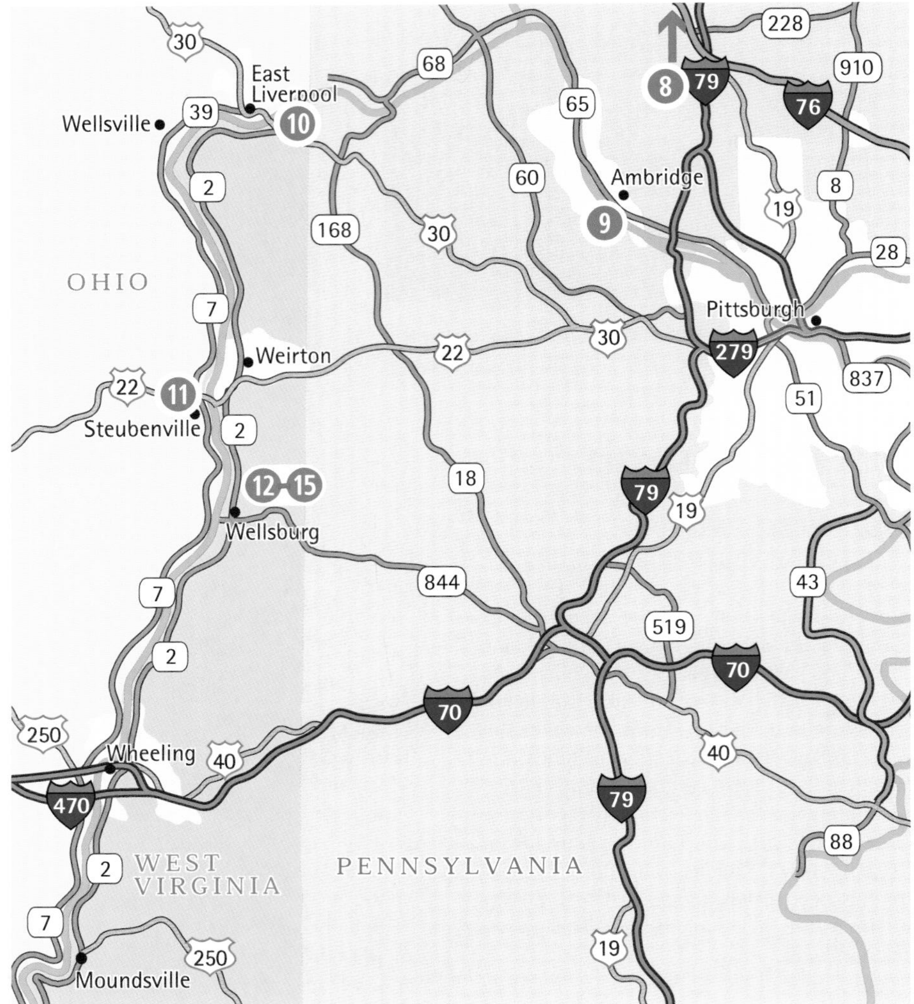

Around the Bend to Wellsburg

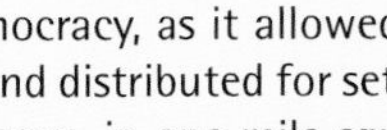

Point of Beginning

The U S land survey system is considered one of the cornerstones of American democracy, as it allowed land to be sold and distributed for settlement, sight unseen, in one mile square section units. Prior to this land sales were determined by "metes and bounds," that is by measuring boundaries from local landmarks on the actual site.

Northwest Territory

The first U S land survey in 1785 divided the land of eastern Ohio into seven ranges, with rectangular grid lines originating at the Point of Beginning Marker.

The entire Northwest Territory was won for the United States by the daring exploits of William Clark's older brother General George Rogers Clark and his volunteer militia in 1779 during the War for Independence. After the war, Revolutionary War veterans were given land grants in recognition of their military service. Both Marietta, Ohio and Clarksville, Indiana were settled by military veterans.

Lewis and Clark

When Lewis and Clark took latitude and longitude measurements at river mouths and significant landmarks, they were collecting the data that would enable the government to continue the gridlines across the continent. The straight line roads and state borders of the modern Lewis and Clark National Historic Trail are a reminder of their initial work as surveyors.

8 HARMONY MUSEUM AND HISTORIC DISTRICT HARMONY PA

218 Mercer Street.

From the *SOUTH* take I-79 N to Exit 87 (Rt. 68). Turn left onto Rte 68. Turn right at Spring St. Go to Mercer St. Turn left. The Museum is just past Main St. From the *NORTH* take I-79 S to Exit 88. Turn right. Go to Mercer Rd. Turn left. Take Mercer Rd to Main St. From the *WEST* take I-76 to I-79 N. then follow *SOUTH* directions. From the *EAST* take I-76 to I-79 N. then follow *SOUTH* directions.

9 OLD ECONOMY VILLAGE AMBRIDGE PA

270 Sixteenth Street.

From the *South* take Rte 65 N. Turn right onto 11th St. Turn left onto Church St. Turn right onto 16th St. Go to Claude St. From the *North* take Rt 65 S. Turn left onto 11th St. Turn left onto Church St. Turn right onto 16th St. Go to Claude St.

10 POINT OF BEGINNING MARKER EAST LIVERPOOL OH

Ohio-Pennsylvania border.

From the *EAST* follow Pennsylvania Route 68 to the state line. From the *WEST* follow Ohio Route 39 to the state line. The marker is on the south side of the highway.

11 OLD FORT STEUBEN AND VISITOR CENTER STEUBENVILLE OH

120 South Third Street.

From the *NORTH* take Ohio Rte 7 South. turn right onto Washington St., Go to 3rd St, turn left. Go past Market St. From the *SOUTH* take Ohio Rte 7 north. turn left onto Washington St., Go to 3rd St, turn left. Go past Market St. From the *east* take US 22 west to Ohio Rte 7. Then follow the *NORTH* directions. From the *WEST* take US 22 East to Ohio Rte 7. Then follow the *NORTH* directions.

12 PATRICK GASS GRAVESITE WELLSBURG WV

23rd Street and Pleasant Avenue.

From Rte 2 head east on 23rd St. Turn left onto Pleasant Avenue.

13 PATRICK GASS BUST WELLSBURG WV

9th Street and Main Street.

From Rte 2 head west on 9th St. past Main St. to the wharf area.

14 BROOKE COUNTY MUSEUM WELLSBURG WV

600 Main Street.

From Rte 2 head west on 6th St to Main St.

15 DROVER'S INN WELLSBURG WV

1001 Washington Pike.

From *Wellsburg* take Rt 27 east for 3.5 miles.

Old Economy Village
Pennsylvania Historical and Museum Commission

Fort Steuben
Old Fort Steuben and Visitor Center

Patrick Gass (1771-1870)
We Proceeeded On, Lewis and Clark Trail Heritage Foundation

2

Around the Bend to Wellsburg

8 HARMONY MUSEUM AND HISTORIC DISTRICT NHL—HARMONY PA

This National Historic Landmark was the first home of the Harmonists, a celibate communal society founded by German immigrants in 1805, who moved to New Harmony, Indiana in 1814. The museum is located in an 1809 warehouse; its exhibits focus on the town's German heritage, and the Harmonist and Mennonite communities which once were located here. Tours are provided by guides in 19th century dress. Exhibits include a gun collection, Native American artifacts, early American furniture, and a wine cellar. Old cemeteries, and several old buildings, including the oldest barn in western Pennsylvania, an 1805 barn, and an early Mennonite meeting house and are part of the historic district.

■ Open daily 1-4. Closed holidays. Free admission.
(888) 821-4822 www.harmonymuseum.org

9 OLD ECONOMY VILLAGE NHL AMBRIDGE PA

The village is a National Historic Landmark, administered by the Pennsylvania Historical and Museum Commission. The Harmonists returned to Pennsylvania and founded their third and final communal village in 1825. It was world famous for both its piety and successful business operations. The substantial buildings of Old Economy include the Museum Building and Feast Hall, Clock and Lock Shop, Communal Kitchen, Society's Store, Mechanics Building, Cabinet Shop and other interesting attractions. The Harmonist Society lasted for 100 years, ending in 1905.

■ Open Tues-Sat 9-5, Sunday noon-5. Closed Mondays and holidays. Admission $7 adults, $6 seniors, and $5 ages 6-17.
(724) 266-4500 www.oldeconomyvillage.org

10 POINT OF BEGINNING MARKER EAST LIVERPOOL, OHIO

The Point of Beginning Marker on the Ohio-Pennsylvania border marks the zero point for the United States Public Land Surveys. The point was determined by Thomas Hutchins, first geographer of the United States, in 1785.

■ Beaver County Historical Research and Landmarks Foundation www.bchrlf.org

11 OLD FORT STEUBEN AND VISITOR CENTER—STEUBENVILLE OH

Fort Steuben was built in 1786 to protect the surveyors who were sent out by the Continental Congress of the United States to map the Northwest Territory—the land which became Ohio, Indiana, Illinois, Michigan, Wisconsin and part of Minnesota. The reconstructed fort depicts the life of the men who opened Northwest Territory for settlement. The Visitor Center houses a museum shop and exhibition hall.

■ Open May-Oct, Mon-Sat 10-4, and Sunday, 11-4. Admission $5 adults, $3 ages 6-12.
(740) 283-1787 www.oldfortsteuben.com

12 PATRICK GASS GRAVESITE WELLSBURG WV

Patrick Gass and his wife are buried in the Brooke County Cemetery. He was one of seven known journal keepers of the expedition; his journal was the first to be published in 1807. Gass was well liked; members of the expedition elected him Sergeant on August 22nd, 1804 at Elk Point after the death of Sgt. Charles Floyd. After the expedition, he settled in Wellsburg, where—except for his service in the War of 1812—he lived for the next 64 years until his death in 1870. He was the longest surviving member of the expedition. The Wellsburg Chamber website has interesting information from local records.

■ (304) 479-2115 www.wellsburgchamber.com

13 PATRICK GASS SCULPTURE BUST WELLSBURG WV

Images of Gass's appearance have survived. In 1859 his biographer and Wellsburg friend, J. G. Jacob described Gass as a sturdy and compact man, who was proud of his ability at age 89 to walk the four miles from his home to Wellsburg "at a pace much faster than men one quarter his age." The sculpture bust, on the Wellsburg wharf across from the County Courthouse, was dedicated during the Lewis and Clark Expedition bicentennial observances in 2003.

■ (304) 479-2115
www.wellsburgchamber.com

14 BROOKE COUNTY MUSEUM WELLSBURG

The county museum on the Wellsburg waterfront is located in a 1797 building originally housing Miller's Tavern and Inn. Patrick Gass was undoubtedly a patron; his friend J. G. Jacob wrote that Gass's robust health could not be attributed to "excessive sobriety" as he was "addicted to a weakness for strong drink."

■ Open April-Oct, Friday and Sunday, 1-5.
(304) 479-2115 www.wellsburgchamber.com

15 DROVER'S INN RESTAURANT AND LODGE— WELLSBURG

Patrick Gass must have also visited here: built in 1848, the three story inn has 16 rooms. It served travelers and drovers, moving their cattle to market. The lodge is an authentically restored 1790 log home adjacent to the inn. The restaurant provides a home-cooked buffet; famous hot wings and sandwiches.

■ Reservations are strongly suggested for the restaurant. Walk-ins are accepted upon availability. Serving Weds-Sat, 5 PM -11 PM, and Sunday, noon to 7 PM.
(304) 737-0188 www.droversinn.net

"A Hero in Humble Life"

In 1831, at age 59, Patrick Gass married a girl more than 40 years younger than himself. His wife Maria died of measles in 1846, leaving him a 75 year old widower with six children, the youngest just 11 months old. His friend J. G. Jacob called him "a hero in humble life."

Gass served as head carpenter on the expedition, in addition to his sergeant's duties and journal keeping. The Lewis and Clark Interpretive Center at Cape Disappointment in Iwalco, Washington displays a razor box carved by Sacagawea as a gift for him; his hatchet, and the Gass family bible. Elk Point, South Dakota holds an annual event honoring his memory in August.

2

Seaman may have looked like this older breed of Newfoundland dog.

Seaman Catches Swimming Squirrels

my dog was of the newfoundland breed very active strong and docile, he would take the squirel in the water kill them and swiming bring them in his mouth to the boat."

—Meriwether Lewis
Sept. 11, 1803 journal entry

This is the first mention of Seaman in the journals: Lewis wrote that as their boats traveled down the Ohio they encountered a great migration of black squirrels swimming across the water, from the west to the east shore. This was in the vicinity of today's Wayne National Forest, northeast of Marietta, Ohio. He set Seaman to work catching them, as they were fat, and "when fryed, a pleasant food."

Newfoundland dogs are a working breed, still employed as water rescue dogs. They are good in the water because of their webbed feet and thick coats of hair. The above illustration is from *We Proceeded On*, (May, 2002) the quarterly publication of the Lewis and Clark Trail Heritage Foundation.

Historian James Holmberg, author of *Dear Brother: Letters of William Clark to Jonathan Clark,* discussed the probable fate of Seaman in another issue of *WPO* (February, 2000). He referred to an article published in 1814 regarding the display of Seaman's dog collar in an Alexandria, Virginia museum. The 1814 article related that Seaman accompanied Lewis on his final journey on the Natchez Trace and "died with grief upon his master's grave."

The inscription on the dog collar (which is now missing) read:

> The greatest traveller of my species. My name is SEAMAN, the dog of captain Meriwether Lewis, whom I accompanied to the Pacifick Ocean through the interior of the continent of North America.

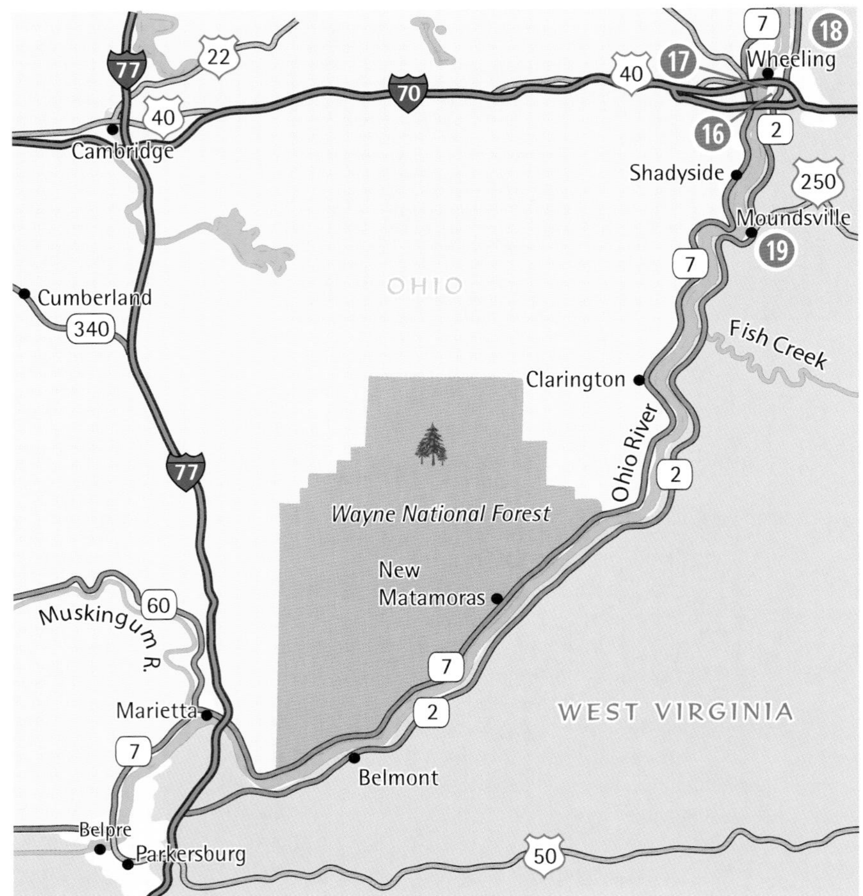

Wheeling and Moundsville

16 WEST VIRGINIA INDEPENDENCE HALL WHEELING WV

1528 Market Street.
From I-70 take exit 1 A, go south on Main Street to 16th Street, turn left onto 16th Street, cross over Market Street, get in the left lane and turn into the parking lot behind the building.

17 WHEELING SUSPENSION BRIDGE WHEELING WV

Wheeling Island to Wheeling.
From *OHIO* take US 40 across the West channel of the Ohio River to South Wabash St on Wheeling Island. Turn right onto Wabash St. Go to Virginia St, turn left. Go 5 blocks to the bridge. From *WEST-VIRGINIA* take I-70 W to exit 1 A. Go south on US 40 to 10th St. Turn right onto the bridge.

18 OGLEBAY MANSION, MUSEUM, AND RESORT WHEELING WV

Oglebay Park on Route 88 North.
From downtown Wheeling take I-70 to exit 2 A. Take exit ramp onto US 40 East. Take US 40 East to Rte 88 (Bethany Pike). Turn left onto Bethany Pike. Go 2.5 miles to Oglebay Park.

19 GRAVECREEK MOUND SITE DELF NORONA MUSEUM MOUNDSVILLE WV

801 Jefferson Avenue.
From I-70 Exit 1 B in Wheeling, go 11 miles south on Rte 2. Rte 2 is named Lafayette Avenue in Moundsville. Turn left (east) onto 12th Street. Go four blocks to Jefferson Avenue. Turn left (north). Go three blocks to the Museum.

Delf Norona Museum
at Gravecreek Mound
Steve Shaluta, WV Tourism

Wheeling Suspension Bridge
Wheeling Convention and Visitors Bureau

2

Great Mound at Grave Creek (c.1848)
Ancient Monuments of the Mississippi Valley

Two Travelers Meet

Lewis arrived at Wheeling on September 8, 1803, where he wrote the President, bought a second pirogue, hired another man, and gave his men a rest day. He spent time with another traveler-journalist, Thomas Rodney. Rodney wrote: "Visited Captain Lewess barge. He shewed us his air gun which fired 22 times at one charge." They dined together at Mr. Zane's.

from *A Journey Through the West: Thomas Rodney's 1803 Journal*

Wheeling and Moundsville

16 WEST VIRGINIA INDEPENDENCE HALL NAT'L HISTORIC LANDMARK—WHEELING

The birthplace of the State of West Virginia, Wheeling Custom House served as home of the Restored Government of Virginia (aligned with the Union) from 1861-1863, which became a state in 1863. Wheeling was the capital city of "Union Virginia." Exhibits display period artifacts and the story of West Virginia's statehood. Film and audio tours available.

■ Open Mon-Sat, 10-4, except state holidays.
(304) 238-1300 www.wvculture.org

 17 WHEELING SUSPENSION BRIDGE NATIONAL HISTORIC LANDMARK

Wheeling Suspension Bridge is the oldest operating suspension bridge in the world built in 1849. The first bridge to span the main channel of the Ohio River, it is 1010 feet in length. Significantly refurbished in 1995, the bridge is also a National Historic Engineering Landmark, and part of the Wheeling National Heritage Area.

The Historic National Road, or US-40 Route and National Scenic Byway, features the bridge. Wheeling was founded by Ebenezer Zane in 1793. When the National Road reached Wheeling in 1818, it followed Zane's Trace, the first road in Ohio, westward. The National Road incorporated many old Indian and pioneer trails, preserving these historic routes for the future.

■ (800) 828-3097 wheelingcvb.com
www.wheelingheritage.com
www.historicwvnationalroad.org
www.scenicbyways.org

 18 OGLEBAY INSTITUTE MANSION MUSEUM AND RESORT WHEELING, WEST VIRGINIA

Oglebay is a unique, 1700 acre family centered, resort, conference center, museum complex, and recreational facility, located 4 miles east of Wheeling.

The Mansion Museum, Stifel Fine Arts Center, Schrader Environmental Center, and Glass Museum at Carriage House Glass are operated by the Oglebay Institute, the largest private arts organization in West Virginia. The Glass Museum showcases over 3000 examples of Wheeling Glass, made from 1829-1939. The Mansion Museum has pioneer artifacts and Victorian treasures. The newest attraction is the Schrader Environmental Center; its Earth Trek Exhibit Hall features 3.4 billion years of the earth's natural history, and promotes good stewardship. The Resort and Conference Center, hosts management and profesional training meetings. Oglebay has two championship golf courses, horse stables and skiing. There are nearly five miles of Discovery Trails.

■ Open daily. Admission: $8 for both Mansion and Glass Museums; $5 for one museum. Ages 12 and under free. Memorial Day-Labor Day, $12.50 wristbands for all day use. Includes museums; zoo, planetarium laser light show, Par 3 golf, miniature golf, tennis, swimming, fishing, pedal boating, trolley, and train ride in zoo. Lodging and dining available at Resort.
(304) 242-7272
www.oglebay-resort.com

 19 GRAVECREEK MOUND SITE AND DELF NORONA MUSEUM MOUNDSVILLE WV

On September 10, 1803 Meriwether Lewis visited "a remarkable artificial mound of earth called by the people in this neighborhood the Indian grave."He noted there were several mounds in the area, but "for this enquire I had not leasure," and so contented himself with a description of the large mound. He measured its "circumpherence" at 310 yards. It was 65 feet high, "terminating in a blont point whose diameter is 30 feet" A ditch ran around the base, 60 feet in width. Near the top of the mound was a giant white oak tree, "whose girth is 13 1/2 feet" and "it's age might resonably calculated at 300 years."

The Gravecreek Mound is one of the largest known conical mounds from the Adena period; and is the most famous of all Adena mounds, It took an estimated 60,000 tons of earth to build. It was constructed from about 250-150 BC, and contains successive layers of burials. The Adena period dates from about 1000 BC to 1 AD. Though they had no horses, and did not use the wheel, they built massive earthworks throughout the Midwest. Artifacts and exhibits interpreting the story of the Adena people are displayed at the adjacent Delf Norona Museum. The West Virginia archaeological collections will be housed in a new addition to the museum.

■ Open daily. Mon-Sat, 10-4:30, Sun 1-5. Closed holidays. A small admission fee.
(304) 843-4128 www.wvculture.orgs

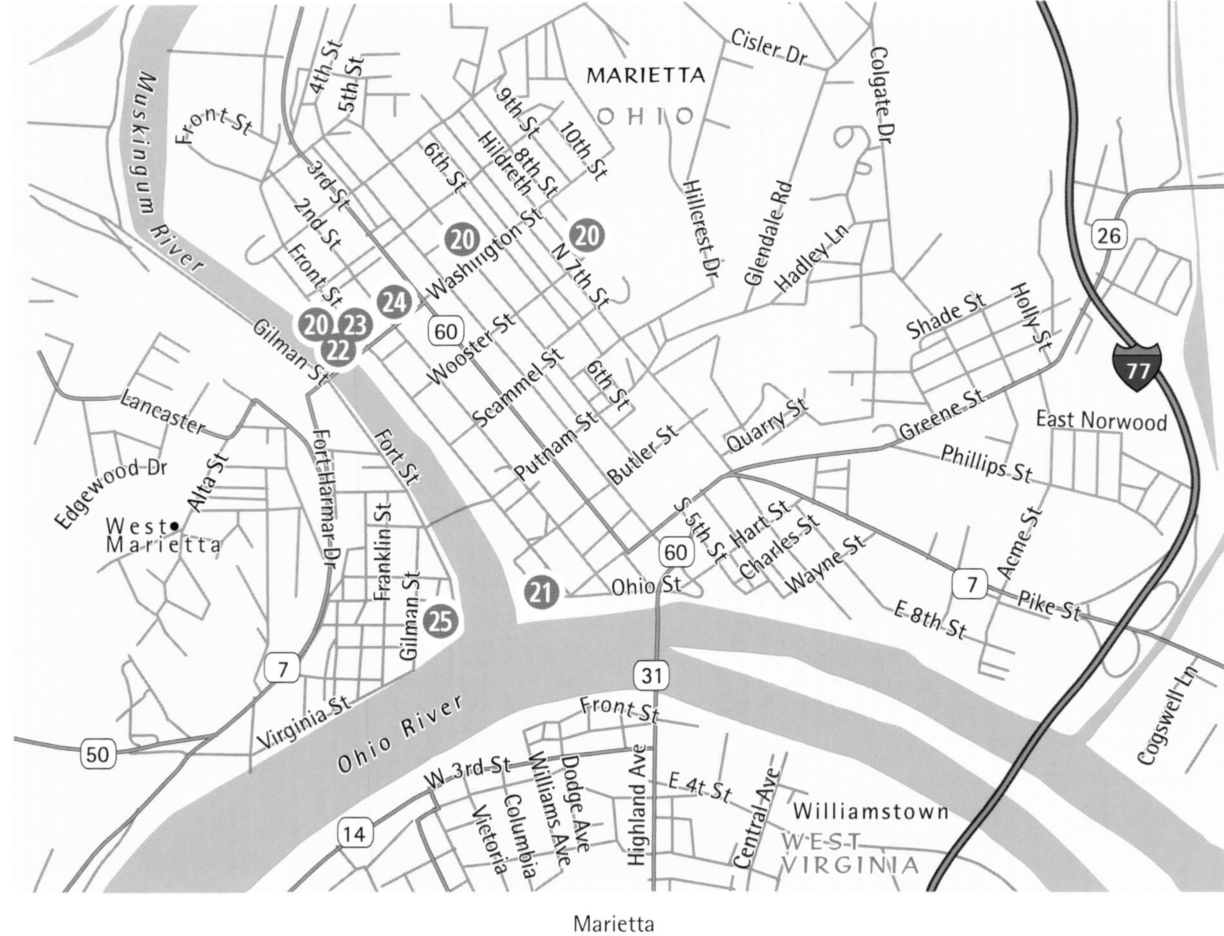

Marietta

20 MOUND CEMETERY AND SACRA VIA EARTHWORKS MARIETTA OH

615 5th Street.

From I-77 Exit 1 take Pike St NW to Greene St. Turn left onto Greene St. Go to 3rd St. Turn right. Go to Washington St. Turn right. Go to 5th St. Turn left. Go 1/2 block to the mound. From the mound continue on 5th St to Warren St. Go left on Warren St to 3rd St. *Sacra Via* runs from 3rd St to the river.

21 CONFLUENCE OF OHIO MUSKINGHUM RIVERS MARIETTA OH

From I-77 Exit 1 take Pike St NW to Greene St. Turn left onto Greene St. Go to Ohio St. Turn right onto Ohio St. Go one block.

22 VALLEY GEM STERNWHEELER–MARIETTA

Washington St Bridge and Front St.

From I-77 Exit 1 take Pike St NW to Greene St. Turn left onto Greene St. Go to 3rd St. Turn right. Go to Washington St. Turn left onto Washington St. Go to landing.

23 OHIO RIVER MUSEUM MARIETTA OH

601 Front Street

From I-77 Exit 1 take Pike St NW to Greene St. Turn left onto Greene St. Go to 3rd St. Turn right. Go to Washington St. Turn left onto Washington St. Go to Front St. Turn right. Go to Saint Clair St.

24 CAMPUS MARTIUS MUSEUM – MARIETTA OH

601 Second Street.

From I-77 Exit 1 take Pike St NW to Greene St. Turn left onto Greene St. Go to 3rd St. Turn right. Go to Washington St. Turn left onto Washington St. Go to 2nd St. Turn right onto 2nd St.

25 FORT HARMAR VILLAGE MARIETTA OH

Market and Gilman Streets.

From I-77 Exit 1 take Pike St NW to Greene St. Turn left onto Greene St. Go to 3rd St. Turn right. Go to Washington St. Turn left onto Washington St. Go across bridge onto Fort Harmar Dr. Go to Market St. Turn left. Go to Gilman St.

Parkersburg

26 BLENNERHASSETT MUSEUM OF REGIONAL HISTORY PARKERSBURG WV

Second and Juliana Streets.

From I-77 take Exit 176 onto US 50 West. Take US 50 (7th St in town) to Juliana St. Turn left onto Juliana St. Go to 2nd. Street.

27 BLENNERHASSETT ISLAND PARKERSBURG WV

In the Ohio River West of Parkersburg.

From I-77 take Exit 176 onto US 50 West. Take US 50 (7th St in town) to Ann St. Turn left onto Ann St. Go to 1st St. Turn right into Point Park, the departure site for sternwheeler rides to the island.

Rufus Putnam's Land Office

Ohio River Museum Flatboat

Sacra Via (Sacred Road)

Campus Martius Museum

2

Marietta & Parkersburg

20 MARIETTA MOUND CEMETERY AND SACRA VIA EARTHWORKS

Marietta was settled at the site of one of America's most famous Native American road networks, the trail connecting the Hopewell Mounds near Chillicothe on the Scioto River to the Marietta Mounds on the Muskingum River. The Great Hopewell Road was about one hundred miles in length. Hopewell Mounds Cultural National Historic Park is located at Chillicothe.

The Marietta Cemetery Mound was built by Adena Indians; it dates to 800 BC-100 AD. A stairway built by early settlers allows visitors to climb to the top. More than 25 Revolutionary War veterans are buried in Mound Cemetery, including General Rufus Putnam, founder of Marietta, and friend of George Washington.

The *Sacra Via*, or Sacred Way, was the name given by settlers in 1788 to the graded thoroughfare leading from the Muskingum River to truncated pyramid mounds. Two of four original mounds remain: the *Quadranaou* mound is located on the west side of Fourth St, north of Warren; the *Capitoleum* elevated square is located at the northwest corner of Washington and Fifth St. The *Sacra Via* and earthworks date from the Hopewell era of 100 BC to 500 AD.

The first settlers were careful to preserve these early prehistoric monuments; but as time went by, much was destroyed. The *Sacra Via*, for instance, was enclosed on both sides by earthern walls, 680 feet long, and 150 feet apart. These walls were 21 feet on their interior sides to the base of the grade, and 8-10 feet on their exterior sides. A local brickmaker used the earth to make bricks in 1843.

The Smithsonian Society's first publication was *Ancient Monuments of the Mississippi Valley*, by Ephraim G. Squier and Edwin H. Davis. Published in 1848, it remains a classic work in American archaeology, and has much information on the Marietta earthworks. Modern archeoastronomers believe the mounds and earthworks were used for celestial observations marking the seasons. The Ohio Historical Society has books and videos on the subject.

■ The Convention and Visitors Bureau at 121 Putnam St has walking tours of the Mounds of Marietta, and the chain saw tree sculptures in the Marietta Parks. (800) 288-2577
(740) 373-5178www.mariettaohio.org
www.ohiohistorystore.org
www.ohiojunction.net/hopewell

21 CONFLUENCE OF OHIO AND MUSKINGHUM RIVERS—MARIETTA

This historic site is located near Picketed Point, a stockade erected to protect early settlers from Indian attacks. The first store and tavern in Northwest Territory were located here. Marquis de Lafayette landed here in 1825.

22 VALLEY GEM STERNWHEELER MARIETTA

The modern sternwheeler riverboat provides a relaxing cruise on the Ohio River. The paddlewheel boat is United States Coast Guard approved and Handicapped Accessible. The lower deck is fully enclosed, with air conditioning/heating, snack bar and restrooms. For over 30 years the Valley Gem has entertained visitors with daytime sightseeing tours and Saturday evening dinner cruises on the Ohio River. During the fall there are tours of the last hand operated lock system on the Muskingum River.

■ 90 minute narrated sightseeing tours, June, July, Aug Tues-Sun at 2:30. Weekends in May and Sept at 2:30. Fares: $9 adults, $8 seniors, $5 ages 3-12. No reservations required.

■ Reservations required for Saturday dinner cruise buffet. 2 hour cruise departs at 5 PM. Fares: $31 adults, $20 ages 3-12.

■ Reservations required for fall foliage locks tours. River conditions permitting, the 1840 locks tour on the Muskingum River is available in the fall on weekends from 1-4. Fares: $16 adults, $10 ages 3-12.
(740) 373-7862
www.valleygemsternwheeler.com

23 OHIO RIVER MUSEUM—MARIETTA

The museum complex consists of three exhibit buildings. featuring the history of steamboat navigation and the ecology and natural history of the Ohio River. Outdoor escorted tours of the *W P Snyder, Jr*, last steam powered sternwheeler towboat in the United States, Also on site is a full scale flatboat reconstruction; and poles showing the height of some of the historic floods at the confluence, reaching 49-60 feet.

■ Open weekends, May 28-Oct 30. Saturdays, 9:30-5; Sundays and holidays 12-5.
Admission: $7 adults, $3 ages 3-12 and students, all ages. Groups by appointment.
((800) 860-0145 or (749) 373-3750 the phone number of the Campus Martius Museum
www.mariettaohio.org

24 CAMPUS MARTIUS MUSEUM MARIETTA

"No colony in America was ever settled under such favorable auspices as that which has just commenced at the Muskingum." George Washington, 1788. To learn the history of the first organized settlement in Northwest Territory visit the Campus Martius Museum. General Rufus Putnam's home and the United States land office, the oldest building in Northwest Territory, are among the displays.

■ Open March 5-Oct 31 Weds-Sun. Hours: Weds-Sat, 9:30-5, and Sun 12-5. Closed Nov 1-March 4. Admission: $7 adults, $3 ages 6-12 and students all ages.
(800) 860-0145 www.mariettaohio.org

25 FORT HARMAR VILLAGE, MARIETTA

Fort Harmar was built at the confluence in 1785, both to protect settlers from Indian attacks and to prevent any more settlers from settling in Ohio before it was legal to do so. Today, Historic Harmar Village is a tourist attraction with shops, 3 small museums and restaurants.

■ Open April-Dec, Tues-Sat 10-5, and Sunday 12-5. Open March, Fri-Sat, 10-5, Sun 12-5.
(800) 288-2577 (740) 373-5178
www.mariettaohio.org

26 BLENNERHASSETT MUSEUM OF REGIONAL HISTORY—PARKERSBURG WV

Three floors of exhibits, ranging from 9,000 year old artifacts, old maps, furniture, guns, jewelry, glassware, autos, farm implements, and other items from the area's rich historic past. The Blennerhassett collection fills 1/4 of a floor.

■ Open Mar 22-Oct 30, Tues-Sat, from 10/11 to 5; and Sunday varying hours. Open wkds in winter. Admission, $2 adult, $1 ages 3-12.
(304) 420-4800 www.blennerhassett.net

27 BLENNERHASSETT ISLAND HISTORICAL STATE PARK—PARKERSBURG WV

The sternwheeler departs from Point State Park for the 20 minute ride to Blennerhassett Island. Allow at least three hours for your visit, including boat rides. (See p. 27 for island mansion history.)

■ Open June-Sept Tues-Fri, 11-4:30; Sat 11-5:30; Sun 1-5:30. Shorter hours spring and fall. Closed Nov 1-Dec 23. Admission: boat ride $8 adult, $7 ages 3-12; mansion tour, $3/$2; wagon ride, $4.75/$2.50. Bike rentals available.
(304) 420-4802 www.blennerhassett.net

Alternative Routes Across Ohio to Cincinnati

28 NATIONAL ROAD MUSEUM ZANESVILLE OH

8850 East Pike, Norwich, Ohio
From I-70 Exit 164 turn onto US 40 East. Go east to Museum.

29 NEWARK EARTHWORKS NEWARK OH

99 Cooper Avenue.
From I-70 Exit 129 go north on Rte 79 (Hebron Road) 9 miles to Great Circle Earthworks at Parkview Dr. From the Great Circle, to go to Octagon Earthworks, take Parkview Dr. north. It becomes 21st St. Turn left (west) on Main St. and go to 33rd St. Turn right (north) for Moundbuilders golf course.

30 OHIO HISTORICAL CENTER COLUMBUS OH

1982 Velma Avenue.
From I-71 Exit 111 go West on 17th Ave to Velma Ave. Turn right onto Velma Ave. Go one block north to the Museum.

31 GARST MUSEUM GREENVILLE OH

205 North Broadway Street.
From I-75 Exit 82 go West on US 36 (Martin St in Greenville) to Broadway St. Turn right onto Broadway St. Go nortwest to the museum at the corner of Broadway and Main. From US 127 turn onto US 36 West (Martin St.). Go west to Broadway St. Turn right onto Broadway St. Go nortwest to the museum at the corner of Broadway and Main.

32 GOLDEN LAMB INN LEBANON OH

27 South Broadway
From I-71 Exit 28 go north on Rte 42 bypass to Rte 123 (Main St). Turn left onto Main St. Go west to Broadway St. Turn right. Go north to the Inn.

33 FORT ANCIENT MUSEUM OREGONIA OH

6123 State Route 350.
From I-71 Exit 36 (Wilmington Rd) take Middleboro Rd South to Rt 350. Turn right onto Rte 350 and go into Fort Ancient.

34 ADENA CHILLICOTHE OH

Adena Road.
US 50 West combines with US 35 as it enters Chillicothe. US 35 diverges from US 50 and continues northwest. Follow US 35 to the exit ramp for Rte 104. Take Rte 104 north for 1/10th of a mile to Pleasant Valley Rd. Turn left onto Pleasant Valley Rd (County Rd 127). Follow it for one-quarter mile to Adena Rd. Turn left onto Adena Rd. Stay on Adena Rd for about one mile (the last half mile is winding).

Hopewell Culture Mounds

35 HOPEWELL CULTURAL NAT'L HISTORICAL PARK CHILLICOTHE OH

16062 State Route 104.
US 50 West combines with US 35 as it enters Chillicothe. US 35 diverges from US 50 and continues northwest. Follow US 35 to the exit ramp for Rte 104. Take Rte 104 north for 1.5 miles to the park.

36 TECUMSEH DRAMA CHILLICOTHE OH

5768 Marietta Road.
US 50 West combines with US 23 as it enters Chillicothe. US 23 diverges from US 50 and continues north. Exit US 23 at Rte 159. Take Rte 159 north to Delano Rd. Go east 1.5 miles to amphitheater.

37 SERPENT MOUND PEEBLES OH

3850 State Route 73.
From Ohio Rte 32 go west on Ohio Rte 73 for six miles to the entrance for Serpent Mound.

Tecumseh Outdoor Drama
Joe E Murray

Garst Museum
Garst Museum, Greenville, Ohio

Moonrise, Octagon Earthworks
Digital representation by CERHAS
Center for the Electronic Reconstruction of Historical and Archaeological Sites

Alternate Routes Across Ohio

28 NATIONAL ROAD MUSEUM AND ZANE GREY MUSEUM—ZANESVILLE

The story of the National Road, from Cumberland MD to Vandalia IL, first promoted by Albert Gallatin in 1806, is told in a 136 foot diorama. US-40 is the Old National Road. Memorabilia, including the recreated writer's study of Zanesville author, Zane Grey, is displayed in the second exhibit. "The father of adult westerns" wrote more than 80 books. Ohio art pottery is featured in the third exhibit.

■ Open May 27-Sept 4, Weds-Sat, 9:30-5; Sundays and holidays, 12-5. Admission: $7 adults, $3 (ages 6-12). (800) 752-2602
www.ohiohistory.org/places/natlroad

29 THE NEWARK EARTHWORKS STATE MEMORIAL—NEWARK, OHIO

The world famous Newark Earthworks, once the largest set of connected geometric earthworks in the world, were built between 100 BC and 500 AD by the Hopewell Culture people. They were part ceremonial, part cemetery, and part astronomical observatory. They originally covered four square miles. The Great Circle is the size of four football fields; the Octagon Earthworks is on the site of the Newark Moundbuilders Country Club golf course.

■ Park grounds at the Great Circle are open Apr 2-Sept 5, Weds-Sun. Octagon earthworks public areas are open daily. For info/tours contact: (800) 600-7178 Great Circle/Ohio Hist Society
www.ohiohistory.org/places/newarkearthworks
www.octagonmoonrise.org

30 OHIO HISTORICAL CENTER—COLUMBUS

The museum was described by the *Smithsonian Guide to Historic America* as "probably the finest museum in America devoted to pre-European history." The Historical Center is also headquarters for the Ohio State Historical Society, which administers 60 historical sites in Ohio. In addition to its premiere archaeology collection, the museum features Ohio history from the ice age to 1970 and Ohio natural history.

■ Open Tues-Sat 9-5; Sun and holidays, 12-5. Admission $7 adults, $3 students.
(800) 686-6124 www.ohiohistory.org/places/ohc

31 GARST MUSEUM—GREENVILLE

The museum features displays on Annie Oakley, the sharpshooter who toured with Buffalo Bill's Wild West Show; and the Treaty of GreenVille. It was at Fort GreenVille that Lewis and Clark first met, when they were officers in the Legion of the United States. The Treaty of Greenville ended the Indian Wars in Ohio in 1795. The Tecumseh Point Walkway along Greenville Creek honors the Shawnee Chief.

■ Open Tues-Sat, 11-5; Sunday, 1-5.
Admission: $3 adults, $2 seniors, $1 ages 6-18.
(937) 548-5250 www.garstmuseum.org

32 GOLDEN LAMB INN—LEBANON

Ohio's oldest inn was established in 1803. It has entertained 12 presidents of the United States. The Golden Lamb continues to welcome guests to its historic restaurant with traditional Ohio fare. 18 historic overnight accomodations.

■ Open daily. Breakfast on weekends. Lunch and dinner daily. (513) 932-5065
www.goldenlamb.com

33 FORT ANCIENT STATE MEMORIAL MUSEUM AT FORT ANCIENT OREGONIA, OHIO

The Fort Ancient State Memorial at Oregonia features 18,000 feet (3.4 miles) of earthern walls built 2000 years ago, enclosing 100 acres. It is the finest example of a hilltop enclosure to be found anywhere in the United States. The Ohio Historical Society estimates it would take 200 miles of construction dump trucks placed end to end to hold the dirt these people hauled up the hill in baskets to build the walls. The fort was also an astronomical site.

The Museum has 9,000 sq. ft. of exhibits, including many interactive ones. It covers 15,000 years of American Indian history in Ohio. The sales shop has many fine American Indian items.

■ Open April-May on wkds, Sat 10-5, Sun 12-5. Late May to early Sept, Weds-Sat, 10-5, Sun 12-5. Sept-Oct, on wkds, Sat 10-5, Sun 12-5. Closed Nov-March. Admission: $7 adult, $3 ages 6-12 and students. $7 per car for park visits.
(800) 283-8904
www.ohiohistory.org/placs/ftancien

34 ADENA MANSION AND GARDENS CHILLICOTHE, OHIO

Adena State Memorial was the 2000 acre estate of Thomas Worthington (1773-1827). The house was designed by Benjamin Henry Latrobe, architect of the U S Capitol. Three acres of terraced gardens. A new museum and education center features daily life at Adena.

■ Open late May-Labor Day, Weds-Sat, 9:30-5; Sun, 12-5. Open wkds in Sept-Oct, and Apr-May, Sat, 9:30-5, and Sun. 12-5. Closed Nov 1-Mar 31. Admission, $7 adults, $3 students.

■ Mansion tours on the hour, 10-4, except noon. (800) 319-7248 or (740) 772-1500
www.ohiohistory.org/places/adena

35 HOPEWELL CULTURAL NATIONAL HISTORICAL PARK—CHILLICOTHE

The national park is a famous archeological site of earthworks and mound complexes, dating from 200 BC-500 AD. The visitor center has exhibits, films, bookstore, and tours.

■ Open daily, 8:30-5. 8:30-6 in June. Admission, $3 adults. From June 1-Sept 9, at 11 AM, 35-45 minutes guided tours of site; at 1:30, a 20-30 patio talk led by a ranger.
(740) 774-1125 www.nps.gov/hocu

36 TECUMSEH OUTDOOR DRAMA CHILLICOTHE

One of America's most famous outdoor shows, *Tecumseh* is the story of the Shawnee Chief, with dramatic battle scenes in the huge outdoor stages of Sugarloaf Mountain Ampitheatre.

■ Season: June-early Sept, Mon-Sat, 8 PM. Admission: $16 adults, $8 ages ten and under.
On Fri and Sat, $18 and $9. Call for reservations.
(866) 775-0700 www.tecumsehdrama.com

37 SERPENT MOUND NATIONAL HISTORIC LANDMARK—PEEBLES

Largest and finest serpent effigy in the US, nearly a quarter of a mile long. Visitor Center.

■ Museum open Apr 1-May 26 on wkds, 10-5; and from May 27-June 30, Weds-Sun, 10-5.
Park open daily, 10-5. Admission $7 cars, $9 RVs
(800) 752-2757
www.ohiohistory.org/places/serpent

River Roads to Cincinnati

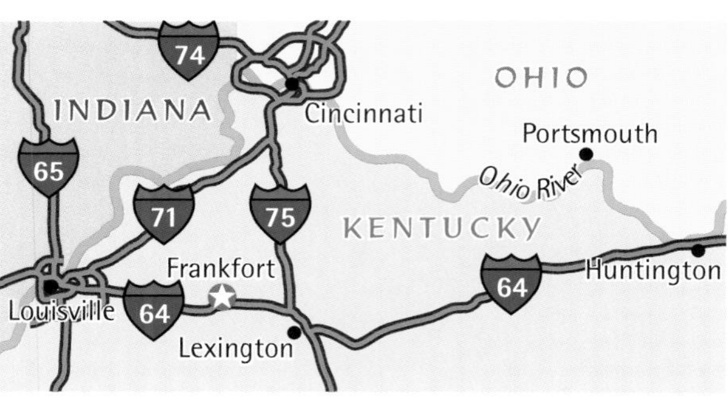

Huntington to Louisville

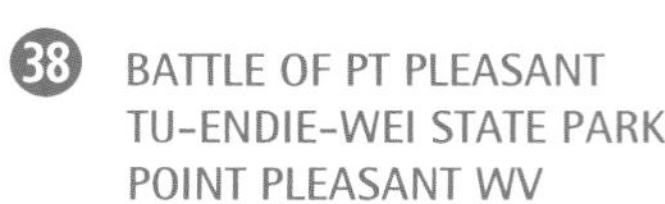

38 BATTLE OF PT PLEASANT
TU-ENDIE-WEI STATE PARK
POINT PLEASANT WV

1 Main Street.
Take US 35 to West Virginia Rte 2. Go North on Rte 2 across the Kanawha River to 1st St. Turn left onto 1st St. Go to Main St. Turn left onto Main St. The park is at the end of the street.

39 OUR HOUSE MUSEUM
GALLIPOLIS OH

432 First Avenue.
Take US 35 to the exit for Ohio Rte 160. Take Rte 160 South (Pine St in Gallipolis) to first Ave. Turn right onto First Ave. Go past Locust Street to the Museum.

40 HERITAGE FARM VILLAGE
AND MUSEUM
HUNTINGTON WV

3300 Harvey Road.
From I-64 take Exit 8 (5th St) to Johnstown Rd, Take Johnstown Rd West to Harvey Rd. Turn left onto Harvey Rd. Go south to the Farm.

41 FLOOD WALL MURALS
PORTSMOUTH OH

Front Street.
From US 52 take US 23 South (Scioto Trail, then Chillicothe St) to Front St. Turn right onto Front St.

42 MOUND PARK
PORTSMOUTH OH

17th St and Grandview Avenue.
From US 52 take US 23 South (Scioto Trail, then Chillicothe St) to 12th St. Turn left. 12th St becomes Robinson Ave. Take Robinson Ave to Grandview Ave. Turn left. Take Grandview Ave to the Park.

43 MUSEUM CENTER
MAYSVILLE KY

215 Sutton Street.
From US 68 turn West onto 2nd St. Go to Sutton St. Turn left.

44 OLD WASHINGTON
WASHINGTON KY

2112 Old Main Street, Maysville.
Washington, now part of Maysville, is 4 miles south of Maysville on US 68. From US 68 turn east onto Old Main St.

45 BIG BONE LICK
STATE PARK
COVINGTON KY

3380 Beaver Road, Union, KY.
From I-71 S take Exit 175 to Rte 338. Go right (west) to US 42. Turn left (south). Go to Rte 338 (Beaver Rd). Turn right (west) onto Beaver Rd. Go 3 miles to Park.

46 CINCINNATI
MUSEUM CENTER
CINCINNATI OH

1301 Western Avenue.
From US 50 West. Follow US 50 west into downtown. Around the stadiums, get into the second lane from the left for the I-75 N exit. From I-75 N, take the first exit on the right, Exit 1H (Liberty St/Ezzard Charles Dr). Merge left at the end of the exit. Turn left at the light and drive straight to the Museum entrance.

The French 500

500 French refuges from the French Revolution came to settle on the Ohio River in 1790. They were Royalists—nobility, professionals, and craftsmen and their families—totally unsuited for life in the American wilderness.

They had been deceived in a land deal by the Scioto Company and were stranded. The citizens of Marietta (named for Queen Marie Antoinette of France) agreed to help settle the Parisians and built homes for them on Ohio Company land at Gallipolis. As soon as they arrived, the new colonists held a dance. Within two years, half of them had relocated to more cosmopolitan surroundings.

The French who remained held a dance twice a week, regardless of their troubles. They made peach brandy for sale, and continued in their accustomed trades, making the finest watches in America, silverware, and other luxury goods. Dr. Antoine Saugrain manufactured thermometers and barometers. He later moved to St Louis, where he was among the friends of Meriwether Lewis who gathered to watch the Discovery Corps set off on their expedition on May 20th, 1804.

Historic Washington, Kentucky
Phyllis Helphenstine

Big Bone Lick State Park

Cincinnati Museum Center
Cincinnati Museum Center at Union Terminal

2

River Roads to Cincinnati

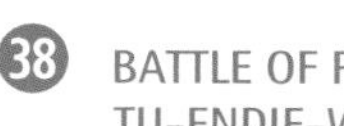

BATTLE OF POINT PLEASANT TU-ENDIE-WEI STATE PARK POINT PLEASANT WV

"Tu Endie-Wei" is a Wyandotte word meaning "point between two waters." It was the scene of a battle in Dunsmore's War of 1774, in which-soldiers commanded by Colonel Andrew Lewis (no relation to Meriwether Lewis) defeated Shawnee warriors commanded by Chief Cornstalk. The Battle of Point Pleasant was recognized by the U S Congress in 1908 as the first battle of the American Revolution, and a 84 ft tall obelisk Battle Monument was placed at the Point. The museum is in a 1796 hewn log house, the oldest in the Kanawa Valley.

■ Point Pleasant Battle Monument State Park is open daily. Mon-Sat, 10-4:30; Sun, 1-4:30. Museum is open May-Oct.
(800) CALL-WVA (225-5982)
www.tu-endi-weistatepark.com

OUR HOUSE MUSEUM GALLIPOLIS OH

The "Our House" Tavern, a three story brick building in Gallipolis ("Galley-police") dates from 1819. In addition to its dining facilities and taproom, it has a large ballroom. In May of 1825, General Lafayette was honored by the local citizens during his triumphal tour of the United States. Many of the early residents were French emigrants; Gallipolis means "French city" in English.

■ Open Memorial Day to Labor Day. Weds-Sat, 10-4, and Sun 1-4. Sept and Oct on wkds only. Admission $4 adults, $3 seniors, $1 students.
(800) 752-2618 www.gallianet.org

HUNTINGTON HERITAGE FARM VILLAGE AND MUSEUM—HUNTINGTON WV

The heritage village has over sixteen buildings showcasing the area's Appalachian heritage. The farm museum has farm implements, machinery, early autos, and one of the largest collections of restored washing machines in the country.

■ Open Mon-Sat, 10-3. Two hour tour: $8 adult, $7 senior, $6 ages 3-12. One hour tour: $6 adult, $5 senior, $5 ages 3-12. Petting Zoo and Nature Walk: $5 each. Bed and Breakfast accomodations available.
(304) 522-1244
www.heritagefarmmuseum.com

PORTSMOUTH FLOOD WALL MURALS PORTSMOUTH OH

The 2000 foot concrete floodwall has murals by artist Robert Dafford portraying the history of the Portsmouth area. Dafford is an internationally known muralist, whose work is on display throughout the United States, Canada and Europe. It is one of the world's largest single mural projects. The Portsmouth murals may be viewed from Front Street near the historic Boneyfiddle District with shops and restaurants.

■ (740) 353-1116 Portsmouth Area CVB
www.portsmouthcvb.org
www.daffordmurals.com
www.historicboneyfiddle.com

MOUND PARK—PORTSMOUTH OH

Horseshoe shaped Indian burial mounds are preserved in the Portsmouth City Park on 17th Street. Portsmouth is only 36 miles southeast of Serpent Mound National HIstoric Landmark near Peebles, Ohio (see #37). Take Highway 73 though Shawnee State Forest to Peebles.

■ (740) 353-1116 www.portsmouthcvb.org

MUSEUM CENTER—MAYSVILLE KY

A marker at Limestone Landing commemorates local resident, John Colter (c. 1775-1813), who enlisted as a private in the Discovery Corp at Maysville on October 15, 1803 with the pay of $5 a month. One of the "Nine Young Men from Kentucky," Colter became one of the most well known members of the Corps bcause of his later adventures in the West. Maysville was known as Limestone originally, and was an early community on the Buffalo Trace Trail.

Kentucky's largest Siberian Elm tree stands at the entrance to the Museum Center, which occupies a historic 1881 museum and library building. It is believed to be the oldest (1878) continuing state historical organization in the US. In 2007 the museum addition will house a new exhibit, the Kathleen Savage Browning Miniatures collection. The story of Simon Kenton, Mason County's pioneer leader and hero, who saved Daniel Boone's life, is also a featured exhibit at the Museum Center.

■ Open Apri-Dec, Mon-Sat, 10-4. Feb-Mar, Tues-Sat, 10-4. Admission $2.50 adults, 50 cents students. (606) 564-5865
www.masoncountymuseum.org

44 OLD WASHINGTON—WASHINGTON KY

Old Washington is older than the state of Kentucky: it was established in 1786, six years before Kentucky became a state. Once a thriving little town of 119 log cabins, it is believed to be the first community named for George Washington. Today it is home to a 1700's living history village, incorporating the old log cabins and other buildings. Attractions include nine museums and almost thirty permanent shops.

■ Open Apr 1 to first wkd in Dec. Mon-Sat, 10-4:30, and Sun, 12-4:30. Closed Dec-Feb. Open wkds only in March. Full historical tour, $10 adult, $4 child. Underground Railroad Tour $6 adult, $4 child. Short video, $1 per person.
(606) 759-7411 or (606) 564-9419
www.washingtonky.com

BIG BONE LICK STATE PARK COVINGTON KY

Over 15,000 years ago a huge ice sheet covered the land north of the Ohio River. Enormous herds of giant mastodons, wooly mammoths and giant sloths visited the warm salt springs that still bubble up today at Big Bone Lick State Park. Big Bone Lick is considered the "Birthplace of American Vertebrate Paleontology." Both Meriwether Lewis and William Clark visited the site to obtain specimens for President Jefferson. Lewis's 1803 shipment was lost when a boat sank; Clark completed the mission in 1807.
The park's outdoor museum has a bog diorama. It also has a real live buffalo herd.

■ General admission to the park is free. RV and tent campgrounds, hiking, recreational activities.
(859) 384-3522 www.parks.ky/stateparks/bb

CINCINNATI MUSEUM CENTER (NHL) CINCINNATI OH

The center is housed in the Cincinnati Union Terminal: the 1933 railroad station is a National Historic Landmark. It is home to the Cincinnati History Museum, Cinergy Children's Museum, the Museum of Natural History and Science, the Historical Society Library, and an Omnimax Theater.

■ Open daily. Mon-Sat, 10-5, Sun 11-6. Admission: $7.25 adults, $6.25 seniors, $5.25 ages 3-12. (800) 733-2077
www.cincymuseum.org

2

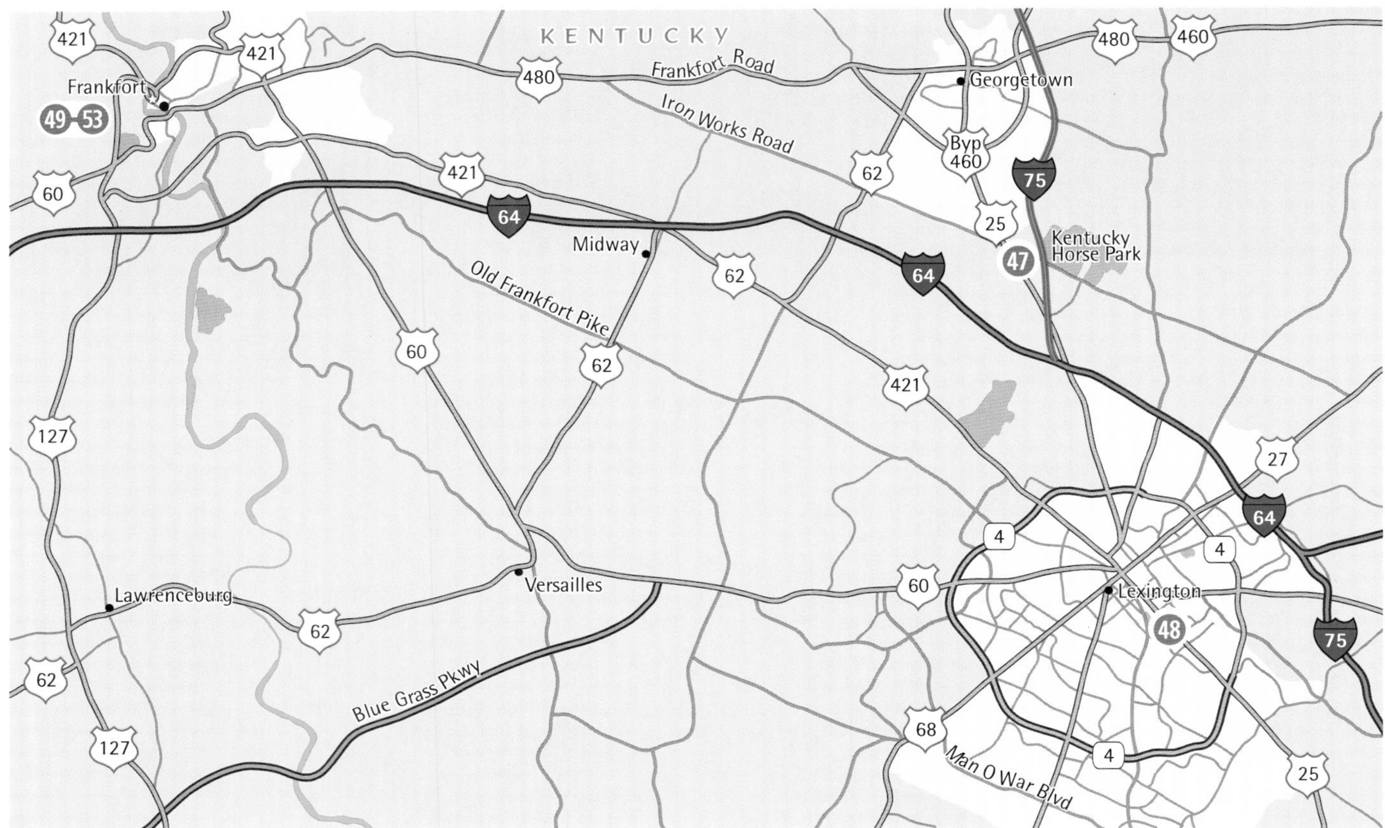

Lexington and Frankfort

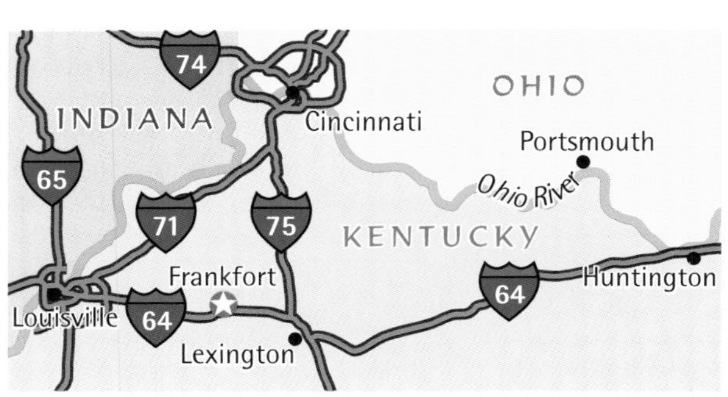

Louisville to Huntington

John Henry smells the roses.
Kentucky Horse Park

47 INT'L MUSEUM OF THE HORSE AND KENTUCKY HORSE PARK—LEXINGTON

4089 Iron Works Parkway.
From I-75 N take Exit 120. Turn right onto Rt 1973 (Iron Works Pike). Take Iron Works Pike to Iron Works Parkway. Turn left into Horse Park.

48 ASHLAND, HENRY CLAY ESTATE—LEXINGTON KY

120 Sycamore Road.
From I-75 S take Exit 118 left to continue on I-75. Then take Exit 115 right to Rt 922 (Newtown Pike). I-75 merges with US 25 (Newtown Pike). Later US 25 makes a left turn and is called Main St, then Vine St, then Main St again, and then Richmond Rd. From Richmond Rd turn right onto Sycamore Rd.

49 KENTUCKY HISTORY CENTER FRANKFORT KY

100 West Broadway.
From I-64 take Exit 58 to US 60 North (Versailles Rd). US 60 then bends left becoming Main St. Stay on Main St to Broadway. Bear right onto Broadway.

50 KENTUCKY MILITARY HISTORY MUSEUM FRANKFORT KY

128 East Main Street.
From I-64 take Exit 58 to US 60 North (Versailles Rd). US 60 then bends left becoming Main St. Stay on Main St to the Museum.

51 KENTUCKY OLD STATE CAPITOL FRANKFORT KY

300 West Broadway.
From I-64 take Exit 58 to US 60 North (Versailles Rd). US 60 then bends left becoming Main St. Stay on Main St to Broadway. Bear right onto Broadway.

52 LIBERTY HALL HISTORIC SITE—FRANKFORT KY

218 Wilkinson Street.
From I-64 take Exit 58 to US 60 North (Versailles Rd). US 60 then bends left becoming Main St. Take Main St to Wilkinson St. Turn left to Liberty Hall.

53 BUFFALO TRACE DISTILLERY FRANKFORT KY

1001 Wilkinson Boulevard.
From I-64 take Exit 58 to US 60 North (Versailles Rd). US 60 then bends left becoming Main St. Take Main St to Wilkinson Blvd. Go right to Distillery.

Kentucky Horse Park

Old Frankfort Pike Gene Burch

Buffalo Trace Distillery
Gene Burch

www.geneburch.com

Ashland, The Henry Clay Estate

Foggy Horse Farm Gene Burch

2

Lexington & Frankfort

47 INT'L MUSEUM OF THE HORSE KENTUCKY HORSE PARK—GEORGETOWN

The 1,023 acre park has two museums, the International Museum of the Horse, the largest museum of its kind in the world; and the American Saddlebred Museum. There is a blacksmith's Farrier Shop, Breeds Barn, Draft Horse Barn, and Hall of Champions. During the season, there are twice daily Parade of Breeds; afterwards visitors may meet and pet the horses and talk with their riders. The racing champions are also shown daily. More than 80 special horse events take place each year at the Horse Park. The Visitor Center has a wide screen, 23 minute film.

■ Open daily, Mar 15-Oct 31, 9-5. Open Weds-Sun, Nov 1-Mar 14, 9-5. Admission: Mar-Oct,$14 adults, $7 ages 7-12. Nov- Mar, $9/$6.

■ Horseback riding: ages 7 and up, must be 48" tall, weight restrictions apply. 45 minute guided trail ride, $15 per person. Pony rides: $5, ages 12 and under. Carriage rides: inquire.

(800) 678-8813 or (859) 233-4303
www.kyhorsepark.com

48 ASHLAND, THE HENRY CLAY ESTATE (NHL) LEXINGTON

Ashland, the home of Henry and Lucretia Clay is a National Historic Landmark. One of the greatest United States Senators, Henry Clay's political career spanned almot half a century from 1803-1851. The original home (1806-1852) was replaced by an 18 room mansion erected by their son in 1857, and remodeled in the Victorian style by their granddaughter. It contains many Clay family antiques and memorabilia. There are six outbuildings on the estate, and formal gardens. The "Henry Clay Walk" is where the Senator often walked and composed his speeches. Henry Clay's 1833 coach has been restored and is on exhibit.

■ Open daily, April-Oct. Mon-Sat,10-4 and Sun, 1-4. Closed January. Open during Feb on wkds and by appt. Closed holidays and Mondays during Nov-March. Admission $7 adults, $3 children. 5 and under free.

■ Guided tours daily. One hour tour starts on the hour. Last tour of day begins at 4 PM. The outdoor patio Ginkgo Tree Cafe is open, weather permitting, April-Oct, Mon-Sat, 11-3.

(859) 266-8581 www.henryclay.org

49 CENTER FOR KENTUCKY HISTORY FRANKFORT

The Kentucky Historical Society has three museums in historic downtown Frankfort: the Center for Kentucky History, the Kentucky Military History Museum, and the Old State Capitol.

The Thomas D. Clark Center for Kentucky History honors the memory of one of America's great historians, Dr.Thomas D Clark (1903-2005), the author of more than 30 books on southern and frontier history during his lifetime. A popular exhibit at the Center is "A Kentucky Journey."

■ Open Tues-Sat 10-5, Sun 1-5. Adults $4, $2 ages 6-18. Tickets are good at all 3 museums.

(502) 564-1792 or (877) 444-7867
www.history.ky.gov

50 KENTUCKY MILITARY HISTORY MUSEUM—FRANKFORT

The museum is operated by the KY National Guard and the KY Historical Society. It emphasizes the history of military volunteers, with an impressive display of weapons and other items, housed in the 1850 Old State Arsenal.

■ Open Tues-Sat 10-5, Sun 1-5. Adults $4, $2 ages 6-18. Tickets are good at all 3 museums.

(502) 564-1792 or (877) 444-7867
www.history.ky.gov

51 KENTUCKY OLD STATE CAPITOL FRANKFORT

The Old State Capitol served as the capitol of Kentucky from 1830-1910. The building is a National Historic Landmark, recognized as a masterpiece of American Architecture in the Greek Revival style. A famous self-supporting stone stairway leads to legislative chambers, restored to their 1850's appearance, with many fine historic paintings.

■ Open Tues-Sat 10-5, Sun 1-5. Adults $4, $2 ages 6-18. Tickets are good at all 3 museums.

(502) 564-1792 or (877) 444-7867
www.history.ky.gov

52 LIBERTY HALL HIST. SITE—FRANKFORT

Two homes, Liberty Hall (c. 1796), built by John Brown, one of Kentucky's first United States Senators and the Orlando Brown home (1835), owned by his son, with an extensive garden. The land was originally owned by General James Wilkinson, who founded Frankfort in 1786.

■ Open Mar 1-mid Dec. House tours are given at 10:30, noon, 1:30, 3:00 on Tues-Sat. On Sun at 12, 1:30 and 3:00. Tours last approximately one hour and involve walking between houses and climbing stairs. $5 adults, $4 seniors, $2 ages 4-18. (888) 516-5101 or (502) 227-2560
www.libertyhall.org

53 BUFFALO TRACE DISTILLERY FRANKFORT

A distillery has operated on this site since 1787. It is the oldest continously operated distillery in the United States. Buffalo Trace makes award winning Kentucky Straight Bourbon, and has won many international awards.

■ Tours start daily on the hour. Mon-Fri, 9-3, Sat 10-2. (800) 654-8471 (502) 696-5926
www.buffalotrace.com

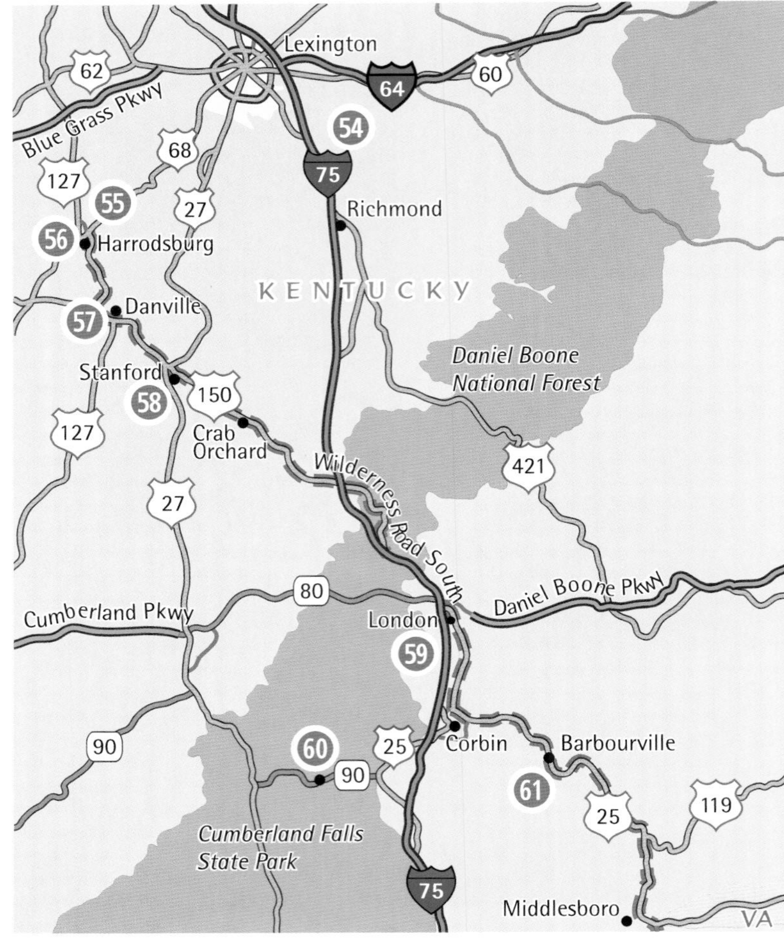

Old Wilderness Roads

Dixie Belle on the Kentucky River
Harrodsburg/Mercer Co. Tourist Commission

McHargue's Mill, Levi Jackson Wilderness Road State Park
Kentucky State Parks

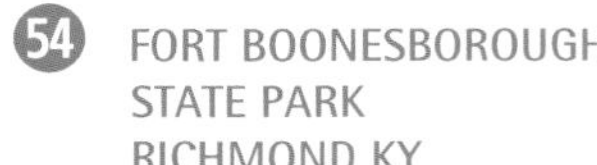

54 FORT BOONESBOROUGH STATE PARK RICHMOND KY

4375 Boonesborough Road.
From I-64 Exit 94 take Rt 1958 Bypass Rd South to Boonesborough Rd (Rt 627). Go right on Boonesborough Rd to the Fort. From I-75 Exit 95 take Boonesborough Rd (Rt 627) Northeast to the Fort.

55 SHAKER VILLAGE OF PLEASANT HILL NAT'L HIST LANDMARK HARRODSBURG KY

3501 Lexington Road.
From I-64 Exit 53 go South on US 127 to US 127 Bypass. Turn left onto Bypass. Go to Lexington Rd (US 68). Turn left onto Lexington Rd.

56 OLD FORT HARROD STATE PARK HARRODSBURG KY

100 South College Street.
From I-64 Exit 53 go South on US 127 to Lexington St in Harrodsburg.

57 CONSTITUTION SQUARE DANVILLE KY

Main Street and Second Street.
From I-64 Exit 53 go South on US 127 to Main St in Danville. Turn left onto Main St. Go East to Second Street.

58 WILLIAM WHITLEY HOUSE STANFORD KY

625 William Whitley Road.
From I-75 Exit 62 go South onto US 25. Turn right (West) onto US 150. Take US 150 to Rt 643 in Crab Orchard.. Turn right onto Rt 1770. Take Rt 1770 to William Whitley Rd. Bear right (Northwest) to William Whitley House.

59 LEVI JACKSON STATE PARK LONDON KY

998 Levi Jackson Mill Road.
From I-75 take Exit 38 East to Rt 192. Take Rt 192 to US 25 (Laurel Rd). Turn right onto Laurel Rd. Take Laurel Rd South to Rt 1006 (Levi Jackson Mill Rd). Turn left (East) onto Levi Jackson Mill Rd.

60 CUMBERLAND FALLS STATE RESORT PARK CORBIN KY

7351 Highway 90.
From I-75 Exit 25 take US 25 W (Cumberland Falls Highway) to Rt 90. Turn right (West) onto Rt 90. Take Rt 90 into Park

61 DR. THOMAS WALKER STATE HISTORIC SITE BARBOURVILLE KY

4929 KY State Route 459.
From I-75 Exit 29 take Rt 709 East straight onto US 25 (Cumberland Gap Parkway). Follow US 25 to Manchester St (about 13.5 miles). Turn right (West) onto Manchester St. In Barbourville turn right from Manchester St onto Matthew St which changes its name to School St. which then changes its name to Sharp Gap Rd (Rt 2423). Sharp Gap Rd runs into Rt 459 which winds about 3 miles to the Walker site.

Cumberland Falls
Kentucky State Parks

William Whitely House
Kentucky State Parks

Shaker Village
Shaker Village of Pleasant Hill, Kentucky

Fort Harrod Visitors
Harrodsburg/Mercer Co.Tourist Commission

2

Old Wilderness Roads

54 FORT BOONESBOROUGH STATE PARK RICHMOND KY

Boonesborough was the first fortified settlement in Kentucky, settled by Daniel Boone in 1775. It was the capitol of the Transylvania Colony. The fort has been reconstructed as a working fort; resident craftsmen demonstrate old time skills. The Kentucky River Museum is located in two restored lock houses and tells the story of river commerce.

RV and tent camping, with many recreational activities, including a junior olympic size swimming pool and water slide.

■ State Park open year round. Tours of the Fort and Kentucky River Museum, April-Oct, 9-5:30. Tour prices, $6 adults, $4 ages 6-12.
(859) 527-3131 www.parks.ky.gov/stateparks

 SHAKER VILLAGE OF PLEASANT HILL NATIONAL HISTORIC LANDMARK HARRODSBURG KY

The restored village of Pleasant Hill is the finest, largest and most completely restored Shaker community in America. Shakers came to Kentucky in 1805; the Shaker name derived from the "shaking" dance they did as part of their religious observances. Shaker music was based on the popular music of the day. As many as 500 people lived at Pleasant Hill; the communal village has 34 restored federal style buildings with living history demonstrations.

There are 80 guest rooms, furnished with Shaker reproductions. Shaker craftsmanship and design style are still a hallmark of excellence. Reproductions and Kentucky-made crafts are available at the two village crafts stores.

The authentic *Dixie Belle* sternwheeler riverboat provides cruises on the Kentucky River along the scenic Kentucky Palisades.

■ Open year round for self-guided tours of 14 restored buildings. April-Oct, from 9:30-5:30. Tour prices: $12.50, adults, $7 ages 12-17, $5, ages 6-11. Nov-March, from 10-4:30. Tour prices: $6.50/$3.50/$2.50.

■ Riverboat excursions are April-Oct at noon, 2 and 4 daily (weather and river conditions permitting). $5 all ages.

■ Reservations are required for lodging and dining; breakfast, lunch and dinner available.
(800) 734-5611 www.shakervillageky.org

 OLD FORT HARROD STATE PARK HARRODSBURG KY

Harrodsburg, established in 1774, was the first permanent English speaking community west of the Allegheny Mountains. After the site was flooded in the spring of 1775, the town was relocated to the higher ground where Fort Harrod was built. Settlers sought the protection of the large fort during Indian attacks for over 20 years, until the Treaty of Greenville ended the Indian Wars in 1795. The old graveyard remains as it was; simple rocks indicate gravesites of some of the more than 500 early pioneers buried here.

The reconstructed fort has crafts people, living history demonstrations and live animals in the stockade during the season. George Rogers Clark planned his campaign to attack Kaskaskia and Vincennes while staying at Fort Harrod. His living quarters have been recreated. A federal monument honors him. Other attractions include the 1813 Mansion Museum; and the Lincoln Marriage Temple, the log cabin where Abraham Lincoln's parents were married in 1806.

■ Open year round (closed last week in December and weekends Dec-Feb.). Open Mid March-Oct, 9-5. Nov-Feb, 8-4:30. Admission: $4.50 adults, $4 seniors, $2.50 ages 6-12.
(859) 734-3314 www.parks.ky.gov/stateparks
(859(734-2364 www.harrodsburgky.com

 CONSTITUTION SQUARE STATE HISTORIC SITE—DANVILLE KY

Ten Kentucky state constitutional conventions took place at Danville during 1784-1792. Buildings on Constitution Square include the Watts-Bell House Museum and replicas of the courthouse, jail, tavern and meetinghouse.

■ Open daily for self guided tours, 9-5. Free admission. The Constitution Square museum store is open Mon-Fri, 9-5.

■ Watts-Bell Museum open April 15-Oct 15, Weds-Sat, 12-4 and Sun, 2-4. Admission: $2 adults, 50¢ children.
(859) 239-7089 www.danville-ky.com

 WILLIAM WHITLEY HOUSE STATE HISTORIC SITE—STANFORD KY

The 1794 house, "Sportsman's Hill," is perhaps the oldest brick home west of the Alleghenies. It was known as "the Guardian of Wilderness Road," with a secret hiding place in case of Indian attack. Visitors to the Whitley house included George Rogers Clark and Daniel Boone. The circular clay race track was the first in the nation. It is believed the American practice of racing counter-clockwise began here. (The British race clockwise.) Costumed tour guide, furnishings of the time period, and a gift shop.

■ Open daily, last wkd May to 1st wkd Sept. 9-4:30; Mar-April, Tues-Sun, 9-4:30; Sept-mid Dec, Tues-Sun, 9-4:30; Jan-Feb, Tues-Fri, 10-3.
(606) 355-2881
www.parks.ky.gov/statehistoricsites/ww

 LEVI JACKSON WILDERNESS ROAD STATE PARK—LONDON

The park's 8 1/2 miles of hiking trails include some parts of the historic Wilderness Road and Boone's Trace trails. Historic attractions are the Defeated Camp Pioneer Burial Ground, McHargue's Mill and Mountain Life Museum outdoor pioneer settlement. McHargue's Mill on the Little Laurel River is a working reproduction mill with authentic interior works. It has the largest display of millstones in the country. RV and tent campgrounds; recreational activities.

■ Open last wkd May-1st wkd Sept. Admission free to State Park. Mill admission is $3.50 adult, $2.50 ages 2-12. (606) 878-8000
www.parks.ky.gov/stateparks/lj

60 CUMBERLAND FALLS STATE RESORT PARK—CORBIN

The falls, called the "Niagara of the South" have a unique "moonbow" on full moon nights. Activities include white water rafting, canoeing, swimming, fishing, boating, and horseback riding. Other attractions are the Visitor Center with exhibits, gift shop and snack bar, and a Nature Preserve. The historic Dupont Lodge has a dining room and museum. There are cottage accomodations and a conference center.

■ Open year round. (800) 325-0063
www.parks.ky.gov/resortparks/cf

61 DR. THOMAS WALKER STATE HISTORIC SITE—BARBOURVILLE KY

Dr Walker, who was a friend of Thomas Jefferson's father, was an agent for the Loyal Land Company. He explorer and named Cumberland Gap in 1750. A replica cabin of "Kentucky's First House" commemorates his expedition, 17 years before Daniel Boone's travels.

■ Open year round. Free admission. Gift shop open Mar-mid Nov. (606) 546-4400
www.parks.ky.gov/statehistoricsites/dt

Region Two: References

BIOGRAPHY

BREAKING WITH BURR: HERMAN BLENNERHASSETT, 1807
edited by Raymond E. Fitch. Ohio University Press (1988)

HENRY CLAY: STATESMAN FOR THE UNION
by Robert V. Remini. W W Norton & Co (1991)

A JOURNEY THROUGH THE WEST: THOMAS RODNEY'S 1803 JOURNAL FROM DELAWARE TO THE MISSISSIPPI TERRITORY
edited by Dwight L. Smith and Ray Swick. Ohio University Press (1997)

KOHKUMTHENA'S GRANDCHILDREN THE SHAWNEE
by Dark Rain Thom. Guild Press of Indiana (1994)

THE JOURNALS OF PATRICK GASS: MEMBER OF THE LEWIS AND CLARK EXPEDITION
edited and annotated by Carol Lynn Mac Gregor. Mountain Press Publishing Company (1997)

THE LIFE AND TIMES OF PATRICK GASS
by J. G. Jacob. Lone Wolf Press (2000)

SERGENT PATRICK GASS, CHIEF CARPENTER; VERSE BY WILLIAM KLOEFKORN
by William Kloefkorn. Spoon River Poetry Press (2002)

THE SHAWNEE PROPHET
by R. David Edmunds. Univ of Nebraska Press (1983)

TECUMSEH A LIFE
by John Sugden. Henry Holt and Company (1997)

TECUMSEH'S LAST STAND
by John Sugden. University of Oklahoma Press (1985)

WARRIOR WOMAN
by James Alexander Thom and Dark Rain Thom. Ballantine Books (2003)

HISTORY

BAYONETS IN THE WILDERNESS: ANTHONY WAYNE'S LEGION IN THE OLD NORTHWEST
by Alan D. Gaff. University of Oklahoma Press (2004)

THE BEGINNING OF THE U. S. ARMY 1783-1812
by James Ripley Jacobs. Princeton Univ Press (1947)

THE BUZZEL ABOUT KENTUCK: SETTLING THE PROMISED LAND
edited by Craig Thompson Friend. University Press of Kentucky (1999)

COUNCIL FIRES ON THE UPPER OHIO
by Randolph C. Downes. University of Pittsburgh Press (1940)

HISTORY

THE FIRST WAY OF WAR: AMERICAN WAR MAKING ON THE FRONTIER
by John Grenier. Cambridge University Press (2005)

FRONTIER KENTUCKY
by Otis K. Rice. Univ Press of Kentucky (1993)

HISTORIC HIGHWAYS OF AMERICA (VOL 2): INDIAN THOROUGHFARES
by Archer Butler Hulbert. Arthur H. Clark Co (1902)

A HISTORY OF KENTUCKY
by Thomas D. Clark. The John Bradford Press (1960)

MEASURING AMERICA: HOW AN UNTAMED WILDERNESS SHAPED THE UNITED STATES AND FULFILLED THE PROMISE OF DEMOCRACY
by Andro Linklater. Walker & Company (2002)

THE MIDDLE GROUND: INDIANS, EMPIRES, AND REPUBLICS IN THE GREAT LAKES REGION 1650-1815
by Richard White. Cambridge University Press (1991)

THE OHIO
by R. E. Banta. The University Press of Kentucky (1998)

THE OHIO FRONTIER: AN ANTHOLOGY OF EARLY WRITINGS
edited by Emily Foster. The University Press of Kentucky (1996)

THE OHIO FRONTIER: CRUCIBLE OF THE OLD NORTHWEST 1720-1830
by R. Douglas Hurt. Indiana University Press (1996)

THE OHIO RIVER: A COURSE OF EMPIRE
by Archer Butler Hulbert. G. P. Putnam's Sons (1906)

THE OLD NORTHWEST: A CHRONICLE OF THE OHIO VALLEY AND BEYOND
by Frederick Austin Ogg. Yale University Press (1921)

ON THE STORIED OHIO: AN HISTORICAL PILGRIMAGE OF A THOUSAND MILES IN A SKIFF, FROM REDSTONE TO CAIRO
by Reuben Gold Thwaites. A. C. McClurg & Co (1903)

THE PATHS OF INLAND COMMERCE: A CHRONICLE OF TRAIL, ROAD, AND WATERWAY (PART 21)
by Archer Butler Hulbert. Kessinger Publishing (1920/2003)

WESTERN LANDS AND THE AMERICAN REVOLUTION
by Thomas Perkins Abernethy. Russell & Russell (1959)

A WAMPUM DENIED: PROCTOR'S WAR OF 1812
by Sandy Antal. Carleton University Press (1997)

VALLEY OF THE OHIO
by Mann Butler. Kentucky Historical Society (1971)

INDIAN MOUNDS

THE FORT ANCIENT EARTHWORKS: PREHISTORIC LIFEWAYS OF THE HOPEWELL CULTURE IN SOUTHWESTERN OHIO
edited by Robert P. Connolly and Bradley T. Lepper. Ohio Historical Society (2004)

HIDDEN CITIES: THE DISCOVERY AND LOSS OF ANCIENT NORTH AMERICAN CIVILIZATION
by Roger G. Kennedy. The Free Press (1994)

INDIAN MOUNDS OF THE MIDDLE OHIO VALLEY: A GUIDE TO MOUNDS AND EARTHWORKS OF THE ADENA, HOPEWELL, COLE, AND FORT ANCIENT PEOPLE
by Susan L. Woodward and Jerry N. McDonald. The McDonald & Woodward Publishing Company (2002)

THE MOUND BUILDERS
by Robert Silverberg. Ohio University Press (1970)

THE MOUNDBUILDERS: ANCIENT PEOPLES OF EASTERN NORTH AMERICA
by George R. Milner. Thames and Hudson (2004)

NATIVE AMERICANS BEFORE 1492: THE MOUND-BUILDING CENTERS OF THE EASTERN WOODLANDS
by Lynda Norene Shaffer. M.E. Sharpe, Inc. (1992)

PATHS OF THE MOUND-BUILDING INDIANS AND GREAT GAME ANIMALS
by Archer Butler Hulbert. Frontier Press, Inc. (1967)

MISCELLANEOUS

THE FIRST AMERICAN WEST: THE OHIO RIVER VALLEY 1750-1829
www.filsonhistorical.org
The Filson Historical Society of Louisville, Kentucky in partnership with the University of Chicago Library has made their joint collection of 15,000 pages of material on "The First American West: The Ohio River Valley, 1750-1820" available on line through the Library of Congress American Memory website. The easiest way to find the website is to visit the home page of the Filson Historical Society and click on the link to the First American West. The direct link to the First American West is:
http://memory.loc.gov/ammem/award99/icuhtml

Of special interest is *Early Western Travel, 1748-1846* a 32 volume set of early travel accounts, edited by Reuben Gold Thwaites, which includes: Maximilian's Journals (1832-34); De Smet's Letters and sketches, 1841-42; Long's Expedition, 1819-20; Brackenridge's Journey Up the Missouri, 1811; Bradbury's Travels in North America, 1809-1811. The 1814 edition of the Lewis and Clark Journals is also available on The First American West.

REGION THREE
LOUISVILLE TO WOOD RIVER CAMP

- Louisville
- Clarksville
- Along the Ohio River
- New Harmony and Vincennes
- Cairo and Cape Girardeau
- Old French Towns
- Cahokia, IL and Cahokia Mounds
- Wood River Camp and Confluence

3

1. Locust Grove, Louisville KY 2. William Clark by Matthew Harris Jouett, Filson Historical Society, Louisville KY 3. Filson Historical Society, Louisville KY 4. Belle of Louisville, Louisville KY 5. Cahokia Mound, Collinsville IL 6. Sacagawea Statue by Glenna Goodacre, Godfrey IL 7. Church of the Holy Family, Cahokia IL 8. Wood River Camp, Hartford IL 9. Lewis and Clark Confluence Tower

Credits: (6) Lewis and Clark Community College, Godfrey IL (8) Lewis and Clark State Historic Site, Hartford IL (9) Lewis and Clark Confluence Tower Foundation, Hartford IL

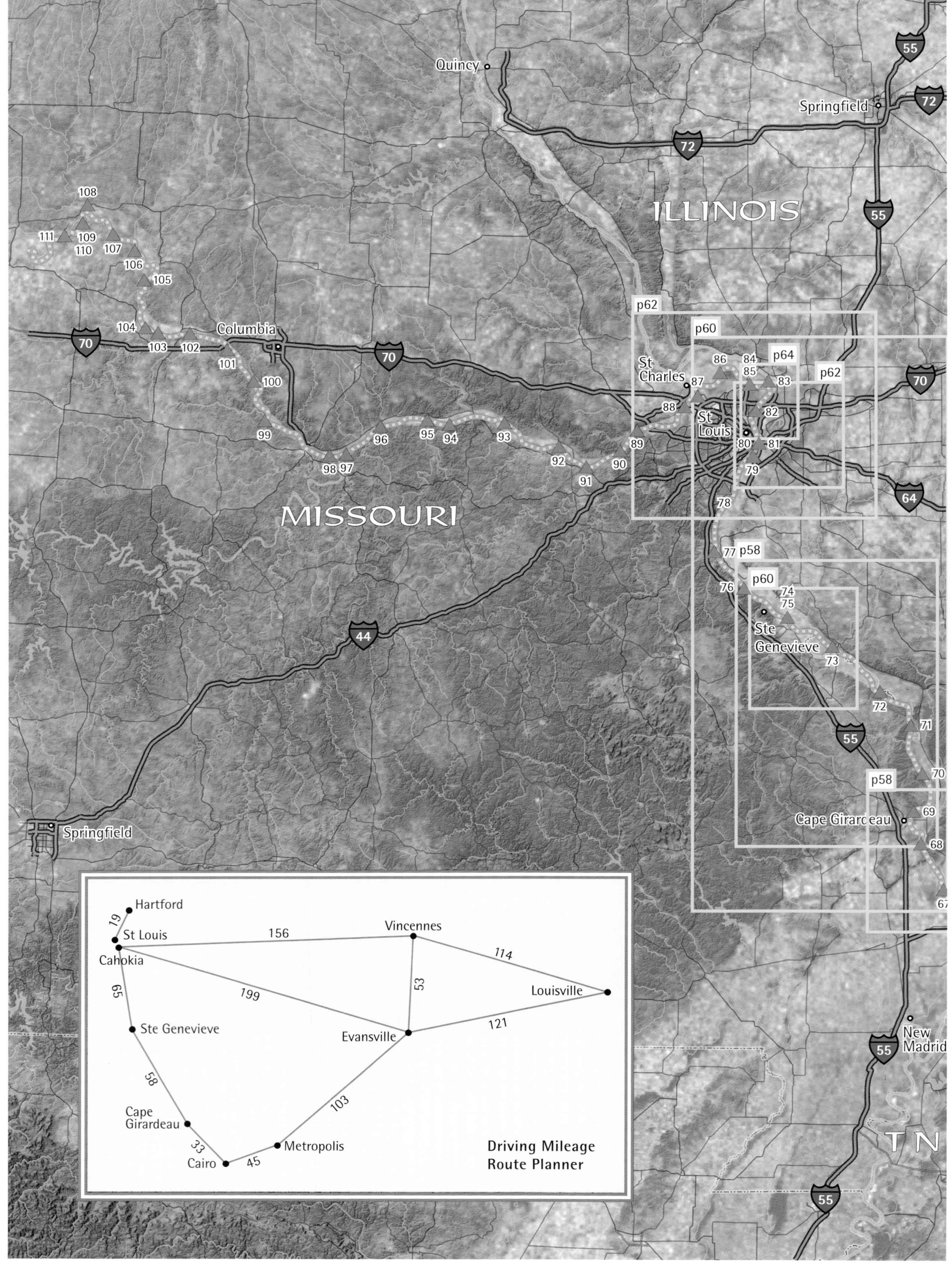
Quincy
Springfield
ILLINOIS
MISSOURI
Columbia
St Charles
St Louis
Ste Genevieve
Cape Girardeau
Springfield
New Madrid
TN
p62
p60
p64
p62
p58
p60
p58
Hartford
St Louis
Cahokia
Ste Genevieve
Cape Girardeau
Cairo
Metropolis
Evansville
Vincennes
Louisville
19
156
114
53
199
65
121
58
103
33
45
Driving Mileage
Route Planner

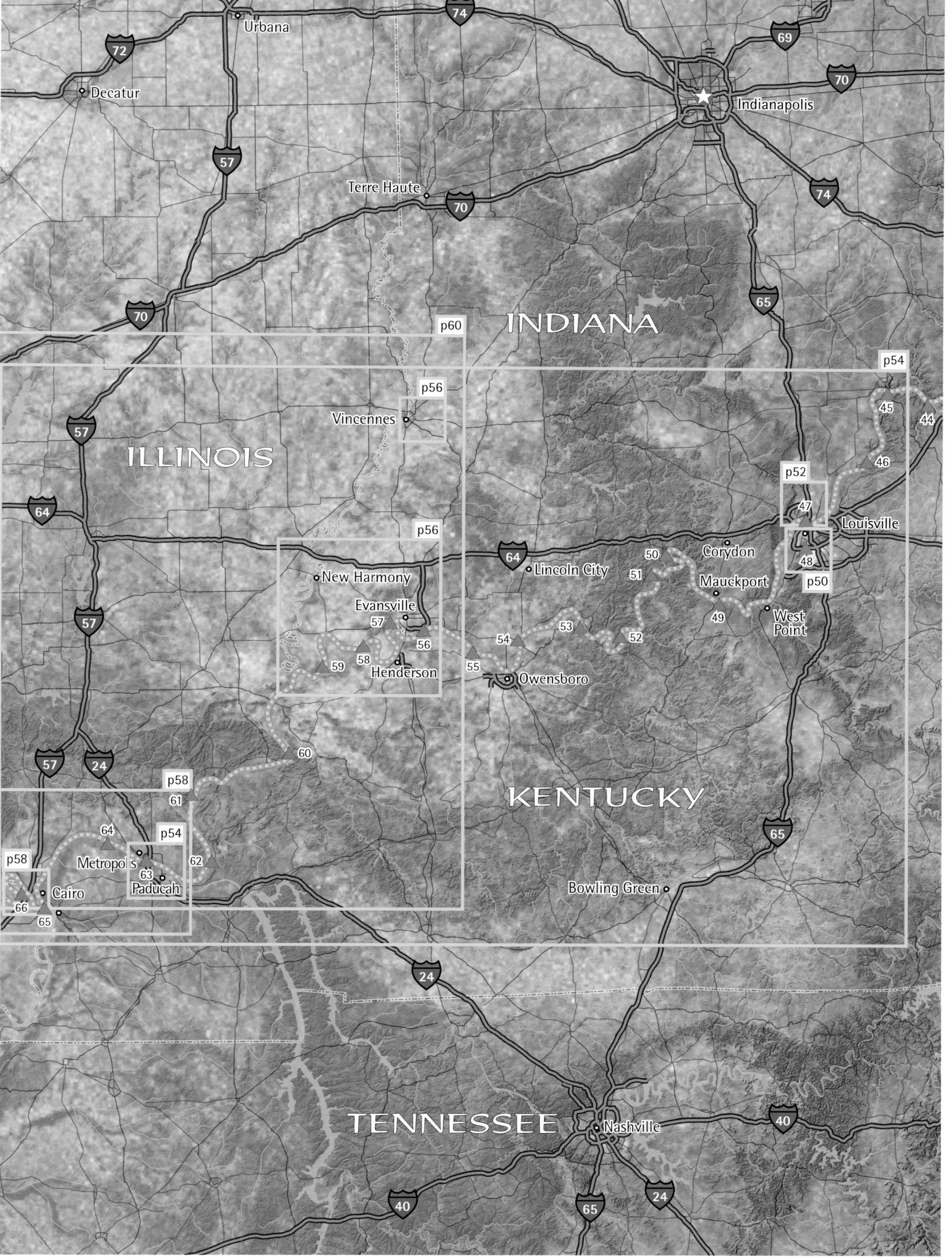
Urbana
Decatur
Indianapolis
Terre Haute
INDIANA
ILLINOIS
Vincennes
Louisville
Corydon
Lincoln City
New Harmony
Evansville
Mauckport
West Point
Henderson
Owensboro
KENTUCKY
Metropolis
Paducah
Cairo
Bowling Green
TENNESSEE
Nashville
p60
p56
p54
p52
p50
p58

3

"Residence of George Rogers Clark on the Indiana Shore, Opposite Louisville from an India Ink sketch by Voustamp" from ***The Ohio River, A Course of Empire*** by Archer B. Hulbert (1906)

3

George Rogers Clark Memorial at Vincennes, Indiana

America 200 Years Ago

The Corps of Volunteers for Northwestern Discovery

Falls of the Ohio—Clarksville, Indiana

Meriwether Lewis arrived at Clarksville at the Falls of the Ohio on October 14th, 1803. He brought with him two of the men who would become members of the Corps of Volunteers for Northwestern Discovery, George Shannon and John Colter. 18 year old Shannon, the youngest member of the Discovery Corps, accompanied him from Pittsburgh. John Colter joined them at Maysville, Kentucky.

William Clark had recruited seven other men. They were: William Bratton, the brothers Reubin and Joseph Field, Charles Floyd, George Gibson, Nathaniel Pryor, and John Shields. Together, they are known as the "Nine Young Men from Kentucky." None of them were army men; they all enlisted into the Corps in October, 1803.

William Clark also had a slave, York, who was his personal servant and companion since childhood. York would go along on the journey to the Pacific and back. He was approximately the same age as Clark. His parents, Old York and Nancy, were slaves in the household of William Clark's parents.

Clark and York were living with his brother General George Rogers Clark at Clarksville, a town founded by his brother, who also founded Louisville, Kentucky. His brother's military exploits during the Revolutionary War had won the entire Northwest Territory for the United States. George Rogers was also a surveyor, scholar and natural scientist. He helped prepare his brother for the expedition—the same expedition George Rogers had been asked by Jefferson to lead twenty years earlier.

Lewis and Clark would serve as Co-Captains on the expedition, as Lewis had promised. However, Clark's captain's commission was denied by the Secretary of War; he was assigned the rank of second lieutenant. They never revealed this to the men. (Clark was posthumously awarded the rank of captain in 2001 at a White House ceremony; York and Sacagawea were made honorary sergeants.)

Fort Massac—Metropolis, Illinois

They left Clarksville on October 26th. Lewis resumed writing in his journal at Fort Massac on November 11th, recording that he had engaged George Drouillard as an Indian Interpreter. Drouillard was half Shawnee-half French; he was hired in a civilian capacity. He was to become one of the most valuable members of the expedition due to his hunting skills and general all around excellence. He was called "Drewyer" in the journals.

Wilkinson-Ville at Cairo, Illinois

On November 14th, Lewis wrote, "passed Wilkinson Ville." Wilkinsonville was a secret military post at the confluence of the Ohio and Mississippi Rivers. No soldiers were at the post in the fall of 1803. In 1801-02 more than half the soldiers in the United States Army were stationed there, in the event that a war with France and/or Spain would start. The number may have been as high as 1500 men. It is unclear how many men who became members of the Corps of Discovery originally came from Wilkinsonville. They were recruited at Kaskaskia, Illinois and from a unit stationed in Tennessee. The records only show who was sworn in the Discovery Corps on January 1, 1804 at Wood River Camp.

General James Wilkinson was the Commanding General of the U S Army and the first Governor of Louisiana Territory. He and Aaron Burr met at Fort Massac to plot their conspiracy to invade Texas. Southern Illinois University has conducted archaeology digs at Wilkinsonville and has a website on these topics: www.southernmostillinoishistory.net.

Cape Girardeau, Missouri

They stopped at Cape Girardeau, a community of 1,111 inhabitants, about equal to the population of St Louis at the time. George Drouillard's uncle, Louis Lorimier, was Commandant of the Cape Girardeau District. Lorimier was a prominent trader from north of Cincinnati, Ohio who had sided with the British during the Revolutionary War. Lorimier, who was married to a Shawnee-French woman, had brought a large number of Shawnee and Delaware Indians to settle in the Spanish-held territory on the west side of the Mississippi River.

Lewis went alone to visit Lorimier. William Clark was unwell. Clark's brother, George Rogers Clark, had destroyed Lorimier's Ohio trading post during the War. Lewis noted the value of the property Lorimier lost was estimated at $20,000, but that he was very prosperous again. When the United States acquired Louisiana

Target Shooting at Wood River Camp, Hartford, Illinois

Brad Winn, Lewis and Clark State Historic Site, Hartford, Illinois

Storage lockers, and the captains' cabin are seen in this view of the keelboat at Onawa, Iowa. Two blunderbusses are attached to the canvas awning supports. The boat is steered by the rudder at the rear of the cabin roof deck. A cannon mounted at the front of the keelboat is not shown.

A keelboat is also on display at the Lewis and Clark Interpretive Center at Hartford IL.. The motorized keelboat which traveled on rivers across the country is at the Boat House Center in St Charles MO.

Lorimier was appointed as an Indian Agent, and one of his sons went to West Point Military Academy. Lewis described Lorimier as very cheerful and remarkable for his hair—his hair was in a single braid, or queue, that fell to his knees. He was at a local horse race. He invited Lewis to stay for supper. Lewis thought his daughter was "much the most descent looking feemale I have seen since I left the settlement in Kentucky, a little below Louisville."

Wood River Camp—Hartford, Illinois

On December 9th Lewis visited the Spanish Commandant of St Louis, who refused them permission to establish a winter camp on the Missouri River. They were already prepared to to stay at Wood River, opposite the confluence of the Missouri and Mississippi Rivers in the "American Bottoms," a flood plain on the east bank of the Mississippi.

William Clark kept the journal during the five months they were at Wood River. Lewis stayed in St Louis and Cahokia, arranging for supplies, gathering information, and preparing for the changeover when the United States would take possession of Upper Louisiana. Clark was in charge of the camp, and getting to know the men. There were fights, and other disciplinary matters. Locals came to visit. There were neighborhood whiskey shops. When both captains were away, Sergeant John Ordway was in charge, and there was trouble with the men not following orders. The men practiced daily target shooting, and lost in shooting matches against the locals. But before they left in May, Clark noted with satisfaction, "Several of the Countrey people In Camp Shooting with the party all git beet and Lose their money."

Lewis came to the camp regularly. Both captains were in St Louis for the ceremonies and celebrations marking the transfer of government on March 9-11, 1804. First the flag of Spain was lowered, and the flag of France was raised for one day. Then the American flag was raised, and Louisiana Territory became part of the United States.

On April 1st, the final selection of men had been completed, and the men enlisted into the army. The Corps of Volunteers for Northwestern Discovery was an elite military unit. Clark described it as "Composed of robust (Young Backwoodsmen of Character) helthy hardy young men, recomended." They had selected three sergeants, John Ordway, Nathaniel Pryor, and Charles Floyd, and 24 privates.

Other soldiers and French engagés would be going along for the first part of the journey; they would return to St Louis with the keelboat in the spring of 1805. The engagés were experienced boatmen, whose skills would be needed. The final composition of the permanent party who went all the way to the Pacific Coast and back was still not established, but it was getting closer.

Preparing to Leave

Clark supervised improvements to the boats. The men built storage lockers running along both sides of the keelboat deck. When their lids were raised, they could became shields in case of attack. They walked on top of them while poling the boat. A bronze cannon and two blunderbusses, were added to the keelboat; each pirogue got a blunderbuss. Blunderbusses were smooth bore weapons that fired grapeshot. The cannon could fire one pound balls or grapeshot. Fifty two lead containers of gunpowder were stored in the hold of the keelboat. Lewis designed the cannisters so that when they were melted down the lead would provide the exact amount of material needed for making the bullets to use the gunpowder.

As spring came to the Mississippi, the goods were stored in the boats, including 21 bales of trade goods for the Indian tribes they would encounter; food supplies (corn, flour, pork, biscuits, beans, lard,"portable soup,"etc); and tools of every description. Keelboat replica builder Butch Bouvier estimates the boat weighed 7-8 tons empty, and its cargo weighed between 10-14 tons.

On May 14th, 1804, the expedition set out at 4 PM, making a short trip of six miles to an island camp. They were on their way to St Charles, 24 miles west of St Louis; where they would wait for Meriwether Lewis, who was still detained on business in St Louis, to join them.

Louisville, Kentucky

1 YORK STATUE, AND RIVERBOAT CRUISES
West River Road.
From I-65 Exit 137 take off-ramp west to West River Road. Go to end of West River Road.

2 FRAZIER HISTORICAL ARMS MUSEUM
828 West Main Street.
From I-65 N Exit 137 turn right onto Franklin St. Then make sharp right turn onto Hancock St. Then turn right onto Main St.

3 FILSON HISTORICAL SOCIETY MUSEUM
1310 South Third Street.
From I-65 N Exit 134B off-ramp turn left onto Saint Catherine Street. Then turn left onto 3rd St.

4 SPEED ART MUSEUM
2035 South Third Street.
From I-65 N Exit 133 off-ramp turn left onto Eastern Parkway (name changes to Cardinal Blvd). From Cardinal Boulevard turn right onto 3rd Street.

5 KENTUCKY DERBY MUSEUM
704 Central Avenue.
From I-65 S Exit 132 off-ramp go straight onto Critenden Dr. Then turn right onto Central Avenue.

6 MULBERRY HILL—CLARK PARK AND CEMETERY
Poplar Level Rd and Thruston Dr.
From I-65 N Exit 133 turn right onto Eastern Parkway. Then turn right onto Poplar Level Rd. Go to Thruston Drive.

7 CAVE HILL CEMETERY
From I-65 N Exit 136A turn right (East) onto Chestnut St. Chestnut St then turns North. At Baxter Ave make a sharp right turn to the Southeast. Go to Cemetery.

8 LOCUST GROVE
561 Blankenbaker Lane.
From I-71 E Exit 2 turn left onto Zorn Ave. Then turn right onto River Rd. Then turn right onto Blankenbaker Lane. Go about one mile to Locust Grove.

9 FARMINGTON HISTORIC HOME
3033 Bardstown Road.
From I-264 Exit 16 go North on Bardstown Rd (US 31, US 150) to Historic Home.

The Story of York

York participated fully as a member of expedition. He had been a companion and body servant to William Clark since they were young boys together. He carried a rifle, he shot game, he cooked. He must have helped in many ways. He was popular with the Indians they encountered. Indians painted themselves black as warriors, and he was real black man. They liked him, and he liked them. They called him "Big Medicine." He fathered a child among the Nez Perce, as did William Clark.

There is an excellent book about York written by Robert Betts called ***In Search of York.*** Betts wrote the book in 1985. An epilog by James Holmberg was added in the 2000 edition, after 47 letters written by William Clark to his brother Jonathan were found. (***Dear Brother: Letters of William Clark to Jonathan Clark*** by James Holmberg).

The letters reveal that York wanted his freedom after they returned from the expedition, and that Clark refused to to grant it.

In 1811, a letter written by Clark's nephew reveals that York had been hired out for some time (perhaps 2 years) as a slave in Louisville so that he "might be with his wife." Clark and York had had some major fallings out. A body servant's work was high status: York was being hired out to strangers as a laborer. He could have worked for others members of the Clark family in Louisville. The letter also states that York's wife was being taken to Natchez by her owner.

Author Washington Irving talked with William Clark in 1832. His notes report that Clark had set three slaves free, including York, whom he set up in business with a large wagon and six horses to haul goods between Nashville and Richmond. Irving says that York couldn't make a go of it and was returning to Clark in St Louis when he died of cholera in Tennessee.

Holmberg reasons that York must have been freed no later than 1815, because slaves could not be freed after they reached the age of 40, and probably died within two or three years of becoming a free man. It is a sad ending to the story of York, but consistent with the realities of the time.

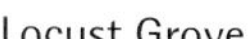

Locust Grove

The marker reads "William Clark, Brother of George Roger Clark..."

Kentucky Derby Museum

Filson Historical Society Museum

Louisville, Kentucky

1 YORK STATUE AND BELLE OF LOUISVILLE STEAMBOAT (NHL)

York's statue, by sculptor Ed Hamilton, is placed in Louisville's historic plaza, "The Belvedere," at 5th St above the steamboat landing. The ***Belle of Louisville*** Steamboat (1914) is a National Historic Landmark and the oldest operating steamboat in the nation. The ***Spirit of Jefferson*** is a diesel-powered riverboat.

■ The ***Belle*** operates between Memorial Day and Labor Day. Fri-Sat, 12-2, and Sun, 2-4. Concession cafe on board. The ***Spirit*** cruises throughout the year, Tues-Sat, 12-2 and 7-9. Fares: $14 adults, $11 seniors, $6 ages 4-12. Lunch tickets are $24, $22, $15 and dinner tickets are $34, $32, and $20. Advance reservations may be made over the phone.
(866) 832-0011 or (502) 574-2992
www.belleoflouisville.org

2 FRAZIER HISTORICAL ARMS MUSEUM

A private collection of important American arms and related artifacts is exhibited with a signficant loan of arms and armor from the Royal Armories in London. The unique, world class museum has three floors of exhibits. Costumed interpreters show how weapons work. Two re-enactment areas include a tournament ring. There are a dozen super realistic tableaus of dramatic warfare episodes. There are feature films, video stations, interactive exhibits and and many very famous weapons.

■ Open daily. Mon-Sat, 9-5. Sun, 12-5. Admission: $9 adults, $7 seniors, $6 students.
(866) 886-7103 www.frazierarmsmuseum.org

3 FILSON HISTORICAL SOCIETY MUSEUM

The Filson Society has one of the most significant Lewis and Clark collections in the nation. Filson Special Collections Curator James Holmberg is the editor of ***Dear Brother: Letters of William Clark to Jonathan Clark.*** The Filson's Museum is located in the carriage house behind the mansion. Their art collection of early portraits is in the Ferguson Mansion.

The museum contains the only known, verifiable, animal object brought back from the expedition, a horn from a bighorn sheep. There are also other treasures of the early frontier in Kentucky, including Daniel Boone's tree carving, "Kill a Bar."

■ Open Mon-Fri, 10-4. Free admission.
(502) 635-5083 www.filsonhistorical.org

4 SPEED ART MUSEUM

Kentucky's oldest and largest art museum has an extensive collection of art, including Egyptian; 17th century Dutch and Flemish art; French art; Renaissance and Baroque tapestries, and contemporary American art and sculpture. African and Native American art are a growing part of the collection.

■ Open Tuesday, Wednesday, Friday 10:30-4; Thursday, 10:30-8; Sat, 10:30-5; Sun, 12-5. Admission is free; $4 donation is suggested.
(502) 634-2700 www.speedmuseum.org

5 KENTUCKY DERBY MUSEUM AND CHURCHILL DOWNS (NHL)

The Kentucky Derby is the oldest, continuously operated race in the United States. It was founded by William Clark's oldest son, Meriwether Lewis Clark in 1875. The Churchills were his mother's brothers, who donated land for the racetrack. The Museum has exhibits and a surround, 360 degree high definition video on the Derby, "The Greatest Race."

■ Open daily, Mar 15-Nov 30, hours are Mon-Sat, 7-5 and Sun 12-5. Winter hours are Mon-Fri, 9-5, and Sun, 12-5. Lunch is available at the Derby Cafe, 11-3, Mon-Fri.

■ Tours are offered from Mar 15-Nov 30, weather permitting (except during Derby, FFA, or Breeder's Cup Week). Tour the backside of the track at 7 AM. Half hour guided tours of the grounds are offered at 8:30 AM, 10 AM, 11:30 AM and 1 PM. Sun at 12:30 PM and 2 PM. Admission: $8 adults, $7 seniors, $3 ages 5-12.
(502) 637-7097 www.derbymuseum.org

6 MULBERRY HILL—CLARK PARK AND FAMILY CEMETERY

The site of the Clark Family home (1785-circa 1900) is now a Louisville city park, a memorial to George Rogers Clark, William Clark's older brother who founded Louisville. The family settled on 256 acres along Beargrass Creek in 1784, where they built their large, two story log cabin called Mulberry Hill. William Clark inherited the property in 1798-99: his parents John Clark and Ann Rogers Clark are buried at the family cemetery along with other family members. A large cypress tree dating from that time remains on the property. There is a public lodge on the park grounds.

■ (502) 456-8171 www.louky.metro.org

7 CAVE HILL CEMETERY

William Clark's family members buried here are his brothers George Rogers Clark and Jonathan Clark (Section P, lot 245); his daughter Mary Margaret (Section D, lot 20-Preston lot); his grandsons Meriwether Lewis Clark, Jr (Section A, lot 699-Churchill lot) and John O'Fallon Clark (Section O, lot 203-Zane lot). Cave Hill is a beautifully landscaped cemetery with fine monuments.

■ Open daily, 8-4:45.
(502) 451-5630 www.cavehillcemetery.com

8 LOCUST GROVE (NHL)

Locust Grove is a National Historic Landmark. William Clark and Meriwether Lewis dined here on November 8, 1806, upon their return from the expedition. It is the only verified remaining structure west of the Appalachian Mountains known to be a stopping point for Lewis and Clark. The home was built by William and Lucy Clark Croghan in 1790. William Croghan was the brother in law and surveying partner of George Rogers Clark. George Rogers spent the last nine years of his life at Locust Grove, from 1809-1818. The site includes the c.1790 Georgian house, the original smoke house and eight other buildings, and formal quadrant gardens. The house is furnished with artifacts belonging to the family and fine examples of Kentucky furniture. There is a museum gallery and gift shop at the Visitor Center.

■ Open daily, Mon-Sat, 10-4:30 and Sun, 1-4:30. Tour began each hour on the quarter hour with the showing of an optional video. Tours of the house and grounds start on the half hour and take approximately 45 minutes. Last tour of the day begans at 3:30. Admission: $6 adults, $5 seniors, $3, ages 6-12.
(502) 897-9845 www.locustgrove.org

9 FARMINGTON HISTORIC HOME

Designed from a plan by Thomas Jefferson, Farmington is an 1816 Federal style mansion. Abraham Lincoln spent about 3 weeks here in 1841, visiting the Speed family. Newly restored, furnished with Kentucky antiques. There is a museum store, garden and other buildings.

■ Open Tues-Sat. 10-4:30. Sun 1:30-4:30. Tours begin on the hour, last tour at 3:45. Sunday tours are 1:30, 2:30, 3:30. Admission: $6 adults, $5 seniors, $3 ages 6-18.
(502) 452-9920 www.historichomes.org

Clarksville and Jeffersonville, Indiana at the Falls of the Ohio

Prince Madoc Exhibit at the Interpretive Center.

10 SOUTHERN INDIANA VISITOR CENTER

305 Southern Indiana Avenue.
From I-65N take the West Court Ave Exit. Turn left (west) onto W Court Ave. Turn left (south) onto Southern Indian Ave. Go 0.1 mile to Visitor Center.

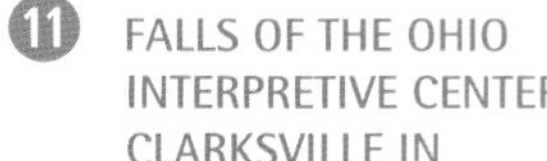

11 FALLS OF THE OHIO INTERPRETIVE CENTER CLARKSVILLE IN

201 West Riverside Drive.
From I-65 N Exit 0 off-ramp turn left (West) onto Court Ave. Court Ave turns left (South) and then merges with US 31. Go South on US 31 to Riverside Dr. Turn right (West). Go to Interpretive Center.

12 CLARK'S CABIN AT CLARK'S POINT CLARKSVILLE IN

Harrison Ave. and Bailey Ave.
From I-65 N Exit 0 off-ramp merge onto US 31. Take off-ramp to Stansifer Ave. Go left to S Clark Blvd. Go right to Harrison Ave. Go left to 1/2 block past Bailey Ave.

13 STEAMBOAT MUSEUM JEFFERSONVILLE IN

1101 East Market Street.
From I-65 N Exit 0 off-ramp turn right (East) onto Court Ave. Turn right (South) onto Spring St. From Spring St turn left (East) onto Market St. Take Market St to the Steamboat Museum.

Prince Madoc and the Welsh Indians

During the time of Lewis and Clark it was widely believed that the Mandan Indians were "white Indians" descended from an expedition of Welshmen who had accompanied Prince Madoc of Wales to the new world in 1170 AD, some 300 years before Columbus. The Welsh Indians were thought to have once lived at the Falls of the Ohio before moving to the Missouri River.

A Welsh explorer, John Evans, went to the Mandan villages in 1796 to discover whether they did indeed speak Welsh, as some had reported. He was a member of a Spanish government sponsored expedition led by the Scottish fur trader James MacKay. The expedition spent the winter of 1796-1797 with the Omaha Indians in Nebraska, while Evans travelled alone to the Mandan villages in North Dakota. He was supposed to continue on to the Pacific on a mission very similar to Lewis and Clark's, but abandoned this unrealistic plan and returned to St. Louis in 1797. Upon his return he proclaimed "there is no such people as the Welsh Indians." He was living as a guest of the Spanish governor in New Orleans when he died of an illness in 1799 at age 29. Welsh claims to the continent had been a matter of contention between Great Britain and Spain since the time of Queen Elizabeth.

The artist George Catlin, who believed they were of different origin than other tribes, painted the Mandans in 1833. He wrote that William Clark "told me before I started for this place, that I would find the Mandans a strange people and half white." (Letter #13, from Catlin's ***North American Indians***, p. 94).

A smallpox epidemic killed between 1600-2,000 Mandans in 1837, leaving only about 200 survivors. Descendants now live on the Three Affiliated Tribes Fort Berthold Reservation in North Dakota.

■ www.madoc1170.com

Reenactors at George Rogers Clark Cabin

Fossil Hunting on the Coral Reef below the Falls of the Ohio Interpretive Center; George Rogers Clark Bridge and Louisville in background. Low water on the Ohio River exposes the fossils in September and October.

Falls of the Ohio Interpretive Center
Kathy Getsinger

3

Clarksville and Jeffersonville Indiana

10 SOUTHERN INDIANA VISITOR CENTER JEFFERSONVILLE, IN

The Visitor Center is located at the first exit of I-65 on Market St, part of the Historic Old Jeffersonville District riverfront area. Jeffersonville was originally laid out in 1802 along a plan proposed by President Jefferson, a checkerboard plan with alternate squares left open for "tree and turf." The streets were redesigned in 1816. The riverfront is a place of restaurants and historic buildings, with parks, flood wall murals, and an Ohio River Overlook. A walking tour brochure is available.

■ Open daily, Mon-Sat, 9-5 and Sun 1-5.
(812) 280-5566 www.sunnysideoflouisville.org

11 FALLS OF THE OHIO INTERPRETIVE CENTER AND STATE PARK CLARKSVILLE, INDIANA

Situated on a bluff overlooking the 430 to 360 million year old fossil beds, the Interpretive Center tells the story of the Falls of the Ohio and the ancient ocean and coral reef that created it. More than 600 types of fossils have been found here. It is the largest exposed fossil bed from the Devonian Period in the world.

The Falls of the Ohio were a two miles series of rapids falling over limestone ledges; the water level dropped 24 feet. These rapids—the only serious navigation obstacle between Pittsburgh and New Orleans—were covered by water when a dam was built in the 1920's. Meriwether Lewis hired a local river pilot to help his boats navigate through the falls safely.

Outside at the front entrance to the Interpretive Center is a bronze statue of Lewis and Clark shaking hands; representing the words of author Stephen Ambrose: "When they shook hands, the Lewis and Clark expedition began." (page 117, ***Undaunted Courage***).

■ Open daily. Mon-Sat, 9-5. Sun, 1-5. Admission: Mon-Thurs, $4 adults, $1 under 19. Fri-Sun and holidays, $5 adults, $2 under 19.
(812) 280-9970 www.fallsoftheohio.org

12 CLARK'S POINT AT FALLS OF THE OHIO STATE PARK—CLARKSVILLE IN

In 1803, General George Rogers Clark built a two story log cabin overlooking the Falls of the Ohio at a place named Point of Rocks. Clark lived there until 1809. His younger brother William Clark and Meriwether Lewis began their expedition from Clark's Point. It was an expedition that George Rogers had been asked to lead in 1783.

The cabin replica, utilizing an old cabin, was built by community volunteers with the involvement of the Falls of Ohio State Park and the Clarksville History Society. It stands on Clark's original lot. The Clarksville Heritage Festival is held during the latter part of October each year. The festival commemorates the departure of the expedition on Oct. 26, 1803.

■ Open Mar-Oct, Mon-Sat, 10-5; Sun, 1-5.
(812) 280-9970 www.fallsoftheohio.org

13 HOWARD STEAMBOAT MUSEUM AND MANSION—JEFFERSONVILLE

This 1894 mansion was the home of the Howard family of Jeffersonville. In 1834 James Howard built his first steamboat, the ***Hyperion***, launched at Jeffersonville. For over a century (1834-1941) the Howard Shipyard and Dock Company were premiere steamboat builders. The mansion has many original furnishings and steamboat memorabilia. The interior was crafted by the same cabinet makers who created the steamboat gothic interiors, using 15 different kinds of wood.

■ Open Tues-Sat, 10-4; Sun 1-4. Personal tours on request. Admission: $5 adults, $4 seniors, and $3 ages 6 through college.
(812) 283-3728 www.steamboatmuseum.org

Note: in the summertime the Louisville and Clarksville areas are both on Eastern daylight savings time.

"Nine Young Men from Kentucky"

The men who enlisted in the army Corps of Volunteers for Northwestern Discovery, at the Falls of the Ohio are called the "Nine Young Men from Kentucky." Two of them came with Meriwether Lewis: 18 year old George Shannon, who joined him at Pittsburgh; and John Colter, at Maysville.

William Clark recruited the others from the local area: cousins Charles Floyd and Nathaniel Pryor; brothers Joseph and Reubin Field; William Bratton; John Shields, and George Gibson. Lewis had asked Clark to find "some good hunters, stout, healthy, unmarried men, accustomed to the woods, and capable of bearing bodily fatigue in a pretty considerable degree."

Charles Floyd came from a prominent family. His father and older brother operated Floyd's ferry across the Ohio from Clarksville to Louisville. Charles was about 20 years old in 1802 (his birthdate is unknown). Despite his youth he held two responsible jobs: he was constable of Clarksville township, and he carried the mail between Louisville and Vincennes, Indiana. Floyd and the Field brothers are recorded as enlisting in August. The others enlisted in October, after Lewis arrived on the 14th.

Both Floyd and Pryor were made sergeants, in charge of squads of the other men. Bratton and Shields were gunsmiths and blacksmiths; Colter and the Field brothers were hunters and scouts; Gibson was a hunter, a fiddler, and good with boats; and young Shannon helped edit the journals for publication. The nine young men from Kentucky proved to be among the best of the best, of the elite army unit known as the Corps of Discovery.

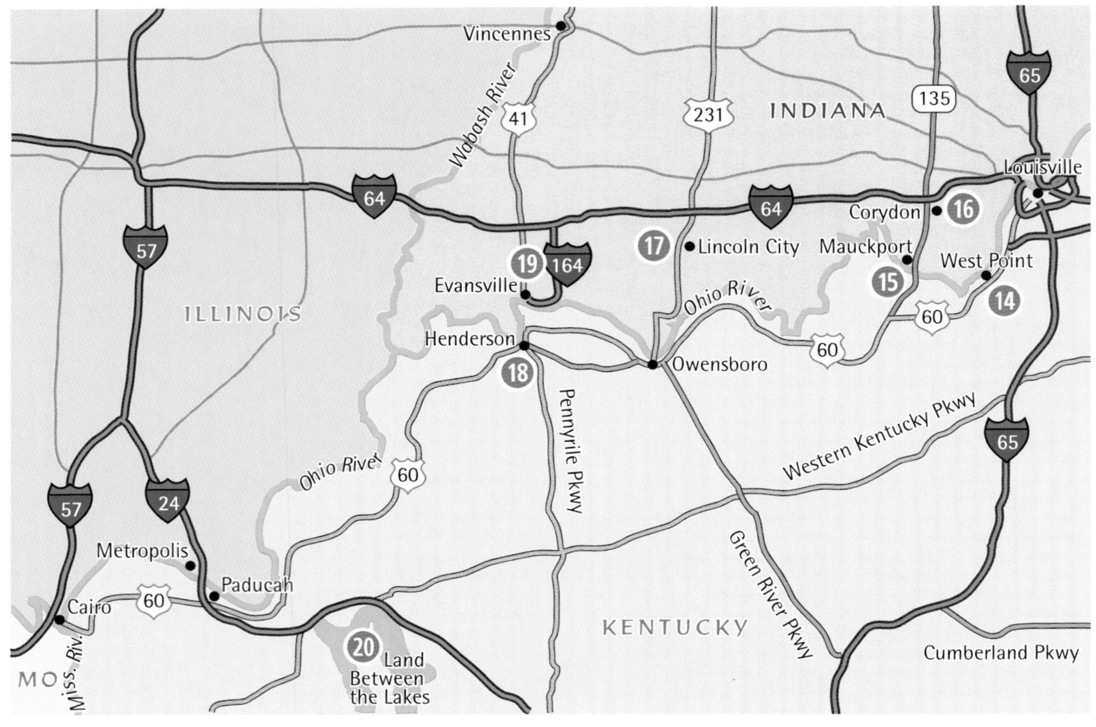

Louisville, Kentucky to Cairo, Illinois

Fort Massac Betty Kluesner

Metropolis, IL and Paducah, KY

14 JOHN SHIELDS MARKER WEST POINT, KENTUCKY

3rd and Elm Streets.
From US 60 turn West onto Main Street. Turn right onto 3rd Street. Go to Elm Street.

15 SQUIRE BOONE CAVERNS MAUCKPORT, INDIANA

100 Squire Boone Road S. W.
From I-64 Exit 105 take Rte 135 South to Watson Rd. Turn left (East). Go to Robins Rd. Turn right (South). Bear left (Southeast) at Squire Boone Rd. Follow Squire Boone Rd to the Caverns.

16 CORYDON STATE CAPITOL CORYDON, INDIANA

200 North Capitol Avenue.
From I-64 Exit 105 take Rte 135 South to Rt 337. Turn left (Southeast). Rt 337 bends South and is named Capitol Ave. in Corydon.

17 LINCOLN BOYHOOD NATIONAL MEMORIAL LINCOLN CITY, INDIANA

State Rt 162 and County Rd 300.
From US 231 turn East on Rte 162. Go to Memorial entrance.

18 AUDUBON MUSEUM AND STATE PARK HENDERSON, KY

3100 US Highway 41.
The park is in the northern ouskirts of Henderson on US 41, a half mile south of the bridge over the Ohio River.

19 ANGEL MOUNDS EVANSVILLE, INDIANA

8215 Pollack Avenue.
From I-164 Exit 5 turn right (East) onto Newburgh Rd. Then turn right (South) onto Stacer Rd. Then turn right (West) onto Pollack Ave.

20 LAND BETWEEN THE LAKES GOLDEN POND, KY

US 68 and Rt. 453.
From I-24 Exit 25 go South onto Purchase Parkway. At Exit 47 go left (Southeast) onto US 68. Go to Rte 453.

21 FLOOD WALL MURALS PADUCAH, KY

North 1st Street.
From I-24 Exit 7 turn right (Northeast) onto US 45. US 45 then turns left (Northwest). From US 45 turn right (Northeast) onto Broadway St. From Broadway St. turn left onto 1st St.

22 MUSEUM OF AMERICAN QUILTERS PADUCAH, KY

215 Jefferson Street.
From I-24 Exit 7 turn right (Northeast) onto US 45. US 45 then turns left (Northwest). From US 45 turn right (Northeast) onto Jefferson Street.

23 FORT MASSAC STATE PARK METROPOLIS, ILLINOIS

1308 East 5th Street.
From I-24 Exit 37 turn West onto US 45. US 45 bends South and is named 5th Street. Follow 5th Street to Fort Massac.

24 SUPERMAN MUSEUM AND STATUE METROPOLIS, IL

611 Market Street.
From I-24 Exit 37 turn West onto US 45. US 45 bends South and is named 5th Street. Follow 5th Street to Market St. Turn left onto Market Street.

Fort Massac Reenactors
Betty Kluesner

Audubon Museum and State Park
Kim McGrew, Audubon Museum

Paducah Flood Wall Murals

Along the Ohio River

14 JOHN SHIELDS MARKER WEST POINT, KENTUCKY

The blacksmith/gunsmith John Shields, one of the most valuable members of the expedition, lived in West Point. A log cabin and marker is located on Elm St near 3rd St. The nearby 1797 Young's Inn, a private residence, has an Audubon marker. The town is near Fort Knox; it is a designated "Preserve America Community."

■ (800) 334-7540 www.radclifftourism.org www.preserveamerica.gov

15 SQUIRE BOONE CAVERNS MAUCKPORT, INDIANA

Squire Boone and his brother, Daniel Boone, discovered these caverns in 1790. When Squire escaped death by hiding in the caves during an Indian attack, he considered the valley and its caverns to be blessed, and settled here with his wife, four sons and their families. John Shields moved to this area after the expedition. Squire Boone's Village has a 200 year old working grist mill and a mine for fool's gold. It has one of the largest rock shops in the Midwest.

■ The Village is open daily last wkd in May to mid-August, and wkds until early Sept. Hours are 10-5 Eastern Daylight Time. Guided one hour tours leave every 30 minutes.

■ Cavern tours operate daily, year round, depending on weather. Tour schedule is 10 AM, noon, 2 PM and 4 PM, Eastern Daylight Time. Admission: $11 adults, $10 seniors, $6.50 ages 6-11. $3 parking during summer months.
(812) 732-4382 www.squireboonecaverns.com

16 CORYDON FIRST STATE CAPITOL CORYDON, INDIANA

Corydon became Indiana's first state capitol in 1813. Prior to that, Vincennes was the capitol of Indiana Territory from 1800-1813. The building was the state capitol from 1816-25.

■ Open April-mid Nov, Tues-Sat, 9-4; and Sun 1-4. Mid Nov-Mar, 12-4 Tues-Sun. Admission $3.50 adults, $3 seniors, $2 children. During Apr-Nov, guided tours of the old state capitol, and 1822 Governor Henrick's home and Porter Law Office are included in admission price. Off season, only the old state capitol is open.
(812) 738-4890 www.indianamuseum.org

■ Scenic Southern Indiana Visitor Center is located in historic Corydon's downtown square. Open daily. (888) 738-2137
www.tourindiana.com (Harrison County CVB)

17 LINCOLN BOYHOOD NAT'L MEMORIAL LINCOLN CITY, INDIANA

The Lincoln Living Historical Farm is a recreated pioneer homestead on the site of the farm where Abraham Lincoln spent his youth, from ages 7 to 21 (1816-1830). National Park Rangers perform activities common to the 1820 era.

■ Open Mar-Nov, 8-5. Dec-Feb, 8-4:30. Admission $3 for 7 days, ages 17+. Maximum of $5 per family.
(812) 937-4541 www.nps.gov/libo

18 AUDUBON MUSEUM AND STATE PARK HENDERSON, KENTUCKY

The museum has the world's largest collection of John James Audubon memorablia, and one of the world's largest collections of his artwork. Audubon lived in Henderson for several years; it is on the Mississippi flyway bird migration route. The park preserves the woods where he walked; there are 5½ miles of nature trails. The nature center has a wildlife observatory. The museum store sells his prints and unique gifts.

■ Open daily, 10-5. Admission $4 adults, $2.50 ages 6-12. (270) 827-1893

■ Cabins, RV and tent camping. Pedal boat and canoe rental. 9 hole golf course. Reservations (270)826-2247 www.hendersonky.org/audubon

19 ANGEL MOUNDS STATE HISTORIC SITE EVANSVILLE, INDIANA

This National Historic Landmark is one of the best preserved prehistoric sites in the United States. Several thousand people lived here from 1100-1450 AD. The museum includes lifelike models of daily life, and an outdoor village.

■ Open Mar-Nov, Tues-Sat, 9-5; Sun, 1-5. Admission, $4 adults, $3.50 seniors, $3 ages 3-12.
(812) 853-3956 www.angelmounds.org

20 LAND BETWEEN THE LAKES NRA GOLDEN POND, KENTUCKY

The Land Between the Lakes (LBL) is managed by the USDA Forest Service. The National Recreational Area is a 37 mile pennisula between Kentucky Lake and Lake Barkley, which has more than two million visitors per year. Attractions include the largest publicly owned buffalo herd east of the Mississippi. There are camping and RV facilities; 26 lake access areas; 300 miles of undeveloped shoreline; 200 miles of hiking/biking trails; hunting and back country permits; camping equipment and canoe and bike rentals; and three visitor centers.

■ Golden Pond Visitor Center open daily, 9-5. Attractions open daily, Apr-Oct; limited hours Mar and Nov; closed Dec-Feb. Admissions: $3 adults, $2 ages 5-12, for Homeplace Living History Farm, Woodland Nature Center, and Planetarium. $3 vehicle fee for Elk and Bison Prairie. Discount pkg: $9 ages 13 and up, $4 ages 5-12.
(270) 924-2233 www.lbl.org

21 RIVER HERITAGE MUSEUM AND FLOOD WALL MURALS—PADUCAH, KY

William Clark founded the town of Paducah in April,1827. The River Heritage Museum is in Paducah's oldest building (1843), restored with period furnishings. Located near the flood wall murals. Video and state of the art interactive models: working lock and dam; dredging exhibit; flood table and other exhibits. Unique gift shop.

■ Open daily, April-Nov, Mon-Sat, 9:30-5; Sun, 1-5. Closed on Sunday Dec-Mar. Admission: $5 adults, $3 under 12. Senior discounts.
(270) 575-9958 www.riverheritagemuseum.org
www.daffordmurals.com

22 MUSEUM OF AMERICAN QUILTER'S SOCIETY—PADUCAH, KENTUCKY

The Society has 70,000 members; they hold a convention in Paducah, "Quilt City U.S.A," during the 3rd week in April.

■ Open April-Oct, Mon-Sat,10-5; Sun, 1-5. Closed Sun in Nov-Mar. Admission: $8 adult, $6 ages 12-18, under 12 free with adult.
(270) 442-8856 www.quiltmuseum.org
www.paducah-tourism.org

23 FORT MASSAC STATE PARK METROPOLIS, ILLINOIS

George Drouillard joined the Discovery Corps here on Nov 11, 1803. A statue of George Rogers Clark overlooks the river on the grounds of this 1802 replica fort. An annual late1700's encampment draws 100,000 visitors in October.

■ Open daily, RV and tent camping. Visitor center, Mon-Sat 9:30-4:30. (618) 524-4712
www.dnr.state.il.us (state parks, fort massac)

24 SUPERMAN MUSEUM AND STATUE METROPOLIS, ILLINOIS

The home of Superman, the Superman Museum Store and the ***Metropolis Planet*** newspaper.

■ Open daily, 9-5. $3 adults, children free with adult. (618) 524-5518 www.supermuseum.com

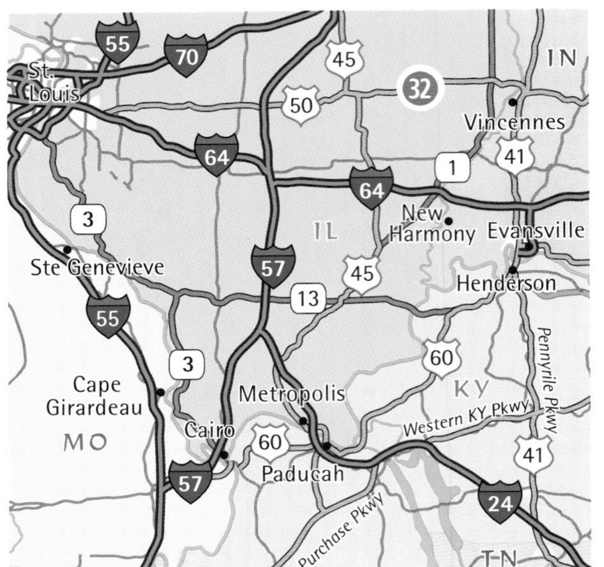

Evansville, Indiana to St Louis, Missouri Area

The Red House, Territory Capitol
Vincennes State Historic Sites

Atheneum/Visitor Center
Historic New Harmony

Halfway House, US Hwy 50

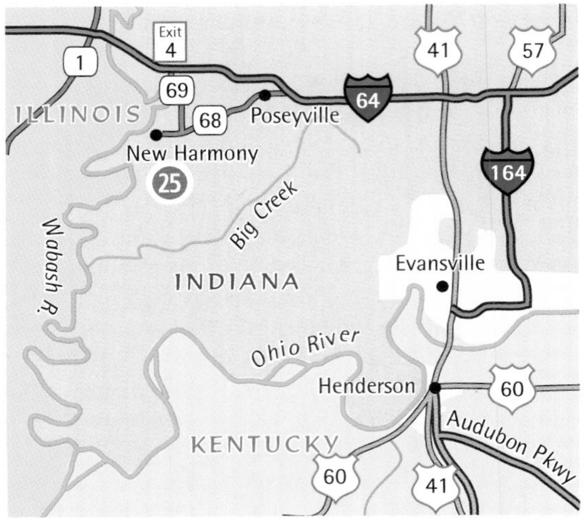

Evansville to New Harmony, Indiana

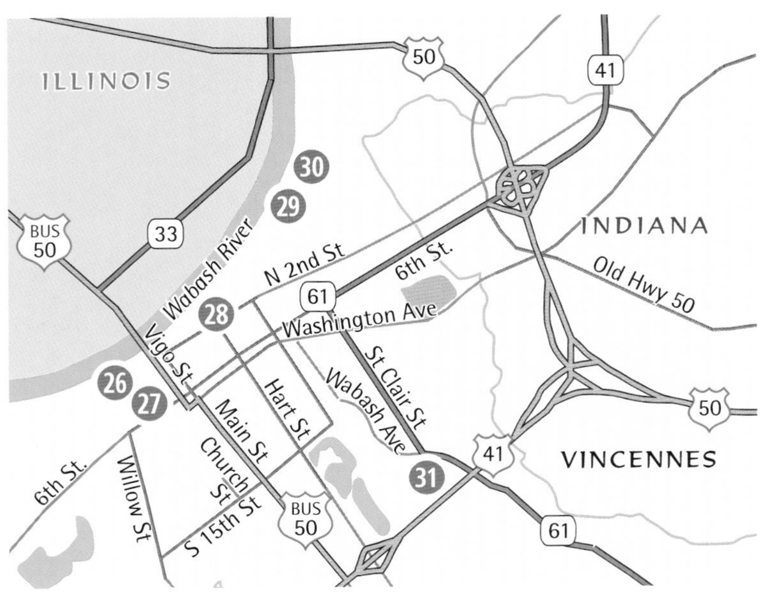

Vincennes, Indiana

25 HISTORIC NEW HARMONY NEW HARMONY, INDIANA

Rt 66 and Rt 69 intersection. From I-64 Exit 4 take Rte 69 to New Harmony.

26 GEORGE ROGERS CLARK NAT'L HISTORICAL PARK VINCENNES, INDIANA

401 S. 2nd St.
From US 50 and from Rte 41 take the 6th St Exit. Go on 6th St to Barnett. Turn right onto Barnett. Go to the Park. From US 41 take the Willow St Exit. Turn right onto Willow. Go to 6th St. Turn right. Go to Barnett St. Turn left and go to the Park.

27 OLD CATHEDRAL COMPLEX VINCENNES, INDIANA

205 Church St.
From US 50 and from Rte 41 take the 6th St Exit. Go on 6th St to Church St. Turn right onto Church St. Go to Cathedral at 2nd St.

28 OLD FRENCH HOUSE AND MUSEUM VINCENNES, INDIANA

1st and Seminary Sts.
From US 50 and from Rte 41 take the 6th St Exit. Go on 6th St to Seminary St. Turn right and go to 1st St.

29 GROUSELAND, WILLIAM HENRY HARRISON MANSION VINCENNES, INDIANA

3 West Scott St.
From US 50 and from Rte 41 take the 6th St Exit. Go on 6th St to Scott St. Turn right and go one block to First St. Turn left and go one block to Scott St. Turn right and go one block to Park St.

30 VINCENNES STATE HISTORIC SITES AND LOG CABIN VISITORS CENTER

1 Harrison St.
From US 50 and from Rte 41 take the 6th St Exit. On 6th St turn right and go on Harrison St to First St.

31 SUGARLOAF MOUND VINCENNES, INDIANA

Wabash Ave and Prospect Ave.
From US 41 take the Hart St Exit. Go North on Hart St to 14th St. Turn right on 14h St and go five blocks to Wabash Ave. Turn right onto Wabash Ave and go to Prospect Ave.

32 GEORGE ROGERS CLARK US 50 ROUTE SOUTHEAST ILLINOIS

From US 45 to Vincennes.

New Harmony Community House #2
Maximilian and Bodmer stayed here.
Historic New Harmony

George Rogers Clark Memorial

Grouseland
Vincennes CVB

New Harmony & Vincennes, Indiana

 NEW HARMONY HISTORIC DISTRICT NATIONAL HISTORIC LANDMARK

The Atheneum/Visitors Center has an orientation film and exhibits. Since its founding in 1814, New Harmony has always been a place of ideas; it continues to hosts visitors and conferences from all over the world.

In 1814 the Harmony Society, a utopian communal society, moved from Harmony, PA near Pittsburgh (Region 2:8) to New Harmony in Indiana. In 1825, they moved back east to Economy, PA (Region 2:9). The Harmonists were originally from Württemberg, Germany.

In 1825 New Harmony's property was sold to Welsh-born industrialist Robert Owen, who established a scientific and educational "think tank" at the village. Distinguished visitors came to live here for months at a time, including Prince Maximilian and artist Karl Bodmer in 1832-33, before they embarked on their journey up the Missouri to Montana.

■ Visitor Center open daily, 9:30-5. Orientation film shown hourly. Mar 15-Dec 30 tours of historic sites at 10 AM and 2 PM daily. Prices: $10 adults, $9 seniors, $5 ages 7-17, and $25 family. 812) 682-4488 www.newharmony.org

■ New Harmony Inn and Conference Center (800) 782-8605 (812) 682-4846 www.newharmonyinn.org

 GEORGE ROGERS CLARK NAT'L HISTORICAL PARK—VINCENNES

The largest national monument outside of Washington DC is located in Vincennes; the granite memorial is a tribute to George Rogers Clark. The Memorial stands on the site where Clark captured the British Fort Sackville from Lt. Governor Henry Hamilton on February 25, 1789. Their heroic march through 240 miles of flooded country—often wading shoulder high in icy water—is considered one of the great military feats of the American Revolution. His army consisted of 172 men: nearly half of whom were French volunteers from the town of Kaskaskia. On July 4, 1788 Lieutenant Colonel Clark and his Virginia frontier militia had captured Kaskaskia without firing a shot. Due to Clark's military victories, Britain ceded Northwest Territory to the United States at the end of the Revolutionary War, doubling the size of the new country.

■ Visitor Center and Memorial open daily, 9-5. Admission: $3 adults, free, ages 17 and under. (812) 882-1776 www.nps.gov/gero

 OLD CATHEDRAL COMPLEX VINCENNES

The Basilica of St Frances Xavier, known as the Old Cathedral, was built in 1826 on the site of the first Catholic parish in Indiana, dating to 1749. Over 4000 early residents of Vincennes are buried in the adjacent French and Indian cemetery. Across the courtyard from the Cathedral is the oldest library in Indiana, containing over 10,000 volumes, dating back to 1319. The library contains records of the history of the Catholic Church in America as well as the history of the Old Northwest.

■ Library open daily, 8-4. Admission $1 adults, 50¢ ages 12 and under.

■ Self-guided tours of Cathedral (except during mass). Visitors welcome at services, 8 AM Mon and Weds; 12 noon Fri; 5:15 PM Sat; 8 and 10:30 AM Sun. Donations 50¢ adults and 25¢ students. (800) 886-6443 www.vincennescvb.org

 OLD FRENCH HOUSE AND INDIAN MUSEUM—VINCENNES

Vincennes is one of the oldest European settlements in the Midwest. It began as the site of a French trading post in 1732. The 1806 home of Michel Brouillet is one of the few remaining upright log style French Creole houses in the United States. It has furnishings of that time period; fur trade, and Indian exhibits.

■ Open last wkd May to 1st wkd Sept. Tues-Sat, 9-12 and 1-5; open Sun 1-5. Admission: $1 adults, 50¢ students. (800) 886-6443 (812) 882-7886 www.vincennescvb.org

 GROUSELAND, WILLIAM HENRY HARRISON MANSION (NHL)

Historian James Holmberg says that Grouseland "may be one of the few extant structures west of the Appalachians that Lewis and Clark visited." He writes that during the War of 1812 Harrison stated "he would rather have Clark with him in the kind of war they were engaged in than any other man in the United States." (page 93, *Dear Brother: Letters of William Clark to Jonathan Clark)*

Grouseland was the home of William Henry Harrison and his family from 1803-1812, when Harrison was Governor of Indiana Territory. The mansion was the first brick house in Indiana Territory; it was called the "White House of the West, " and includes a Council Room where Harrison met with Indian tribes. Grouseland was named for the grouse game bird that Harrison loved to hunt.

Harrison served as Commander of the Army in the Northwest during the War of 1812; and in 1840 was elected the 9th President of the United States. He died in office in 1841, after serving only 31 days.

■ Open Mar-Dec, Mon-Sat, 9-5 and Sun, 11-5; Jan-Feb, 11-4 on Sat-Sun.
Admission: $5 adults, $3 high school, college students, $2 students.
(800) 886-6443 www.vincennescvb.org

 LOG CABIN VISITORS CENTER VINCENNES STATE HISTORIC SITES

The Log Cabin Visitor Center has information on Vincennes history. It administers the Vincennes State Historic Sites:
1811 "Red House" Territory Capitol
1804 Print Shop of Elihu Stout replica
1838 Old State Bank
1840 Maurice Thompson birthplace
1801 Jefferson Academy replica
1803-1811 Fort Knox II site (3 miles north)
Tours start at the Log Cabin Visitor Center.

■ Open mid Apr-mid Nov, Tues-Sat, 9-5 and Sun 1-5. Admission: $3.50 adult, $3 senior, $2 children.
(812) 882-7422 www.vincennescvb.org

 SUGARLOAF MOUNDS—VINCENNES

The Sugarloaf Mounds are named for their resemblance to old fashioned sugarloafs. The lower sugarloaf mound is now called Pyramid Mound; artifacts dating from 900 AD are displayed at Grouseland. The Buffalo Trace Road from Louisville passed near the mounds. (Charles Floyd must have taken this road on his mail route from Louisville to Vincennes.)

■ (812) 882-7886 www.vincennescvb.org

32 GEORGE ROGERS CLARK US 50 ROUTE

The National Park Service is studying a proposal to create a "George Rogers Clark Northwest Campaign Trail." The route of US Hwy 50, going east from junction with US Hwy 45, follows the last 50 miles of so of Clark's march to Vincennes in February, 1779.

The complete George Rogers Clark Memoir of the Campaign is available at the Indiana Historical Bureau website:
www.statelib.lib.in.us/www/ihb/resources

Confluence of the Ohio and Mississippi
Betty Kluesner

Cape Girardeau Mural: MeriwetherLewis meets Louis Lorimier at the horse race. (Mississippi River Tales Mural)
Cape Girardeau CVB

3

Cape Girardeau to St. Genevieve, Missouri

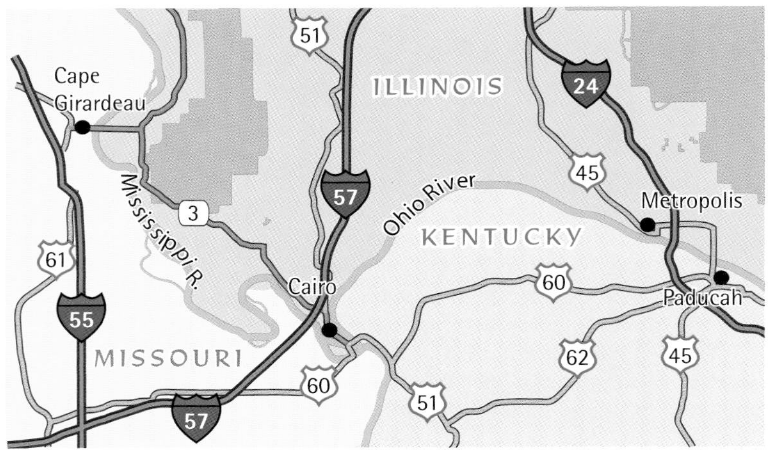

Metropolis, Illinois to Cape Girardeau, Missouri

33 FT DEFIANCE STATE PARK, CONFLUENCE OF OHIO AND MISSISSIPPI RIVERS CAIRO, ILLINOIS

Fort Defiance Road.
From I-57 Exit 1 turn East onto Rt 3. Keep straight onto to US 51 (Sycamore St, then Washington Ave). US 51 bends South. Keep straight onto US 60/US 62. Go 1/10th mile to Fort Defiance Rd. Follow Fort Defiance Rd Southeast to the confluence.

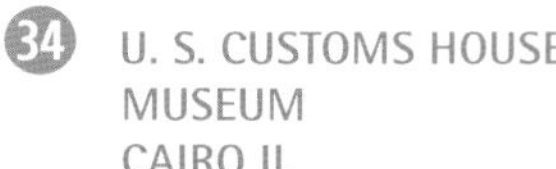

34 U. S. CUSTOMS HOUSE MUSEUM CAIRO IL

1400 Washington Ave.
From I-57 Exit 1 turn East onto Rt 3. Keep straight onto to US 51 (Sycamore St, then Washington Ave). Go to 1400 Washington Ave.

35 TYWAPPITY BOTTOMS AND RIVER RIDGE WINERY COMMERCE, MO

850 County Rd 321.
From I-55 Exit 80 turn West onto Rt 77. Then turn right (Notheast) onto Rt E. Follow Rte E into Commerce. Rt E turns left (North). Follow Rt E to Rt 321. Turn left (West) onto Rt 321. Follow Rte 321 1.8 miles (just before Riverview Dr) to the Winery.

36 RED HOUSE INTERPRETIVE CENTER CAPE GIRARDEAU, MO

128 South Main St
From I-55 Exit 96 turn east onto William St.Turn left (north) onto Main St. Go 0.1 mile to the Red House Interpretive Center.

37 CAPE ROCK PARK CAPE GIRARDEAU, MO

83 E Cape Rock Dr.
From I-55 Exit 96 turn East onto William St. Then turn left (North) onto US 61. Then turn right (East) onto Independence St. Then turn left (North) onto Main St. Then turn right (East) onto Cape Rock Dr. Follow Cape Rock Dr to the Park.

38 CAPE GIRARDEAU MURALS CAPE GIRARDEAU, MO

Convention and Visitors Bureau
100 Broadway St.
From I-55 Exit 96 turn East onto William St. Then turn left (North) onto US 61. Then turn right (East) onto Independence St. Then turn left (North) onto Main St. Go to Broadway St.

39 SOUTHEAST MISSOURI REGIONAL MUSEUM CAPE GIRARDEAU, MO

One University Plaza.
From I-55 Exit 96 turn East onto William St. Then turn left (North) onto US 61. Then turn right (East) onto Independence St. Then turn left (North) onto Henderson Ave. Then turn right (east) when you come to the intersection of Henderson Ave and Rockwood Dr.

40 TRAIL OF TEARS STATE PARK JACKSON, MO

429 Moccasin Springs.
From I-55 Exit 105 take US 61 North. Then turn right (East) onto Rte 177. Rte 177 turns right (South). Just before the the intersection with Rte V, turn left (East) into the Park entrance.

41 TOWER ROCK AND TOWER ROCK WINERY ALTENBURG, MO

10769 Hwy A.
From I-55 Exit 117 take Rte KK East. Then turn left (North) onto US 61. Then turn right (East) onto Rte A. Follow Rte A through Altenburg to the Winery.

Cairo Custom House Museum
SIU School of Architecture

The Red House Interpretive Center
Cape Girardeau Convention and Visitors Bureau

Tower Rock
Tower Rock Winery

Cairo and Cape Girardeau Area

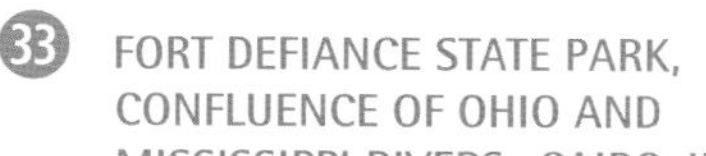

33 FORT DEFIANCE STATE PARK, CONFLUENCE OF OHIO AND MISSISSIPPI RIVERS—CAIRO, IL

An observation tower viewing platform gives visitors a view of where the two largest rivers in North America meet. For five days Lewis and Clark practiced their skills in celestial observation and land surveying here.

Southern Illinois educational institutions, with funding from the Library of Congress, have done archaeological and historical research; developed a website; and created a compass design sculpture for the confluence state park.

The confluence also marks the start of a mapping project by the Geography Dept of the University of Missouri, which has an atlas and website devoted to Lewis and Clark campsites along the Mississippi and Missouri Rivers. Due to land accretion along the river, the modern location of their campsite at the confluence is thought to be just north of 4th St on Ohio St in Cairo.

■ http://lewisclark.geog.missouri.edu
(800) 248-4373 Fort Defiance State Park
www.shawneecc.edu/sihcc

34 CUSTOMS HOUSE MUSEUM—CAIRO, IL

Congress in 1854 made Cairo a Port of Delivery. A customs officer inspected goods and collected fees after ships had passed the Point of Entry at New Orleans. The Custom House Museum, and the public library across the street, both have interesting architecture and exhibits. General Ulysses S Grant made Cairo his headquarters for 6 months during the Civil War.

■ Open Mon-Fri, 10-noon and 1-3. Donations welcomed. (681) 734-9632 Call the library to arrange tours by appt. (618) 734-1840
www.southernmostillinoishistory.net

35 TYWAPPITY BOTTOMS AND RIVER RIDGE WINERY—COMMERCE, MO

Sgt John Ordway returned to settle near Commerce in 1809. George Drouillard, Alexander Willard and Reuben Field all bought land in the Cape Girardeau District.The River Ridge Winnery is located just 1.8 miles north of Commerce in the hills near the Mississippi River. The Winery has a tasting room, gift shop and fine dining.

■ Open daily 11-6. Call (573) 264-2747 for reservations. www.riverridgewinery.com

36 RED HOUSE INTERPRETIVE CENTER CAPE GIRARDEAU, MO

The Red House replica was completed in 2003 as a Lewis and Clark Bicentennial project. Meriwether Lewis visited Louis Lorimier, the Spanish Commandant of the Cape Girardeau District, at the Red House on Nov. 23, 1803. The commandant was the uncle of George Drouillard, the civilian hunter and interpreter they had just hired at Fort Massac. Drouillard's mother was the sister of Lorimier's wife; the sisters were Shawnee-French, and their husbands were French-Canadians. (See pages 48-49 for more on Lorimier.) The Shawnee and Delaware Indians had settled along Apple Creek north of Cape Girardeau at Shawneetown. The Absentee Shawnee and the Delaware Tribes now live in Oklahoma.

■ The Red House is open March-December on Saturdays from 10-4. Admission: $3 adults, $1 students. Contact the Convention and Visitor's Bureau to schedule a tour.
Email: info@visitcape.com (800) 777-0068 or (573) 335-1631 www.visitcape.com

37 CAPE ROCK PARK

The original Cape Rock that identified Cape Girardeau is a rock point where the French trader Jean Baptiste Girardot established a trading post in the 1730's. Cape Rock Park is about 3 miles north of the Red House; it has a magnificent view of the river. A bronze plaque commemorates the site of the trading post.

■ www.cityofcapegirardeau.org
(573) 335-5421

38 CAPE GIRARDEAU MURALS

The Great Murals Tour of Cape Girardeau provides a fun way to explore the city's history. Many murals are located north of the Red House in the city's historic downtown district, near the shops and restaurants. The ***Missouri Wall of Fame*** has 45 famous people born in Missouri; the ***Mississippi River Tales*** flood wall murals by Thomas Melvin have local history; there are 13 different mural attractions in all.

■ A Murals Tour map may be downloaded at www.visitcape.com, or pick one up at the Convention and Visitors Bureau at 100 Broadway.
(800) 777-0068 (573) 335-1631
www.thomasmelvin.com

39 SOUTHEAST MISSOURI REGIONAL MUSEUM—CAPE GIRARDEAU, MO

The museum has one of the finest collections of prehistoric Mississippian artifacts in the US; a collection of Southwestern Indian arts and crafts; and life size sculpture and bas relief from the 1904 St Louis World's Fair. The museum will be expanded to include a steamboat museum and other new exhibits when it moves to new quarters at the River Campus in 2007.

■ Open daily: Mon-Fri 9-4 and wkds 12-4. Closed on school holidays.
(573) 651-2260 www5.semo.edu/museum

40 TRAIL OF TEARS STATE PARK AND NATIONAL HISTORIC TRAIL JACKSON, MISSOURI

Lewis and Clark camped here on Nov. 24, 1803. The Trail of Tears State Park is a memorial to the Cherokee Indians who were forced to leave their homelands in the southeastern United States and relocate to Indian Territory in Oklahoma during the winter of 1838-39. Seventeen groups of 1000 Cherokee people made the 800-1000 mile journey on foot. It is estimated that over 4000 people died along the way. Nine of these groups crossed the Mississippi River at this state park, where two miles of the historic trail are preserved. The Visitor Center has both Trails of Tears and nature exhibits.The 3415 acre park has a wild area similiar to the Appalachian Mountains; hiking trails, picnic areas, a man made lake, and RV and tent campgrounds.

■ (573) 334-1711 www.mostateparks.com
www.nps.gov/trte

41 TOWER ROCK AND TOWER ROCK WINERY—ALTENBURG, MO

Lewis and Clark measured and mapped Tower Rock and the surrounding area. The famous river landmark is called the "Plymouth Rock of the Missouri Synod Lutheran Church," founded here in 1839 by German immigrants from Saxony.

Tower Rock Winery has a garden, lake and vinyard. Music, food and wine festival on 3rd wkds, May-Oct. Light fare is served. Their website has good Tower Rock and local history.

■ For info on Tower Rock, call the forest office at (573) 824-5479. The Winery is open Tues-Sun, 12-6, year round. (573) 824-5479
www.tower-rock-winery.com

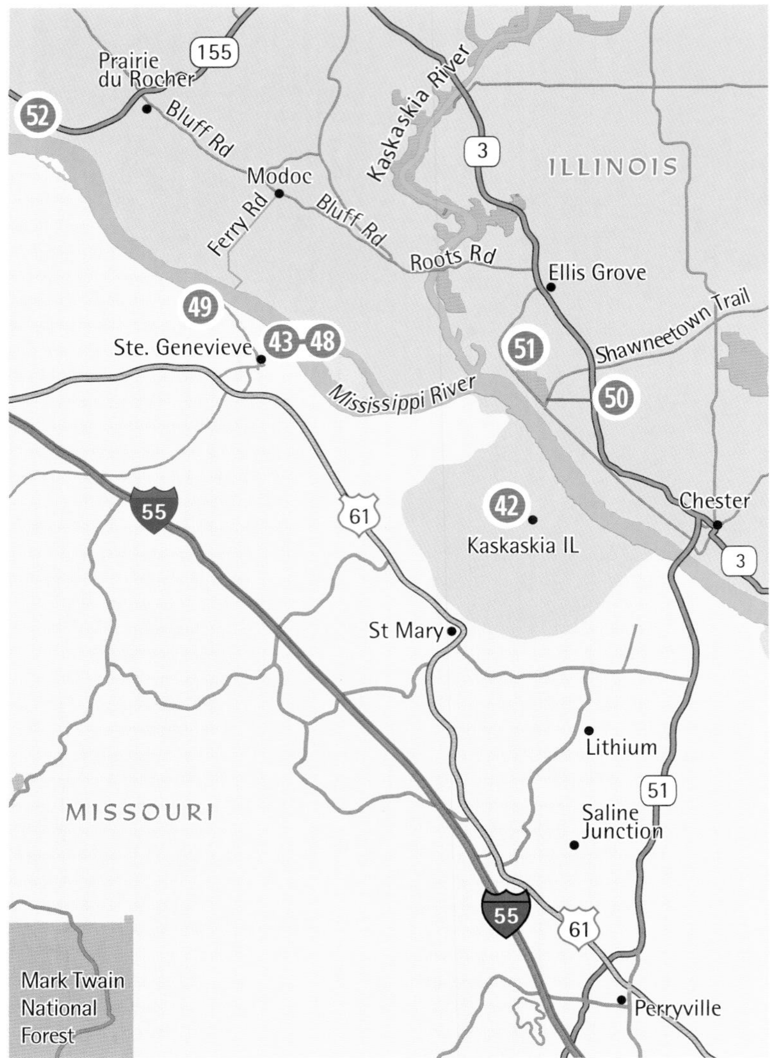

Kaskaskia to Ste Genevieve

Ste Genevieve Area Locator Map

Ste Gen-Moduc Ferry

42 KASKASKIA BELL
KASKASKIA ISLAND, IL

Kaskaskia Island.

From I-55 Exit 141 take Rte Z East. Then turn left (Northeast) onto US 61. US 61 turns left (Northwest). Then turn right (Northeast) onto Rt 15. Rte 15 runs Northwest then turns Northeast. Go past Grabe Rd to the Bell.

43 GREAT RIVER ROAD INTERPRETIVE CENTER
STE GENEVIEVE, MO

66 South Main St.

From I-55 Exit 154 take Rt O to US 61. Turn right (Southeast). Then turn left (East) onto Market St. Then turn left (North) onto Main St.

44 BOLDUC HOUSE MUSEUM
STE GENEVIEVE, MO

123 South Main St.

From I-55 Exit 154 take Rte O to US 61. Turn right (Southeast). Then turn left (East) onto Market St. Then turn right (South) onto Main St.

45 BOLDUC LA MEILLEUR HOUSE
STE GENEVIEVE, MO

Market and Main Streets.

From I-55 Exit 154 take Rte O to US 61. Turn right (Southeast). Then turn left (East) onto Market St. Then turn right (South) onto Main St.

46 FELIX VALLE HOUSE
STE GENEVIEVE, MO

2nd and Merchant Streets.

From I-55 Exit 154 take Rte O to US 61. Turn right (Southeast). Then turn left (East) onto Market St. Then turn left (north) onto Second St. Go to Merchant St.

47 LA MAISON GUIBOURD-VALLE
STE GENEVIEVE, MO

4th and Merchant Streets.

From I-55 Exit 154 take Rte O to US 61. Turn right (Southeast). Then turn left (East) onto Market St. Then turn left (north) onto 4th St. Go to Merchant St.

48 STE GENEVIEVE MUSEUM
STE GENEVIEVE, MO

DuBourg and Merchant Streets.

From I-55 Exit 154 take Rte O to US 61. Turn right (Southeast). Then turn left (East) onto Market St. Then turn left (north) onto DuBourg Place. Go to Merchant St.

49 STE GEN-MODUC FERRY
STE GENEVIEVE, MO

Modoc Ferry Landing.

From I-55 Exit 154 take Rte O to US 61. Turn right (Southeast). Then turn left (East) onto Market St. Then turn left (North) onto Main St. Continue to the end of Main St.

50 PIERRE MENARD HOME
ELLIS GROVE, IL

4230 Kaskaskia St.

From I-55 Exit 141 go Northeast on Rte Z. Next turn left (North) onto US 61. Next turn right (Southeast) onto Rte H. Next turn left (North) onto Rte 51. Rte 51 bends Northeast and crosses the Mississippi River. Turn left (Northwest) onto Kaskaskia St. Continue to the Pierre Menard Home.

51 FORT KASKASKIA SITE
ELLIS GROVE, IL

From I-55 Exit 141 go Northeast on Rte Z. Next turn left (North) onto US 61. Next turn right (Southeast) onto Rte H. Next turn left (North) onto Rte 51. Rte 51 bends Northeast and crosses the Mississippi River. Turn left (Northwest) onto Kaskaskia St. Follow Kaskaskia St to Shawneetown Trail. Turn right (Northeast). Go to Park Rd. Turn left (north). Continue to Fort.

52 FORT DE CHARTRES II
PRAIRIE DU ROCHER, IL

1350 State Route 155.

From Rte 3 at Roma, IL take Rte 155 through Prairie du Rocher to Fort de Chartres.

Felix Valle House, Ste Genevieve
greatriverroad.com

Fort Kaskaskia Site

Pierre Menard Home

Old French Towns on the Mississippi

42 KASKASKIA BELL STATE HIST. SITE AND OLD KASKASKIA VILLAGE NATIONAL HISTORIC LANDMARK KASKASKIA ISLAND, ILLINOIS

The town of Kaskaskia, Illinois which once was the capitol of old Illinois on the eastern side of the Mississippi River, is now on the western side. The Kaskaskia Bell, cast in France in 1741, is eleven years older and only slightly smaller than the U S Liberty Bell in Philadelphia. It was a gift of King Louis XV to the people of Illinois Country. On July 4, 1778 it rang long and loud when George Rogers Clark captured Kaskaskia for the United States. It is called the "Liberty Bell of the West."

■ Open daily, 8-5. (618) 859-3741
www.state.il.us/hpa/hs/Kaskaskia.htm

43 GREAT RIVER ROAD INTERPRETIVE CENTER—STE GENEVIEVE, MO

Ste Genevieve's historic district is a National Historic Landmark and Missouri's oldest town. Founded c. 1735, it contains the largest group of French colonial houses in the U S, more than 150 pre-1825 structures. The tourist information center has a walking tour video, an art gallery and other exhibits and a gift shop.

■ Open daily, 9-4. (573) 883-7097
www.ste-genevieve.com/tourism.htm

44 BOLDUC HOUSE MUSEUM NATIONAL HISTORIC LANDMARK STE GENEVIEVE, MO

The Bolduc House is the winner of the ***2005 Preserve America Presidential Award.*** The 1770 house was moved to its present site in 1784, after the flood of 1783 destroyed the earlier community of Ste Genevieve. It is the most authentically restored French Creole house in the U S; with original 18th century furnishings and an herb garden. The Bolduc-LeMeilleur House is included in the admission price; both homes and garden are on the tour.

■ Open daily, Apr-Oct, Mon-Sat,10-4; Sun11-5. Admission: $4 adult, $2 student.
(573) 883-3105 www.bolduchouse.com

45 BOLDUC LA MEILLEUR HOUSE STE GENEVIEVE, MO

Louis Bolduc's granddaughter's home is a mixture of French and American styles, built in 1820. Included with the Bolduc House Museum.

46 FELIX VALLE STATE HISTORIC SITE STE GENEVIEVE, MO

The site contains several buildings. The Valle house was built in 1818 in the federal style by its original owner, who operated a trading post on the premises. The Valle family acquired it in 1824. The business firm of Menard and Valle dealt with the Indian trade in Missouri and Arkansas; Felix Valle owned a mining firm and iron works. Guided tours are given.

The Amoreux House (c. 1792) is part of the state historic site. It is open Apr-Oct, and is included with admission to the Felix Valle site. It is located near the Big Common Field on St. Marys Road.

■ Open year round, Tues-Sat, 10-4 and Sun, 12-5. Admission: $2.50 adults, $1.50 students.
(573) 883-7102 www.greatriverroad.com

47 LA MAISON GUIBOURD-VALLE STE GENEVIEVE, MO

The house dates from 1806-07, and is of vertical log construction. The home was aquired in the 1930's by members of the Valle family who furnished it with family antiques dating from the Louis XV and Louis XVI periods. A foundation maintains the house and its lovely gardens and gift shop.

■ Open daily, Apr-Oct, 10-5. Nov-Mar, 12-4. $2 adults, 50¢ children. (573) 883-3461
www.greatriverroad.com

48 STE GENEVIEVE MUSEUM STE GENEVIEVE, MO

The Ste Genevieve Museum is located on historic Dubourg Place, near the Church of Ste Genevieve founded in 1759. (Ste. Genevieve is the patron saint of Paris.) The church bells still ring the hour. The town square in a French river town was called the "Place des Armes" where the church, civil and military authorities were all located together near the waterfront.

The museum was built on the square in 1935 as the town's bicentennial commemoration. It contains displays relating to the area's earliest industry, salt mining at Saline Spring; weapons; prehistoric and historic Native American artifacts; old documents and other memorabilia.

■ Open daily: Apr-Oct, 9-11 and 12-4. Nov-Mar, 12-4. Admission $2 adults, $1 students.
(573) 883-3461 www.greatriverroad.com

49 STE GENEVIEVE-MODUC FERRY STE GENEVIEVE, MO

The Ste Genevieve-Moduc Ferry holds about nine vehicles. Foot passengers may also use the car ferry. When pulling up to the ferry landing, blink your car lights; if the boat is across the river, they will come and get you. The ferry takes ten minutes to cross the Mississippi.

■ Ferry hours: daily, Mon-Fri, 6 AM-6 PM; Sat, 6 AM-7 PM; Sun, 8 AM-7 PM. Standard car fare is $7 each way, $12 roundtrip. Inquire for pedestrian rates and other vehicles.
(573) 883-7415 www.greatriverroad.com

50 PIERRE MENARD HOME NATIONAL HISTORIC LANDMARK STATE HISTORIC SITE ELLIS GROVE, IL

The home is the grandest French colonial home in the Mississippi Valley, built c. 1815 for fur trader and entrepeneur Pierre Menard. Menard and his partner William Morrison helped fund the first expedition back up the Missouri River in 1807, the Lisa-Drouillard Expedition. The mansion is furnished in family heirlooms and period pieces. Audio-visual program and museum on ground floor. Tour of house and grounds and other buildings on property.

■ Open daily, Weds-Sun, 8-4.
Suggested donation: $2 adults, $1 children.
(618) 859-3031
www.state.il.us/hpa/hs/Menard.htm

51 FORT KASKASKIA STATE HISTORIC SITE ELLIS GROVE, IL

While at Kaskaskia, the expedition gained more members from US Army units stationed in the area. The Fort Kaskaskia site consists of the bluff overlook of Old Kaskaskia, and Garrison Hill Cemetery. RV and tent campground.

■ Open daily, 6 AM-10 PM.
(618) 859-3741
www.state.il.us/hpa/hs/Kaskaskia.htm

52 FORT DE CHARTRES II NATIONAL HISTORIC LANDMARK PRAIRIE DU ROCHER, IL

Fort de Chartres, is a stone fort c. 1750, which has been partially reconstructed with a museum. Popular reenactments and living history, 1st wkd in June and 1st wkd Oct.

■ Open Weds-Sun, 9-5. Donations suggested.
(618) 284-7230
www.state.il.us/hpa/DeChartres.htm

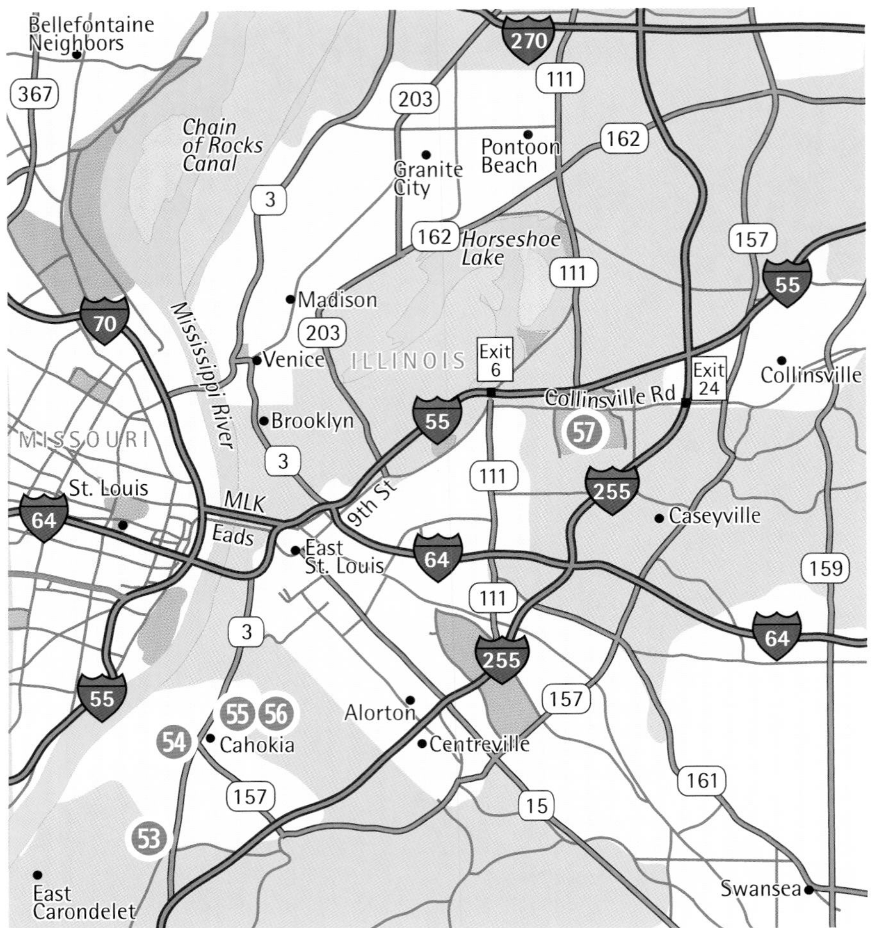

Town of Cahokia, Illinois and Cahokia Mounds at Collinsville

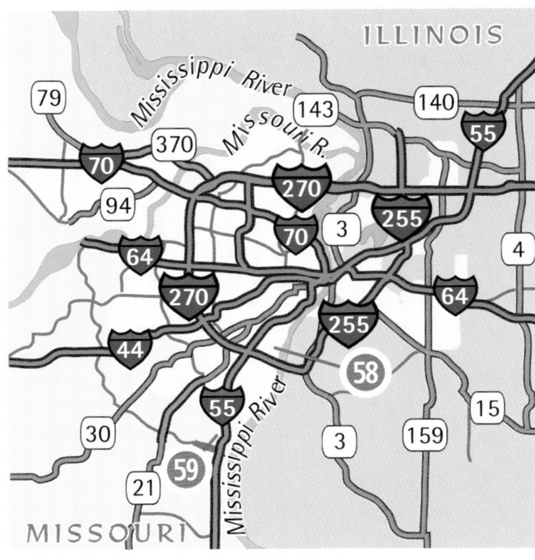

Greater St Louis Interstate Network

53 BOISMENUE HOUSE
EAST CARONDELET, IL

2110 First St.
From I-255 Exit 10 merge onto Rte 3 heading North. Turn left (West) onto Stolle Rd. Then turn right (north) onto Water St. Go to First Street.

54 CAHOKIA COURTHOUSE
CAHOKIA, ILLINOIS

107 Elm St.
From I-255 Exit 10 merge onto Rte 3 heading North. Turn left (West) onto First St. Go to Elm Street.

55 JARROT MANSION
CAHOKIA, ILLINOIS

124 E. First St.
From I-255 Exit 10 merge onto Rte 3 heading North. Turn right (East) onto First St. Go past Church St.

56 HOLY FAMILY LOG CHURCH
CAHOKIA, ILLINOIS

116 Church St.
From I-255 Exit 10 merge onto Rte 3 heading North. Turn right (East) onto First St. Go to Church St.

57 JEFFERSON BARRACKS
ST LOUIS , MO

533 Grant Rd.
From I-55 Exit 199 go East on Reavis Barracks Rd. Then bear right (South) onto Telegraph Rd. Then turn left (Northeast) onto Kingston Dr (Rte 231). Then turn right (South) onto Broadway which changes name to Grant Rd.

58 MASTODON SITE AND MUSEUM
IMPERIAL, MO

1050 Museum Drive.
From I-55 Exit 186 go right (west) on Imperial Main St. Then turn right (north) onto W Outer Rd. Then turn left (west) onto Museum Drive.

59 CAHOKIA MOUNDS
COLLINSVILLE, IL

30 Ramey.
From I-70/I-55 Exit 9 turn South onto Fairmont Ave. The turn right (West) onto Collinsville Rd. Then turn left (South) onto Ramey.

Pompey's 1809 Baptism

On December 28, 1809 Jean Baptiste Charbonneau, the son of Sacagawea and Toussaint Charbonneau, was baptized at the Catholic log church in St Louis. The Old Cathedral now stands on the site near the Gateway Arch. Pompey was 4½ years old. His parents had brought him to St Louis, fulfilling William Clark's request that he be allowed to raise their son and provide for his education.

Neither William Clark nor Meriwether Lewis was present. Lewis had tragically met his death on the Natchez Trace in Tennessee on October 11th, just weeks earlier. Clark was in Washington DC, having left in September; he had intended to meet his friend in Washington.

In their place stood one of the most powerful men in St. Louis, Auguste Chouteau, the co-founder of St. Louis and his twelve year old daughter, who would be godfather and godmother to the little boy.

At this time, St Louis had no resident priest. A Trappist monk, Father Urbain Guillet, traveled from Cahokia Mounds to celebrate Christmas Mass and perform the baptism. The Trappists were originally from Switzerland. They erected about a dozen buildings on a mound where they operated a school for boys ages 10-14. They went back to Switzerland in 1813.

The Charbonneau family had come down river to St Louis with Pierre Chouteau, who had finally, successfully, managed to return the Mandan Chief Big White (Sheheke) to the Mandan Villages in North Dakota. Clark sold Charbonneau some land in Florissant where they lived in 1810-1811; in August, 1811 they went back up river with Manuel Lisa, returning to their home on the Knife River.

Source: "Pompey's Baptism" by Bob Moore in ***We Proceeded On***, Feb, 2000 (vol 26:1) the quarterly publication of the Lewis and Clark Trail Heritage Foundation. Bob Moore is historian at www.nps.gov/jeff

Cahokia Courthouse Museum

Nicholas Jarrot Mansion

The Great Cahokia Monks Mound

Cahokia, Illinois & Cahokia Mounds

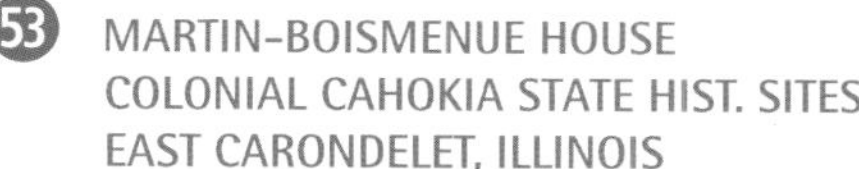

53 MARTIN-BOISMENUE HOUSE COLONIAL CAHOKIA STATE HIST. SITES EAST CARONDELET, ILLINOIS

In the time of Lewis and Clark, the sixty mile stretch between Cahokia and the Kaskaskia/Ste Genevieve area was heavily populated; the 1790 Martin-Boismenue ("bwah-me-noo") house was right on the main road. Built in the French Creole vertical log style, it is one of the oldest known residences in Illinois.

■ The house is open during the Colonial Mardi Gras in February and open by appointment. (618) 332-1782 www.greatriverroad.com

54 CAHOKIA COURTHOUSE VISITOR CENTER COLONIAL CAHOKIA STATE HIST. SITES CAHOKIA, ILLINOIS

Meriwether Lewis lived in Cahokia during the winter of 1803-04; he often conducted his business at the Courthouse; the postmaster John D. Hay was his friend. The courthouse was the judicial and administrative center for an area stretching to the Canadian border.

The Courthouse Visitor Center administers and arranges tours for Colonial Cahokia State Historic Sites: the Cahokia Courthouse, Martin-Boismenue House, Jarrot Mansion, and Holy Family Log Church

■ Open daily, last wkd in May to 1st wkd in Sept, 9-5. Sept-May hours: Weds-Sun, 9-5.
(618) 332-1782
www.state.il.us/HPA/hs/Courthouse.htm

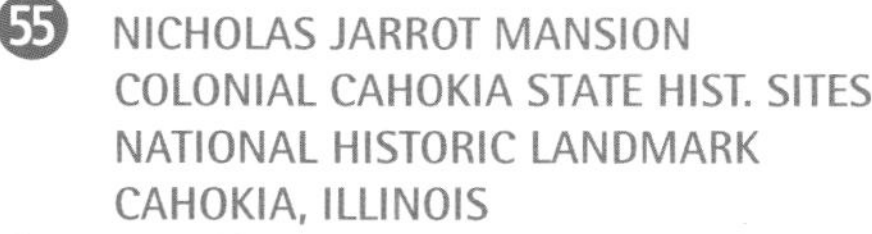

55 NICHOLAS JARROT MANSION COLONIAL CAHOKIA STATE HIST. SITES NATIONAL HISTORIC LANDMARK CAHOKIA, ILLINOIS

The Jarrot Mansion was built between 1807-1810; it is the oldest brick building in Illinois and a rare example of frontier Federal style American architecture; for many years it was one of the finest homes in the St Louis area. The mansion is currently undergoing extensive interior and exterior restoration and is open by appointment.

Nicholas Jarrot was a French emigrant, who married well, speculated in land, and engaged in the fur trade. Jarrot was the wealthiest man in the region. He owned as much as 25,000 acres including Cahokia Mounds and Wood River Camp where the expedition spent the winter. When Meriwether Lewis was in Cahokia, he most likely was a guest of the Jarrot family.

■ (618) 332-1782 www.greatriverroad.com

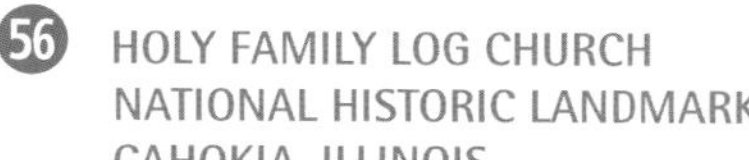

56 HOLY FAMILY LOG CHURCH NATIONAL HISTORIC LANDMARK CAHOKIA, ILLINOIS

Cahokia is the oldest town on the Mississippi River, dating back to the establishment of the Holy Family Parish in 1699 when the log church was built. Undoubtedly some of the members of the Corps of Discovery worshipped here during the time they were at Wood River Camp. The church had been newly rebuilt in 1799; replacing an earlier building which was destroyed in a fire. The church is the only church built of upright logs still standing in the United States.

■ Open daily, June-August, 10-4. Staffed by parish volunteers. Open by appt at other times. (618) 332-1782 www.greatriverroad.com

■ A traditional Latin Mass is celebrated at the log church on Sundays at 9 AM. Arrive early. www.diobelle.org/parishes (681) 337-4548

57 JEFFERSON BARRACKS COUNTY PARK ST LOUIS COUNTY, MISSOURI

Jefferson Barracks was established in 1826 as the country's first infantry school, and remained in operation until 1946. A National Cemetery is located here. There are two museums, the Ordnance Room and Powder Magazine Museums, and a Visitor Center. Audio tour available.

□ Open Feb-Dec, Weds-Sun, 12-4. Suggested donation, $2. 12 and under free. Audio tour rental, $4.
(314) 638-2100 www.co.st-louis.mo.us/parks

58 MASTODON STATE HISTORIC SITE AND MUSEUM—IMPERIAL, MO

This was a famous early paleontological site, the Kimmswick Bone Bed. Bones of mastodons and other creatures were found here in the early 1800's. A full size replica of a mastodon skeleton is displayed at the museum, along with the first Clovis spear point (c 14,000-10,000 years ago) found in direct association with mastodon bones. The Clovis point was discovered in 1979. An audio-visual program tells the story of the site and its significance. There is a half mile trail to the bone beds, and two other hiking trails.

■ Open Mar-Nov, Mon-Sat, 9-4:30; Sun, 12-4:30. Dec-Feb, closed Tues and Weds. Hours are 9-4 and 12-4 Sundays. Admission $2.50 ages 15 and up. 14 and under free. (636)464-2976
www.mostateparks.com/mastodon.htm

Cahokia Mounds Museum

59 CAHOKIA MOUNDS STATE HIST. SITE NATIONAL HISTORIC LANDMARK WORLD HERITAGE SITE COLLINSVILLE, IL

Cahokia Mounds is located across the river from St Louis. It preserves the remains of the central section of 2200 acres of the only prehistoric Indian city north of Mexico. The city was inhabited from 700 AD to 1400 AD, and grew to a population of 10,000-20,000 by 1100 AD. Sixty nine of the original one hundred and twenty earthern mounds are still preserved.

At the center is Monks Mound (c.1050-1200 AD), which at one hundred feet tall is the largest prehistoric platform temple mound north of Mexico. Monks Mound got its name from a group of Trappist monks who lived nearby at mound #48 between 1809-1813. Prior to that, a Catholic mission chapel had been built on the lower terrace of the mound itself, ministering to Cahokia-Illinois Indians from 1732-1752.

More than two hundred mounds have survived in the greater St Louis area. St Louis had an early nickname of "Mound City." There are also structures known as "woodhenges" at the Cahokia Mounds site. Six woodhenge sites, consisting of poles with a central pole, have been identified. These "sun circles" were used to mark the seasons. The state historic site offers educational programs on weekends close to equinoxes and solstices at a reconstructed woodhenge at Cahokia Mounds.

The Interpretive Center is a state of the art facility. Don't miss the unique 15 minute audio visual presentation in the Orientation Theater. The museum displays and exhibits are first class; as is the gift shop. If you plan to climb the mounds, consider the weather and avoid the mid-day heat.

■ Open April-1st wkd Sept, daily, 9-5. Sept-March, closed Mon-Tues. Suggested donation: $2 adults, $1 children. Grounds are open 8 AM til dusk. (618) 346-5160
www.cahokiamounds.com

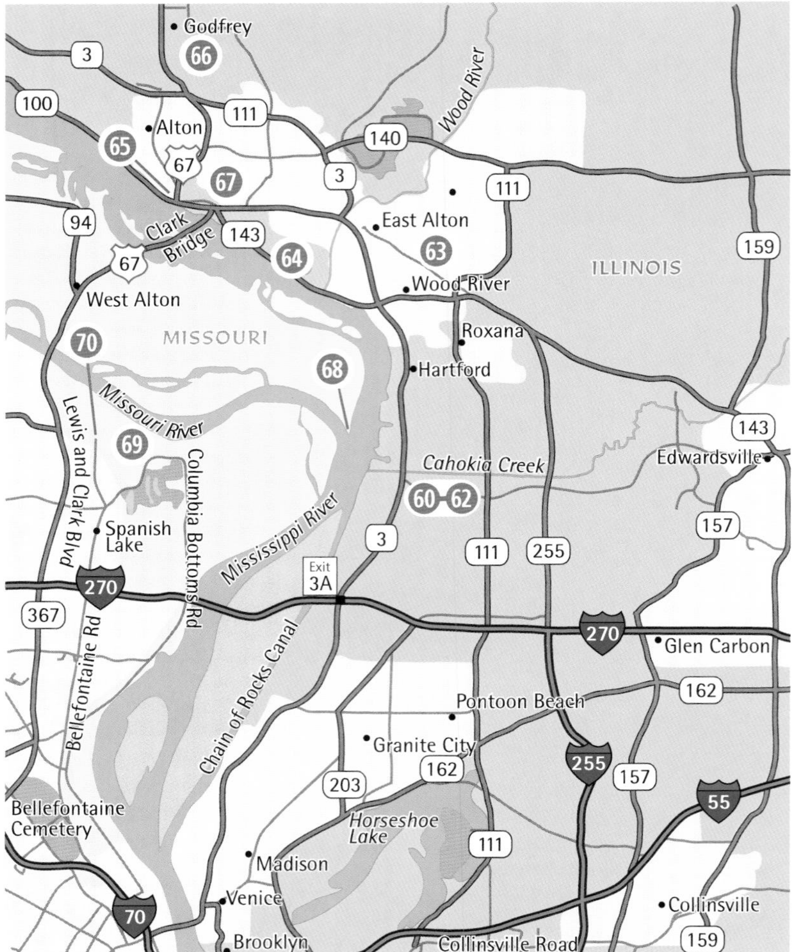

Hartford and Wood River, Illinois at the Confluence of the Mississippi and Missouri Rivers

Confluence of the Mississippi and Missouri Rivers
United States Army Corps of Engineers

Meeting of the Great Rivers National Scenic Byway Bike Trail
Alton Regional Convention and Visitors Bureau

The "Missouri" Delta Blues?

The Missouri is the longest river in the United States: 2,565 miles from its origin at the Three Forks in Montana to the Mississippi at St Louis. However, its length should include the 1,175 miles from St. Louis to New Orleans; making it, at 3,740 miles, the fourth longest river system in the world.

The Mississippi is 1,175 miles long from its origin in northern Minnesota to its junction with the Missouri (1,390 miles shorter than the Missouri). Logically, then, the Mississippi should be considered a tributary of the much longer Missouri. But historically the Mississippi was explored first, by Marquette, LaSalle and Joliet in 1673-82.

60 LEWIS AND CLARK INTERPRETIVE CENTER HARTFORD, IL

One Lewis and Clark Trail.
From I-255 N Exit 3 take New Poag Rd west. Go past Rte 3 to Levee Rd on the south side of the canal. Follow Levee Rd to the Center.

61 LEWIS AND CLARK MEMORIAL TOWER HARTFORD, IL

From Rt 255 N Exit 3 take New Poag Rd west. Go past Rte 3 to Levee Rd on the north side of the canal. Follow Levee Rd to the Tower.

62 MEETING OF GREAT RIVERS SCENIC BYWAY

Rts 3, Rte 43 and Rte 100.
From Rt 3 at New Poag Rd go north to Rte 143. Turn left (west). Take Rte 143 to Rte 100. Turn left (west) onto Rte 100. Follow Rte 100 about 30 miles.

63 WOOD RIVER MUSEUM AND VISITOR CENTER WOOD RIVER, IL

40 West Ferguson.
From Rt 255 N Exit 6 take Rte 143 west. Then turn right (north) onto Wood River Ave. Then immediately turn left (west) onto Ferguson.

64 NATIONAL GREAT RIVERS MUSEUM AND #1 LOCK AND DAM EAST ALTON, IL

31 Lock and Dam Way.
From Rte 255 N Exit 6 take Rte 143 (Berm Hwy) west to Museum.

65 BALD EAGLES MIGRATION ALTON, IL

Alton Regional Convention and Visitors Bureau, 200 Plasa St, Alton, Il.
From Rt 255 N Exit 6 take Rte 143 west. In Alton keep straight onto Landmarks Blvd which bends right (north) onto Plasa St.

66 SACAGAWEA STATUE LEWIS AND CLARK COLLEGE GODFREY, IL

5800 Godfrey Rd.
From Rt 255 N Exit 6 take Rte 143 west. Keep straight onto US 67 which bends north and heads into Godfrey where it is named Godfrey Rd. The College is just past Tolle Lane.

67 CLARK BRIDGE ALTON, ILLINOIS

US 67.
The Clark Bridge runs between Illinois and Missouri on US 67.

68 CONFLUENCE POINT STATE PARK—WEST ALTON, MO

1005 Riverlands Way.
At West Alton take US 67 north. Just before Clark's Bridge turn right (east) onto riverlands. Go to the Park.

69 COLUMBIA BOTTOM CONSERVATION AREA ST LOUIS COUNTY, MO

Strodtman Rd.
From I-270 Exit 34 go north on Columbia Bottom Rd to Strodtman Rd.

70 FT BELLE FONTAINE PARK ST LOUIS COUNTY, MO

13002 Bellefontaine Rd.
From I-270 Exit 32 take Bellefontaine Rd north to the north end.

Hartford Lewis and Clark Center
Lewis and Clark Interpretive Center, Hartford

Clark Bridge over the Mississippi River
Alton Regional Convention and Visitors Bureau

National Great Rivers Museum
Alton Regional Convention and Visitors Bureau

Wood River Camp and Confluence

60 LEWIS AND CLARK INTERPRETIVE CENTER AND CAMP RIVER DUBOIS ILLINOIS STATE HISTORIC SITE HARTFORD, IL

The Interpretive Center and the replica of Camp River Dubois, are located near today's confluence of the Missisippi and Missouri Rivers. The original location of Lewis and Clark's winter camp at Wood River is about five miles north near Wood River and East Alton, Illinois.

The Interpretive Center has a full scale "cutaway" replica of the keelboat; four exhibit galleries, a theater, and a gift shop. The reconstructed Camp River Dubois is adjacent to the Center (River Dubois means Wood's River in French.) Guided tours of the camp are held on the hour. Events commemorating the Corps' arrival and departure are held in Dec and May; other events in March, Sept, and Oct.

■ Open daily mid April-Oct, 9-5. Nov-April, Weds-Sun, 9-5. Free admission. Donations are appreciated and help support the reenactors. (618) 251-5811 www.campdubois.com

61 LEWIS AND CLARK MEMORIAL TOWER HARTFORD, IL

The Memorial Tower will be open in September, 2006. It is right across the canal from the Interpretive Center. The two connected towers are 180 feet tall; one has a stairway, the other has an elevator. There are three observation decks, at 50, 100, and 150 feet above the tower base. Fountains, public restrooms, gift shop.

■ (618) 251-5811 (Interpretive Center)
www.hartfordillinois.net

62 MEETING OF GREAT RIVERS NATIONAL SCENIC BYWAY—HARTFORD, IL

A scenic byway auto route and paved bike trail go along the Mississippi River on the Illinois side from the Interpretive Center north to Pere Marquette State Park; limestone bluffs, eagles, historic villages, antique shops and magnificent scenery. The distance is about 30 miles to the park, the largest state park in Illinois. The bike trail connects to both the St Louis and confluence bike trails across the river by way of the Chain of Rocks Bridge.

■ (618) 465-6676 www.visitalton.com
www.byways.org www.trailnet.org

63 WOOD RIVER MUSEUM AND VISITOR CENTER—WOOD RIVER, IL

The Wood River Museum was founded in 1997; it features early area history and the history of the local Standard Oil Company. It also has a replica Camp Dubois, which is occasionally open to visitors. Gift shop.

■ Open Sun-Fri, 1-4; Saturday, 10-4.
Free admission, donations suggested.
(618) 254-1993
www.woodriverheritagecouncil.org

64 NATIONAL GREAT RIVERS MUSEUM AND #1 LOCK AND DAM—EAST ALTON, IL

This is the first of eleven planned Corps of Engineer regional visitor centers. The story of the Mississippi River and state of the art interactive exhibits; working models of locks and dams. Exhibits on the Great Flood of 1993. Bird watching platforms: eagles congregate here in the winter. The bike trail runs right past the museum.

■ Open daily 9-5. Free admission. Melvin Price Lock and Dam tours at 10, 1, and 3.
(877) 462-6979 www.greatriverroad.com

65 BALD EAGLE AND PELICAN MIGRATIONS—EAST ALTON, ILLINOIS

The region is known as "Eagle Country" during December-February, when bald eagles migrate south from Canada and the northern U S to catch fish in the River Bend Region. Pelicans come through twice a year, mid to late March and mid October. Bring binoculars and cameras. Stop at the Alton Visitor Center, or check the website for the latest bird news. Lots of antique shops and historic towns to visit.

■ (800) ALTON-IL (258-6645)
www.visitalton.com

66 SACAGAWEA STATUE LEWIS AND CLARK COLLEGE GODFREY, IL

Sculptor Glenna Goodacre, who created the image of Sacagawea for the $1 coin, created this statue using the same model. The college started as the Monticello Female Seminary in 1838. It became the Lewis and Clark Community College in 1969.

■ Open daily. (618) 466-2798 www.lc.edu
www.glennagoodacre.com

67 CLARK BRIDGE—EAST ALTON, ILLINOIS

This multi-award winning bridge, named for William Clark, was completed in 1994, and has four traffic lanes and two bike lanes. It links some of the most important sites on the trail, including Camp River Dubois and Fort Bellefontaine. The Lewis Bridge crosses the Missouri going south on 67. Highway 94 goes across the Portage des Sioux floodplain to St. Charles. This is where William Clark held the Portage des Sioux Treaty Councils with Indian tribes in 1815, at the end of the War of 1812.

■ www.greatriverroad.com
www.figgbridge.com

68 PAT AND EDWARD "TED" JONES CONFLUENCE POINT STATE PARK

Visitors can watch the Missouri and Mississippi merge at their confluence from ground level. The state park is a flood plain and natural wetlands. Restoration is underway in the 1,118 park to restore forests, prairies and marshes, and preserve native plants. This a great place to watch the bird migrations. No camping or boat access. Hiking paths and trails.

■ Day use only. Free admission.
(800) 334-6946 (636) 899-1135
www.mostateparks.com/confluence.htm

69 COLUMBIA BOTTOM CONSERVATION AREA—ST LOUIS COUNTY, MO

This 4,318 acre urban conservation area is another flood prone area being restored and managed. Boat ramps. Five miles of hiking and biking trails, and an observation platform for the confluence. Visitor Center.

■ Open Weds-Fri, 8-5; Sat 8-4.
(314) 877-6015 www.mdc.mo.gov/areas

70 FORT BELLE FONTAINE PARK ST LOUIS COUNTY, MISSOURI

Built in 1805, the first US military fort and trading post for local Indian tribes in Louisiana Territory. The expedition came to end here on Sept 22,1806. They bought new clothes at the post store, and proceeded into town to celebrate.
Visitors can still see the stone staircase and natural spring of Belle Fontaine.

■ (800) 735-2966 (314) 544-5714
www.stlouisco.com/parks

Region Three: References

3

BIOGRAPHY

AUDUBON: THE KENTUCKY YEARS
by L. Clark Keating. University Press of Kentucky (1976)

BACKGROUND TO GLORY: THE LIFE OF GEORGE ROGERS CLARK
by John Bakeless. J. B. Lippincott Company (1957)

THE CONQUEST OF THE ILLINOIS: GEORGE ROGERS CLARK
edited by Milo Milton Quaife. Southern Illinois University Press (2001)

DEAR BROTHER: LETTERS OF WILLIAM CLARK TO JONATHAN CLARK
edited by James J. Holmberg. Yale University Press (2002)

GEORGE DROUILLARD: HUNTER AND INTERPRETER FOR LEWIS AND CLARK, AND FUR TRADER 1807-1810
by M. O. Skarsten. Arthur H. Clark Company (2003)

HOW GEORGE ROGERS CLARK WON THE NORTH-WEST; AND OTHER ESSAYS IN WESTERN HISTORY
by Reuben Gold Thwaites. Books For Libraries Press (1968)

IN SEARCH OF YORK: THE SLAVE WHO WENT TO THE PACIFIC WITH LEWIS AND CLARK
by Robert B. Betts. Colorado Associated University Press (2000)

JOHN JAMES AUDUBON: THE MAKING OF AN AMERICAN
by Richard Rhodes. Alfred A. Knopf (2004)

THE LEGEND OF PRINCE MADOC AND THE WHITE INDIANS
by Dana Olson. Olson Enterprises (1987)

LONG KNIFE: THE STORY OF A GREAT AMERICAN HERO, GEORGE ROGERS CLARK
by James Alexander Thom. Ballantine Books (1994)

MADOC AND THE DISCOVERY OF AMERICA: SOME NEW LIGHT ON AN OLD CONTROVERSY
by Richard Deacon. George Braziller (1966)

MADOC: THE LEGEND OF THE WELSH DISCOVERY OF AMERICA, THE MAKING OF A MYTH
by Gwyn A. Williams. Oxford University Press (1987)

NEW HARMONY, INDIANA: ROBERT OWEN'S SEEDBED FOR UTOPIA
by Donald F. Carmony and Josephine M. Elliott. Indiana Magazine of History (1999)

REPORT ON A JOURNEY TO THE WESTERN STATES OF NORTH AMERICA; AND A STAY OF SEVERAL YEARS ALONG THE MISSOURI (DURING THE YEARS 1824, '25, '26, 1827)
by Gottfried Duden. University of Missouri Press (1980)

BIOGRAPHY

ROBERT OWEN: OWEN OF NEW LANARK AND NEW HARMONY
by Ian Donnachie. Tuckwell Press (2000)

THOMAS SAY, NEW WORLD NATURALIST
by Patricia Tyson Stroud. University of Pennsylvania press (1992)

SIGN-TALKER: THE ADVENTURE OF GEORGE DROUILLARD ON THE LEWIS AND CLARK EXPEDITION
by James Alexander Thom. Ballantine Books ((2000)

HISTORY

AMERICAN MONSTER: HOW THE NATIONS FIRST PREHISTORIC CREATURE BECAME A SYMBOL OF NATIONAL IDENTITY
by Paul Semonin. New York University Press (2000)

ANCIENT ANIMALS LOCKED IN LOUISVILLE'S ROCKS: A GUIDE FOR FOSSIL HUNTERS
by Larry Steinrock, James E. Conkin, and Barbara Conkin. University of Louisville (1995)

ARCHAEOLOGY AT FRENCH COLONIAL CAHOKIA
by Bonnie L. Gums. Illinois Historic Preservation Agency (1988)

THE CALENDAR AND QUARTERMASTER'S BOOKS OF GENERAL GEORGE ROGER'S CLARK'S FORT JEFFER-SON, KENTUCKY 1780-1781
compiled and edited by Kenneth C. Carstens. Heritage Books, Inc. (2000)

CAHOKIA: MIRROR OF THE COSMOS
Sally A. Kitt Chappell. University of Chicago Press (2002)

COLONIAL STE. GENEVIEVE: AN ADVENTURE ON THE MISSISSIPPI FRONTIER
by Carl J. Ekberg. The Patrice Press (1996)

FRENCH FOLKLIFE IN OLD VINCENNES
by Ronald L. Baker. Vincennes Historical and Antiquarian Society (1998)

THE FRENCH IN THE HEART OF AMERICA
by John Finley. Pelican Publishing Company (1998)

FRENCHMEN AND FRENCH WAYS IN THE MISSISSIPPI VALLEY
edited by John Francis McDermott. University of Illinois Press (1969)

FRONTIER ILLINOIS
by James E. Davis. Indiana University Press (1998)

LEWIS AND CLARK IN THE ILLINOIS COUNTRY: THE LITTLE-TOLD STORY
by Robert E. Hartley. Xlibris & Sniktau Publications (2002)

HISTORY

NEW HARMONY AS SEEN BY PARTICIPANTS AND TRAVELERS
by William Pelham, Karl Bernhard, and Victor Colin Duclos. Porcupine Press (1975)

NEW HARMONY'S FIRST UTOPIANS, 1814-1824
by Donald E. Pitzer and Josephine M. Elliott. University of Southern Indiana (2002)

NOTES ON OLD CAHOKIA: TRICENTENNIAL COMMEMORATIVE EDITION
by Charles E. Peterson. Jarrot Mansion Project (1999)

OPENING THE OZARKS: A HISTORICAL GEOGRAPHY OF MISSOURI'S STE. GENEVIEVE DISTRICT 1760-1830
by Walter A. Schroeder. University of Missouri Press (2002)

THE STORY OF OLD STE. GENEVIEVE: AN ACCOUNT OF AN OLD FRENCH TOWN IN UPPER LOUISIANA; ITS PEOPLE AND THEIR HOMES
by Gregory M. Franzwa. The Patrice Press (1998)

TWO HUNDRED YEARS AT THE FALLS OF THE OHIO: A HISTORY OF LOUISVILLE AND JEFFERSON COUNTY
by George H. Yater. The Heritage Corporation (1979)

VISIONARIES, ADVENTURERS, AND BUILDERS: HISTORICAL HIGHLIGHTS OF THE FALLS OF THE OHIO
by Carl E. Kramer. Sunnyside Press (2000)

MISCELLANEOUS

■ Maurice Thompson's 1901 best selling novel, *Alice of Old Vincennes,* may be read at www.authorsclassicnovels.com

The Filson Society has collaborated with the University of Chicago in digitalizing 15,000 pages of documents on the Appalachian West. See "The First American West: The Ohio River Valley 1750-1820" on the Library of Congress American Memories website, at www.loc.gov.

REGION FOUR
ST LOUIS TO KANSAS CITY

- Old St Louis Riverfront
- St Louis
- St Charles and Florissant
- River Route to Jefferson City
- Columbia Area
- Kansas City
- Leavenworth and St Joseph Area

4

1. Lewis and Clark American Restaurant, St Charles MO 2. Three Flags Over St Louis, March 2004 Bicentennial
3. Nat'l Frontier Museum, Independence MO 4. William Clark Gravesite Monument, Bellefontaine Cemetery, St Louis MO
5. Old Courthouse and the Gateway Arch, St Louis MO; 6. Lewis and Clark Statue, Kansas City MO 6. Fort Osage, Sibley MO
7.Discovery Expedition Keelboat at Jefferson City 8. Native American Heritage Museum, Highland KS

Credits: (1) (3) (7)Betty Kluesner; (3) National Frontier Museum; (8) St Joseph, MO Convention and Visitors Bureau

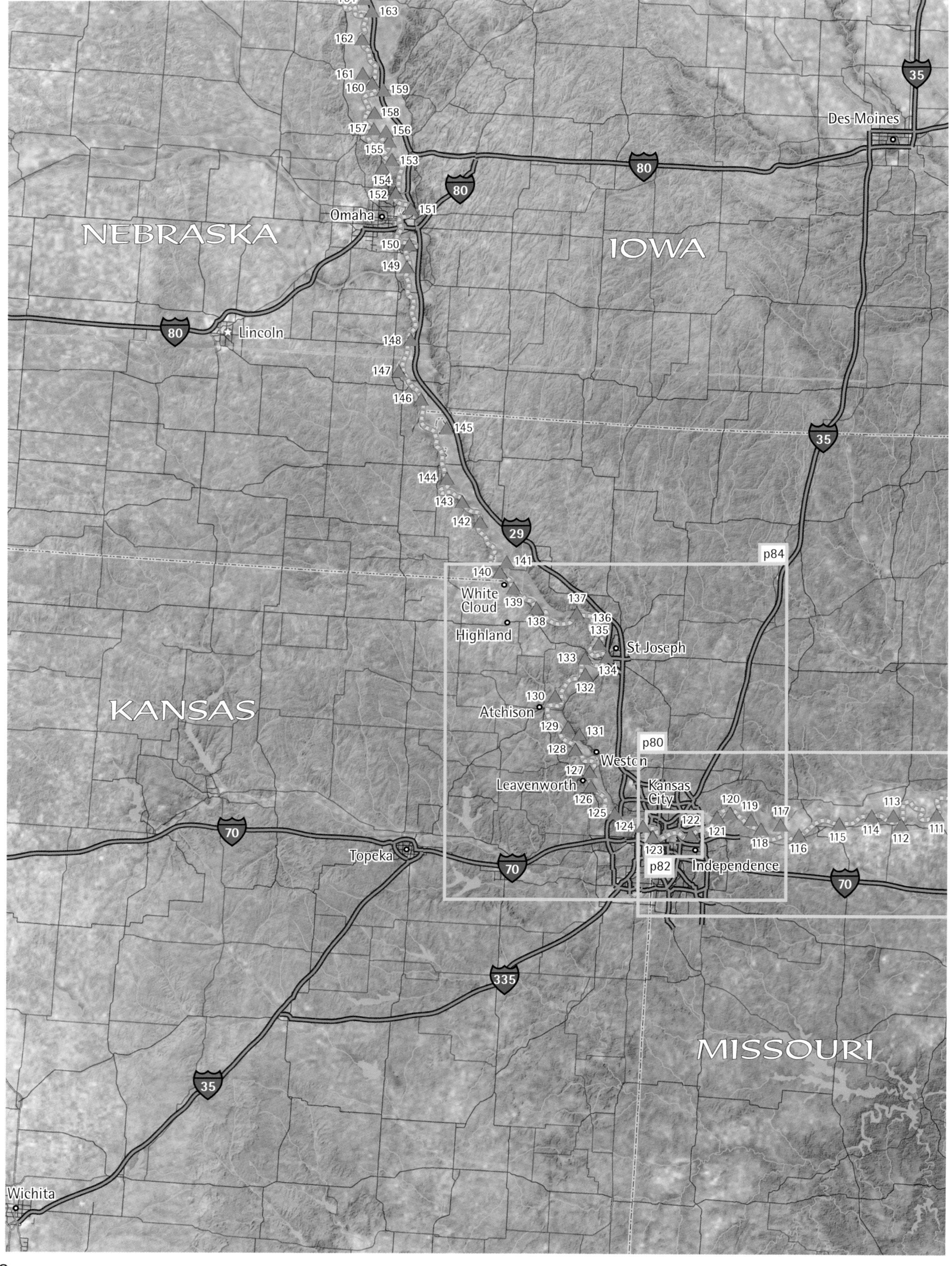
NEBRASKA
IOWA
KANSAS
MISSOURI
Omaha
Lincoln
Des Moines
White Cloud
Highland
St Joseph
Atchison
Weston
Leavenworth
Kansas City
Independence
Topeka
Wichita
p84
p80
p82

4

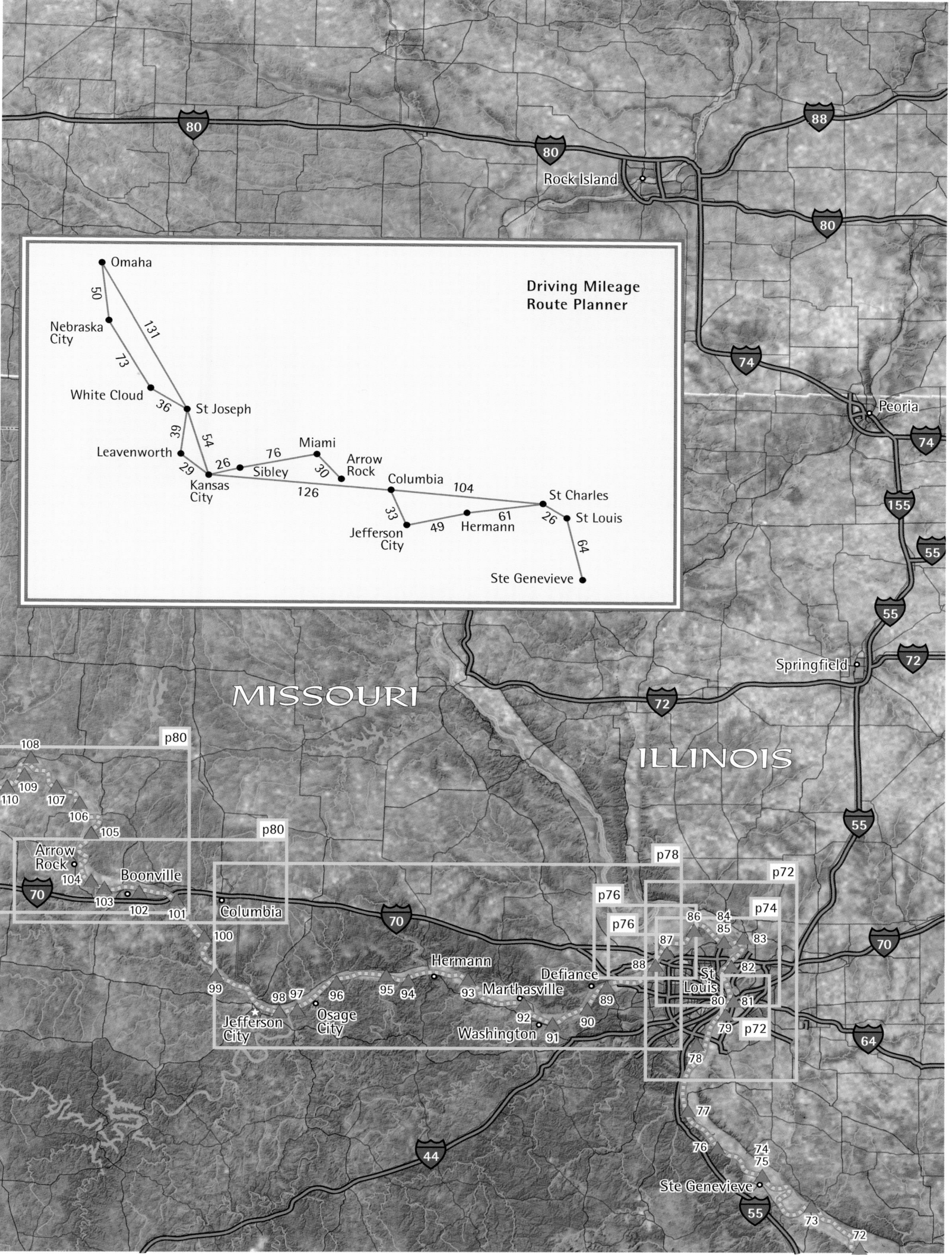

Driving Mileage
Route Planner
Omaha
Nebraska City
White Cloud
St Joseph
Leavenworth
Kansas City
Sibley
Miami
Arrow Rock
Columbia
Jefferson City
Hermann
St Charles
St Louis
Ste Genevieve
50
131
73
36
39
54
29
26
76
30
126
104
33
49
61
26
64
MISSOURI
ILLINOIS
Rock Island
Peoria
Springfield
Boonville
Columbia
Hermann
Defiance
Marthasville
Washington
Osage City
St Louis
p80
p78
p76
p72
p74

4

The Gateway Arch superimposed on a view of old St Louis from an 1817 Banknote

Capt. William Clark dined with the Duquettes in May, 1804 on these premises. (Later, the Sacred Heart Academy, St Charles MO)
Betty Kluesner

Log Church Construction Site
Betty Kluesner

4

America 200 Years Ago

Lewis and Clark in Missouri

St Charles Farewell

William Clark and the men waited for Meriwether Lewis, who was detained at St Louis on business, to join them at St Charles. The small town on the west side of the Missouri River was known as Petite Côte or "Little Hill." Its inhabitants were mostly poor people, French speaking, whose men worked in the fur trade. Clark described the villagers as being "extreemly kind," and as "poor, polite and harmonious." There were two dances held during the seven days they were there. Clark was invited to dine with the Duquette family. The men attended services at St Charles Borromeo Catholic Church. (The original log church is being reconstructed as an interpretive center .)

The delay was providential because they needed to reload the keelboat. The keelboat had run into logs three times on the first day; it had nearly capsized, being improperly loaded. On the Missouri River, weight was needed in the front of the boat, to absorb the shock of hitting logs hidden underwater. They had put the weight in the rear, not knowing any better.

On May 16th, Clark hired two experienced Missouri River boatmen, and enlisted them in the U. S. Army: Pierre Cruzatte and François Labiche, who were both half-French, half-Omaha Indian. Cruzatte was a one-eyed fiddle player; Labiche also served as an interpreter.

On May 20th Lewis and a group of the leading citizens of St Louis arrived in a heavy rain. The next day, on Monday, May 21st the expedition set off at 3 o'clock in the afternoon, after a rainy day parade down Main Street.

Hard Rains and Falling Banks

It rained a lot during the first weeks of the expedition. On the second day when they ran into the logs, Clark noted that it had rained all night; the river was "excessively rapid" and "Banks falling in." It would continue to rain for weeks as they struggled up the river.

The Missouri was lined on both sides with giant cottonwood trees. The force of the current going into a river bend would eventually cause the riverbank to collapse and trees to fall into the water. Stuck in the river bottom, the trees were called "snags" or "planters." Submerged trees which emerged suddenly with a "sawing" motion were called "sawyers." Huge sawyers or groups of trees might come floating down the river. Or a fallen tree might remain attached to the river bank, collecting driftwood against it, called an "embarass." The river current was affected by these conditions. Sand bars formed and disappeared within hours.

Expert judgement and experience were needed to navigate through these hazards. Boats would seek the slower parts of the current on the sides of the river. The central current was very fast (5½-7 miles per hour) until it got past the mouth of the Platte River, 600 miles upstream. The Platte was dumping large amounts of sand and water into the Missouri. After passing it, the current dropped to 3-3½ miles per hour.

Proceeding on

On May 26th, the Captains separated the men into five messes, or working units. The men who were members of the Discovery Corps, or the permanent party, formed into three squads under Sergeants Nathaniel Pryor, Charles Floyd and John Ordway. They manned the keelboat. The French engagés (hired hands) manned the red pirogue; and the soldiers who were going to return to St Louis with the keelboat manned the white pirogue. The messes ate and worked together. Men from the keelboat also rotated onto the pirogues as needed. Lewis and Clark, Drouillard, York and others had a separate mess. It has been estimated that there may have been as many as 50-55 men on the expedition as they brought the keelboat and pirogues up river.

Privates Cruzatte and Labiche stayed at the bow (rhymes with wow), or front of the boat, sharing the duties of "bows-man," and larboard (left) bow oar. They decided the path the three boats would take through the water. In time of danger they would both act as bows-men, and someone else would take the front oar.

Fiddle playing and singing were associated with being a bows-man, as music set the work pace for the rowers and entertained them. The French were famous singers. Their songs were

William Clark, Governor of Missouri Territory, official portrait at State Capitol in Jefferson City
Mark W Kelly

Keelboat at Jefferson City
Betty Kluesner

First Missouri State Capitol
Betty Kluesner

Missouri State Capitol
Betty Kluesner

4

were nonsensical or romantic, with many verses, often with a lead singer and chorus responses. It was so much a part of river life that Clark only noted when they had music and dancing at night, and the men were "in high spirits."

They endured much hardship and danger as they traveled through Missouri. Captain Lewis almost fell to his death climbing a 300 foot hill at Tavern Cave near Washington, Missouri. He stopped his fall at 20 feet with the aid of his knife. It rained constantly, the river rose many inches, there were mosquitoes and ticks; it got very hot; and the men had fevers and skin boils (bacterial infections of cuts and scrapes).

The boats narrowly escaped sinking several times. On June 9th, at Arrow Rock, the keelboat got caught up in some hidden driftwood and snags and turned around. Clark wrote that it was a "disagreeable and Dangerous Situation, particularly as immense large trees were Drifting down and we lay immediately in their Course." But the men moved quickly, swam ashore and pulled the boat out of danger using ropes. Clark commented proudly, "I can say with Confidence that our party is not inferior to any that was ever on the waters of the Missoppie."

They had a court martial when John Collins and Hugh Hall broke into the whiskey barrel and got drunk at the mouth of the Kansas River. Court martial punishments were whippings on the bare back. Clark wrote the men were "always found verry ready to punish Such Crimes." They celebrated the Fourth of July at a creek they named "Independence Creek" near Atchison, Kansas on the 28th anniversary of the Declaration of Independence.

They hunted bear, deer, and elk; saw "emence number of Parrot-quetes" in the Kansas City area; ate ripe grapes and berries; and evaluated the land they were passing through with the eyes of farmers and pioneers. Did the captains ever dream that most of the rest of their lives would be spent in Missouri?

Missouri in the Later Years

Upon their return from the Pacific Coast, President Jefferson appointed Meriwether Lewis to be Governor of Louisiana Territory; and William Clark to be Superintendent for Indian Affairs and Brigadier General of the Militia for Louisiana Territory. Lewis was governor for only two years, ending with his death in 1809.

After Louisiana became a state in 1812, Louisiana Territory, headquartered in St Louis, was renamed Missouri Territory. Missouri itself became a state in 1821. During these intervening years, from 1813-1821, William Clark was appointed Governor of Missouri Territory, while retaining his other posts. He was the most powerful man in the West.

To the Indians, St Louis was known as "Red Head's Town," for Clark's red hair. He served as Superintendent for Indian Affairs for over 30 years, until his death in 1838. The Indians always trusted him. He established an Indian Council Chamber and Museum adjacent to his home, where he displayed his Indian artifacts. His skills as a diplomat helped to maintain peace with many Indian tribes.

War of 1812

The Missouri frontier was very much a part of the War of 1812 with Great Britain. The United States invaded Canada, and the British gave military aid to Indians who wanted to establish an Indian state in the Old Northwest Territory. Residents of Missouri defended themselves through local militia and neighborhood forts, where families could seek shelter. Clark had established Fort Osage in 1808 for trade with the Osage Indians, but it was abandoned during the war due to its isolated position. The Boones, the Chouteaus, Clark and Manuel Lisa all played active roles in defending Missouri Territory against Indian attacks.

Sacagawea died of an illness at Fort Manuel in South Dakota in December, 1812, leaving a baby girl named Lizette. Manuel Lisa brought the baby to St Louis where William Clark adopted both her and her older brother, Pompey, who was already attending school in St Louis. Clark himself, tragically, had two wives die, and three of his seven children die. His home and Indian museum were located directly north of where the Gateway Arch stands today, a lasting memorial to the days of old St Louis.

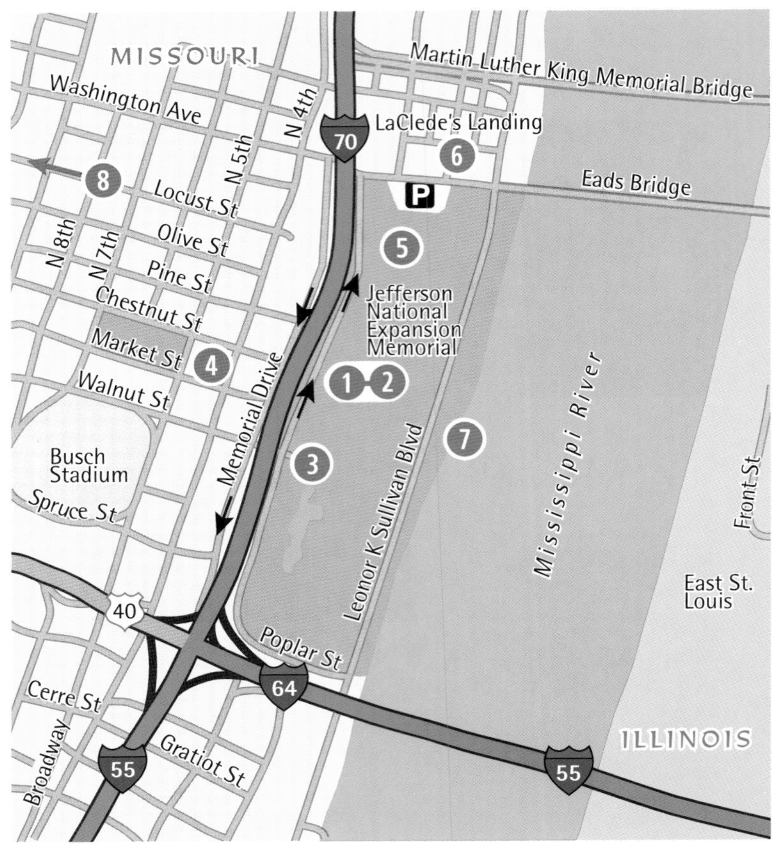

Old St Louis Riverfront Area

Old St Louis Riverfront

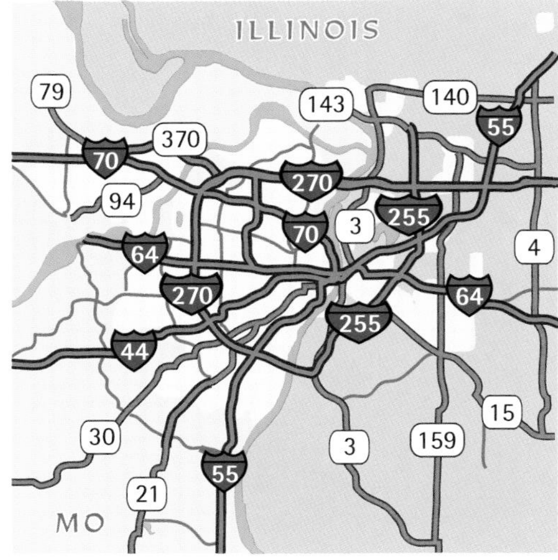

St Louis Metro Area Interstates

❶ GATEWAY ARCH

50 S Leanor K Sullivan Blvd.
From I-70 E take Exit 250B south onto Memorial Dr (one-way south). Go past the Pine St stoplight to Chestnut St. Turn left (east) and cross under the highway. Then turn left (north) onto Memorial Dr (one-way north). Stay in the right lane and turn right (east) onto Washington Ave. The parking garage is on the right.

❷ MUSEUM OF WESTWARD EXPANSION GATEWAY ARCH

30 N Leanor K Sullivan Blvd.
From I-70 E take Exit 250B south onto Memorial Dr (one-way south). Go past the Pine St stoplight to Chestnut St. Turn left (east) and cross under the highway. Then turn left (north) onto Memorial Dr (one-way north). Stay in the right lane and turn right (east) onto Washington Ave. The parking garage is on the right.

❸ OLD CATHEDRAL MUSEUM

209 Walnut St.
The museum is at the east end of Market St. past Memorial Dr. From I-70 E take Exit 250B south onto Memorial Dr (one-way south). Go past the Pine St stoplight to Chestnut St. Turn left (east) and cross under the highway. Go past Memorial Dr.

❹ OLD COURTHOUSE MUSEUM

440 Market St.
From I-70 E take Exit 250B south onto Memorial Dr (one-way south). Go to Market St. Turn right.

❺ WILLIAM CLARK HOUSE AND INDIAN MUSEUM SITE

Jefferson National Expansion Memorial.
The site of Clark's house is on the grounds of the Arch Memorial; north of the arch. From I-70 E take Exit 250B south onto Memorial Dr (one-way south). Go past the Pine St stoplight to Chestnut St. Turn left (east) and cross under the highway. Then turn left (north) onto Memorial Dr (one-way north). Stay in the right lane and turn right (east) onto Washington Ave. The parking garage is on the right.

❻ LACLEDE'S LANDING

Memorial Dr and Washington Ave.
From I-70 E take Exit 250B south onto Memorial Dr (one-way south). Go past the Pine St stoplight to Chestnut St. Turn left (east) and cross under the highway. Then turn left (north) onto Memorial Dr (one-way north). Stay in the right lane and turn right (east) onto Washington Ave.

❼ GATEWAY ARCH RIVERBOAT CRUISES

Riverfront wharf east of the Arch.
From I-70 E take Exit 250B south onto Memorial Dr (one-way south). Go past the Pine St stoplight to Chestnut St. Turn left (east) and cross under the highway. Then turn left (north) onto Memorial Dr (one-way north). Stay in the right lane and turn right (east) onto Washington Ave. The parking garage is on the right.

❽ CAMPBELL HOUSE MUSEUM

1508 Locust Street.
From I-70 E take Exit 250B south onto Memorial Dr (one-way south). Go to Pine St. Turn right (west). Go to 15th St. Turn right (north). Go to Locust St.

Old Cathedral
Thomas C Danisi

Old Courthouse

Clark's home and Indian Museum site north of the Gateway Arch

Old St Louis Riverfront

4

1 GATEWAY ARCH—JEFFERSON NATIONAL EXPANSION MEMORIAL

The Gateway Arch is the symbol of St Louis; a 630 feet tall stainless steel arch that stands at the heart of Old St Louis. The "Gateway to the West" also symbolizes Thomas Jefferson's plans for National Expansion. The Arch was designed by Eero Saarinen in 1947. It took almost twenty years to solve the engineering and construction issues before the Arch was completed in 1965. The tram ride to the top of the Arch with the panoramic view at the top is one of the world's great tourist attractions.

Arch attractions include the Museum of Westward Expansion, a gift shop, and three paid attractions (tram ride and two films). A parking garage is located north of the Arch. Be sure to allow enough time for the security screening process.

■ Open daily. last wkd in May to 1st wkd Sept, 8 AM-10 PM; Sept-May, 9 AM-6 PM.

■ The tram ride takes approximately 60 minutes, and departs every ten minutes. You may stay as long as you wish at the top. Tram tickets sometimes sell out: reserve in advance.

■ "Monument to The Dream,"a documentary on the Arch, is shown hourly, 10-5. (35 minutes)

■ The *National Geographic* giant screen film, "Lewis and Clark: Great Journey West" is shown on the half hour: 9:30-7:30 in the summer; 9:30-4:30 in the winter. (45 minutes)

■ There is a one time National Park Entrance fee of $3 per adult (no more than $6 will be charged per family unit) for paid attractions.

■ Ticket for tram ride: $10 adult, $7 with Nat'l Park Passport, $7 ages 13-16, $3 ages 3-12.

■ Ticket for one film: $7 adult, $4 with Nat'l Park passport, $4 ages 13-16, $2.50, ages 3-12

■ Discounts for tram ride and one film: $14 adult, $11 with Nat'l Park passport, $11 ages 13-16, $5.50 ages 3-12.

■ Discount for two films: $4 additional.

■ Tickets may be purchased in advance. Place order on the website, or by phone, with a credit card; $3 processing fee per order. Pick up tickets on arrival at Arch.

■ Parking fee is $6 for 9 hours. 75¢ each add'l hour. Early bird special, $4, 6 AM-9 AM.
(877) 982-1410 www.gatewayarch.com

2 MUSEUM OF WESTWARD EXPANSION

Exhibits feature the history of America's westward expansion in the 1800's, from the time of the Louisiana Purchase to the close of the frontier.

Visit the JNEM website. It is the single best website on Lewis and Clark history. Scroll down to the bottom of the web page to find the Lewis and Clark link.

■ Open last wkd May to 1st wkd Sept, 8 AM-10 PM; Sept-May, 9 AM-6 PM. Free admission.
(877) 982-1410 www.nps.gov/jeff

3 OLD CATHEDRAL AND OLD CATHEDRAL MUSEUM

Pope John XXIII declared the Old Cathedral a Basilica in 1961. The founder of St Louis, Pierre Laclede, dedicated this site to the Catholic Church of St Louis in 1764. Pompey was baptized here in 1809, in a log church. The Cathedral was dedicated in 1834. From 1826-43 its diocese covered nearly half of America, from Louisiana to the Pacific Northwest. It was the first Catholic Cathedral west of the Mississippi. William Clark would have attended services here in the last years of his life.

■ Open daily. Daily Mass, Mon-Fri, 7 AM and 12:10 PM; Sat, 7 AM; Sun, 8, 10:30, noon and 5 PM. Weekend Vigil, 5:30 PM.
(314) 231-3250 www.explorestlouis.com

4 OLD COURTHOUSE MUSEUM

The Old Courthouse was built between 1845-1862. It is part of Jefferson National Expansion Memorial. Many historic events took place in the Courthouse, including the Dred Scott decision of 1857. Many fine exhibits, dioramas and murals. Gift shop.

■ Open daily, 8-4:30. Free admission.
(314) 655-1700 www.nps.gov/jeff

5 WILLIAM CLARK HOUSE AND INDIAN MUSEUM SITE

William Clark created the first museum west of the Mississippi, when he built a two story home, with an Indian council chambers and museum next to it in 1816. The museum was 100 feet long and 30 feet wide. He proudly displayed the many Indian artifacts he owned and other items of interest. As Superintendent of Indian Affairs, he hosted Indian Councils and other public and private events here. Many famous people visited the museum, including George Catlin, Prince Maximilian and Karl Bodmer. Clark's home and museum were located on the north triangle, the grassy spot between the Arch and the Parking Garage.

The JNEM website has a interactive map of Old St Louis. Look at the "Circa 1804" link in the Lewis and Clark site. Clark's second home is in Block 12 (the 1816 home and museum). His first home is in Block 9A. www.nps.gov/jeff

6 LACLEDE'S LANDING

LaClede's Landing is just north of the Arch. The old industrial district is the center of restaurants and entertainment in the downtown area. Horse drawn carriages operate after 4 PM. Fees: $25-$85, 2 passengers, 15-60 minutes.
www.stlouiscarriagecompany.com
(314) 621-3334 (carriages)
(314) 241-5875 www.lacledeslanding.org

7 GATEWAY ARCH RIVERBOAT CRUISES

Replica steamboats, the *Tom Sawyer*, and the *Becky Thatcher*, at the riverfront near the Arch. One hour narrated sight seeing cruises; programs given by National Park Service rangers. Dinner cruises include jazz.

■ Sightseeing cruises daily. 10:30 AM, noon, 1:30, 3, 4:30. Fares: $10 adult, $4 ages 3-12. Dinner cruises: board at 7 PM, depart 7:30, return 9:30. $37 adult, $18 ages 3-12.
Reservations for dinner cruises: (877) 982-1410
www.gatewayarchriverboats.com

8 CAMPBELL HOUSE MUSEUM

The 1851 home of Robert Campbell, who made his fortune in the fur trade. One of the most accurately restored Victorian homes in the US. Hundreds of original family possessions. The museum exhibits feature the fur trade, and other subjects relating to early St Louis history. Robert Campbell (1804-1879) was in the Rocky Mountain fur trade from 1824-35.

■ Open Weds-Sat, 10-4 and Sun 12-4. Admission: $6 a person, children 12 and under free.
www.stlouis.missouri.org (314) 421-0325

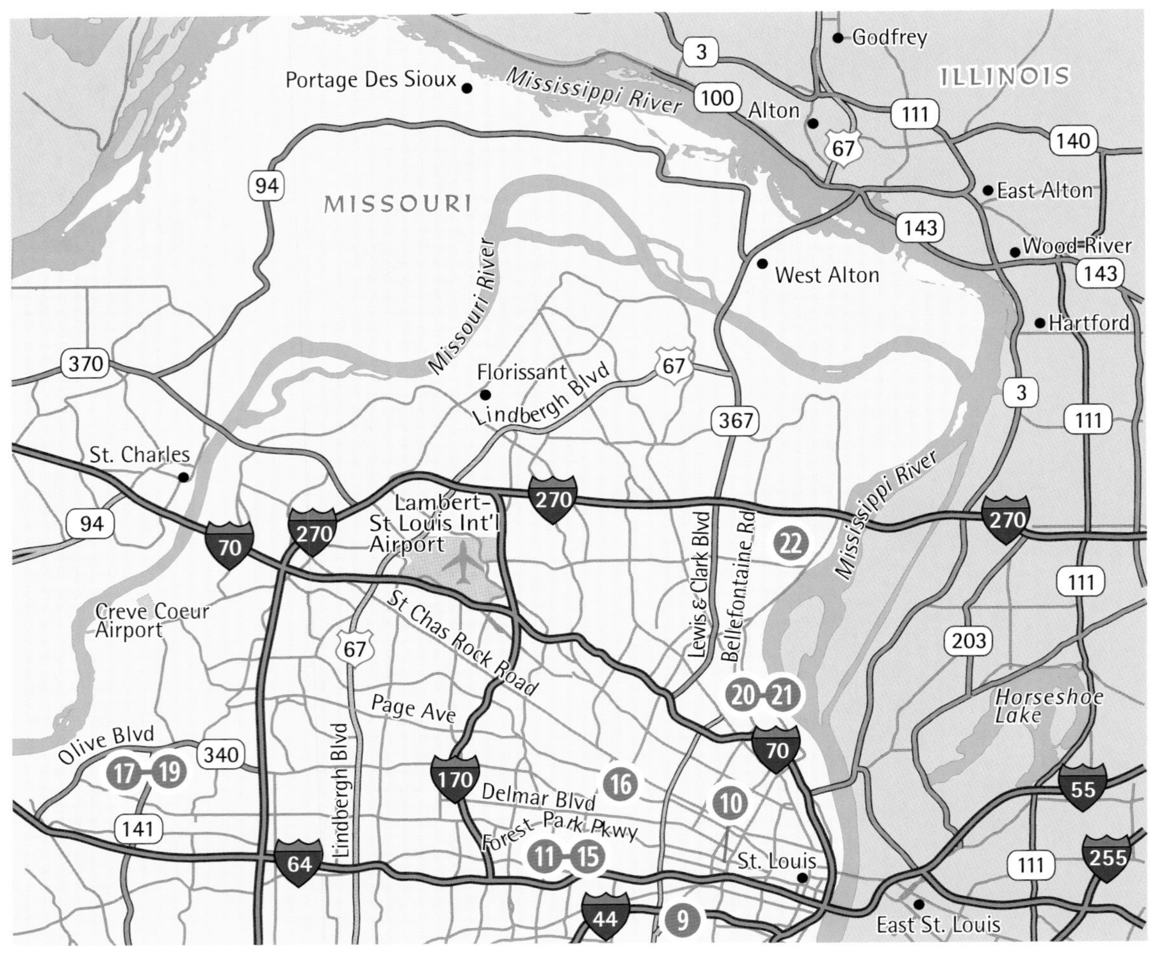

St Louis Metro Area

9 MISSOURI BOTANICAL GARDENS

4344 Shaw Blvd.
From I-44 Exit 28 B turn onto Vandeventer Ave. Turn left (east) onto Shaw Blvd. Continue to Botanical Gardens.

10 ST LOUIS UNIVERSITY MUSEUM OF ART

3663 Lindell Blvd.
From I-64 E take Exit 37A. Turn left (north) onto Grand Blvd. Then turn left (west) onto Lindell Blvd. From I-64 W take Exit 38 A. Continue onto Forest Park Ave. Turn right (north) onto Grand Blvd. then turn left (west) onto Lindell Blvd.

11 MISSOURI HISTORY MUSEUM FOREST PARK

5700 Lindell Blvd.
From I-64 E Exit 36 A take ramp around to Kingshighway north. Go to Lindell Blvd. Turn left (west) From I-64 W take Exit 36 B. Turn right (north) onto Kingshighway Blvd. Go to Lindell Blvd. Turn left (west).

12 ST LOUIS ZOO FOREST PARK

From I-64 E take Exit 34 D ramp to Concourse Dr (Hampton Ave). Turn right (north). Go to Wells Dr. Turn left (west).

13 ST LOUIS SCIENCE CENTER FOREST PARK

5050 Oakland Ave.
From I-64 E take Exit 36 A east to Kingshighway Blvd. Then immediately turn right (west) onto Oakland Ave for half a block.

14 ST LOUIS ART MUSEUM FOREST PARK

One Fine Arts Drive.
From I-64 E take Exit 34 D ramp to Concourse Dr (Hampton Ave). Turn right (north). Then turn left (west) onto Washington Dr. Then turn left (west) onto Government Dr. Go right onto Fine Arts Dr.

15 FOREST PARK JEWEL BOX/TREE WALK

Jewel Box
From I-64 E take Exit 34 D ramp to Concourse Dr (Hampton Ave). Turn right (north). Go to Wells Dr, turn right (east). Then turn left (north) onto McKinley Dr. Located east of the Zoo.

16 ST LOUIS WALK OF FAME UNIVERSITY CITY, MO

Delmar Blvd; Skinker Boulevard to Kingsland Avenue.
From I-64 W, Exit 33 E, turn right (north) onto McCausland Ave which becomes Skinker Blvd. Go to Delmar Blvd.

17 HISTORIC VILLAGE FAUST COUNTY PARK

15185 Olive Blvd, Chesterfield, MO.
From I-64 W Exit 19 B turn right onto Olive Blvd (Rt 340).

18 THORNHILL ESTATE OF FREDERICK BATES FAUST COUNTY PARK

15185 Olive Blvd, Chesterfield, MO.
From I-64 W Exit 19 B turn right onto Olive Blvd (Rt 340).

19 BUTTERFLY HOUSE FAUST COUNTY PARK

15193 Olive Blvd, Chesterfield, MO.
From I-64 W Exit 19 B turn right onto Olive Blvd (Rt 340).

20 WILLIAM CLARK GRAVESITE BELLEFONTAINE CEMETERY

4947 W Florissant Ave.
From I-70 W Exit 245 B bear right (nortwest) onto Florissant Ave. Clark's tomb is in the north corner of the cemetery on Meadow Ave.

21 NEZ PERCE WARRIORS MEMORIAL CALVARY CEMETERY

5239 W Florissant Ave.
From I-70 W Exit 245 B bear right (nortwest) onto Florissant Ave.

22 BISSELL HOUSE

10225 Bellefontaine Rd.
From I-270 Exit 32 turn right (south) onto Bellefontaine Rd.

Missouri History Museum

Butterfly House in Faust County Park
Missouri Botanical Gardens

William Clark Gravesite

St Louis

9 MISSOURI BOTANICAL GARDENS NATIONAL HISTORIC LANDMARK

Founded in 1859, the Gardens include 79 acres of horticultural display, including a 14 acre Japanese strolling garden, the Climatron® conservatory, and the 1850 estate home of Henry Shaw. The Gardens are near "The Hill" neighborhood of fine Italian restaurants and stores.

■ Open daily, 9-5. Morning walk hours, Weds and Sat, 7-9 AM. Free public tours by garden guides at 1 PM daily. Narrated tram rides from Apr-Oct, $3. Admission: $8 adults, free ages 12 and under. (800) 642-8842 www.mobot.org

10 ST LOUIS UNIVERSITY MUSEUM OF ART

The art museum contains Jesuit western history artifacts, including items relating to Father Pierre Jean De Smet, SJ (1801-73), the famous Indian missionary. Other exhibits include Asian netsukes, Santos art, and the Cartier Collection.

■ Open Tues-Sat, 11-4. Free admission.
(314) 977-3399 www.sluma.slu.edu

11 MISSOURI HISTORY MUSEUM

An exhibit on St Louis history includes the desk of William Clark and his portrait. The building itself was the nation's first memorial to Jefferson, built in 1913. Another exhibit features the St Louis World's Fair of 1904, the Louisiana Purchase Exposition. The Fair was held in Forest Park, where the history museum, art museum, science center and zoo, plus other attractions are located today. Meriwether's, the museum's restaurant, located in the modern Emerson Center has good food and a view of Forest Park.

■ Open daily, 10-6. Tues, 10-8. Free admission. Meriwether's serves lunch 11-2, and Sunday brunch 10-2. Self serve during other hours.
(314) 361-7313 www.mohistory.org

12 ST LOUIS ZOO—FOREST PARK

The state of the art biopark has more than 3000 animals. Attractions include Jungle of the Apes, Big Cat Country, and Emerson Electric Children's Zoo. The River's Edge, a 27 million dollar, 10 acre immersion environment, has animals from all over the world. The Monsanto Insectarium has a geodesic flight dome among other exhibits. The 1904 World's Fair Flight Cage is home the Love Conservation Foundation Cypress Swamp. A miniature Zooline Railroad takes visitors around the zoo. Passengers may get on and off the train to see exhibits.

■ Open daily, 9-5. Extended hours, last wkd in May to 1st wkd in Sept, 8-7. General zoo admission is free. Railroad fare is $4. The Insectarium is $2 admission, and free from 9-10 AM.
(800) 966-8877 www.stlzoo.org

13 ST LOUIS SCIENCE CENTER

The Science Center is located just across from the Planetarium in Forest Park via a walkway over Highway 64. Outdoor physics interactive exhibits at Science Park. Glided Segway human transporter tours on weekends in Forest Park ($65-80 2½-3 hours); 1 hour classes ($10).

■ Open 9:30-4:30, Mon-Thurs and Sat. Fri, 9:30-9:30, Sun 11:30-4:30. Free admission.
(800) 456-7572 or (314) 289-4400
www.slfp.com

14 ST LOUIS ART MUSEUM—FOREST PARK

The museum was the Palace of Fine Arts for the 1904 World's Fair, standing on top of "Art Hill."

■ Open Tues-Sun, 10-5, and Friday, 10-9. Free admission. Free one hour tours at 1:30 daily.
(314) 721-0072 www.stlouis.art.museum

■ Audio walking tours of the Art Hill area are available at the Visitor Information Center.
www.forestparkforever.org

15 FOREST PARK JEWEL BOX/TREE WALK

The Tree Walk is adjacent to the Art Deco 1936 floral conservatory, the Jewel Box, which has been restored to its original beauty.

■ Open 9-4 daily. Admission $1. Free from 9-12 on Mon and Tues. Self guided tree walk.
(314) 289-5300 www.slfp.com/ForestPark

16 ST LOUIS WALK OF FAME

Brass stars and plaques set in the sidewalks of Delmar Boulevard, honor 110 famous people associated with St. Louis. William Clark's star is at 6619 Delmar Blvd. The neighborhood is known as "The Loop," with shops and restaurants.

■ www.stlouiswalkoffame.org

17 HISTORIC VILLAGE—FAUST COUNTY PARK

The historic village is a collection of eleven rescued old buildings, set in Faust County Park. Weekend festivals in late Sept and Dec.

■ Open daily. 7 AM to half hour after sunset. Free admission. (636) 532-7298
www.co.st-louis.mo.us/parks

18 THORNHILL ESTATE —FAUST COUNTY PARK

The 1819 estate of Frederick Bates (1777-1825), Missouri's second governor. The estate has outbuildings, and gardens. Bates served under Meriwether Lewis as Secretary of the Territory; they were bitter enemies.

■ Visitors may explore the grounds. House tours by appointment: $3 adult, $1.50 children.
(636) 532-7298 ww.co.st-louis.mo.us/parks

19 BUTTERFLY HOUSE—FAUST CO PARK

More than a thousand butterflies flutter around in native and tropical habitat environments; operated by the Missouri Botanical Gardens. The St Louis Carousel is at Faust Park also.

■ Open daily, last wkd in May-1st wkd in Sept, 9-5. Open Sept-May, Tues-Sun, 9-4. Admission: $6 adult, $4.50 senior, $4 ages 4-12.
(636) 530-0076 www.butterflyhouse.org

20 WILLIAM CLARK GRAVESITE BELLEFONTAINE CEMETERY

William Clark (1770-1838) is buried here. His gravesite is located in the northeast corner of the cemetery. Stay to the left after passing the the main gate and office at Florissant Avenue. Look for the obelisk monument.

■ Open daily 8-5. Office open Mon-Fri, 8-4. Map and self guided tour available.
www.findagrave.com (314) 381-0750

21 NEZ PERCE WARRIORS MEMORIAL CALVARY CEMETERY

Two of the four Nez Perce warriors who came to visit William Clark in 1831 died in St Louis and were baptized Catholic before they died. In 2000, Nez Perce tribal members participated in ceremonies honoring these men and dedicated a monument to their memory. Stay to the left after the main gate on Florissant Avenue and ;ook for the giant feather monument in the northeast section.

■ Open daily, 8-5. Office hours: Mon-Fri, 8:30-4, and Sat, 8:30-12:30. (314) 381-1313
www.stlcathcem.com

22 GENERAL DANIEL BISSELL HOUSE

One of St Louis' oldest homes, built c.1823-28. Many Bissell family early 19th century furnishings are displayed. Call the curator at Jefferson Barracks to arrange a tour.
(314) 544-6224 www.mostateparks.com

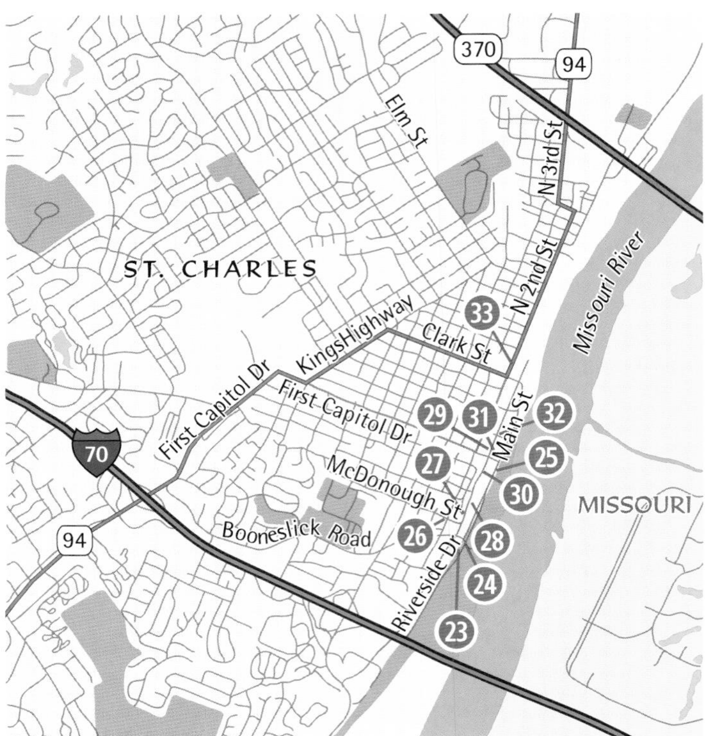

St Charles

St Charles and Florissant

French Colonial Duplex House

23 LEWIS AND CLARK BOAT HOUSE AND NATURE CENTER
1050 S Riverside Drive.
From I-70 W Exit 229 B go right (north) onto 5th St. Then bear right (northeast) onto Booneslick Rd. Go left (north) onto Riverside Dr.

24 KATY TRAIL
99 E Chauncey St
From I-70 W Exit 229 B go right (north) onto 5th St. Then bear right (northeast) onto Booneslick Rd. Go left (north) onto Riverside Dr.

25 TRAILHEAD BREWERY IN OLD GRIST MILL (BOONE'S LICK TRAILHEAD)
921 S Riverside Drive
From I-70 W Exit 229 B go right (north) onto 5th St. Then bear right (northeast) onto Booneslick Rd. Go left (north) onto Riverside Dr.

26 SPANISH COMMANDANT'S HOUSE AND DANCE SITE
119 McDonough St.
From I-70 W Exit 229 B go right (north) onto 5th St. Turn right (east) onto McDonough St.

27 LEWIS AND CLARK STATUE AND EXPEDITION DEPARTURE SITE MARKER
810 S Main Street.
From I-70 W Exit 229 B go right (north) onto 5th St. Then bear right (northeast) onto Booneslick Rd. Go left (north) onto Main St. The marker is at Main and Water Sts. The statue is in Frontier Park.

28 FRENCH COLONIAL DUPLEX HOUSE
719 South Main St.
From I-70 W Exit 229 B go right (north) onto 5th St. Then bear right (northeast) onto Booneslick Rd. Go left (north) onto Main St.

29 LEWIS AND CLARK'S RESTAURANT AND PUB
217 S Main St.
From I-70 W Exit 229 B go right (north) onto 5th St. Then bear right (northeast) onto Booneslick Rd. Go left (north) onto Main St.

30 ST CHARLES BORROMEO LOG CHURCH
401 S Main St.
From I-70 W Exit 229 B go right (north) onto 5th St. Then bear right (northeast) onto Booneslick Rd. Go left (north) onto Main St.

31 FIRST MISSOURI STATE CAPITOL
200-216 S Main St.
From I-70 W Exit 229 B go right (north) onto 5th St. Then bear right (northeast) onto Booneslick Rd. Go left (north) onto Main St.

32 ST CHAS CO HIST SOC
101 S Main St
From I-70 W Exit 229 B go right (north) onto 5th St. Then bear right (northeast) onto Booneslick Rd. Go left (north) onto Main St.

33 MOTHER DUCHESNE SHRINE
619 N Second St.
From I-70 W Exit 229 B go right (north) onto 5th St. Turn right (east) onto Clark St. Then turn left (north) onto 2nd St.

34 OLD ST FERDINAND SHRINE
1 Saint Francois St.
Florissant, MO
From I-270 W Exit 25 A-B bear right (northeast) onto US 67 (Lindbergh Blvd). Turn right (southwest) onto Rue St Charles. Turn right (northwest) onto Rue St Francois.

35 CASA ALVAREZ
289 Rue St Denis
Florissant, MO
From I-270 W Exit 25 A-B bear right (northeast) onto US 67 (Lindbergh Blvd). Turn right (southeast) onto Rue St Denis.

St Charles Main Street
All St Charles photos by Betty Kluesner

Lewis and Clark Boat House

Lewis and Clark's Restaurant

St Charles and Florissant

23 LEWIS AND CLARK BOAT HOUSE AND NATURE CENTER–ST CHARLES

The Boat House is the permanent home of the Discovery Expedition of St Charles and their keelboat and pirogues. The Discovery Expedition retraced the route of Lewis and Clark across the country in 2003-2006, and these are the boats they used. The Center has displays of Indian tribes, the men of the expedition with their equipment and artifacts, a walk through forest; and a Trading Post gift shop.

■ Open daily, Mon-Sat, 10-5; Sun, 12-5.
(636) 947-3199 www.lewisandclark.net

24 KATY TRAIL–ST CHARLES

The 225 mile hiking and biking trail's eastern trailhead is at St. Charles. The Boathouse Center parking lot is a favorite parking area. 165 miles are designated as an official segment of the Lewis and Clark National Historic Trail, from St Charles to Boonville. The trail is the longest rails-to-trail project in the US, and one of the most popular. Bike day rentals are available through hotels and cycle shops.

■ (800) 334-6946 Katy Trail State Park info
www.mostateparks.com/katytrail
www.bikekatytrail.com
www.mometumcycles.com (636) 946-7433

25 TRAILHEAD BREWERY–ST CHARLES

The Trailhead Brewing Co is located in the renovated Old Grist Mill at the corner of Boone's Lick Road and Main Street. With a seating capacity of 300 inside and 100 outside, the restaurant has beer and American fare.

It stands at the eastern end, or trail head of the "Booneslick Trail" between St Charles and Daniel Boone's Salt Lick (near present day Boonville). The Booneslick Trail was the main travel road west for many years; it parallels the route of today's I-70. Parts of the Old Grist Mill date back to the founding of St Charles.

■ Open daily, Mon-Sat, 11 AM-1:30 AM; Sun, 11 AM to midnight. (636) 946-2739
www.trailheadbrewing.com

26 SPANISH COMMANDANT'S HOUSE AND EXPEDITION DANCE SITE

The men of the expedition attended a ball on Saturday evening, May 19th, at the Spanish Commandant's house. This is the site of the house, but not the original house. The house is c. 1820. The ground floor was the dance hall.

■ Lewis and Clark Boat House for info
(636) 947-3199 www.lewisandclark.net

27 LEWIS AND CLARK STATUE AND EXPEDITION DEPARTURE SITE

The marker reads "On Monday Morning, May 21, Under Stormy Skies, The Expedition Left St Charles By Boat On Their Journey To The Unknown And To Immortality." The statue of Lewis and Clark with Seaman is located in Frontier Park, where the Lewis and Clark Encampment and Festival is held annually on a weekend near the 21st of May.

■ Lewis and Clark Boat House for info
(636) 947-3199 www.lewisandclark.net

28 FRENCH COLONIAL DUPLEX HOUSE

What did the village look like in 1803? This French colonial duplex at 719 South Main St might date back to the 1790's. The village was called *Les Petites Côtes*, or the Little Hills, at that time. Lewis wrote that there were about 450 residents and 100 dwellings. Many of the buildings would have looked like this one: duplexes with large porches, often used as combination homes and businesses. But most would would have had vertical log construction; this building is brick, covered with native walnut.

■ Karen's River Cabin gift shop is located here. Gifts and collectibles by Missouri artists.
(636)-724-4206 www.historicstcharles.com

29 LEWIS AND CLARK'S AMERICAN RESTAURANT AND PUB–ST CHARLES

The Trailhead and Lewis and Clark's are under the same ownership. This is one of the most popular restaurants in the St Louis area. The menu is American fare. Over one hundred years old, the 3 story building has patio seating overlooking Main Street.

■ Open daily, Mon-Sat, 11 AM-1:30 AM, and Sun, 11 AM-midnight.(636) 947-3334
www.lewisandclarksrestaurant.com

30 ST CHARLES BORROMEO LOG CHURCH–ST CHARLES

Clark wrote: "Send 20 men to church today." The log church where the men worshipped on Sunday, May 20th, 1803 is being rebuilt as a Educational and Visitor Center. There will be a small chapel on the premises.

The original vertical log church was built by Louis Blanchette, the founder of St Charles, in 1776. The church was dedicated in 1791, and the village was renamed St Charles in honor of the Spanish Monarch Carlos IV.

■ (636) 946-1893 St Charles Borromeo Church
www.historicstcharles.com

31 FIRST MISSOURI STATE CAPITOL STATE HISTORIC SITE

Completely restored and furnished as it appeared in 1821-26, when it was the home of the Missouri State Legislature. The Pecks Bros Dry Goods Store on the ground floor level has also been restored. Two floors of exhibits and an orientation film.

■ Open daily, Mon-Sat, 9-4 and Sun 11-5. Free admission. Guided tours on the hour. Tour price, $2.50 adult, $1.50 ages 12 and under.
(314) 946-9282 www.historicstcharles.com

32 ST CHARLES COUNTY HISTORICAL SOCIETY ARCHIVES

Located in the Old Market House, part of which dates to 1832. The Archives has a small museum of local artifacts. Their website has over 10,000 photos and geneaological material. Bookstore.

■ Open Mon, Weds, Fri 10-3; and 2nd and 4th Saturdays, 10-3.
(636) 946-9828 www.scchs.org

33 MOTHER DUCHESNE SHRINE

William Clark dined here at the Duquette home on the day of their departure. In 1818 the Duquettes gave their log house to Phillippine Duchesne, who founded the first free school west of the Mississippi in the house, the beginnings of the Academy of the Sacred Heart. The Shine of St Rose Phillippine Duchesne, the 4th United States saint, has a museum with exhibits of frontier St Charles, and an 1835 convent.

■ Open daily, 9-4. Guided tours on Tues, Thurs, Fri at 9-11 and 1-3; Sat, 10-12, and 1-3; and Sun, 12-3. (636) 946-6127
www.ash1818.org

34 OLD ST FERDINAND SHRINE HISTORIC DISTRICT–FLORISSANT, MO

The 1821 church is thought to be the oldest church between the Mississippi and the Rockies. The 1819 convent wing once had a school for Indian children taught by Mother Duchesne.

■ Open Sundays, 1-4. Tours by appointment at other times. (314) 837-2110
www.florissantmo.com

35 CASA ALVAREZ–FLORISSANT, MO

The only building in the St Louis area directly connected to Spanish colonial government is the 1790 home of Eugenio Alvarez, the Spanish storekeeper of the Royal Treasury. The home is now a private residence.
www.florissantmo.com

River Route: St Charles to Columbia

36 WORLD BIRD SANCTUARY VALLEY PARK, MO

125 Bald Eagle Ridge Road.
From I-44 Exit go north on Rte 141 to the first available right turn which leads to the I-44 north outer road. Turn left and go west to the Sanctuary.

37 SHAW NATURE RESERVE GRAY SUMMIT, MO

From I-44 Exit 253 turn left (south) onto Hwy 100. Go under I-44. Turn right (east) and continue on Hwy 100 past Gray Summit Rd to Reserve entrance.

38 DANIEL BOONE HOME AND BOONESFIELD VILLAGE DEFIANCE, MO

1868 Highway F.
From Rte 94 at Defiance, MO go north to Rte F. Turn left (west). Go to Daniel Boone Home.

39 GARY LUCY GALLERY WASHINGTON, MO

231 West Main Street.
From I-44 Exit 251 turn west onto Rte 100. Go to Jefferson St in Washington. Turn right (north). Go to Main St. Turn left (northwest). onto Main St.

Students at Daniel Boone's Grave
Lindenwood University

40 DANIEL BOONE GRAVE MARTHASVILLE, MO

240 Boone Monument Road.
From I-44 Exit 247 go west on US 50. Turn right (north) onto Rte 47. Turn right (north) onto Boone Monument Road.

41 JOHN COLTER MEMORIAL NEW HAVEN, MO

Main and Miller Streets.
From I-44 Exit 247 go west on US 50. Turn right (north) onto Rte 47. Turn left (west) onto Rte 100. Turn Right (north) onto Miller St. Go to Main St.

42 DEUTSCHHEIM STATE HISTORIC SITE HERMANN, MO

109 West Second Street.
From I-44 Exit 247 go west on US 50. Turn right (north) onto Rte 47. Turn left (west) onto Rt 100. Rt 100 is 1st St in Hermann. Turn left (south) onto Market St. Turn right (west) onto 2nd St.

From I-70 it is 15.5 miles from Exit 175 to Hermann on Rte 19.

43 GERMAN SCHOOL MUSEUM HERMANN, MO

4th and Schiller Streets.
From I-44 Exit 247 go west on US 50. Turn right (north) onto Rte 47. Turn left (west) onto Rt 100. Rt 100 is 1st St in Hermann. Turn left (south) onto 4th St. Go to Schiller St.

From I-70 it is 15.5 miles from Exit 175 to Hermann on Rte 19.

44 STONE HILL WINERY AND RESTAURANT HERMANN, MO

1110 Stone Hill Highway.
From I-44 Exit 247 go west on US 50. Turn right (north) onto Rte 47. Turn left (west) onto Rte 100. Rt 100 is 1st St in Hermann. Turn left (south) onto Market St. Bear right (southwest) onto Rte 100. Turn right (west) onto 14th St. Turn left (south) onto Goethe St. Turn right (west) onto 16th St. Turn right (north) onto Jefferson St. Turn left (northwest) onto Stone Hill Hwy.

From I-70, it is 15.5 miles from Exit 175 to Hermann on Rte 19.

Katy Trail near Hermann
MO Dept Natural Resources

45 CLARK'S HILL OSAGE CITY, MO

1700 Osage Hickory Street.
From US 50 in Jefferson City turn left (northeast) oto Old Rte J. Turn left (north) onto Osage 4th St. Road changes name to Osage Hickory St. Go to end of road.

46 STATE CAPITOL/MUSEUM JEFFERSON CITY, MO

201 West Capitol Avenue.
From US 50 W take Jefferson City Exit. Turn right (northeast) onto Jackson St. Turn left (northwest) onto Capitol Ave.

47 JEFFERSON LANDING JEFFERSON CITY, MO

2 Jefferson Street.
From US 50 W take Jefferson City Exit. Turn right (northeast) onto Jackson St. Turn left (northwest) onto Capitol Ave. Turn right onto Jefferson St.

Daniel Boone Home
Lindenwood University

Hermann, "Rhineland on the Missouri"
Hermann Area Chamber of Commerce

Jefferson Landing
MO Dept Natural Resources

River Route to Jefferson City

4

36 WORLD BIRD SANCTUARY VALLEY PARK, MO

The World Bird Sanctuary was founded by ornithologist Walter C Crawford, Jr. The Sanctuary is one of North America's largest facilities for conservation of birds; it has a particular emphasis on birds of prey (raptors) and parrots. Walk the trails and view the birds. Educational programs and gift shop.

■ Open daily, 8-5. Visitor Information Center is open 11-3. Please call if weather is bad; the roads may be closed. Free admission.
(636) 861-3225 www.worldbirdsanctuary.org

37 SHAW NATURE RESERVE GRAY SUMMIT, MO

The 2500 acre Nature Reserve is part of the Missouri Botanical Gardens. It serves as an outdoor laboratory for many research and educational progams. There are 13 miles of hiking trails through Ozark Border landscapes, including a 5 acre wildflower garden.

■ Open daily, 7 AM-sunset. Visitor Center hours are Mon-Fri, 8-4:30 and Sat-Sun, 9-5. Admission: $3 ages 13 and over, $2 seniors/
(636) 451-3512 www.shawnature.org

38 DANIEL BOONE HOME AND BOONESFIELD VILLAGE—DEFIANCE, MO

The Boone home is an imposing, four story building built by Nathan Boone, Daniel Boone's son, between 1804-1810. It was the last home of Daniel Boone, who died here at age 85 in 1820. Lindenwood University of St Charles manages the property and the adjacent Boonesfield Village. Students earn course credits by participating in the living history village, and studying history and traditional skills.

■ Open Mar-Thanksgiving wkd (late Nov). Mon-Sat, 9-5 and Sun 12-5. Admission: one hour tour, $7 adults, $6 seniors, $4 ages 4-11; two hour tour, $12 adults, $10 seniors, $6 ages 4-11. Tours every hour on the half hour. Call to confirm hours, varies by daylight savings time.
(636) 798-2005 www.lindenwood.edu/boone

39 GARY LUCY STUDIO—WASHINGTON, MO

Artist Gary Lucy paints Lewis and Clark, wildlife, and Missouri riverboat scenes. His studio has riverboat models on display, and many Lewis and Clark items for sale. It is located in historic Washington's district of restaurants, galleries and shops.

■ (800) 937-4944 www.garylucy.com

40 DANIEL BOONE GRAVE MONUMENT MARTHASVILLE, MO

It is a matter of dispute whether Daniel Boone is buried here, or in Frankfort, Kentucky. This is his original 1820 burial place, chosen by him. Or was he reinterred in Frankfort in the 1840's? You can visit both gravesites to pay your respects. There are 14 standing gravestones at the Monument overlooking Touque Creek.

Marthasville, established in 1817, is one of the oldest communities on the Missouri River. La Charette, the last town the expedition passed on their way west, was located near here. The citizens of La Charette welcomed them back with a round of gun fire and a "harty Cheer" on Sept 20, 1806.

■ www.moriver.org

41 JOHN COLTER MEMORIAL NEW HAVEN, MO

When John Colter finally realized he had had enough of narrow escapes in the West, he got married and settled down here. The Visitor Center and Colter Museum has exhibits, a small gift shop, and a river walk along the levee with interpretive signs.

■ Open April-Oct, Weds-Sat, 10-4; Sun, 12-4.
(537) 237-3830 ww.newhavenmo.com

42 DEUTSCHHEIM STATE HISTORIC SITE HERMANN, MO

"Deutsch Heim" (German Home) was the term German writers used to describe Missouri in the 1820's-50's. Germans emigrated in large numbers to Missouri in the 1800's, and Hermann with its rolling hills was a favorite area, called the "Rhineland on the Missouri." The state historic site has the Pommer-Gentner House, the Strehly House and Winery, the Print Shop, historic garden and grapevines, half-timbered barn, and a museum shop.

■ Open daily, Mar-Dec, 8-4; Jan-Feb, Weds-Sun, 8-4. Tours at 10, 12:30 and 2:30. Admission: $2
(573) 486-2200 www.mostateparks.com

43 HISTORIC HERMANN MUSEUM HERMANN, MO

The German School (1871-1955) is now a museum and gift shop operated by Historic Hermann. Early memorabilia, a gift shop, and volunteer staff to welcome you. Festivals are held in Hermann in March, May, October and December, and vinyard tours in July. Hermann has nearly 50 bed and breakfasts and other lodging for visitors.

■ Museum open April-Oct, Tues-Sun, 10-4. Open by appointment, Nov-March.

■ Visitor Center is open daily, 312 Market St, Apr-Oct, 9-5; Nov-Mar, 9:30-4:30; and Sunday, all year 10-4. (800) 932-8687
www.hermannmo.info

44 STONE HILL WINERY AND RESTAURANT—HERMANN, MO

Stone Hill Winery is Missouri's oldest, and most award-winning winery; it is one of the most popular tourist attractions in Missouri. Guided tours of the winery's underground cellars, modern production facilty and wine tasting rooms are offered. The Vintage Restaurant serves German and American fare.

■ Open daily, Mon-Fri, 8:30 AM to 5:30 or 7:30 depending on season. Sunday, 10-6. Tours: $1.50 adults, 50¢ ages 6-12.
(800) 909-WINE (9463)
www.stonehillwinery.com

45 CLARK'S HILL/NORTON SITE OSAGE CITY, MO

The expedition camped near the base of Clark's Hill, June 1-3, 1803. A 1½ mile hiking trail with interpretive signs leads to a bluff overlook, with a view of the Osage and Missouri Rivers.

■ (573) 449-7402 www.mostateparks.com

46 STATE CAPITOL AND MISSOURI STATE MUSEUM—JEFFERSON CITY

The Missouri State Museum is located on the ground floor of the State Capitol, with a History Hall and Resources Hall for Missouri's agricultural, forestry and mining industries. Dioramas, and exhibits. Free guided tours of the State Capitol are offered daily. The House lounge on the third floor features Thomas Hart Benton's mural, "A Social History of Missouri."

■ Open daily, 8-5. Tours Mon-Sat, on the hour except noon. Sunday, tours at 10,11,2 and 3.
(573) 751-2854 www.mostateparks.com

47 JEFFERSON LANDING—JEFFERSON CITY

Jefferson Landing is located one block from the State Capitol on the riverfront. The 1839 Lohman building is a Visitor Center with exhibits on transportation. The 1855 Union Hotel houses the Elizabeth Rozier Gallery.

■ Open Tues-Sat, 10-4. Guided tours every hour on the hour.
(573) 751-2854 www.mostateparks.com

Columbia, Rocheport, Boonville and Boone's Lick

Canoeing at Rocheport
Brett Dufur

4

Arrow Rock to Fort Osage

48 ANTHROPOLOGY MUSEUM UNIV OF MO-COLUMBIA

100 Swallow Hall.
From I-70 go south on US 63 to Stadium Blvd. Go west on Stadium Blvd to College Ave. Turn right (north). Go to University Ave. Turn left (west). Go to 9th St. Parking garage on University Avenue.

49 JEFFERSON'S ORIGINAL GRAVE MARKER/STATUE MIZZOU BOTANICAL GARDEN UNIV OF MO-COLUMBIA

From I-70 go south on US 63 to Stadium Blvd. Go west on Stadium Blvd to College Ave. Turn right (north). Go to University Ave. Turn left (west). Go to 9th St. On the west the grave marker is between the Residence on the Quad and the Columns.

50 WALTERS-BOONE MUSEUM—COLUMBIA

3801 Ponderosa Street.
From I-70 go south on US 63 to the exit for US 63 Bus.. At the end of the exit turn right (west) onto Old US 63. Immediately turn left (south) onto Nilfong Blvd. Follow Nilfong Blvd 0.3 miles to Ponderosa St. Turn left (southeast).

51 LE BOURGEOIS ROCHEPORT, MISSOURI

From I-70 Exit 115 go north to the junction with Rte BB.

52 MIGHTY MO CANOE RENTALS AND KATY TRAIL BIKE RENTALS—ROCHEPORT

205 Central Street.
From I-70 Exit 115 go north on Rte BB. Turn right (north) onto Central St.

53 HERITAGE PARK BOONVILLE, MISSOURI

Main and Morgan Streets.
From I-70 Exit 103 go north on Main St (Rte B) to Morgan St.

54 HARLEY PARK RIVER OVERLOOK BOONVILLE, MISSOURI

Parkway Drive.
From I-70 Exit 101 go northeast onto US 40. Turn left (northwest) onto Sombart Rd. Turn right (northeast) onto Santa Fe Trail. Turn left (northwest) onto Parkway Drive.

55 BOONE'S LICK BOONESBORO, MO

From I-70 Exit 101 go northeast onto US 40. Turn left (west) onto Rte 87. Turn left (west) onto Rte 187. Travel southwest to the park.

56 ARROW ROCK MUSEUM AND VISITOR CENTER

From I-70 Exit 98 go north on Rte 41 to Van Buren St in Arrow Rock. Turn right (east). Go to 4th St. turn right (south) to museum.

57 HISTORIC ARROW ROCK TAVERN

3rd and Main Street.
From I-70 Exit 98 go north on Rte 41 to Main St in Arrow Rock. Turn right (east).

58 ARROW ROCK WALKING TOURS

1st and High Streets.
From I-70 Exit 98 go north on Rte 41 to High St in Arrow Rock. Turn right (east).

59 LEWIS AND CLARK TRAIL ARROW ROCK

Overlook Drive.
From I-70 Exit 98 go north on Rte 41 to Main St in Arrow Rock. Turn right (east). Go past the end of Main St.

60 VAN METER STATE PARK OLD FORT – MIAMI, MO

From I-70 Exit 78 go north on US 65. Turn right (north) onto Rte 41. Turn left (west) onto Rt 122. Follow Rt 122 to the park.

61 FORT OSAGE—SIBLEY, MO

134 Osage Street.
From I-70 Exit 24 take Rte BB north. In Buckner road name changes to Sibley St, then Tarsney Rd. Turn left (west) onto Chicago St. Turn right (north) onto Santa Fe St. Turn right (east) onto 4th St. Turn left (north) onto Osage St.

Boone's Lick State Park
MO Dept of Natural Resources

Boone's Lick

On June 6, 1804 the Corps of Discovery passed Salt Creek in the vicinity of today's Boonville. Clark noted the water was so salty that "one bushel of water is said to make 7 lb. of good Salt."

The sons of Daniel Boone established a business at the Salt Lick in 1805. For many years pioneers traveled on the Boone's Lick Trail from St Charles to settle here, or to continue farther west.

They settled here because the land was good and the salt industry was prosperous. Salt was necessary to preserve meat in an era before refrigeration, and to tan hides in making leather. It was shipped back to St Louis by keelboat.

Salt is also a necessity of life for hoofed animals. Domestic animals—horses, cattle and sheep—need salt. And for countless generations, wild animals—such as deer and buffalo—and those who hunt them, have visited salt licks.

Interstate 70 is the modern version of the Boone's Lick Road, but travelers may wish to explore the route of US Highway 40.

Hannah Cole
Hope Photo, Boonville MO

Fort Osage Nat'l Historic Landmark
Betty Kluesner

Thomas Jefferson, Botanical Gardens
University of Missouri-Columbia

Arrow Rock Tavern
MO Dept of Natural Resources

Columbia Area

48 MUSEUM OF ANTHROPOLOGY UNIVERSITY OF MISSOURI–COLUMBIA

The museum's collection focuses on North American cultures; and Missouri history from 11,200 years ago to the present. It also has the world's largest archery collection. Gift shop.

■ Open Mon-Fri, 9-4. Free admission. Tours by appointment. (573) 882-3573 anthromuseum.missouri.edu

49 JEFFERSON'S ORIGINAL GRAVE MARKER-BOTANICAL GARDEN UNIVERSITY OF MISSOURI–COLUMBIA

A living museum of plants and sculptures, the botanical garden has Jefferson's grave marker, a statue of Thomas Jefferson by George Lundeen, and garden plants of the type found in Jefferson's Monticello gardens. The area is located directly north of the Anthropology Museum.

■ Open Mon-Fri, 7:30-5. Free admission. (573) 884-3160 gardens.missouri.edu

50 WALTERS–BOONE MUSEUM COLUMBIA, MISSOURI

The museum and visitors center tells the story of the Boone's Lick Trace, the pioneers who settled here, and the development of Boone County. "Old Time Fiddlers" gather regularly to make music. Fine Arts Gallery and Gift Shop.

■ Open Apr-Oct, Tues-Fri, 12-4, wkds, 1-5. Nov-Mar, Wed and Fri, 12-4, and wkd, 1-5. Admission: $3. (573) 443-8936 members.sockets.net/~bchs

51 LES BOURGEOIS RESTAURANT AND WINERY–ROCHEPORT, MISSOURI

Les Bourgeois Restaurant and Winery is located half way between Kansas City and St Louis on a high bluff overlooking the Missouri River. Full service restaurant. Winegarden and picnic area. Tours, wine tasting and gift shop.

■ Open Mar-Oct, Tues-Sat,11-9 and Sun,11-3. Nov-Feb, Tues-Thurs, 11-8; Fri-Sat, 11-9, and Sun, 1-3. Weekend winery tours at 1, 2 and 3. (573) 698-2613 www.missouriwine.com

52 MIGHTY MO CANOE RENTALS AND KATY TRAIL BIKE RENTALS ROCHEPORT, MISSOURI

Brett Dufur, author and publisher of *The Complete Katy Trail Guidebook*, offers canoe and kayak rentals and excursions from his bookstore in Rocheport. The historic town of Rocheport on the Katy Trail has bed and breakfasts, antique shops and restaurants. Many options for canoe/bike/travel transportation back and forth.

■ Canoe and kayak trips, May-Oct, 1 PM on Saturdays: $30 a person. Reserve in advance. (573) 698-3903 www.mighty-mo.com

■ Bike rentals at Trailside Cafe. (573)698-2702 www.trailsidecafebike.com

■ Historic Rocheport www.rocheport.com

53 HERITAGE PARK–BOONVILLE, MO

The downtown heritage park has a larger than life size bronze statue of Hannah Allison Cole, a widow with nine children, who founded Boonville in 1810. Hannah Cole was granted a license to operate a ferry in 1817. Six bronze busts of others associated with the Boonville area will complete the heritage project.

■ (660) 882-7977 www.boonvillemo.org

54 HARLEY PARK RIVER OVERLOOK BOONVILLE, MISSOURI

The city park was established in 1887. It provides a view of Boone's Lick Country and the Missouri River. It has four earthern mounds (100 BC-500 AD) and interpretive signage.

■ (660) 882-7977 www.boonvillemo.org

55 BOONE'S LICK STATE HISTORIC SITE NEAR BOONVILLE, MISSOURI

Boone's Lick still has an iron boiling kettle left over from the days of salt making, wooden cribs, and a salty creek. Interpretive exhibits and a picnic shelter. Some artifacts from the site are on display at the Arrow Rock State Historic Site Visitor Center. There is no longer a ferry across the river to Arrow Rock.

■ Open daily from sunrise to sunset. (660) 837-3330 www.mostateparks.com

56 ARROW ROCK NATIONAL HISTORIC LANDMARK AND STATE HISTORIC SITE –ARROW ROCK, MO

The state administers a modern visitor center, several historic buildings, and an RV and tent campground. The center has a 20 minute video, gift shop, and an extensive collection of artifacts and interesting exhibits. Arrow Rock is also the start of the historic 1820's Sante Fe Trail.

■ Visitor Center open daily, Mar-Nov, 10-4; June-Aug, 10-5. Open Fri-Sun, Dec-Feb, 10-4. (660)-837-3330 www.mostateparks.com

57 HISTORIC 1834 ARROW ROCK TAVERN ARROW ROCK, MISSOURI

The Arrow Rock Huston Tavern is probably the oldest continuously operating restaurant west of the Mississippi. It serves traditional, hearty fare. Reservations are strongly recommended, but walk-ins are welcome.

■ Open June-Oct, Tues-Sun for lunch, 1-3; Tues-Sat for dinner, 5-8. Open on weekends the rest of the year, Fri-Sun, 1-3 and Fri-Sat, 5-8. (660) 837-3200 www.arrowrock.org

58 ARROW ROCK WALKING TOURS

Two tours: (a) Huston Tavern, George Caleb Bingham house, Sappington Museum and Court House; or (b) Huston Tavern, Lodge Hall, Print Shop, Sites Gun Shop, and Victorian House. Bingham is one of America's great artists, and Sappington's anti-fever pills with quinine were the first effective treatment for malaria.

■ Tours start at the boardwalk. Daily in summer, weekends in spring and fall. Tour times are 10, 11:30, 1:30, 3, and 4. $5 adults, $1.50 children. (660) 837-3231 www.arrowrock.org

59 LEWIS AND CLARK TRAIL OF DISCOVERY–ARROW ROCK, MO

A one mile hiking trail along the old river wharf and ferry landing site allows visitors to view the river and the bluffs. Graveled hiking path. (660) 837-3330 www.mostateparks.com

60 VAN METER STATE PARK EARTHWORKS AND OLD FORT–MIAMI, MISSOURI

The Missouri Indians once lived here. The Visitor Center interprets their history, the landscape, and ancient earthworks which are still visible.

■ Open daily, May-Sept, Mon-Sat, 1-4 and Sun, 1-5. Oct-April, Thurs-Sun, 10-4. (660) 886-7537 www.mostateparks.com

61 FORT OSAGE NATIONAL HISTORIC LANDMARK–SIBLEY, MO

Fort Osage was planned and built by William Clark in 1808. It played an important role in frontier history for 19 years serving as both a fort and trading post for the Osage Indians. A new Education Center for all ages opens in 2007. Living history interpreters year round.

■ Open Mar-Nov 15, Tues-Sun, 9-4:30. Rest of the year on weekends, 9-4:30. Admission: $5 adults, $3 seniors, $3 ages 5-13. (816) 650-5737 www.historicfortosage.com

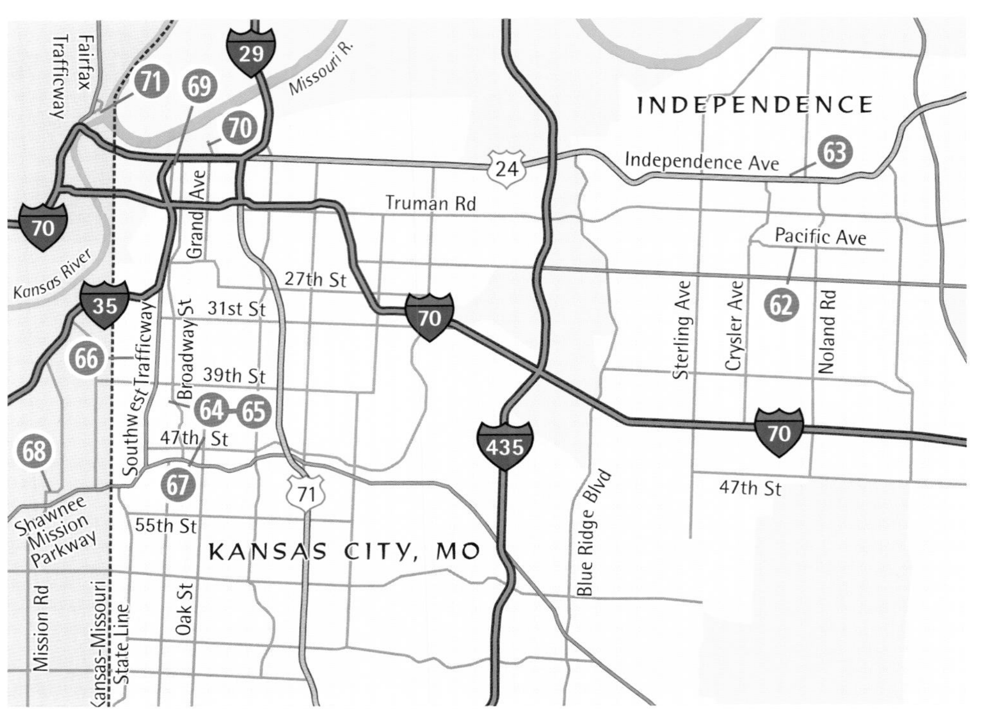

Kansas City, Kansas; Kansas City, Missouri; Independence. Missouri

Nelson-Atkins Museum of Art
Nelson Atkins Museum of Art

62 NAT'L FRONTIERS TRAIL MUSEUM INDEPENDENCE, MO

318 West Pacific Avenue.
From I-70 Exit 12 take Noland Rd north. Turn left (west) onto Linden Ave. Turn right (north) onto Main St. Turn left (west) onto Pacific Ave.

63 TRUMAN LIBRARY AND MUSEUM INDEPENDENCE, MO

US Highway 24 and Delaware St.
From I-70 Exit 12 take Noland Rd north. Turn left (west) onto Independence Ave (US 24).

64 PIONEER PARK IN WESTPORT KANSAS CITY, MO

Westport Rd and Broadway Rd.
From I-235 S, Exit 1 A, keep straight onto Souhwest Trafficway. Turn left (east) onto Mill St. Turn left (east) onto Westport Rd. Go to Broadway Rd.

65 KELLY'S WESTPORT INN KANSAS CITY, MISSOURI

500 Westport Road.
From I-235 S, Exit 1 A, keep straight onto Souhwest Trafficway. Turn left (east) onto Mill St. Turn left (east) onto Westport Rd. Go to Pennsylvania Avenue.

Clark's Point

66 THOMAS HART BENTON HOME AND STUDIO KANSAS CITY, MISSOURI

3616 Belleview Avenue.
From I-235 S, Exit 1 A, keep straight onto Souhwest Trafficway. Turn right (west) onto Valentine Rd. Turn right (north) onto Belleview Avenue.

67 NELSON-ATKINS MUSEUM OF ART KANSAS CITY, MO

4525 Oak Street.
From I-235 S, Exit 1 A, keep straight onto Souhwest Trafficway, road changes name to Belleview Ave. Turn left (east) onto Ward Parkway. Bear left (east) onto Volker Blvd. Turn left (north) onto Oak Street. Go to Warwick Boulevard.

68 SHAWNEE INDIAN MISSION KANSAS CITY, MO

3403 West 53rd Street.
From I-35 S, Exit 233 A, go south on MIssion Road. Turn right (west) onto 53rd Street.

69 CLARK'S POINT KANSAS CITY, MO

611 West 8th Street, Case Park.
From I-35 N, Exit 2 Y, merge onto 6th Street (US 169). Turn right (south) onto Broadway Boulevard. Turn right (west) onto 7th Street. Turn left (south) onto Pennsylvania Avenue. Turn right (west) onto 8th Street.

70 STEAMBOAT ARABIA MUSEUM KANSAS CITY, MO

400 Grand Boulevard.
From I- 70 W/I-35 S, Exit 2 D merge west onto Independence Avenue. Turn right (north) onto Delaware Street. Turn right (east) onto 5th Street. Turn left (north) onto Grand Boulevard.

71 KAW POINT KANSAS CITY, KANSAS

Levee Road.
From I-70 E, Exit 423 ramp (northeast) bear left (north) onto James Street. Take James Street past first stop sign and follow signs to Fairfax Boulevard. The bottom of the ramp is # 1 Fairfax Boulevard. Look for the KAW POINT sign to your right. Turn right after the KAW POINT sign into the parking lot. Head through the parking lot to the concrete flood wall.

Education Pavilion, Kaw Point
Friends of Kaw Point Park

Kaw Point

The expedition camped at the mouth of the Kansas River from June 26th to 29th, where they observed a great number of "Parrot queets" (the extinct Carolina parakeet). Fearing an Indian attack, they built a defensive breastwork from one river to the other, using logs and bushes six foot deep. They made latitude and longitude observations, repaired a pirogue, and dried out their wet goods.

This was also the time they court martialed John Collins and Hugh Hall for raiding the whiskey barrel while on night guard duty. The punishments were 100 lashes and 50 lashes on the bare back.

On June 29th, as they left, they came very close to sinking the keelboat. Clark wrote, "the Sturn of the Boat Struck a moveing Sand and turned within 6 inches of a large Sawyer, if the Boat had Struck the Sawyer, her Bow must have been Knocked off and in Course She must hav Sunk in the Deep water below."

National Frontier Trails Museum
National Frontier Trails Museum

Thomas Hart Benton Studio
Missouri Dept of Natural Resources

The Discovery Keelboat at Kaw Point in 2005
Friends of Kaw Point Park

Kansas City

4

62 NATIONAL FRONTIERS TRAIL MUSEUM INDEPENDENCE, MISSOURI

The museum features the great trails of westward expansion: the Lewis and Clark Trail, the Sante Fe, Oregon, Mormon, and California Trails; the role of fur trappers and traders; and the transcontinental railroad. Most visitors take about 1-1½ hours to tour the exhibits and view the award-winning film. Independence, Missouri was the great "jumping off place" for western travel. Wagon train ruts can be still seen across the street.

■ Open daily, Mon-Sat, 9-4:30; Sun,12:30-4:30. Admission: $4 adults, $3.50 seniors, $2.50 ages 6-17. (816) 325-7575
www.frontiertrailsmuseum.org

■ Pioneer Trails Adventures offers covered wagon tours of historic Independence. 15-20 minute tour: $6; 30-35 minute tour, $12 adults, $6 ages 12 and under; one hour tour, $20 adults, $6 ages 12 and under. Children 2 and under are always free. Reservations:
(816) 254-2466, (816) 204-5372
www.pioneertrailsadventures.com

63 HARRY TRUMAN PRESIDENTIAL MUSEUM AND LIBRARY—INDEPENDENCE

Thomas Hart Benton, one of America's great artists, painted a mural for the Harry Truman Presidential Library and Museum, called "Independence and the Opening of the West." The President took part in planning the mural, which covers the years 1817-47. The two men became life long friends. Museum exhibits include both the presidential years and Truman's life, family, and times.

■ Open daily, Mon-Sat, 9-5; Sun, 12-5. Admission: $7 adults, $5 seniors, $3 ages 6-18.
(800) 833-1225 www.trumanlibrary.org

64 PIONEER PARK IN WESTPORT KANSAS CITY, MISSOURI

Pioneer Park is located in the heart of the old Westport tourist area, near Kelly's Inn. Heroic bronzes of Jim Bridger, Alexander Majors and John Calvin McCoy, and a giant terrazo map of western trails, commemorate Westport's role in settling the American West. A self-guided walking tour and map of Westport are available on the historical society's website.

■ (816) 926-9397 www.westporthistorical.org

65 KELLY'S WESTPORT INN KANSAS CITY, MISSOURI

This is one of the oldest buildings in Kansas City. It was owned by a grandson of Daniel Boone's, Albert Gallatin Boone, from 1854-60. The building next door, 504 Westport Road, also dates to 1850-51, and was owned by Jim Bridger. Kelly's is known as the anchor of Westport, and has a great pub menu.

■ Open daily until 3 AM. (816) 561-5800
www.kellyswestportinn.com

66 THOMAS HART BENTON HOME AND STUDIO STATE HISTORIC SITE KANSAS CITY, MISSOURI

Born in Neosha MO in 1889, Thomas Hart Benton is one of America's most well known regionalist painters; he painted historical and cultural themes in a vivid and dramatic style. Several of his paintings and sculptures are on display in the house. His studio is just as it was in 1975, the year he died.

Benton was named after his great-great uncle, the U S Senator from Missouri, Thomas Hart Benton (1782-1858), who was a champion of westward expansion. Benton and William Clark were sometimes political allies in early Missouri and national politics.

Knowledgeable interpreters conduct guided tours of his home and studio. Each tour takes about 45 minutes and is offered when you arrive.

■ Open daily. Mon-Sat, 10-4 year round. Sundays from Apr-Oct, 12-5 and from Nov-Mar, 11-4. Guided tours: $2.50 adults, $1.50 ages 6-12, family rate maximum of $12.
(816) 931-5722 www.mostateparks.com

67 NELSON-ATKINS MUSEUM OF ART KANSAS CITY, MISSOURI

The museum is one of the nation's leading art institutions, with an emphasis on Asian art; it is especially well known for its collection of Chinese art. Modern sculpture, featuring the monumental sculptures of Henry Moore, ancient art, decorative arts, African and Native American art are also noteworthy.

■ Hours: Tues-Thurs, 10-4. Fri, 10-9, Sat 10-5, and Sun, 12-5. Free admission. Guided tours on Tues-Sat at 11 AM and 1 PM. On Sun at 1:30 and 2:30. (816) 561-4000
www.nelson-atkins.org

68 SHAWNEE INDIAN MISSION NATIONAL HISTORIC LANDMARK STATE HISTORIC SITE—FAIRWAY, KS

A manual training school for the Shawnee, Delaware and other Indian tribes was conducted here from 1839 until 1862, when it became a Union Army camp. It also served as territorial capitol (the 1854-55 bogus legislature) and as a supply point for the Sante Fe and Oregon Trails.

■ Open, Tues-Sat, 10-4. (call for further info)
(913) 262-0867 www.kshs.org

69 CLARK'S POINT—KANSAS CITY, MO

William Clark noted this site would make a "butifull place for a fort."Instead it is home to a monumental bronze by Eugene Daub honoring Lewis, Clark, York, Sacagawea, the baby Jean Baptiste and Seaman the dog.
www.experiencekc.com

70 STEAMBOAT ARABIA MUSEUM KANSAS CITY, MISSOURI

The *Arabia* Steamboat sank in 1856 bound for the gold fields of Montana. A family of treasure hunters located the boat in a Missouri farm field, and excavated it in 1987. The Hawley family established a museum for the *Arabia* and its cargo in Kansas City's River Market District. There are both reconstructed and salvaged sections of the steamboat and paddle wheel on display; a short video; well-designed exhibits; and a working preservation lab, where visitors can watch the cleaning process and ask questions. Half the cargo is on display; the remaining 100 tons will take an estimated 25 years to clean. The family is continuing to search for more sunken steamboats. They are often at the museum, leading tours and welcoming visitors.

■ Open Mon-Sat, 10-5:30; last tour at 4. Open Sun, 12-5; last tour at 3:30. Tours start every half hour. Admission: $12.50 adults, $11.50 seniors, $4.75, ages 4-12.
(816) 471-4030 www.1856.com

71 LEWIS AND CLARK HISTORIC PARK KAW POINT—KANSAS CITY, KANSAS

An open-air pavilion, riverfront boardwalk, Confluence of Nations Plaza, mural, and other public art; and interpretive exhibits at the confluence of the Kansas and Missouri Rivers.
www.lewisandclarkwyco.org

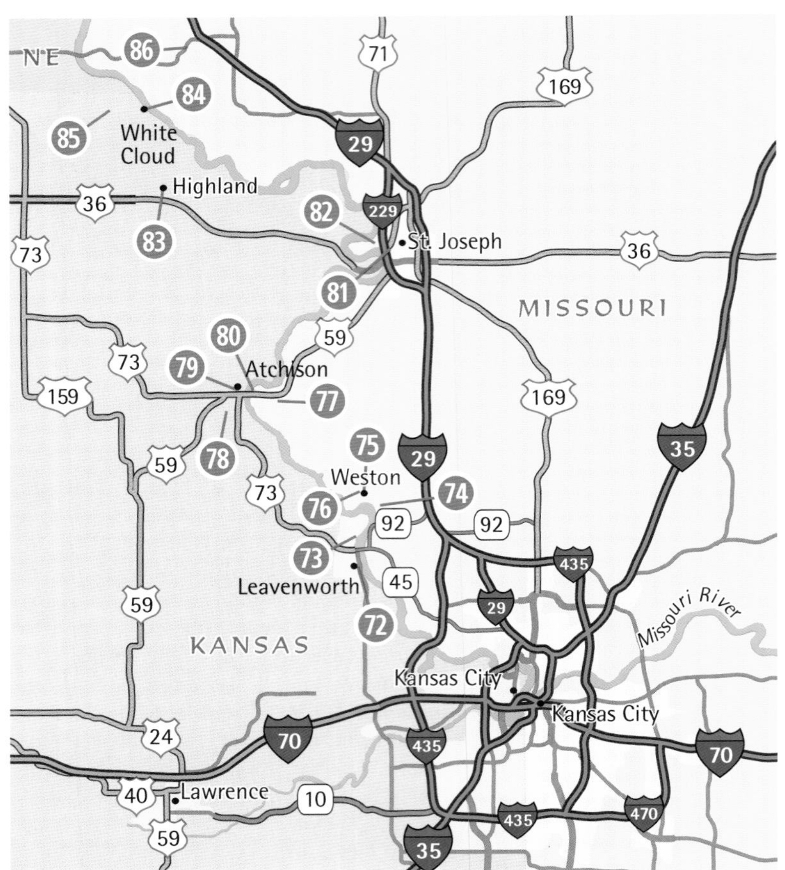

Joseph Robidoux

Joseph Robidoux (1783-1868)

Lewis and Clark "met young Mr. Bobidoux" on Sept 16, 1806 while he was going up river, near today's St Joseph. Robidoux, who came from a fur trade family, traded with the Otoe, Pawnee and Ioway. He had a trading post in old Council Bluffs from 1809-22, and established a post in the Blacksnake Hills (St Joseph) in 1826.

72 FRONTIER ARMY MUSEUM FORT LEAVENWORTH, KANSAS

7th St and Metropolitan Ave.
To Fort Leavenworth. From I-70 W, Exit 224, go right (north) onto Rte 7; road changes name to US 73. Turn left (west) onto Metropolitan Ave. To Frontier Army Museum within Fort Leavenworth. From Metropolitan Ave go north on Grant Ave to Reynolds Ave. Turn right (east). Go one block to Gibbons Ave. The museum is on the left (north).

73 LEAVENWORTH LANDING PARK LEAVENWORTH, KANSAS

Cherokee and Esplanade Streets.
From I-70 W, Exit 224, go right (north) onto Rte 7; road changes name to US 73. Turn right (east) to Cherokee St. Go to Esplanade St.

74 WESTON MUSEUM AND WALKING TOUR WESTON, MISSOURI

601 Main Street.
From I-29 Exit 20 go west onto Rte 273 (Elm Grove Rd). To stay on Rte 273 turn right (northwest). Later road changes name to Rte JJ and still later to Walnut St.. Turn left (southwest) onto Main St.

75 O'MALLEY'S PUB AND RESTAURANT—WESTON, MO

500 Welt Street.
From I-29 Exit 20 go west onto Rte 273 (Elm Grove Rd). Later road changes name to Rt JJ and still later to Walnut St.. Turn left (southwest) onto Welt St.

76 WESTON BEND STATE PARK

16600 Highway 45.
From I-29 Exit 20 go west onto Rte 273 (Elm Grove Rd). To stay on Rte 273 turn right (northwest). Turn left (south) onto Rt 45.

77 LEWIS AND CLARK LAKE AND PARK—RUSHVILLE, MO

801 Lakecrest Boulevard.
From I-29 Exit 20 go west onto Rte273 (Elm Grove Rd). To stay on Rte 273 turn right (northwest). Turn right (north) onto Rte 45. Turn left (west) onto CR 251. Road changes name to Lakecrest Blvd.

78 VISITOR CENTER AND MUSEUM—ATCHISON, KS

200 South 10th Street.
From I-29 Exit 30 go southwest onto Rte H. Turn right (north) onto Rte 371. Turn left (west) onto Rte 116. Turn left (south) onto CR 253. Turn right (north) onto CR 249. Turn left (west) onto US 59. Turn right (north) onto 10th St.

79 INTERNATIONAL FOREST OF FRIENDSHIP ATCHISON, KANSAS

South side of Warnock Lake.
From I-29 Exit 30 go southwest onto Rte H. Turn right (north) onto Rte 371. Turn left (west) onto Rte 116. Turn left (south) onto CR 253. Turn right (north) onto CR 249. Turn left (west) onto US 59. Turn left (south) onto Rawlins Rd. Turn right (southwest) onto 274th Rd. Turn left (south) onto Pratt Rd. Turn left (east) onto Warnock Lake Rd. Turn right (south) onto Allenham Dr.

80 RIVERFRONT PARK ATCHISON, KANSAS

Commercial St and River Road.
From I-29 Exit 30 go southwest onto Rte H. Turn right (north) onto Rt 371. Turn left (west) onto Rt 116. Turn left (south) onto CR 253. Turn right (north) onto CR 249. Turn left (west) onto US 59. Turn right (north) onto 4th St. Turn right (east) onto Commercial St.

81 ROBIDOUX ROW MUSEUM ST JOSEPH, MISSOURI

Third and Poulin Streets.
From I-229 N Exit 6 B go straight onto US 59. Turn right (east) onto Poulin St. Go to 3rd St.

82 ST JOSEPH MUSEUM AND GLORE PSYCHIATRIC MUSEUM ST JOSEPH, MISSOURI

3406 Frederick Avenue.
From I-29 N Exit 47 turn west onto Frederick Ave.

83 NATIVE AMERICAN HERITAGE MUSEUM HIGHLAND, KANSAS

1737 Elgin Road.
From I-229 S, US 36 Exit, merge onto US 36 west. Bear right (northwest) onto Rte 7. At Sparks bear left (northwest) onto 240th Rd. Go west to Elgin Rd.

84 FOUR-STATE LOOKOUT WHITE CLOUD, KANSAS

From I-229 S, US 36 Exit, merge onto US 36 west. Bear right (northwest) onto Rte 7. In White Cloud turn left (southwest) onto Main St. Turn right (northwest) onto 3rd St and climb hill to lookout.

85 WHITE CLOUD CASINO WHITE CLOUD, KANSAS

770 Jackpot Drive, Iowa Indian Reservation.
From I-229 S, US 36 Exit, merge onto US 36 west. Bear right (northwest) onto Rte 7. Continue past White Cloud on Rte 7 to 330th St on the reservation. Turn left (west). Go past Thrasher Rd to Jackpot Dr.

86 SQUAW CREEK WILDLIFE REFUGE MOUND CITY, MISSOURI

Highway 159 South.
From I-29 Exit 79 go southwest on US 159 about 2.5 miles to Refuge.

Amelia Earhart Statue
Int'l Forest of Friendship

Lewis and Clark Pavilion
Atchison Chamber of Commerce

St Joseph Museum and Glore Psychiatric Museum
St Joseph Museums

Native American Heritage Museum
Kansas State Historical Society

Leavenworth & St Joseph Area

4

72 FRONTIER ARMY MUSEUM FORT LEAVENWORTH, KANSAS

Fort Leavenworth is the oldest (1827) continuously operating Army fort west of the Mississippi River. The museum has one of the finest collection of 19th century military artifacts in the country. Historic buildings and Wayside Tour exhibits on fort grounds.

■ Picture ID required upon entering the Fort. Open Mon-Fri, 9-4; Sat, 10-4. Free admission (913) 684-3186 www.leavenworth.army.mil

73 LEAVENWORTH LANDING PARK LEAVENWORTH, KANSAS

Leavenworth established in 1854 is the "First City of Kansas." The historic riverboat landing is a beautiful walking trail with sculptures and Wayside Tour exhibits along the riverfront.

■ (913) 682-4113 www.leavenworth-net.com

74 WESTON HISTORICAL MUSEUM AND WALKING TOUR—WESTON, MO

Weston once was the second busiest port on the Missouri, second only to St Louis. It has many old buildings, and is a popular antiquing town. The museum showcases Weston history; self guided walking tours. A Lewis and Clark campsite marker is located at the foot of Main St.

■ Open Mon-Fri, 9-4; Sat, 1-4. Free admission. (816) 640-2650 www.westonmo.com

75 O'MALLEY'S 1842 IRISH PUB AND RESTAURANT—WESTON, MO

Nationally known Irish entertainers perform regularly at O'Malley's, located in 3 vaulted limestone cellars of the 1842 Royal Brewery. Upstairs dining in the American Bowman restaurant. The patio and courtyard have annual music festivals throughout spring, summer and fall featuring many musicial genres.

■ Pub has live music on weekends. Check schedule at www.westonirish.com

■ Open for lunch, Tues-Sun, 11:30-3:30 and for lunch and dinner, Fri-Sat, 11:30-9. (816) 640-5235 www.westonmo.com

76 WESTON BEND STATE PARK

Five old tobacco barns remain in this state park. Tobacco growing is still a part of the area's economy. RV and tent campgrounds, 3 mile paved loop trail, beautiful scenic overlook.

■ (816) 640-5443 www.mostateparks.com

77 LEWIS AND CLARK LAKE AND STATE PARK—RUSHVILLE, MISSOURI

"great quantities of fish and Gees and Goslings" still may be found in this peaceful state park. RV and tent campgrounds, picnic tables. River overlook trail and interpretive signage.

■ (816) 579-5564 www.mostateparks.com

78 VISITOR CENTER AND COUNTY HISTORICAL MUSEUM—ATCHISON, KS

The old Sante Fe Depot has visitor information and museum exhibits. Lewis and Clark, Amelia Earhart and rare guns are featured. Departure point for hour long trolley tours.

■ Open daily year round. Mon-Fri, 8-5; Sat 9-5; Sun 11-5.Wkd winter hours: Sat 1-4, Sun 12-4. (800) 234-1854 or (913) 367-2427 visitor info

■ Trolley tours operate May-Oct on weekends and certain weekdays; departs on the hour: $4 adults, $2 ages 4-12. (800) 234-1854 www.atchisonkansas.net

79 INT'L FOREST OF FRIENDSHIP AND FIRST NATIONAL RECREATION TRAIL ATCHISON, KANSAS

A living memorial to those who have been involved in aviation and aerospace. Trees and flags from all 50 states and over 35 countries represent over 700 honorees, whose names are placed on a memorial sidewalk. Pioneer aviator Amelia Earhart (1897-1937) was born in Atchison. Her birthplace home is a museum (www.ameliaearhartmuseum.org).

■ Open daily. (913) 367-1419 www.ifof.org

80 ATCHISON RIVERFRONT PARK

Lewis and Clark Pavilion on the riverfront; a ten mile hiking/biking trail; keelboat replica play area; river overlook and boat ramps.
(916) 367-5500 www.atchisonkansas.net

81 ROBIDOUX ROW MUSEUM ST JOSEPH, MISSOURI

Joe Robidoux incorporated the town of St Joseph in 1843; around 1850 he built row apartments as temporary living quarters for families moving to St Joseph. After his wife died, he moved into an apartment himself, where he lived until his death in 1868. His apartment has been restored, with some of his original belongings. The St Joseph Historical Society is located in another section with exhibits and gift shop.

■ Open May-Sept, Tues-Fri, 10-4; Sat and Sun, 1-4. Oct-April, Tues-Fri, 12-4; Sat, 1-4. Closed in January. Admission includes guided tour: $
(816) 232-5861 www.ci.st-joseph.mo.us

82 ST JOSEPH MUSEUM AND GLORE PSYCHIATRIC MUSEUM—ST JOSEPH, MO

The St Joseph Museum has moved in with the Glore Psychiatric Museum and the Black Archives of St Joseph. The Museum has an over 3,000 Indian artifacts collected by a local man prior to 1923; natural history and other exhibits. The Psychiatric Museum feature 400 years of "modern" psychiatric care; artifacts, audio visual displays. The Black Archives documents the history of African Americans in St Joseph.

■ Open daily, Mon-Sat, 10-5; Sun, 1-5. Admission for all 3 museums: $3 adults, $1 ages 7-18. (800) 530-8866 www.stjosephmuseum.org

83 NATIVE AMERICAN HERITAGE MUSEUM STATE HISTORIC SITE—HIGHLAND, KS

.The award winning museum, housed in an 1855 Presbyterian Mission, has exhibits on the Ioway, Sac and Fox tribes; and features a bark house and arts and crafts of present day descendants.

■ Open Weds-Sat, 10-5; Sun, 1-5. Admission: $3 adults, $2 seniors and students.
(785) 442-3304 www.kshs.org

84 FOUR STATE LOOKOUT WHITE CLOUD, KANSAS

Lewis and Clark pavilion and viewing platform at White Cloud, near the Ioway Reservation. www.dpcountykansas.com

85 WHITE CLOUD CASINO

The Ioway Tribe of Kansas and Nebraska Casino has a restaurant.

■ Open Sun-Thurs, 9 AM-1 AM, Fri-Sat, 9 AM-3 AM. (877) 652-6115 or (785) 595-3430 www.dpcountykansas.com

86 SQUAW CREEK NATIONAL WILDLIFE REFUGE—MOUND CITY, MISSOURI

More than half million birds, mostly snow geese and ducks, and many bald eagles visit in late fall (last two weeks in Nov are prime).

■ Open daily, sunrise to sunset. Refuge hdqtrs open Mon-Fri, 7:30-4. (660) 442-3187 www.fws.gov/midwest/squawcreek

Region Four: References

BIOGRAPHY

BEFORE LEWIS AND CLARK: THE STORY OF THE CHOUTEAUS, THE FRENCH DYNASTY THAT RULED AMERICA'S FRONTIER
by Shirley Christian. Farrar, Straus and Giroux (2004)

DANIEL BOONE: AN AMERICAN LIFE
by Michael Lofaro. University Press of Kentucky (2003)

DANIEL BOONE: MASTER OF THE WILDERNESS
by John Bakeless. University of Nebraska Press (1989)

4

DANIEL BOONE: THE LIFE OF AN AMERICAN PIONEER
by John Mack Faragher. Henry Holt and Co. (1992)

DUKE PAUL OF WUERTTEMBERG ON THE MISSOURI FRONTIER: 1823, 1830 AND 1851
by Hans von Sachsen-Altenburg and Robert L. Dyer. Pekitanoui Publications (1998)

THE FIRST CHOUTEAUS: RIVER BARONS OF EARLY ST. LOUIS
by William E. Foley and C. David Rice. University of Illinois Press (1983)

THE FOUNDING FAMILY OF ST. LOUIS
by Mary B. Cunningham and Jeanne C. Blythe. Midwest TechnicalPublications (1977)

MANUEL LISA AND THE OPENING OF THE MISSOURI FUR TRADE
by Richard Edward Oglesby. University of Oklahoma Press (1963)

MANUEL LISA: WITH HITHERTO UNPUBLISHED MATERIAL
by Walter B. Douglas. Argosy Antiquarian Ltd (1964)

MY FATHER, DANIEL BOONE: THE DRAPER INTERVIEWS WITH NATHAN BOONE
edited by Neal O. Hammon. University Press of Kentucky

NATHAN BOONE AND THE AMERICAN FRONTIER
by R. Douglas Hurt. University of Missouri Press (1998)

OLD BULLION BENTON: SENATOR FROM THE NEW WEST.
by William Nisbet Chambers. Little, Brown and Company (1956)

THE ROBIDOUS: A BREED APART
by Clyde M. Rabideau. Clyde M. Rabideau (1998)

WILDERNESS JOURNEY: THE LIFE OF WILLIAM CLARK
by William E. Foley. University of Missouri Press (2004)

WILLIAM CLARK: JEFFERSONIAN MAN ON THE FRONTIER
by Jerome O. Steffen. Univ of Oklahoma Press (1977)

HISTORY

AN ACCOUNT OF UPPER LOUISIANA
edited by Carl J. Ekberg and William E. Foley. University of Missouri Press (1989)

ALONG THE BOONE'S LICK ROAD: MISSOURI'S CONTRIBUTION TO OUR FIRST TRANSCONTINENTAL ROUTE - U. S. 40
by Dan A. Rothwell. Young at Heart Publishing Co (1999)

ALONG THE OLD TRAIL (VOLUME 1): PIONEER SKETCHES OF ARROW ROCK AND VICINITY
by T. C. Rainey. The Friends of Arrow Rock Inc. (1971)

ANNALS OF ST. LOUIS IN ITS EARLY DAYS UNDER THE FRENCH AND SPANISH DOMINATIONS 1764-1804
by Frederic L. Billon. Arno Press (1971)

ANNALS OF ST. LOUIS IN ITS TERRITORIAL DAYS FROM 1804 TO 1821
by Frederic L. Billon. Arno Press (1971)

ARROW ROCK: WHERE WHEELS STARTED WEST
by Jean Tyree Hamilton. Freinds of Arrow Rock, Inc (1972)

ATLAS OF LEWIS AND CLARK IN MISSOURI
by James D. Harlan and James M. Denny. University of Missouri Press (2003)

BEFORE LEWIS AND CLARK: DOCUMENTS ILLUSTRATING THE HISTORY OF THE MISSOURI, 1785-1804 (2 VOLUMES)
edited by A. P. Nasatir. University of Nebraska Press (1990)

BEYOND THE FRONTIER: A HISTORY OF ST. LOUIS TO 1821
by Frederick A. Hodes. The Patrice Press (2004)

BOURGMONT: EXPLORER OF THE MISSOURI 1698-1725
by Frank Norall. University of Nebraska Press (1988)

DR. JOHN SAPPINGTON OF SALINE COUNTY, MISSOURI 1776-1856
by Thomas B. Hall, Jr., and Thomas B Hall III. The Friends of Arrow Rock, Incorporated (1986)

EXPLORING LEWIS AND CLARK'S MISSOURI
by Brett Dufur. Pebble Publishing, Inc. (2004)

THE GENESIS OF STATEHOOD OF MISSOURI: FROM WILDERNESS OUTPOST TO STATEHOOD
by William E. Foley. University of Missouri Press (1989)

HERMANN, MISSOURI: THE GERMAN SETTLEMENT SOCIETY OF PHILADELPHIA AND ITS COLONY
by William G. Bek. American Press, Inc. (1984)

HISTORICAL SAINT CHARLES, MISSOURI
compiled by Edna McElhiney Olson. St. Charles County Historical Society (1998)

HISTORY

A HISTORY OF MISSOURI (VOLUME 1): 1673-1820
by William E. Foley. Univ of Missouri Press (1999)

A HISTORY OF MISSOURI (VOLUME 2): 1820-1860
by Perry McCandless. Univ of Missouri Press (2000)

THE IMPERIAL OSAGES: SPANISH-INDIAN DIPLOMACY IN THE MISSISSIPPI VALLEY
by Gilbert C. Din and Abraham P. Nasatir. University of Oklahoma Press (1983)

LEWIS AND CLARK IN MISSOURI
by Ann Rogers. Meredco (1981)

LION OF THE VALLEY: ST. LOUIS, MISSOURI
by James Neal Primm. Pruett Publishing Company (1981)

MARKING MISSOURI HISTORY
edited by James W. Goodrich and Lynn Wolf Gentzler. The State Historical Society of Missouri (1998)

MARK TWAIN IN ST. LOUIS: A BIOGRAPHICAL TOUR THROUGH BELLEFONTAINE CEMETERY
by Manuel Garcia. Manuel Garcia

MISSOURI: A HISTORY OF THE CROSSROADS STATE
by Edwin C. McReynolds. University of Oklahoma Press (1962)

OLD ST. CHARLES
by Sue Schneider. The Patrice Press (1993)

THE OSAGE IN MISSOURI
by Kristie C. Wolferman. University of Missouri Press (1997)

PEOPLE OF THE TROUBLED WATER: A MISSOURI RIVER JOURNAL
by Nancy M. Peterson. Renaissance House (1988)

SAINT LOUIS: AN INFORMAL HISTORY OF THE CITY AND ITS PEOPLE, 1764-1865
by Charles Van Ravenswaay, edited by Candace O'Connor. Missouri Historical Society Press (1991)

THE VALLEY OF THE MISSISSIPPI ILLUSTRATED
by Henry Lewis. Minnesota Historical Society (1967)

WILLIAM CLARK AND THE SHAPING OF THE WEST
by Landon Y. Jones. Hill and Wang (2004)

MISCELLANEOUS

THE COMPLETE KATY TRAIL GUIDEBOOK: AMERICA'S LONGEST RAILS-TO-TRAILS PROJECT
by Brett Dufur. Pebble Publishing (2003)
Follow in the footsteps of Lewis and Clark. Guide to services, towns, people, places and history along Missouri"s Katy Trail. Wineries, B and Bs, camping, photos, and maps.

REGION FIVE
NEBRASKA AND IOWA

- Nebraska City Area
- Plattsmouth and Bellevue Area
- Omaha and Council Bluffs
- North Omaha to Missouri Valley
- Onawa to Sioux City
- Northeastern Nebraska

5

1. Old Baldy, Lynch NE 2. Second Council, Fort Calhoun NE 3. Buffalo Crossing, Omaha NE 4. Children's Art Wall, Bellevue NE 5. Joslyn Art Museum, Omaha, NE 6. Keelboat, Onawa IA 7. Omaha Dancer's Regalia, Omaha NE 8. Western Historic Trail Center, Council Bluffs IA 9. National Park Service Regional Office, Headquarters of the National Historical Lewis and Clark Trail, Omaha NE 10. Sgt. Floyd Monument, Sioux City IA

Credits: (1) Lee Myers

5

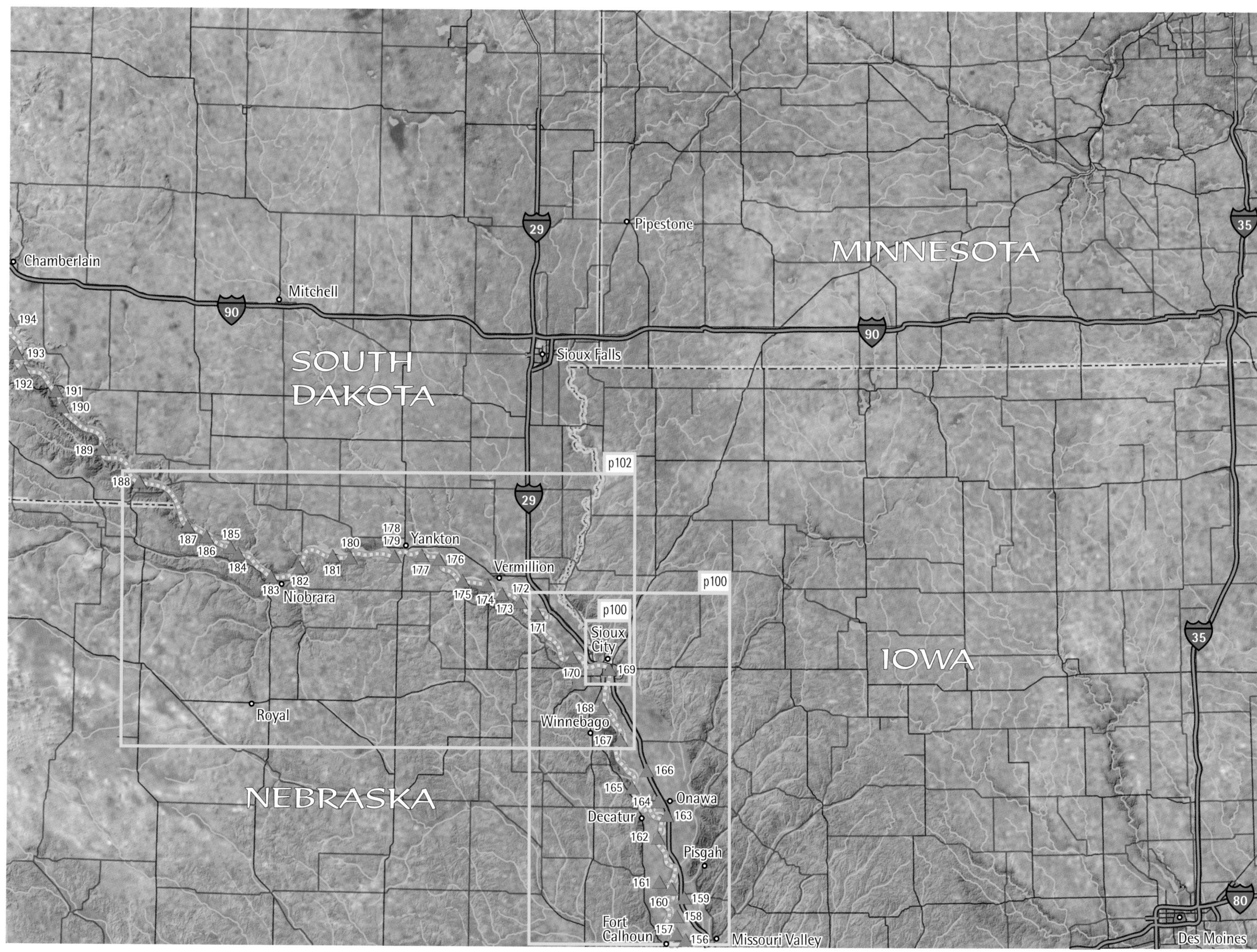

MINNESOTA
IOWA
SOUTH DAKOTA
NEBRASKA
35
80
90
29
Des Moines
Pipestone
Sioux Falls
Mitchell
Chamberlain
Vermillion
Yankton
Niobrara
Royal
Sioux City
Winnebago
Decatur
Onawa
Pisgah
Missouri Valley
Fort Calhoun
p100
p102
156
157
158
159
160
161
162
163
164
165
166
167
168
169
170
171
172
173
174
175
176
177
178
179
180
181
182
183
184
185
186
187
188
189
190
191
192
193
194

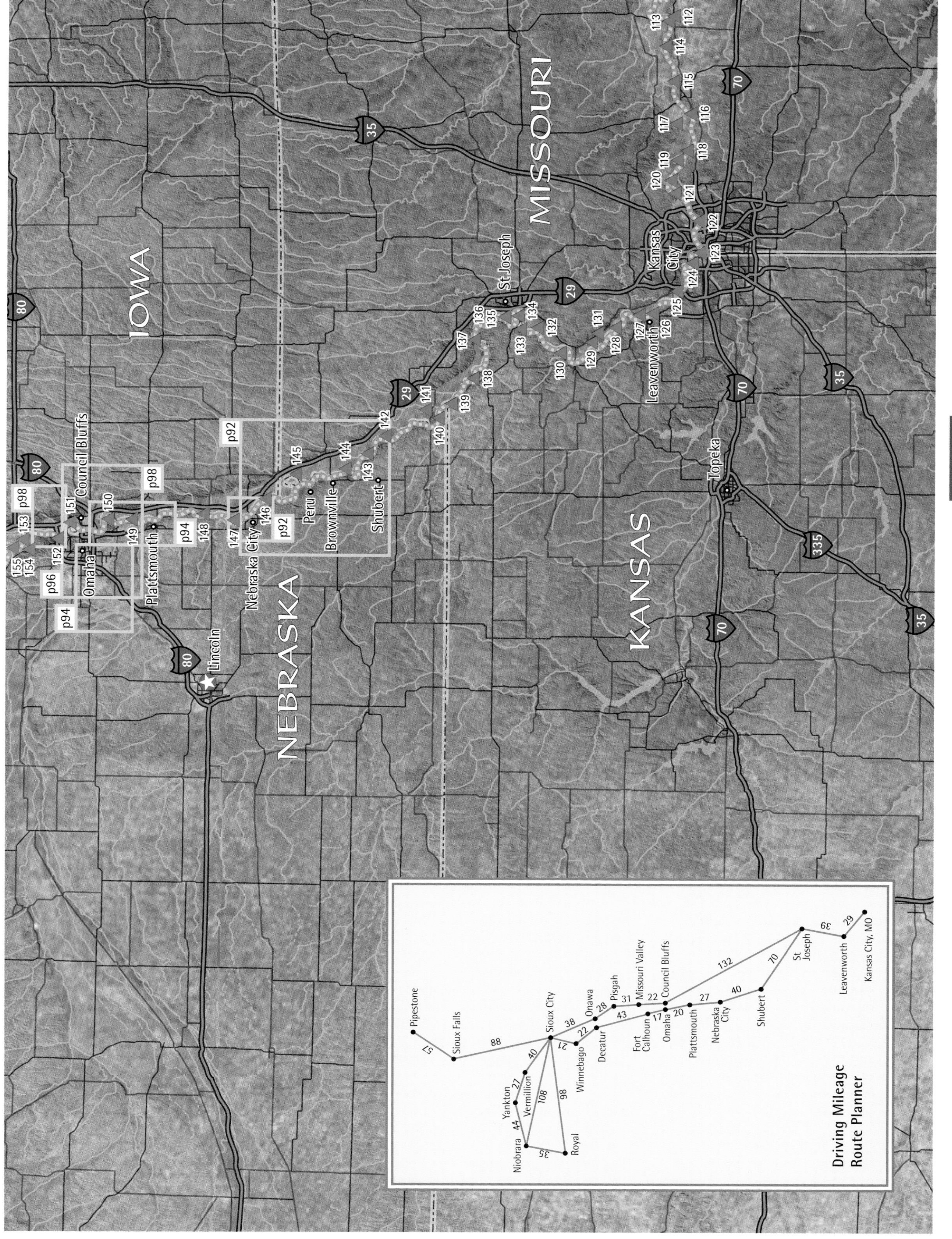
IOWA
MISSOURI
NEBRASKA
KANSAS
Council Bluffs
Omaha
Plattsmouth
Nebraska City
Peru
Brownville
Shubert
Lincoln
St Joseph
Kansas City
Leavenworth
Topeka
p92
p94
p96
p98
Driving Mileage Route Planner
Pipestone
Sioux Falls
Sioux City
Yankton
Vermillion
Niobrara
Royal
Winnebago
Decatur
Onawa
Pisgah
Missouri Valley
Council Bluffs
Fort Calhoun
Omaha
Plattsmouth
Nebraska City
Shubert
St Joseph
Leavenworth
Kansas City, MO

5

First Council with the Otoe Indians, August 3, 1804
Patrick Gass Journal Woodcut

Bat Shunatona and Peyton "Bud" Clark, at the Bicentennial Council on August 3, 2004. Otoe dancers came from Oklahoma to visit their old homeland.

5

America 200 Years Ago

Early Council Bluffs

For many years, land on both sides of the Missouri north of its junction with the Platte was called "Council Bluffs," in honor of Lewis and Clark's first council with Indians living in the newly acquired Louisiana Territory. Today, only Council Bluffs, Iowa retains the name. Fort Calhoun, about 20 miles north of Omaha, Nebraska, is the actual site where the council was held.

President Jefferson had instructed Lewis and Clark to meet with the Otoe Indians, who lived near the junction of the Platte and Elkhorn Rivers. The men rested at White Catfish Camp from July 22nd-26th, 1804 and made new oars, while Drouillard and Cruzatte were sent out to invite the Otoe chiefs to come in for a council. They found the earth lodge village deserted: the Otoe were away on their annual buffalo hunt.

On July 28th the expedition was proceeding on, disappointed at not finding the Otoe at home, when the vicinity of today's Lewis and Clark Monument they heard gunfire. It was a hunting party of Missouria Indians and a French trader, who knew where the Otoe could be found. Drouillard and *la Liberte*, a French boatman, were sent to invite the Otoe to come in for a council further up the Missouri.

The Council at Council Bluffs

The expedition waited for the Otoe at a bluff in today's Fort Calhoun, Nebraska. Several members of the expedition must have known the area well. The expedition at this time consisted of about fifty five men A dozen or more were French engagés, who were experienced travelers on the Missouri. Two members of the permanent party, Pierre Cruzatte and Francois Labiche were half Omaha-half French. Cruzatte went out with Drouilliard in search of the Otoe, and Labiche went out another time.

The Otoe and Missouri Chiefs arrived on August 2nd, bearing gifts of "water Millions" (watermelons). The next day speeches were made and medals and presents were given out. Lewis and Clark agreed to help the Otoe make a peace between themselves and the Omaha Indians. It was arranged that they would meet again at a second council at the Omaha Indian village about 80 miles north.

Local Indians

The Omaha claimed land down to the Platte River as their hunting grounds. The Otoe also claimed the land around the Platte and south of it. Both tribes had the same name for the Platte, "Ne-brath-ka, " which means flat or shallow water; Platte is the French word for flat.

On July 27th, Clark explored the area of today's downtown Omaha, examining some mounds covering "2 or 300 acres." The mounds were the remains of an Otoe earth lodge village from the 1770's. Their earth lodges, made out of grass sod, were about 40 feet in diameter. They had a life of about 15-20 years; when they collapsed they looked like small hills or mounds. Pioneer settlers made their own homes out of earth, called sod houses.

Clark saw an old Ioway Indian village site near the Lewis and Clark Monument bluff in Council Bluffs, Iowa. The Ioway, Otoe and Missouria tribes were originally from the Great Lakes region, and are related to the Winnebago. They spoke Chiwere Sioux. In the 1770's the Ioway moved back east to the Des Moines River. The Missouria formerly lived on the Grand River in Missouri; in 1798, after their population had been severely reduced by warfare and disease, they came to live with the Otoe. Today, the Otoe-Missouria have a reservation at Red Rock, Oklahoma.

The Omaha and Ponca tribes in northeastern Nebraska are Dhegiha Sioux; they were originally from the Cahokia Mounds empire in the Mississippi valley. The Osage, Quapaw, and Kansa Indians are related to them.

White Pelicans and River Bends

The expedition proceeded on up the river. There were a couple of memorable experiences. On August 8th, they encountered three miles of white feathers floating down the Missouri. The feathers covered the entire width of the river, about 200 feet. Eventually they found "in credible" numbers of white pelicans, molting their feathers, near the mouth of the Little Sioux River. Lewis shot one and measured the capacity of its beak to hold water. It took five gallons of water to fill the pouch attached to the underside of the beak.

The keelboat replica at Blue Lake in Onawa, Iowa, and a very old cottonwood tree, which may date back to the time of Lewis and Clark visit .

Sgt Floyd Monument, America's First National Historic Landmark, Sioux City

5

The next episode, on August 9th, was measuring the distance between walking across the land at a river bend, and poling, rowing and dragging the three boats around the same bend. The distance walking was 3/4 of a mile. The distance around the bend was 17 1/2 miles. In addition, Clark wrote, "Musquetors worse this evening than ever I have Seen them."

The Missouri River often formed large bends. Eventually it would cut through a new channel, taking the same direct route as Lewis had done by walking. The old bend would then become known as a "cut-off lake" or a "horseshoe bend lake." Blue Lake at Lewis and Clark State Park in Onawa, where the keelboat replica is docked, is an old cut-off lake. The August 9th, 1804 campsite is located there.

Blackbird Hill

On August 11th they reached Blackbird Hill, where "the late King of the mahar who Died 4 years ago and 400 of his nation with the Small pox was buried." The Omaha Chief Blackbird had been a powerful chief The smallpox had killed about one quarter of the Omaha tribe. The captains and tēn men, climbed the hill and raised a flag, a white flag bound with blue, white and red at Chief Blackbird's grave. This grave was a famous landmark on the Missouri. All travelers stopped to visit it. It was painted by Karl Bodmer and George Catlin in the 1830's. Unfortunately, within a few days. it would be joined by another gravesite on a hilltop, the grave of Sergeant Charles Floyd, the only man to die on the expedition. At this time, they only knew that Floyd hadn't been feeling well. The boats proceeded on up the "verry Crooked" river. This time the distance was 974 yards by land, and around the bend was 18 3/4 miles.

On August 13th they formed a camp on a large sandbar north of "Tonwantonga" which means "Big Village" in the Omaha language. The Omaha were Dhegiha Sioux, related to the Ponca who lived north of them. Like the Otoe, the Omaha were away on a buffalo hunt. The deserted village was devastated by the recent smallpox deaths; they had burned their homes in an attempt to limit the spread of the disease, and there were many burial mounds.

Fish Camp at Homer

They called this August 13th-19th campsite "Fish Camp" where they set up "bush drags" (a kind of barrier made of brush) and caught upwards of 800 fish at a time, including 490 catfish. They were waiting for the Otoe to arrive, and the Omaha to return home. They were also waiting for a search party to return with two men who had deserted from the expedition. One was *la Liberte*, the French boatman who had gone with Drouillard to find the Otoe on their buffalo hunt; the other was Moses Reed, a private who had deserted on August 4th after the first council. Drouillard's party caught both men, but returned to camp with only Reed; ***la Liberte*** had escaped again. The Otoe chiefs were traveling with Drouillard's party. Reed was punished and dismissed from the corps. He returned to St Louis with the keelboat party in the spring.

On August 18th, it was Meriwether Lewis's 30th birthday; they had a dance and extra whiskey. On the 19th, the second council with the Otoe and Missouri chiefs took place. The Omaha had not returned, so there was no opportunity to meet with them. Big Horse, one of the principal chiefs of the Otoe, was present at this meeting. His descendant, Bat Shunatona, met with Peyton Clark, a descendant of William Clark, at Fort Atkinson, 200 years to the day after the first council.

The Death of Sergeant Floyd

Sergeant Charles Floyd, age 22, was very unwell on the evening of the 19th. Clark wrote, "Serjeant Floyd is taken verry bad all at onc with a Beliose Chorlick we attempt to relieve him without Success as yet, he gets wordse and we are muc allarmed at his Situation, all attention to him." The next day, on August 20, 1804, as the expedition was proceeding on, he died of a ruptured appendix. He was buried on a high hill with full military honors, and a cedar post was erected at his grave. His modern monument at Sioux City, Iowa was chosen as America's first National Historic Landmark.

5

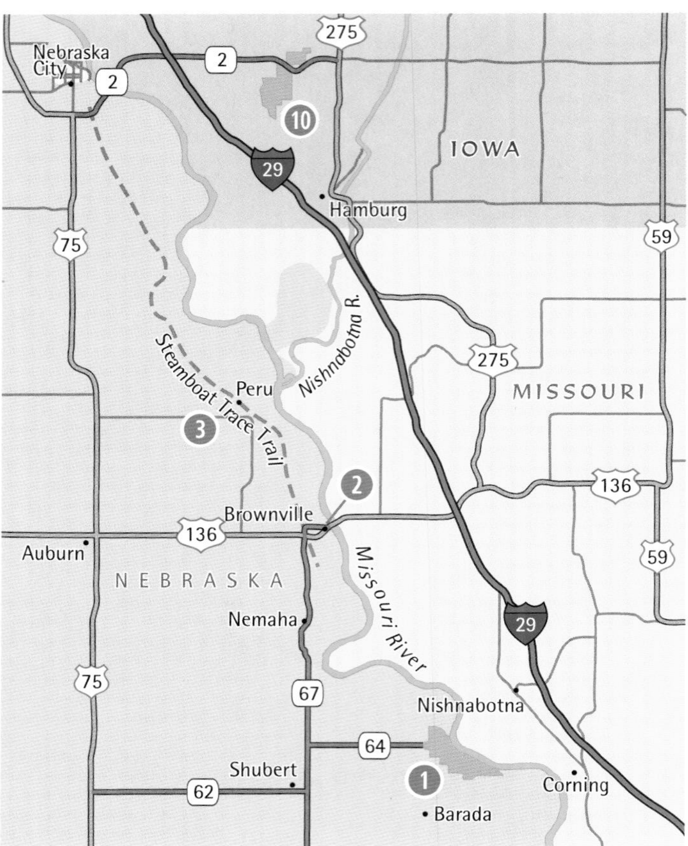

Indian Cave State Park to Nebraska City

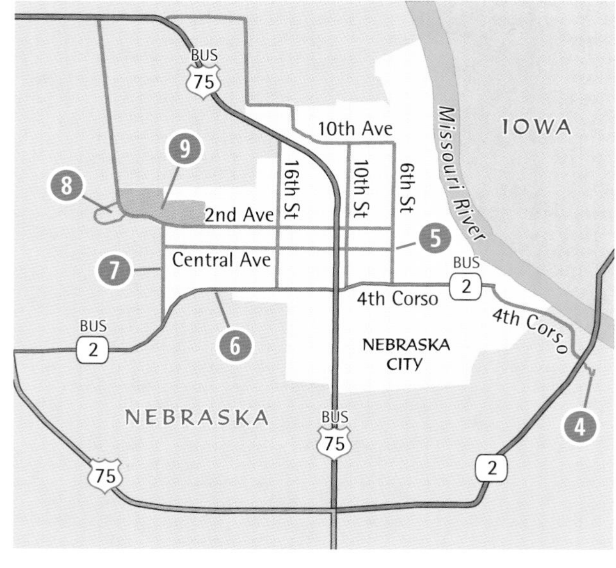

Nebraska City

1 INDIAN CAVE STATE PARK AND ST DEROIN SHUBERT, NEBRASKA

From I-29 Exit 110 go west on US 136. Turn left (south onto Rte 67. Turn left (east) onto Rte 64. Take Rte 64 to the park entrance.

2 CAPTAIN MERIWETHER LEWIS DREDGE BROWNVILLE, NEBRASKA

Brownville State Recreation Area.
From I-29 Exit 110 go west on US 136. Turn left (south) onto 1st St. Turn left onto East Water Street. Go to the end of East Water Street.

3 STEAMBOAT TRACE TRAIL BROWNVILLE TO NEBRASKA CITY, NE

Nebraska Ave and Allen St.
From I-29 Exit 110 go west on US 136. Turn left (south) onto Wharf St. Road Changes name to Nebraska Ave. Continue to Allen St.

4 MISSOURI RIVER BASIN LEWIS AND CLARK CENTER NEBRASKA CITY, NE

100 Valmont Drive.
From I-29 Exit 10 go west on Iowa Rte 2. Cross Missouri River. Continue on Nebraska Rte 2. Take first left turn past bridge onto Valmont Drive.

5 RIVER COUNTRY NATURE CENTER NEBRASKA CITY, NE

114 South 6th Street.
From I-29 Exit 10 go west on Iowa Rte 2. Cross Missouri River. Continue on Nebraska Rt 2. Turn right (north) onto 4th Corso. 4th Corso turns left (west). Turn right (north) onto 6th St.

6 MAYHEW CABIN NEBRASKA CITY, NE

2012 4th Corso.
From I-29 Exit 10 go west on Iowa Rte 2. Cross Missouri River. Continue on Nebraska Rte 2. Turn right (north) onto 4th Corso. 4th Corso turns left (west). Go past 19th St.

7 LIED LODGE AND CONFERENCE CENTER NEBRASKA CITY, NE

2700 Sylvan Road.
From I-29 Exit 10 go west on Iowa Rte 2. Cross Missouri River. Continue on Nebraska Rt 2. Turn right (north) onto 4th Corso. 4th Corso turns left (west). Then 4th Corso curves to the southwest. Turn right (north) onto Steinhart Park Road. Go to Sylvan Road.

8 ARBOR DAY FARM NEBRASKA CITY, NE

100 Arbor Avenue.
From I-29 Exit 10 go west on Iowa Rte 2. Cross Missouri River. Continue on Nebraska Rte 2. Turn right (north) onto 4th Corso. 4th Corso turns left (west). Then 4th Corso curves to the southwest. Turn right (north) onto Steinhart Park Road. Steinhart Park Rd changes name to Arbor Ave and curves westward to the farm.

9 ARBOR LODGE NEBRASKA CITY, NE

2300 2nd Avenue.
From I-29 Exit 10 go west on Iowa Rte 2. Cross Missouri River. Continue on Nebraska Rte 2. Turn right (north) onto 4th Corso. 4th Corso turns left (west). Turn right (north) onto 11th St. Turn left (west) onto 2nd Ave Go to park entrance at southeast corner of the park.

10 WAUBONSIE STATE PARK HAMBURG, IOWA

2585 Waubonsie Park Road.
From I-29 Exit 10 go east on Rte 2. Go right (southwest) onto Rte 239. Rte 239 connects to park trails.

Keelboat at Lewis and Clark Center
Missouri River Basin Lewis and Clark Center

Arbor Lodge State Historical Park
J. Nabb, Nebraska DED

Steamboat Trace Trail
J. Nabb, Nebraska DED

Missouri River Basin Lewis and Clark Center

Nebraska City Area

1 INDIAN CAVE STATE PARK AND ST DEROIN—SHUBERT, NEBRASKA

Attractions include: Lewis and Clark overlook deck; petroglyphs; the old St Deroin Cemetery, and the reconstructed village of St Deroin.

In 1853, trader Joseph Deroin set up a village for the half breed Otoe families and 111 orphans left behind by French traders. Heritage program of old time crafts during summer months.

■ RV and tent camping. 22 miles of hiking and biking trails in the 3000 acre park. $3.35 daily park permit fee. Open year round.
(402) 471-0641 www.ngpc.state.ne.us

2 CAPTAIN MERIWETHER LEWIS DREDGE BROWNVILLE, NEBRASKA

National Historic Landmark steamboat dredge named for Meriwether Lewis houses the Museum of Missouri River History. The Corps of Engineers boat was built in 1932 and was in service until 1969, working to channelize the Missouri River. Volunteers called the "River Rats Reunion" staff the dredge museum.

■ Open Memorial Day to Labor Day, daily, 1-5 . $3 adults, $1 ages 6-12. (402) 825-4131
www.meriwetherlewisfoundation.org

3 STEAMBOAT TRACE TRAIL BROWNVILLE TO NEBRASKA CITY, NE

21 miles of an old Burlington Northern Railroad corridor has been made into a hiking and biking trail of crushed limestone. The trail passes through Peru, home of Nebraska's oldest college (1867), Peru State College, "the Campus of a Thousand Oaks." The trail features limestone bluffs, woodlands, and riverbanks.

Lewis and Clark were in the area from July 15-19, 1804. They saw "great quantity of Cerres, Plums, Grapes and Berries." They were entering the land of the "ball pated Prarie," the Loess Hills of Iowa located across the river.

■ The trail is closed during hunting season from mid-November through January.
(402) 335-3325 www.nemahanrd.org

4 MISSOURI RIVER BASIN LEWIS AND CLARK INTERPRETIVE CENTER NEBRASKA CITY, NEBRASKA

The center sits high on a bluff near the Highway 2 bridge across the Missouri. The 3 story building focuses on the 178 plants and 122 animals described in the Lewis and Clark Journals. Dr. Gary Moulton, editor of the Journals, was the center's first scholar-in-residence.

The Great Hall of Large Animals and the keelboat and white pirogue used in making the IMAX film, *Great Journey West,* are special attractions. Visitors may row the pirogue and explore the keelboat. The most unusual attraction is the center's pet prairie dog, "P D." A reconstructed 48 foot Indian earth lodge is located near the center and may be visited; another trail leads to a river overlook deck.

■ Open daily. Free admission. March-Oct hours are 9-6 Mon-Sat, and 9-5 Sunday. Nov-Feb hours are 9-5 Mon-Sat and 12-5 Sunday.
(402) 874-9900
www.mrb-lewisandclarkcenter.org

5 RIVER COUNTRY NATURE CENTER NEBRASKA CITY, NEBRASKA

A local taxidermist's collection of 100 rare and exotic chickens, illustrates the loss of diversity in agricultural species; plus over 300 other native Nebraska birds, mammals, fish, amphibians, and reptiles in natural habitat replicas.

■ Open 10-4 on Saturday and Sunday, year round. Call for extended summer hours.
(800) 514-9113 or (402) 873-6654
www.nebraskacity.com

6 MAYHEW CABIN AND HISTORICAL VILLAGE—NEBRASKA CITY, NE

Nebraska's only Underground Railroad Network to Freedom Site. The 1855 cabin and cave have a hideaway and underground passage used to free runaway slaves by members of John Brown's abolitionists group. Strategically located between free and slave states, it was an important stop on the Underground Railroad. The historical village includes an indoor display of ten early shops, a gift shop, and several outdoor building exhibits.

■ Open May 30-Oct 30. Hours: Mon-Sat 10-6 and Sunday, 12-5. Admission, $6 adults, $5 seniors, $3 ages 2-12.
(402) 873-3115 www.mayhewcabin.com

7 LIED LODGE, RESTAURANT AND CONFERENCE CENTER—NE CITY

The Lied Lodge and Conference Center is a non profit facility of the Arbor Day Foundation. It hosts conferences on sustainability and the environment. Its dining room and lodging facilities are open to the general public.

■ The Lied Lodge dining room serves breakfast, lunch and dinner. Inquire about room rates.
(402) 873-8733 www.liedlodge.org

8 ARBOR DAY FARM TREE ADVENTURE NEBRASKA CITY, NE

Original farm buildings and apple orchards from the estate of J. Sterling Morton. The Farm Tree Adventure includes Lied Greenhouse with over 100,000 tree seedlings, and Pavilion. A 2/3 mile walking trail leads to the Canopy Tree House, with an observation deck and handicap accessible ramp. The Apple House gift shop and snack bar is located in the old Morton barn.

■ Arbor Day Farm is open daily. June-August, Mon-Sat, 9-7 and Sunday, 11-7. Sept-Oct (fall harvest), 9-7 daily. Nov-May, Mon-Sat, 9-5 and Sunday, 11-5. Admission: $6 adults, $4, ages 4-12. Free tree seedling and tree guide.
(888) 448-7337 www.arbordayfarm.org

9 ARBOR LODGE NATIONAL HISTORIC LANDMARK AND ARBORETUM NEBRASKA CITY, NE

J Sterling Morton's home is a state historic site. The neo-colonial mansion has many original furnishings. Morton and his wife Carrie's tree plantings led to the founding of Arbor Day in 1885 by the Nebraska Legislature. Arbor Day is observed around the world with tree plantings on April 22nd. Osage orange trees in the park date to the 1850's.

■ Arboretum open daily, 8 AM to sunset. $3.35 daily park permit fee required for vehicles. Mansion self-guided tours, Apr 15-May 27, 11-5; May 27-Sept 5, 10-5; Sept 6-Oct 24, 11-5. Admission is $5 adults, $1 ages 3-12.
(402) 873-7222 www.nebraskacity.com

10 WAUBONSIE STATE PARK HAMBURG, IOWA

An Iowa state park in the Loess Hills named for Pottawattamie Chief Waubonsie. RV and tent campgrounds; seven miles of trails along steep ridges, mature woodlands, ridgetop prairies.
(712) 382-2786 www.iowadnr.com

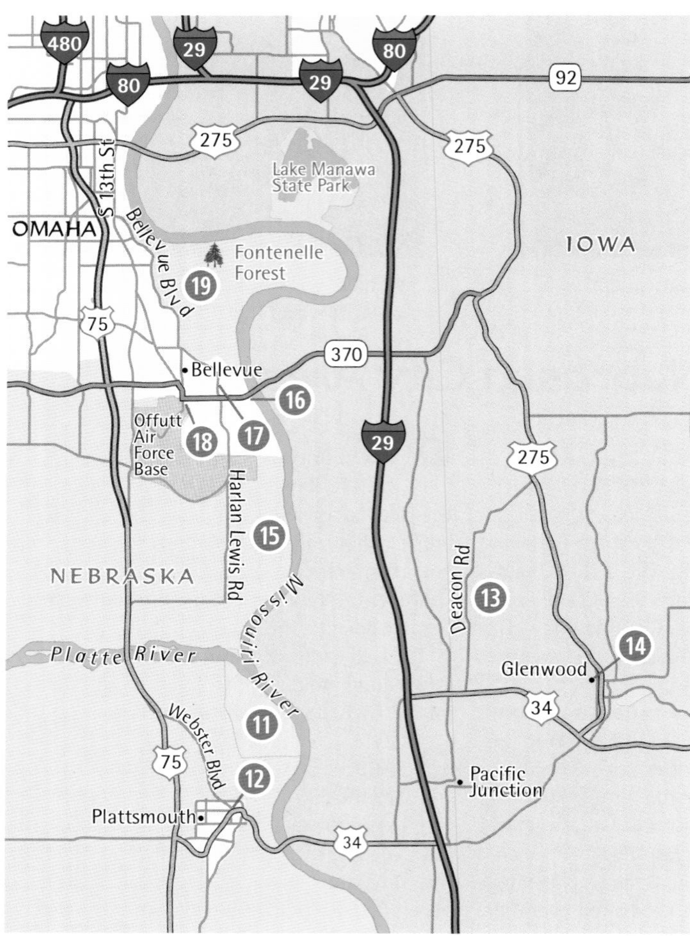

Plattsmouth and Bellevue, Nebraska and Glenwood, Iowa

Mouth of the Platte to Two Rivers

11 MOUTH OF THE PLATTE PLATTSMOUTH, NE

17614 Schilling Refuge Road.

From I-29 Exit 32 go west onto US 34. Crossing a toll bridge enter Nebraska US 34 on Livingston Rd which swings right (north); then left (west) into 2nd Ave; then right (north) as 3rd St. Turn right (east) onto Main St. Turn left (north) onto Schilling Refuge Rd.

12 CASS COUNTY MUSEUM PLATTSMOUTH, NE

646 Main Street.

From I-29 Exit 32 go west onto US 34. Crossing a toll bridge enter Nebraska US 34 on Livingston Rd which swings right (north); then left (west) into 2nd Ave; then right (north) as 3rd St. Turn left (west) onto Main St.

13 PONY CREEK LOOP, GLENWOOD, IOWA

From I-29 Exit 35 take US 34 east to US 275. Go north on US 275 to Deacon Rd. Turn left (west) onto Deacon Rd which swings south and heads back to US 34.

14 GLENWOOD PUBLIC LIBRARY–GLENWOOD, IA

109 North Vine Street.

From I-29 Exit 35 take US 34 east to US 275. Go north on US 275 (Locust St in Glenwood). Turn right (east) onto Sharp St. Turn left (north) onto Vine St.

15 CATFISH LAKE RESTAURANT BELLEVUE, NE

1006 Cunningham Road.

From I-29 Exit 42 go west on Rte 370 across the Missouri River onto Mission Ave in Bellevue. Turn left (south) onto Hancock St (name changes to Harlan Lewis Rd). Turn left (east) onto Cunningham Rd.

16 CHILDREN'S ART WALL BELLEVUE, NE

Haworth Park.

From I-29 Exit 42 go west on Rte 370 to Mission Ave in Bellevue. Turn left (south) onto Payne Dr.

17 THE OLD CABIN–BELLEVUE, NE

1805 Hancock Street..

From I-29 Exit 42 go west on Rte 370 to Mission Ave in Bellevue. Turn right (north) onto Hancock St.

18 SARPY COUNTY MUSEUM BELLEVUE, NEBRASKA

2402 Clay Street.

From I-29 Exit 42 go west on Rt 370 to Mission Ave in Bellevue. Turn left (south) onto Calhoun St. Turn (right) onto 24th Ave. Turn left (south) onto Clay St.

19 FONTENELLE FOREST NATURE CENTER–BELLEVUE

1111 North Bellevue Boulevard.

From I-80 W Exit 452 take Kennedy Freeway (US 75) south. Go left (east) onto Chandler Rd. Turn right onto Bellevue Blvd. Go 0.6 mile to the entrance on the left.

20 STRATEGIC AIR AND SPACE MUSEUM–ASHLAND, NE

28210 West Park Highway.

From I-80 W Exit 426 go right (northwest) on Rte 66 to museum.

21 WILDLIFE SAFARI PARK ASHLAND, NE

From I-80 W Exit 426 go left (southeast) onto Rte 66. Turn left (northeast) onto Platteview Dr.

22 AK-SAR-BEN AQUARIUM GRETNA, NE

21501 West Highway 31

From I-80 W Exit 432 go left (south) on Rte 31 for 5 miles.

23 TWO RIVERS WATERLOO, NE

27702 F Street.

From I-80 W Exit 445 go right (west) on US 275 (West Center Rd). Trun left (south) onto CR 96 (264th St). Turn right (west) onto F St.

Mouth of the Platte and Camp White Catfish

On July 21st, the expedition passed the mouth of the Platte with "great difficuelty," estimating the current to be "at least 8" miles an hour. The force of the Platte, entering a channel 1/3 its size, caused sandbars to rise and disappear within hours in a "boiling motion." The expedition had poled, rowed, and dragged their way up the Missouri from St Louis against a current of 5 1/2 to 7 miles an hour. After passing the Platte, the current dropped to about 3 1/2 miles. They camped that night at Papillion Creek.

The next day they went only ten miles up river to camp opposite the hills of today's Fontenelle Forest. They needed to rest, send messengers to the Otoe Indians, make new oars, and dry out their provisions. The camp was called "White Catfish" in honor of the channel catfish they caught.

This July 22nd-26th campsite is now on the Nebraska side of the Missouri River, due to a change in the river channel. The Great Marsh of Fontenelle Forest is the old river bed; the campsite location is on Gifford Point near the Wetlands Learning Center. It is also the original site of Trader's Point.

The name "Nebraska" means "flat water" in both the Otoe and Omaha languages. They called the Platte River by this name. (Platte means "flat" in French.) Though the Platte was too shallow to navigate, its wide banks became the great travel route of the western trails, the railroad, and Interstate 80.

Wildlife Safari Park

Mouth of the Platte

Children's Lewis and Clark Art Wall

Plattsmouth and Bellevue Area

11 MOUTH OF THE PLATTE PLATTSMOUTH, NEBRASKA

The mouth of the 990 mile long Platte River empties into the Missouri at the Schilling Wildlife Management Area, located east of Plattsmouth's Main Street Historic District.

■ Open daily, April 1-Oct 14, 7 AM - 9 PM. (402) 296-0041 www.visitcasscounty.com www.nps.gov/rivers/waterfacts.html

12 CASS COUNTY HISTORICAL SOCIETY MUSEUM—PLATTSMOUTH, NE

The museum tells the story of the historic river town of Plattsmouth and Cass County which opened for settlement in 1854.

■ Hours: April-Oct, 12-4, Tues-Sunday; Nov-March,12-4,Tues-Saturday
(402) 296-4770 www.plattsmouthchamber.com

13 PONY CREEK LOOP LOESS HILLS NATIONAL SCENIC BYWAY GLENWOOD, IOWA

Pony Creek is a major archaeology site. The hills along this scenic byway were once dotted with earthlodges, dating back to A.D. 1000-1300.

The Loess ("luss") Hills stretch for 200 miles along Iowa's western border. In the time of Lewis and Clark they were "bald-pated" due to the Indian practice of annual fire burnings to create grasslands for the animals they hunted.

■ www.uiowa.edu/~osa/archaeologyle.htm www.iowadnr.com/forestry/loesshills.html

14 GLENWOOD PUBLIC LIBRARY GLENWOOD, IOWA

Donald Jackson, editor of the ***Letters of the Lewis and Clark Expedition***, was born and raised in Glenwood. He called the Glenwood Public Library his "own personal Library of Congress." A collection of his books and writings may be seen here. His archives are located at Colorado College in Colorado Springs.

■ Open Mon-Sat. (712) 527-5252 www.publiclibraries.com/iowa.htm www.coloradocollege.edu/library

15 CATFISH LAKE RESTAURANT BELLEVUE, NEBRASKA

Rustic family dining restaurant out in the country, with catfish holding ponds; serving fish, chicken, steak. Lewis and Clark campsite marker.

■ Open Tues-Sunday, 11 AM-9:30 PM and Monday, 5-9:30. (402)292-9963

16 LEWIS AND CLARK CHILDREN'S ART WALL—BELLEVUE, NEBRASKA

Lewis and Clark artwork by 710 children from ten states. Located in Haworth Park, south of Hwy 34 toll bridge. R V and tent campgrounds.

■ www.bellevuenebraska.com

17 THE OLD CABIN, BELLEVUE

Bellevue is the second oldest United States town west of the Missouri, established in 1822: Pierre, South Dakota is the oldest, established in 1818. The log cabin is thought to date from 1835 when Dr. Marcus Whitman went out West with the fur trade caravan, and saved the life of Lucien Fontenelle and others during a cholera epidemic at Bellevue. He recommended moving cabins up from the river onto the bluff. Other places to see include: the 1823 Peter A. Sarpy trading post site; 1848 Presbyterian Otoe and Omaha Indian Mission site, which also served as the first Nebraska Territorial government building; 1856 Bellevue Pioneer Cemetery and Omaha Chief's Big Elk's gravesite; 1856 Fontenelle Bank; 1856 Presbyterian Church; and 1856 home of Reverend William Hamilton.

■ (402) 292-1880 Sarpy County Museum www.bellevuenebraska.com

18 SARPY COUNTY HISTORICAL MUSEUM BELLEVUE, NEBRASKA

The museum has Native American artifacts and period room displays. There is also a large scale model of historic Fort Crook, established in 1894-96, and Offutt Air Field. Kira Gale's historical booklets are sold in the gift shop.

□ Open Tues-Sun, 9-4. Closed Mondays. Admission: $2 adults, $1 srs, 50 cents, children. (402) 292-1880 www.sarpymuseum.com

19 FONTENELLE FOREST NATURE CENTER BELLEVUE, NEBRASKA

Fontenelle Forest Nature Association owns land both in Bellevue and along River Road in North Omaha. A one mile boardwalk trail extends out from the Nature Center building. Over 70 earth lodge sites have been found on the 1400 acres owned by this private nature association. The hills of the forest were once called the Côtes á Quesnelle (French for "Fish Dumpling Hills"). Inquire at the Nature Center for directions to the 1822 trading post site, about a 3 mile roundtrip hike on hilly forest trails. The Wetlands Learning Center is located two miles south of the Nature Center, and has a 3/8 mile boardwalk trail to the Great Marsh.

■ Open daily 8-5. Admission: $7 adults, $6 srs. and $5 ages 3-11. Admission sticker required. (402) 731-3140 www.fontenelleforest.org

20 STRATEGIC AIR AND SPACE MUSEUM ASHLAND, NEBRASKA

The nation's foremost museum devoted to aviation and aerospace exhibits. The 300,000 square foot building has a glass atrium, aircraft hangers, exhibits, and an aircraft restoration area. Stratcom, the nation's Strategic Air Command Headquarters, is located in Bellevue.

■ Open daily 9-5. Admission: $7 adults; $6 seniors and military; $3 ages 5-12.
(402) 827-3100 www.strategicairandspace.com www.strategic-air-command.com

21 WILDLIFE SAFARI PARK —ASHLAND, NE

The Wildlife Safari Park is located near the Air and Space Museum on I-80. It is one of the few places along the Lewis and Clark Trail that visitors are almost certain to see buffaloes; in larger conservation areas buffalos often roam far from the road. See elk, cranes, pronghorn antelope, and deer from your car window on a four mile drive through the Park. Bears, wolves, an aviary, hiking trails, and a visitor center are also attractions.

■ Open daily, 9:30-5, from April 1-Oct 31. Open weekends 9:30-5, Nov-Mar, depending on the weather. Admission: $5 adults, $4 seniors, and $3, ages 5-11.
(402) 738-2007 www.omahazoo.com

22 AK-SAR-BEN AQUARIUM—GRETNA, NE

A white catfish is on display, along with other native Nebraska fish at Schramm Park's Aquarium on the Platte River.

■ Open daily Memorial-Labor Day, 10-4:30 weekdays, 10-5 weekends. Call for other times of year. Admission: $1 adults, 50 cents ages 6-15. (402)332-3901 www.outdoornebraska.org

23 TWO RIVERS STATE RECREATIONAL AREA—WATERLOO, NEBRASKA

Site of the Otoe-Missouria earth lodge village at the Platte and Elkhorn Rivers. RV and tent campgrounds, and railroad caboose accomodations. Fishing, bike rentals, hunting.

■ Daily park vehicle permit fee, $3.35.
(402) 359-5165 www.visitnebraska.org

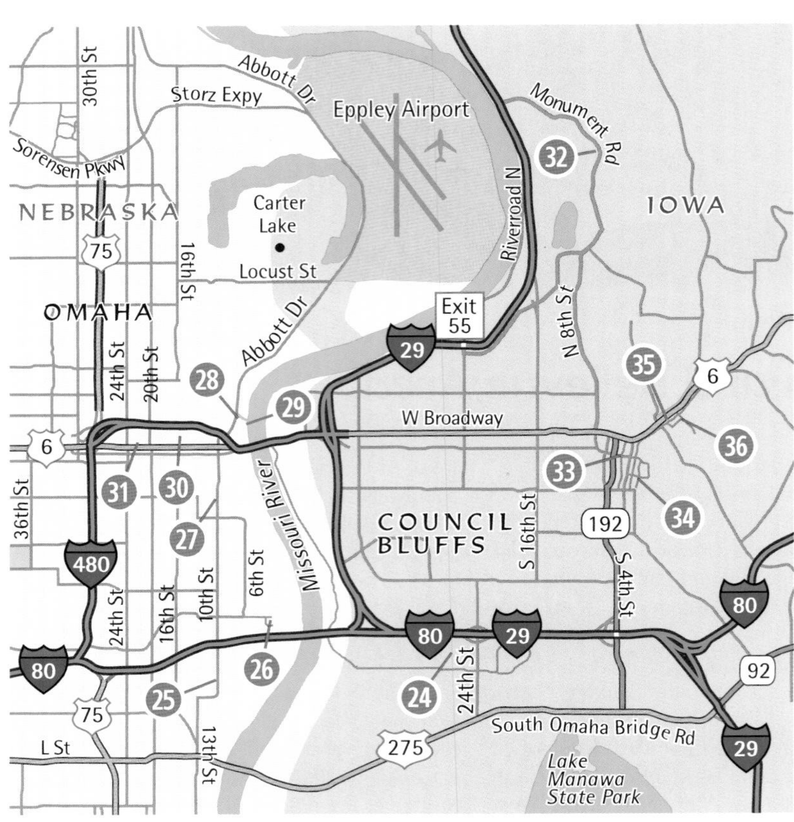

Omaha, Nebraska and Council Bluffs, Iowa

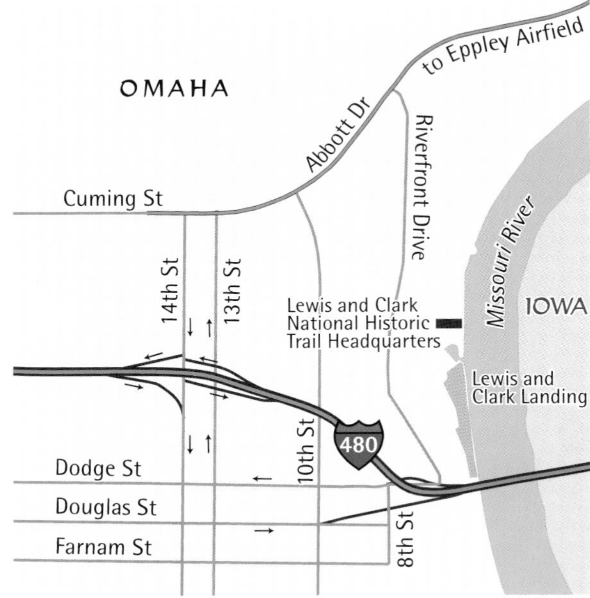

Lewis and Clark Landing, Omaha Riverfront

Lewis and Clark Monument
Council Bluffs

24 WESTERN HISTORIC TRAILS CENTER–COUNCIL BLUFFS, IA

3434 Richard Downing Avenue.
From I-80 E/I-29 S, Exit 1 B go right (south) onto 24th St. Go 1/6 mile. Turn right (west) onto service road. Go 1.25 miles to Center.

25 HENRY DOORLY ZOO OMAHA, NE

3701 South 10th Street.
From I-80 E take Exit 454. Turn right (south) onto 13th St. Go two blocks. Turn left (east) onto Bert Murphy Ave. Turn left (north) onto 10th St.

26 LAURITZEN GARDENS OMAHA, NE

100 Bancroft Street.
From I-80 E take Exit 454. Turn left (north) onto 13th St. Turn right (east) onto Bancroft St.

27 DURHAM WESTERN HERITAGE MUSEUM–OMAHA

801 South 10th Street.
From I-480 E Exit 4 turn right (south) onto 14th St. Turn left (east) onto Douglas St. Turn right (south) onto 10th St.

28 LEWIS AND CLARK TRAIL NAT'L HDQTRS–OMAHA

601 Riverfront Drive.
From I-480 E Exit 4 turn right (south) onto 14th St. Turn left (east) onto Douglas St. Turn left (north) onto 10th St. Turn right (east) onto Dodge St. Go to 8th St. turn left (north). Go beneath the interstate to Riverfront Dr. Go left (north) 0.4 mile.

29 LEWIS AND CLARK LANDING–OMAHA, NE

345 Riverfront Drive.
From I-480 E Exit 4 turn right (south) onto 14th St. Turn left (east) onto Douglas St. Turn left (north) onto 10th St. Turn right (east) onto Dodge St. Go to 8th St. turn left (north). Go beneath the interstate to Riverfront Dr. Go left (north) 1/4 mile.

30 SPIRIT OF NEBRASKA'S WILDERNESS–OMAHA

The sculpture park is located between 14th and Capitol and 16th and Dodge Sts. From I-480 E Exit 4 go right (south) on 14th St to Capitol Ave.

31 JOSLYN ART MUSEUM OMAHA, NE

2200 Dodge Street.
From I-480 E Exit 3 go right (south) onto 20th St. Turn right (west) onto Dodge St.

32 LEWIS AND CLARK MONUMENT-COUNCIL BLUFFS

19962 Monument Road.
From I-29 N Exit 55 turn right (south) onto 25th St. Immediately turn left (east) onto Avenue N which changes name to Nash Blvd. Bear right (east) onto Big Lake Rd. Turn left (northeast onto Mynster Springs Rd. Go left (north) onto Monument Rd for 0.8 miles.

33 UNION PACIFIC RAILROAD MUSEUM–COUNCIL BLUFFS

200 Pearl Street.
From I-480 E, Broadway Exit, go east on Broadway for 3 miles. Turn right (south) onto Pearl St.

34 GENERAL DODGE HOUSE COUNCIL BLUFFS. IA

605 Third Street.
From I-480 E, Broadway Exit, go east on Broadway for 3 miles. Turn right (south) onto 4th St. Turn left onto Story St. Turn right (south) onto 3rd St.

35 KANESVILLE TABERNACLE COUNCIL BLUFFS, IA

222 East Broadway.
From I-480 E, Broadway Exit, go east on Broadway for 3.5 miles.

36 DE SMET MISSION MARKER–COUNCIL BLUFFS

Pierce and Union Streets.
From I-480 E, Broadway Exit, go east on Broadway for 3.6 miles. Turn right (southeast) onto Union St. Go to Pierce St.

Buffalo Crossing at 15th and Capitol
Omaha

Western Historic Trails Center
Council Bluffs

National Park Service , Lewis and Clark
National Trail Headquarters, Omaha

Omaha and Council Bluffs

24 WESTERN HISTORIC TRAILS CENTER COUNCIL BLUFFS, IOWA

The "Path of Names" sidewalk entrance has many Lewis and Clark Trail names. Lewis and Clark Study Group meets here from Sept-May, on Tuesdays from 9-11; visitors are welcome to attend. Old time music on Thursdays from 1-4 year round. Travel information and exhibits on all the western trails, plus a big gift shop.

• White Catfish Festival, 3rd weekend July

■ Open daily, May-Sept, 9-6; Oct-April, 9-5.
(712) 366-4900 www.iowahistory.org
Study Group: www.mouthoftheplatte.org

25 HENRY DOORLY ZOO—OMAHA, NE

The zoo has the Lied Jungle, the world's largest indoor rain forest; and the geodesic Desert Dome, the world's largest indoor desert. The saltwater aquarium, orangutan forest, and IMAX Theater are other attractions. The zoo's Wildlife Safari Park, located 30 miles west of Omaha, has North American animals. (See page 95)

■ Open daily, 9:30-5. Admission: $10.25 adults, $8.75 seniors, $6.50 ages 5-11.
(402) 733-8400 www.omahazoo.com

26 LAURITZEN GARDENS—OMAHA, NE

Omaha's Botanical Center has 100 acres of outdoor exhibits, a visitor center and cafe. The adjacent Kennefick Park has two Union Pacific locomotives, Centennial #6900, the largest diesel-electric ever built, and Big Boy #4023, the largest steam locomotive ever built.

■ Open daily 9-5. Admission: $6 adults, $3 children. One hour narrated tram tours of the gardens are available, May-Oct for $2 per person. The cafe is open from 10-2 daily. The exhibits at Kennefick Park are free.
(402)346-4002 www.omahabotanicalgardens.org

27 DURHAM WESTERN HERITAGE MUSEUM OMAHA, NEBRASKA

The museum is located in the 1931 art deco Union Train Station in Omaha's Old Market area. Its famous Byron Reed coin and document collection includes the very rare 1804 dollar, the "King of American Coins," and a complete collection of all peace medal types ever issued. There are many interesting exhibits, a gift shop and old fashioned soda fountain.

■ Open Tues-Sat, 10-5; Sun 1-5. Admission: $6 adults, $5 seniors, $ 4 ages 3-12.
(402) 444-5071 www.dwhm.org

28 LEWIS AND CLARK NATIONAL HISTORIC TRAIL HEADQUARTERS—OMAHA

The Midwest Regional Office of the National Park Service administers the Lewis and Clark National Historic Trail from its headquarters on Omaha's riverfront. A book store and gift shop are located on the main floor. The Lewis and Clark Interpretive Trail along the Missouri River passes right by the building.

■ Open Mon-Fri 8:30-4:30 in winter; seven days a week during summer months, 9-5.
(402) 661-1804 www.nps.gov/lecl

29 LEWIS AND CLARK LANDING—OMAHA

Lewis and Clark Landing is the site of what once was the largest lead refinery plant in the world. The Asarco plant closed in 1997, and a 23 acre park was created. A statue near the NPS building commemorates the refinery workers. Lewis and Clark Study Group suggested the name for the landing and put up a marker. A Lewis and Clark Icon is located near Rick's Cafe.
www.mouthoftheplatte.org
www.omaha.lib.ne.us/earlyomaha

30 SPIRIT OF NEBRASKA'S WILDERNESS AND WAGON TRAIN PARK—OMAHA

The Spirit of Nebraska's Wilderness is a group of 58 bronze and stainless steel Canada geese in flight and 3 bison sculpted by Kent Ullberg as part of a monumental public sculpture group and park sponsored by First National Bank. A pioneer wagon train group by sculptors Blair Buswell and Ed Fraughton will complete the project, which stretches for several blocks near the First National Tower Center in downtown Omaha. The 40 story building is the tallest between Chicago and Denver.
www.firstnational.com www.visitomaha.com

31 JOSLYN ART MUSEUM—OMAHA

Joslyn Art Museum is a 1931 art deco building. Its internationally famous Western American Collection features art by Karl Bodmer, who accompanied Prince Maximilian up the Missouri in 1834; and art by Alfred Jacob Miller, George Catlin, John James Audubon and others. Copies of William Clark's maps are part of the Maximilian collection.

■ Open Tues-Sat, 10-4; Sun, noon-4. Admission: $6 adult, $4 seniors and college students, $3.50 ages 5-17. Free admission, Sat 10-noon.
(402) 342-3300 www.joslyn.org

32 LEWIS AND CLARK MONUMENT COUNCIL BLUFFS, IOWA

The Monument bluff is across the river from Eppley Airfield, where Lewis and Clark camped on July 27th and combatted the "Misquiters." Clark noted an old Ioway village site in today's Big Lake Park below the bluff.

■ (800) 228-6878 www.councilbluffsiowa.com

5

33 UNION PACIFIC RAILROAD MUSEUM COUNCIL BLUFFS, IOWA

The Union Pacific is America's largest railroad. Its headquarters are in Omaha, but its history is equally shared with Council Bluffs. The museum is located in the old Carnegie Library.

■ Open Tues-Sat, 10-4. Admission:
(712) 329-8307 www.up.com

34 GENERAL DODGE HOUSE (NHL) COUNCIL BLUFFS. IOWA

Major General Grenville Dodge's family were pioneer settlers in Omaha and Council Bluffs. After the Civil War, General Dodge became Chief Engineer of the Union Pacific Railroad; 10,000 men laid track westward from the Missouri River for the first transcontinental railroad. His home was built in 1869.

■ Open Tues-Sat, 10-5; Sunday 1-5
Admission: $7, adults, $5 srs, $3 ages 6-16
(712) 322-2406 www.dodgehouse.org

35 KANESVILLE TABERNACLE COUNCIL BLUFFS, IOWA

A replica of the log church where over 1000 Mormons witnessed Brigham Young become Second Prophet and President of The Church of Jesus Christ of Latter-Day Saints in 1847. The Mormon outfitting town of Kanesville became Council Bluffs in 1853.

■ Open daily, April-Sept 9:30-7; Oct-March 10-5. Free admission. Visitor Center, exhibits.
(712) 322-0500 www.mormon.org

36 FATHER DE SMET MISSION MARKER COUNCIL BLUFFS, IOWA

Jesuit Pierre-Jean De Smet began his career as an Indian missionary here in 1838. The Prairie Band of Potawatami had a five million acre reservation in Missouri and southwestern Iowa from 1837-1846, when they moved to Kansas.
www.pbindiantribe.com

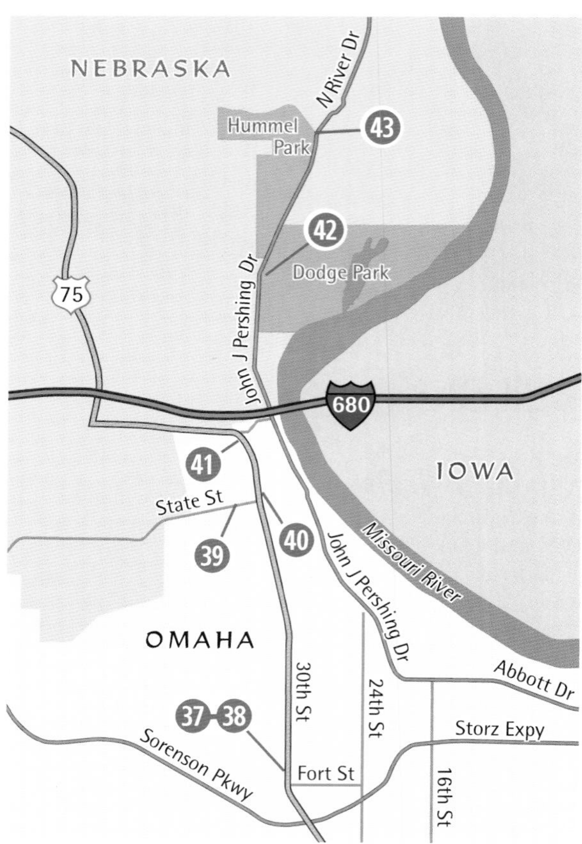

North Omaha to River Road

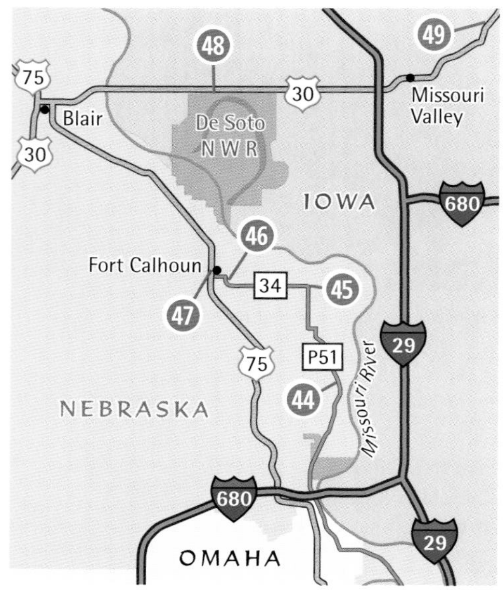

Omaha to Missouri Valley

Cabanne-Lisa Marker

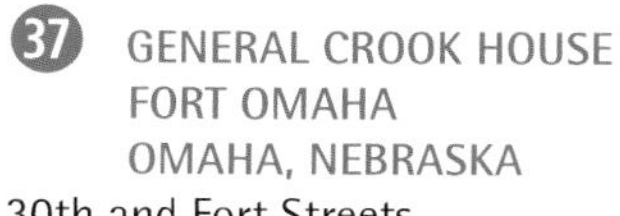

37 GENERAL CROOK HOUSE
FORT OMAHA
OMAHA, NEBRASKA

30th and Fort Streets.
From I-680 E, Exit 13 turn right (south) onto 31st St which then runs onto 30th St. At Fort St turn right (west) onto South Rd. Turn right (north) onto West Rd. Go to North Rd.

38 FORT OMAHA
STANDINGBEAR MEMORIAL
AND WALKING TOUR
OMAHA, NEBRASKA

30th and Fort Streets.
From I-680 E, Exit 13 turn right (south) onto 31st St which then runs onto 30th St. At Fort St turn right (west) onto South Rd. Turn right (north) onto East Rd. Go to Middle Rd.

39 MORMON TRAIL CENTER
OMAHA, NEBRASKA

3215 State Street.
From I-680 E, Exit 13 turn right (south) onto 31st St which then runs onto 30th St. Turn right (west) onto State St.

40 FLORENCE BANK
OMAHA, NEBRASKA

8502 North 30th Street.
From I-680 E, Exit 13 turn right (south) onto 31st St which then runs onto 30th St. Go to Willit St.

41 FLORENCE MILL
OMAHA, NEBRASKA

9102 North 30th Street.
From I-680 E, Exit 13 turn right (south) onto 31st St. Immediately turn left (east) onto McKinley St. Turn left (north) onto 30th St.

42 LEWIS AND CLARK ICON
AT N P DODGE PARK
OMAHA, NEBRASKA

11005 Pershing Drive.
From I-680 E, Exit 13 turn right (south) onto 31st St. Immediately turn left (east) onto McKinley St (road changes name to Dick Collins Rd). Turn left (north) onto Pershing Dr. Turn right (east) onto Dodge Park Rd.

43 CABANNE AND LISA
MARKER AT HUMMEL PARK
OMAHA, NEBRASKA

12560 Pershing Drive.
From I-680 E, Exit 13 turn right (south) onto 31st St. Immediately turn left (east) onto McKinley St (road changes name to Dick Collins Rd). Turn left (north) onto Pershing Dr.

44 NEALE WOODS
WASHINGTON COUNTY, NE

14423 Edith Marie Avenue.
From I-680 E, Exit 13 turn right (south) onto 31st St. Immediately turn left (east) onto McKinley St (road changes name to Dick Collins Rd). Turn left (north) onto Pershing Dr (road changes name to River Dr). Go 2.7 miles. Turn left (north) onto White Deer Lane. Turn left (west) onto Edith Marie Ave.

45 BOYER CHUTE REFUGE
WASHINGTON COUNTY, NE

From I-680 E, Exit 12 turn left (north) onto US 75 for 8 miles. Turn right (east) on to Madison St in Fort Calhoun. Go to stop sign at "T" intersection. Turn right (south) onto CR 34. Go 3 miles east to refuge main gate.

46 FORT ATKINSON S H P
FORT CALHOUN, NE

7th and Madison Streets.
From I-680 E, Exit 12 turn left (north) onto US 75 for 8 miles. Turn right (east) on to Madison St in Fort Calhoun. Go 1/2 mile to park entrance.

47 WASHINGTON CO MUSEUM
FORT CALHOUN, NEBRASKA

102 N 14th Street.
From I-680 E, Exit 12 turn left (north) onto US 75 for 8 miles to Monroe St.

48 DE SOTO BEND REFUGE AND
STEAMBOAT MUSEUM
MISSOURI VALLEY, IOWA

1434 316th Lane.
From I-29 Exit 75 go west on US 30 for 5 miles to refuge entrance.

49 HISTORICAL VILLAGE
AND WELCOME CENTER
MISSOURI VALLEY, IOWA

2931 Monroe Avenue.
From I-29 Exit 75 go east on US 30 for 5 miles to Monroe Ave.

General Crook House

Fort Atkinson

De Soto NWR/Steamboat Bertrand

North Omaha to Missouri Valley

37 GENERAL CROOK HOUSE MUSEUM FORT OMAHA–OMAHA, NE

Major General George Crook served in both the Civil War and Indian Wars. Though considered the army's greatest Indian fighter, he was well regarded by Indians as a man of his word. He was Commander of the Dept of the Platte at Fort Omaha from 1875-82 and from 1886-88. The historical archives of Douglas County and the National Indian Wars Library are located next door to this restored Victorian home, heirloom garden, and gift shop.

■ Open Mon-Fri, 10-4, Sat and Sun 1-4
Admission $5 adults ($6 mid Nov-Dec); $4 students, and $3 ages 6-12.
(402) 455-9990 www.omahahistory.org

38 FORT OMAHA STANDING BEAR MEMORIAL AND WALKING TOUR

The Trial of Ponca Chief Standing Bear took place at Fort Omaha in 1879 in the US District Court. It established for the first time that Native Americans had rights protected by the US Constitution. Chief Standing Bear was protesting a forced moved from the Niobrara region in northeastern Nebraska to Oklahoma Indian Territory. Many Ponca died the first winter; Standing Bear wanted to bury his son in Nebraska, but was arrested when he returned. General Crook and others supported him in bringing this matter to trial. As a result of the court decision, the Ponca were allowed to return to their homeland. (See page 103 for Ponca Tribe)

■ The Standing Bear Memorial is near the parade ground flag pole. The walking tour brochure is available at General Crook House.
(402) 455-9990 www.omahahistory.org

39 MORMON TRAIL CENTER AT HISTORIC WINTER QUARTERS–OMAHA

In 1846-47 over 3000 Mormons camped at Winter Quarters in the Florence Area of North Omaha, preparing to move on in the spring to Salt Lake City in Utah Territory. A total of about 7000 Mormons emigrants were in the immediate area. An estimated one in ten died that winter; many are buried in Mormon Pioneer Cemetery across the street from the Trail Center. The Mormon Trail, or Council Bluffs Road, went along the north side of the Platte River.

■ Open daily, 9 AM to 9 PM. Free admission.
Guided tours and a short film
(402) 453-9372 www.placestovisit.lds.org

40 FLORENCE BANK–OMAHA

The 1856 bank is the oldest bank in Nebraska. The bank issued its own "wildcat currency" in the early days of land speculation, and closed sometime before 1860.

■ May-Sept, Tues-Sunday, 1-5. Donation jar.
(402) 453-4280 www.historicflorence.org

41 FLORENCE MILL–OMAHA

The oldest mill in Nebraska, built at Winter Quarters under the supervision of Brigham Young; it began operating as a grist mill in March,1847. The mill was modernized several times and continued in operation until the. It is now a mill museum and art gallery.

■ Open during summer months.
(402) 551-1233 www.historicflorence.org

42 LEWIS AND CLARK ICON AT N P DODGE PARK–OMAHA

Lewis and Clark Interpretive Trail Icon Sculptures are located at 16 interpretive sites. The expediton camped here on July 28th, 1804, the day they met Missouria Indian elk hunters who knew where the Otoe were on their buffalo hunt. N P Dodge Park has RV and tent campgrounds, athletic fields, fishing, and boating.
(402) 444-5900 www.mouthoftheplatte.org
www.ci.omaha.ne.us/parks

43 CABANNE AND LISA MARKER AT HUMMEL PARK AND HISTORIC RIVER ROAD–WASHINGTON COUNTY

The brick marker is at the north entrance to Hummel Park near Ponca Road. Prince Paul and Prince Maximilian visited Cabanne's Post. The Cabanne trading post site was located on both sides of Ponca Creek across from Ponca and River Roads. It has been the subject of an archaelogy dig. Fort Lisa's location is unknown.
(402) 455-9990 www.omahahistory.org

44 NEALE WOODS NATURE CENTER WASHINGTON COUNTY, NEBRASKA

Hike in the hills and forests of the historic River Road area. Neale Woods Nature Center has nine miles of rugged trails. The Krimlofski Tract Addition on River Road is also part of Neale Woods.

■ Open Saturday, 8-5 and Sunday,12-5
Admission $5 adults, $4 seniors, $3 ages 3-11
(402) 453-5615 www.fontenelleforest.org

45 BOYER CHUTE NATIONAL WILDLIFE REFUGE–WASHINGTON COUNTY, NE

The Boyer Chute is a restored 2½ mile river channel off the Missouri River, like the braided network in Lewis and Clark's time. Eight miles of walking trails and wildlife habitat.

■ Day use only. Gate locked at dusk. Closed during deer hunts. No camping, no boating.
(402) 468-4313 http://boyerchute.fws.gov

46 FORT ATKINSON STATE HISTORICAL PARK–FORT CALHOUN, NEBRASKA

Lewis and Clark's First Council with the Otoe is commemorated with a sculpture. The Visitor Center has quality artifacts, and the reconstructed 1820's fort is open for exploration. (See "Early Council Bluffs" page 90)

■ Open daily, 10-5, Memorial Day-Labor Day.
$3.35 daily vehicle permit fee.
Living history on first weekends of month, check schedule on www.fortatkinsononline.org
(402) 468-5611 www.outdoornebraska.org

47 WASHINGTON COUNTY MUSEUM FORT CALHOUN, NEBRASKA

The oldest county museum in Nebraska has prehistoric artifacts, fort relics, Lewis and Clark, and pioneer exhibits.

■ Open Mon, Weds, Thurs, Fri, 9-4, and
Sat and Sun, 1-4. Donation $2 adult, $1 child
(402) 468-5740 www.newashcohist.org

48 DE SOTO NAT'L WILDLIFE REFUGE STEAMBOAT BERTRAND MUSEUM MISSOURI VALLEY, IOWA

Hundreds of thousands of snow geese visit the Refuge from mid Oct to late Nov. The Steamboat Bertrand sank in 1865 and was buried in a field until 1968. Over 200,0000 artifacts were recovered. Many are on display in the museum.

■ Visitor Center open daily 9-4:30.
Grounds open 6 AM-10 PM, April 15-Sept 30
Vehicle fee, $3. Closed Thanksgiving, Christmas
New Year's (712) 642-2772
http://midwest.fws.gov/desoto

49 HISTORICAL VILLAGE AND WELCOME CENTER–MISSOURI VALLEY, IOWA

1800's Village complex and Iowa Welcome Center

■ Center open daily 9-5 Mon-Sat, 12-5 Sun.
Village open daily mid April-November
Admission to village, $2 adults, 75 cents 6-12
(712) 642-2114 www.harrisoncountyparks.org

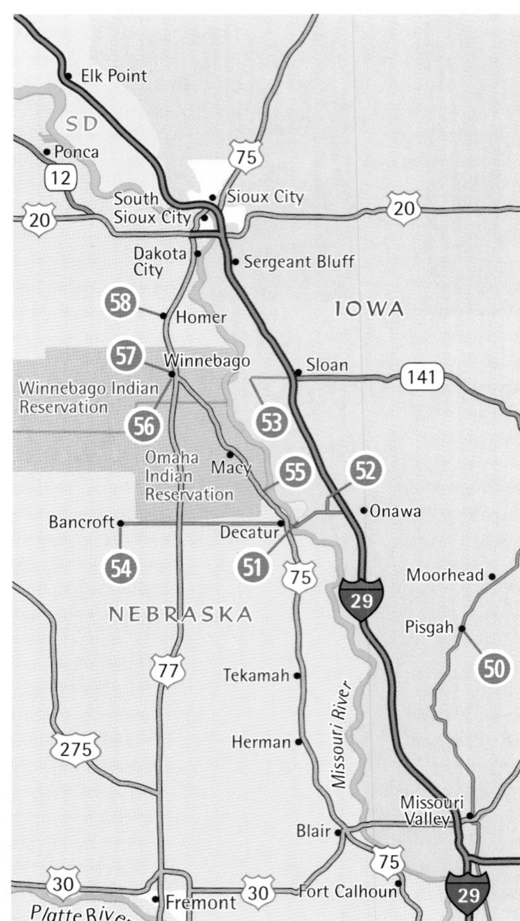

Fort Calhoun to Sioux City

Sioux City, Iowa and South Sioux City, Nebraska

50 LOESS HILLS VISITOR CENTER—PISGAH, IOWA
201 Polk Street.
From I-29 Exit 95 go east on Rte 301. Turn left (north) onto CR F 20. Turn left (north) onto Polk St.

51 CASINO OMAHA—ONAWA, IA
1 Blackbird Bend Boulevard.
From I-29 Exit 112 take Rte 175 west 5 miles to casino.

52 KEELBOAT—ONAWA, IOWA
21914 Park Loop.
From I-29 Exit 112 go west on Rte 175. Turn right (north) onto Rte 324.

53 WINNAVEGAS CASINO SLOAN, IOWA
1500 330th Street.
From I-29 Exit 127 go west on CR K 35 (330th St) 3 miles to casino.

54 NEIHARDT CENTER BANCROFT, NEBRASKA
306 W Elm Street.
From I-29 Exit 112 go west on Rte 175 to toll bridge across Missouri River. Go west on Rte 51. Turn left (south) onto US 75. Turn right (west) onto Rte 51. Bear right (northeast) onto Rte 16. Turn left (west) onto Elm St.

55 BLACKBIRD HILL MACY, NEBRASKA
From I-29 Exit 112 go west on Rte 175 to toll bridge across Missouri River. Go west on Rte 51. Turn right (north) onto US 75. Go 3 miles past Decatur.

56 WINNEBAGO MUSEUM WINNEBAGO, NE
Winnebago Indian Reservation.
From I-29 Exit 112 go west on Rte 175 to toll bridge across Missouri River. Go west on Rte 51. Turn right (north) onto US 75. Go 20 miles to Reservation.

57 ALLNATIVE STORE WINNEBAGO, NEBRASKA
503 Ho-Chunk Plaza.
From I-29 Exit 112 go west on Rte 175 to toll bridge across Missouri River. Go west on Rte 51. Turn right (north) onto US 75. Go 20 miles to Reservation. Store is at north end of town.

58 TONWANTONGA HOMER, NEBRASKA
From I-129 in South Sioux City, NE take Exit 1 to US 75 south. Go 8 miles to Village site.

59 SGT FLOYD MONUMENT SIOUX CITY, IOWA
From I-29 N Exit 143 go right (east), then immediately turn left (north) onto Lewis Blvd. Go 2.2 miles to Monument.

60 SOUTHERN HILLS MALL SIOUX CITY, IOWA
4400 Sergeant Rd.
From I-29 Exit 144 go east on US 20 to Lakeport St Exit. Go north to Sergeant Rd. Go left (west) to mall.

61 **62** SERGEANT FLOYD RIVERBOAT MUSEUM/ INTERPRETIVE CENTER SIOUX CITY, IOWA
900/1000 Larsen Park Road
From I-29 W Exit 149 take Larsen Park ramp south, then east.

63 PUBLIC MUSEUM SIOUX CITY, IOWA
2901 Jackson Street.
From I-29 N Exit 147 B go north on Nebraska St. Turn right on 29th St.

Sergeant Charles Floyd

Charles Floyd was born on the Kentucky frontier about 1782. In 1799 his family moved across the Ohio River to Clarksville, Indiana where his father and older brother operated a ferry at the Falls of the Ohio.

In 1802, 20 year old Charles was appointed town constable, and awarded the contract to deliver the mail between Clarksville and Vincennes, a 220 mile weekly roundtrip on horseback.

William Clark lived with his brother at Clark's Point overlooking the Falls of the Ohio. After receiving Lewis's invitation to co-lead the expedition, William chose Charles Floyd and the Field brothers from Louisville as his first three recruits for the Corps of Discovery.

Despite his youth, Charles was picked to be one of three sergeants. He kept a journal until two days before his death on August 20, 1804. He most likely died from a ruptured appendix. Clark wrote about his young friend, "he was buried with the Honors of War much lamented," and added"—This Man at all times gave us proofs of his firmness and Deturmined resolution to doe Service to his Countrey and honor to himself."

The cedar post that marked his gravesite on the hill was a landmark for many years before the Monument was built.

Omaha Dancer's Regalia

Keelboat at Lewis and Clark Park

Lewis and Clark Interpretive Center

Sergeant Floyd Monument

Onawa Area and Sioux City

50 LOESS HILLS STATE FOREST VISITOR CENTER–PISGAH, IOWA

The Pisgah Visitor Center has interesting exhibits. Preparation Canyon State Park has an huge observation deck called "the spot" by locals.

■ Visitor Center open daily May-Oct, Mon-Fri, 8-4, Sat and Sun 1-4. Nov-April, Mon-Fr, 8-4. (712) 456-2924 www.state.ia.us/dnr

■ The Loess Hills Center in Moorhead arranges step-on guided tours, hospitality, and has a gift shop. (712) 886-5441 www.loesshillstours.com

51 CASINO OMAHA AND RESTAURANT ONAWA, IOWA

The Omaha Tribe gained a casino on the Iowa side of the river when the river changed its course. The restaurant has a prime rib buffet and a snacks and yogurt bar.

■ Open daily. Sun-Thurs, 8 AM-2 AM, Fri Sat, 24 hours.(402) 837-5308 www.onawa.com www.500nations.com casinos

52 KEELBOAT AT LEWIS AND CLARK STATE PARK–ONAWA, IOWA

Keelboat builder Butch Bouvier has been building replicas across America. This is the third generation of the original replica at Blue Lake. Visitors are welcome to go on board.

• Lewis and Clark Festival, 2nd weekend June

■ Open year round. Camping, trails, fishing, boating on Blue Lake. www.keelboat.com (712) 423-2829 www.iowadnr.com

53 WINNA VEGAS CASINO, INN AND RESTAURANT–SLOAN, IOWA

The WinnaVegas Casino has a motel and accomodations for large RVs on its grounds.

■ The Flowers Island Family Restaurant is open from 7AM-10PM. The Casino is open 24/7.

■ Winna Vegas Inn call (800) 256-7545 (712) 428-9466 www.winnavegas.biz

54 JOHN G NEIHARDT CENTER BANCROFT, NEBRASKA

John G. Neihardt is the author of *Black Elk Speaks* and many other works. Neihardt's Study and Sacred Hoop Garden are on the grounds.

• Spring Conference, last Saturday in April
Neihardt Day, first Sunday in August

■ Open March-Nov, Mon-Sat, 9-5 and Sun 1:30-5. Dec-Feb, Mon-Fri, 9-5
(402) 648-3388 www.neihardtcenter.org

55 BLACKBIRD HILL SCENIC OVERLOOK MACY, NEBRASKA

Omaha Chief Blackbird died in an 1800 smallpox epidemic which killed 400 Omaha. On August 11, 1804 the captains and 10 men raised a flag at his gravesite on Blackbird Hill. The overlook interpretive shelter is near Blackbird Hill.

■ www.omahatribeofnebraska.com

56 WINNEBAGO CULTURAL CENTER AND MUSEUM–WINNEBAGO, NE

The museum is on the campus of Little Priest Tribal College; its director is the tribal historian. Exhibits feature Winnebago artifacts and the history of the tribe. In 1865 the Omaha Nation shared its reservation land with the Winnebago. Winnebagos (the Ho-Chunk Nation) also live in Wisconsin, their original homeland.

■ Open Tues-Fri, 9-12 and 1-4
(402) 878-3313 www.winnebagotribe.com

57 ALLNATIVE STORE AND BISON HERD WINNEBAGO, NEBRASKA

The Winnebago tribe's Ho-Chunk, Inc. is developing non-gaming business ventures, including an online store, catalog, and two retail outlets selling Indian made goods. The AllNative store is near the new 40 acre housing development. The bison herd is across the highway. (The other store is in the Southern Hills Mall in Sioux City.)

■ Open Mon-Fri 9 AM-7 PM, Sat 10-6
(402) 878-2400 www.allnative.com
www.hochunkinc.com

58 TONWANTONGA VILLAGE SITE HOMER, NEBRASKA

The site of the Omaha Big Village and the expedition's "Fish Camp" of Aug 13-19, 2004. Also the site of the MacKay-Evans 1795-97 Fort Charles. (See page 53) (866) 494-1307

■ www.visitsouthsiouxcity.com

59 SGT FLOYD MON'T (NHL)-SIOUX CITY, IA

22 year old Sgt Charles Floyd was the only man to die on the expedition. He died of a ruptured appendix on August 22nd, 1804. He is buried on the bluff where the Monument now stands. The 100 foot tall stone obelisk was dedicated on Memorial Day, 1901; it is the First National Historic Landmark.

■ (712) 279-0198 www.siouxcitymuseum.org www.siouxcityhistory.org www.cr.nps.gov/nhl

60 SOUTHERN HILLS MALL LEWIS AND CLARK MURALS AND ALLNATIVE STORE SIOUX CITY, IOWA

38 original wall murals portray the story of the expedition from start to finish. The Mall is the only commerical site to be selected as a National Trail site by the National Park Service. It also has a Lewis and Clark children's play area; interpretive markers; and AllNative store owned by the Winnebago Tribe.

■ Open Mon-Sat 10- 9, Sunday 12-6
(712) 274-0109 www.southernhillsmall.com

61 SGT FLOYD RIVER MUSEUM AND STATE WELCOME CENTER (NHL) SIOUX CITY, IOWA

The museum and welcome center is located in the *Sergeant Floyd* tugboat. The Corps of Engineers used the historic boat from 1932-75.

There is a forensic reconstruction of a life size model of Sgt. Charles Floyd. A plaster cast of the skull and other body measurements were obtained when an earlier gravesite washed away, and the Monument was built. In addition, one of America's largest collections of scale model steamboats and keelboats is on display.

■ Open daily, 9-5. Free admission.
(712) 279-0198 www.siouxcitymuseum.org
http://sgtfloyd.com

62 LEWIS AND CLARK INTERPRETIVE CENTER–SIOUX CITY, IOWA

The Interpretive Center is located near the Riverboat Museum on the waterfront. It has life size dioramas portraying many aspects of the expedition; audio-visual and hands-on interactive displays; and a large bookstore and gift shop. Outdoors, a heritage garden and prairie serve as "living history."

■ Open Tues-Sat, 9-5 and Sun 12-5.
Free admission. (712) 224-5242
www.siouxcitylcic.com

63 SIOUX CITY PUBLIC MUSEUM SIOUX CITY, IOWA

The Museum has a large collection of Native American and prehistoric artifacts. It also has natural history and local history exhibits, and a gift shop.

■ Open Tues, 9-8, Weds-Sat, 9-5, and Sun 1-5.
Free admission. (712) 279-6174
www.siouxcitymuseum.org

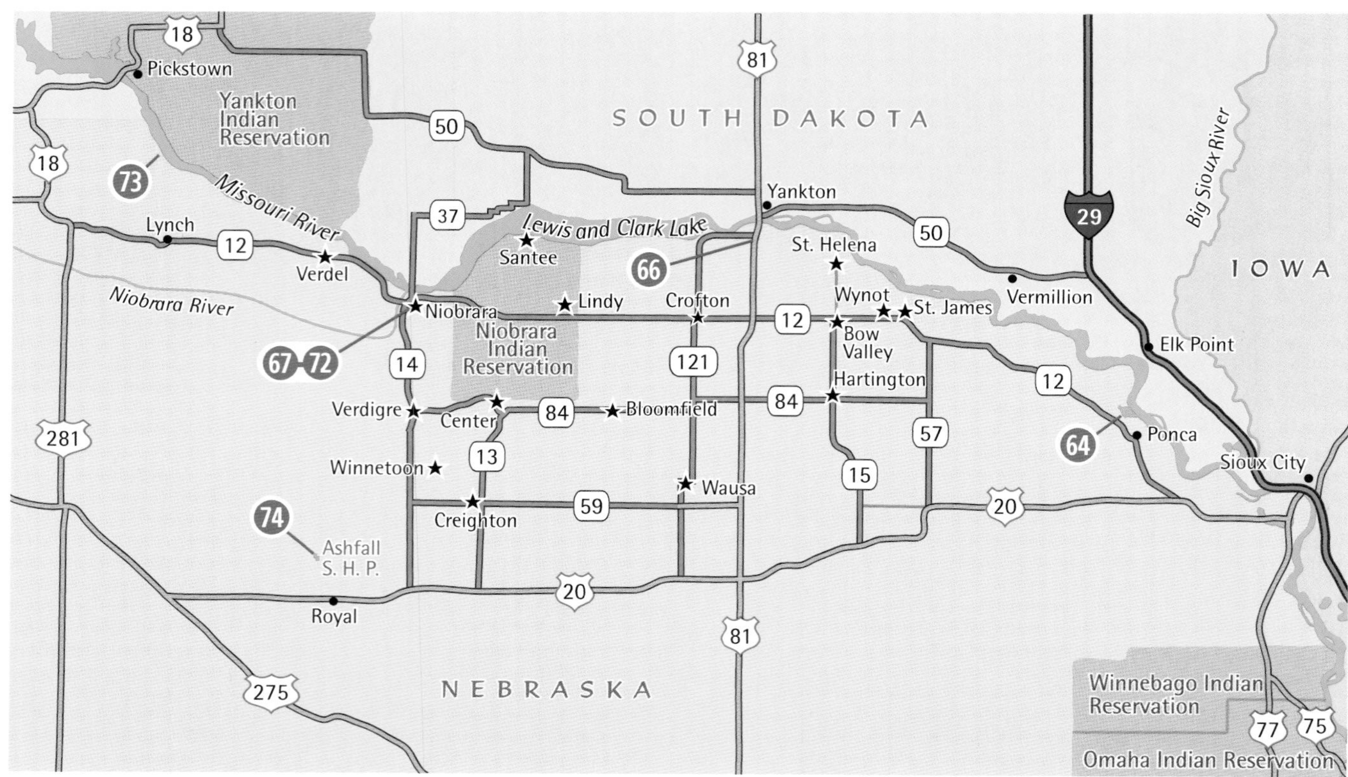

Northeastern Nebraska

64 MISSOURI RIVER VISITOR CENTER PONCA STATE PARK
88090 Spur 26-E.
From US 20 - Rte 12 Jct go northwest on Rte 12 to Ponca. Turn right (north) onto Nebraska St. Turn right (east) onto 3rd St. Turn left (north) onto Union St/Rte 26 E. Road changes name to 26 E Spur.

65 SHANNON TRAIL NORTHEAST NEBRASKA
Verdigre, Center, Winnetoon, Creighton, Wausa, Bloomfirld, Hartington, Bow Valley, St. James, Wynot, St. Helena, Crofton, Lindy, Santee, Niobrara, Verdel. Shannon Trail, east-west, 56 miles.

66 NORTHEAST NEBRASKA CORPS OF DISCOVERY WELCOME CENTER
89705 Highway 81, Crofton, NE.
From US 20 - US 81 Jct go north 34 miles to Welcome Center.

67 PONCA TRIBAL MUSEUM NIOBRARA, NEBRASKA
254 Park Avenue.
From US 20 - Rte 14 Jct go north. Turn right (east) onto Rte 12. Turn right (south) onto Spruce Ave, then immediately turn left (east) onto Park Ave which then jogs south and east.

68 SANTEE TRIBAL MUSEUM SANTEE, NEBRASKA
108 Spirit Lake Avenue.
From US 20 - Rte 13 Jct go north on Rte 13. Bear left (northwest) onto Rt 84. Continue north on 531 Ave and then Rte 12. Turn right (east) onto Rte S 54D. In Santee turn left (west) onto Spirit Lake Ave.

69 OHIYA CASINO NIOBRARA, NEBRASKA
52946 Highway 12.
From US 20 - Rte 13 Jct go north on Rte 13. Bear left (northwest) onto Rt 84. Continue north on 531 Ave . Turn right (east) onto Rte 12.

70 CHIEF STANDING BEAR MEMORIAL BRIDGE NIOBRARA, NEBRASKA
Spans Missouri River between NE Rte 14 and SD Rte 37.
From US 20 - Rte 14 Jct go north to Rte 12 in Niobrara. Turn right (east). Turn left (north) onto Rte 14. Go to bridge.

71 NIOBRARA STATE PARK NIOBRARA, NEBRASKA
89261 522 Avenue.
From US 20 - Rte 14 Jct go north to Rte 12 in Niobrara. Turn left (west) onto Rte 12. Go to park entrance at 522 Ave.

72 KREYCIK RIVERVIEW ELK AND BUFFALO RANCH NIOBRARA, NEBRASKA
88971 517 Ave.
From US 20 - Rte 14 Jct go north to Rte 12 in Niobrara. Turn left (west) onto Rte 12. Turn left (south) onto 522 Ave. Bear right (west) onto 891 Rd. Turn left (south) onto 519 Ave. Turn right (west) onto 890 Rd. Turn left (south) onto 517 Ave.

73 OLD BALDY LYNCH, NEBRASKA
From US 20 - US 281 Jct go north to Rte 12. Go east to Lynch. Turn north on 4th St. Continue north 5.8 miles. to junction with local road on right. Go east 0.4 mile to road fork. Go north 0.7 mile.

74 ASHFALL FOSSIL BEDS ROYAL, NEBRASKA
86930 517th Avenue.
From US 20 in Royal go west 2 miles. Go north 6.6 miles to Ashfall Rd.

TRIBAL POW WOWS	www.indianaffairs.state.ne.us
Nebraska Indian Affairs Commission	(402) 471-2311
Santee Pow Wow—Santee, NE	3rd wkd in June
Winnebago Pow Wow—Winnebago, NE	last full wkd in July
Omaha Harvest Pow Wow—Macy, NE	mid August
Ponca Pow Wow—Niobrara, Ne	mid August
FORT OMAHA INTERTRIBAL POW WOW	www.mccneb.edu/intercultural
Metropolitan Community College	
Fort Omaha Campus Intercultural Office	(402) 457-2400
Fort Omaha Pow Wow—Omaha, NE	mid September

Pow wows are Native American social events and family reunions. Please learn pow wow etiquette.
www.gatheringofnations.com/powwows

George Shannon at Bloomfield
Shannon Trail Promoters

Old Baldy
Lee Myers

Niobrara River
Lee Myers

Ashfall Fossil Beds
Mike Voorhies

Northeastern Nebraska

64 PONCA STATE PARK MISSOURI RIVER VISITOR CENTER—PONCA, NEBRASKA

The Missouri National Recreational River is what the river was like 200 years ago, before it was channelized. This relatively wild stretch of river is divided into two sections: 59 miles from Ponca State Park to Gavins Point Dam; and 39 miles from the Standing Bear Bridge to Fort Randall Dam. It is a favorite destination for canoeing and float trips.

The MNRR has a Resource and Education Center at Ponca State Park with exhibits and meeting room facilities. The park has cabins, camping, guided trail rides on horseback, other trails and recreational activities.

■ Open daily. Vehicle fee $3.35
(402) 755-2284 www.outdoornebraska.org

65 PRIVATE GEORGE SHANNON TRAIL 16 COMMUNITIES

The youngest member of the Lewis and Clark Expedition, 19 year old George got lost while out hunting the expedition's horses in the vicinity of Wynot, Nebraska on August 26, 1804. Though search parties were sent out for him, he was moving ahead of the boats, instead of behind them. Clark wrote that he almost starved to death "for want of Bulletes or Something to kill his meat." He ate grapes and shot a rabbit with a stick in his gun. He was found on September 11th, 16 days later, 140 miles up river.

Find 13 chainsaw carvings of Shannon and his companions in the rolling hills of the "Czech Alps" as they are known locally.

■ Participating communities are:
(1) Verdigre, (2) Center, (3) Winnetoon, (4) Creighton, (5) Wausa, (6) Bloomfield, (7) Hartington, (8) Bow Valley, (9) St James Marketplace, (10) Wynot, (11) St Helena, (12) Crofton, (13) Lindy, (14) Santee-Ohiya Casino, (15) Niobrara, (16) Verdel.
(402) 667-6557 www.shannontrail.com

66 CORPS OF DISCOVERY WELCOME CENTER—CROFTON, NE

Trained staff and volunteers provide travel information about Nebraska and South Dakota. Exhibits, markers, programs, gift shop. Walking trails in the panoramic Missouri River Valley.

■ Open daily. Memorial Day-Labor Day, 9-6. Sept-May, 10-4. (402) 667-6557
www.crofton-ne.com/discover
e-mail for info: cdwc@byelectric.com

67 PONCA TRIBAL MUSEUM NIOBRARA, NEBRASKA

Ponca tribal history and artifacts. Adjacent to Niobrara Museum in downtown Niobrara. Earth lodge and bison herd tours available.

■ Open Mon-Fri, 8-4:30. Free admission.
(402) 857-3519 www.poncatribe-ne.org

68 SANTEE SIOUX TRIBAL MUSEUM SANTEE, NEBRASKA

Santee Sioux history and artifacts in a museum at tribal headquarters.

■ Open Mon-Fri. 8-4:30. Free admission.
(402) 857-2772 www.santeedakota.org

69 OHIYA CASINO AND RESTAURANT NIOBRARA, NEBRASKA

Private George Shannon's statue may be found here at the Santee "Oh-hee-ya" Casino. The restaurant is a salad, soup and desert bar.

■ Open daily 8 AM - Midnight. (402) 857-3860
www.santeedakota.org

70 CHIEF STANDING BEAR MEMORIAL BRIDGE—NIOBRARA, NEBRASKA

An annual "Bridging the Shores" festival in late August commemorates the building of this bridge near the junction of the Missouri and Niobrara Rivers. (See page 99 for the Memorial to Chief Standing Bear at Fort Omaha)
www.niobrarane.org www.poncatribe-ne.org

71 NIOBRARA STATE PARK NIOBRARA, NEBRASKA

Niobrara is an Indian word which means "Running Water." Its junction with the Missouri is a peaceful place of sloughs and sandbars and islands. The Cramer Interpretive Center overlooks a 15 star flag site marking the Lewis and Clark camp of September 4, 1804. A railroad bridge over the Niobrara has been turned into a walking path.

■ Cabins, RV and tent camping. Reservations start being taken on January 1st for Nebraska State Parks. Vehicle entrance fee, $ 3.35
(402) 755-2284 www.outdoornebraska.org

72 KREYCIK RIVERVIEW ELK AND BUFFALO RANCH—NIOBRARA, NE

A working elk, bison and cattle ranch which has 2 hour covered wagon tours on summer weekends. An online and ranch gift shop sells everything made from elk and buffalo.

■ Tours May 15-Sept 30, and by appointment. Saturday tours at 10, 2 and 4; Sunday tours at 2 and 4. No tours on Memorial Day, 4th of July, and Labor Day. $6.50 per person, plus tax.
www.nebraskaelktours.com
elkranch@bloomnet.com or write to:
88971 517 Ave, Niobrara NE 68760-6016

73 OLD BALDY—LYNCH, NEBRASKA

On September 7, 1804 the expedition discovered its first prairie dog town as they explored Old Baldy (also called The Towers). The prairie dog village covered about four acres of ground on and around the hill. The men poured five barrels of water down a burrow hole until they managed to catch one. Eventually this little creature was sent back east in the spring of 1805 to visit President Jefferson at Monticello and then to live at Peale's Museum in Philadelphia. An area sewing group makes "the Lynch Dawg," a stuffed animal souvenir of the Trail; a Lynch Dawg has watched over the production of this book.

■ (800) 337-2706 www.lynchne.com

74 ASHFALL FOSSIL BEDS STATE HISTORICAL PARK—ROYAL, NEBRASKA

Nearly 12 million years ago a volcano erupted in southwestern Idaho causing a down pouring of volcanic ash here. Countless animals seeking refuge at a water hole were suffocated and buried in one to two feet of powdered glass. The skeletons of these animals are preserved intact, and in rounded form. The animals include 10 foot rhinos; tiny three-toed horses; dogs; saber toothed cats; saber toothed deer; and mastodons. Visitors may watch paleontologists at work in the Rhino Barn shelter and at the Visitor Center. The *National Geographic* has described it as the "Pompeii of prehistoric animals." Fossils similar to those seen by Lewis and Clark are on display at the Visitor Center: part of a long necked plesiosaur, a horned dinosaur, and a large predatory fish. They are from the world famous collection of the University of Nebraska State Museum in Lincoln.

■ Open May 1 to 2nd weekend in October. Hours: Memorial Day-Labor Day, Mon-Sat 9-5, and Sun 11-5. Before Memorial Day, closed on Sunday and Monday, open 10-4 Tues-Sat. After Labor Day, closed Monday, open 10-4 Tues -Sat and Sunday 1-4.
(402) 893-2000 www.outdoornebraska.org
http://ashfall.unl.edu

Region Five: References

BIOGRAPHY

ADVENTURES OF THE OJIBBEWAY AND IOWAY INDIANS IN ENGLAND, FRANCE, AND BELGIUM BEING NOTES OF EIGHT YEARS' TRAVELS AND RESIDENCE IN EUROPE WITH HIS NORTH AMERICAN INDIAN COLLECTION (2 VOLUMES)
by Geo. Catlin. Digital Scanning, Inc. (1852/2001)

BRIGHT EYES: THE STORY OF SUSETTE LA FLESCHE, AN OMAHA INDIAN
by Dorothy Clarke Wilson. McGraw-Hill Book Company (1974)

A CYCLE OF THE WEST: THE SONG OF THREE FRIENDS, THE SONG OF HUGH GLASS, THE SONG OF JED SMITH, THE SONG OF THE INDIAN WARS, THE SONG OF THE MESSIAH
by John G. Neihardt. University of Nebraska Press (2002)

5

GENERAL HENRY ATKINSON: A WESTERN MILITARY CAREER
by Roger Nichols. University of Oklahoma Press (1965)

IRON EYES FAMILY: THE CHILDREN OF JOSEPH LA FLESCHE
by Norma Kidd Green. Johnsen Publishing Company (1969)

JOSHUA PILCHER: FUR TRADER AND AGENT
by John E. Sunder. University of Oklahoma Press (1968)

THE PONCA CHIEFS: AN ACCOUNT OF THE TRIAL OF STANDING BEAR
by Thomas Henry Tibbles. University of Nebraska Press (1972)

TALKING INDIAN: REFLECTIONS ON SURVIVAL AND WRITING
by Anna Lee Walters. Firebrand Books (1992)

TRAVELS IN NORTH AMERICA 1822-1824
by Paul Wilhelm, Duke of Wurttemberg, edited by Savoie Lottinville. University of Oklahoma Press (1973)

UP THE MISSOURI WITH AUDUBON: THE JOURNAL OF EDWARD HARRIS
edited by John Francis Mc Dermott. University of Oklahoma Press (1951)

THE WEST OF WILLIAM H. ASHLEY: THE INTERNATIONAL STRUGGLE FOR THE FUR TRADE
edited by Dale H. Morgan, Fred A. Rosenstock Old West Publishing Company (1964)

HISTORY

AMERICA LOOKS WEST: LEWIS AND CLARK ON THE MISSOURI
Nebraskaland Magazine Volume 80, Number 7: August-September 2002

HISTORY

AN UNSPEAKABLE SADNESS: THE DISPOSSESION OF THE NEBRASKA INDIANS
by David J. Wishart. University of Nebraska Press (1994)

ARCHAEOLOGY AND ETHNOHISTORY OF THE OMAHA INDIANS: THE BIG VILLAGE SITE
by John M. O'Shea and John Ludwickson. University of Nebraska Press (1992)

BETRAYING THE OMAHA NATION, 1790-1916
by Judith Boughter. University of Oklahoma Press (1998)

BLESSING FOR A LONG TIME: THE SACRED POLE OF THE OMAHA TRIBE
by Robin Ridington and Dennis Hastings. University of Nebraska Press (1997)

DEFENDING THE WESTERN FRONTIER: MANUEL LISA AND THE WAR OF 1812 IN THE COUNCIL BLUFFS AREA
by Kira Gale. River Junction Press (2000)

DIPLOMATS IN BUCKSKINS: A HISTORY OF INDIAN DELEGATIONS TO WASHINGTON CITY
by Herman J. Viola. Revilo Books (1995)

EARLY DAYS AT COUNCIL BLUFFS
by Charles H. Babbitt. Walsworth (1916/1990)

THE FONTENELLE AND CABANNE TRADING POSTS: THE HISTORY AND ARCHEOLOGY OF TWO MISSOURI RIVER SITES 1822-1838
by Richard E. Jensen. Nebraska State Historical Society (1998)

FORT ATKINSON ON THE COUNCIL BLUFFS: THE SIXTH'S ELYSIAN FIELDS
by Sally A. Johnson. Nebraska State Historical Society (1972)

FORT ON THE PRAIRIE: FORT ATKINSON, ON THE COUNCIL BLUFF 1819-1827
by Virgil Ney. Command Publications (1978)

FROM PITTSBURGH TO THE ROCKY MOUNTAINS: MAJOR STEPHEN LONG'S EXPEDITION 1819-1820
edited by Maxine Benson. Fulcrum Inc. (1988)

"LA BELLE VUE": STUDIES IN THE HISTORY OF BELLEVUE, NEBRASKA
edited by Jerold L. Simmons. Walsworth (1976)

LEWIS AND CLARK AT COUNCIL BLUFF
by Kira Gale. River Junction Press (1999)

LEWIS AND CLARK ON THE GREAT PLAINS: A NATURAL HISTORY
by Paul A. Johnsgard. University of Nebraska Press (2003)

LOVE SONG TO THE PLAINS
by Mari Sandoz. University of Nebraska Press (1966)

HISTORY

THE MISSOURI EXPEDITION 1818-1820: THE JOURNAL OF SURGEON JOHN GALE WITH RELATED DOCUMENTS
edited by Roger L. Nichols. University of Oklahoma Press (1969)

THE MORMON BATTALION: U. S. ARMY OF THE WEST, 1846-1848
by Norma Baldwin Ricketts. Utah State University Press (1996)

MORMONS AT THE MISSOURI, 1846-1852 "AND SHOULD WE DIE..."
by Richard E. Bennett. University of Oklahoma Press (1987)

THE NATURAL HISTORY OF THE LONG EXPEDITION TO THE ROCKY MOUNTAINS 1819-1820
by Howard Ensign Evans. Oxford University Press (1997)

THE OMAHA TRIBE (2 VOLUMES)
by Alice C. Fletcher and Francis La Flesche. University of Nebraska Press (1992)

THE OTOES AND MISSOURIAS: A STUDY OF THE INDIAN REMOVAL AND THE LEGAL AFTERMATH
by Berlin Basil Chapman. Times Journal Publishing Company (1965)

PETER A. SARPY AND EARLY BELLEVUE
by Kira Gale. River Junction Press (1999)

PEOPLE OF THE MOONSHELL: A WESTERN RIVER JOURNAL
by Nancy M. Peterson. Renaissance House (1984)

THE PONCA TRIBE
by James H. Howard. University of Nebraska Press (1995)

PROLOGUE TO LEWIS AND CLARK: THE MACKAY AND EVANS EXPEDITION
by W. Raymond Wood. University of Oklahoma Press (2003)

RETRACING MAJOR STEPHEN H. LONG'S 1820 EXPEDITION: THE ITINERARY AND BOTANY
by George J. Goodman and Cheryl A. Lawson. University of Oklahoma Press (1995)

RULO TO LYNCH WITH LEWIS AND CLARK: A GUIDE AND NARRATIVE
by Orville Menard. Lamplighter Press (2003)

STEPHEN LONG AND AMERICAN FRONTIER EXPLORATION
by Roger L. Nichols and Patrick L. Halley. University of Oklahoma Press (1995)

WHEELBOATS ON THE MISSOURI: THE JOURNALS AND DOCUMENTS OF THE ATKINSON-O'FALLON EXPEDITION, 1824-26
edited by Richard E. Jensen and James S. Hutchins. Montana State Historical Society Press (2001)

REGION SIX
SOUTH AND NORTH DAKOTA

■ River Route: Sioux City to Chamberlain ■ Native American Scenic Byway: Chamberlain to Pierre

■ Pierre and Fort Pierre ■ Native American Scenic Byway: Pierre to Bismarck

■ Interstate Route: Sioux City to Bismarck ■ Bismarck and Mandan

■ Fort Mandan and Knife River Villages to Parshall

■ New Town and The Confluence ■ North Dakota Badlands

1. Lewis and Clark Riverboat, Bismarck ND, 2. Buffalo, Houck Ranch, Fort Pierre SD, 3. Fort Mandan, Washburn ND, 4. Lewis and Clark Visitor Center, Yankton SD, 5. On-A-Slant Indian Village, Mandan ND. 6. Sunflowers, North Dakota, 7. Lower Brule Buffalo Interpretive Center, Fort Pierre SD, 8. United Tribes International Pow Wow, Bismarck ND

CREDITS: (1) (6) (8) North Dakota Tourism, Dawn Charging; (5) North Dakota Tourism, Pat Hertz (2) (7) South Dakota Tourism; (4) Lee Myers

6

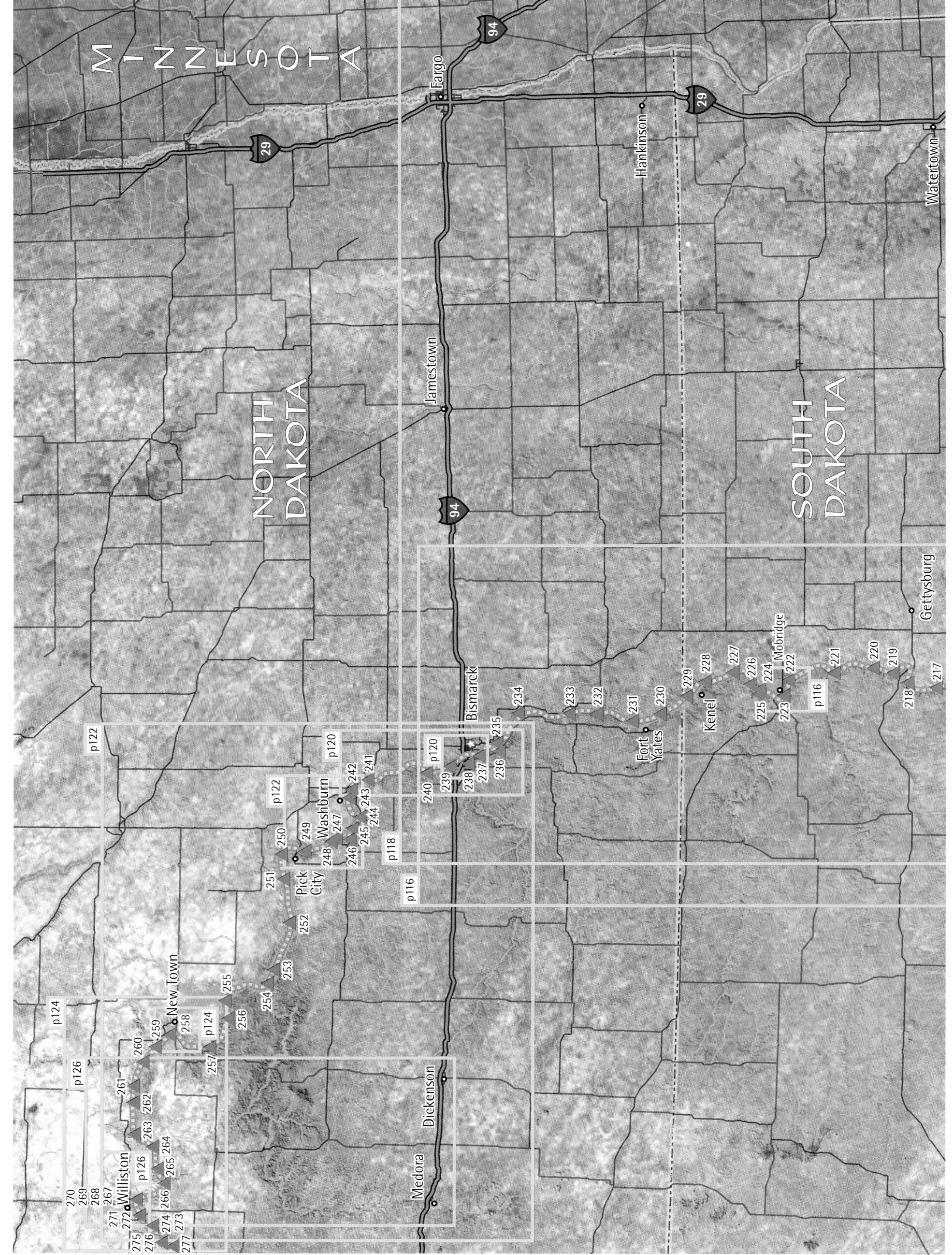

MINNESOTA
NORTH DAKOTA
SOUTH DAKOTA
94
29
Fargo
Hankinson
Watertown
Jamestown
Gettysburg
Mobridge
Kenel
Fort Yates
Bismarck
Washburn
Pick City
New Town
Williston
Dickenson
Medora
p116
p118
p120
p122
p124
p126
217
218
219
220
221
222
223
224
225
226
227
228
229
230
231
232
233
234
235
236
237
238
239
240
241
242
243
244
245
246
247
248
249
250
251
252
253
254
255
256
257
258
259
260
261
262
263
264
265
266
267
268
269
270
271
272
273
274
275
276
277

6

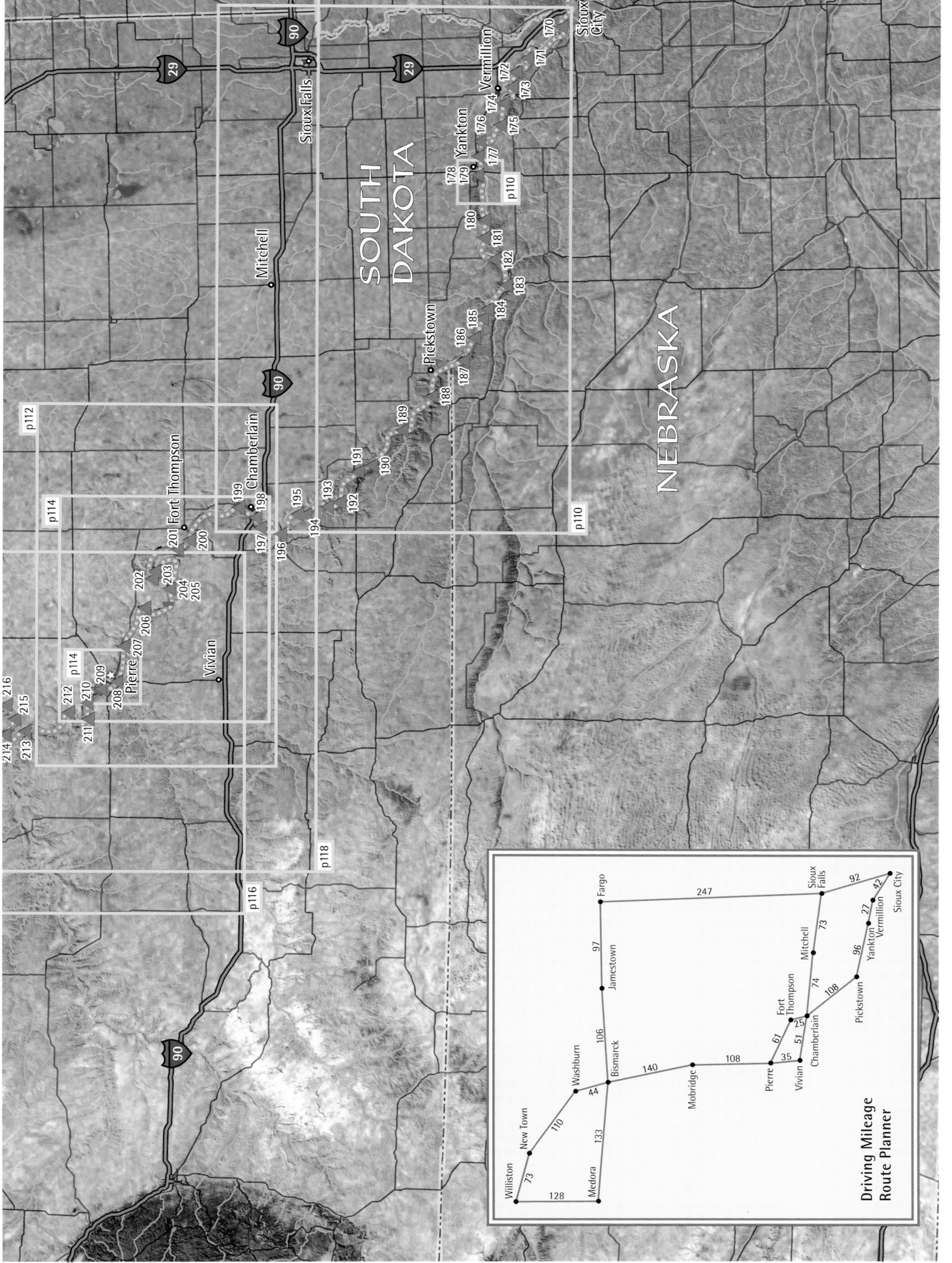
SOUTH DAKOTA
NEBRASKA
Sioux Falls
Mitchell
Chamberlain
Fort Thompson
Pickstown
Yankton
Vermillion
Sioux City
Vivian
Pierre
29
90
p110
p112
p114
p116
p118
170
171
172
173
174
175
176
177
178
179
180
181
182
183
184
185
186
187
188
189
190
191
192
193
194
195
196
197
198
199
200
201
202
203
204
205
206
207
208
209
210
211
212
213
214
215
216
Driving Mileage
Route Planner
Williston
New Town
Washburn
Medora
Bismarck
Jamestown
Fargo
Mobridge
Pierre
Vivian
Fort Thompson
Chamberlain
Mitchell
Sioux Falls
Pickstown
Yankton
Vermillion
Sioux City
73
110
44
128
133
106
97
247
140
108
35
61
51
25
74
73
108
96
27
42
92

Buffalo Herd at *Dances With Wolves* Triple U Ranch
South Dakota Tourism

Highway 1806 in North Dakota
North Dakota Tourism

Bad River Reenactment
South Dakota Tourism

6

America 200 Years Ago

Lewis and Clark in Indian Country

STRANGERS IN A STRANGE LAND

President Jefferson wrote to Lewis while he was still in St Louis that there was one Indian tribe, the Sioux, on whom "we wish most particularly to make a friendly impression, because of their immense power, and because we learn they are very desirous of being on the most friendly terms with us." When the Corps of Discovery entered the Dakotas, they met both the roving bands of the Sioux, and the village Indian tribes, the Arikara, Mandan, and Hidatsa, who lived along the Missouri River. All of these tribes had existing relationships with British fur trading companies in Canada.

One of Lewis and Clark's main duties was to establish diplomatic relations with the Indians, by holding councils, and by arranging for delegations of chiefs to visit Jefferson in Washington. They were to begin establishing economic relationships. And they were to provide answers to a very long list of questions Jefferson had given them regarding all aspects of Indian life. They also needed practical help in surviving as "strangers in a strange land."

ADVENTURES

On August 22nd at Elk Point SD the men elected carpenter Patrick Gass as sergeant, to replace Charles Floyd, who died two days earlier. Gass was popular both then and now; his journal was the first to be published upon their return, and he lived a very long and interesting life.

On August 25th, the captains and 11 men set out on an excursion to visit a "mountain of evel Spirits" they had heard about from the Indians. The mound was said to have little 18 inch tall people, or devils, who resided there. The walk was long, and they were hot and thirsty; but they satisfied their curiosity and climbed Spirit Mound, north of Vermillion, South Dakota.

The next adventure was much more serious; On August 27th, 19 year old George Shannon, the youngest member of their expedition, got lost. He rambled ahead of the boats on the left side of the Missouri River as it bends northwards, traveling in both Nebraska and South Dakota. The men eventually figured out he was moving ahead of the boats, and caught up with him on September 11th before he starved to death, having eaten only grapes and one rabbit.

While George was lost they encountered their first prairie dog town, caught a live prairie dog; saw their first buffalo herds and killed their first buffalo; and saw the backbone of a 45 foot long prehistoric fish embedded in a hillside. They also held a council with the Yankton Sioux.

YANKTON SIOUX

On August 27th, near the James River, they set the prairie on fire to signal their arrival in the area to the Yankton Sioux. The captains had recruited a well known French trader, Pierre Dorion Sr, to come back up river with them and serve as a Sioux interpreter, when they met him on the Missouri on June 12th. Dorion had lived with the Yankton for over 20 years. The captains asked Dorion to remain with the Yankton in order to escort a group of chiefs to Washington in 1805. It was to prove a fateful decision, because they lost the services of their skilled Sioux interpreter.

The Yankton chiefs counciled with Lewis and Clark at Calumet Bluff from August 29th-31st. Dorion was to arrange as many peace talks as he could between the Yankton and their enemies. The Yankton chiefs told them they were "only at peace with 8 Nations, and agreeable to their Calculation at war with 20 odd." Clark learned the Yankton were part of the Dakota Sioux, who were divided "into 20 tribes possessing Sepperate interest." It was estimated the Dakota tribes had 2000-3000 warriors, and at least 40 traders living among them. They roamed the prairies and grew no corn, but relied on hunting and digging prairie turnips to eat, and trading for food with the village Indians.

NATIVE AMERICAN SCENIC BYWAY

As the Discovery Corps proceeded up the Missouri they began to see absolutely immense herds of animals—buffalo, antelope, deer and elk—thousands at a time, as far as the eye could see. Lewis saw antelope run so fast, that he compared it to the flight of birds. He measured a rabbit's leap at 21 feet; and saw a prairie dog town half a mile square on a side.

Fort Manuel, where Sacagawea died in 1812, is the newest historic attraction on the Native American Scenic Byway. It is located on the Standing Rock Reservation, 7 miles south of the North Dakota/South Dakota border.
South Dakota Tourism

Earth Lodge at Knife River Villages National Historic Site where Sacagawea and her family lived.
North Dakota Tourism

Sacagawea or Sakakawea?
In North Dakota the official spelling of her name is Sakakawea. Either spelling is acceptable. It means "Bird Woman" in Hidatsa.

South Dakota Tourism

6

They reached the "Grand Detour" or the Big Bend of the Missouri River on September 20th. It took two days to go around the bend; it was 30 miles by water, and one mile by land. The Big Bend still exists, and is located on the Lower Brulé and Crow Creek Indian Reservations on the Native American Scenic Byway. Tours may be arranged through the Lower Brule tribe. The National Byway begins at Chamberlain, SD and goes north through the Cheyenne River and Standing Rock Sioux Reservations.

CONFRONTATION WITH THE TETON SIOUX

On September 24th in the vicinity of Pierre SD, John Colter's horse was stolen by some Teton (Brulé) Sioux. That night one third of the men did guard duty; the rest remained on the boats. They held a council with Brulé chiefs, including Black Buffalo and Partisan, the next day. Their island camp that night was named "Bad-Humoured Island." The next few days were tense, mixed with the customary visiting. The two chiefs were rivals for power, and Clark noted, "Black Buffalo Said to be a good man." The lack of an nterpreter was a real handicap.

The Brulé had recently been in a battle with the Omaha, and had killed 75 warriors, and taken 48 women and children prisoner. Pierre Cruzatte learned from the Omaha that the Sioux planned to "Stop our progress and if possible rob us." They didn't sleep that night, and left the next day. Black Buffalo accompanied them on board the keelboat for two days. His support, and the captains' resolve and show of force, had prevented any further trouble.

Eight years later during the War of 1812, William Clark and Manuel Lisa persuaded Black Buffalo to keep the Dakota tribes neutral and out of the war. Their personal knowledge and respect for one another made the difference.

THE ARIKARA VILLAGES

They reached the three Arikara Villages near the Grand River on October 8th, where the Lake Oahe Reservoir is located today. The Arikara, who are related to the Pawnee, spoke a Caddoan language. They lived in earth lodges in fortified villages, and raised corn, beans, squash, pumpkins, watermelon and tobacco, which they traded for goods from the Sioux. The captains were now entering the complex trading network of the village Indians.

The Arikara were devastated by smallpox epidemics that began in the 1780's; they had lost about 75% of their population, which once numbered 25,000-30,000 people. Neighboring village tribes had been similiarly stricken. The villages were the combined remnants of many different tribal bands.

The captains believed they could act as peace makers between the Arikara, Sioux, and their neighbors to the north, the Mandan and Hidatsa. Instead, they would be involved in difficulties with them for years to come.

WINTER AT FORT MANDAN

The expedition wintered at the Mandan and Hidatsa Indian villages, north of present day Bismarck, North Dakota. The Mandans numbered about 1250 people, and lived in two villages on the Missouri. A few miles to the north, the Hidatsa lived in three villages along the Knife river. They numbered about 2700 people. On November 7th, the Corps begin building Fort Mandan near the first village of the Mandans, Big White's (Sheheke's) Village. Big White would accompany them to Washington to meet the President on their return journey in 1806.

The five villages were the major trading center of the northern plains. Several British traders were in residence. A French trader Toussaint Charbonneau and his two Shoshone wives lived with the Hidatsas. The captains knew they needed to obtain horses from the Shoshones to cross the Rocky Mountains, so they arranged for Charbonneau and one of his wifes, Sacagawea, to come with them as interpreters. On February 11, 1805 Sacagawea gave birth to her first child, Jean Baptiste, at Fort Mandan. Meriwether Lewis helped deliver the baby.

On April 6th, the expedition departed for the Pacific Coast. The keelboat was sent back to St Louis with treasures for President Jefferson including reports, specimens, and one live prairie dog. They proceeded on in the two pirogues and six dugout canoes. The permanent party numbered 34 individuals, including the baby.

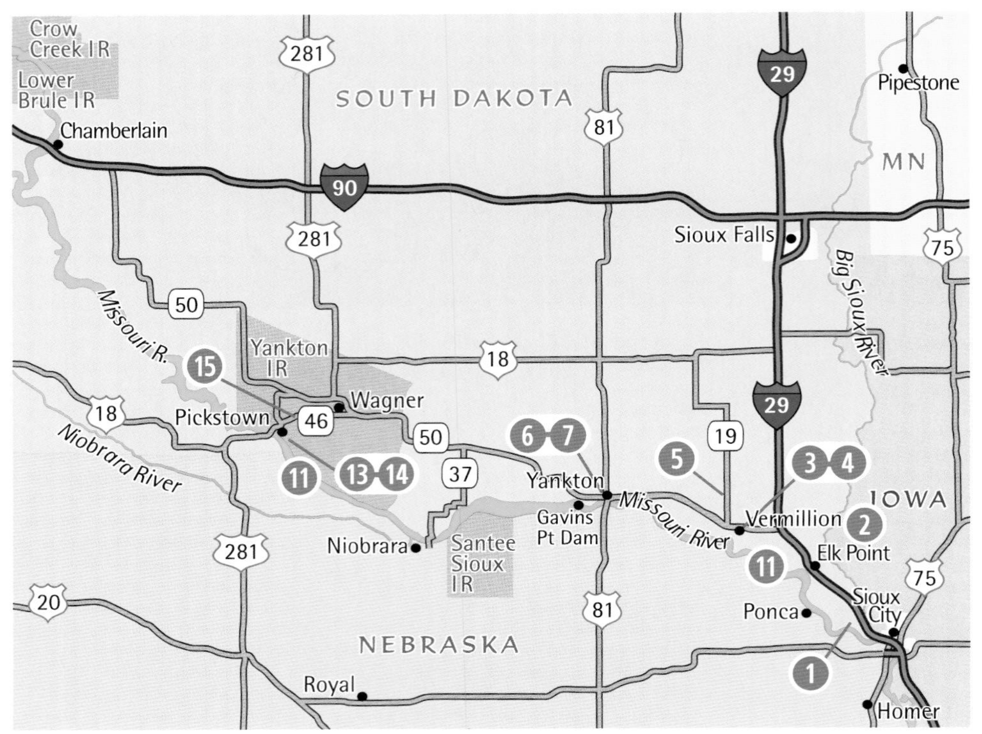

Sioux City, Iowa to Chamberlain, South Dakota

Festivals and Pow Wows

Elk Point Lewis and Clark Heritage Days Festival 3rd wkd in August. Annual Gass Election August 22nd. www.elkpoint.org (605) 356-3336

Vermillion Lewis and Clark Festival 2nd to last wkd in August. W H Over Museum (800) 809-2071 www.usd.edu/whover

Yankton Lewis and Clark Festival 4th wkd in August. (800) 888-1460 www.lewisandclarkfestival.org

Fort Randall Traditional pow wow 1st full wkd in August at Lake Andes near Wagner. (605) 384-5836 www.yanktonsiouxtourism.com

6

1 ADAMS HOMESTEAD AND NATURE PRESERVE McCOOK LAKE SD
272 Westshore Drive.
From I-29 Exit 4 go west on Rte 23 (Northshore Dr). Bear left (south) onto Westshore Dr.

2 ELK POINT HERITAGE PARK ELK POINT SD
From I-29 Exit 18 go right (southeast) onto Main St. Turn right (southwest) onto Harrison St.

3 W H OVER MUSEUM VERMILLION SD
1110 Ratingen Street.
From I-29 Exit 26 go west on Rte 50 for 7 miles. Turn left (south) onto Ratingen St

4 NATIONAL MUSIC MUSEUM VERMILLION SD
414 East Clark Street.
From I-29 Exit 26 go west on Rte 50 for 7 miles. Turn left (south) onto Pine St. Turn right (west) onto Clark St. Go to Yale St.

5 SPIRIT MOUND VERMILLION SD
Rte 19 and 313th St.
From I-29 Exit 31 go west on Rte 11 road changes name to 313th St. Turn right (north) onto Rte 19. Go 0.3 mile to Mound.

6 PIERRE DORION GRAVE YANKTON SD
West 2nd St and Riverside Drive.
From I-29 Exit 26 go west on Rte 50 for 32 miles. Entering Yankton Rte 50 bends left (southwest). Turn right (west) onto 2nd St. 2nd St ends at Riverside Dr.

7 DAKOTA TERRITORIAL MUSEUM YANKTON SD
610 Summit Street.
From I-29 Exit 26 go west on Rte 50 for 32 miles. Entering Yankton Rte 50 bends left (southwest). Turn right (west) onto 4th St Turn right (north) onto Summit St.

8 GAVINS POINT DAM AND POWERPLANT YANKTON SD
From US 81 - Rte 50 Jct in Yankton go south across the Missouri River on US 81. Turn right (west) onto Rte 121. Go 4 miles.

9 GAVINS POINT FISH HATCHERY/ AQUARIUM YANKTON SD
From US 81 - Rte 50 Jct in Yankton go west on Rte 52 (4th St). Rte 52 (Summit St) turns right (northwest) and then north. Rte 52 then turns left (west) on 8th St. Go 3.5 miles to the Fish Hatchery Rd. Turn left (south).

Fort Randall Dam to Gavins Point Dam, Yankton SD

10 LEWIS AND CLARK VISITOR CENTER HISTORIC CALUMET BLUFF
From US 81 - Rte 50 Jct in Yankton go south across the Missouri River on US 81. Turn right (west) onto Rte 121. Go 4 miles.

11 MISSOURI NATIONAL RECREATIONAL RIVER
39 miles from Fort Randall Dam to Running Water SD (Standing Bear Bridge), and 59 miles from Gavins Point Dam to Ponca State Park.

12 LEWIS AND CLARK RECREATION AREA YANKTON SD
From US 81 - Rte 50 Jct in Yankton go west on Rte 52 (4th St). Rte 52 turns northwest, then north, then west. Go 8 miles west on 8th St.

13 FORT RANDALL DAM AND VISITOR CENTER PICKSTOWN SD
From the junction of US 281 and US 18 in Pickstown take US 281/18 west 0.6 mile to the Fort Randall Dam Visitor Center.

14 OLD FORT RANDALL MILITARY POST PICKSTOWN SD
From Pickstown take US 281/18 west 1.5 miles to local road that descends south to the base of the dam. Go one mile to the old Fort.

15 FORT RANDALL CASINO, HOTEL AND RESTAURANT WAGNER SD
Located on Rte 46 three miles east of Fort Randall Dam on the Yankton Sioux Reservation.

Eugene Gass Painter, great grandson of Patrick Gass at Elk Point Evelyn Orr

Spirit Mound
South Dakota Tourism

Lewis and Clark Visitor Center at Calumet Bluff Lee Myers

Fort Randall Casino and Hotel
South Dakota Tourism

Sioux City to Chamberlain

1 ADAMS HOMESTEAD AND NATURE PRESERVE– NORTH SIOUX CITY SD

Several restored buildings, an 1872 farmhouse, barn, log cabin, church and school, with more than 10 miles of hiking/biking trails. The 1500 acre nature preserve is along one of the last free flowing segments of the Missouri River.

■ Open year round. Call ahead for visitor hours. Golf cart guided tours for visitors with physical limitations. Free admission.
(605) 232-0873 www.sdgfp.info

2 ELK POINT HERITAGE PARK ELK POINT SD

On August 22, 1804 Patrick Gass was elected Sergeant to replace Sgt. Charles Floyd. A bust of Patrick Gass and interpretive panels are displayed in the city park, as well as the flags of seven Indian tribes who once lived here.

■ Elk Point Heritage Days are held around August 22nd with a Rendezvous Camp, Native American dancing and more. Free admission.

■ Campground with electrical hookups, $10 a day, first come, first served.
(605) 356-3336 or 356-2164
www.elkpoint.org

3 W H OVER MUSEUM–VERMILLION SD

The museum hosts an annual Lewis and Clark Festival in late August. The museum has the largest natural and cultural history collections in South Dakota; it has outstanding exhibits of Sioux artifacts, and over 500 photographs of territorial days (1869-1883) by Stanley Morris. Gift shop.

■ Open daily. Mon-Fri, 9-5;Sat, 9:30-4:30; Sun,1-4:30. Free admission.Donations welcome.
(605) 677-5228 www.usd.edu/whover

4 NATIONAL MUSIC MUSEUM VERMILLION SD

The museum is world famous for its collection of more than 10,000 musical instruments, from all cultures and all time periods; it attracts visitors and researchers from all over the world. The Center is part of the Univ of SD's Vermillion campus. There are frequent concerts and conferences, and Friday noon brown bag lunches. A free self-guided audio tour with 50 stops is highly recommended.

■ Open daily. Mon-Sat, 9-5; Sun, 2-5. Suggested donation: $7 adults, $3 students.
(605) 677-5306 www.usd.edu/smm

5 SPIRIT MOUND HISTORIC PRAIRIE VERMILLION SD

On August 25th, 1804 Lewis and Clark led a small expedition to investigate Spirit Mound, where little 18 inch devils with big heads were supposed to live; armed with sharp arrows, they killed all those who dared to approach the hill. What they found was a beautiful landscape with a view of buffalo and elk herds in every direction. A 3/4 mile hiking trail leads to the summit of Spirit Mound today.

■ Open year round. (605) 987-2263
www.sdgfp.info

6 PIERRE DORION GRAVE–YANKTON SD

The French-Canadian trader, who had a Yankton Sioux wife, was the first white settler in the Yankton area. He served as interpreter at the Calumet Bluff Council, and escorted tribal delegations to Washington DC in 1805. His son, Pierre Jr. went with the Hunt-Astorian Expedition to Oregon in 1811.

■ (800) 888-1460 www.yanktonsd.com

7 DAKOTA TERRITORIAL MUSEUM YANKTON SD

Yankton was capital of Dakota Territory from 1861-83. The complex has the Main Museum, a reconstructed Territorial Council building, railroad depot, one-room schoolhouse, and old caboose. Plus a collection of fishing tackle and General Custer's band instruments.

■ Open last wkd May-1st wkd Sept, Tues-Sat, 10-5, and Sun, 12-4. Off season hours are Tues-Fri, 1-5. (605) 665-3898
www.lewisandclarktrail.com

8 GAVINS POINT DAM–YANKTON SD

■ Powerplant tours are given last wkd in May to 1st wkd in Sept, on Fri, Sat, Sun and holidays from 10-6. and by appt. (402) 667-7873
www.nwo.usace.army.mil

9 GAVINS POINT FISH HATCHERY AND AQUARIUM–YANKTON SD

Gavins Point raises the endangered pallid sturgeon and paddlefish, and 12-16 other species of sport fish. 36 outdoor ponds and an aquarium.

■ Aquarium open daily May-Sept. and on weekdays during April and October. Hatchery open year round. Admission donation 25¢.
(605) 665-3352
www.r6.fws.gov/gavinspoint

10 LEWIS AND CLARK VISITOR CENTER

The Visitor Center on Calumet Bluff has exhibits and films, a large bookstore, wayside exhibits, and the Dorian Prairie Garden. An annual Lewis and Clark Festival is held in late August on the shores of Lake Yankton below the dam. Reenactors and Native Americans commemorate the Calumet Bluff Council.

■ Open daily last wkd May to 1st wkd Sept, from 8-6 (8-7 on Fri-Sat). Off season open weekdays, 8-4:30. (402) 667-2546
www.now.usace.army.mil

11 MISSOURI NAT'L RECREATIONAL RIVER

Two sections of the river endure in a relatively natural state: 59 miles from Ponca State Park to Gavins Point Dam, and 39 miles from Fort Randall Dam to Running Water SD. The Lewis and Clark Visitor Center has information.

■ (402) 667-2546 www.nps.gov/mnrr

12 LEWIS AND CLARK LAKE NE AND SD STATE RECREATION AREAS

A very popular resort lake, with motels, cabins, campgrounds, rent-a-campers, and recreation.

■ (605) 665-2680 Lewis and Clark Resort
(605) 668-2985 South Dakota SRA
(800) 826-7275 Nebraska SRA
www.sdgfp.info www.outdoornebraska.org

13 FORT RANDALL DAM AND VISITOR CENTER– PICKSTOWN SD

■ Powerplant tours, last wkd May-1st wkd Sept, daily at 10, 1, and 3. Visitor Center open last wkd May-1st wkd Sept, daily, 8:30-6.
(605) 487-7847 x 3223
www.nwo02.usace.army.mil

14 OLD FORT RANDALL MILITARY POST–PICKSTOWN SD

The old chapel ruins, cemetery, and an interpretive trail are all that are left of this 1856 fort. The nearby visitor center has exhibits.

■ Use Fort Randall Visitor Center contact info

15 FORT RANDALL CASINO, HOTEL AND RESTAURANT–WAGNER SD

The Yankton Sioux welcome visitors. A 3-story hotel adjoins the casino and restaurant. They also offer step-on guided tours. Check their website for several annual pow wows.

■ (800) 362-6333 hotel/casino
www.fortrandall.com

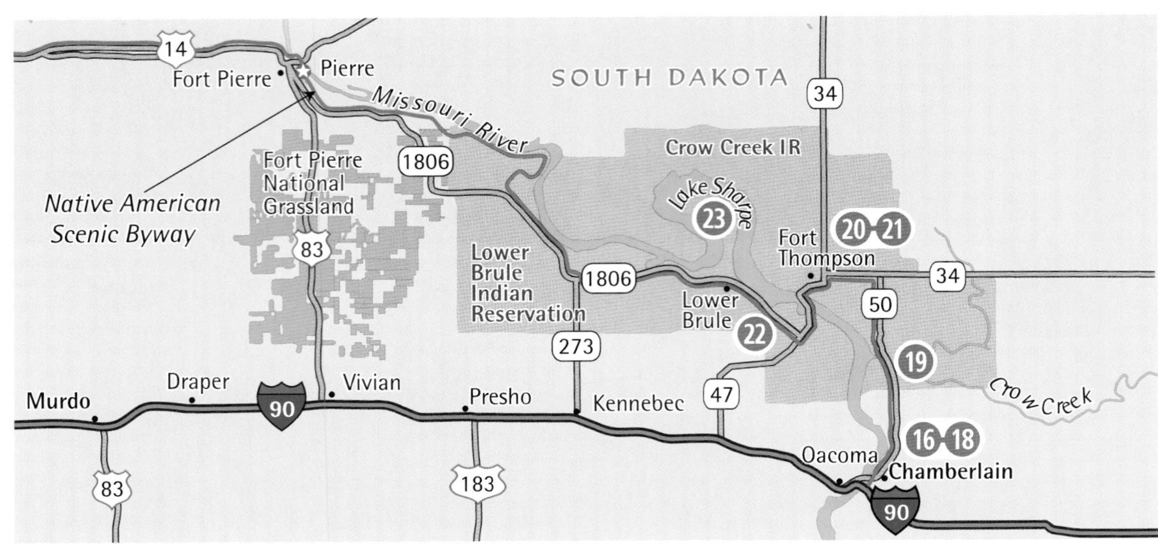

National Native American Scenic Byway (red line) from Chamberlain to Pierre

6

16 LEWIS AND CLARK INFORMATION CENTER
I-90
CHAMBERLAIN, SD

The Interpretive Center is in the Chamberlain Rest Area Facility on I-90 between Exits 263 and 265.

17 AKTA LAKOTA MUSEUM AND CULTURAL CENTER
CHAMBERLAIN, SD

Red Cloud Drive.
From I-90 Exit 263 go north onto Main St. Follow Main St 1.5 miles to Joseph St. Turn left (north). Go 0.2 mile to Red Cloud Dr. Turn left (west) to Museum.

18 SOUTH DAKOTA HALL OF FAME
CHAMBERLAIN, SD

1480 South Main Street.
From I-90 Exit 263 go north onto Main St. The Hall of Fame is on the south end of Main St.

19 SIOUX CROSSING OF THE THREE RIVERS
CROW CREEK SIOUX RESERVATION
SOUTH DAKOTA

Crow, Wolf, and Campbell Creeks.
From I-29 Exit 263 go north 16 miles on Rte 50 to BIA 4.

20 BIG BEND DAM AND POWER PLANT
LAKE SHARPE
FORT THOMPSON, SD

Route 34 and Route 47.
From I-90 Exit 248 go 18 miles north on Rte 47 to Dam site.

21 LODE STAR CASINO, RESTAURANT AND HOTEL
FORT THOMPSON, SD

Route 34 and Route 47.
From I-90 Exit 248 go 21 miles north on Rte 47 to junction with Rte 34.

22 GOLDEN BUFFALO CASINO, RESTAURANT AND MOTEL
LOWER BRULE, SD

321 Sitting Bull Street.
From I-90 Exit 248 go 6.6 miles north on Rte 47. Turn left (north) onto BIA 10. Go 7.1 miles. Turn left (north) onto Rte 1806. Go 0.7 mile. Turn left (west) to stay on Rte 1804. Go 0.4 mile. Turn right (north) onto Iron Nation St.. Go three blocks to the Casino.

23 LOWER BRULE SIOUX BUFFALO INTERPRETIVE CENTER
LOWER BRULE, SD

29349 Highway 1806.
From I-90 Exit 235 Go 12.6 miles north on Rte 273. Turn left (west onto Rte 1806. Go 16 miles. to the Buffalo Interpretive Center.

National Native American Scenic Byway

The National Native American Scenic Byway starts at Oacoma-Chamberlain in South Dakota and heads north on back roads from Interstate 90; it generally following the route of Highway 1806 in South Dakota and North Dakota. The Byway ends in Bismarck ND.

In 1976, both states commemorated the Lewis and Clark Expedition by designating various highway segments as 1806 on the west side of the Missouri River, and 1804 on the east side of the river. The Byway route takes travelers through four reservations of the Great Sioux Nation: the Crow Creek and Lower Brule in SD; and the Cheyenne River and Standing Rock on the SD/ND border and ND.

Lower Brule and Crow Creek Pow Wows

The Lower Brule Wacipi, Fair and Rodeo is held on the 2nd weekend in August. There are hundreds of dancers and over 20 drums present.

The Crow Creek Wacipi and Fair is held on the 3rd weekend in August. It features a nationally recognized Native American Art Show and Auction.

Everyone is welcome to attend these pow wows. Wacipi is pronounced "wa chee pee" and is the Lakota word for pow wow. Please visit the Alliance of Tribal Tourism Advocates to learn more about pow wows.

- www.attatribal.com
- www.lbst.org

Adventures on the Big Bend

The Big Bend of the Missouri River was also called the "Grand deTour" by Lewis and Clark. They measured it as 30 miles around by water, and about one mile across by land at the neck of the bend. On the night of Sept. 21st, 1804 while they were camping on a sandbar on the Big Bend, the segeant on guard duty realized that the sand bar was giving away. They quickly got on board the boats and shoved off. They had not got to the opposite shore before part of their campsite fell into the river.

As the traveled around the Big Bend Clark described the scene: "a butifull inclined Plain in which there is great numbers of Buffalow, Elk and Goats (antelopes) in view feeding and Scipping on these Plains." The prairies had "Great qts. of Prickley Pear."

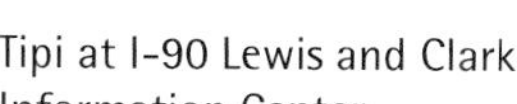

Tipi at I-90 Lewis and Clark Information Center

Trail Rider
South Dakota Tourism

Akta Lakota Museum
South Dakota Tourism

Lower Brule Buffalo Interpretive Center
South Dakota Tourism

Big Bend Country: Chamberlain to Pierre on the National Native American Scenic Byway

16 LEWIS AND CLARK INFORMATION CENTER AT I-90—CHAMBERLAIN

The Visitor Information Center at Exit 265 sits high on a bluff above the river. The building has a 30 foot glass wall, with the stern of a replica keelboat coming through it to serve as an outdoor observation deck. Exhibits show the supplies the expedition brought with them and camp life. Lewis and Clark and other audio travel tapes and CDs are available at all South Dakota's Interstate Information Centers.

■ Open daily from May-Oct, 8 AM-8 PM. Free admission.
(605) 734-4562 information center
(605) 734-4416 www.chamberlainsd.org

17 AKTA LAKOTA MUSEUM AND CULTURAL CENTER—CHAMBERLAIN

Akta Lakota means "to honor the people." The museum is part of the St. Joseph's Indian School, and is located on its campus. The museum, which attracts visitors from all over the world, features a renowned collection of art by Lakota, Dakota and Nakota artists, and unique cultural displays. Large gift shop and bookstore.

■ Open daily from last wkd in May to 1st wkd in Sept. Mon-Sat, 8-6; Sun, 9-5. Open 8-5 during off season, and closed weekends.
(800) 798-3452 or (605) 734-3452
www.aktalakota.org www.stjo.org

18 SOUTH DAKOTA HALL OF FAME CHAMBERLAIN

The private museum honors people who have lived some portion of their lives in South Dakota. It includes a Wells Fargo Theater, interactive displays, Indian artifacts and a Walk of Fame. Sitting Bull and Crazy Horse are among the honorees.

■ Open daily from last wkd May to 1st wkd Sept. Hours, Mon-Fri, 10-5, Sat, 10-4 and Sun, 1-4. (Closed Sat-Sun, Sept-April). Free admission, donations are helpful.
(800) 697-3130 or (605) 734-4216
www.sdhalloffame.com

19 SIOUX CROSSING OF THE THREE RIVERS HWY 50, CROW CREEK SIOUX RESERV.

On September 19th, 1804 Clark wrote: "I walked on Shore to See this great Pass of the Sioux and Calumet ground." He explained that it was "the place that all nations who meet are at peace with each other. Called the Seaux pass of the 3 rivers." Even if rival or enemy tribes crossed the Missouri River at the area of the three creeks, it was a guaranteed neutral zone. Pipestone Quarry in southwestern Minnesota, which supplies the soft red stone for peace pipes (calumets) was another neutral ground. The three creeks are Wolf Creek, Crow Creek and Campbell Creek.

■ (605) 245-2221 Crow Creek Sioux Tribe

20 BIG BEND DAM/LAKE SHARPE RECREATION AREA AND CROW CREEK/ LOWER BRULE RESERVATION TOURS

The Big Bend is the biggest, naturally occurring, bend of any river in the US. The Big Bend Dam, located at Fort Thompson, creates the 80 mile Lake Sharpe Reservoir that goes north past Pierre to Oahe Power Plant. Lake Sharpe has 24 different Recreation Areas campgrounds; Left Tailrace, two miles from Fort Thompson, is a highly developed RV campground on the Crow Creek Reservation with 81 campsites.

Fort Thompson is tribal headquarters for the Crow Creek Reservation. The tribe's wildlife department offers guided fishing and hunting trips. The tribe maintains a buffalo herd that grazes north of Fort Thompson. Buffalo tours and visits to historic sites are provided. The "Spirit of the Circle" Monument commemorates the Dakota and Winnebago warriors imprisoned at Fort Thompson at the end of Dakota Minnesota Uprising in 1862.

The Lower Brule Reservation is located on the western side of the river, which provides access to the "Narrows" of the Big Bend. They offer a variety of tours including hunting and fishing guided tours; "Heart of the Sioux Nation" cultural tours in the summer which include overnight tipi accomodations; and guided tours to the "Narrows," located 3½ miles north of the tribal offices in the town of Lower Brule.

■ Power plant tours daily, last wkd May to 1st wkd Sept, between 10 AM-1 PM. Tours by appt may be scheduled. (605) 245-2255
■ Left Tailrace Recreation Area. 81 campsites. (605) 245-2255 www.sdgfp.info
■ Crow Creek Reservation tours; and guided fishing/hunting trips. (605) 245-2221
■ Lower Brule Reservation and the Narrows tours: (605) 473-0561
Hunting/fishing tours: (605) 473-5666

21 LODE STAR CASINO, RESTAURANT AND HOTEL—FORT THOMPSON

The casino restaurant is the place for dining while enjoying the recreational opportunities in the area. The hotel has over 50 rooms and a conference room.

■ Open daily. Mon-Fri, 7 AM-2 AM; Sat-Sun, 7 AM-4AM. Restaurant: Mon-Fri, 7 AM-10 PM; Sat-Sun, 7 AM-11 PM.
info@lodestar.com
(888) 268-1360 or (605) 245-6000

22 GOLDEN BUFFALO CASINO, RESTAURANT AND MOTEL—LOWER BRULE

The casino, restaurant, 38 room motel and convention center are located along the Native American Scenic Byway on the Missouri River.

■ Open daily: 8 AM-midnight. Restaurant: 8 AM-10 PM. (605) 473-5577 www.lbst.org
Motel reservations: (605) 473-5577

23 LOWER BRULE SIOUX BUFFALO INTERPRETIVE CENTER—LOWER BRULE

The Buffalo Center is located seven miles east of Fort Pierre on Hwy 1806. It has interpretive exhibits, and a gift shop. The Center has a buffalo herd, which occasionally can be seen. The tribe has three buffalo herds.

■ Open Mar-Oct, Mon-Fri, 8-5. Call to inquire about possible weekend hours.
(605) 473-5561 www.lbst.org

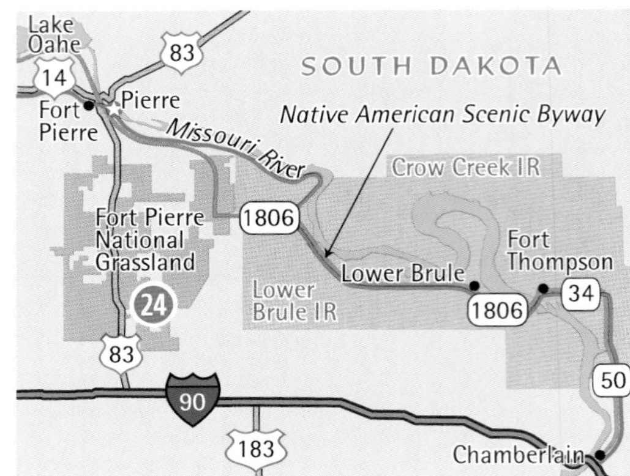

I-90 Route to Pierre

South Dakota Tourism

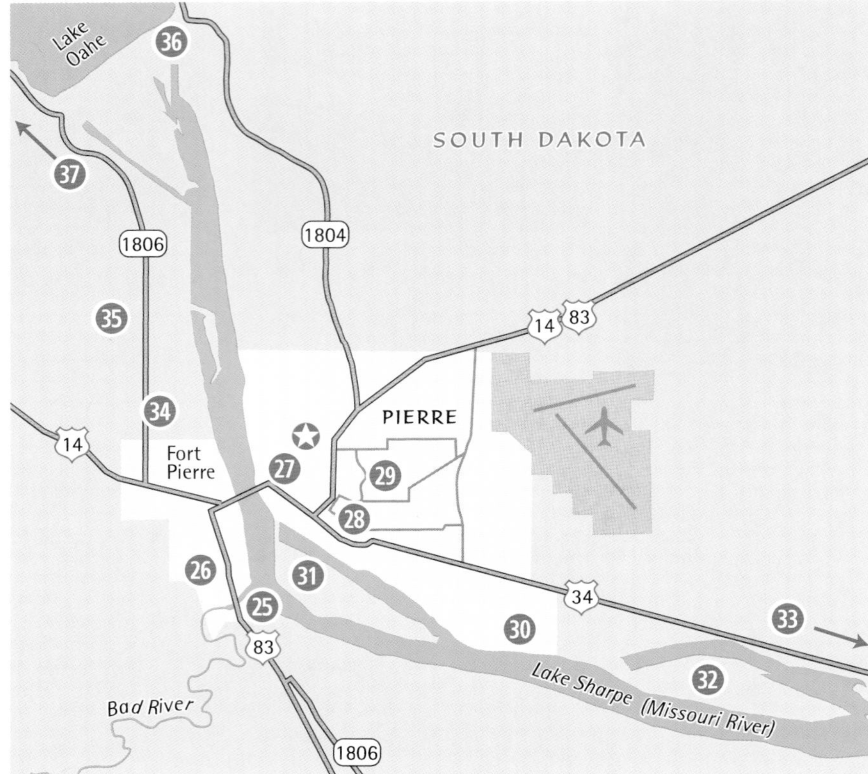

Fort Pierre and Pierre

24 FORT PIERRE NATIONAL GRASSLANDS, SD
US 83 running between I-90 and Rte 34 is the main highway through the grasslands.

25 LILLY PARK
FORT PIERRE, SD
From US 83 in Fort Pierre go east on Cedar Ave. Turn left, go about a block, and turn right onto Ash Lane which ends at Lilly Park.

26 VERENDRYE MONUMENT
FORT PIERRE, SD
From US 83 in Fort Pierre go west on Main St to 2nd St. Turn right and follow the road around to the left and up the hill.

27 SD DISCOVERY CENTER AND AQUARIUM
PIERRE, SD
805 West Sioux Avenue.
In Pierre, at the intersection of W Sioux Ave (US 83/US 14) and James St.

28 SOUTH DAKOTA STATE CAPITOL AND CAPITOL LAKE
PIERRE, SD
500 East Capitol Avenue.
From the intersection of US 83 (Sioux Ave) and US 14 (Pierre St) take Pierre St to Pleasant Dr. Turn right . Go to Euclid St. Turn left. Go to Capitol Ave. Turn right. Go two blocks.

29 SOUTH DAKOTA CULTURAL HERITAGE CENTER AND MUSEUM
PIERRE, SD
900 Governors Drive.
From the intersection of US 83 (Sioux Ave) and US 14 (Pierre St) take Pierre St to Pleasant Dr. Turn right . Go to Euclid St. Turn left. Go to Broadway Ave. Turn right. Go to Governors Dr. Turn left . Go 0.3 mile to Museum.

30 PIERRE NATIVE PLANT ARBORETUM AND NATURE AREA
PIERRE, SD
From the intersection of US 83 (Sioux Ave) and US 14 (Pierre St) follow Sioux Ave southeast to Jackson Ave. Turn right. Go to Missouri Ave. Turn left. Go one mile to the Arboretum.

31 LA FRAMBOISE ISLAND
PIERRE, SD
From the intersection of US 83 (Sioux Ave) and US 14 (Pierre St) follow Sioux Ave northwest to Poplar Ave. Turn left. Go to the end of Poplar Ave. Take walking trails onto La Framboise Island.

32 FARM ISLAND STATE PARK VISITOR CENTER
PIERRE, SD
1301 Farm Island Road.
From the intersection of US 83 (Sioux Ave) and US 14 (Pierre St) follow Sioux Ave southeast to Washington Ave. Turn left. Go to Wells Ave. Turn right. Go southeast 1.9 miles on Wells Ave (Rte 34) to Farm Island Rd. Turn right.

33 MEDICINE KNOLL OVERLOOK
PIERRE, SD
From the intersection of US 83 (Sioux Ave) and US 14 (Pierre St) follow Sioux Ave southeast to Washington Ave. Turn left. Go to Wells Ave. Turn right. Go southeast 11.5 miles on Wells Ave (Rte 34) to Medicine Creek Rd.

34 FORT PIERRE CHOUTEAU NAT'L HIST. LANDMARK
FORT PIERRE, SD
From the intersection of US 83 (Sioux Ave) and US 14 (Pierre St) follow Sioux Ave northwest across the river to Rte 1806. Go west one mile then north 1.25 miles to Fort Chouteau Rd. Turn right.

35 SCOTTY PHILIP CEMETERY
FORT PIERRE, SD
From the intersection of US 83 (Sioux Ave) and US 14 (Pierre St) follow Sioux Ave northwest across the river to Rte 1806. Go west one mile then north two miles to CR 908. Go left 0.4 mile.

36 OAHE DAM/OAHE LAKE VISITOR CENTER
PIERRE, SD
From the intersection of US 83 (Sioux Ave) and US 14 (Pierre St) take Pierre St to Pleasant Dr. Turn right . Go to Euclid St Turn left. Go northeast then north onto Rte 14. Go left onto Rte 1804. Go north 6 miles to the Visitor Center.

37 TRIPLE U BUFFALO RANCH
FORT PIERRE, SD
26314 Tatanka Road.
From the intersection of US 83 (Sioux Ave) and US 14 (Pierre St) follow Sioux Ave northwest across the river to Rte 1806. Go 31 miles north to Ranch entrance. Go west 4 miles to Ranch headquarters.

State Capitol of South Dakota
South Dakota Tourism

Cultural Heritage Center/Museum
South Dakota Tourism

Lilly Park, Black Buffalo Plaque
South Dakota Tourism

Oahe Chapel
South Dakota Tourism

Pierre and Fort Pierre

24 FORT PIERRE NATIONAL GRASSLAND

The 116,000 acre mixed grass prairie may be seen from State Road 83 en route to Pierre.
■ Primitive camping. (308) 432-0309
www.fs.fed.us www.trailsandgrasslands.org

25 LILLY PARK—FORT PIERRE

Fischers Lilly Park in Fort Pierre commemorates where the expedition's confrontation with the Teton Sioux took place on September 24-28,1804 at the mouth of the Bad River. It has been developed as a Lewis and Clark National Historic Trail site with modern amenities, and a walking bridge over the Bad River. The park has 6 RV pads, first serve basis with no stay limit.
.■ (605)223-7679 www.fortpierre.com

26 VERENDRYE MONUMENT NATIONAL HISTORIC LANDMARK—FT PIERRE

The great Canadian explorers, the Verendryes, claimed this land (the entire Louisiana Purchase) for France in 1743 by burying a lead plate on this scenic overlook. A group of teenagers found the plate in 1913, which now is on exhibit at the South Dakota Cultural Heritage Center and Museum in Pierre. The Verendrye Plate is considered one of the most historically significant finds in the northwestern US.
.■ www.fortpierre.com (605) 223-7679
www.laverendryetrail.mb.ca

27 SOUTH DAKOTA DISCOVERY CENTER AND AQUARIUM—PIERRE

A science playground for all ages which provides over 60 interactive exhibits and activities.
■ Open Memorial Day to Labor Day, 1-5, Sunday-Friday, and 10-5 Saturday. Open Labor Day to Memorial Day, 10-5, Mon-Sat, and 1-5 Sun. Admission: $4 adult; $3, 3-12; under 3, free. (605) 224-8295 www.sd-discovery.com

28 SOUTH DAKOTA STATE CAPITOL AND CAPITOL LAKE—PIERRE

The population of Pierre is about 14,000. The population of Fort Pierre across the Missouri River (Lake Sharpe) is about 2,000. The public buildings in South Dakota's capital city are magnificent. The capitol was built in 1910 and restored in time for the state's centennial celebration in 1989. Capitol Lake is visited by migratory birds in the fall, and is the home of three war veteran memorials and a perpetual flame honoring veterans.
■ Open daily, 8 AM-10 PM. Self guided tour brochures are available at the Capitol; call several days in advance for guided tours.
(605) 773-3765
www.travelsd.com/parks/capitol

29 SOUTH DAKOTA CULTURAL HERITAGE CENTER AND MUSEUM—PIERRE

The museum documents the heritage of the diverse ethnic populations that settled South Dakota and has a large collection of Sioux artifacts beautifully displayed. The SD Historical Society is headquartered here. Gift shop.
■ Open daily. Last wkd in May to 1st wkd Sept, Mon-Sat, 9-6:30; Sun, 1-4:30. Off season, Mon-Sat, 9-4:30 and Sun, 1-4:30. Admission: $4, adults; $3 seniors; free, ages 17 and under. (605) 773-3458 www.sdhistory.org

30 PIERRE NATIVE PLANT ARBORETUM AND NATURE AREA-PIERRE

Miles of hiking paths follow the Missouri River in this mixed flood plain arboretum. Early morning walks reveal many kinds of wildlife.
■ www.pierrechamber.com. Contact the urban forestry ranger for tours at (605) 773-3594.

31 LA FRAMBOISE ISLAND—PIERRE

The tree covered island which Lewis and Clark named "Good Humored Island" has seven miles of hiking/biking trails and wildlife. Joseph La Framboise had a trading post here from 1817-1822. It was the beginning of Pierre, the oldest continuous white settlement west of the Missouri River. They named another island "Bad humoured Island" (today's Marion Island) after the encounter with the Sioux at today's Fischers Lilly Park.
■ (800) 962-2034 or (605) 224-7361
www.pierrechamber.com

32 FARM ISLAND RECREATION AREA AND LEWIS AND CLARK CENTER—PIERRE

John Colter camped on this island (which is no longer an island) and killed 4 elk (Sept. 23, 1804). Later it served as a farm for Fort Pierre.
■ Swimming; hiking trail to La Framboise Island; campsites and cabins. Bicycle, canoe and paddleboat rentals. (605) 224-5605
www.sdgfp.info/parks Call (800) 710-2267 for campground reservations, www.campSD.com

33 MEDICINE KNOLL OVERLOOK—PIERRE

A marker commemorates Sept. 22, 1804, when three Sioux boys swam the river to the expedition camp opposite Medicine Creek to tell them the 140 lodges of the Teton Sioux were located a short distance above.
■ (800) 962-2034 or (605) 224-7361
www.pierrechamber.com

34 FORT PIERRE CHOUTEAU NATIONAL HISTORIC LANDMARK FORT PIERRE

The American Fur Company's Fort Pierre was in operation from 1832-55, replacing an earlier Fort Tecumseh. Fort Pierre's stockade enclosed over 100,000 square feet, making it the largest fur trading post on the Upper Missouri.
■ Volunteers are welcome at archeology digs every summer. www.sdhistory.org
(605) 394-1936 or Mike.Fosha@state.sd.us

35 SCOTTY PHILIP CEMETERY—FT PIERRE

The great buffalo herds which once roamed North America are estimated to have numbered 60 million. Today there are estimated 400,000 buffalo thanks to the work of Scotty Philip, a local cattle rancher, and others, both Indian and white, who began raising buffalo when there were only about 1000 left in the late 1800's. Scotty Philip (1858-1911) is buried here.
■ (605) 223-7679 www.fortpierre.com
www.bisoncentral.com

36 OAHE DAM AND POWERPLANT OAHE LAKE VISITOR CENTER—PIERRE

Lake Oahe is the 14th largest man-made reservoir in the world. The Visitor Center and campground are staffed by local volunteers. The old Oahe Chapel is near the dam.
■ Daily powerplant tours: last wkd May-1st wkd Sept; Visitor Center, 9:30, 1 and 3. Bring photo ID. Off season call (605) 224-5862.
■ Visitor Center open last wkd May-1st wkd Sept. Mon-Thurs, 9-5; Fri-Sat, 9-8; Sun, 9-5.
(605) 224-5862 www.nwo.usace.army.mil

37 TRIPLE U BUFFALO RANCH—FT. PIERRE

The 1990 award-winning film *Dances with Wolves* was made here. Home to 3500 buffalo and 60,000 acres of natural prairie. Ranch house lodging. Hunting, Oct-Jan. Gift shop with buffalo souvenirs, meat, and other products. Visitors welcome.
■ (605) 567-3625 www.tripleuranch.com

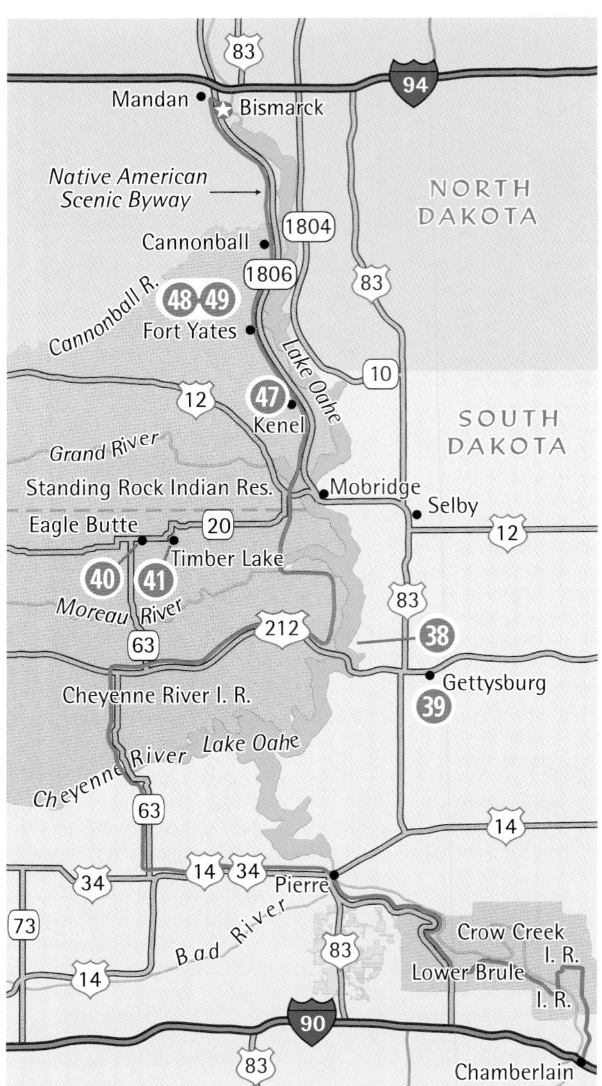

Pierre to Bismarck: Native American Scenic Byway

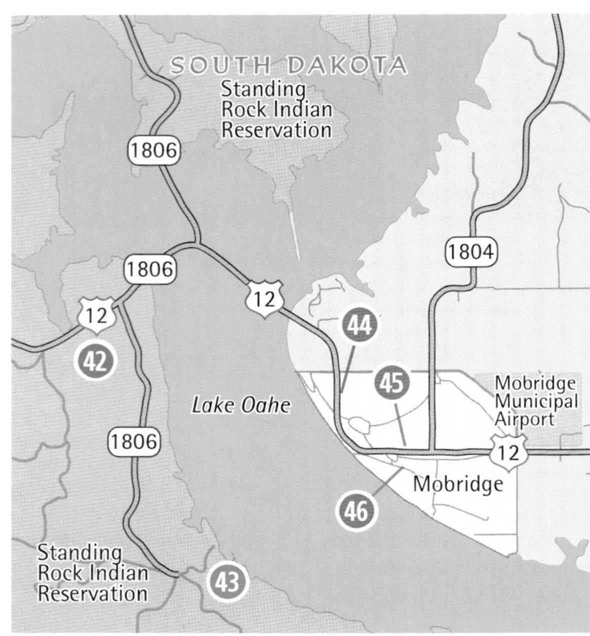

Standing Rock Reservation and Mobridge SD

Prairie Knight Casino and Resort
North Dakota Tourism

Holy Hill of the Mandans
Standing Rock Reservation

38 ARIKARA LODGE/ WHITLOCK RECREATION AREA GETTYSBURG SD

16157A West Whitlock Road.
From US 83 and US 212 Jct go west on US 212. Turn right (north) onto Rte 1804/298 Ave. Turn left (west) onto 160 St. Turn left (south) onto West Whitlock Recr Area Rd.

39 DAKOTA SUNSET MUSEUM GETTYSBURG SD

205 West Commercial Avenue.
From US 83 and US 212 Jct go east on US 212 (Garfield Ave). Turn right (south) onto Main St. Go to Commercial Ave.

40 H V JOHNSTON LAKOTA CULTURAL CENTER EAGLE BUTTE SD

US 212 and Route 19 B.
From US 83 and US 212 Jct go west 65 miles to Rte 19 B.

41 TIMBER LAKE AND AREA MUSEUM—TIMBER LAKE SD

800 Main Street.
From US 12 and Rte 1804 Jct go west, then north, then west across the Missouri River on US 12 for 8.5 miles. Turn left (south) onto Rte 20. Follow Rte 20 for 29.4 miles to Timber Lake. Turn left (south) onto F St. Go 4 blocks. Turn left (east), Go one block to Main St.

42 GRAND RIVER CASINO AND BAY RESORT—MOBRDIGE SD

From US 12 and Rte 1804 Jct go west, then north, then west across the Missouri River on US 12 for 6.6 miles.

43 SITTING BULL AND SACAGAWEA MONUMENTS MOBRIDGE SD

From US 12 and Rte 1804 Jct go west, then north, then west across the Missouri River on US 12. Turn left (south) onto Rte 1806.. Go 3.6 miles. Turn left onto local roads.

44 KLEIN MUSEUM MOBRIDGE SD

1820 West Grand Crossong.
From US 12 and Rte 1804 Jct go west, then north on US 12.

45 INDIAN PRAYER ROCKS MOBRIDGE SD

Mobridge City Park.
From US 12 and Rte 1804 Jct go west 3 blocks on E Grand Crossing. Turn right (north) onto 1st Ave. Go 2 blocks. Turn left (west) onto 7th St.. Go one block to Park.

46 OSCAR HOWE MURALS MOBRIDGE SD

212 North Main Street.
From US 12 and Rte 1804 Jct go west 4 blocks on E Grand Crossing. Turn left (south) onto Main St. Go 3 blocks to the City Auditorium.

47 FORT MANUEL KENEL SD

From US 12 and Rte 1804 Jct go west, then north, then west across the Missouri River on US 12. Turn right (north) onto Rte 1806.. Go 21.6 miles to local road 3/4 mile south of Kenel. Turn left (west).

48 PRAIRIE KNIGHT CASINO AND RESORT FORT YATES ND

7932 Route 24.
From US 12 and Rte 1804 Jct go west, then north, then west across the Missouri River on US 12. Turn right (north) onto Rte 1806.. Go 48.2 miles to 92nd St. Turn right (east). Go 0.8 mile to the Casino.

49 SITTING BULL BURIAL STATE HISTORIC SITE STANDING ROCK RESERV. FORT YATES ND

From US 12 and Rte 1804 Jct go west, then north, then west across the Missouri River on US 12. Turn right (north) onto Rte 1806.. Go 48.2 miles to 92nd St. Turn right (east). Go 1.8 miles. Turn left (north). Go to Burial Site.

Arikara Lodge
South Dakota Tourism

Fort Manuel
South Dakota Tourism

Standing Rock Monument
Standing Rock Reservation

Sitting Bull Monument

Pierre to Bismarck on the National Native American Scenic Byway

38 ARIKARA LODGE, WEST WHITLOCK RECREATION AREA—GETTYSBURG SD

A reconstructed earth lodge stands where there once was an Arikara Village. The Arikara ("Ah-rik-ara") lived and farmed here, supplying garden produce to other tribes in trade. West Whitlock Recreation Area is a popular fishing spot and campground on Lake Oahe.

■ Open year round. Campsites May-Sept. Cabins year round. $5 daily vehicle entrance fee.
(800) 710-2267 or www.CampSD.com
for reservations. (605) 765-9410
www.sdgfp.info/Parks/Regions/OaheSharpe

39 DAKOTA SUNSET MUSEUM GETTYSBURG SD

The museum was built around the 40 ton Medicine Rock sacred to the Lakota people; two murals by Lakota artist Del Iron Cloud portray the Medicine Rock and the museum's big game collection. A 100 year complete blacksmith's shop is also part of this award-winning museum's extensive collections.

■ Open daily, last wkd in May to 1st wkd in Sept, 1-5. Off season, Tues-Sat, 1-5. Free tours are given. Donations welcome. (605) 765-9480
www.venturecomm.net/~dakotasunset

40 H V JOHNSTON LAKOTA CULTURAL CENTER AND CHEYENNE RIVER SIOUX TRIBE RESERVATION TOURS EAGLE BUTTE SD

The Center serves as a local activity center as well as a museum and gift shop. The museum contains a collection of historical artifacts from the Cheyenne River Sioux tribe, including murals, old photographs, beadwork and painting.

Wildlife, eco and culture tours of the reservation, including the bison herd, numbering over 900 buffalo, and elk herd, are available through the nearby Cheyenne River Sioux Tribe Game, Fish and Parks Department.

■ Lakota Center open
(605) 964-2542 www.travelsd.com/history

■ CRSTGFP tours are available for the tribal Buffalo Range and/or the tribal Elk Range. The Elk Range has wild horses also. All tours must be arranged at least two weeks in advance. Overnight tipi stays are optional.
(605) 964-7812 www.crstgfp.com/tours

41 TIMBER LAKE AND AREA MUSEUM TIMBER LAKE SD

One of the finest collections of ammonite fossils in the world is found here. (Ammonites were sea creatures with beautiful ribbed, spiral shells.) The museum has a dinosaur exhibit; Lakota traditional clothing; a working blacksmith shop; and early reservation-era photos and art. Cheyenne River and Standing Rock Sioux materials and other local history items are featured. The museum has a nice gift shop.The historical society across the street has a major collection of documents and photographs.

■ Open Mon-Fri, 9-5. Evenings and weekends by appointment. Free admission.
(605) 865-3553 www.tlsd.us

42 GRAND RIVER CASINO AND BAY RESORT STANDING ROCK RESERVATION SD

The Casino has a new Lodge and restaurant with an all-you-can-eat buffet. The Bay Resort at Grand River is located just northwest of Mobridge; it has cabins and an RV campground. Casino and lodge are 2 miles west of Mobridge.

■ Casino is open 24/7. Dining: 7 AM-11 AM, breakfast menu; 5 PM-10 PM, all-you-can-eat buffet. (800) 475-3321 or (605) 845-7106 for lodging. (605) 845-7104 for gaming.
www.grandrivercasino.com

43 SITTING BULL AND SACAGAWEA MONUMENTS—MOBRIDGE SD

The monument to Sitting Bull, the great Chief of the Hunkpapa Teton Sioux, who was shot and killed on Dec. 15, 1890 on the Standing Rock Reservation after the Masacre at Wounded Knee was carved by the great sculptor Korczak Ziolkowski, the Crazy Horse mountain sculptor. The Sacagawea monument is nearby.

■ www.sittingbullmonument.org
www.crazyhorse.org www.mobridge.org

44 KLEIN MUSEUM—MOBRIDGE SD

The Klein Museum has a distinguished collection of early Indian beadwork and head dresses, clothing, tools and early photographs. There are room displays of early pioneer artifacts. They also have a display of "cannonball rocks" from the Cannonball River. The museum gift shop has authentic Native American beadwork, and and locally produced arts and crafts.

■ Open April-Oct. Mon-Fri from 9-noon and 1-5; Saturdays, 1-5. Closed on Tuesdays in April, May, Sept and Oct.
(605) 845-7243 www.mobridge.org

45 INDIAN PRAYER ROCKS AT CITY PARK MOBRIDGE SD

Indians would take an oath of initiation by placing their hand in the hand prints found in these rocks in the Mobridge City Park. The rocks were dedicated to the public in 1910.
www.mobridge.org

46 OSCAR HOWE MURALS—MOBRIDGE SD

Ten murals painted in 1942 by one of America's most famous Native American artists, Oscar Howe. The murals in the Mobridge City Auditorium Scherr-Howe Arena depict Sioux ceremonies and history. The Oscar Howe Art Gallery is located in Mitchell, SD.

■ (605) 845-3700 (City Auditorium)
www.mobridge.org www.dakotadiscovery.com

47 FORT MANUEL—KENEL SD

Fort Manuel, where Sacagawea died of putrid fever in December of 1812 (see pages 108-109) has been reconstructed near its original site.

■ Open daily May-Oct, 10 AM-6 PM.
(701) 854-8500 www.standingrocktourism.com
www.kenel.org

48 PRAIRIE KNIGHTS CASINO AND RESORT—FORT YATES ND

Deluxe accomodations at the Casino Lodge. Restaurant and buffet. High stakes gaming.

■ Casino open 24/7. Dining: Sun-Thurs, 7 AM-10:30 PM; Fri-Sat, 7:30 AM-11:30 PM.
(800) 425-8277 x 7704 reservations
www.prairieknights.com

49 SITTING BULL BURIAL STATE HISTORIC SITE —FORT YATES RESERVATION TOURS

The Lewis and Clark Legacy Trail, along the bluffs of the Missouri River starts at the Prairie Knights Marina. Tours of the reservation are arranged through the Tourism office. The original gravesite of Sitting Bull is located one mile from the highway. The Standing Rock monument is near the tribal headquarters.

■ Tribal tourism: (701) 854-7214 x 186
www.standingrocktourism.org

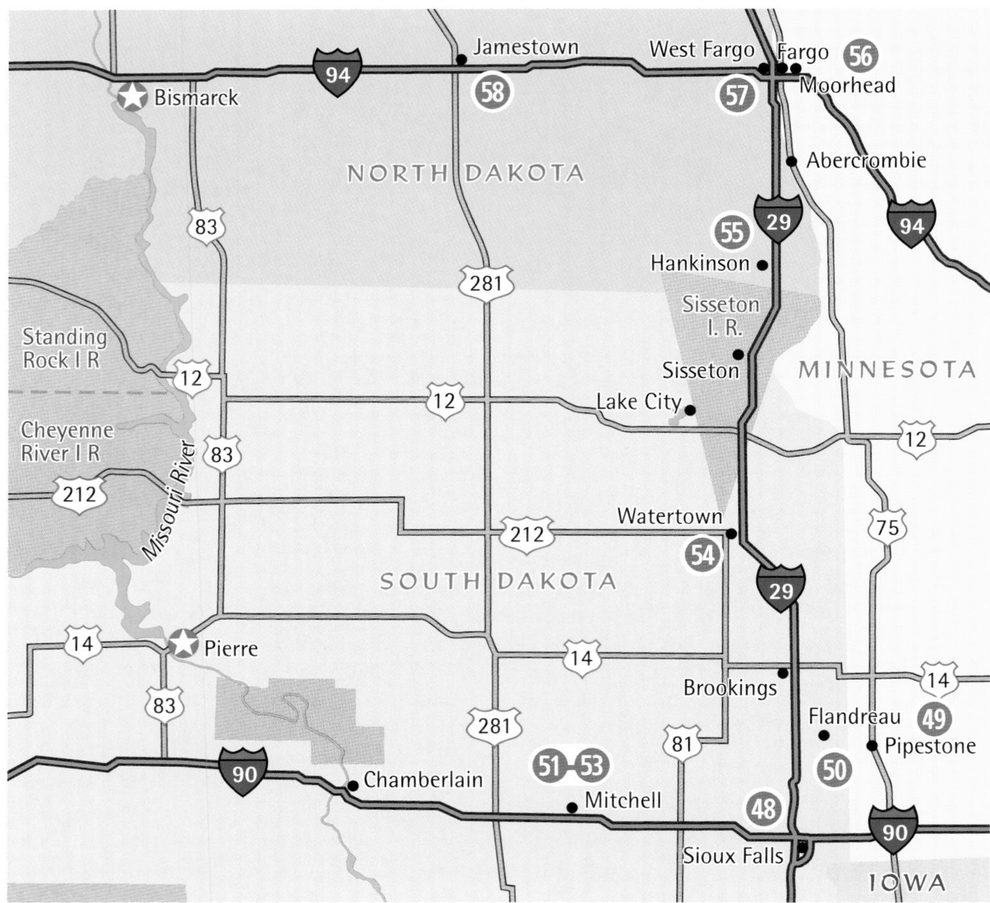

Interstate Routes 29, 90 and 94

50 DELBRIDGE MUSEUM AND GREAT PLAINS ZOO SIOUX FALLS SD

805 South Kiwanis Avenue.

From I-29 Exit 79 go east onto Rte 42 (12th St). Turn right (south) onto Kiwanis Ave. Go three blocks to the Museum.

51 PIPESTONE NATIONAL MONUMENT PIPESTONE MN

36 Reservation Avenue.

From I-29 Exit 109 go east on Rte 34. At state line road changes name to Rte 30. Go to US 75 (8th Ave). Turn left (north). Go to 4th St. Turn left (west). Go to 2nd Ave. Turn right (north) into the Monument.

52 ROYAL RIVER CASINO AND HOTEL FLANDREAU SD

607 South Veterans Street.

From I-29 Exit 114 go east on Rte 32 to Flandreau. Turn right (south) on Veterans St. Go 0.4 mile to Royal River Casino.

53 CORN PALACE MITCHELL SD

604 North Main St.

From I-90 Exit 332 go north onto Burr St. Turn left (west) onto Havens St. Turn right (north) onto Sanborn Blvd. Turn right (east) onto 6th Ave. Go to Main St.

54 MIDDLE BORDER MUSEUM OSCAR HOWE ART CENTER MITCHELL SD

1300 East University Street.

From I-90 Exit 332 go north onto Burr St. Turn left (west) onto Norway Ave. Turn right (north) onto University Ave. Go two blocks to the Museum.

55 MITCHELL PREHISTORIC INDIAN VILLAGE MITCHELL SD

3200 Indian Village Road.

From I-90 Exit 33 go north onto Ohlman St. Go 3.2 miles. Turn right (east) onto Indian Village Rd. Go 0.3 mile to the Village.

56 DAKOTA SIOUX CASINO AND HOTEL WATERTOWN SD

16415 Sioux Conifer Road.

From I-29 Exit 185 go west on 164th St (CR 6). Go 4.6 miles. Turn left (south) on Sioux Conifer Rd. Go 0.1 mile to Casino.

57 DAKOTA SIOUX MAGIC CASINO AND HOTEL HANKINSON ND

46102 Highway 10.

From I-29 Exit 232 go east on Rte 10 (119th St) to the Casino.

58 HERITAGE HJEMKOMST CENTER MOORHEAD MN

202 First Avenue North.

From I-29 Exit 65 go east on US 10 (Main Ave). Turn left (north) onto 2nd St N. Go to First Avenue N.

Mitchell Prehistoric Indian Village

59 BONANZAVILLE USA WEST FARGO ND

1351 Main Avenue W.

From I-94 Exit 343 go east two blocks on Main Ave W to the Bonanzaville Museum.

60 NATIONAL BUFFALO MUSEUM AND FRONTIER VILLAGE JAMESTOWN ND

500 17th Street SW.

From I-94 Exit 258 go north three blocks on US 281 to to 17th St. Turn right (east) and go 0.1 mile to Museum entrance.

Nicollet Marker
Pipestone National Monument

World's Largest Buffalo, Jamestown
N D Tourism, Dawn Charging

Corn Palace
South Dakota Tourism

Heritage Hjemkomst Center
N D Tourism, Dawn Charging

Interstate Route: Sioux City to Bismarck

50 DELBRIDGE MUSEUM AND GREAT PLAINS ZOO—SIOUX FALLS SD

The museum has about 150 mounted specimens of birds and mammals in naturalistic settings representing five continents. They were donated to the museum by Henry Brockhouse, an avid hunter, who created one of the largest collections in the world. Revolving exhibits also.

The museum is located at the Great Plains Zoo. The Zoo is an accredited member of the American Zoo and Aquarium Association and has over 500 animals from around the world. There is an Asian Cat habitat, Bear Canyon, and African Savannah, plus a Children's Zoo.

■ Open daily, Apr-Sept 9-7; Oct-Mar 10-5. Admission: $6.75 adult, $6 senior, $3.75 ages 3-12. (605) 367-7059 www.siouxfallscvb.com

51 PIPESTONE NATIONAL MONUMENT PIPESTONE, MINNESOTA

The pipestone quarries have been a sacred ground for Native Americans for many generations. The soft red stone is used to carve peace pipes and other items. American Indians of all tribes are the only people allowed to quarry stone at the National Monument. Stone specimens and handcrafted items may be purchased in the gift store, where there are craft demonstrations from April-October.

Lewis and Clark knew they were in the vicinity of the quarries, and mentioned it the day after Sgt. Floyd died on August 21, 1804. Clark wrote that it was "a place of Peace with all nations." The Nicollet Expedition exploring the Upper Mississippi carved their initials in the stone in 1838. Pipestone is also known as catlinite; it was named for William Clark's friend, George Catlin, the American artist who painted at the quarries in 1836. Catlin's Indians paintings are on exhibit at the Renwick Gallery in Washington DC. (catlinclassroom.si.edu)

■ Open daily. last wkd May-1st wkd Sept 8-6; Sept-May, 8-5. Admission: $3 individual, $5 family. (507) 825-5464 www.nps.gov/pipe

■ The "Song of Hiawatha Pageant" is presented annually in an outdoor amphitheater on the last two weeks in July, and first weekend in August. (800) 430-4126 (507) 825-4126 www.pipestoneminnesota.com

52 ROYAL RIVER CASINO AND HOTEL, RESTAURANT AND RV PARK—FLANDREAU SD

Owned by the Santee Sioux tribe. There is an award-winning buffet and snack bar. The hotel has murals by the noted Hunkpapa Sioux artist Del Iron Cloud.

■ Casino always open. Restaurant open daily from 7 AM-10 PM.
(800) 833-8666 www.royalrivercasino.com

53 CORN PALACE—MITCHELL SD

The exterior of the Corn Palace is decorated with fresh murals created out of corn and harvest grains every year. Thousands of bushels of corn, grain, grasses, wild oats, brome grass, blue grass, rye, straw and wheat are used. The Corn Palace is a multi-use center in the center of a tourist area.

■ Open daily. Last wkd May-1st wkd Sept 8 AM-9 PM; Apr-May and Sept-Oct, 8-5.
Open Nov-Mar, Mon-Fri 8-5. Free admission.
(866) 273-2676 www.cornpalace.org

54 DAKOTA DISCOVERY CENTER MITCHELL, SOUTH DAKOTA

Lewis and Clark statues greet you at the door of this five building museum complex. Four historic buildings. Exhibit galleries include the Oscar Howe Art Gallery, Middle Border History Gallery, changing exhibits, and many works by well known South Dakotan artists. Gift shop and online store.

■ Open May-Sept Mon-Sat 9-6 Sun 1-4; Oct-Apr Mon-Fri 10-4 Sat 1-4. Admission: $5 adult, $4 senior, $2 ages 6-18.
(605) 996-2122 www.dakotadiscovery.com

55 MITCHELL PREHISTORIC INDIAN VILLAGE NATIONAL HISTORIC LANDMARK

The museum has a video, a model of the village as it appeared a 1000 years ago, a walk through lodge, and many exhibits. Visitors watch from the gallery as archaeologists conduct a dig in the air-conditioned Thomsen Center Archaedome. Outdoor interpretive trail.

■ Open daily: Apr Mon-Fri 9-4; May 9-4; Memorial wkd-Labor Day 8-6; Sept 9-4. Open Mon-Fri 9-4 in Oct, Nov-Mar by appointment. Admission: $6 adult, $5 senior,$4 ages 6-18.
(605) 996-5473 www.mitchellindianvillage.org

56 DAKOTA SIOUX CASINO AND HOTEL WATERTOWN SD

Owned by the Sisseton-Wahpeton Tribe. The Rose Restaurant serves a buffet at 11, Mon-Thurs; at 5:30 on Fri-Sat; and Sun at 10 AM. Full service restaurant. Nightly menu specials also.

■ Casino and restaurant open all day every day. (800) 658-4717 or (605) 882-2051
www.dakotanationgaming.com

57 DAKOTA SIOUX MAGIC CASINO AND HOTEL—HANKINSON ND

Owned by the Sisseton-Wahpeton Tribe. One mile from the SD-ND border. Hotel rooms have data ports on phones, cable tv, other amenities. Seven Fires Restaurant Grill open 24/7.

■ Casino and restaurant open all day every day. (800) 325-6825 or (701) 634-3000
www.dakotanationgaming.com

58 HERITAGE HJEMKOMST CENTER MOORHEAD, MINNESOTA

Another kind of wooden boat, The Hjemkomst Norwegian Viking Ship; Hopperstad Stave Church Replica; and Red River Valley Exhibit.

■ Open Mon 9-5 Tues 9-8 Wed-Sat 9-5 Sun 12-5. Admission: $6 adult, $5 senior, $5 college student, $4 ages 5-17 (218) 299-5511
www.hjemkomst-center.com

59 BONANZAVILLE USA—WEST FARGO ND

A Museum and Historic Village; with one of the region's largest collections of Native American artifacts. Telephone museum; 20 aircraft; 80 cars and other old machinery and buildings.

■ Museum open May Mon-Fri 9-5; Jun-Sept Mon-Sat 10-5 Sun 12-5; Oct-Dec Mon-Fri 12-5 Historic Village open May-Sept.
(701) 282-2822 www.bonanzaville.org

60 NATIONAL BUFFALO MUSEUM AND FRONTIER VILLAGE—JAMESTOWN ND

Home of a sacred white (albino) buffalo and buffalo herd. Buffalo exhibits, art, and a gift shop. Historic Frontier Village.

■ Open last wkd May-1st wkd Sept daily 9-8; Sept-Oct Mon-Fri 9-5 Sat 10-5 Sun 12-5; Nov-Apr Mon-Fri 9-5 Sat 10-5; May Mon-Fri 9-5 Sat 10-5 Sun 12-5. (800) 807-1511 (701) 252-8648
www.buffalomuseum.com

Fort Abraham Lincoln Blockhouse
North Dakota Tourism, Rebecca Pedersen

On-A-Slant Village Arikara Earth Lodge

Double Ditch Shelter Overlook
Kathy Getsinger

The United Tribes International Pow Wow is held the weekend after Labor Day at the United Tribes Technical College in Bismarck, ND. Events start on Thursday and go through Sunday. ■ Admission: $15 weekend pass; $8 one day pass. Elders (60 and over) and children under 5 are free. Free camping on grounds.
(701) 255-3285 www.unitedtribespowwow.com

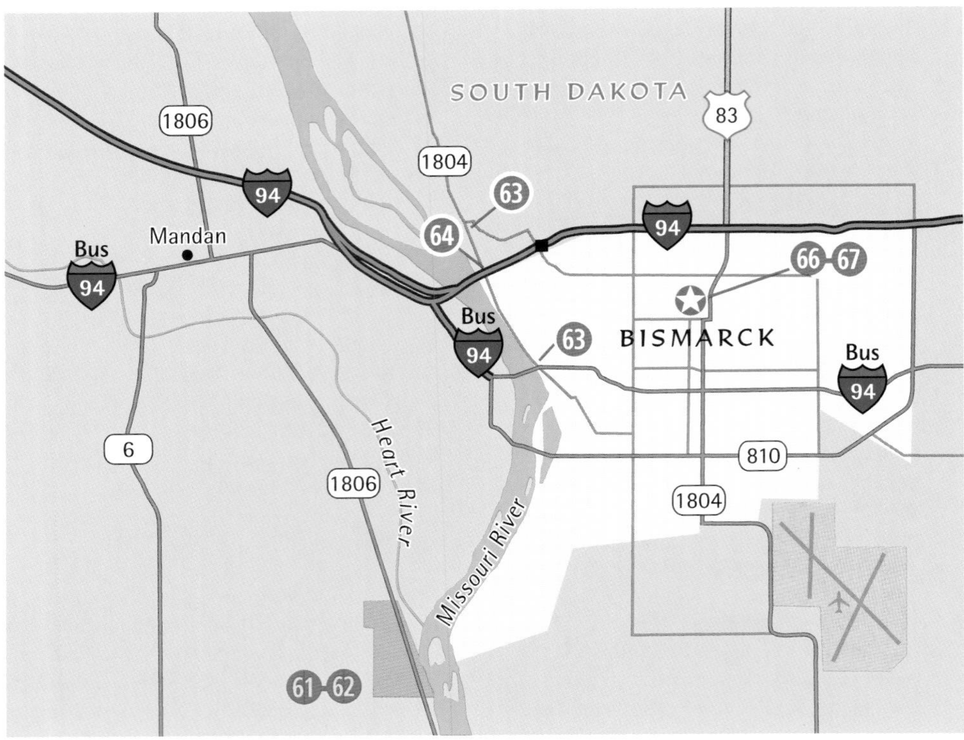

Bismarck, Mandan and Fort Abraham Lincoln State Park

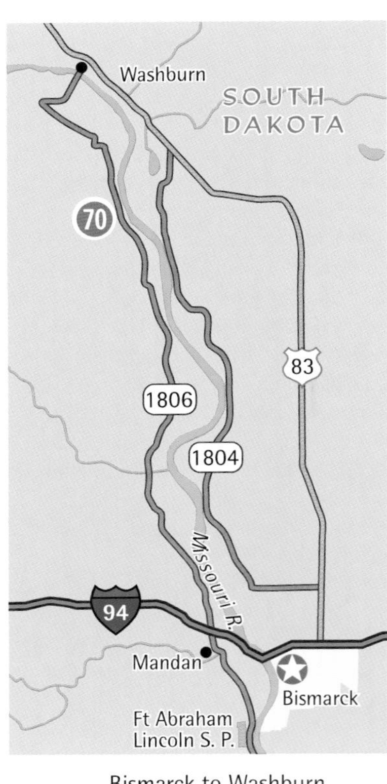

Bismarck to Washburn

61 FORT ABRAHAM LINCOLN STATE PARK AND ON-A-SLANT VILLAGE BISMARCK ND

4480 Fort Lincoln Road.
From I-94 Exit 153 go southeast onto Mandan Ave. Turn right (west) onto Main St. Turn left south onto 6th Ave (Rte 1806). Bear left on Fort McKeen Rd (Rte 1806). Go 1.6 miles to Fort Abraham Lincoln.

62 FIVE NATIONS ARTS MANDAN ND

401 West Main St.
From I-94 Exit 153 go southeast onto Mandan Ave. Go 0.7 mile. Turn right (west) onto Main St. Go 1.1 miles to Five Nations Arts.

63 CHIEF LOOKING'S VILLAGE RIVER OVERLOOK BISMARCK ND

From I-94 Exit 157 go west on Burnt Boat Dr. Turn left (south) onto Broadview Lane. Turn right (west) onto North Grandview Lane.

64 LEWIS AND CLARK RIVERBOAT AND KEELBOAT PARK BISMARCK ND

2300 River Drive.
From I-94 Exit 157 take Tyler Parkway northwest. Turn left (west) onto Burnt Boat Drive. Turn left (south) onto River Road. Go 0.7 mile to Riverboat.

65 CAPTAIN MERIWETHERS BISMARCK

1700 River Road
From I-94 Exit 157 take Tyler Parkway northwest. Turn left (west) onto Burnt Boat Drive. Turn left (south) onto River Road. Go 1.7 mile to restaurant.

66 NORTH DAKOTA STATE CAPITOL BISMARCK ND

600 E Boulevard Avenue.
From I-94 Exit 159 go south onto State Street (Rte 1804). turn right (west) onto E Boulevard Ave.

67 ND HERITAGE CENTER AND SAKAKAWEA STATUE BISMARCK ND

619 E Boulevard Avenue.
From I-94 Exit 159 go south onto State Street (Rte 1804). turn right (west) onto E Boulevard Ave.

68 DOUBLE DITCH INDIAN VILLAGE BISMARCK ND

From I-94 Exit 157 take Tyler Parkway northwest. Turn left (west) onto Burnt Boat Drive.Turn righ (north) onto River Road. Keep straight onto Route 1804. Go 4.7 miles to Double Ditch Indian Village.

Lewis and Clark Riverboat, Bismarck
North Dakota Tourism, Dawn Charging

Five Nations Art Museum
North Dakota Tourism, Dawn Charging

Sakakawea Statue, State Capitol
North Dakota Tourism

Bismarck and Mandan

61 FORT ABRAHAM LINCOLN STATE PARK ON-A-SLANT VILLAGE MANDAN, NORTH DAKOTA

Fort Abraham Lincoln:
The reconstructed Victorian-style residence of General George Armstrong Custer and his wife Libbie is a major attraction at Fort Abraham Lincoln State Park, North Dakota's oldest state park. The Custers lived here from 1873-1876. General Custer died in the Battle of the Little Bighorn on May 17, 1876, in which Custer and his entire 7th Cavalry of 210 men were killed. The commissary, barracks and other buildings have also been reconstructed.
On-A-Slant Mandan Village:
There were about 15,000 Mandans living in 7-9 fortified towns near the Heart River in the mid 1700's. It was one of the largest population centers in the country. On-A-Slant Village was the most famous; it was established about 1575 according to archeological evidence. Today the village site, located on sloping ground near the mouth of the Heart River, is part of Fort Abraham Lincoln State Park. There are four reconstructed earth lodges and guided tours. The park's visitor center and museum has exhibits on the Mandan. The Lewis and Clark Expedition camped near the old village site on October 20, 1804; and across the river on August 18, 1806.

■ Open daily, May-Sept, 9-5. Extended season hours 9-7, from last wkd May-1st wkd Sept. Admission: $5 vehicle daily entrance fee. $6 adults/$4 students, touring fee for historic buildings and Mandan Village.

■ 50 minute guided tours of the Mandan Village every half hour during season

■ 40 minute Living History guided tours of Custer House, every half hour during season.

■ One hour trail rides, $12 person, call the Commissary store to make reservations. (701) 667-6385.

■ Campground reservations start first Tuesday in April: call (800) 807-4723. Campgrounds and picnic areas are open year round. Electrical hook-ups, etc are available during the season and may be at other times. There are events and weekend programs throughout the season from last wkd in May to 1st wkd in Sept.
(800) 807-4723 or 701) 667-6380
www.fortlincoln.com www.ndparks.com

62 FIVE NATIONS ARTS MANDAN, NORTH DAKOTA

The finest Native American art store in North Dakota provides a market for native artists from five Indian nations of the Northern Plains. The store is located in the former Northern Pacific Railway Depot in Mandan. Merchandise includes art and jewelry in all price ranges; music CD's and cassettes; and locally produced scented soap. Gifts and souvenirs.

■ Open daily. May to Sept, Mon-Sat, 9-7; Sunday, 12-5. Oct-April, Mon-Sat, 9-5; Sun, 12-5.
(701) 663-4663 www.fortlincoln.com

63 CHIEF LOOKING'S VILLAGE RIVER OVERLOOK,–BISMARCK,

A Mandan Village was once located on this bluff overlooking the Missouri River. Today, visitors can take a self guided tour, and see ancient earth lodge depressions and a fortification ditch. The Bismarck-Mandan Convention and Visitor Bureau and Genuine Dakota Gift Shop is located on Burnt Boat Drive, just before the turn off into the park where the overlook is.

■ (701) 222-4308
www.bismarckmandancvb.com

64 LEWIS AND CLARK RIVERBOAT AND KEELBOAT PARK

Keelboat Park has scale replicas of a keelboat and steamboat that may be climbed on. There are metal sculptures of Lewis and Clark and Sacakawea, and Thunderbirds created by United Tribes Technical College students.

The 150 passenger Lewis and Clark Riverboat is docked at the Historic Port of Bismarck. Tickets are purchased at the Gift Shop on the dock. Arrive 30 minutes before departure.

■ Cruise season is from Memorial Day to Labor Day, and wkds in May and Sept. Gift shop open Mon-Sat, 10 AM to 9 M; Sun, noon to 8 PM.
Excursion Cruises (1½ hrs): Tues-Sun, 2:30; and Weds-Fri, 6 PM. $15 adults, $10 ages 4-11.
Sunset Cruises (1½ hrs), Tues-Sat, 8:30, $15/$10
Free Pizza Cruises, Sun-Mon, 6 PM $15/$10
Famous Dave's Ribs /Chicken, Tues, 6 PM $30/$22
Gourmet Dinner Cruise (2 hrs), Sat, 6 PM $40/$30
(701) 255-4233
www.lewisandclarkriverboat.com

65 CAPTAIN MERIWETHERS RESTAURANT–BISMARCK

Upscale dining in a casual atmosphere on the riverfront. Nautical and Lewis and Clark themes. Main dining room has river rock fireplaces; enclosed patio or deck dining for warmer months. Live music on some weekends.

■ Open daily, Mon-Sat, 11 AM-1 AM; Sun 10 AM-2 PM. Average main course price, $15. Salads and sandwiches also.
(701) 258-0666 www.captainmeriwethers.com

66 NORTH DAKOTA STATE CAPITOL

The 19 story Art Deco State Capitol, built in 1933, has unique woods and materials from many states and countries.

■ Open daily. last wkd May-1st wkd Sept, hourly tours, 8-11 and 1-4. Sat tours, 9-11 and 1-4. Sun tours, 1-4. Off season, tours are offered Mon-Fri, 8-11, 1-4. (701) 328-2471
www.ndtourism.com www.nd.gov/fac

67 NORTH DAKOTA HERITAGE CENTER AND SAKAKAWEA STATUE

The Heritage Center, State Historical Society, and Research Library and Archives are located in the North Dakota Heritage Center on the State Capitol grounds. The Heritage Center has exhibits on North Dakota history, a museum store; many public events and changing exhibitions. The Sakakawea Statue stands near the Heritage Center. A replica of this statue is in the Statuary Hall in the Nation's Capitol.

■ Open daily. May 16-Sept 15, 8-5. Off season, open Mon-Fri, 8-5; Sat 9-5, Sun 11-5.
(701) 328-2666 www.nd.gov/hist

68 DOUBLE DITCH INDIAN VILLAGE STATE HISTORIC SITE

There are ongoing archeology digs at this site where a very large Mandan Village once stood. New evidence indicates it may date back to the 1400's. As many as 3,000 people may have continuously occupied the site for three centuries. There are at least four defensive ditches, rather than a "double ditch."

■ See North American Database of Archaeological Geophysics www.cast.uark.edu/nadag
www.ndtourism.com

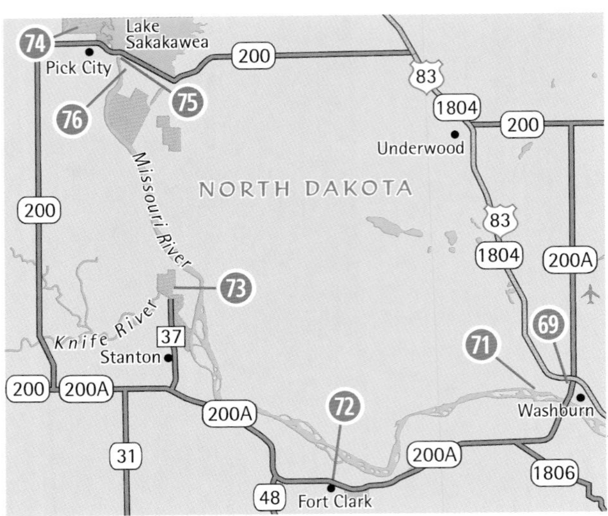

Fort Mandan and the Knife River Villages Area

Knife River Village Earth Lodge

Knife River

Fort Clark Site

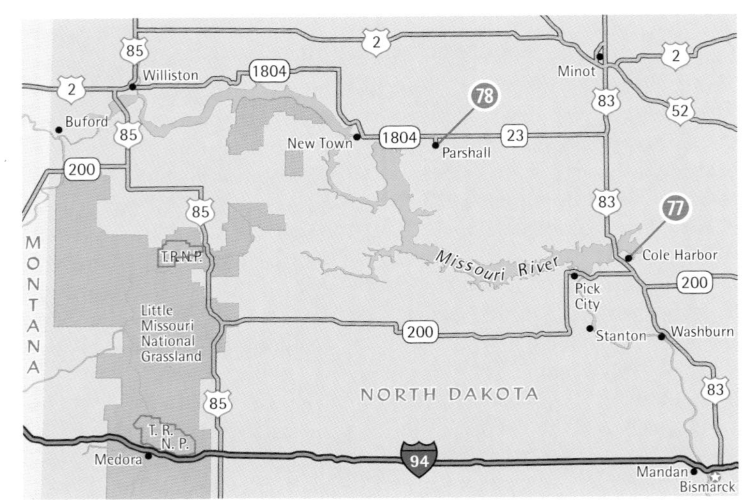

Bismarck to Williston

6

69 NORTH DAKOTA LEWIS AND CLARK INTERPRETIVE CENTER WASHBURN ND

From I-94 Exit 159 in Bismarck go north on Rte 1804 for 39 miles to the junction with Rte 200 A.

70 CROSS RANCH STATE PARK SANGER ND

From I-94 Exit 153 in Washburn bear right (north) onto Mandan Ave. Turn left (west) onto Old Red Trail. Turn right (north) onto Rte 1806. Go 11.5 miles to Cross Ranch State park at Sanger.

71 FORT MANDAN WASHBURN ND

From I-94 Exit 159 in Bismarck go north on Rte 1804 for 35.7 miles. Turn left (south) onto Rte 200 A. Immediately turn right (west) onto County Road 17. Go 2,5 miles to Fort Mandan.

72 FORT CLARK TRADING POST STATE HISTORIC SITE HIGHWAY 200 ALTERNATE

From the junction of Rte 1804 and 200 A in Washburn follow 200 A south and then west for 13.7 miles. Turn right (north) on local road. Go 0.8 mile to Fort Clark.

73 KNIFE RIVER VILLAGES STANTON ND

From I-94 Exit 127 go north on Rte 31 for 30.5 miles. Turn right (east) onto Rte 200 A. Go 1.7 miles. Turn left (north) onto County Road 37. Go 0.5 miles to Village. Turn right.

74 LAKE SAKAKAWEA STATE PARK PICK CITY ND

From US 83 and Route 200 (Route 1806) Junction go west 14 miles on Route 1806 to Pick City. Turn right (north) onto local road. Go one mile to Lake Sakakawea State Park.

75 GARRISON DAM PICK CITY ND

From US 83 and Route 200 (Route 1806) Junction go west 11 miles on Route 200 past Riverdale. At Garrison Dam turn left (west) onto local road over the Dam. Go 1.8 miles to Powerhouse.

76 GARRISON DAM FISH HATCHERY PICK CITY ND

From US 83 and Route 200 (Route 1806) Junction go west 11 miles on Route 200 past Riverdale. At Garrison Dam turn left onto local road. Go southeast 0.2 mile Turn right (south). Go 0.2 mile to Fish Hatchery.

77 AUDUBON NATIONAL WILDLIFE REFUGE COMPLEX COLE HARBOR ND

From US 83 and Route 200 (Route 1806) Junction go northwest on US 83 (Route 1804) for 6.6 miles. Turn right (east) onto 11 Street NW. Go 0.5 mile. Turn left (northeast) on 33rd Avenue NW. Go 0.2 miles.

78 BROSTE ROCK MUSEUM PARSHALL ND

508 North Main Street.
From US 83 and County Road From US 83 and Route 23 Junction go west on route 23 for 39 miles to Parshall. Turn left (south) onto Route 1804 (72nd Avenue NW). Turn right (west) onto 75th Avenue NE. Go one Block. Turn left (south) onto Main Street. Go two blocks to the Museum.

Rock Museum

Fort Mandan

Lewis and Clark Interpretive Center
North Dakota Tourism, David Borlaug

Fort Mandan and Knife River Villages to Parshall

69 NORTH DAKOTA LEWIS AND CLARK INTERPRETIVE CENTER—WASHBURN

The Lewis and Clark Interpretive Center provides an overview of the Lewis and Clark Expedition, as well the time they spent at Fort Mandan. The replica of Fort Mandan is only a few miles down the road from the Center. The Center has one of only four complete collections of artist Karl Bodmer's prints, portraying Missouri River and Indian life in 1834. There is a gift shop and bookstore. Lewis and Clark Days are held on the first full weekend in June.

■ Open daily. Last wkd May-1st wkd Sept 9 AM-7 PM. Off season, 9-5. Admission: $7.50 adults, $5 students. (877) 462-8535
(701) 462-8535 www.fortmandan.com

70 CROSS RANCH STATE PARK SANGER, ND

Located along 7 miles of some of the last free flowing waters of the Missouri River, the park has an undeveloped 5,000 acre nature preserve with an extensive trail system; a boat ramp; canoe and cabin rentals. The River Peoples Visitor Center has displays about the river. The Sanger Campground has RV and tent camping. Back country area camping also. Many activities and events, music concerts, during the summer.

■ Open daily. $5 vehicle entrance fee.
(800) 807-4723 reservations
(701) 328-5357 www.ndparks.com

71 FORT MANDAN—WASHBURN, ND

This replica fort is one of the finest and most interesting attractions on the Lewis and Clark Trail; it is built near the site where the original fort was located in the winter of 1804-05. The rooms have been furnished with the equipage the Lewis and Clark Expedition would have had. Interpreters provide year-round tours of the fort and programs.

The Headwaters Fort Mandan Visitor Center is inspired by a Mandan earth lodge and has exhibits, classroom facilities, and a gift shop. The expedition began building Fort Mandan on Nov. 3, 1804, and left for the Pacific Coast on April 8, 1805.

■ Open daily. Last wkd May-1st wkd Sept 9 AM-7 PM. Off season, 9-5. Admission: $7.50 adults, $5 students. (877) 462-8535
(701) 462-8535 www.fortmandan.com

72 FORT CLARK TRADING POST STATE HISTORIC SITE—HWY 200 ALTERNATE

This is one of the most historically significant sites in North Dakota. Fort Clark, named for William Clark, was established in 1830-31, near a Mandan village. Both George Catlin and Karl Bodmer painted scenes here. A journal kept by Francis Chardon details the tragic year in 1837 when smallpox killed 90% of the Mandan population. The Arikara lived here afterwards and they suffered epidemics of cholera and smallpox. More than 100 earth lodge depressions and 800 graves are located on this site, which has been nominated as a National Historic Landmark.

■ Open daily, May 16-Sept 15. Self guided tour brochures available at the rock shelter kiosk at the site. Interpretive signs.
(701) 794-8832
www.state.nd.us/HIST/ftClark

73 KNIFE RIVER VILLAGES NATIONAL HISTORIC SITE—STANTON NATIONAL HISTORIC SITE—STANTON

Another remarkable historic site is the Knife River Villages, the Hidatsa villages where Sakakawea and her family lived. A Hidatsa earth lodge near the Visitor Center is filled with interesting exhibits. Wheelchair accessible trails lead to the three village sites along the Knife River. A ranger driven golf-cart ride to the village sites is available upon request for people with mobility impairments. (when staffing permits). The Visitor Center has a museum, and a 15 minute orientation film; a gift shop and bookstore. There are 14 miles of trails.

Archaeological investigation has revealed the site has been inhabited, not for hundreds of years, but for thousands of years.

■ Open daily, last wkd May-1st wkd in Sept, 7:30 AM-6:00 PM. Off season, 8-4:30 Mountain Standard Time. Free admission.
(701) 745-3300 www.nps.gov/knri

74 LAKE SAKAKAWEA STATE PARK PICK CITY, ND

Located on the south shore of Lake Sakakawea near Garrison Dam, the state park offers a wide range of water-based recreational activities, including boat rentals, fishing guides, and a full service marina. The lake is one of the three largest man made lakes in the United States, extending 178 miles from Garrison Dam to Williston, ND. RV and tent campgrounds. Boat and camper storage.

■ Open daily. $5 vehicle entrance fee.
Full service season, May 20-Sept 30. Reduced services seasons Oct-mid May.
For reservations call (800) 807-4723.
(701) 487-3315 www.ndparks.com/Parks/LSSP

75 GARRISON DAM/LAKE SAKAKAWEA PICK CITY HISTORIC SITE

Garrison Dam is the fifth largest rolled-earth dam in the world. Exhibits in the power plant lobby tell the story of the construction of the dam in 1947-54.

■ Power Plant Tours, from last wkd in May to 1st wkd in Sept: Weds-Sat, at 12 and 3 PM.
Off season tours by appointment.
(701) 654-7441 www.nwo.usace.army.mil

76 GARRISON DAM NATIONAL FISH HATCHERY—PICK CITY, ND

Tour the 64 fish rearing ponds where fish are raised, and the Visitor Center with aquarium displays of the many fish species found in the Missouri River. There is a wetland hiking trail.

■ Hatchery open year round. Visitor Center open last wkd May-1st wkd Sept, 8-3:30. Free.
(701) 654-7451 www.r6.fws.gov/garrisondam

77 AUDUBON NAT'L WILDLIFE REFUGE COMPLEX—COLE HARBOR, ND

Almost 100 islands are found in Lake Audubon, named for the naturalist and artist, John James Audubon, who spent the winter of 1843 in North Dakota. The 14,735 acrea refuge is an important nesting grounds and flyway for waterfowl, including the Giant Canada goose. 7.5 mile auto tour. One mile interpretive walking trail. Fishing and hunting in season.

■ Open year round. (701) 442-5474
www.r6.fws.gov/refuges/audubon

78 PAUL BROSTE ROCK MUSEUM PARSHALL, ND

One of the finest rock collections in the U S, displayed in unusual ways, and housed in a rock building. Also atlatl spears and arrowheads.

■ Open May-Oct, Tues-Sun, 10-5. Admission $4 adults, $2 students.
(701) 862-3264
www.parshallndak.com

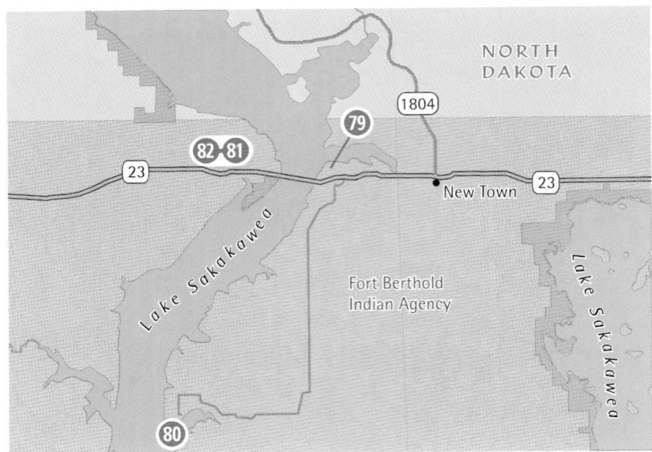

New Town

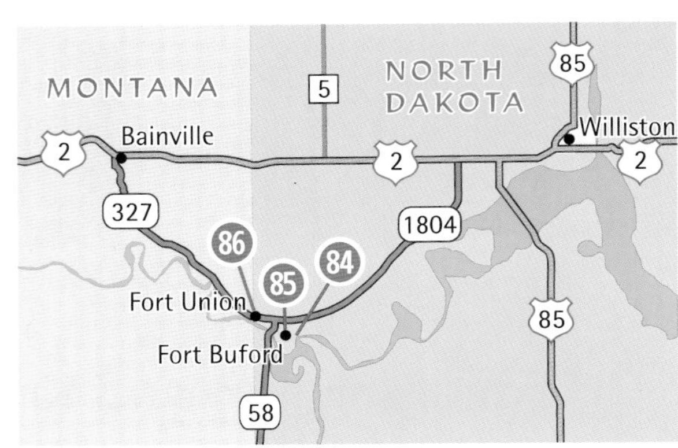

Confluence of the Missouri and Yellowstone

New Town to Williston

New Town, Big Bend on the Upper Missouri North Dakota Tourism

Lewis and Clark State Park
North Dakota Tourism, Dawn Charging

The Three Affiliated Tribes Little Shell Pow Wow is held the 2nd weekend in August at New Town. The Nux Baa Ga Pow Wow is held the 3rd weekend in August at Parshall. www.ndtourism.com

79 CROW FLIES HIGH BUTTE NEW TOWN ND

From the Route 1804 and Route 23 Junction in New Town go west on Route 23 for 2.3 miles. The local road going to Crow Flies High Butte is on the right, just after passing 2nd St NW on the left. Go 0.3 mile on the local road.

80 REUNION POINT BAY NEW TOWN ND

From the junction of Rte 1804 and Rte 23 Junction in New Town go south on West Street (changes name to 89th Avenue NW) for 3.1 miles. Turn right (west) onto 36th Street NW. Go 3 miles. Turn left (south) onto 92nd Street SW. Go two miles. Turn right (west) onto local road. This road winds 1.6 miles westward to Reunion Bay.

81 FOUR BEARS CASINO AND LODGE NEW TOWN ND

202 Frontage Road.
From the Route 1804 and Route 23 Junction in New Town go west on Route 23. Go across the Missouri River over The Four Bears Bridge. After 4 miles arirve at Frontage Road. Go left (south) on Frontage Road to the Casino.

82 THREE TRIBES MUSEUM NEW TOWN ND

Frontage Road.
From the Route 1804 and Route 23 Junction in New Town go west on Route 23. Go across the Missouri River over The Four Bears Bridge. After 4 miles arrive at Frontage Road. Go left (south) on Frontage Road to the Mueum which is next door to the Four Bears Casino.

83 LEWIS AND CLARK STATE PARK EPPING ND

4904 119th Road NW.
From the US 85 and Route 1804 Junction in Williston go east on Route 1804. After 1.5 miles Route 1804 jogs left (north) for one block at Main Street. Continue east on Route 1804 for 17.2 miles. Turn right (south) onto County Road 15. Go 2.9 miles to Lewis and Clark State Park.

84 MISSOURI AND YELLOWSTONE CONFLUENCE CENTER WILLISTON ND

From the US 85 and US 2 Junction in Williston take US 2 west. Go 5.3 miles. Turn left (south) onto Route 1804. Go 15.3 miles. Turn left (south) onto 153rd Avenue (County Road 5). Go 0.9 mile to the Confluence Center.

85 FORT BUFORD STATE HISTORIC SITE WILLISTON ND

From the US 85 and US 2 Junction in Williston take US 2 west. Go 5.3 miles. Turn left (south) onto Route 1804. Go 15.8 miles.. Turn left (south) onto Fort Bufrod Historic Site Road. Go 0.8 mile to the Fort.

86 FORT UNION TRADING POST NATIONAL HISTORIC SITE WILLISTON ND

From the US 85 and US 2 Junction in Williston take US 2 west. Go 5.3 miles. Turn left (south) onto Route 1804. Go 17.6 miles to state line. Continue west on Montana State Route 327. Go 0.1 mile. Turn left (south) onto local Road. Go 0.2 mile to Fort entrance.

Four Bears Bridge, New Town
North Dakota Dept of Transportation

Confluence Center
North Dakota Tourism

Fort Union
NPS Photo by Linda Gordon Rokosz

New Town and The Confluence

79 CROW FLIES HIGH BUTTE LOOKOUT NEW TOWN, ND

Crow Flies High Butte is located three miles west of town, north of Four Bears Bridge, overlooking Lake Sakakawea. The Lookout Point has a fine view of the lake and surrounding area.

In the 1870's the Hidatsa Chief Crow Flies High and his band fled to the abandoned Fort Union area and lived there and then moved to the mouth of the Knife River, where they continued traditional ways. In 1894, as the last hold-outs, they moved back to the Fort Berthold Reservation and accepted land allotments and government food rations.

■ (701) 627-4812 www.newtownnd.com www.cr.nps.gov/mwac/garden_coulee

80 REUNION POINT BAY— NEW TOWN

Reunion Bay is where the Captains reunited on August 12th, 1806 after parting at Traveler's Rest on July 3, 1806. Dramatic events had taken place: Lewis' party had killed two Blackfeet; Clark's party had their entire herd of 50 horses stolen. Just the day before, on August 11th, Lewis had been shot by Pierre Cruzatte when they were out hunting. Cruzatte had mistaken Lewis, who was wearing leather clothing, for an elk. Lewis received a flesh wound in his buttock which would take a month to heal.

■ (701) 627-4812 www.newtownnd.com

 81 FOUR BEARS CASINO AND LODGE AND JET BOAT EXCURSIONS NEW TOWN, NORTH DAKOTA

The Casino has a 97 room hotel and RV Park, and The Cache Restaurant, offering both buffet and full menu items.

■ Casino open Fri-Sat 24hrs; Sun-Thur 8 AM-4 AM. Restaurant hours: 7 AM-11:30 AM, 12-3:30 PM, 4-9 PM.
(800) 294-5454 www4bearscasino.com

■ Jet boat excursions depart from the 4 Bears Marina, 1/4 mile southeast of the Casino. The two hour boat rides are at: 7 AM, 9:30 AM, 12 noon, 2:30 PM, 5 PM, 7:30 PM. Price: $35 adult, $30 ages 7-12. Six and under free. Reservations: (701) 627-2628 or (800) 294-5454 www.4bearscasino.com

 82 THREE TRIBES MUSEUM NEW TOWN, ND

Exhibits feature the history and artifacts of the Three Affiliated Tribes, the Mandan, Hidatsa, and Arikara. The Mandan and the Hidatsa were living at the Knife Rivers Villages during the time of Lewis and Clark. The Arikaras were south of them. The Mandan and Hidatsa, devastated by small pox epidemics, began living together in 1845 at Like-a-Fishhook Village, where the Arikara joined them in 1862. The tribes had very successful farming and ranching operations until the Garrison Dam project flooded their lands in the late 1940's. This is how "New Town" came into being on the Fort Berthold Reservation.

Reservation Tours can be arranged through the museum. The Museum has a gift shop.

■ Open Apr-Nov daily 10-6. Admission: $3 adult, $2 senior, $2 age 12-18. (701) 627-4477 www.newtownnd.com

 83 LEWIS AND CLARK STATE PARK HIGHWAY 1804

Lake Sakakawea is almost 200 miles long. This state park is located at the western end, where occasionally pallid sturgeons and paddlefish may be found. The park has a campstore with fishing gear and well developed marina facilities. RV Campground, cabins. There is a self guided nature trail.

■ Open year round. Entry fee; $5 vehicle-day (701) 859-3071 www.ndparks.com

 84 MISSOURI AND YELLOWSTONE CONFLUENCE INTERPRETIVE CENTER WILLISTON, NORTH DAKOTA

The beautiful new Confluence Center tells the story of the confluence of the Missouri and its largest tributary, the Yellowstone River; the geography and geology of the area; its prehistory; Lewis and Clark; the fur trade era, and western expansion. The outdoor setting remains much as it was when the Lewis and Clark were here in 1805-06.

■ Open May 16-Sept 15 daily 8-6, Sept 16-May 15 Wed-Sun 9-4. Admission (also covers Fort Buford): $5 adult, $2.50 child, free under 5. (701) 572-9034 www.willistondtourism.com

 85 FORT BUFORD STATE HISTORIC SITE WILLISTON, ND

Chief Sitting Bull surrendered at Fort Buford in 1881, five years after Custer's Defeat at the Battle of the Little Bighorn. Chief Joseph was also imprisoned here after his defeat at the Battle of the Bear Paw Mountains in 1877.

Fort Buford was in operation between 1866-1895. It is located just below the confluence wit the Yellowstone and 2½ miles below Fort Union. The museum is housed in the original field officers quarters. The stone powder magazine building also is original. Both date back to the 1870's.

■ Open May 16-Sept 15 daily 8-6. Admission (also covers Missouri-Yellowstone Confluence Center): $5 adult, $2.50 child, free under 5. (701) 572-9034 www.willistondtourism.com

 86 FORT UNION TRADING POST NATIONAL HISTORIC SITE

Fort Union was the most important post on the Upper Missouri from 1828 to 1867. It has been partially restored. The Trade House has a ranger, dressed as a fur trader, who presents living history programs using historic replicas of items used in trade with the Native Americans who brought in furs. The Bourgeois House is where Kenneth McKenzie the trading post commander lived in lavish style. Indians who traded here included the Assiniboine, Cree, Crow, Blackfeet, Ojibwa, Hidatsa, Mandan and Arikara tribes.

The Yellowstone Steamboat reached Fort Union in 1832. It was the destination of many distinguished visitors: Prince Maximilian and artist Karl Bodmer; George Catlin; John James Audubon; Rudolph Kurz and Father Pierre-Jean De Smet.

The Visitor Center has exhibits, a video slide program, a hands-on fur exhibit, and a gift shop and bookstore.

■ All hours Central Time. Bourgeois House open daily last wkd May-1st wkd Sept 8-8. Off-season 9-5:30. Trade House open daily last wkd May-1st wkd Sept 10-5:45. Free admission. (701) 572-9083 or (701) 572-7622 www.nps.gov/fous

Medora Musical North Dakota Tourism, Bruce Wendt

The Medora Musical is a two hour musical variety show, with national acts, offered nightly at the Burning Hills Ampitheater. The Ampitheater is carved into a Badlands canyon at the edge of Medora. It has reserved seating for 2,900; a 7 story escalator is built into a rock butte.

■ Nightly, 8:30 PM, Mountain Standard Time, 1st wkd in June to the 1st wkd in Sept. Tickets: $30-24, adult; $15.50-13, grades 2-12. Preschool free. Behind the Scenes Tour at 7 PM: $5.58 adult, $2.79 student. Reservations: (800) 633-6721 www.medora.com

Theodore Roosevelt

Theodore Roosevelt first came to the Badlands in 1883 on a hunting trip. He invested in the Maltese Cross Ranch cattle business; it was the start of a lifelong commitment to the American West. He authored numerous books including ***The Winning of the West***, before becoming Vice President of the United States in 1900. Roosevelt became President after the assassination of President William McKinley in 1901. During his presidency he established the U S Forest Service; the first national monuments, 18 in number; 5 national parks; 51 wildlife refuges; and 150 national forests. He founded the National Conservation Commission in 1908.

Confluence of Yellowstone and Missouri and Little Missouri National Grasslands

 THEODORE ROOSEVELT NATIONAL PARK NORTH DAKOTA

North Unit.
From the US 85 and Route 1804 Junction in Williston go west on US 2/US 85 for 3 miles. Turn left (south) onto US 85. Follow US 85 south for 24.4 miles. Turn left (east) to stay on US 85. Go 17 miles. At Main St in Watford City turn right (south) to stay on US 85. Go south 14.9 miles. Turn right (southwest) to the North Unit Visitor Center.
South Unit.
From I-94 Exit 24 go right (southeast) onto 3rd Avenue. Go 1.5 miles. Turn left (east) to stay on 3rd Avenue. Go two blocks. Turn left (north) onto Third Street. Go 2 blocks to the Medora Visitor Center.

88 CHATEAU DE MORES STATE HISTORIC SITE MEDORA ND

From I-94 Exit 24 go right (southeast) onto 3rd Avenue. Go 1.2 miles. Turn left (south) onto local road. Go 0.1 mile to the Chateau.

 JOACHIM MUSEUM DICKINSON ND

1226 Sims Street.
From I-94 Exit 61 go south onto 3rd Avenue West. Turn left (east) onto Museum Drive (12th Street). Go to the Museum on Sims Street.

 DAKOTA DINOSAUR MUSEUM DICKINSON ND

200 East Museum Drive.
From I-94 Exit 61 go south onto 3rd Avenue West. Turn left (east) onto Museum Drive). Go 0.4 mile to the Dinosaur Museum.

Trail Ride, Theodore Roosevelt Nat'l Park
North Dakota Tourism, Dawn Charging

Bully Pulpit: Best New Affordable Public Golf Course, 2005 (*Golf Digest*)
North Dakota Tourism, Dawn Charging

Sunset, North Dakota Badlands
North Dakota Tourism, Bruce Wendt

Theodore Roosevelt Maltese Cross Ranch Cabin, Medora North Dakota Tourism

Chateau de Mores, Medora
North Dakota Tourism, Bruce Wendt

North Dakota Badlands

 THEODORE ROOSEVELT NATIONAL PARK—MEDORA

The National Park encompasses the Little Missouri Badlands, which are located in the Little Missouri National Grasslands. It is one of the few remaining areas that resembles the Great Plains as Lewis and Clark saw it. The Park has three units: North Unit, South Unit, and Elkhorn Ranch. Elkhorn Ranch is the historic site of Roosevelt's second ranch. There are signs, but no remaining buildings. It is located 35 miles north of the Medora (South Unit) Visitor Center. Ask at a Visitor Center before going there.

The North Unit is located near Watford City (about 50 miles from I-94 Belfield Exit 42). The Visitor Center is at the park entrance. It has exhibits and a movie. There is a 14 mile Scenic Drive, with pullouts and a number of self-guided nature trails. An auto tour guide and maps are sold at the Visitor Centers.

The South Unit is located at Medora (I-94 Exits 24 and 27). The South Unit has a paved, 36 mile scenic loop road with signage. It has a museum with personal items of Theodore Roosevelt. The Maltese Cabin, which is located behind the Visitor Center, is open for tours; and there are daily ranger programs in the summer.

The Painted Canyons, about 7 miles east of Medora, has a Visitor Center and Overlook at I-94 Exit 32. The views are spectacular at sunset.

The Park has buffalo and prairie dogs, as well other kinds of wildlife. Visitors are warned to be cautious around them: to stay far away from the buffalo; and not to feed or tease the prairie dogs. Their bite may result in a serious infection.

The park has 3 campgrounds. Two are operated on a first-come, first-served basis. They do not have trailer hookups. The third campground may be reserved, and accomodates horses. Guided trail rides are offered at the park.

■ Medora Visitor Center: Open daily, year round. Last wkd May-1st wkd Sept, 8-8, Mountain Standard Time. Off season, 8-4:30. North Visitor Center open daily 8-5 from last wkd May to 1st wkd in Sept. Off season when staff is available.Entry fee: $10 maximum - 7 days. $5 per person $10 maximum per vehicle.
(701) 623-4466 (South Unit)
(701) 842-2333 (North Unit)
www.nps.gov/thro
www.medorand.com

 CHATEAU DE MORES STATE HISTORIC SITE—MEDORA

The Chateau de Mores was the home of a 24 year old French aristocrat, the Marquis de Mores, who came to the Badlands in 1883 to start a business of shipping range cattle back east in refrigerated rail cars. The Marquis and his wealthy father-in-law built a packing plant; opened a stage line and invested in ranches. Their short-lived business empire collapsed in 1886. The town was named for his wife, Medora. The Chateau is a 26 room mansion overlooking the town. Theodore Roosevelt was a guest at the home. The home has an interpretive center, exhibits, video and museum store.

■ Open May 16 - Sept 15 daily 8:30-6:30. Admission: $6 adult, $3 age 6-15. (701) 328-2666
www.state.nd.us/hist/chateau/chateau.htm
www.medorand.com

89 JOACHIM MUSEUM—DICKINSON

The Joachim Museum complex has a museum, machinery building and historical village. The museum has exhibits on local heritage and the history of Southwest North Dakota. The Machinery Building has pioneer horse-drawn machinery; a blacksmith shop exhibit; a miniature farm; household items, and many other displays. The Prairie Outpost Park has an oil derrick; a Scandanavian Stabbur; a pioneer stone house built by the Germans from Russia Heritage Society; and a collection of old buildings from the late 1800's-early 1900's.

■ Open last wkd May-1st wkd Sept Mon-Sat 10-5. Free admission. (701) 456-6225
www.joachimmuseum.org

 DAKOTA DINOSAUR MUSEUM DICKINSON

The museum is a 13,400 square foot facility dedicated to displaying a sampling of the several thousand geological and paleontological specimens collected by Larry and Alice League from all over the world. The Leagues began digging for dinosaurs in 1984 near Dickinson. They serve as the museum director and curator.

There are 10 full scale dinsaurs; rhinoceros and bison; rock and mineral collection; fluorescent minerals; mammal skulls; vertebrate and invetebrate fossils; seashells and sea life. 91% of the exhibits are real. There is a complete real Triceratops skeleton. Wall murals portray dinosaurs, rhinoceos and bison. Museum store.

■ Open May 1-1st wkd Sept daily 9-5. Admission: $6 age 13 and older, $3 age 3-12. (701) 577-0131 www.dakotadino.com

Region Six: References

BIOGRAPHY

BUFFALO BIRD WOMAN'S GARDEN: AGRICULTURE OF THE HIDATSA INDIANS
as told to Gilbert L. Wilson. Minnesota Historical Society Press (1987)

CHARDON'S JOURNAL AT FORT CLARK, 1834-1839: DESCRIPTIVE OF LIFE ON THE UPPER MISSOURI; OF A FUR TRADER'S EXPERIENCES AMONG THE MANDANS, GROS VENTRES, AND THEIR NEIGHBORS; THE RAVAGES OF THE SMALL POX EPIDEMIC OF 1837
edited by Annie Heloise Abel. University of Nebraska Press (1997)

EARTH LODGE TALES FROM THE UPPER MISSOURI: TRADITIONAL STORIES OF THE ARIKARA, HIDATSA, AND MANDAN
edited by Douglas R. Parks, A. Wesley Jones, and Robert C. Hollow. University of Mary (1978)

INTERPRETERS WITH LEWIS AND CLARK: THE STORY OF SACAGAWEA AND TOUSSAINT CHARBONNEAU
by W. Dale Nelson. Univ of North Texas Press (2003)

6

JOSEPH N. NICOLLET ON THE PLAINS AND PRAIRIES: THE EXPEDITIONS OF 1838-39 WITH JOURNALS, LETTERS, AND NOTES ON THE DAKOTA INDIANS
edited by Edmund C. Bray and Martha Coleman Bray. Minnesota Historical Society Press (1976)

JOURNAL OF RUDOLPH FRIEDERICH KURZ: AN ACCOUNT OF HIS EXPERIENCES AMONG FUR TRADERS AND AMERICAN INDIANS ON THE MISSISSIPPI AND THE UPPER MISSOURI RIVERS DURING THE YEARS 1846 TO 1852
edited by J. N. B. Hewitt. US Gov't Printing Office (1937)

LETTERS AND NOTES ON THE MANNERS, CUSTOMS AND CONDITIONS OF THE NORTH AMERICAN INDIANS: WRITTEN DURING EIGHT YEARS' TRAVEL (1832-1839) AMONGST THE WILDEST TRIBES OF INDIANS IN NORTH AMERICA (2 VOLUMES)
by George Catlin. Dover Publications (1973)

THE LOST GUIDE: THE MAN BEHIND THE LEWIS AND CLARK EXPEDITION
by Richard Hetu. East Village Press (2004)

ON THE UPPER MISSOURI: THE JOURNAL OF RUDOLPH FRIEDERICH KURZ, 1851-1852
edited by Carla Kelly. University of Oklahoma Press (2005)

SACAGAWEA'S SON: THE LIFE OF JEAN BAPTISTE CHARBONNEAU
by Marion Tinling. Mountain Press Publishing Co (2001)

TABEAU'S NARRATIVE OF LOISEL'S EXPEDITION TO THE UPPER MISSOURI
edited by Annie Heloise Abel. Univ of Oklahoma Press (1939)

BIOGRAPHY

THREE YEARS AMONG THE INDIANS AND MEXICANS
by Thomas James. University of Nebraska Press (1846/1894)

SACAGAWEA'S CHILD: THE LIFE AND TIMES OF JEAN BAPTISTE (POMP) CHARBONNEAU
by Susan M. Colby. The Arthur H. Clark Co. (2005)

SHEHEKE MANDAN INDIAN DIPLOMAT: THE STORY OF WHITE COYOTE, THOMAS JEFFERSON, AND LEWIS AND CLARK
by Tracy Potter. Farcountry Press and Fort Mandan Press (2003)

TRAVELS IN THE INTERIOR OF AMERICA IN THE YEARS 1809, 1810 AND 1811
by John Bradbury. University of Nebraska Press (1986)

VIEWS OF LOUISIANA: TOGETHER WITH A JOURNAL OF A VOYAGE UP THE MISSOURI RIVER, IN 1811
by Henry Marie Brackenridge. Quadrangle Books (1962)

HISTORY

AMERICAN INDIANS IN U. S. HISTORY
by Roger L. Nichols. University of Oklahoma Press (2003)

THE ARIKARA WAR: THE FIRST PLAINS INDIAN WAR, 1823
by William R. Nester. Mountain Press Publishing Company (2001)

CORN AMONG THE INDIANS OF THE UPPER MISSOURI
by George F. Will and George E. Hyde. University of Nebraska Press (1964)

AN ETHNOHISTORICAL INTERPRETATION OF THE SPREAD OF SMALLPOX IN THE NORTHERN PLAINS UTILIZING CONCEPTS OF DISEASE ECOLOGY
by Michael K. Trimble. J & L Reprint Company (1986)

FIVE INDIAN TRIBES OF THE UPPER MISSOURI: SIOUX, ARICKARAS, ASSINIBOINES, CREES, CROWS
by Edwin Thompson Denig and edited by John C. Ewers. University of Oklahoma Press (1961)

FORT UNION AND THE UPPER MISSOURI FUR TRADE
by Benton H. Barbour. University of Oklahoma Press (2001)

FORT UNION TRADING POST: FUR TRADE EMPIRE ON THE UPPER MISSOURI
by Erwin N. Thompson. Fort Union Association (2003)

THE DIPLOMACY OF LEWIS AND CLARK AMONG THE TETON SIOUX 1804-1807
by Harry H. Anderson.
South Dakota History. Vol. 35, No. 1, Spring 2005

HISTORY

EARLY FUR TRADE ON THE NORTHERN PLAINS: CANADIAN TRADERS AMONG THE MANDAN AND HIDATSA INDIANS, 1738-1818. THE NARRATIVES OF JOHN MACDONELL, DAVID THOMPSON, FRANCOIS-ANTOINE LAROQUE, AND CHARLES MCKENZIE
edited by W. Raymond Wood and Thomas D. Theissen. University of Oklahoma Press (1985)

A HISTORY OF THE DAKOTA OR SIOUX INDIANS: FROM THEIR EARLIEST TRADITIONS AND FIRST CONTACT WITH WHITE MEN TO THE FINAL SETTLEMENT OF THE LAST OF THEM UPON RESERVATIONS AND THE CONSEQUENT ABANDONMENT OF THE OLD TRIBAL LIFE
by Doane Robinson. Ross and Haines (1904/1956)

THE INDIAN FRONTIER 1763-1846
by R. Douglas Hurt. University of New Mexico Press (2002)

INDIAN LIFE ON THE UPPER MISSOURI
by John C. Ewers. University of Oklahma Press (1988)

JOURNAL OF A FUR TRADING EXPEDITION ON THE UPPER MISSOURI 1812-1813
by John C. Luttig, edited by Stella M. Drum. Argosy Antiquarian Ltd. (1964)

KINSMEN OF ANOTHER KIND: DAKOTA-WHITE RELATIONS IN THE UPPER MISSOURI VALLEY, 1650-1862
by Gary Clayton Anderson. Minnesota Historical Society Press (1997)

PIPESTONE: A HISTORY OF PIPESTONE NATIONAL MONUMENT, MINNESOTA
By Robert A. Murray. Pipestone Indian Shrine Association (1965)

A SIOUX CHRONICLE
by George F. Hyde. University of Oklahoma Press (1993)

ROADSIDE HISTORY OF SOUTH DAKOTA
by Linda Hasselstrom. Mountain Press Publishing Company (1994)

THE VILLAGE INDIANS OF THE UPPER MISSOURI: THE MANDANS, HIDATSAS, AND ARIKARAS
by Roy W. Meyer. University of Nebraska Press (1977)

VOYAGES OF THE STEAMBOAT YELLOWSTONE: THE LIFE AND TIMES OF AN EARLY-AMERICAN STEAMBOAT AS IT PIONEERED ON THE UPPER MISSOURI RIVER AND PLAYED A MAJOR ROLE IN THE WAR FOR TEXAS INDEPENDENCE
by Donald Jackson. University of Oklahoma Press (1987)

THE YANKTON SIOUX
by Herbert T. Hoover and Leonard R. Bruguier. Chelsea House Publishers (1988)

REGION SEVEN
MONTANA TO THE ROCKIES

- Fort Peck to Havre on the Hi-Line Highway ■ Fort Benton to Lima
- Central Montana ■ Great Falls ■ Great Falls Portage Route
- Blackfeet Reservation and Glacier National Park
- Gates of the Mountain, Helena and Butte ■ Three Rivers Valley
- Bozeman, Livingston and Yellowstone National Park
- Billings, Cody, Crow Indian Reservation ■ Pompeys Pillar to Sidney

1. Beaverhead Rock, Dillon MT 2. Lewis and Clark Statue, Great Falls MT 3. Ryan Dam and the Great Falls, Great Falls MT 4. Giant Springs, Great Falls MT 5. Little Rockies Express Dance Troupe, Rocky Boy Reservation MT 6. Old Faithful, Yellowstone National Park 7. Museum of the Rockies, Bozeman MT 8. Hornaday Buffalo, Museum of the Northern Great Plains, Fort Benton MT 9. Fort Peck Dam, Fort Peck MT 10. Clark Canyon Reservoir, Dillon MT 11. Pompey's Pillar National Monument, Pompeys Pillar MT

Credits: (1) (2) (3) (4) (10) Betty Kluesner; (3) Upper Missouri River Keelboat Company; (5) (6) (8) Travel Montana

7

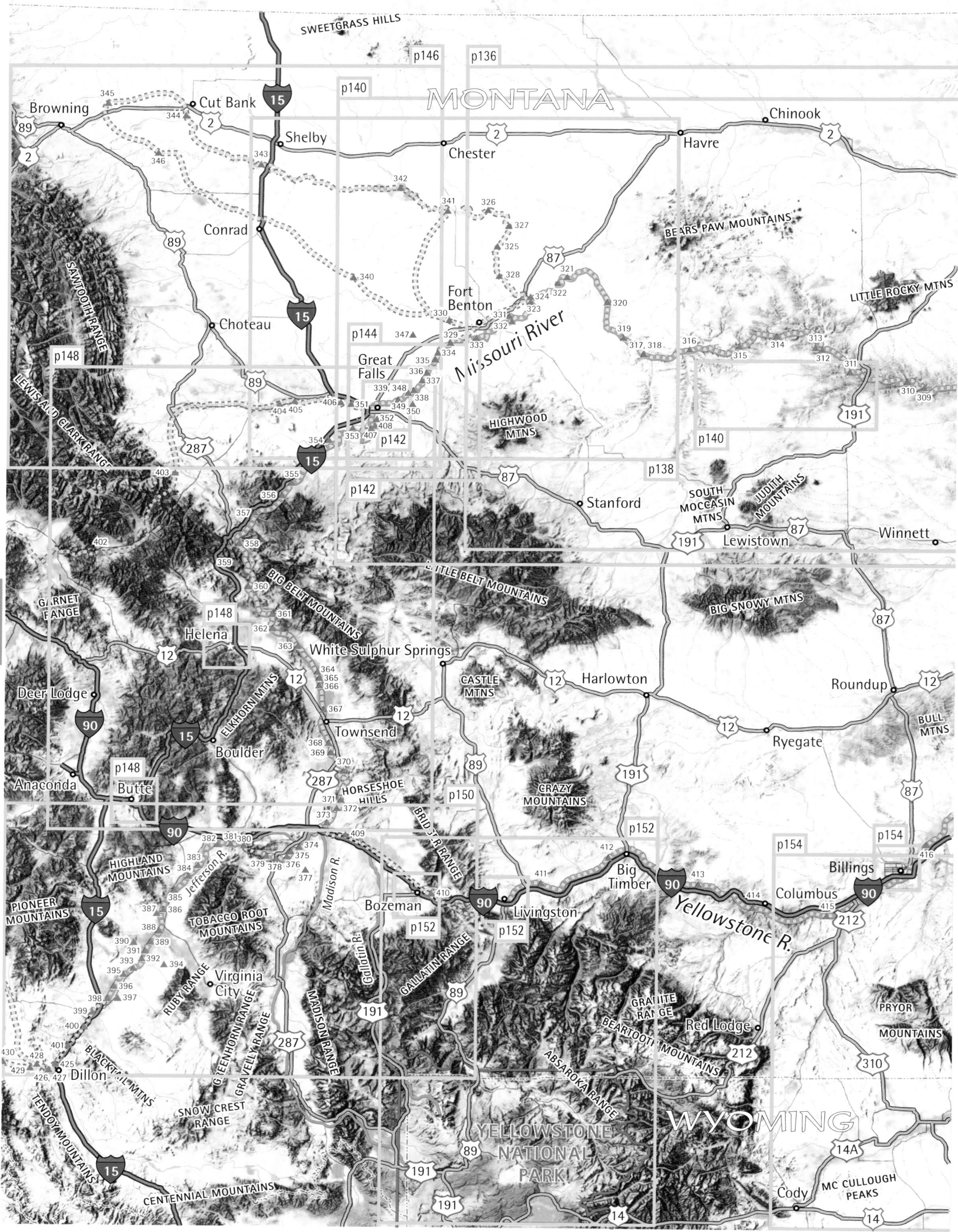

SWEETGRASS HILLS
MONTANA
WYOMING
Browning
Cut Bank
Shelby
Chester
Havre
Chinook
Conrad
Choteau
Fort Benton
Great Falls
Missouri River
BEARS PAW MOUNTAINS
LITTLE ROCKY MTNS
SAWTOOTH RANGE
LEWIS AND CLARK RANGE
HIGHWOOD MTNS
Stanford
SOUTH MOCCASIN MTNS
JUDITH MOUNTAINS
Lewistown
Winnett
LITTLE BELT MOUNTAINS
BIG BELT MOUNTAINS
BIG SNOWY MTNS
GARNET RANGE
Helena
White Sulphur Springs
CASTLE MTNS
Harlowton
Roundup
BULL MTNS
Deer Lodge
ELKHORN MTNS
Townsend
Boulder
Ryegate
Anaconda
Butte
HORSESHOE HILLS
CRAZY MOUNTAINS
HIGHLAND MOUNTAINS
Jefferson R.
Madison R.
BRIDGER RANGE
Big Timber
Billings
Columbus
PIONEER MOUNTAINS
Bozeman
Livingston
Yellowstone R.
TOBACCO ROOT MOUNTAINS
Gallatin R.
GALLATIN RANGE
GRANITE RANGE
BEARTOOTH MOUNTAINS
Red Lodge
PRYOR MOUNTAINS
Virginia City
RUBY RANGE
GREENHORN RANGE
GRAVELLY RANGE
MADISON RANGE
ABSAROKA RANGE
Dillon
BLACKTAIL MTNS
SNOW CREST RANGE
TENDOY MOUNTAINS
YELLOWSTONE NATIONAL PARK
CENTENNIAL MOUNTAINS
Cody
MC CULLOUGH PEAKS
p136
p138
p140
p142
p144
p146
p148
p150
p152
p154

7

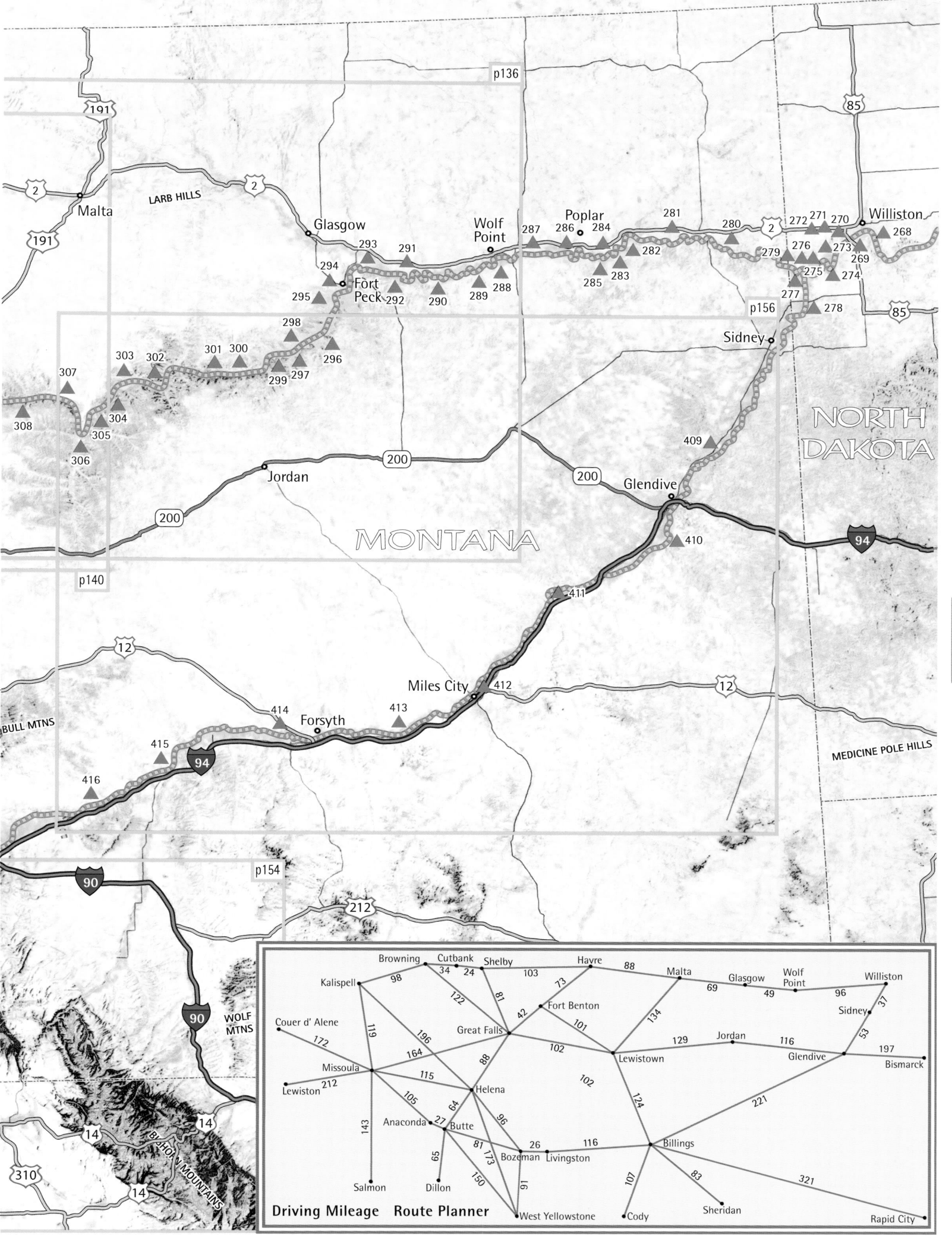

p136
p140
p154
p156
Malta
LARB HILLS
Glasgow
Wolf Point
Poplar
Williston
Fort Peck
Sidney
Jordan
Glendive
MONTANA
NORTH DAKOTA
Miles City
Forsyth
BULL MTNS
MEDICINE POLE HILLS
WOLF MTNS
BIGHORN MOUNTAINS
Driving Mileage Route Planner
Browning
Cutbank
Shelby
Havre
Malta
Glasgow
Wolf Point
Williston
Kalispell
Fort Benton
Sidney
Couer d' Alene
Great Falls
Jordan
Lewistown
Glendive
Bismarck
Missoula
Lewiston
Helena
Anaconda
Butte
Bozeman
Livingston
Billings
Salmon
Dillon
West Yellowstone
Cody
Sheridan
Rapid City

Decision Point, the Confluence of the Marias and Missouri Rivers
Travel Montana

Dugout on Wheels
Betty Kluesner,
Discovery Expedition of St Charles

Buffalo Nickel Buffalo at Fort Benton
Travel Montana

America 200 Years Ago

Reaching the Headwaters of the Missouri

DECISION POINT AND THE GREAT FALLS

When the expedition reached the confluence of the Missouri and Marias Rivers on June 3rd,1805 they had to make a momentous decision: which river was the Missouri, and which was the Marias? If they guessed wrong, there was no hope that they could get over the Rocky Mountains in the season of good weather. They made camp at Decision Point.

7

The north fork of the river looked like the muddy Missouri River they had been traveling on. The south fork was clear and transparent. Exploring parties went out. The captains were in the minority in believing the Missouri was now a clear mountain river, and the muddy river was a tributary. Clark took a party south, and Lewis took a party north. When they returned the captains were convinced, but the men were not. Lewis set out on the south river with an advance party to discover the Great Falls, which would be conclusive proof they were on the Missouri. The others followed behind. On June 13th, Lewis first heard the roaring noise and then saw the "sublimely grand specticle" of the Great Falls of the Missouri River.

THE PORTAGE ROUTE

They would spend three weeks portaging their canoes and gear around the Great Falls, from June 21st to July 14th. They endured rain, sleet, snow, hail and wind, dragging the canoes on wheels across hills covered with prickly pear cactus. They encountered rattle snakes and grizzly bears. Sacagawea became very ill at the Lower Portage Camp. Clark and the Charbonneau family almost drowned in a flash flood that filled a ravine they had taken refuge in during one violent storm. The men with the canoes were battered and bruised by giant hail stones. Sometimes the men were so fatigued dragging the canoes they fainted. And "yet no one complains, all go on with cheeerfulness" Lewis wrote. At times it was so windy they rigged sails to move the canoes over dry land.

As they made the 18 mile portage back and forth between the camps, they saw innumerable herds of buffalo in all directions. Clark reported that he "saw at least ten thousand at one view." At White Bears Islands, the Upper Portage Camp, they had many close calls with grizzly bears, or "white bears" as they called them. Seaman was in a "constant state of alarm" barking at them through the night.

THE IRON BOAT "THE EXPERIMENT"

On June 23rd, at the Upper Portage Camp past the Great Falls, Lewis began assembing the iron frame boat he called "The Experiment." For the next 17 days, Lewis and some of the men worked on bolting the boat frame together and covering it with elk and buffalo skins. This was the boat he had designed—probably together with Thomas Jefferson—and which was made at Harpers Ferry National Armory. By July 2nd the portage of the canoes and baggage was completed, but the iron boat was not ready.

There were several mistakes made. The worst mistake was not having realized they would be unable to find any pine tar to use as glue to seal the edges of the skins together. Other mistakes were shaving the skins, and using large needles to sew them together. In short, the boat would not float. It leaked, and then it sank. Lewis was "mortifyed." On July 10th, Clark set out with a party to find some large trees to build more canoes. The two pirogues had been "cached" at Decision Point and Lower Portage Camp to be used on the return journey. The purpose of the iron boat was supposed to be that it was light enough to carry over the Rocky Mountains, and then it could be used as a substitute for the pirogues in carrying goods on the rivers flowing to the Pacific.

THE THREE FORKS OF THE MISSOURI

Clark and a party of four men set out overland "in pursute of the Snake Indians" on July 23, 1805. "Snake Indians" was their name for Sacagawea's people, the Lemhi-Shoshone. They hoped a small party would not intimidate the Indians, on whom all their plans depended for obtaining horses to cross the Rocky Mountains. On July 25th they reached the Three Forks of the Missouri, where they explored the surrounding countryside but had no luck in finding the Shoshone and their horses.

Lewis and the main party arrived by canoes at the Three Forks on July 27th. Clark's party joined them there. Clark was worn out by his travels on blistered feet wounded by prickly pear thorns, and by the strain of rescuing Charbonneau from drowning the day before. All of the expedition members were fatigued from the exertion of traveling against fast moving current as they approached the headwaters.

The captains named the Three Forks, the Jefferson, the Madison and the Gallatin Rivers for President Thomas Jefferson; Secretary of State James Madison; and Secretary of the Treasury Albert Gallatin. They knew from earlier advice Indians had given them that the Jefferson, the westernmost river, would lead to the ultimate source of the Missouri. They rested at Three Forks and took latitude and longitude

Three Forks of the Missouri
Betty Kluesner, Discovery Expedition of St Charles

Rainbow Dam and Rainbow Falls
Betty Kluesner,
Discovery Expedition of St Charles

Lewis and Clark Statue, Great Falls
Don Peterson

Beaverhead Rock
Betty Kluesner
Discovery Expedition of St Charles

Blackfeet Heritage Center and Art Gallery
Siyeh Corporation

readings. On July 30th, they proceeded on to explore the Jefferson River and began their ascent of the Rocky Mountains.

Near Beaverhead Rock, at Twin Bridges, Montana, the Jefferson River divides again into three rivers. The captains named the western fork, the Wisdom River (now called the Big Hole River), and the eastern fork the Philanthropy River (now called the Ruby River). The central Jefferson River changes its name here to the Beaverhead River.

Sacagawea recognized the landmark on August 8th. She told them her nation called the hill the Beaver's Head, and assured them they were near "the summer retreat of her nation on a river beyond the mountains which runs to the west." Sacagawea had been kidnapped from her homeland by Hidatsa Indians three or four years earlier. Now she was returning home with her husband, Toussaint Charbonneau, and their 7 month old baby, Pompey. She was probably about16 years old in 1805.

THE END OF THE "ENDLESS MISSOURI"

The expedition experienced many dramatic events in Montana east of the Rocky Mountains; but one of the most significant was reaching Horse Prairie Creek near the Continental Divide. Lewis described it as "the most distant fountain of the waters of the mighty Missouri in surch of which we have spent so many toilsome days and wristless nights." On August 12, 1805 Hugh McNeal placed his feet on either side of the tiny stream and "thanked his god that he had lived to bestride the mighty and heretofore deemed endless Missouri." In fact the actual source waters of the Missouri flow into the Beaverhead River not from Horse Prairie Creek but from the Red Rock Lakes in the Centennial Mountains, near where I-15 crosses the border between Montana and Idaho about 85 miles southeast.

The search for the Shoshone and their adventures crossing the mountains are found on pages 162-163 in Region Eight.

THE RETURN JOURNEY

Returning east in 1806, the captains made the decision to split up and explore two major tributaries of the Missouri River, the Marias and the Yellowstone. Lewis went north to explore the Marias; and Clark went back south towards the Yellowstone. Both expeditions split up once again at the Missouri, and Clark's party split one more time at the Yellowstone. There were five separate parties traveling in eastern Montana in July of 1806. Eventually they all reunited at Reunion Bay south of New Town, North Dakota on August 12th.

THE FIGHT WITH THE BLACKFEET

Lewis set out to explore the Marias River to determine how far north it extended. He hoped to increase the territorial claims of the United States to 50° north latitude, about 100 miles north of the present border between Canada and the United States. Part of his group remained at the Great Falls to retrieve the white pirogue from its cache site. Plans were made to reunite at Decision Point, the cache site of the red pirogue. Lewis, the two Field brothers and George Drouillard went north, following the Marias. On July 26th, he realized that Cut Bank Creek, a tributary of the Marias, was not going anywhere. He named their campsite, "Camp Disappointment." They were on their way back to Decision Point when they met a group of eight young Piegan Blackfeet Indians.

From the start, they had been worried about meeting any Blackfeet. The Blackfeet controlled the buffalo hunting grounds and beaver country of the Montana plains because they were supplied with guns and ammunition by British-Canadian fur traders. Lewis and Clark had been entering into trade agreements with other tribes, promising to supply them with guns and ammunition. Now Lewis had encountered the Blackfeet at Two Medicine River.

An incident happened. In much the same way that an incident happened with George Washington in 1754 in western Pennsylvania, at the start of the French and Indian War. It was a situation ready to explode. The United States of America, all seventeen of them, were ready to claim their control over a continent. The prize was the Pacific Northwest.

The young Piegan warriors attempted to steal their guns and their horses, the morning after they camped together on July 27th. In the ensuing fight, two Indians were killed. Lewis left a peace medal "about the neck of the dead man that they might be informed who we were." Lewis and his party rode hard well into the night to reach Decision Point and warn their companions of the danger.

THE AFTERMATH

In the years to come, George Drouillard, John Colter, John Potts and Peter Weiser would return to the Bighorn and Yellowstone Rivers on the Montana plains with Manuel Lisa and the Missouri Fur Company. In a famous encounter with the Blackfeet at Three Forks in 1809, Colter escaped by "running for his life" after Potts was killed. In another encounter with the Blackfeet in 1809 east of Three Forks, George Drouillard lost his life.

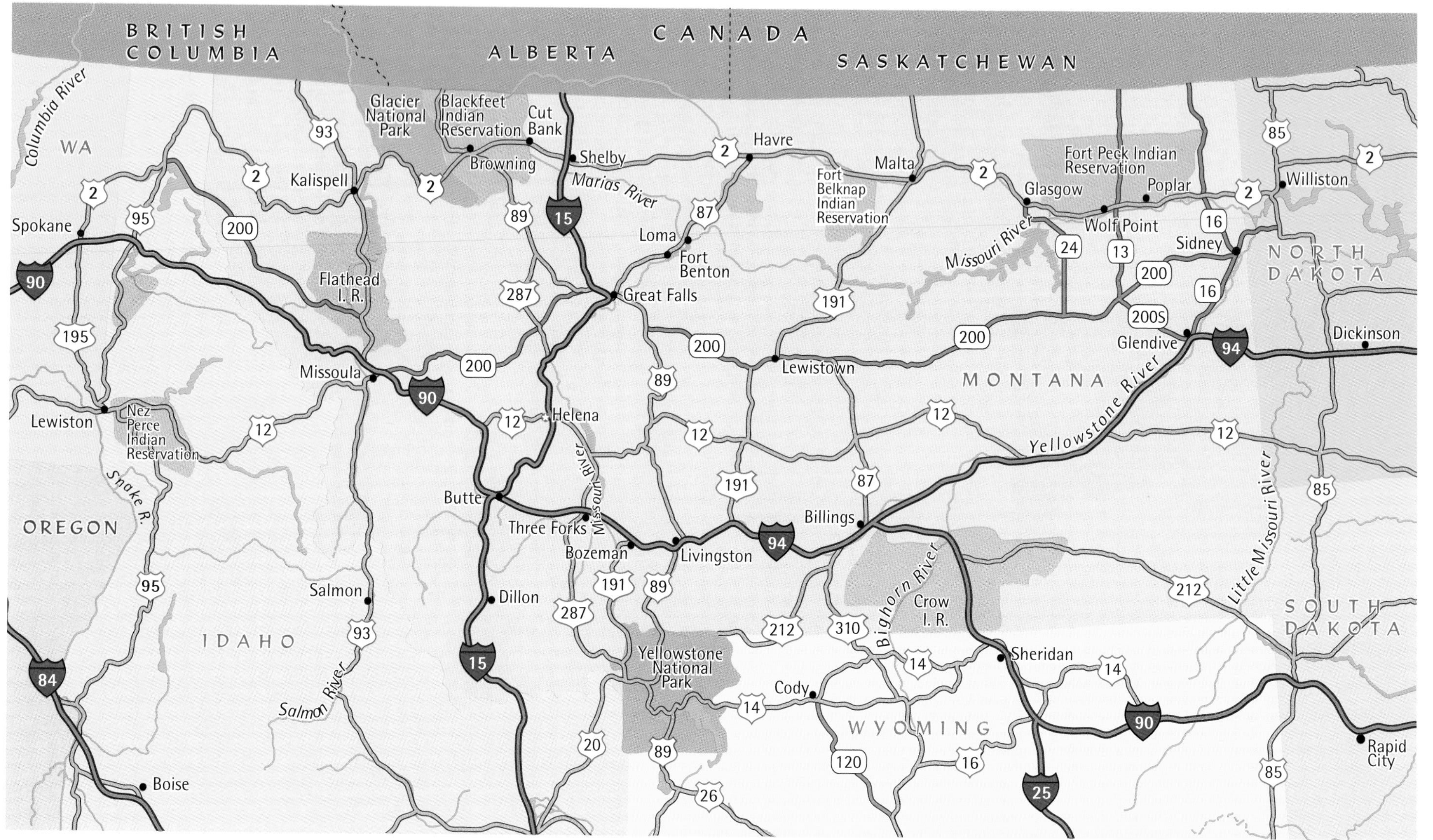
BRITISH COLUMBIA
ALBERTA
CANADA
SASKATCHEWAN
WA
Columbia River
Spokane
Kalispell
Glacier National Park
Blackfeet Indian Reservation
Browning
Cut Bank
Shelby
Marias River
Havre
Fort Belknap Indian Reservation
Malta
Fort Peck Indian Reservation
Glasgow
Poplar
Wolf Point
Williston
Sidney
NORTH DAKOTA
Missouri River
Loma
Fort Benton
Great Falls
Flathead I.R.
Lewistown
Glendive
Dickinson
MONTANA
Missoula
Helena
Lewiston
Nez Perce Indian Reservation
Snake R.
OREGON
Butte
Three Forks
Bozeman
Livingston
Billings
Yellowstone River
Little Missouri River
Salmon
Dillon
Bighorn River
Crow I.R.
SOUTH DAKOTA
IDAHO
Yellowstone National Park
Sheridan
Cody
Salmon River
WYOMING
Boise
Rapid City

Region Seven Highway Route Planner

Great Falls Lewis and Clark Interpretive Center

Montana is the fourth largest state in the union. It is about 630 miles from its eastern border to its western border, and about 280 miles from its northern border to its southern border. Its name means "mountain" in Spanish: there are over 77 named mountain ranges in the state, of which more than fifty are located in the Rocky Mountains. Many more tourists come to Montana each year than there are residents: its population in the year 2000 was 902,195. Only six states have less population.

About 60% of the state is part of the Great Plains region of the North American continent: this is the area covered in Region Seven of ***Lewis and Clark Road Trips***. The next section, Region Eight, covers the routes across the Rocky Mountains and the Bitterroot Mountains to the cities of Lewiston, Idaho and Clarkston, Washington.

Looking at the map on the opposite page, the routes of the Lewis and Clark Expedition can be sorted out in terms of highways and rivers. Region Seven has eleven areas containing 109 destinations in eastern Montana. Montana has 166 Lewis and Clark campsites; more than any other state, or 29% of the total number of 573 campsites.

OUTBOUND JOURNEY

The expedition entered Montana at the junction of the Missouri and Yellowstone Rivers near Williston, North Dakota; then they traveled on the Missouri River to its Three Forks headwaters near Dillon. A modern traveler on today's highways can choose a number of ways to reach Dillon from Williston.

Option One: Mostly Interstate
Williston to Dickinson on US-85
Dickinson to Billings to Butte on I-94
Butte to Dillon on I-15
This route takes you through the spectacular scenery of Theodore Roosevelt National Park and the North Dakota Badlands. The expedition did not follow this route, but Clark's return party did travel on the Yellowstone River along today's Interstate 90. It contains Pompeys Pillar National Monument, and Headwaters State Park at Three Forks. Butte was the copper mining capitol of the world at one time.

Option Two: The Classic Route
Willston to Havre on US-2
Havre to Great Falls on US-87
Great Falls to Helena on I-15
Helena to Three Forks on US-287
Three Forks to Butte on I-94
Butte to Dillon on I-15
This is the classic route, as it has Decision Point at Loma, Fort Benton, and Great Falls and the Portage Route. Great Falls is a major Lewis and Clark destination. Helena is the state capitol. US-287 follows the path of the Missouri River to the Three Forks Headwater Region.

Option Three: Most Direct Route
Williston to Glendive on US-85 and SR-16
Glendive to Butte on I-94
Butte to Dillon on I-15
Glendive is the home of Makoshika State Park and dinosaurs. The interstate route has many attractions and side trip destinations, including the Little Bighorn National Battlefield and Yellowstone National Park.

Option Four: Least Traveled Route
Williston to Sidney on US-85 and SR-16
Sidney to Lewiston on SR-200
Lewiston to Great Falls on SR-200
State Route 200 from Lewiston to Great Falls is part of the country that Charlie Russell made famous with his paintings.

RETURN JOURNEY

On the return journey in 1806, the expedition split up into several smaller parties. Meriwether Lewis took a group northwards to explore the Marias River, to determine how far north it went, and then had a fight with Blackfeet Indians at Two Medicine River on today's Blackfeet Reservation.

William Clark took a group to explore the Yellowstone River, the largest tributary of the Missouri. At the Yellowstone, Sgt Nathaniel Pryor and a small group went overland, but had their horses stolen by Crow Indians on today's Crow Indian Reservation and turned back to the Yellowstone. Other parties went from Great Falls to New Town, North Dakota. Everyone reunited at Reunion Bay, south of New Town, on today's Three Affiliated Tribes Reservation (Mandan, Arikara and Hidatsa).

Option Five: Clark's Return Route
Yellowstone River
Dillon to Twin Bridges on SR-41
Twin Bridges to Whitehall on SR-41 and 55
Whitehall to Billings on I-94
Billings to New Town on I-94, SR-16, US-85 and US-2.
This route takes you from Dillon to the town of Twin Bridges where three rivers come together to form the Jefferson River (the Ruby, Beaverhead and Big Hole Rivers). The Jefferson River itself is one of three rivers that come together to form the Three Forks of the Missouri River. The Three Forks are the Jefferson, Gallatin and Madison Rivers.

SR-41 follows the path of the Jefferson River up to I-94. At Three Forks Clark's larger party split up, and one group took the canoes north to Great Falls. Clark and a party of ten rode on horseback to the Yellowstone River where they made canoes at Park City. From there, Sgt. Nathaniel Pryor and three men went overland with the horses intending to reach the Mandan Villages. When their horses were stolen by Crow Indians Pryor's party returned to the Yellowstone; made bull boats and caught up with Clark's canoes.

In following Clark's return route, it makes sense to explore as much of the Three Forks Valley and Yellowstone National Park as you have time for. Bozeman is home to the Museum of the Rockies and Montana State University. Livingston is the gateway to Yellowstone National Park. Billings is the largest city in Montana with a population of about 91,000.

Option Six: Pryor's Return Route
Crow Indian Reservation
Billings to Pryor on US-212 and US-314
Pryor to Lovell on US-314
Lovell to Cody on US-14A
Lovell to Sheridan on US-14A
Sheridan to Billings on US-87
Attractions on this route include the Chief Plenty Coups Museum in Pryor, the Pryor Mountain Wild Horse Refuge, the Bighorn Medicine Wheel, the Little Bighorn Battlefield and a side trip to Cody, Wyoming, site of the Buffalo Bill Historical Center.

Option Seven: Meriwether Lewis' Return Route
Blackfeet Indian Reservation
Great Falls to Browning on US-89
Browning to Glacier National Park on US-2
Browning to Shelby on US-2
Shelby to New Town on US-2
Lewis and his party of three rode north from Great Falls following the Marias River. They went as far north as Lewis' Camp Disappointment nine miles east of Browning on US-2, and then they turned back. The fight with the young Blackfeet took place at Two Medicine River on today's Blackfeet Reservation. US-89 from Great Falls to Browning runs near the most ancient Indian path on the North American continent, the Old North Trail, located along the eastern edge of the Rocky Mountains. It is thought to be at least 12,000 years old.

Take some time to see the Blackfeet Indian Reservation and Glacier National Park, which are some of the most popular attractions in the American West. Then head east on Highway 2 to follow Lewis' return route to Reunion Bay south of New Town, North Dakota.

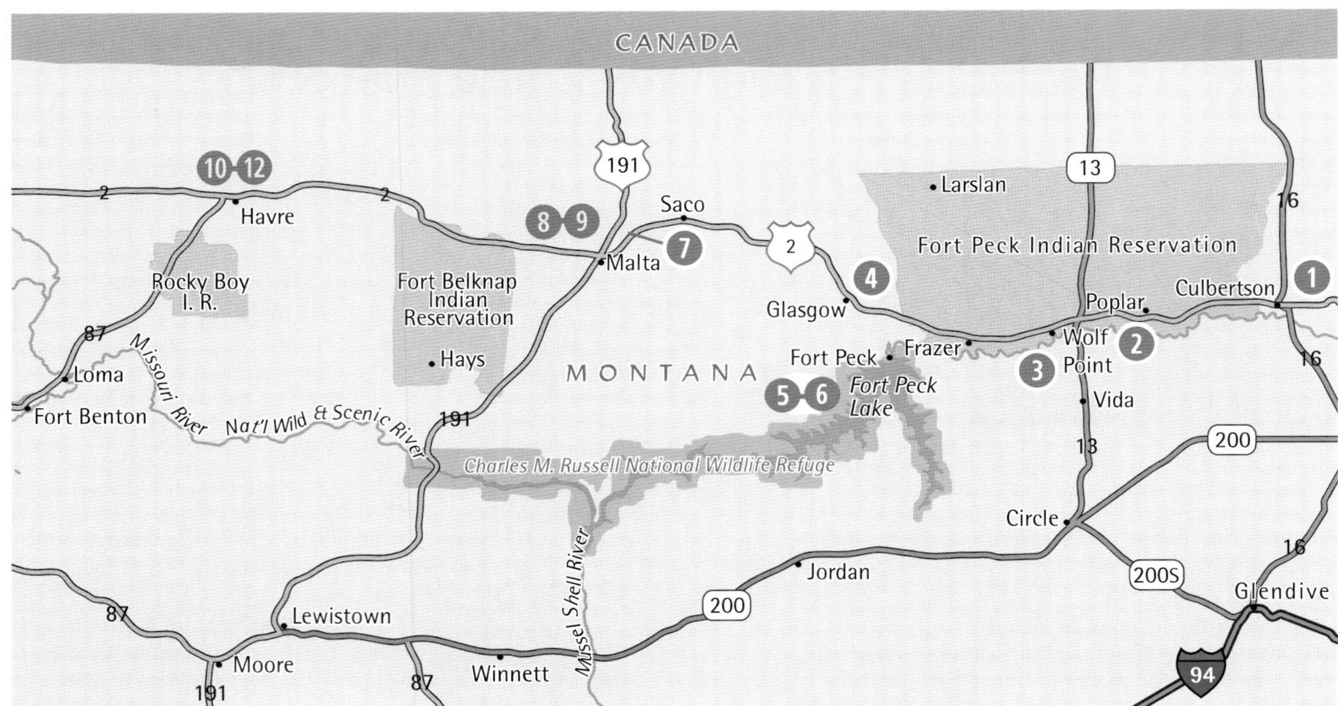

Culbertson to Havre on the Hi-Line Highway

Fort Berthold Reservation Buffalo Herd
Travel Montana

Fort Peck Dam

1 CULBERTSON MUSEUM
CULBERTSON MONTANA

3/4 mile east of Culbertson on the north side of US Highway 2.

2 FORT PECK
TRIBAL MUSEUM
POPLAR MONTANA

3rd Avenue and US 2.
73 miles west of Williston, North Dakota on US 2.

3 WOLF POINT MUSEUM
WOLF POINT MONTANA

220 2nd Avenue South.
94 miles west of Williston, North Dakota on US 2. From US 2 turn south onto 4th Avenue. 4th Avenue veers southeast and changes name to 3rd Avenue. Go south to Benton Street. Turn left (west). Go to 2nd Avenue.

4 VALLEY COUNTY
PIONEER MUSEUM
GLASGOW MONTANA

816 US Highway 2 West.
143 miles west of Williston, North Dakota on US 2. Between 8th and 9th Avenues.

5 DINOSAUR FIELD STATION
FORT PECK MONTANA

40 Deer Born Road.
The turn-off for the Field Station is 129 miles west of Williston, North Dakota on US 2. Go south 8.6 miles on Route 117. Turn left (east) onto Deer Born Road. The Field Station is (east) opposite the Fish Hatchery.

6 FORT PECK DAM
INTERPRETIVE CENTER
AND MUSEUM
FORT PECK MONTANA

The turn-off for the Museum is 129 miles west of Williston, North Dakota on US 2. Go south 9.6 miles on Route 117. Bear left (southeast) onto Yellowstone Road. Go past the Downstream Recreation Area to the Interpretive Center.

7 SLEEPING BUFFALO STONE
AND RESORT–MALTA

The Sleeping Bufalo Stone is located between Saco and Malta on Hwy 2 (about 10 miles west of Saco and 18 miles east of Malta). The resort is about one mile north of the stone, near Nelson Reservoir. Take the local road next to the stone or SR 203, located 0.5 mile west of the stone, to the resort.

8 PHILLIPS COUNTY MUSEUM
MALTA MONTANA

431 1st Street E.
From the US191 and US 2 intersection go east 0.3 miles to the Museum.

9 DINOSAUR FIELD STATION
MALTA MONTANA

4 S 1st St E.
The Dinosaur Field Station is just south of the intersection of US 191 ans US 2, and north of the railroad overpass.

10 HAVRE BENEATH THE
STREETS
HAVRE MONTANA

120 Third Avenue.
In Havre US 2 is 1st Street. Go to Third Avenue. Turn south. Go to 120 Third Avenue.

11 H EARL CLACK MUSEUM
HAVRE MONTANA

306 Third Avenue.
In Havre US 2 is 1st Street. Go to Third Avenue. Turn south. Go past Third Street to 120 Third Avenue.

12 WAHKPA CHU'GN
BUFFALO JUMP SITE
HAVRE MONTANA

From the intersection of US 2 and State Route 232 (7th Avenue N) go north one block. Turn left (west) onto Main Street (Main Street changes name to 1st Street). Go 1.3 miles to the Buffalo Kill Site.

Fort Peck Assiniboine and Sioux Cultural Center and Museum

Phillips County Museum
Travel Montana

Havre Beneath the Streets
Travel Montana

Fort Peck to Havre on the Hi-Line Highway

1 CULBERTSON MUSEUM AND VISITOR CENTER–CULBERTSON

The museum welcomes visitors to Montana's Hi-Line Country. Displays of cowboy, pioneer and homesteader artifacts are a reminder of the area's colorful past. Tourist information.

■ Open daily. Jun-Aug 8AM-8 PM. May and Sept 9-6. Free tours daily and by appointment Apr and Oct. (406) 787-5271
www.culbertsonmt.com

2 FORT PECK ASSINIBOINE AND SIOUX CULTURAL CENTER AND MUSEUM AND POPLAR MUSEUM/GIFT SHOP–POPLAR

About 6,000 Assiniboine and Sioux live on the Fort Peck Reservation. The Tribal Museum has exhibits featuring heritage, arts and crafts and wildlife exhibits. The Poplar Museum, across Highway 2 has historic displays and has intricate beadwork and quillwork for sale.

■ Tribal Museum is open Mon-Fri 8-4:30. Free admission. Weekends by appointment.
(406) 768-5155 www.indiannations.visitmt.com
■ Poplar Museum is open June-Sept, 11-5. Free admission. (406) 768-5223

3 WOLF POINT MUSEUM AND ASSINIBOINE CULTURAL VILLAGE

Located in the basement of the county library, the museum has exhibits on fur trapping, cattle ranching and a rifle collection. A traditional Assiniboine teepee village at the Missouri River welcomes visitors. The Wild Horse Stampede Rodeo, held for three days in mid-July, is the oldest rodeo in Montana. The Red Bottom Celebration Pow Wow, in mid-June in nearby Frazer, has been held since 1903.

■ Museum is open Jun-Aug, Mon-Fri 10-5. Free admission (406) 653-2411
■ Assiniboine Cultural Village (406) 653-1009
■ Wild Horse Stampede (406) 653-2012
■ Red Bottom Celebration (406) 768-3710
www.visitmt.com search for Wolf Point

4 VALLEY COUNTY PIONEER MUSEUM GLASGOW

Assiniboine collection, Lewis and Clark, wildlife, dinosaurs, Fort Peck dam exhibits. From jet plane to vintage tractors and railroad exhibits. Gift shop.

■ Open last wkd May-1st wkd Sept. Mon-Sat 9-7, Sun 1-5. Free admission. (406) 228-8692
www.valleycountymuseum.com

5 FORT PECK PALEONTOLOGY, INC. AND DINOSAUR FIELD STATION–FORT PECK

Paleontologists research, prepare, mold and cast fossil finds at the facility. "Peck's Rex" at the Fort Peck Dam Museum was made here. Gift shop.

■ Open Mon-Fri 8-4. Admission: $4.00 adult, $1.00 child. Tours by appointment.
(406) 526-3539 www.pecksrex.com

6 FORT PECK DAM INTERPRETIVE CENTER AND MUSEUM–FORT PECK

World-class Interpretive Center with exhibits on wildlife, paleontology and cultural history of the Fort Peck area. Two versions of Peck's Rex, a famous Tyrannosaurus Rex, are on exhibit. Giant aquariums feature native and introduced species of fish in Fort Peck Lake and the Missouri River. A "star" attraction on the Montana Dinasour Trail, which has 12 other facilities.

■ Open last wkd May-last wkd Sept. Daily 9:30 AM-9:00 PM. Free admission.
(406) 526-3411 www.fortpeckpaleo.com

7 SLEEPING BUFFALO STONE AND SLEEPING BUFFALO RESORT AND HOT SPRINGS–SACO/MALTA

Touching the Sleeping Buffalo Stone was considered to bring good luck to Indians who once hunted buffalo on these plains.

The Sleeping Buffalo Resort and Hot Springs, one mile north of the stone, has mineral baths and water slides; hotel, cabins, cafe, bar, 9 hole golf, and world-class fishing. (406) 527-3370

■ www.visitmt.com Search for Saco, MT

8 PHILLIPS COUNTY MUSEUM–MALTA

The Judith River was named by William Clark for the girl who was to become his wife. Now some of the most exciting discoveries of dinosaurs ever made are coming from the Judith River area. The Museum displays dinosaur finds made by the Judith River Dinosaur Institute. It also has Native American, pioneer, gold mining, stagecoaches, old cars, and early outlaw exhibits.

■ Open mid May-mid Sept. Mon-Sat 10-5, Sun 12:30-5. Free admission. 406) 654-1037
www.maltachamber.com/museum

9 DINOSAUR FIELD STATION–MALTA

The world's best preserved dinosaur, "Leonardo" is on display at the Dinosaur Field Station. The 77 million year old Brachylophosaurus is covered with skin, scales, muscle, foot pads. He was a plant eating dinosaur, with a duck bill and a short crest on his head. No other fossil like Leonardo has ever been found in 200 years of dinosaur digs. He was discovered in the year 2000 on a Judith River Dinosaur Institute dig, led by Dr. Nate Murphy, the paleontologist in charge of the field station. Dinosaur digs are offered in the summer at a cost of $1,495 or $895 for serious volunteers.

■ Open May-Sept. Mon-Sat 10-5. Limited winter hours. Free admission. (406) 654-5300
www.montanadinosaurdigs.com
www.mummydinosaur.com

10 HAVRE BENEATH THE STREETS

A saloon, laundry, opium den, bordello, bakery and other businesses are located beneath the streets of Havre in a hundred year old underground mall. Reservations (406) 265-8888.

■ Daily tours. May-Sept 9-5. Oct-Apr, Mon-Sat, 10-4. Admission: $10 adult, $9 senior, $7 student. www.havremt.com/attractions

11 H EARL CLACK MUSEUM–HAVRE

Located in the old post office in the Holiday Village Mall, the museum has dioramas, dinosaur eggs and embryos; Native American, Buffalo Jump and Fort Assiniboine artifacts; and old machinery. Tourist information, and guided tours of the Buffalo Jump. Tours of Fort Assinniboine near the Bear Paw Mountains by appointment. Art Gallery and Gift Shop.

■ Open daily last wkd May-1st wkd Sept 11-6. Oct-Apr Wed-Sun 1-5. Free admission.
(406) 265-4000 www.theheritagecenter.com

12 WAHKPA CHU'GN BUFFALO JUMP ARCHAEOLOGICAL SITE–HAVRE

(Pronounced "walk-pa-che-gun") One hour walking tour of one of the best preserved buffalo jump sites on the plains. Bison kill and campsite deposits have been left in place at various sites up to 20 feet below the surface, and enclosed in five wooden display houses. Prehistoric Indians drove buffalo over these cliffs to their death, 2000-600 years ago.

■ Tours last wkd May-1st wkd Sept. Mon-Sat 10-5 and 7 PM, and by appointment, weather permitting. Admission: $6 adult, $5 senior, $3 student, children free.
(406) 265-6417 www.buffalojump.org

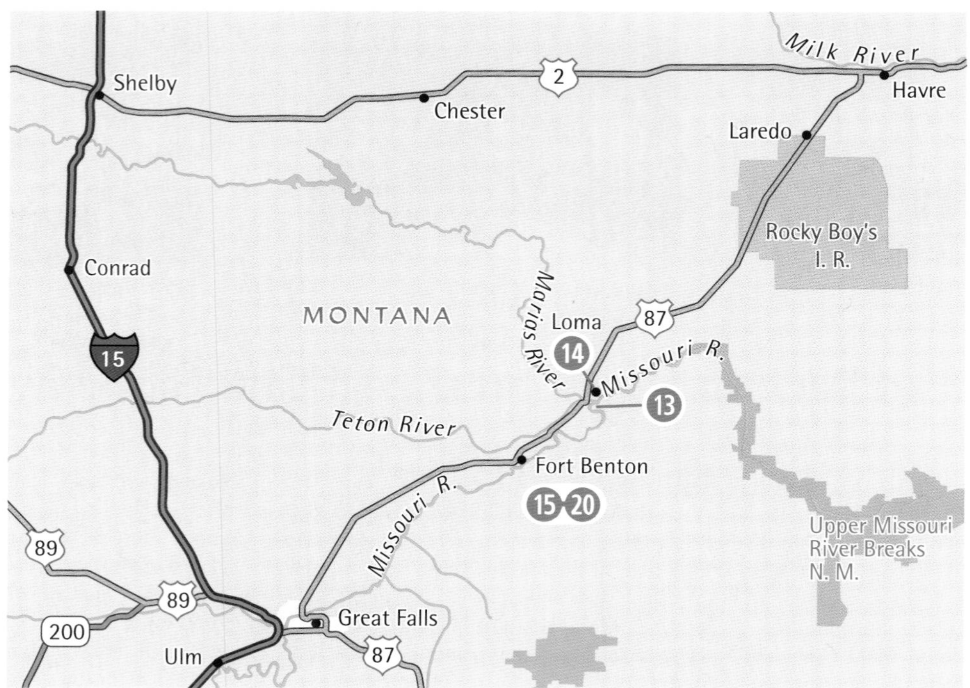

Fort Benton and Loma

Fort Benton Levee Walk:
The *Mandan* Keelboat

Upper Missouri River Breaks National Monument Interpretive Center

13 DECISION POINT
LOMA MONTANA

From 3rd Street in Loma go south on US 87 for 0.6 mile. Cross the Marias River. Turn left (south) onto Loma Ferry Road. Go 0.7 mile. Go left (east) to Decision Point Overlook.

14 EARTH SCIENCE MUSEUM
LOMA MONTANA

106 Main Street.
From US 87 go two blocks east on 3rd Street to Main Street. Turn right.(south) one block to the Earth Science Museum.

15 UPPER MISSOURI RIVER BREAKS NAT'L MONUMENT
FORT BENTON MONTANA

701 Seventh Street.
From US 87 go east onto State Route 80. Route 80 merges with Saint Charles Street. Turn left (southeast) on 13th St. Go five blocks to Front St. Turn right (southwest). Go six blocks to the Visitor Center.

16 LEVEE WALK AND OLD FORT BENTON BRIDGE
FORT BENTON MONTANA

From US 87 go east onto State Route 80. Route 80 merges with Saint Charles Street. Turn left (southeast) onto 18th Street. Go five blocks to Front Street. The walking tour begins at the Museum of the Upper Missouri on 18th Street and goes four blocks south along Front Street to the Grand Union Hotel on 13th Street. Walk east on 13th Street to cross the river on the Old Fort Benton Bridge.

17 "OLD" FORT BENTON
FORT BENTON

18h Street and Front Street.
From US 87 go east onto State Route 80. Route 80 merges with Saint Charles Street. Turn left (southeast) onto 18th Street. Go five blocks to Front Street. Turn left (northeast) onto Front Street. The "Old" Fort is in the park, to the north of the Museum of the Upper Missouri.

18 MUSEUM OF THE UPPER MISSOURI
FORT BENTON MONTANA

18h Street and Front Street.
From US 87 go east onto State Route 80. Route 80 merges with Saint Charles Street. Turn left (southeast) onto 18th Street. Go five blocks to Front Street. The Museum is in the park on the left.

19 MUSEUM OF THE NORTHERN GREAT PLAINS AND HOMESTEAD VILLAGE
FORT BENTON MONTANA

1205 20th Street.
From US 87 go east onto State Route 80. Route 80 merges with Saint Charles Street. Turn left (southeast) onto 19th Street. Go two blocks to Washington Street. Turn left (northeast). Go one block to 20th Street.

20 GRAND UNION HOTEL
FORT BENTON MONTANA

1 Grand Union Square.
From US 87 go east onto State Route 80. Route 80 merges with Saint Charles Street. Turn left (southeast) on 13th St. Go five blocks to Front St. The hotel is on the right.

Historic "Old" Fort Benton
Travel Montana

Decision Point
Travel Montana

The Buffalo Nickel Buffalo
Travel Montana

Faithful Shep on the Levee Walk

General Wm. Ashley 38 foot replica keelboat
Upper Missouri River Keelboat Co.

Fort Benton and Decision Point

13 DECISION POINT—LOMA

Decision Point was an important decision for the Corps of Discovery: which of the two rivers was the Missouri? They spent 9 days at the confluence of the Marias (Ma-rye-as) and Missouri Rivers, from June 3-11, 1805. After sending out several exploring parties, they correctly decided to follow the Missouri River to the south.

Lewis wrote that "Capt. C and myself stroled out to the top of the hights in the fork of these rivers from whence we had an extensive and most inchanting view." There were innumerable herds of buffalo in every direction on the plains surrounded by "their shepperds the wolves." There were antelopes and elks. Wild roses were in full bloom along the river bottoms.

Today a short 1/4 mile sidewalk allows visitors to stroll to the top of the hill and take in the view. The expedition camped below, and cached supplies and the red pirogue to be retrieved on their return journey the next year.

Lewis named the river Maria's for his cousin Maria, and on June 8th he indicated that he felt the river would be an "object of contention between the two great powers of America and Great Britin." It would affect the boundary line between the United States and Canada, and be commercially important in the fur trade. In July of 1806, he would lead an exploring expedition up the Marias to determine its source.

■ www.visitmt.com Search for Decision Point

14 EARTH SCIENCE MUSEUM—LOMA

Many boat floats depart from and arrive at Loma's recreational area. The Earth Sciences Museum is located in a storefront in this tiny town. It has a wide collection of gems, minerals, fossils and Native American artifacts from the surrounding area.

This and the Doll Museum in Loma are considered two of the best small museums in the Northwest. Both are free.

■ Open daily, last wkd May-1st wkd Sept, from 10-5. (406) 739-4224
www.russell.visitmt.com/attractions/museums

15 UPPER MISSOURI RIVER BREAKS NAT'L MONUMENT INTERPRETIVE CENTER—FORT BENTON

The Bureau of Land Management has a new Interpretive Center in Fort Benton for the Upper Missouri Breaks, which it manages. The Missouri Breaks has been designated a Wild and Scenic River; it extends for about 150 miles from Fort Benton to Fort Peck Dam and includes the famous White Cliffs area and Badlands. The White Cliffs can only be seen by riverboat. The Interpretive Center has Lewis and Clark exhibits, river exhibits and artifacts; and a 13 minute video on the Missouri Breaks.

The Interpretive Center is a major contact point for information about floating the river, outfitters and guides, and river safety. The Fort Benton website has links to outfitters. river tours, and shuttle services.

■ Open daily, mid May-mid Sept, from 8-5. Off season by appointment. Free admission. (406) 622-3392 www.mt.blm.gov
www.fortbenton.com

16 LEVEE WALK AND OLD FORT BENTON BRIDGE—FORT BENTON MONTANA

The four block Levee Walk is home to the Lewis and Clark Memorial and the Shep sculpture by Bob Scriver; the ***Mandan*** Keelboat from the 1952 film, ***The Big Sky;*** and other statues. Fort Benton became the head of steamboat navigation on the Missouri in 1860. The old Fort Benton Bridge, now a walking trail, provides a nice view of the Missouri River.

■ (406) 622-3864 www.fortbenton.com

17 "OLD" FORT BENTON NATIONAL HISTORIC LANDMARK

The American Fur Company built Fort Benton in 1846; it was named for Senator Thomas Hart Benton of Missouri. Fort Benton was Montana's most important city until the railroads came in 1883. Its National Historic Landmark designation honors the role it played in western expansion. The blockhouse, the oldest building in Montana, still stands on the riverfront. The fort is currently being reconstructed.

■ Open daily. May-Sept, 10-5; and by appointment off season. Admission: $4 adult, $1 child. Admission price includes Museum of the Upper Missouri and Museum of the Northern Great Plains and Homestead Village.

■ Daily tours of the Fort at 10:30 AM, 1 PM and 3 PM. Sunday tours, 1 PM and 3 PM
(406) 622-5316 www.fortbenton.com

18 MUSEUM OF THE UPPER MISSOURI FORT BENTON

The history of Fort Benton, the "Birthplace of Montana,"is told in historical sequence in this interesting museum, located next to old Fort Benton. Gift shop.

■ Open daily, 10-5, May-Sept. 3 for 1 admission, see Old Fort Benton.

19 MUSEUM OF THE NORTHERN GREAT PLAINS AND HOMESTEAD VILLAGE FORT BENTON

The Museum has the Hornaday Buffalo, a premier exhibit at the Smithsonian for 70 years. The big bull posed for many government coins, stamps, and other iconic images. The Montana Agricultural Center complex describes the evolution of farming practices by three generations of farm families. Homestead Village has restored buildings from the early 1900's.

■ Open daily, 10-5, May-Sept. 3 for 1 admission, see Old Fort Benton.

20 GRAND UNION HOTEL—FORT BENTON

Montana's oldest operating hotel, built in 1882. was restored to its original splendor in 1999. Located on Fort Benton's historic riverfront, it has a gift and book shop; restaurant. and brew pub. Guest rooms and suites have historic furnishings; elevator access; and are smoke-free.

■ Restaurant open daily Jun-Oct 5-10 PM. Nov-May Wed-Sun 5-10 PM. Brewpub open daily Jun-Oct 5-10 PM. (888) 838-5985
(406) 622-1882 www.grandunionhotel.com

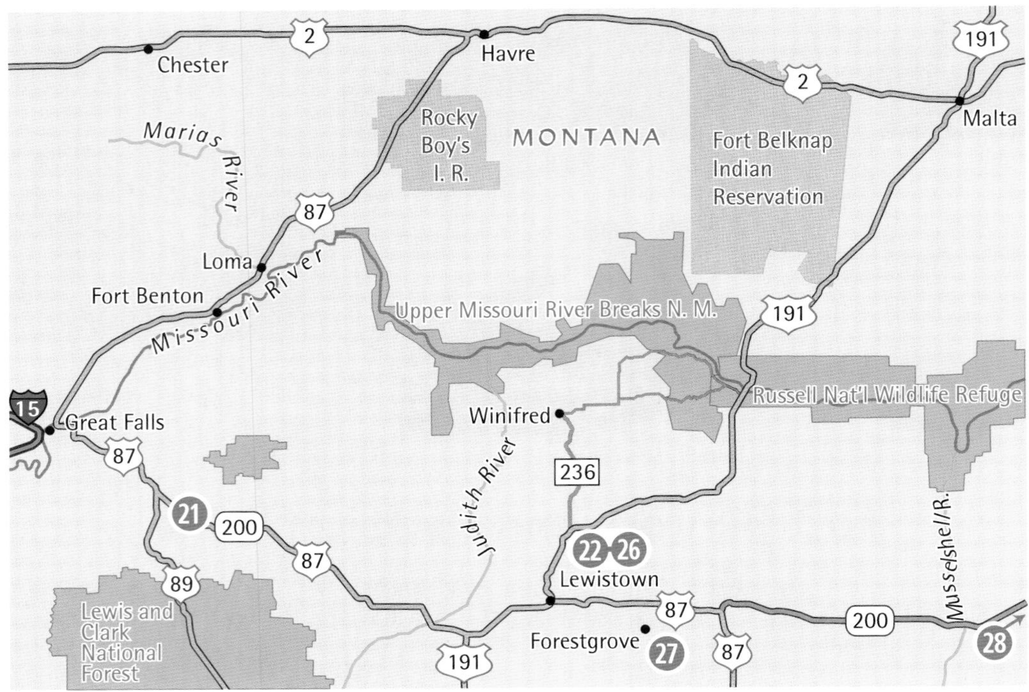

Lewistown Area

Bear Gulch Pictographs

Chokecherry Festival

Lewistown, the Chokecherry Capital of Montana, holds an annual Chokecherry Festival on the Saturday after Labor Day. Chokecherries grow in abundance along Upper Spring Creek. Native Americans considered these grounds to be sacred, and held them in common, as they did the Pipestone Quarries in southwestern Minnesota.

21 CHARLES M RUSSELL MEMORIAL TRAIL MONTANA

US Highway 87 between Great Falls and Lewistown; 101 miles.

22 CENTRAL MONTANA MUSEUM LEWISTOWN MONTANA

408 Northeast Main.
From the US 191 and US 87 Junction go northeast on Main Street seven blocks to the Museum.

23 BIG SPRINGS TROUT HATCHERY LEWISTOWN MONTANA

From the Us 191 and US 87 Junction go south 0.4 mile. Keep straight on State Route 238. Go 4.2 miles. Bear right (southeast) onto State Route 266. Go two miles to the Fish Hatchery.

24 CHARLIE RUSSELL CHEW-CHOO LEWISTOWN MONTANA

From the US 191 and US 87 Junction go north on US 191 for 2.5 miles. Turn left (west) onto State Route 505. Go 5.6 miles. Turn left (west) onto Hanover road. Go 0.2 mile to Kingston Junction.

25 CHARLES M RUSSELL NATIONAL WILDLIFE REFUGE AUTO TOUR

From the US 191 and US 87 Junction in Lewistown go north on US 191 for 42.8 miles. Turn right (east) onto Russell Auto Tour Road. Go 5.8 miles. Follow Auto Tour Road northwest for 1.4 miles, then northeast for 1.5 miles. Then go northwest for 10.7 miles returning to US 191.

26 MISSOURI BREAKS NATIONAL BACK COUNTRY BYWAY AUTO TOUR

From the US 191 and US 87 Jct in Lewistown go north on US 191 for 14.5 miles. At Hilger, go north on CR 236 for 23.8 miles to Winifred. Go east then north on Cleveland Rd for 1.8 miles. Turn right (east) onto Knox Ridge Rd. Knox Ridge Rd winds north and east for 11.9 miles to an intersection that is the beginning of a loop. At this point Knox Ridge Rd is heading north and meets the start of Upper Two Calf Rd which continues north and then east for 13.2 miles. Then go southeast on Lower Two Calf Rd for 18.6 miles. Then follow Knox Ridge Rd 21.8 miles back to the intersection with Upper Two Calf Rd completing the loop.

27 BEAR GULCH PICTOGRAPHS FOREST GROVE MONTANA

From Lewistown go south on Rte 238 for 8 miles. Turn left (east) onto Forest Grove Rd. Go 13 miles. Turn right (south) onto Fairview Rd. Go 2.7 miles to Pictographs.

28 GARFIELD COUNTY MUSEUM JORDAN MONTANA

The Garfield County Museum is at the east end of Jordan on State Route 200.

Charlie Russell Studio in Great Falls
Travel Montana

C M Russell National Wildlife Refuge
Travel Montana

Charlie Russell Chew Choo
Travel Montana

Central Montana

21 CHARLES M RUSSELL MEMORIAL TRAIL AUTO TOUR

Twenty five interpretive markers are placed-along Hwy 87 from Great Falls to Lewistown, officially designated as the "Charles M Russell Trail;" and on gravel roads going south along the Judith River to the Lewis and Clark National Forest. They mark places immortalized in Charlie Russell's paintings. A very nice auto tour booklet with illustrations and maps is available from the Lewistown Chamber of Commerce. The contents of the booklet may be seen on the Lewistown website under "places to see."

Charlie Russell (1864-1926), "America's Cowboy Artist," came to Montana at age 16 in 1880 and worked as a cowboy for 11 years in the Judith Basin area before becoming a full time artist. Buffalo herds and Indian hunters were still a way of life when he first arrived. Within three years the buffalo herds were gone. He was a friend of Native Americans and many of his paintings portray their old way of life.

His studio and home are located in Great Falls at the C M Russell Museum complex.

■ Lewistown Chamber of Commerce
(406) 535-5436 www.lewistownchamber.com

 CENTRAL MONTANA MUSEUM LEWISTOWN

The museum has pioneer, cowboy, and Native American artifacts. Cattle and sheep ranching, gold and sapphire mining, and homesteading all played a role in the region's history. Lewistown was not named for Meriwether Lewis, but rather for a temporary military post in 1874, "Camp Lewis," named for an army major.

■ Daily 9-5. (406) 535-3642 www.visitmt.com Search for Central Montana Museum

 BIG SPRINGS TROUT HATCHERY LEWISTOWN

Big Spring in the foothills of the Snowy Mountains, is one of the largest fresh water springs in the world, and one of the purest springs in the United States. More than three million trout are raised annually at the state fish hatchery here. There is a large display area and interpretive signage.

■ Open all year during daylight hours. Lewistown Chamber of Commerce
(406) 535-5436 www.lewistownchamber.com

 CHARLIE RUSSELL CHEW-CHOO

Montana's premier dinner train goes through some of the most scenic landscape in central Montana, scenery which inspired Charlie Russell's paintings. The train crosses three trestle bridges and goes through one tunnel. Prime rib dinner is served on the Chew-Choo. Wildlife is often seen from the train.

■ Train tours Jun-Oct; ten Saturdays at 4,5, or 6 PM. Dec; six dates 13 tours Fri, Sat, Sun 5:00 PM and 7:30 PM. Tickets: $90 adult regular, $125 adult V.I.P., $50 child regular, $70 child V.I.P. (800) 860-9646
www.charlierussellchoochew.com

25 CHARLES M RUSSELL NATIONAL WILDLIFE REFUGE AUTO TOUR

This is prime Lewis and Clark Missouri River country. The 20 mile drive through the grasslands and scenic visitas of the Missouri Breaks (Badlands) takes approximately two hours for the entire route, marked by 13 signs. The tour route begins and ends at US-191. It enters the refuge just past James Kipp State Park and the bridge across the Missouri, follows the river east and then heads north to exit at US-191. A one hour shorter tour going east along the river (and then doubling back) is also recommended.

The refuge is the second largest in the continental United States. It has one of the largest prairie herds of elk; pronghorn antelope, deer and prairie dogs; and birds in abundance. The area was a traditional hunting ground for the Crow, Blackfeet and Sioux Indians. The best time for wildlife viewing is early morning and late evening.

On May 23-25, 1805 Lewis wrote that he saw a "large assemblage of the burrows of the Burrowing Squirrel" and "several gangs of the big horned Anamals on the face of the steep bluffs " in the area of the refuge.

The refuge is jointly managed by the U S Fish and Wildlife Service and the Bureau of Land Management offices in Lewistown.

■ FWS office is located on Airport Road in Lewistown. Open 7:30-4:30, Mon-Fri.
(406) 538-8706 http://cmr.fws.gov

■ BLM office is located on 920 NE Main St in Lewistown. Open 7:45-4:30, Mon-Fri.
(406) 538-1900 www.mt.blm.gov

26 MISSOURI BREAKS NATIONAL BACK COUNTRY BYWAY AUTO TOUR

The "Back Country Byway" is recommended for four wheel drives and high clearance vehicles. The byway consists of gravel roads and unimproved roads that become total, impassable, "gumbo" roads when wet. Check the weather and do not attempt to travel the byway when wet weather is threatening.

Lewis and Clark called it the "Deserts of America." Fur traders called it the "Badlands." The route is a 73 mile loop trail, which begins and ends in Winifred. It is part of both the Lewis and Clark and the Nez Perce National Historic Trails. Contact the BLM office in Lewistown for a booklet on driving the Back Country Byway.

■ BLM office is located on 920 NE Main St in Lewistown. Open 7:45-4:30, Mon-Fri.
(406) 538-1900 www.mt.blm.gov

7

 BEAR GULCH PICTOGRAPHS FOREST GROVE

About 2,000 prehistoric pictographs (paintings) and petroglyphs (etchings) on rock walls in the foothills of the Little Snowy Mountains are found on the ranch. Visitors of all ages are welcome. Campgrounds and a new visitor center. Volunteers are welcome to help with the work of site documentation, recording, artifact excavation, and site construction.

■ Remote site tours depart daily at 10 AM.
$15 per person or $25 per family

■ (406) 428-2185 www.beargulch.net

 GARFIELD COUNTY MUSEUM JORDAN

Paleontologist Chris Morrow at the Garfield County Museum works with PaleoWorld Research Foundation of Virginia to bring kids, families, students, and dinosaur enthusiasts to summer digs for dinosaurs in the Badlands of Montana. Weekly digs, or "Dig-for-a-Day." Ages 18 and up, unless accompanied by a guardian. The museum has a full size Triceratops, other fossils, and homestead exhibits.

■ Open last wkd May-1st wkd Sept Mon-Fri 1-5. Free admission. (406) 557-2517
www.visitmt.com Search for Garfield Co Museum

■ (941) 473-9511 www.paleoworld.org
Weekly costs: $700 adult, $350 ages 15 and under. Family rates available. Daily: $100/$50

Statues at Broadwater Bay
Betty Kluesner, Discovery Expedition of St Charles

Great Falls Downtown Area

Great Falls, Montana

29 LEWIS AND CLARK NATIONAL TRAIL INTERPRETIVE CENTER GREAT FALLS MONTANA

4201 Giant Springs Road.
From I-15 Exit 280 go east across the river on Central Ave. Turn left (north) onto River Drive. Keep left (east) onto Giant Springs Road. Go 0.8 miles to the Center.

30 GIANT SPRINGS HERITAGE PARK GREAT FALLS MONTANA

4600 Giant Springs Road.
From I-15 Exit 280 go east across the river on Central Ave. Turn left (north) onto River Drive. Keep left (east) onto Giant Springs Road. Go 1.5 miles to the Springs.

31 BROADWATER OVERLOOK PARK VISITOR CENTER GREAT FALLS, MONTANA

15 Upper River Drive.
From I-15 Exit 278 go east across the river on the US-89 Bridge. Immediately after crossing turn right (south) onto Overlook Drive. Look for the huge flag at Overlook Park.

Ulm Pishkun Buffalo Jump
Betty Kluesner DESC

32 C M RUSSELL MUSEUM COMPLEX GREAT FALLS, MONTANA

400 13th Street North.
From I-15 Exit 280 go east across the river on Central Ave (road changes name to 1st Ave). Turn left (north) onto 13th St. Go 4 blocks to the Museum.

33 PARIS GIBSON SQUARE MUSEUM OF ART GREAT FALLS, MONTANA

1400 1st Avenue North.
From I-15 Exit 280 go east across the river on Central Ave (road changes name to 1st Ave). Go to 14th Street.

34 HERITAGE CENTER GREAT FALLS, MONTANA

422 2nd Street South.
From I-15 Exit 280 go east across the river on Central Ave (road changes name to 1st Ave). Go to 4th Street. Turn right (south). Go past 4th Avenue to the Center.

35 LEWIS AND CLARK TRAIL HERITAGE FOUNDATION GREAT FALLS, MONTANA

600 Central Avenue.
From I-15 Exit 280 go east across the river on Central Ave (road changes name to 1st Ave). Go to 7th Street. Turn right (south). Go one block to Central Avenue and turn right (west). Go one block.

36 RIVER'S EDGE TRAIL AND GRIZZLY BEAR MARKER GREAT FALLS, MONTANA

From I-15 Exit 280 go east to 3rd St West. Turn left. Proceed north on 3rd St NW Bypass. 1.1 miles. Turn right on 17thAve NE (at the Goodyear Store and the Feed Lot). Continue on 17th Ave NE and turn right on 4th St NE (Gendco) cross the RR tracks and turn right on the gravel drive. Continue on the gravel drive for 0.4 miles and select a convenient turnout. Look for the interpretive sign near the river along the paved trail.

37 ULM PISHKUN STATE PARK ULM, MONTANA

Ulm Pishkun is 10 miles south of Great Falls. From I-15 Exit 270 (Ulm Exit) turn north onto Ulm Vaughn Rd. Go 3.5 miles.

Lewis and Clark National Historic Trail Interpretive Center
USDA Forest Service

Paris Gibson Square
Travel Montana

River's Edge Trail, Grizzly Bear Marker
Don Peterson

Great Falls

29 LEWIS AND CLARK NAT'L HISTORIC TRAIL INTERPRETIVE CENTER

The 25,000 square foot Center sits high on a bluff overlooking the Missouri River near Giant Springs. It features the expedition's portage around the Great Falls of the Missouri. Exhibits trace the 8,000 mile route of the expedition, and the Indian cultures they encountered.

A self-guided audio tour is available in five languages. Plan for a two hour visit. A 30 minute film by Ken Burns, shown on the hour, provides a brief introduction to the Lewis and Clark story. The Center hosts programs year round; and has living history at River Camp on the riverfront in summer months.

■ The Library Archives of the Lewis and Clark Trail Heritage Foundation is located at the Center and is open by appointment. To set up an appointment, call (406) 454-1234, or send an e-mail to: library@lewisandclark.org

■ The Portage Cache Store has merchandise and books. They also have an online store: www.lewis-clarkstore.com

■ Lewis and Clark Institutes are held on Saturdays in the summer; activities include camping with the Corps; blacksmithing; canoeing; horseback riding; and history tours.
(406) 452-5661 www.lewisclarkia.com

■ An annual Lewis and Clark Festival is held on the last week and weekend in June.
(406) 452-5661 www.lewisclarkia.com

■ The Center is open daily, last wkd May-1st wkd Sept, 9-6. From Oct-May, Tues-Sat 9-5, Sun 12-5. Admission: $5 adult. Free for ages 15 and under accompanied by an adult.
(406) 727-8733
www.fs.fed.us/r1/lewisclark/lcic

30 GIANT SPRINGS HERITAGE PARK

Giant Springs Heritage State Park has a large-freshwater spring, discharging 156 million gallons of water per day, via one of the world's shortest rivers, the 200 foot long Roe River, into the longest river in the United States, the Missouri River. The Missouri River, combined with the Mississippi River flowing to the Gulf, is 3900 miles long. You can also feed the fish at the trout hatchery, and enjoy a walk along the River's Edge Trail.

■ Visitor Center open all year Mon-Fri 8-5. Admission: $5 vehicle pass, $1 walk-in.
(406) 454-5840
www.visitmt.com Search for Giants Springs

31 BROADWATER OVERLOOK PARK VISITOR CENTER

The Great Falls Visitor Center is located at the confluence of the Sun River and the Missouri River. It has a gift shop and tourist information, and a Lewis and Clark Memorial statue by the noted Montana sculptor, Bob Scriver.

■ Open spring-summer daily 9-6, fall-winter daily 10-4. Free admission.
(800) 735-8535 www.travel.mt.gov

32 C M RUSSELL MUSEUM COMPLEX NATIONAL HISTORIC LANDMARK

The museum has a large collection of original Russell paintings and personal objects. It also includes works by other noted western artists, and a Browning Firearms Collection. Russell's log cabin studio, built in 1903, adjacent to his home is filled with the cowboy gear and the Indian artifacts he used as references.

■ Museum open May-Sept daily 9-6, Oct-Apr Tues-Sat 10-5. Russell Studio open May-Sept daily 10-5, Oct-Apr Sun 1-5. Russell Home open May-Sept daily 10-5. Admission: $8 adult, $6 senior, $3 student.
(406) 727-8787 www.cmrussell.org

33 PARIS GIBSON SQUARE MUSEUM OF ART

The 1895 high school building, built out of sandstone, has been turned into a Museum of Art. A permanent collection features self-taught art from the Northwest and Native American art. Changing exhibits, programs and classes.

■ Open Mon-Fri 10-5, Tues evening 7-9, Sat 12-5. Admission: $5 adult. (406) 727-8255
www.the-sq.org

34 HIGH PLAINS HERITAGE CENTER

Cascade County Historical Society Museum has arrowheads, Indian artifacts, and Montana heritage exhibits. The Trolley Tour departs daily, June-Sept, from the Center and local hotels.

■ Open last wkd May-1st wkd Sept Mon-Sat 10-5 Sun 12-5. Oct-Apr Mon-Fri 10-5 Sat 12-5.
(406) 761-3805 www.highplainsheritage.org

■ Trolley: One Hour City Tours, Mon-Thurs, 9 and 4 ; Fri-Sun, 9, 1, and 4. Cost $12 adult, $5 ages 5-12. Two Hour Historic Tours, daily, at 10 AM. $20 adult, $5 ages 5-12.
(888) 707-1100 (406) 771-1100
www.greatfallshistorictrolley.com

35 LEWIS AND CLARK TRAIL HERITAGE FOUNDATION OFFICE

Trail Heritage Foundation members are "Keepers of the Story and Stewards of the Trail." The foundation was started in 1969 to support the Lewis and Clark National Historic Trail, the first National Historic Trail created by Congress. The foundation has forty chapters across America, and encourages the formation of new chapters. A quarterly publication, ***We Proceeded On,*** is a benefit of membership. Members participate in Trail Stewardship projects, and hold chapter meetings. An annual meeting is held in August at different locations around the country. The annual meetings are a mix of fellowship, programs, and touring. New comers are welcomed. Altogether, the foundation maintains both a commitment to scholarship and encouragement of interest at all levels. The foundation maintains a library and archives at the Interpretive Center. (See #29) It has published a curriculum guide used by many schools; and has an online "Ask A Question" form and other resources.

Membership is: $30 student; $40 individual, library, non-profit; $55 family, international, business; and donor categories. You may join on line. The office is currently located in downtown Great Falls. Call to confirm.

■ Open Mon-Fri 9-5. (888) 701-3434
(406) 454-1234 www.lewisandclark.org

 36 RIVER'S EDGE TRAIL AND GRIZZLEY BEAR MARKER

The 25 mile trail goes along the Missouri River. Imagine what it was like when it was crowded with buffalo and grizzly bears. This is place where Meriwether Lewis jumped in the river to save his life when pursued by a grizzly bear on June 14th, 1805.

■ (406) 788-3313 www.thetrail.org

37 ULM PISHKUN STATE PARK—ULM

This is possibly the largest buffalo kill site in North America. For thousands of years Native Americans stampeded herds of buffalo over the cliffs, and then butchered them below. The Visitor Center has exhibits and a gift shop. The view from the cliffs is worth it. Plan for a two hour visit.

■ Open May-Sept daily 8-6 Oct-April Wed-Sat 10-4 Sun 12-4. Admission: day-use pass, $2 adult, $1 ages 6-12. (406) 866-2217
fwp.mt.gov/lands/site_282807.aspx

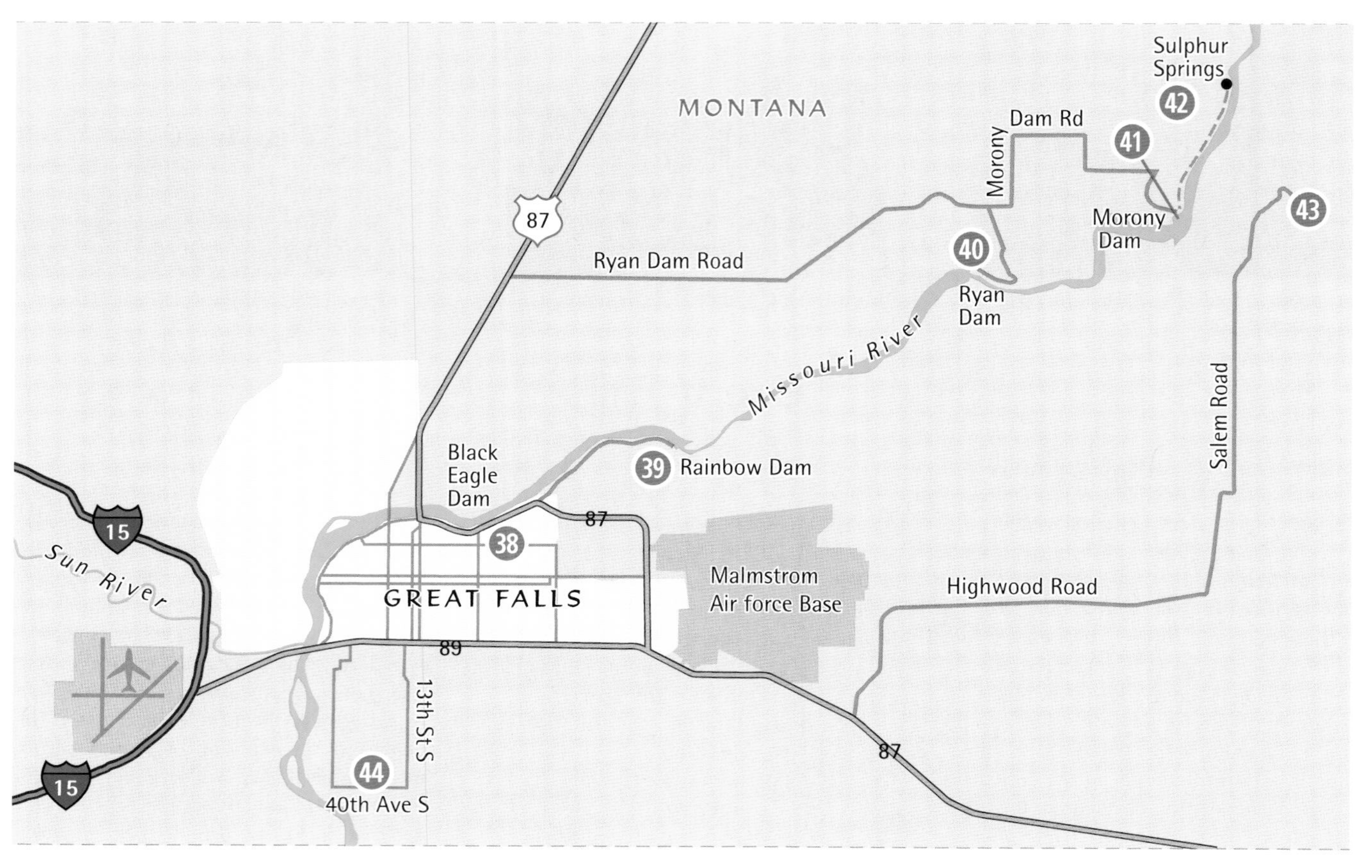

Portage Route

7

Rainbow Dam and Rainbow Falls
Betty Kluesner Discovery Expedition of St Charles

 BLACK EAGLE FALLS AND DAM OVERLOOK

From I-15 Exit 280 go east across the river on Central Avenue. Turn left (north) onto River Drive. Go 3.5 miles to Falls and Overlook.

To go from Black Eagle Dam to Rainbow Dam go 2.2 miles east on Giant Springs Road.

 RAINBOW FALLS AND LEWIS AND CLARK OVERLOOKS

From I-15 Exit 280 go east across the river on Central Avenue. Turn left (north) onto River Drive. Keep left onto Giant Springs Road. Go 2.5 miles to the Overlooks.

Black Eagle Overlook is on River Drive North, 3/4 mile of a mile west of the Giant Springs Road intersection.

Prickley Pear Cactus

Ryan Dam and the Great Falls
Betty Kluesner Discovery Expedition of St Charles

40 RYAN DAM

Drive to 15th St (US-87) in Great Falls and head north across the Missouri River. Just before Milepost #6, turn right (east) onto Morony Dam Road. Go 6.9 miles. Turn right (south) onto Ryan Dam Road. Follow it south and then west for 1.8 miles to the Dam.

To go from Ryan Dam to Morony Dam take Ryan Dam road east and then north 1.8 miles. Turn right (east) onto Morony Dam Road. Go 4.8 miles to Morony Dam.

 MORONY DAM

Drive to 15th St (US-87) in Great Falls and head north across the Missouri River. Just before Milepost #6, turn right (east) onto Morony Dam Road. Go 13 miles to the Dam.

42 SULPHUR SPRINGS TRAIL

The trailhead to Sulphur Springs is on your left just before you reach the Morony Dam area.

 LOWER PORTAGE CAMP INTERPRETIVE SITE

From I-15 Exit 278 go east on US-87 for 6 miles. Turn left (north) onto Highwood Road (State Route 228). Go north then east for 6 miles. Turn left (north) onto Salem Road. Go 5.6 miles to the Interpretive Site.

 UPPER PORTAGE CAMP OVERLOOK

From I-15 Exit 278 go east across the river on US 89. There US 89 is 10th Avenue S. Turn right (south onto 13th Street S. Go 2 miles. Turn right (west) onto 40th Avenue S. Go 0.5 mile to the Overlook.

To go from Upper Portage Camp to Lower Portage Camp go east on 40 Avenue S. Turn left (north) onto 13th Street S. Go 3 miles. turn right (east) onto 10th Avenue S (US 89). Turn left (north) onto Highwood Road (State Route 228). Go north then east for 6 miles. Turn left (north) onto Salem Road. Go 5.6 miles to the Interpretive Site.

Iron Boat at the Upper Portage Camp Site
Bob Pawloski

Portage Route

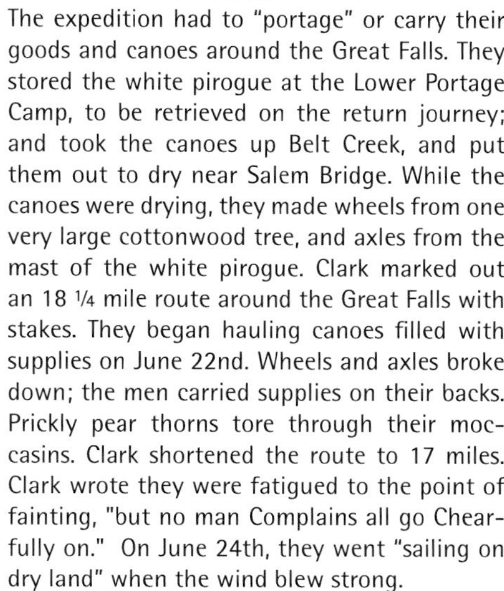

Dugout with Wheels
Betty Kluesner
Discovery Expedition of St Charles

Salem Bridge and Portage Creek
Don Peterson

Lewis and Clark Interpetive Center
Betty Kluesner, DESC

Lewis & Clark Portage Route

38 BLACK EAGLE FALLS AND DAM OVERLOOK

A black eagle had built her nest on a cottonwood tree on an island near these falls. Lewis visited the falls on June 14th, 1805, before being chased by the grizzly bear into the river. He climbed a hill near the falls and saw the river which the Indians called Medicine River; and wrote "in the valley just below me immence herds of buffaloe are feeding." He estimated the herd at "at least a thousand buffaloe."

■ (406) 727-8733 www.fs.fed.us
Search for Lewis and Clark

39 RAINBOW FALLS AND DAM, CROOKED FALLS, LEWIS AND CLARK OVERLOOK

Three falls were once located near today's Lewis and Clark Overlook: Crooked Falls, Rainbow Falls and the now submerged Colter's Falls, which were all at the same bend in the river. Lewis, who had a hard time between the "two great rivals for glory," decided that Rainbow Falls was "pleasingly beautifull," while the Great Falls he had seen the day before was "sublimely grand." The Lewis and Clark Overlook is near the Interpretive Center and Giant Springs.

■ (406) 727-8733 www.fs.fed.us
Search for Lewis and Clark

40 RYAN DAM

The Great Falls of the Missouri that Lewis first saw on June 13th are located here. First he heard "roaring too tremendious" to be anything other than the Great Falls. He declared it to be "the grandest sight I ever beheld," and tried to draw it, but this drawing has not survived. Words seemed inadequate to describe it, and he wished he had brought a camera obscura, to trace the image for an accurate drawing.

■ (406) 727-8733 www.fs.fed.us
Search for Lewis and Clark

41 MORONY DAM

Morony Dam is not part of the Great Falls, it is located about 4 1/2 miles river miles below the Falls and about 1 1/4 river miles above Belt Creek, where Lower Portage Camp was located. (Lewis and Clark called it Portage Creek in the Journals.) From the Morony Dam Overlook, if you look to the north, you will see the area where they camped and Sulphur Springs.

■ (406) 727-8733 www.fs.fed.us
Search for Lewis and Clark

42 SULPHUR SPRINGS TRAIL

On June 15th, as Clark and the main party were approaching the Great Falls he wrote "our Indian woman Sick and low Spirited." When Lewis joined the party he was greatly concerned about Sacagawea, who was "extreemly ill,"not only for herself "with a young child in her arms," but for the fact that she was their "only dependence for a friendly negotiation with the Snake Indians on whom we depend for horses."

Lewis had noticed a sulphur springs, near a large creek on the opposite shore from their campsite and resolved to try the mineral waters as a cure. He gave her "two dozes of barks and opium" and mineral water to drink. Two days later she was free of pain and fever, and eating heartily of broiled buffalo meat and soup.

There is a 3.6 mile round trip trail to Sacagawea's Sulphur Springs. The area is still the same as when the expedition was here: there are prickly pear cactus and yucca plants, and rattlesnakes. Watch out for rattlesnakes sunning themselves on rock ledges. Wear hiking boots, or sturdy walking shoes, (no sandals!) and bring layers of clothing, as the weather is changeable in Montana. In the summer bring sun protection gear and water.

■ (406) 727-8733 www.fs.fed.us
Search for Lewis and Clark

43 LOWER PORTAGE CAMP INTERPRETIVE SITE

The expedition had to "portage" or carry their goods and canoes around the Great Falls. They stored the white pirogue at the Lower Portage Camp, to be retrieved on the return journey; and took the canoes up Belt Creek, and put them out to dry near Salem Bridge. While the canoes were drying, they made wheels from one very large cottonwood tree, and axles from the mast of the white pirogue. Clark marked out an 18 1/4 mile route around the Great Falls with stakes. They began hauling canoes filled with supplies on June 22nd. Wheels and axles broke down; the men carried supplies on their backs. Prickly pear thorns tore through their moccasins. Clark shortened the route to 17 miles. Clark wrote they were fatigued to the point of fainting, "but no man Complains all go Chearfully on." On June 24th, they went "sailing on dry land" when the wind blew strong.

On June 29th Clark and the Charbonneau family almost died when they took shelter in a deep ravine during a hail storm, and a flash flood and rock slides filled the ravine. At the last moment, Clark rescued Sacagawea and the baby and Charbonneau. The portage crew were bloody and bruised from the hail stones. Finally, the portage was completed on July 2nd.

■ (406) 727-8733 www.fs.fed.us
Search for Lewis and Clark

44 UPPER PORTAGE CAMP OVERLOOK

Even though the portage was completed on July 2nd, they didn't resume their journey until July 14th, as they were dealing with the problems of the iron boat. When you visit the Lower Portage Camp site near Salem Bridge, imagine that as you drive along the roads near the Portage Route that you are surrounded by tens of thousands of buffalo. When you are at Upper Portage Camp, imagine that you are surrounded by dozens of grizzly bears. For more on the story of the Portage Route, see the Introduction of pages 132-133, or better yet, go online and read about it on the University of Nebraska Press website.

■ www.unp.unl.edu Search under digital projects for Journals of Lewis and Clark

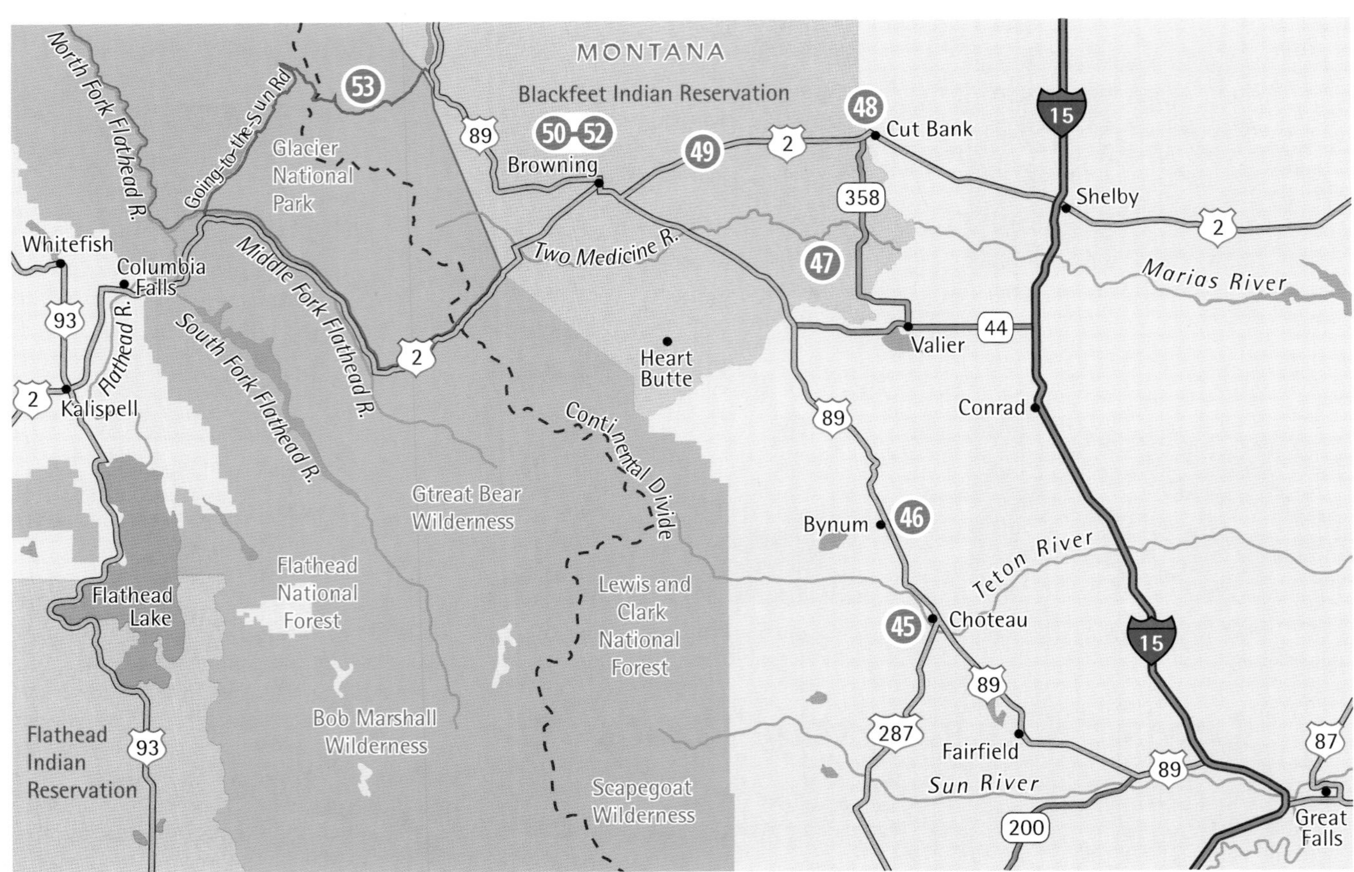

Blackfeet Indian Reservation and Glacier National Park

7

Museum of the Plains Indian
Travel Montana

North American Indian Days Pow Wow is held the 2nd weekend in July in Browning. The neighboring village of Heart Butte has a Pow Wow on the 2nd weekend in August. Make room/tipi/campground reservations well in advance.
www.blackfeetcountry.com

45 OLD TRAIL MUSEUM CHOTEAU MONTANA

823 North Main Avenue.
From I-15 Exit 313 go west on Route 221 for 23.5 miles to Choteau. Bear left (southwest) onto 1st Street NE. Go 0.5 mile. Turn right (northwest) onto Main Avenue (US 89). Go 0.5 mile to the Museum.

46 TWO MEDICINE DINOSAUR STATION BYNUM MONTANA

128 2nd Avenue South.
From I-15 Exit 313 go west on Route 221 for 23.5 miles to Choteau. Bear left (southwest) onto 1st Street NE. Go 0.5 mile. Turn right (northwest) onto (US 89). Go 13.7 miles to Bynum. Turn left (west) onto 2nd Avenue South.

47 TWO MEDICINE FIGHT SITE BLACKFEET INDIAN RESERVATION MONTANA

From Choteau.
From the US 287 and US 89 Junction go north 54.7 miles to Piegan. The Fight Site is about 9 miles east-northeast.
From Cut Bank.
From US 2 in Cut Bank go northwest then southwest for 2 miles to State Route 358. Turn left (south). Go 10.4 miles to the bridge over the Two Medicine River. The Fight Site is about 6 miles west.

48 GLACIER COUNTY MUSEUM CUTBANK MONTANA

107 Old Kevin Highway.
From I-15 Exit 363 go west on US 2 for 21 miles. Turn right (north) onto Old Kevin Highway. Go 0.6 mile. Turn right (east) to Museum.

49 CAMP DISAPPOINTMENT BROWNING MONTANA

From I-15 Exit 363 go west on US 2. Go 45 miles (2.3 miles beyond State Route 444). Just past the 236 mile marker on US 2 turn right (north) onto local road. Go 0.3 mile to the Camp Disappointment Obelisk.

50 MUSEUM OF THE PLAINS INDIAN BROWNING MONTANA

124 2nd Avenue NW.
From I-15 Exit 363 go west on US 2. Go 54 miles. Turn right (northwest) to continue On US 2/US 89. Go 3.5 miles. Turn left (west) to stay on US 2/US 89. Go one block. Turn right (north) onto Piegan Street. Go two blocks. Turn left (west) onto 2nd Avenue. Go to Museum.

51 BLACKFEET NATION HERITAGE CENTER AND ART GALLERY BROWNING MONTANA

333 Central Avenue West.
From I-15 Exit 363 go west on US 2. Go 54 miles. Turn right (northwest) to continue On US 2/US 89. Go 3.5 miles. Turn left (west) to stay on US 2/US 89. Go 0.4 mile to the Store.

52 GLACIER PEAKS CASINO

209 North Piegan Street.
From I-15 Exit 363 go west on US 2. Go 54 miles. Turn right (northwest) to continue On US 2/US 89. Go 3.5 miles. Turn left (west) to stay on US 2/US 89. Go one block. Turn right (north) onto Piegan Street. Go one block to the Casino.

53 GOING-TO-THE-SUN ROAD GLACIER NATIONAL PARK MONTANA

West Glacier to Saint Mary.
The south end of Going-to-the-Sun Road begins at West Glacier on US 2. The north end of Going-to-the-Sun Road begins at Saint Mary on US 89.

Glacier National Park
Travel Montana

North American Indian Days, Browning
Travel Montana

Blackfeet Heritage Center and Art Gallery
Siyeh Corporation

Blackfeet Indian Reservation and Glacier National Park

45 OLD TRAIL MUSEUM—CHOTEAU

The museum is located in the Rocky Mountain Front region near the oldest prehistoric trail in North America. Exhibits feature fossils, dinosaurs, Native American artifacts, grizzly bears and the colorful local history of Choteau.

■ Open May 15-1st wkd Sept daily 10-5. Oct-Apr Tues-Sat 10-3. Admission: $3.00 adult, $2.00 child, free under 7. (406) 466-5332 www.visitmt.com Search for Old Trail Museum (800) 823-3866 www.choteaumontana.com

46 TWO MEDICINE DINOSAUR STATION BYNUM

The museum has the world's longest dinosaur model on display, a Seismosaurus skeleton, and the first baby dinosaur ever found. Timescale Adventures, a non-profit, offers hands-on seminars ranging from 3 hour introductions to 1-10 days of field work. Indoor programs during winter months; outdoor programs, May-Sept, weather permitting. Minimum of 3 adult enrollment fees for any seminar. Fees range from $45 (3 hours) to $900 (10 days).

■ Open last wkd May-1st wkd Sept daily 9-6. Oct-Apr Mon-Thur 9-5. Admission: $4.00 adult, $3.00 senior, $3.00 child. (800) 238-6873 or (406) 469-2211 www.tmdinosaur.org www.timescale.org

 TWO MEDICINE FIGHT SITE BLACKFEET INDIAN RESERVATION

The fight between Lewis' party and the Blackfeet happened along the Two Medicine River on the eastern edge of the Blackfeet Reservation. If you take either US-89 or SR-358 you will cross the Two Medicine River. The site is located between the two roads, and is not open to visitors unless by permission. An interpretive marker and sculpture is located on SR-358 south of Cutbank. Curly Bear Wagner offers tours to this and other Lewis and Clark sites.

■ (406) 338-2058 www.curlybear.org

48 GLACIER COUNTY MUSEUM—CUTBANK

The museum features exhibits on the area's oil well industry; Native American artifacts; and homestead history. Tipis, a sheepherder's wagon, oil pumps and an old caboose.

■ Open last wkd May-1st wkd Sept Tues-Sat 10-5. Oct-May, Tues-Sat, by chance or by appointment. Admission free. (406) 873-4904 www.glaciercountymt.org/museum

 CAMP DISAPPOINTMENT NATIONAL HISTORIC LANDMARK BROWNING

Lewis named this campsite "Disappointment" because his hope of adding 100 miles north of the present border with Canada to the territory United States (50° latitude) was "disappointed." If he had chosen to explore the Milk River, instead of the Marias, he would have found it did indeed go further north than today's boundary line, but not by a 100 miles. To arrange a Blackfeet guided tour, contact Curly Bear Wagner.

The Meriwether Meadows campground is located nearby and accomodates all sizes of RV's, trailers and campers.

■ (406) 338-7737 www.mericamp.com
■ (406) 338-2058 www.curlybear.org

 MUSEUM OF THE PLAINS INDIAN BROWNING

The museum has a permament gallery devoted to the historic cultures of the Northern Plains. Traditional clothing is displayed on life size figures from many different tribes: Blackfeet, Crow, Northern Cheyenne, Sioux, Assiniboine, Arapaho, Shoshone, Nez Perce, Flathead, Chippewa and Cree. Other displays feature arts and ceremonies. Two exhibition galleries feature contemporary Native American arts and crafts from the Northern Plains. Gift Shop.

■ Open Jun-Sept daily 9-4:45. Oct-May Mon-Fri 10-4:30. Admission: summer $4 adult, $1 child; winter free. (406) 338-2230 www.browningmontana.com/museum

 BLACKFEET HERITAGE CENTER AND ART GALLERY—BROWNING

The Blackfeet Heritage Center and Art Gallery and its online store are 100% owned by the Blackfeet Nation. They sell the Lewis and Clark commemorative coins, and Blackfeet and other Native American high quality arts and crafts. The Center is housed in the former studio of the late Montana sculptor Bob Scriver. The head of the center, Loren Bird Rattler, returned to the reservation after spending three years with the National Museum of the American Indian in Washington DC. The Center's goal is to promote as many Native American cultures through tribal art as possible.

■ Open daily, May-Oct, 9-6. Nov- Apr, Mon-Fri 10-4. (406) 338-5661 www.blackfeetnationstore.com

52 GLACIER PEAKS CASINO AND RESTAURANT—BROWNING

The Blackfeet Siyeh Corporation manages several enterprises, including Lewis and Clark commemorative coins, the Heritage Center, and the new Glacier Peaks Casino and Restaurant opening in the summer of 2006. They run the smaller Discovery Lodge Casino in Cutbank also.

■ (406) 338-5669 www.siyehdevelopment.com

 GLACIER NATIONAL PARK, GOING-TO-THE-SUN-ROAD, BLACKFEET TOURS, AND TIPI VILLAGE

The Park covers over one million acres, with 700 miles of trails. It is one of North America's most popular attractions. Going-to-the-Sun Road is a spectacular 52 mile road which crosses the Continental Divide at Logan Pass (normally open from mid-June to mid-Oct). Campgrounds and historic lodging are available at the Park.

The Blackfeet offer tours of both Glacier National Park and Blackfeet Reservation tours. The Lodgepole Art Gallery and Tipi Village offers tipi accomodations near the Park.

■ Glacier National Park visitor facilities open late May to mid-Sept; not available in winter. Admission: 7-day vehicle permit May-Nov $25.00 Dec-Apr $10 (406) 888-7800 www.nps.gov

■ Sun Tours provides all day tours on Going-to-the-Sun Road in Glacier National Park with Blackfeet guides. 25 passenger, air-conditioned buses with a perfect safety record. $65 per person. (800)786-9200 www.browningmontana.com

■ Blackfeet Historical Sites Tour provides $50 half day and $100 full day mini-bus tours on the reservation with Blackfeet guides; tours depart from the Museum of the Plains Indian. Contact Curly Bear Wagner at (406) 338-2058. www.curlybear.org

■ Lodgepole Gallery and Tipi Village has a tipi village and art gallery 2½ miles west of Browning on Hwy 89. Overnight tipi stays cost $40 first person, $12 each additional person. (406)338-2787 www.blackfeetculturecamp.com

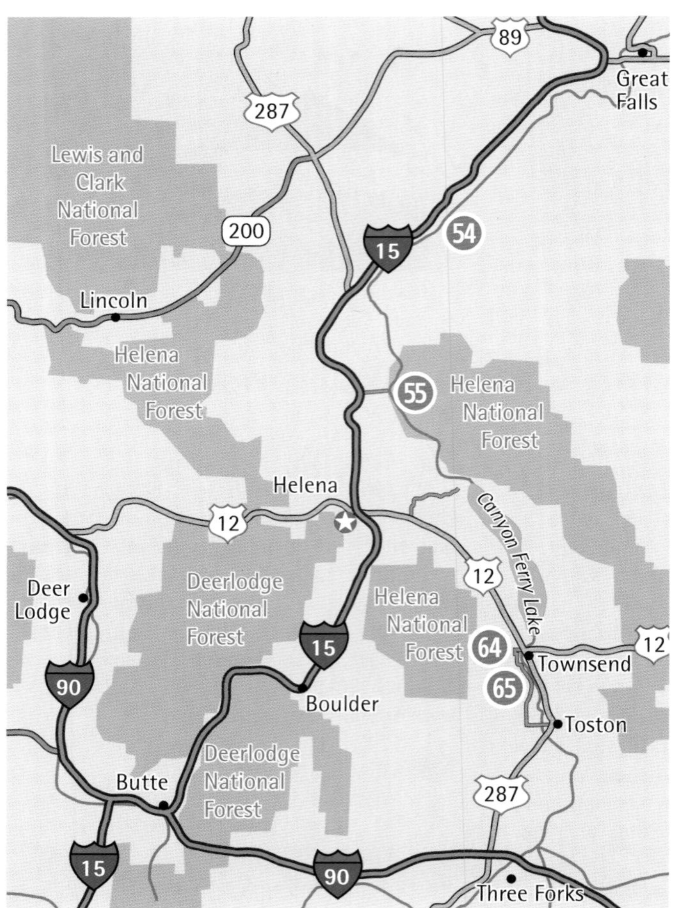

Great Falls to Helena, Butte and Three Forks

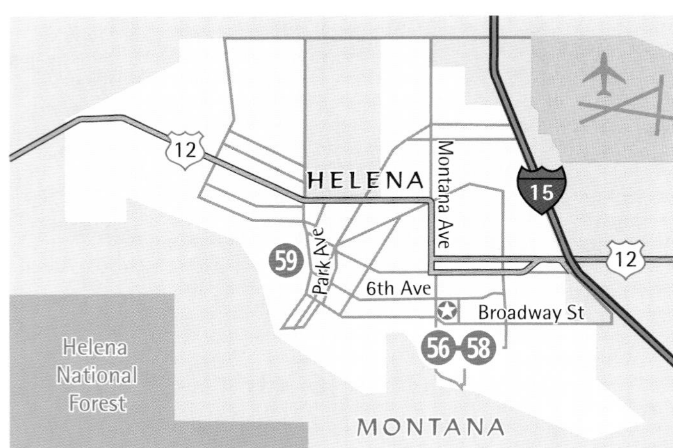

Helena, State Capital of Montana

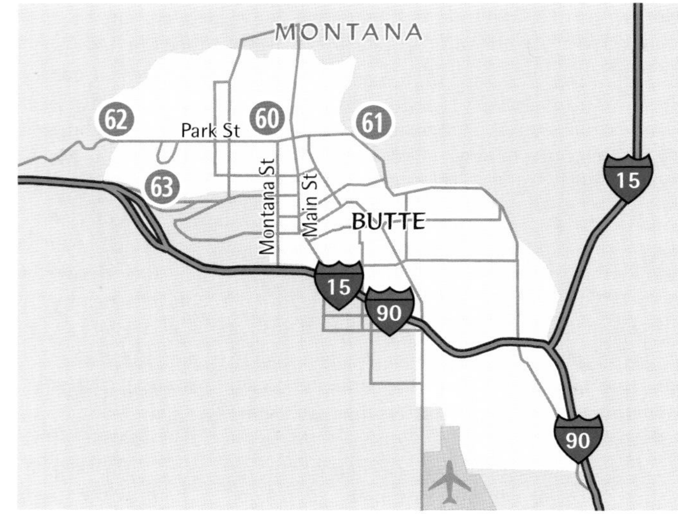

Butte

7

54 TOWER ROCK STATE PARK MONTANA

From I-15 Exit 247 go southwest on Old US 91 for 0.7 mile.

55 GATES OF THE MOUNTAINS BOAT TOURS UPPER HOLTER LAKE MT

From Helena go 15 miles north on I-15 to Exit 209. Go 2.8 miles east to marina on Upper Holter Lake.

56 STATE CAPITOL BUILDING HELENA MONTANA

1301 East 6th Avenue.
From I-15 Exit 192 go west on Prospect Ave for 0.7 mile. Turn left (south) onto Roberts St. Go four blocks to the Capitol grounds.

57 MONTANA STATE MUSEUM HELENA MONTANA

225 North Roberts Street.
From I-15 Exit 192 go west on Prospect Ave for 0.7 mile. Turn left (south) onto Roberts St. Go four and a half blocks (past 6th Ave) to the Historical Society grounds on the left (west).

58 LAST CHANCE TOUR TRAIN HELENA MONTANA

6th Avenue and Roberts Street.
From I-15 Exit 192 go west on Prospect Ave for 0.7 mile. Turn left (south) onto Roberts St. Go four and a half blocks (past 6th Ave). The Tour Train departs from the Montana State Historical Society.

59 MASONIC MUSEUM HELENA MONTANA

425 North Park Avenue.
From I-15 Exit 192 go west on Prospect Ave for 0.9 mile. Go left (south) one block on Montana Ave. Turn right (west) onto Cruse Ave. Go west then northwest 0.8 mile. Continue northwest 0.2 mile on Neill Ave. Turn left (south) onto Park Ave. Go 0.2 mile to Museum.

60 PICCADILLY MUSEUM OF TRANSPORTATION BUTTE MONTANA

20 West Broadway Street.
From I-90/I-15 Exit 126 go north onto Montana St. 1.5 miles. Turn right (east) onto Broadway St. Go 0.1 mile to the Museum.

61 BERKELEY OPEN-PIT MINE BUTTE, MONTANA

From I-90/I-15 Exit 126 go north onto Montana St. 0.8 mile. Turn right (east) onto Park St. Go 0.8 mile. Turn right (southeast) onto Continental Dr. Follow signs to Berkeley Pit viewing stand.

62 MINERAL MUSEUM BUTTE, MONTANA

1300 West Park Street.
From I-90/I-15 Exit 126 go north onto Montana St. 0.8 mile. Turn left (west) onto Park St. Go 0.8 mile. Turn left (south) west of the Student Union Building. Follow signs to museum parking.

63 WORLD MUSEUM OF MINING BUTTE, MONTANA

155 Museum Way.
From I-90/I-15 Exit 126 go north onto Montana St. 0.8 mile. Turn left (west) onto Park St. Go 1.1 miles. Turn left (south) onto Museum Way. Go 0.2 mile to Museum.

64 BROADWATER COUNTY MUSEUM TOWNSEND, MONTANA

133 North Walnut.
From I-15 Exit 192 at Helena go east on US 12/US 287 for 32.1 miles. Turn left (east) onto Broadway St. Go 5 blocks. Turn left (north) onto Walnut St.

65 CRIMSON BLUFFS AUTO TOUR —TOWNSEND TO TOSTON, MONTANA

From Townsend, go northwest on US-287 about 1.5 mile. Cross the Missouri River Bridge. Turn on Indian Creek Road, immediately after crossing the bridge. Then cross railroad tracks, and turn south on River Road. Turn left (east) onto State Rte 285, the road into Tosten. Rejoin US-287 and continue south to I-90 and the Three Forks area.

If you pick up a map at the Forest Service office there is a longer tour route to follow.

Tower Rock
Don Peterson

Gates of the Mountains
Betty Kluesner

State Capitol, Helena
Travel Montana

Gates of the Mountains, Helena and Butte

54 TOWER ROCK STATE PARK

On July 16th Meriwether Lewis named and climbed Tower Rock and saw a "most pleasing view" and immense herds of buffalo. Montana's newest state park has not yet been developed for public access.

■ (406) 454-5840 www.fwp.mt.gov/lands Serach for Tower Rock

55 GATES OF THE MOUNTAINS BOAT TOURS—HELENA

One of the most popular attractions on the Lewis and Clark Trail, the riverboats make daily 105 minute cruises. May-June: 11 and 2 on weekdays; 10, 12, 2, 4 on wkds and holidays. July-Aug: 11, 1, 3 on weekdays; every hour, 10-4 on wkds, holidays. Sept: Weds-Fri, 11 and 2, and 11, 1 and 3 on Sat-Sun, holidays.

■ Tours last wk May-last wk Sept. Fares: $10 adult, $9 senior, $6 child, free under 4. (406) 458-5241 www.gatesofthemountains.com

56 STATE CAPITOL BUILDING—HELENA

Open for self-guided tours. Guided tours hourly, May-Sept Mon-Sat, 9-3; Sun 12-4. Call for other tour hours. Charlie Russell's monumental (25 ft x 12 ft) painting of Lewis and Clark's meeting with the Flathead Indians at Ross' Hole hangs in the Montana House of Representative's Chamber.

■ Open daily 9-5. Closed Sundays durirng winter season. (406) 444-2694 www.montanacapitol.com

57 MONTANA HISTORICAL SOCIETY MUSEUM—HELENA

The museum is located across the street from the State Capitol. It has one of the major collections of Charles M Russell art, over 200 pieces; and the life work of Montana sculptor Bob Scriver. "Big Medicine," the sacred white buffalo who lived to an advanced age on the National Bison Range on Montana's Flathead Reservation resides here as a taxidermy exhibit. A large Native American collection; and old firearms. Exhibits portray Montana's history spanning 12,000 years. Gift shop and book store.

■ Open daily May-Sept 9-5. Oct-Apr Tues-Sat 9-5. Admission: $5.00 adult, $1.00 child. (406) 444-2694 www.montanahistoricalsociety.org

58 LAST CHANCE TOUR TRAIN HELENA

Last Chance Tours has been operating for over 50 years in Helena. Take an hour and explore the capital city on this tour train. It departs from the Montana State Historical Society, Mondays through Saturdays. May 15-30, 11, 1, 3; June, 10, 11 1, 2, 3; July-Aug, 10, 11, 1, 2, 3,4, 6; and Sept., 11, 1, 3.

■ Tours mid-May - mid-Sept. Fares: $7 adult and teen, $6.50 senior, $6 child, free under 4. (406) 423-1023 www.lctours.com

59 MASONIC MUSEUM HELENA

The Grand Lodge of Montana has Meriwether Lewis' Masonic apron on display. It was found on Lewis' body at the time of his death. During the bicentennial years it was loaned to the National Bicentennial Exhibition.

■ Open Mon-Fri 9-4. Free admission. (406) 442-7774 www.grandlodgemontana.org

60 PICCADILLY MUSEUM OF TRANSPORTATION—BUTTE

The museum has transportation memorabilia and advertising art from over 100 countries around the world. It's late founder was one of the few people to travel to the more than 3,800 counties in the United States. License plates, highway signs, and road art.

■ Open last wkd May-1st wkd Sept Mon-Sat 10-5. Oct-Apr open by appointment. Free admission. (406) 723-3034 www.picadillymuseum.com

61 BERKELEY OPEN-PIT MINE—BUTTE

Butte is one of the largest National Historic Landmark districts in the United States with 4,500 buildings. 22 billion dollars of minerals were mined from Butte Hill, mostly copper. At its peak, more than 200 mines operated in Butte; its population grew to over 100,000 in the 1920's. The Berkeley Pit was the largest truck-operated open-pit copper mine in the United States. It is now a 1700 hundred foot hole in the ground, filled with acidic water.

■ Open daily Mar-Nov. Admission $2 (406) 723-3177 www.visitmt.com Search for Berkeley Pit

62 MINERAL MUSEUM—BUTTE

The Mineral Museum is located in a building on the Montana Tech campus, near the World Museum of Mining. Exhibits display over 1,300 minerals. The Centennial Gold Nugget, weighing over 2 pounds is on display, and some of Montana's famous saphires and agates.

■ Open last wkd May-1st wkd Sept daily 9-6. May, Sept, Oct Mon-Fri 9-4 Sat-Sun 1-5. Free admission. (406) 496-4414 www.mbmg.mtech.edu/museum

63 WORLD MUSEUM OF MINING—BUTTE

The outdoor museum has a historic village, "Hell Roaring Gulch"; an Underground Exhibit; the Orphan Girl Mine; mineral collections; and the Mine Yard with more than 66 exhibits. Living history and live music; and a coffee shop, candy shop, and gift shop. Many visitors might want to spend most of a day here.

■ Open daily, Apr 1 - May 26, 9-5:30. May 27 - Sept 5, 9 AM-9 PM. Sept 5 - Oct 31, 9-5:30. Admission: $7 adults, $6 seniors, $5 ages 13-18, $2 ages 5-12. Family rate: 2 adults and children ages 12 and under, $15. (406) 723-7211 www.miningmuseum.org

64 BROADWAY COUNTY MUSEUM TOWNSEND

The museum, located in Townsend near the south end of Canyon Ferry Reservoir, has a half scale Lewis and Clark dugout canoe. Exhibits include homestead days; early rural electrication; barbed wire; and other local history.

■ Open daily May 15 - Sept 15 1-5. Free Admission. (406) 266-5252 www.visitmt.com Search for Broadwater County Museum

65 CRIMSON BLUFFS AUTO TOUR AND YORK ISLANDS SCENIC ROUTE

The Auto Tour goes along River Road where interpretive markers have been placed. Lewis saw the "remarkable bluff of a crimson coloured earth" on July 24th. Clark identified York's Islands on the map he drew. This scenic route along the path of the Missouri River and about 15 miles from Townsend to Tosten, is a nice way to approach the Three Forks area.

■ (406) 266-3425 USDA Forest Service office, 415 S Front St, Townsend, has Auto Tour maps. www.visitmt.com Search for Crimson Bluffs

7

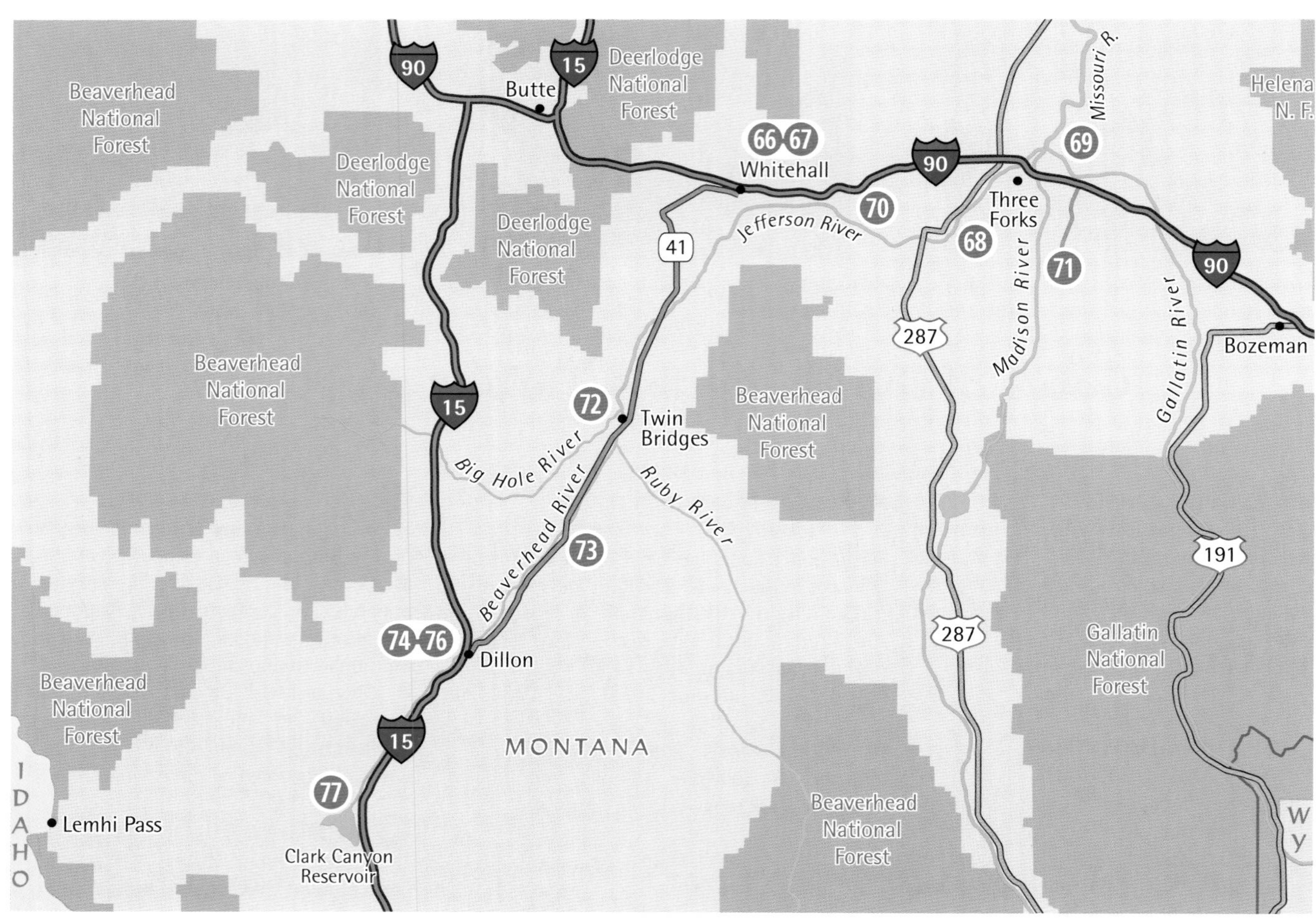

Three Forks Valley: Jefferson, Madison and Gallatin Rivers

66 LEWIS AND CLARK MURALS WHITEHALL MT

From I-90 Exit 249 go south on Whitehall St to Legion Ave. Go left (east) to murals.

67 JEFFERSON VALLEY MUSEUM WHITEHALL MT

303 South Division Street.
From I-90 Exit 249 go south on Whitehall St to Legion Ave. Go left (east) to Division St. Go two blocks. Turn right (south). Go three blocks to the Museum.

68 HEADWATERS HERITAGE MUSEUM THREE FORKS MT

202 Main Street.
From I-90 Exit 278 go soutwest on Frontage Rd/Railroad Ave to Main St. Go south to Cedar St.

69 MISSOURI HEADWATERS STATE PARK THRFEE FORKS MT

From I-90 Exit 278 go east on Rte 205 for 1.3 miles. Turn left (north) onto Pyfer Rd. Go 1.1 miles north then east. Turn left (north) onto Rte 286. Go 1.3 miles to Park.

70 LEWIS AND CLARK CAVERNS THREE FORKS MT

From I-90 Exit 256 go south and then east on Rte 2 for 7.4 miles to Lewis and Clark State Park.

71 MADISON BUFFALO JUMP STATE PARK BOZEMAN MT

From I-90 Exit 283 (Logan Exit) go south on Buffalo Jump Rd. for 6.7 miles on gravel roads to Madison Buffalo Jump State Park.

72 MADISON COUNTY LEWIS AND CLARK INTERPRETIVE CENTER TWIN BRIDGES MT

Madison County Fairgrounds.
From Rte 2 at Twin Bridges go west on 4th Ave across the river bridge. Go to the Fairgrounds entrance on the left (south).

73 BEAVERHEAD ROCK STATE PARK DILLON MT

From Twin Bridges go 12.8 miles south on Rte 2. Beaverhead Rock can be seen 0.3 miles to the west.

74 CLARK'S LOOKOUT STATE PARK DILLON MT

From I-15 Exit 63 go south 0.5 mile on ramp to I-15 Bus. Go 0.6 mile east. Turn left (north) onto Old State Highway 91. Go 0.4 mile. Turn left (west) onto Lovers Leap Road. Go 0.1 mile to Lookout.

75 LEWIS AND CLARK VISITOR CENTER DIORAMA DILLON MT

125 South Montana Street.
From I-15 Exit 62 go on I-15 Bus southeast then northeast for 0.5 mile. Keep straight on Atlantic St for 0.7 mile. Turn left (northwest) onto Glendale St. Go four blocks to Montana St. Turn left (southwest).

76 BEAVERHEAD COUNTY MUSEUM DILLON MT

15 South Montana Street.
From I-15 Exit 62 go on I-15 Bus southeast then northeast for 0.5 mile. Go straight on Atlantic St for 0.7 mile. Turn left (northwest) onto Glendale St. Go four blocks to Montana St. Turn right (northwest).

77 CAMP FORTUNATE CLARK CANYON RESERVOIR MT

From I-15 Exit 44 go west on Rte 324 for 2.6 miles. Turn left (south) onto local road. Go 0.5 mile to the Overlook.

Clark Canyon Reservoir
Betty Kluesner
Discovery Expedition of St Charles

Compass Checking at Clark's Lookout, Betty Kluesner, DESC

Madison River
Betty Kluesner, DESC

Interpretive Plaza
Missouri Headwaters State Park

Three Forks Missouri Headwaters

66 LEWIS AND CLARK OUTDOOR MURALS WHITEHALL

Twelve murals by Kit Mather are placed around the town of Whitehall, commemorating the Lewis and Clark Expedition. The "City of Murals" is located in the Jefferson River Valley. The Lewis and Clark Caverns are located nearby. Whitehall is home to the Golden Sunlight Mine, the largest gold mine in Montana.

■ (610) 432-4130 www.whitehall-ledger.com

67 JEFFERSON VALLEY MUSEUM–WHITEHALL

The museum is located in a 1914 barn. Exhibits feature Native American history of the area, and other local history. Interactive exhibits include a Victrola music machine that still plays, a player piano, and a telephone that rings.

■ Open last wkd May-1st wkd Sept Tues-Sun 12-4. Free admission. (406) 287-7813 www.whitehall-ledger.com

68 HEADWATERS HERITAGE MUSEUM SACAJAWEA STATUE AND HOTEL THREE FORKS, MT

The museum is located in the town of Three Forks, six miles from Missouri Headwaters State Park. Thousands of historical artifacts from the surrounding area are displayed, including an anvil from the 1808-10 trading post of the Missouri Fur Company. A statue of Sacajawea, dedicated for the bicentennial, is located in front of the Sacajawea Hotel, a historic 1910 inn, bar, and restaurant at Main and Ash Streets.

■ Museum is open June-Sept, Mon-Sat 9-5. Free admission. (406) 285-4778 www.threeforksmontana.com/attractions

■ Sacajawea Hotel (406) 285-6515 www.sacajaweahotel.com

69 MISSOURI HEADWATERS STATE PARK–THREE FORKS

Located at the confluence of the Jefferson, Madison and Gallatin Rivers, the Three Forks of the Missouri River, Missouri Headwaters State Park has a primitive campground ($12 a night); interpretive panels with audio narrations, a visitor contact station, and park naturalists. A summer series of talks is held on Saturday evenings at 7 PM in June, July and August.

■ Park facilities, $5 vehicle day use fee. (406) 994-4042 www. fwp.mt.gov/lands

70 LEWIS AND CLARK CAVERNS STATE PARK–THREE FORKS

Lewis and Clark Caverns is one of the largest limestone caverns in the Northwest. The 2 hour long cavern tours have two miles of walking, bending and stooping in 48° temperature. The park has a visitor center, displays, campgrounds and cabins; summer evening programs.

■ Open all year. $5 vehicle day-use fee. Cavern tour fee, $10 adult, $5 ages 6-11. (Day use fee waived if taking cavern tour.) Cavern tours daily from May-Sept. First tour starts at 9; last tour at 4:30, May-June 14 and Sept; and last tour at 6:30, from June 15-1st wkd in Sept. (406) 287-3541 www.fwp.mt.gov/lands

71 MADISON BUFFALO JUMP STATE PARK BOZEMAN

The buffalo jump was used by Natives Americans for 2,000 years to stampede buffalo off the cliffs to their death ,where they were butchered below.

■ Open all year. $5 vehicle day use fee. (406) 994-4042 www.fwp.state.mt.us/lands

72 MADISON COUNTY LEWIS AND CLARK INTERPRETIVE PARK–TWIN BRIDGES

A statue of Sacajawea, her son Pompey, and the Newfoundland dog, Seaman are the focal point of the park, which also has a tipi, dugout canoe, interpretive signage, and picnic tables. The park is located at the Madison County Fairgrounds, which has 7 historic log buildings, designed by the architect who did Yellowstone's log buildings.

■ Open all year. (406) 684-5824 www.twinbridgeschamber.com

73 BEAVERHEAD ROCK STATE PARK DILLON

When they saw Beaverhead Rock on August 8th, Sacajawea told them they were near her people, the Shoshone. This was a familiar landmark. Her people spent the summer over the mountains at a river running to the west. Lewis wrote he would "pass the mountains to the Columbia" and proceed on until he found either the Shoshone or other Indians with horses to trade, so they could get their supplies over the mountains. Beaverhead Rock is an undeveloped state park.

■ Open all year. No fees. (406) 834-3413 www.visitmt.com Search for Beaverhead Rock

74 CLARK'S LOOKOUT STATE PARK–DILLON

Clark's Lookout is a 70 foot hill overlooking the Beaverhead River one mile north of Dillon. On August 13th, William Clark hiked to the top to see what lay ahead for the expedition. Moderately steep trail, with interpetive signage. This is one of the few places you can be guaranteed to stand at the same place Clark stood.

■ Open all year. (406) 834-3413 www.fwp.state.mt.us/lands

75 LEWIS AND CLARK DIORAMA VISITOR CENTER–DILLON

The Visitor Center displays a wonderful diorama that was on display for many years at the Montana State Historical Society Museum at Helena. The diorama depicts the departure of Lewis and his party on the morning of August 9, 1805 to find the Shoshone. The exhibit, which was cut in pieces and placed in storage for years, has been restored and repaired by local volunteers.

■ Open daily Jun-Aug 8-8, May and Sept daily 9-5, Oct-Apr Mon-Fri 9-5. (406) 683-5511 www.exploredillon.com

76 BEAVERHEAD COUNTY MUSEUM DILLON

The museum is housed in a log building complex next door to the visitor center. Here you can see a homesteader's cabin, the first flush toilet outhouse in Dillon, mining and agricultural equipment, and other local history.

■ Open all year Mon-Fri 8-5. Last wkd May-1st wkd Sept also Sat 1-4. Free Admission. (406) 683-5027 www.visitmt.com Search for Beaverhead County

77 CAMP FORTUNATE CLARK CANYON RESERVOIR

On August 13th, Lewis' party made contact with the Shoshone. On August 17th, Clark's party arrived with Sacagawea. First Sacagawea had a joyful reunion with a girlfriend. Then when Sacagawea was translating, she recognized the chief, Cameahwait, as her brother. For this reason, the camp was named "Camp Fortunate." The site is under water at the Clark Canyon Reservoir, but an overlook has interpretive signage.

■ Open all year. (406) 683-2307 www.exploredillon.com

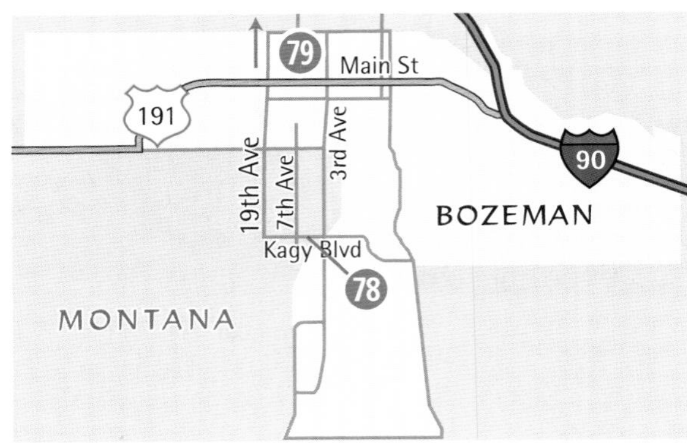

Bozeman, Montana

Livingston, Montana

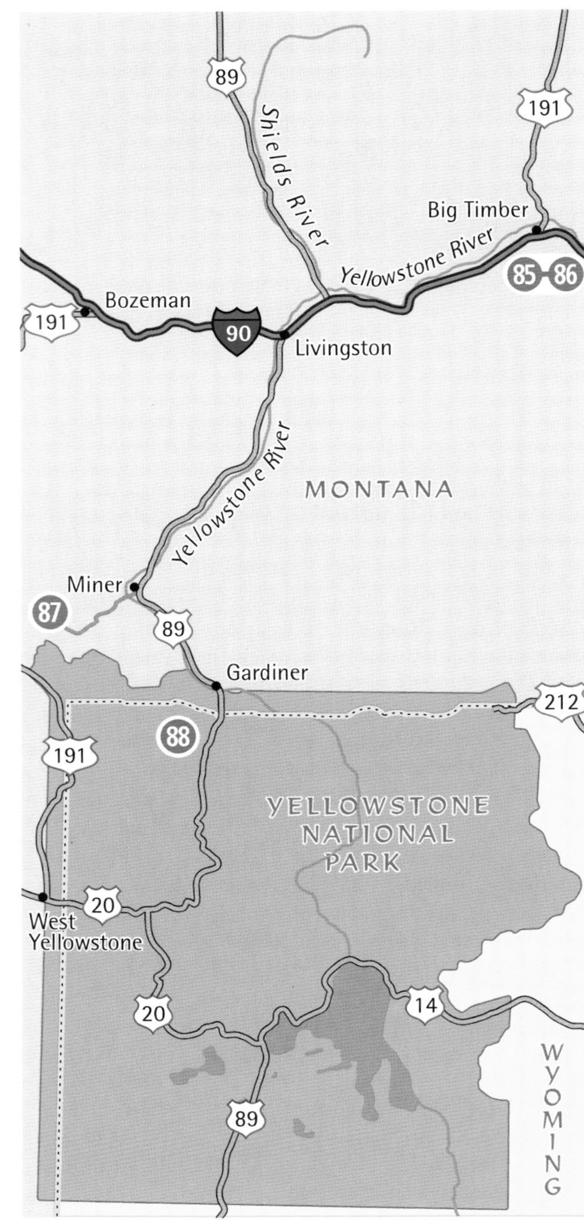

Bozeman, Livingston and Yellowstone National Park

78 MUSEUM OF THE ROCKIES BOZEMAN MT

600 West Kagy Boulevard.
From I-90 Exit 306 turn right (south) onto 7th Avenue. Go 1.1 miles. Turn right (west) onto Main Street. Go 0.8 mile. Turn left (south) onto 19th Ave. Go 1.3 miles. Turn left (east) onto Kagy Boulevard. Go one mile to the Museum.

79 AMERICAN COMPUTER MUSEUM AND VIDEO GAME HALL OF FAME AND MUSEUM BOZEMAN MT

2304 North 7th Ave
From I-90 Exit 306 go north on 7th Ave 0.5 mile to the museum.

80 YELLOWSTONE GATEWAY MUSEUM LIVINGSTON MT

118 West Chinook Street.
From I-90 Exit 333 go north then northeast on US 89 for 1.5 miles to Main Street. Turn left (northwest) onto Main Street. Immediately turn left again then right. Go 0.2 miles to Chinook Street. Go left (southwest) to the Museum.

81 FLY FISHING DISCOVERY CENTER LIVINGSTON MT

215 East Lewis Street.
From I-90 Exit 333 go north then northeast on US 89 for 1.5 miles to B Street. Turn right (southeast). Go two blocks. Turn left (northeast) onto Lewis St. Go to the Museum.

82 LIVINGSTON DEPOT LIVINGSTON MT

200 West Park Street.
From I-90 Exit 333 go north then northeast on US 89 for 1.3 miles to Second Street.

83 SACAJAWEA PARK AND STATUE LIVINGSTON MT

From I-90 Exit 333 go north then northeast on US 89 for 1.3 miles to Yellowstone Street. Turn right (southeast). Go five blocks (0.5 mile) to the Park.

84 LEWIS AND CLARK INTERPRETIVE SIGN LIVINGSTON, MT

Six miles west of Livingston on I-90 East, coming from Bozeman, between Exit 324 and Livingston.

85 CRAZY MOUNTAIN MUSEUM BIG TIMBER MT

From I-90 E Exit 367 go east on the Frontage Road. The Museum is adjacent to the cemetery.

86 GREYCLIFF PRAIRIE DOG TOWN STATE PARK BIG TIMBER MT

From I-90 Exit 377 go east to the Greycliff Frontage Road. Go right (south) 0.1 mile to the Park.

87 PETRIFIED FOREST GALLATIN NAT'L FOREST MINER MT

From I-90 Exit 333 go south on US 89 for 31.9 miles. Turn right (west) onto Old Yellowstone Trail. Go south 5.8 miles. Turn right (west) onto Tom Miner Creek Road. Go 10.3 miles to the Gallatin Petrified Forest Trailhead.

88 YELLOWSTONE NAT'L PARK

Three entrances to Yellowstone National Park are in Montana. The North Entrance is from Gardiner on US 89.. The West Yellowstone Entrance is at the junction of US 191 and US 20. The Northeast Entrance is via US 212.

Yellowstone River
Betty Kluesner
Discovery Expedition of St Charles

Museum of the Rockies Dinosaur

Gateway to Yellowstone
Travel Montana

Old Faithful, Yellowstone
Travel Montana

Bozeman, Livingston and Yellowstone National Park

78 MUSEUM OF THE ROCKIES—BOZEMAN

The region's biggest natural history museum has many fascinating exhibits. The world-reknowned Dr. Jack Horner has finished the first phase of the new dinosaur complex: the Hall of Horns and Teeth; and a full size recreation of the "good mother lizard" dinosaur nesting colonies found on "Egg Mountain" near Choteau; and the world's largest T-Rex skull. Other exhibits are "Enduring Peoples," the story of prehistoric people and the 12 Montana Indian tribes who descended from them; and Lewis and Clark and the mountain men and fur trade era. There is an eleven acre living history farm during summer months. There is also an excellent geology exhibit. T-Rextaurant open June 14-Sept 1 on on Bair Plaza in front of the museum. Gift shop.

■ Open mid-Jun-1st wkd Sept daily 8-8. 1st wkd Sept-mid-Jun Mon-Sat 9-5 Sun 12:30-5. Admission: $9.50 adult, $8.50 senior, $6.50 age 5-18. (406) 994-2251
www.museumoftherockies.org

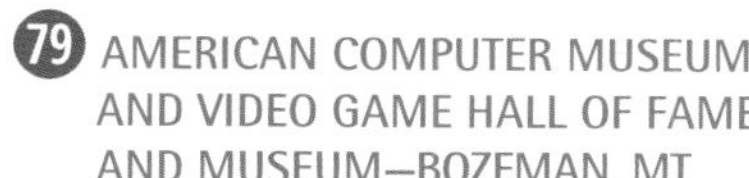

79 AMERICAN COMPUTER MUSEUM AND VIDEO GAME HALL OF FAME AND MUSEUM—BOZEMAN, MT

The world's oldest computer museum, open to the public since 1990. Displays appeal to beginners and experts. Regularly scheduled tours led by friendly guides. Over 1,000 artifacts presented in a timeline fashion of over 20,000 years of history. The Video Game Hall of Fame and Museum is the newest addition.

■ Open daily, June-Aug, 10-4 (Thurs until 8). Sept-May, Tues, Weds, Fri, Sat, 12-4 and Thursday, 4-8. Admission: $4 adult, $2 ages 6-12.
(406) 582-1288 www.compustory.com

80 YELLOWSTONE GATEWAY MUSEUM LIVINGSTON

The Museum has Ice Age artifacts from the oldest burial site in North America, and other prehistoric artifacts. Yellowstone Park, Railroad, Pioneer and Old West History.

■ Open daily Jun-Aug, 10-5. Sept, Tues-Sat 10-4. Oct-May by appointment. Admission: $4 adult, $3.50 senior. $3 ages 6-12.
(406) 222-4184 www.livingstonmuseums.org

81 FLY FISHING DISCOVERY CENTER BOZEMAN

An exhibit on Lewis and Clark's fish discoveries is one of the attractions in this interesting museum. 10,000 fishing flys, a tackle room, murals, and a pallid sturgeon, the boneless fish, on display. From June 1-1st wkd in Sept, the FFDC offers free fly-casting lessons from 5-7 PM on Tuesdays and Thursdays. Equipment is provided. The Center is owned by the Federation of Fly Fishers.

■ Open Jun-Sept Mon-Sat 10-6 Sun 12-5. Oct-May Mon-Fri 10-5. Admission: $3 adult, $2 senior, $1 ages 7-14.
(406) 222-9639 www.livingstonemuseums.org

82 LIVINGSTON DEPOT

The 1902 Northern Pacific Railroad Depot was the access to Yellowstone National Park until 1979. The Depot Museum has historic exhibits and cultural programs during summer months. There are 14 art galleries in Livingston.

■ Open Jun-Sept Mon-Sat 9-5 Sun 1-5. Admission: $3 adult, $2 senior, $2 ages 6-12.
(406) 222-2300 www.livingstonemuseums.org

83 SACAJAWEA PARK AND STATUE LIVINGSTON, MONTANA

The Discovery Corps visited the Livingston area on July 15, 1806. This lovely, larger-than-life size, statue by Mary Michaels is the only sculpture that shows Sacajawea on horseback, and shows Pompey as a 17 month old toddler, instead of as an infant.

■ (406) 222-0850 www.sacajaweapark.com

84 LEWIS AND CLARK I-90 INTERPRETIVE MARKER—LIVINGTSTON

Just west of Livingston, the Great Bend of the Yellowstone Lewis and Clark Heritage Commission has put up an exhibit on Interstate 90.

■ (406) 222-0850
www.yellowstone-chamber.com

85 CRAZY MOUNTAIN MUSEUM BIG TIMBER, MT

Exhibits and paintings on Sweet Grass County history. A collection of old chaps in an aspen tack room; Walk Through Time: ancient rocks, minerals and arrowheads along a timeline. Sheep and wool exhibits, miniature town exhibit, rodeo history, cattle and horse brands. Norwegian artifacts in a "stabbur," or Norwegian storehouse, are house in a separate building with a one room school house and a Lewis and Clark exhibit. Native Plants Garden.

■ Open last wkd May-1st wkd Sept Wed-Sun 1-4:30. Winter by appointment. Free admission.
(406) 932-5126 www.sweetgrasscounty.com

86 GREYCLIFF PRAIRIE DOG TOWN STATE PARK— BIG TIMBER, MT

See these entertaining, blacktailed prairie dogs at Greycliff Prairie Dog Town State Monument. Pets must be on a leash.

■ Open all year. Day use fee May-Sep $2.
(406) 247-2940 www.fwp.mt.gov/lands

87 PETRIFIED FOREST GALLATIN NATIONAL FOREST

The Gallatin Petrified Forest is between 35 and 55 million years old. It is unique because many of its trees are in an upright position, in as many as 80 layers, one on top of another. There is a half mile interpretive trail, which climbs up an 11-13% grade. Once you know what petrified wood looks like you may collect small amounts as souvenirs. Stop in the USDA Forest Service Ranger District office on Highway 89 in Gardiner to obtain a free permit to collect them.

■ (406) 848-7375 wwwfs.fed.us/r1/gallatin

88 YELLOWSTONE NATIONAL PARK

Yellowstone is the world's first national park, established in 1872. It contains more than 2.2 million acres of scenic vistas, waterfalls, and steamings geysers. It is the world's largest area of geyser activity. It is also the largest wildlife area in the United States. Most park roads are closed between November and May. There are five entrances to the park. Mammoth Hot Springs Visitor Center is open year round. 12 campgrounds, 5 visitor centers.

■ Entrance fee $20 - 7days Hotel and cabin accomodations, June to Sept: (307) 344-7311; campground reservations: (307) 344-7311
(406) 344-7381 www.nps.gov/yell

Clark and Pryor's Parties

Clark's Yellowstone Exploration party camped near Park City, from July 19-23rd, 1806. They made two small canoes, to switch from horse to river travel. While there, Indians stole 24 of their horses. Clark sent Sergeant Nathaniel Pryor and 3 others overland with the remaining 17 horses, to be delivered to the Mandan Villages in North Dakota to be used for trading. Pryor's group started out south of Billings on the 24th, on a route paralleling I-90, when the Indians stole all the rest of the horses on the very first night they camped, a few miles west of Hardin. Pryor's party made two bull boats out of skins, and caught up with Clark on the Yellowstone on August 8th.

www.lewis-clark.org Search for Yellowstone River Return/Nathaniel Pryor's Mission

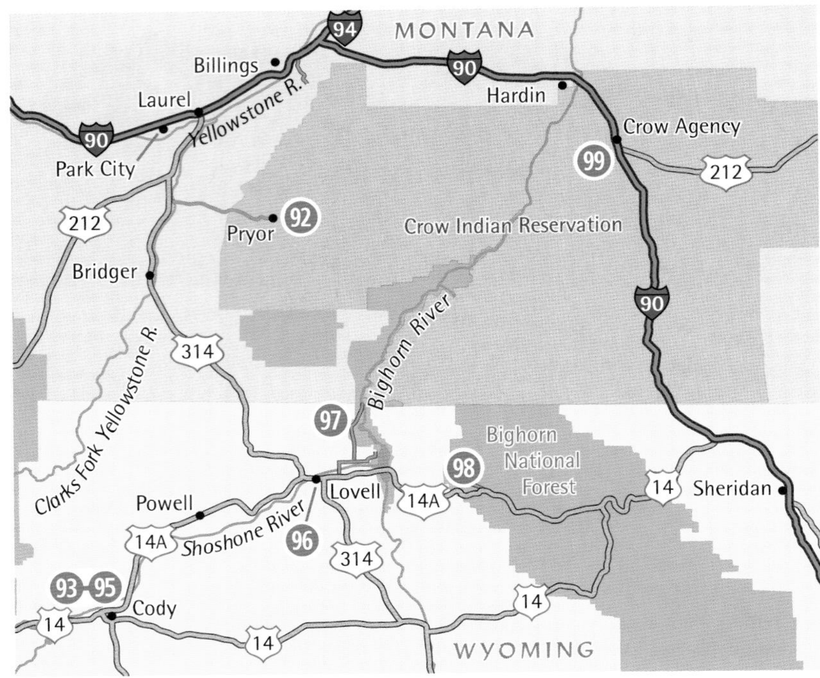

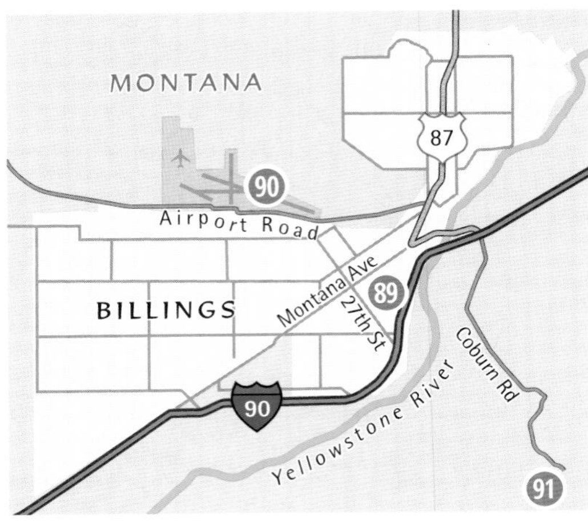

89 WESTERN HERITAGE CENTER BILLINGS MT

2822 Montana Avenue.

From I-90 Exit 450 go northwest on 27th St (Rte 3) for 1.3 miles. Turn left (southwest) onto Minnesota Ave. Go two blocks. Turn right (northwest) onto 29th St. Go one block. Turn right (northeast) onto Montana Ave.

90 YELLOWSTONE COUNTY MUSEUM BILLINGS MT

1950 Terminal Circle.

From I-90 Exit 450 go northwest on 27th St (Rte 3) for 3.5 miles to Logan International Airport. Drive into the airport, past the front of the terminal, around the west parking lots and follow the road as it curves east. The museum is just before the exit on the right.

91 PICTOGRAPH CAVE BILLINGS MT

From I-90 Exit 452 go southeast on Old Hardin Rd. Immediately go south on Coburn Rd. for 5.3 miles.

92 CHIEF PLENTY COUPS MUSEUM PRYOR MT

From I-90 Exit 434 in Laurel go south on US 212 for 11.6 miles. Turn left (south) onto US 310 for 4 miles. turn left (east) onto Pryor Rd. Go 16.8 miles to Chief Plenty Coups State Park.

93 BUFFALO BILL HISTORICAL CENTER CODY WY

720 Sheridan Avenue.

From the junction of US 14 Alt and US 14 in Cody go west 0.8 mile on Sheridan Ave to the Center.

94 COLTER'S HELL TRAIL CODY WY

1138 Demaris Street.

From the junction of US 14 Alt and US 14 in Cody go west 0.8 mile on Sheridan Ave. Turn left (south) onto 8th Street. Go 0.5 mile. Turn right (west) onto North Fork Hwy. Go 1.8 miles. Colter's Hell Trail is in front of Old Trail Town.

95 OLD TRAIL TOWN AND MUSEUM OF THE OLD WEST CODY WY

1138 Demaris Street.

From the junction of US 14 Alt and US 14 in Cody go west 0.8 mile on Sheridan Ave. Turn left (south) onto 8th Street. Go 0.5 mile. Turn right (west) onto North Fork Hwy. Go 1.8 miles to Old Trail Town.

96 BIGHORN CANYON VISITOR CENTER LOVELL WY

From the junction of US 314 and US 14 Alt in Lovell 60 go 0.3 mile northeast on on US 14 Alt to the Visitor Center.

97 PRYOR MOUNTAIN WILD HORSE REFUGE LOVELL WY

From the junction of US 314 and US 14 Alt in Lovell go 0.3 mile northeast then east on on US 14 Alt for 2.7 miles. Turn left (north) onto state Route 37. Go 14 miles to a paved road that parallels the lip of the Bighorn Canyon.

98 BIGHORN MEDICINE WHEEL US 14 A

From the junction of US 314 and US 14 Alt in Lovell go east 34 miles to local road. Turn left (northwest) onto local road. Go 2.9 miles to the Medicine Wheel. The local road is 1/3 mile west of Forest Service Road 13.

99 LITTLE BIGHORN BATTLEFIELD CROW AGENCY

At I-90 Exit 510.

The annual Clark Bottom Rendezvous, a Lewis and Clark and Mountain Men gathering, is held 10 miles west of Billings at Laurel during the third week of July. The rendezvous is held where people have always camped: at the confluence of the Yellowstone and Clarks Fork of the Yellowstone Rivers. (Not to be confused with the Clark Fork River of Montana and Idaho.) If you want to visit the site, take I-90 Laurel Exit 434 and go south 0.7 mile over the Yellowstone River bridge; turn left to go the confluence campgrounds.

www.visitmt.com Search for Clark Bottom Rendezvous

7

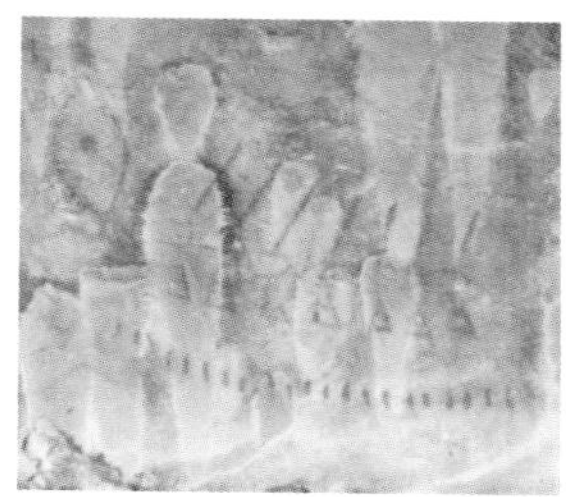

Pictograph Cave State Monument, National Historic Landmark
Betty Kluesner, Discovery Expedition of St Charles

Chief Plenty Coups State Park
Travel Montana

Crow Fair
Travel Montana

Billings, Cody and Crow Indian Reservation

89 WESTERN HERITAGE CENTER—BILLINGS

The Center, located in the old Billings public library, is an accredited museum and an affiliate of the Smithsonian; it "tells the stories of the peoples of the Yellowstone River Valley." It has recently developed oral history projects and exhibitions with the Crow and Northern Cheyenne tribes. It's extensive collection of artifacts includes over 1,000 photographs. Changing exhibits are featured.

■ Open Tues-Sat, 10-5. Free admission.
(406) 256-6809 www.ywhc.org

90 YELLOWSTONE COUNTY MUSEUM BILLINGS, MONTANA

Entrance to the Yellowstone County Museum is through an 1892 wealthy cattleman's log cabin located at the Billings Logan International Airport. It is much larger than it looks, as it has an extensive display area in a lower level; the collection includes more than 15,000 cowboy, Native American, and western artifacts. The cabin area has a Lewis and Clark Fur Trading Post Gift Shop, and an exhibit area devoted to Lewis and Clark and the fur trade. Its Landmarks Gallery has work by local artists and/or museum artifacts.

■ Open all year Mon-Fri 10:30-5; Sat 10:30-3. Free admission. (406) 254-6031
www.yellowstonecountymuseum.org

91 PICTOGRAPH CAVE STATE MONUMENT NATIONAL HISTORIC LANDMARK BILLINGS, MONTANA

Located six miles south of Billings, the cave complex used by prehistoric peoples has evidence of habitation dating back to 4500 years ago. The pictographs date back to over 2200 years ago. There is a 1.000 foot walking trail that is not handicapped accessible. Bring binoculars to view the pictographs.

■ Open daily, April-last wkd May, 10-7; last wkd in May to 1st wkd Sept, 8 AM - 8 PM; and from then to Oct 15, 10-7.
Vehicle day use fee $5. (406) 247-2940
www.pictographcave.org

 CHIEF PLENTY COUPS MUSEUM AND STATE PARK—PRYOR, MT

The most famous of Crow Chiefs, Chief Plenty Coups, gave his homestead to Montana in 1928 to be used as a memorial to the Crow people. It is the only museum dedicated to the Crow Nation. The chief lived in a tipi and entertained in a house. He also had a store. The museum, home, store and tipi site are located in the state park near a sacred spring.

■ Open May-Dec. Museum daily 10-5. Park daily 8-8. Winter by appointment Day use fee $2 adult, $1 ages 6-12.
(406) 252-1289 www.plentycoups.org

 BUFFALO BILL HISTORICAL CENTER CODY, WYOMING

This is one of the great museum centers of the United States. The complex includes five museums: Buffalo Bill Museum; Whitney Gallery of Western Art; Plains Indian Museum; Cody Firearms Museum; and Draper Museum of Natural History. Buffalo Bill founded the town of Cody.

■ Open daily Apr 10-5 May-Sept 15 8 AM-8 PM Sept 16-Oct 8-5. Nov-Mar Tues-Sun 10-3. Admission: $15 adult,313 senior, $10 student, $6 ages 5-12, $40 family (307) 587-4771
www.bbhc.org

94 COLTER'S HELL TRAIL—CODY, WY

When expedition member John Colter returned to the area with the Lisa-Drouillard 1807 party of fur traders, he discovered the boiling pots of mud and steaming geysers along the Shoshone River at Cody. His companions found his stories incredible and called it "Colter's Hell." For many years it was mistakenly assumed he had discovered the geysers of Yellowstone National Park. A walking trail with historic markers is located at the site.

■ (307) 587-2777 www.codychamber.org

 OLD TRAIL TOWN AND MUSEUM OF THE OLD WEST—CODY, WY

Old Trail Town is located across the highway from Colter's Hell Trail. It is a collection of 26 historic frontier buildings dating from 1879-1901, including the Rivers Saloon and the Hole in the Wall gang's cabin. It also has 100 horse drawn vehicles and an extensive collection of Shoshone, Gros Ventre and Crow artifacts. Small gift shop.

■ Open daily May-Sept, 8 AM-8 PM. Admission: $7 adult, $6 senior, $3 (ages 6-12)
(307) 587-5302
www.museumoftheoldwest.org

96 BIGHORN CANYON NATIONAL RECREATIONAL AREA—LOVELL, WY

The north end of Bighorn Canyon is on the Crow Reservation. Please stay on the road. The south end is open to hiking biking, and horseback riding. Bighorn Lake, created by the 1966 Yellowtail Dam, extends for 60 miles in Wyoming and Montana; 55 of which are in the spectacular Bighorn Canyon. Visitor Centers are located in Lovell and in Fort Smith, Montana.

■ Lovell Visitor Center is open daily. last wkd May-1st wkd Sept, 8-6. 1st wkd Sept-last wkd May 8:30-4:30. Entrance fee $5 - day.
(406) 666-2412 or (307) 548-2251.
www.nps.gov/bica

97 PRYOR MOUNTAIN WILD HORSE REFUGE LOVELL, WYOMING

The first nationally designated area for wild horses, is along the Bighorn Canyon. The small herd of 120 Pryor Mountain Mustangs, are thought to be of Spanish ancestry. Enjoy the horses from a safe distance. Do not attempt to get close or feed them. Camping and cabin available through BLM office in Billings.

■ (406) 896-5013 www.mt.blm.gov/bifo

98 BIGHORN MEDICINE WHEEL NATIONAL HISTORIC LANDMARK—HIGHWAY 14 A

The Medicine Wheel is located at 9,642 feet on Medicine Mountain in the Bighorn Range. The wheel is an ancient sacred site to Native Americans; it is aligned with the summer solstice sunrise, and many ceremonies are held here.

■ (307) 548-6541 www.fs.fed.us/r2/bighorn

99 LITTLE BIGHORN BATTLEFIELD NATIONAL MONUMENT—CROW AGENCY

The Crow Fair Powwow, Rodeo and Race Meet is one of the largest pow wows in the country, held each year on the 3rd weekend in August. More than 45,000 spectators attend. The campgrounds are a short distance from the Battlefield National Monument. The Little Bighorn Battlefield is the site of Custer's Defeat in 1876. Walking trails, and a 5 mile auto tour route.

■ Open daily: last wkd May-Jul 8 AM-9 PM Aug -1st wkd Sept 8-8 Sept-Oct 8-6 Nov-Mar 8-4:30 Apr-May 8-6. Entry fee $10.
(406) 638-3204 www.nps.gov/libi
www.friendslittlebighorn.com

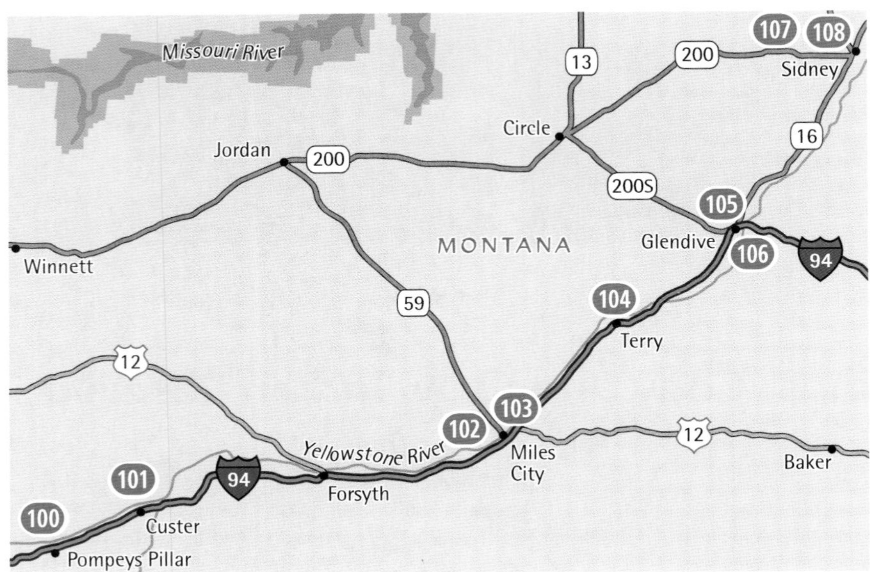

Pompeys Pillar to Sidney

100 POMPEYS PILLAR
From I-94 Exit 23 go west on Route 312 0.8 mile to the Pillar Monument.

101 FORT MANUEL LISA
CUSTER MT
From I-94 Custer Exit 47 go north on Rte 47. Immediately turn right (east) onto Old Highway 10. Go 2.1 miles to the Manuel Lisa Fishing Access Site.

102 RANGE RIDERS MUSEUM
MILES CITY MT
From I-94 Exit 135 go north on I-94 Bus/US12 for two miles to the Range Riders Museum.

103 PIROGUE ISLAND
STATE PARK
MILES CITY MT
From I-94 Exit 135 go north on I-94 Bus/US12 for 2.8 miles. Turn left (northwest) onto Rte 22. Go 2.2 miles. Turn right (northeast) onto Kinsey Rd. Go 2.2 miles. Turn right (southeast) onto local road. Go two miles to Pirogue Island State Park.

104 PRAIRIE COUNTY
MUSEUM
TERRY MT
101 South Logan.
From I-94 Exit 176 go north on Route 253 for four blocks. Turn left (west) onto Spring Street. Go 0.5 mile to Logan Avenue. Turn right (north). Go to the Museum.

105 MAKOSHIKA DINOSAUR
MUSEUM
GLENDIVE MT
111 West Bell Street.
From I-94 Exit 213 go south on Lewis and Clark Trail 0.7 mile. Turn left (west) onto I-94 Bus (Towne Street). Go 1.1 miles. Turn right (southwest) onto Merrill Avenue. Go one block. Turn right (northwest) onto Bell Street. Go to the Dinosaur Museum.

106 MAKOSHIKA STATE PARK
GLENDIVE MT
From I-94 Exit 215 go southwest on Merrill Avenue for one mile. Turn left (southeast) onto Allard Street. Go 0.2 mile. Turn right (southwest) onto Sargent Avenue. Go 1.4 miles. Turn left (southeast) onto Snyder Street. Go 0.5 mile to Makoshika State Park.

107 LEWIS AND CLARK CENTER
SIDNEY MT
909 South Central Avenue.
From Rte 200 go northeast on Rte 16 (Central Ave) for 1.8 miles to the Visitor Center.

108 MONDAK CENTER
SIDNEY MT
120 3rd Avenue SE.
From Route 200 go northeast on Route 16 (Central Avenue) for 2.3 miles to Main Street. Turn right (east). Go two blocks. Turn right (south) to the Heritage Center on 3rd Avenue.

Manuel Lisa's Forts

Manuel Lisa (1772-1820) was the first trader with a large expedition up the river in 1807 after the Lewis and Clark Expedition. George Drouillard accompanied him, representing the financial interests of Menard and Morrison of Illinois. Lisa established Fort Raymond, named for his son, at the confluence of the Bighorn and Yellowstone Rivers in the heart of beaver country.

Lisa returned to St Louis with furs at the end of the summer of 1807. George Drouillard and John Colter were exploring the region. Colter discovered "Colter's Hell" at Cody. Then, over the winter of 1807-08, Colter was with Flathead Indians when they were attacked by the Blackfeet and fought on the side of the Flatheads. In the early autumn of 1808, Colter and others were trapping beaver at Three Forks. The Blackfeet killed John Potts (a member of the Lewis and Clark Expedition), and arranged a sport of allowing a naked Colter to run for his life from pursuing Indians. Colter escaped.

In 1809 William Clark became president of Manuel Lisa's fur company. Clark remained in St Louis while Lisa's expedition of 1809 returned Mandan Chief Sheheke to his village. In 1810 their men established a fort at Three Forks, where George Drouillard was killed by the Blackfeet. Partner Alexander Henry abandoned the fort and established Fort Henry at Henry's Fork on the Snake River in Idaho. Colter retired from the fur trade.

In 1812, while at war with Great Britain, Lisa and Clark sent another expedition up the river to Fort Manuel at Kenel SD. Sacagawea died of putrid fever at the fort in December, 1812. Lisa enlisted the support of Teton Chief Black Buffalo to remain neutral during the war; built Fort Lisa at Council Bluffs; and brought Sacagawea's baby girl, Lizette, to St. Louis to be adopted by William Clark, along with Pompey.

Lisa was at his Council Bluffs fort in the winter of 1819-20 when the Stephen Long Exploring Expedition was there and Fort Atkinson was built. He died in St Louis in 1820 after a fight with a man whom he had accused of stealing 1,800 pounds of beaver pelts from his warehouse on the riverfront. He left provisions for all of his children, both white and Indian, in his will and is buried at Belle Fontaine Cemetery in St Louis near William Clark's gravesite.

William Clark's Name

Pompeys Pillar

Range Rider Museum
Travel Montana

Makoshika State Park
Travel Montana

Pompey's Pillar to Sidney

100 POMPEYS PILLAR NATIONAL HISTORIC LANDMARK BILLINGS, MONTANA

William Clark carved his name on this sandstone bluff on July 25, 1806. It can still be seen today, located on the rock face near the top of the boardwalk trail staircase. This is the only on-site physical evidence of a Lewis and Clark Expedition campsite.

Clark named this 150 foot tall landmark bluff for Sacagawea and Toussaint Charbonneau's little son, Pompey, then 17 months old. He called it Pompy's Tower, but the editor of the journals, Nicholas Biddle changed it to Pompeys Pillar. Pompey means "little chief" in the Shoshoni language.

The Clark on the Yellowstone Interpretive Center located at Pompeys Pillar has exhibits and a gift shop. Annual Clark Days are held on the last weekend in July.

■ Open daily last wkd May-1st wkd Sept. 1st wkd, 8-8. Sept, 9-5. Entry fee $3 per vehicle. Off season: gate closed, walk-ins are permitted, one mile walk to monument.
(406) 875-2223 www.pompeyspillar.org

101 FORT MANUEL LISA HISTORICAL SITE MARKER AND MANUEL LISA STATE FISHING ACCESS SITE—CUSTER, MT

Clark's party camped here on July 26th, 1806 at the confluence of the Bighorn and Yellowstone Rivers. In 1807 it became the site of Fort Manuel Lisa (aka Fort Raymond), the first building erected by white men in Montana. Today it is a fishing access site with a boat ramp and primitive camping. The Bighorn is considered to be one of the world's finest trout fishing streams.

■ (406) 247-2940 www.fwp.state.mt.us
No fees. Seasonal. Call for dates.

102 RANGE RIDERS MUSEUM MILES CITY, MONTANA

Miles City was named for General Nelson Miles who established Fort Keogh just west of Miles City in 1876, after Custer's defeat at the Battle of the Little Bighorn.

Range Riders museum has nine buildings, preserving the diversified history of the Miles City area—military history, livestock industry, cattle drives, wagon trains, homesteaders, riverboats, railroad history, Native American. Exhibits include: a gun collection with over 400 firearms; early photographs; a frontier town with 11 buildings; Charles Russell Gallery; Carol's Hattery; Fort Keogh's Officer Quarters; Native American artifacts; ranch replicas, and art. It is the largest western museum in the area.

■ Open daily. May-Oct, 8-6. Admission: $5 adult, $4 senior, $1 student, 50¢ ages 6-12. (406) 232-6146 www.mcchamber.com

103 PIROGUE ISLAND STATE PARK MILES CITY

Clark's party camped on this island on July 29th, near the confluence of the Tongue River and the Yellowstone. He noted that "Beaver is very plenty on this part of the Rochejhone" (French for Yellowstone). Pirogue Island is covered with cottonwood trees, and is a haven for waterfowl, bald eagles and deer. Visitors can look for moss agates, and hike around its 269 acres.
Boat floaters can access the island, but crossing to the island is not recommended if water is flowing.

■ Open all year. No entry fee. (406) 234-0900
www.visitmt.com Search for Pirogue Island

104 PRAIRIE COUNTY MUSEUM AND CAMERON GALLERY—TERRY

On the edge of the scenic badlands and home of the moss agate, the Prairie County Museum has a complex that includes the only steam heated outhouse this side of the Mississippi; a train depot; a red wooden caboose; bank building; pioneer homestead; and other buildings.

The Cameron Gallery is devoted to the photographs of "Lady" Evelyn Cameron, a British woman who moved to Prairie County with her husband, a naturalist. She took photographs of ranch life and wildlife in the late 1800's-early 1900's with a 5x7 Graflex camera. The gallery has large, crisp copies of the photos that made her famous.

Evelyn Cameron's life and work was documented in a PBS special in 2005, and is also the subject of a book: ***Photographing Montana 1894-1928: The Life and Work of Evelyn Cameron,*** by Donna Lucey. Prints, PBS video, original photographs and postcards may be purchased from the Evelyn Cameron Foundation.

■ Open last wkd May-1st wkd Sept Wed-Mon 9-3. Free admission. (406) 635-4040
www.visitmt.com Search for Prairie County
www.evelyncameron.com

105 MAKOSHIKA DINOSAUR MUSEUM GLENDIVE, MONTANA

Makoshika Dinosaur Museum showcases fossils and dinosaurs from around the world. The museum plans to expand its Dinosaur Hall to 13,000 square feet in 2006-2007, with a new Dinosaur Walk and Time of the Titans. It offers ranch vacations and dinosaur digs.

■ Open May-Sept Tues-Sat 10-5; Oct-Apr Wed-Sat 12-5. Admission $3 adult, $2 senior, $2 student. (406) 377-1637
www.makoshika.com

106 MAKOSHIKA STATE PARK GLENDIVE, MONTANA

Makoshika is a Lakota word for "badlands." It is the largest of Montana's state parks, with 11,531 acres. Attractions include: campgrounds; visitor center; scenic drives; biking trails; and two hiking trails, each about half a mile long. Fossils from ten different species of dinosaurs have been found here. The center has many exhibits relating to the prehistory of the area. Trailers and motorhomes are not recommended past the first two miles of paved road in the park.

■ Open all year last wkd May-1st wkd Sept 10-6; 1st wkd Sept-last wkd May 9-5. $5 vehicle day use fee

■ June-July, 7 PM Thursdays campfire programs.
(406) 377-6256 www.midrivers.com
www.visitmt.com Search for Glendive

107 LEWIS AND CLARK VISITOR CENTER SIDNEY, MONTANA

The Lewis and Clark Visitor Center welcomes tourists, provides information, and has souvenirs and Lewis and Clark materials for sale.

■ Open all year Mon-Fri 8-5.
(406) 433-1916 www.sydneymt.com

108 MONDAK HERITAGE CENTER AND MUSEUM, SIDNEY, MT

The MonDak Heritage Centers covers a seven county area in Montana and North Dakota. Sidney is located on the Lewis and Clark Trail following the Yellowstone River along State Road 16 up to its confluence with the Missouri near Williston, ND. The center has local art exhibits, and local art for sale. The museum has a frontier town Main St exhibit. Gift and book shop.

■ Open all year Tues-Fri 10-4 Sat 1-4. Admission: $3 adult, $1 child.
(406)-433-3500 www.richland.org

Region Seven: References

BIOGRAPHY

COLTER'S HELL & JACKSON'S HOLE
by Merrill Mattes. Yellowstone Library and Museum Association and the Grand Teton Natural History Association (1962)

COURAGEOUS COLTER AND COMPANIONS
by L. R. Colter-Frick. L. R. Colter-Frick (1997)

THE DISCOVERY OF YELLOWSTONE PARK: JOURNAL OF THE WASHBURN EXPEDITION TO THE YELLOWSTONE AND FIREHOLE RIVERS IN THE YEAR 1870
by Nathaniel Pitt Langford. University of Nebraska Press (1972)

JOHN COLTER: HIS YEARS IN THE ROCKIES
by Burton Harris. University of Nebraska Press (1993)

FUR TRADERS, TRAPPERS, AND MOUNTAIN MEN OF THE UPPER MISSOURI
edited by LeRoy R. Hafen. University of Nebraska Press (1971)

A LIFE WILD AND PERILOUS: MOUNTAIN MEN AND THE PATHS TO THE PACIFIC
by Robert M. Utley. Henry Holt and Company (1997)

MANUEL LISA AND THE OPENING OF THE MISSOURI FUR TRADE
by Richard Edward Oglesby. University of Oklahoma Press (1963)

MANUEL LISA: WITH HITHERTO UNPUBLISHED MATERIAL
by Walter B. Douglas and annotated and edited by Abraham P. Nasitir. Argosy-Antiquarian Ltd. (1964)

THE MOUNTAIN MEN: THE DRAMATIC HISTORY AND LORE OF THE FIRST FRONTIERSMEN
by George Laycock. Lyons & Burford, Publishers (1998)

THE SAGA OF HUGH GLASS: PIRATE, PAWNEE, AND MOUNTAIN MAN
by John Myers Myers. University of Nebraska Press (1963)

THOSE WHO GO AGAINST THE CURRENT
by Shirley Seifert. J. B. Lippincott Company (1943)

TRAPPERS OF THE FAR WEST: SIXTEEN BIOGRAPHICAL SKETCHES
edited by LeRoy R. Hafen. University of Nebraska Press (1972)

THE TRAVELS OF JEDEDIAH SMITH: A DOCUMENTARY OUTLINE INCLUDING THE JOURNAL OF THE GREAT AMERICAN PATHFINDER
by Maurice M. Sullivan. University of Nebraska Press (1992)

HISTORY

ACROSS THE WIDE MISSOURI
by Bernard DeVoto. Houghton Mifflin Company (1947)

AFTER LEWIS AND CLARK: MOUNTAIN MEN AND THE PATHS TO THE PACIFIC
by Robert M. Utley. University of Nebraska Press (2004)

THE BATTLE FOR BUTTE: MINING AND POLITICS ON THE NORTHERN FRONTIER, 1864-1906
by Michael P. Malone, Montana Historical Society Press (1981)

COMPETITIVE STRUGGLE: AMERICA'S WESTERN FUR TRADING POSTS 1764-1865
by R. G. Robertson. Tamarack Books, Inc. (1999)

COPPER CAMP: THE LUSTY STORY OF BUTTE, MONTANA, THE RICHEST HILL ON EARTH
by Writers Project of Montana. Riverbend Publishing (1970)

FORT BENTON: WORLD'S INNERMOST PORT
by Joel Overholser. River & Plains Society (1987)

FRENCH FUR TRADERS AND VOYAGEURS IN THE AMERICAN WEST
edited by LeRoy R. Hafen. University of Nebraska Press (1993)

THE FUR TRADE OF THE AMERICAN WEST 1807-1840: A GEOGRAPHICAL SYNTHESIS
by David J. Wishart. University of Nebraska Press (1979)

THE FUR TRADE ON THE UPPER MISSOURI 1840-1865
by Paul L. Hedren. University of Oklahome Press (1993)

LEWIS AND CLARK EXPLORATION OF CENTRAL MONTANA: MARIAS RIVER TO THE MOUNTAINS
by Ella Mae Howard. Lewis and Clark Interpretive Association, Inc. (1993)

LEWIS AND CLARK IN THE THREE RIVERS VALLEYS, MONTANA 1805-1806. FROM THE ORIGINAL JOURNALS OF THE LEWIS AND CLARK EXPEDITION
Edited by Donald E. Nell and John E. Taylor. The Patrice Press (1996)

LEWIS & CLARK ON THE UPPER MISSOURI
by Jean Clary, Diana Ladd, Pat Hastings, Jeanne O'Neill, Katie White, Riga Winthrop. Stoneydale Press Publishing Company (1999)

MONTANA: A HISTORY OF TWO CENTURIES
Michael P. Malone, Richard B. Roeder, and William L. Lang. University of Washington Press (1991)

MISCELLANEOUS

DALE BURK'S MONTANA
by Dale A. Burk. Stoneydale Publishing Company (2002)

MAGNIFICENT JOURNEY: A GEOLOGIC RIVER TRIP WITH LEWIS AND CLARK THROUGH THE UPPER MISSOURI RIVER BREAKS NATIONAL MONUMENT
by Otto L. Schumacher and Lee A. Woodward. Woodhawk Press (2004)

MONTANA'S HISTORICAL HIGHWAY MARKERS
compiled by Glenda Clay Bradshaw from original text by Robert H. Fletcher: updated by Jon Axline. Montana Historical Society Press (1999)

MONTANA PLACES: EXPLORING BIG SKY COUNTRY
by John B Wright. New Mexico Geographical Society (2000)

MOON HANDBOOKS: MONTANA
by W. C. McRae and Judy Jewell. Avalon Travel (2002)

SCENIC DRIVING MONTANA
by S. A. Snyder. Falcon Publishing (1995)

A TRAVELER'S COMPANION TO MONTANA HISTORY
by Carroll Van West. Montana Historical Society Press (1986)

YELLOWSTONE TREASURES: THE TRAVELERS COMPANION TO THE NATIONAL PARK
by Janet Chapple. Granite Peak Publications (2002)

LEWIS & CLARK'S PORTAGE OF THE FALLS
Audio tour of the portage around the great falls.
Casette tape and map.
Portage Route Chapter of the Lewis and Clark Trial Heritage Foundation.

REGION EIGHT
WESTERN MONTANA AND IDAHO

■ Highway Route Planner ■ Across the Divide to Salmon ■ Bitterroot Valley, Hwy 93 ■ Missoula at the Crossroads ■ Blackfoot River Corridor, Hwy 200 ■ Mission Valley, Hwy 93 ■ I-90 and Hwy 95 to Lewiston ■ Lolo Pass Trail, Hwy 12 ■ Nez Perce Country, Hwy 12 ■ Nez Perce Country, Hwy 95 ■ Lewiston and Clarkston

1. Clearwater River near Orofino 2. Nez Perce NHP Visitor Center and Museum 3. Sacajawea Statue at Salmon 4. Historic St Mary's Mission 5. Canoes on the Clearwater 6. Indian Tipi, Sacajawea Center 7. Jet Boat, Hells Canyon 8. Tipi frames at Big Hole National Battlefield 9. DeVoto Memorial Grove at Lochsa River, Lolo Trail 10. Bitterroots

Credits: (2) (7) Mike McElhatton; (3) (6) Idaho Tourism; (5) Betty Kluesner, Discovery Expedition of St Charles; (8) TravelMT

8

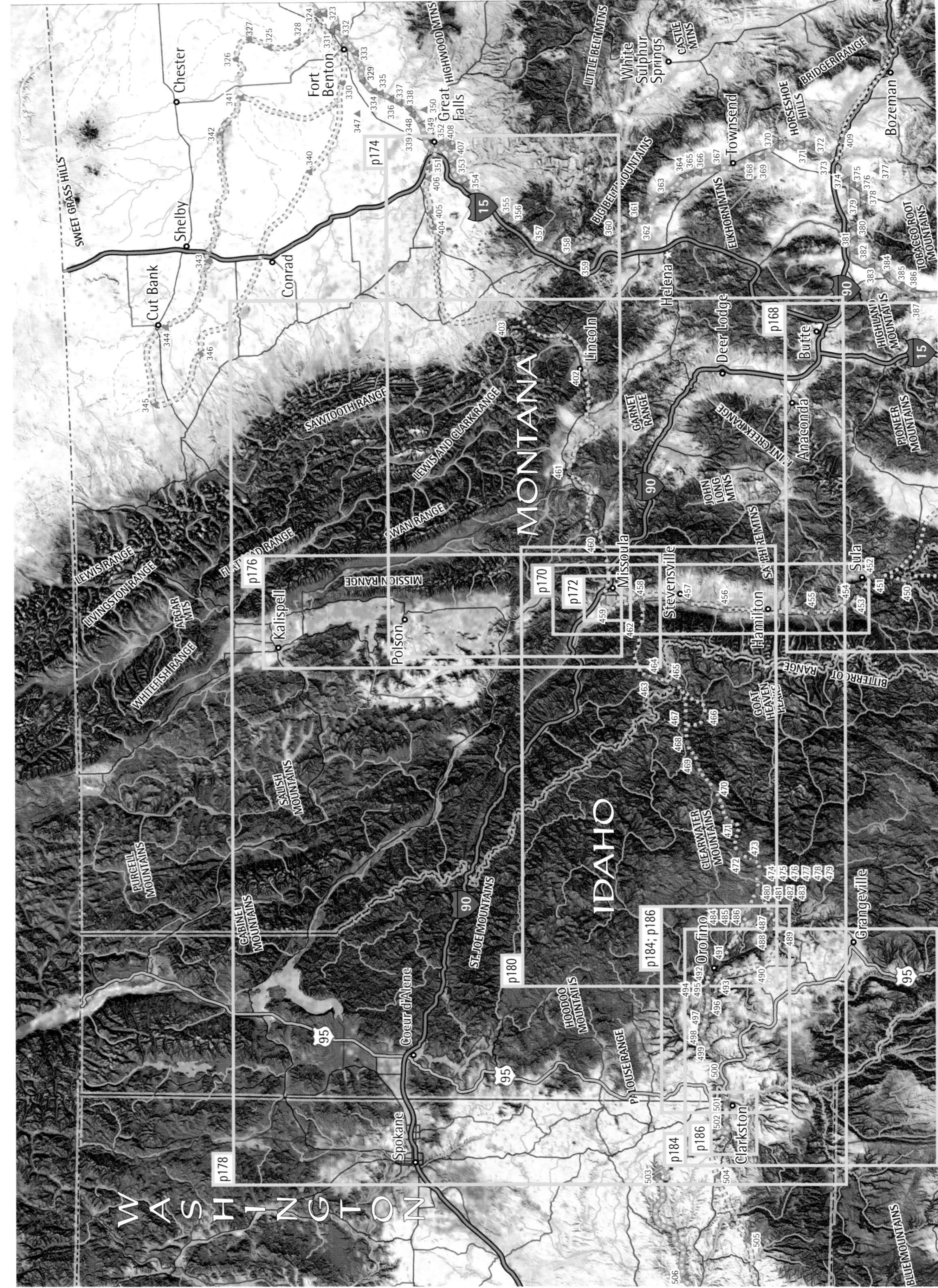
SWEET GRASS HILLS
Chester
Shelby
Cut Bank
Conrad
Fort Benton
Great Falls
HIGHWOOD MTNS
LITTLE BELT MTNS
White Sulphur Springs
CASTLE MTNS
BRIDGER RANGE
HORSESHOE HILLS
Townsend
Bozeman
BIG BELT MOUNTAINS
ELKHORN MTNS
TOBACCO ROOT MOUNTAINS
Helena
Lincoln
Deer Lodge
Butte
HIGHLAND MOUNTAINS
PIONEER MOUNTAINS
Anaconda
FLINT CREEK RANGE
GARNET RANGE
JOHN LONG MTNS
SAWTOOTH RANGE
LEWIS AND CLARK RANGE
MONTANA
SWAN RANGE
LEWIS RANGE
LIVINGSTON RANGE
WHITEFISH RANGE
MISSION RANGE
Kalispell
Polson
Missoula
Stevensville
Hamilton
Sula
BITTERROOT RANGE
GOAT HEAVEN PEAKS
IDAHO
CLEARWATER MOUNTAINS
SALISH MOUNTAINS
PURCELL MOUNTAINS
CABINET MOUNTAINS
ST. JOE MOUNTAINS
HOODOO MOUNTAINS
PALOUSE RANGE
Coeur d'Alene
Spokane
Orofino
Grangeville
Clarkston
WASHINGTON
BLUE MOUNTAINS
p168
p170
p172
p174
p176
p178
p180
p184; p186
p184
p186
15
90
95

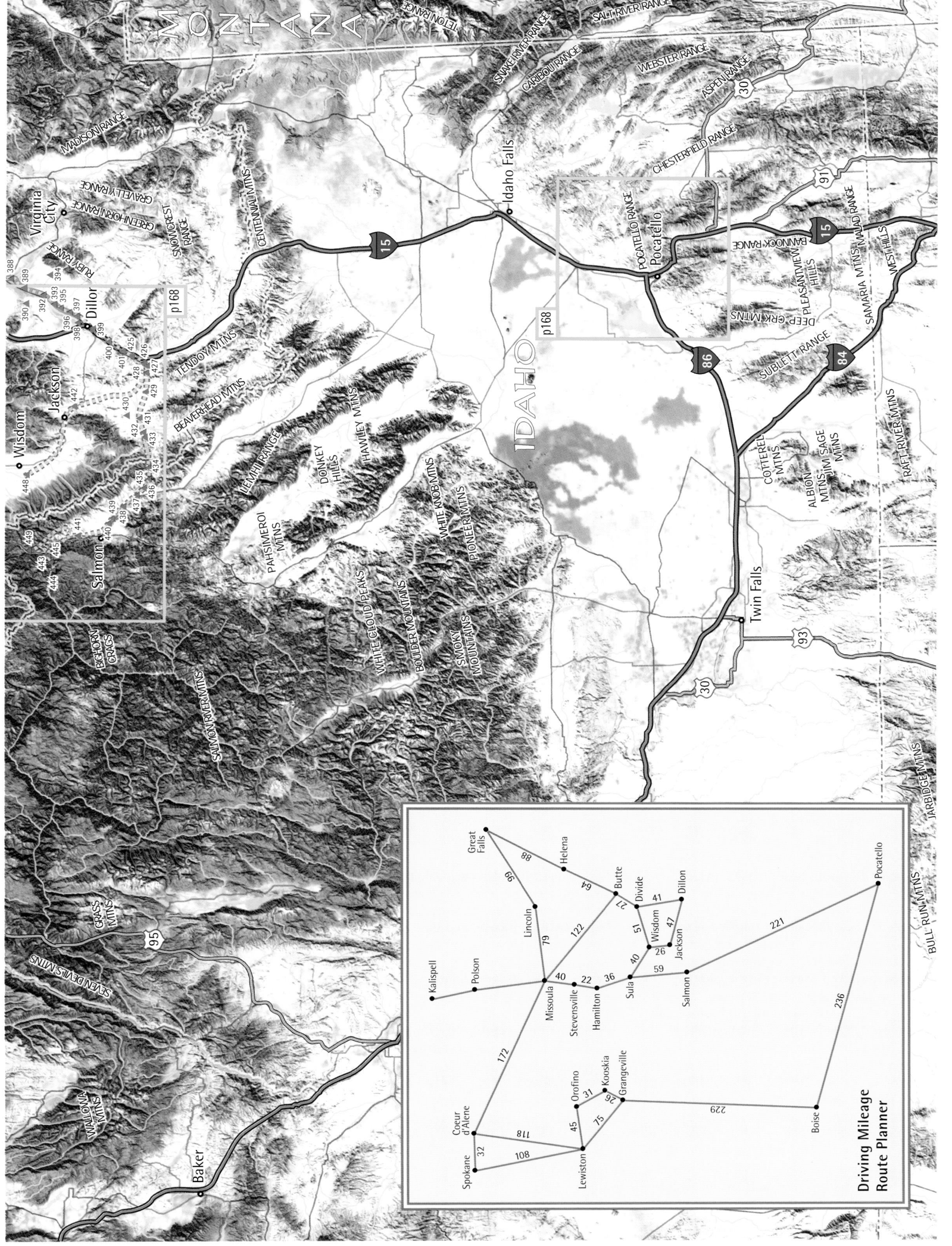
MONTANA
IDAHO
Virginia City
Dillon
Jackson
Wisdom
Salmon
Idaho Falls
Pocatello
Twin Falls
Baker
MADISON RANGE
GRAVELLY RANGE
GREENHORN RANGE
RUBY RANGE
SNOWCREST RANGE
CENTENNIAL MTNS
TENDOY MTNS
BEAVERHEAD MTNS
LEMHI RANGE
DONKEY HILLS
HAWLEY MTNS
PAHSIMEROI MTNS
WHITE KNOB MTNS
PIONEER MTNS
WHITE CLOUD PEAKS
BOULDER MOUNTAINS
SMOKY MOUNTAINS
BIGHORN CRAGS
SALMON RIVER MTNS
SEVEN DEVILS MTNS
WALLOWA MTNS
GRASS MTNS
TETON RANGE
SNAKE RIVER RANGE
SALT RIVER RANGE
CARIBOU RANGE
WEBSTER RANGE
ASPEN RANGE
CHESTERFIELD RANGE
POCATELLO RANGE
BANNOCK RANGE
PLEASANTVIEW HILLS
DEEP CRK MTNS
SUBLETT RANGE
SAMARIA MTNS
MALAD RANGE
WEST HILLS
COTTEREL MTNS
ALBION MTNS
JIM SAGE MTNS
RAFT RIVER MTNS
JARBIDGE MTNS
BULL RUN MTNS
p168
p168
15
15
86
84
30
30
91
93
95
Driving Mileage Route Planner
Great Falls
Helena
Butte
Divide
Dillon
Lincoln
Wisdom
Jackson
Kalispell
Polson
Missoula
Stevensville
Hamilton
Sula
Salmon
Pocatello
Spokane
Coeur d'Alene
Lewiston
Orofino
Kooskia
Grangeville
Boise
88
99
64
27
41
51
47
79
122
26
40
40
22
36
59
221
236
172
32
108
118
45
75
31
26
229

View from Lemhi Pass
Betty Kluesner, Discovery Expedition of St Charles

Shoshone Indians on Horseback
Sacajawea Interpretive Center, Idaho Tourism

Across the Mountains to the Snake River

8

MEETING THE SHOSHONE

On August 9, 1805 in the vicinity of Beaverhead Rock, Lewis took three of his best men to scout a route over the mountains following an old Indian path. On the 11th Lewis saw an Indian on an "eligant horse without a saddle" coming towards them. Lewis was certain he was a Shoshone, the Indian tribe they had to make contact with to supply them with horses to cross the mountains. Lewis approached him shouting "tab-ba-bone" which he thought was the Shoshone word for "whiteman." However, it meant "stranger." The Indian rode off, avoiding them. Though they had taken Sacagawea on the expedition because she was a Shoshone, they had not taken her along.

On August 13th, they crossed the Continental Divide at Lemhi Pass. South of Salmon, Idaho near the Lemhi River they met an old Shoshone woman and a young girl. Lewis repeated his "tab-ba-bone" and pulled up his shirt sleeve to show his white skin. He gave them presents and painted their faces with red vermillion. Sacagawea had told him this was the sign of peace. He asked the women to take them to their camp. Two miles down the road, sixty warriors rode up; after consulting the women, the men greeted them with the "national hug."

When Clark and the others joined them on August 17th, Sacagawea was reunited with her tribe. As she was translating for the captains she realized the Chief of the Shoshone, Cameahwait, was her brother. "She jumped up, ran and embraced him and threw her blanket over him and cried profusely" Clark later reported to Nicholas Biddle, the editor of the journals.

The language chain was as follows: the captains spoke English to Labiche, who spoke French to Charbonneau, who spoke Hidatsa to Sacagawea, who translated it into Shoshone. The captains needed pack horses and a guide for their travels over the mountains. In return they promised to supply trade goods and firearms to the Shoshone in the future.

THE SHOSHONES HELP THE CORPS

On August 21st Clark recorded these observations about the Shoshone:

> "Those Indians are mild in the disposition appear Sincere in their friendship, punctial, and decided. kind with what they have, to Spare. They are excessive pore, nothing but horses there Enemies which are noumerous on account of there horses and Defenceless Situation, have Deprived them of tents and all the Small Conveniances of life. . . .
> The women are held Sacred and appear to have an equal Shere in all Conversation, which is not the Case in any other nation I have seen. their boyes and Girls are also admited to Speak except in Councils, the women doe all the drugery except fishing and takeing care of the horses, which the men apr. to take upon themselves."

The Shoshone delayed leaving to go on their annual buffalo hunt because of the Corps of Discovery. The people were starving. On August 24th the Shoshone women began carrying the baggage of the Corps of Discovery across the Continental Divide from Camp Fortunate to the Lemhi River. On August 30th they finally left to go east through the mountains to where tens of thousands of buffalo could be found on the Montana plains.

Fires were set in the valleys to notify other Shoshone bands and the Flathead Indians that it was time for the hunt. They hunted together to prevent being attacked by their enemies. Cameahwait's band had only four poor guns in their possession, unlike their enemies the Gros Ventres who were supplied with weapons by British-Canadian fur traders.

MEETING THE FLATHEADS (SALISH)

The Corps of Discovery, with 29 horses acquired from the Shoshone, started north along the North Fork of the Salmon River accompanied by a Shoshone guide "Old Toby" and his son. Against Toby's advice, they decided to take the shortest route over the first range of the Bitterroot Mountains near today's Lost Trail Pass at the Montana-Idaho border and US-93. The route had no trails. Steep mountainsides enclosed a creek bed they called "the dismal swamp," forcing them to climb mountains in very dense timber. Their horses slipped and fell down the mountain sides and several were injured. There was snow, and rain, and sleet. Their last thermometer got broken.

On September 4th, the expedition followed a route they saw mountain sheep taking, and descended into the mountain valley later called "Ross's Hole," where they encountered the Salish, or Flathead Indians. There were about 400 Indians, and over 500 horses in the valley. The Indians gave them blankets, and shared their chokecherry harvest with them. The Flatheads traded their fine horses for the expedition's poor horses, and the expedition now had 40 good pack horses and three colts.

The Salish spoke in a "gurgling kind of language" and Sergeant Ordway speculated they might be the Welsh Indians. He wrote in his journal they have a "brogue on their tongue" and "they are the likelyest and honestest we

DESC Canoes on the Clearwater
Betty Kluesner, Discovery Expedition of St Charles

Hellsgate Canyon
near Missoula

National Bison Range
Flathead Reservation
TravelMT

Centennial Mall Sculptures at Lewis-Clark State College in Lewiston, Idaho

Chief Timothy Park on the Snake River
Maya Lin Sculpture Site Bill Sigglekow

have seen and are verry friendly to us." Oddly enough, the Flatheads most likely got their name because they were normal looking. It was the western Indians who flattened, or deformed, the heads of their infants to achieve pointed skulls, who called the Salish "flatheads."

The Salish have lived in the Pacific Northwest since the end of the last Ice Age, as recorded in Salish oral tradition, and by archaeological evidence. The Confederated Salish and Kootenai Tribes now live on the Flathead Reservation in the Mission Valley north of Missoula. They have published one of the most important books to come out of the Lewis and Clark Bicentennial: ***The Salish People and the Lewis and Clark Expedition.***

TRAVELERS' REST AND THE LOLO TRAIL

Old Toby had told them about the160 mile long Indian Trail through the Bitterroot Mountains, which would later become known as the Lolo Trail. The Nez Perce used it to travel east for buffalo, berries, and roots; the Salish used it to travel west for camus roots and salmon.

The Corps spent September 9-11, 1805 at the old Indian campground they named "Travelers' Rest," located south of Missoula, Montana on the eastern edge of the Lolo Trail. They returned there on June 30-July 2, 1806, before splitting into separate exploring parties.

In 2002 an archaeology dig was conducted on the site looking for traces of mercury. The expedition used "Dr. Rush's Thunderbolt" medicine consisting of 60% mercury as a general cure-all for a variety of gastro-intestinal ailments. Mercury was also used as a treatment for syphyllis. Concentrations of mercury were found in an area where military regulations would dictate the Corps should place their latrine ditch; establishing Travelers' Rest as one of the few verified expedition campsites.

Highway 12 goes along the Lochsa and Clearwater River valleys. It has many Lewis and Clark Trail interpretive sites, including a grove of cedar trees honoring the western historian Bernard De Voto. Travelers today can to travel the "Lolo Motorway," an old logging and forest service road along parts of the old Lewis and Clark route over the mountains.

Traveling across the Bitterroot Mountains into Idaho was one of the most difficult times they endured on the whole expedition. They took wrong trails on steep paths blocked by fallen timber. They were starving. It snowed eight inches on September 16th, obscuring the trail along the mountain ridges. Finally, on September 20th, Clark's advance party came to the end of the trail at the Nez Perce Village at Weippe Prairie.

THE NEZ PERCE

Zoa L. Swayne, a writer who lived in Orofino, Idaho, gathered material from1934-1989; from her friends among the Nez Perce and from Nez Perce stories of the Lewis and Clark Expedition in historical records. Her book, *Do Them No Harm,* is an account of the expedition's time with the Nez Perce told from the point of view of the Nez Perce.

The Nez Perce, like the Salish, have always lived in this area. And like the Salish and Shoshone they needed firearms to defend themselves against Blackfeet and Atsina (Gros Ventre) attacks when they entered the Montana plains to hunt buffalo. In 1805 they had just obtained their first guns by traveling to the Hidatsa Villages at Knife River. They knew of the expedition, and welcomed them.

8

"Do them no harm" is what an elderly Nez Perce told her people. As a young woman she had been captured by other Indians; and then lived among whites who had treated her well. Both William Clark and York fathered sons with Nez Perce women. Clark's Nez Perce descendants met with Peyton "Bud" Clark, great-great-great grandson of William Clark, and leader of the Discovery Expedition of St Charles re-enactors retracing the expedition's journey, in 2005.

From Sept 27-Oct 6, they camped on the Clearwater River ("Kooskooske") near Orofino and made the dugout canoes that would take them on the Clearwater, Snake and Columbia Rivers to the Pacific Ocean. Now, for the first time on their journey, they would be traveling with the current instead of against it. Two Nez Perce chiefs accompanied them as guides, and stayed with them until October 25th when they were on the Columbia River. The Corps of Discovery returned to spend over a month with the Nez Perce from May 5-June 15, 1806, waiting for the snows in the mountains to melt, and grass to grow for their horses.

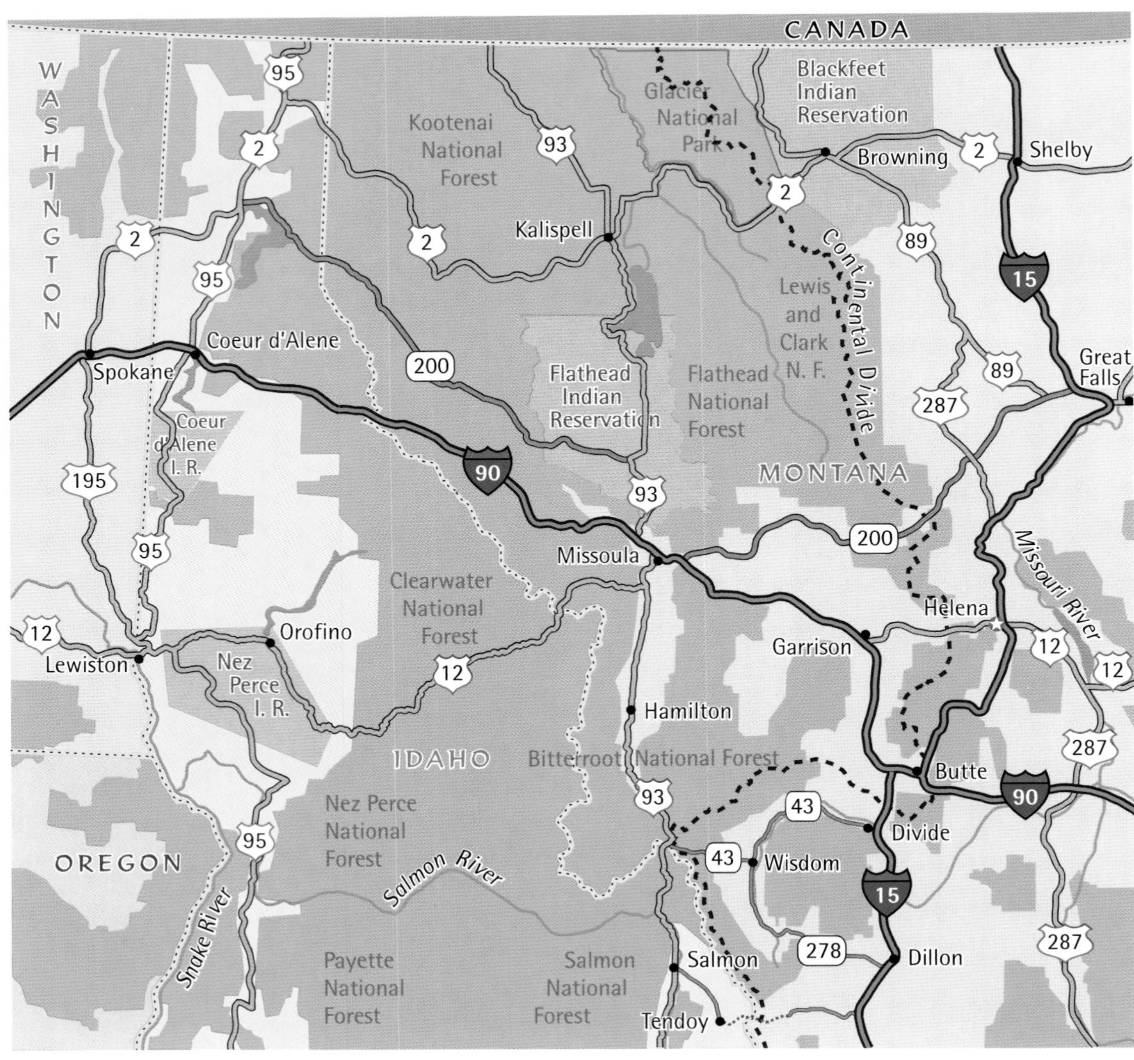

Highway Routes Across the Mountains to Missoula and Lewiston

Route 1 (206 miles)
Clark Canyon Reservoir→Lemhi Pass → Back Country Byway→Tendoy→Salmon → Lost Trail Pass → Missoula

pages
Across the Divide to Salmon, Idaho 166-67
Bitterroot Valley, Highway 93 168-69
Missoula at the Crossroads 170-71

Route 1 is the route the expedition took over Lemhi Pass in 1805. It is single lane gravel road much of the way. The roads open when the snow melts in June, and close due to snow in November. There is no potable water, and cell phone service is limited.

The Sacajawea Memorial is located at the top of the Pass on the Continental Divide, at the state boundary between Montana and Idaho. The road down to Tendoy is known as the Back Country Byway, with two alternate routes.

This is the route to take if you want to explore Sacajawea's homeland, and the adventure of going over the Continental Divide on a gravel road. It was the "high point" of the Lewis and Clark journey; and many consider the Lemhi Pass, a National Historic Landmark, to be the high point of exploring the modern Lewis and Clark Trail.

Route 2 (194 miles)
Dillon → Badger Pass → Bannack → Big Hole Pass → Jackson → Wisdom → Chief Joseph Pass →Lost Trail Pass → Missoula

pages
Three Rivers Valley 150-51
Across the Divide to Salmon, Idaho 166-67
Bitterroot Valley, Highway 93 168-69
Missoula at the Crossroads 170-171

Route 2 is part of Clark's Return Route in 1806. It will take you over the Continental Divide on paved roads from Dillon. The ghost town of Bannack and Hot Springs at Jackson are special features. It goes to the Big Hole National Battlefield, on the Nez Perce Nat'l Historic Trail.

Route 3 (171 miles)
Divide → Wisdom → Chief Joseph Pass → Lost Trail Pass → Missoula

pages
Across the Divide to Salmon, Idaho 166-67
Bitterroot Valley, Highway 93 168-69
Missoula at the Crossroads 170-171

Locals generally take Route 3. It runs along the path of the Big Hole River, and also goes to the Big Hole National Battlefield.

Route 4 (122 miles)
Butte → Missoula

pages
Gates of the Mountains, Helena and Butte . . . 148-49
I-90 and US-95 Route to Lewiston, Idaho . . . 176-77
Missoula at the Crossroads 170-71

Route 4 is the Interstate 90, divided-lane highway route. This is the only interstate route across the mountains in Montana.

Route 5 (115 miles)
Helena → MacDonald Pass → Garrison → Missoula

pages
Gates of the Mountains, Helena and Butte . . . 148-49
I-90 and US-95 Route to Lewiston, Idaho 176-77
Missoula at the Crossroads 170-71

Route 5 is about 50 miles of US-12 through the mountains and 65 miles of Interstate 90, a nice compromise.

Spiral Highway, Lewiston

Road to Lemhi Pass
Betty Kluesner, DESC

Lewis and Clark Back Country Byway
Idaho Travel Council

Lolo Pass, Highway 12
Janet Sproull

Lewis and Clark
Jean-Michel Huctin

Nez Perce Trail Marker

Mullan Road Monument

Hell Gate Canyon

Route 6 (167 miles)
Great Falls → Rogers Pass → Missoula

	pages
Great Falls	142-43
Blackfoot River Corridor, Highway 200	172-73
Missoula at the Crossroads	170-71

Route 6 is Lewis's Return Route in 1806 along the Blackfoot River corridor on Highway 200. The locals have gone to real effort to mark and promote this trail. This is a scenic route which includes a hiking trail to Lewis and Clark Pass on the Continental Divide, and the old ghost town of Garnet on a back country byway.

Route 7 (348 miles)
Great Falls →Browning → East Glacier Park → Marias Pass → Kalispell →Missoula

	pages
Great Falls	142-43
Blackfeet Reservation and Glacier Nat'l Park	146-47
Flathead Reservation, Highway 93	174-75
Missoula at the Crossroads	170-71

Route 7 takes you through dinosaur country, the Blackfeet Indian Reservation and Glacier National Park, and brings you out at the north end of Flathead Lake and the Flathead Reservation. This is part of Lewis's route exploring the Marias River, and the fight with the Blackfeet.

Route 8 (217 miles)
Missoula → Lolo Pass → Orofino → Lewiston

	pages
Missoula at the Crossroads	170-71
Lolo Trail on Highway 12	178-79
Nez Perce Country, Highway 12	180-81

Route 8 through the Bitterroot Mountains on Highway 12 across the Lolo Pass is a "must see" for many Lewis and Clark fans. The actual Lolo Trail route of the Corps of Discovery is up on the ridge tops on the Lolo Trail Motorway. The highway follows the path of the Lochsa and Clearwater Rivers through the mountains. The distance from Lolo, Montana to East Kamiah, Idaho is only about 140 miles. If you stop to visit Lewis and Clark sites, though, plan on spending 6-7 hours. Remember that daylight hours are in shorter supply down in mountain valleys.

Make lodging arrangements in advance in the Orofino area, or go 50 miles on Highway 12 to Lewiston-Clarkston and plan to return the next day to explore the area. This is where the Corps of Discovery met the Nez Perce Indians, who extended genuine hospitality to them on their outbound and return journeys.

Route 9 (291 miles)
Missoula → Lookout Pass → Mullan → 4th of July Pass → Coeur d'Alene → Lewiston

	pages
Missoula at the Crossroads	170-71
I-90 and US-95 Route to Lewiston, Idaho	176-77

Route 9 is for travelers who prefer to use Interstate 90 and US highways. It takes you along the route of the old military Mullan Road built between Fort Walla Walla and Fort Benton by Lt. John Mullan in 1859-60.

Route 10 (310 miles)
Missoula → Lookout Pass → Mullan → 4th of July Pass → Coeur d'Alene → Spokane → Lewiston

	pages
Missoula at the Crossroads	170-71
I-90 and US-195 Route to Lewiston, Idaho	176-77

Route 10 is a variation of Route 9. If you go 20 miles past Coeur d'Alene you can stay in Spokane, and then take US-195 down to Lewiston. Both 195 and 95 will take you to the Three State Lookout, where you might consider the alternative of winding the rest of your way down to Lewiston on the Spiral Highway (see photo above).

What is the Continental Divide?

The Continental Divide is the dividing ridge of land where water flows downward in opposite directions to different oceans. There are other divides, which are also called "watersheds." The Continental Divide of North America is formed by a series of mountain ranges, mostly in the Rocky Mountains. Lewis and Clark called them the Stoney Mountains, or the Shining Mountains for their snow-covered peaks.

- Be aware that cell phone service is limited in the mountains.
- Montana
  Call (800) 226-ROAD (7623) for current road and weather conditions.
  www.mdt.mt.gov/travinfo
- Idaho
  In Idaho call 511 for current road and weather conditions and travel info.
  www.511.idaho.gov

Mountain Weather Conditions

Summer months are mid-June to September; nighttime temperatures are often at freezing or near freezing levels. North from Highway 200 and Rogers Pass snowfall may happen anytime of the year.

Mountain Driving Tips

- Don't use cruise control while driving if there are icy conditions. Ice patches may occur on mountains roads which don't receive much sunlight. Slow down around curves. Water often crosses the road around curves and may form ice patches.
- Don't ride your brakes descending a long hill. Shift to a lower gear.
- Take frequent breaks. Mountain driving can be tiring.

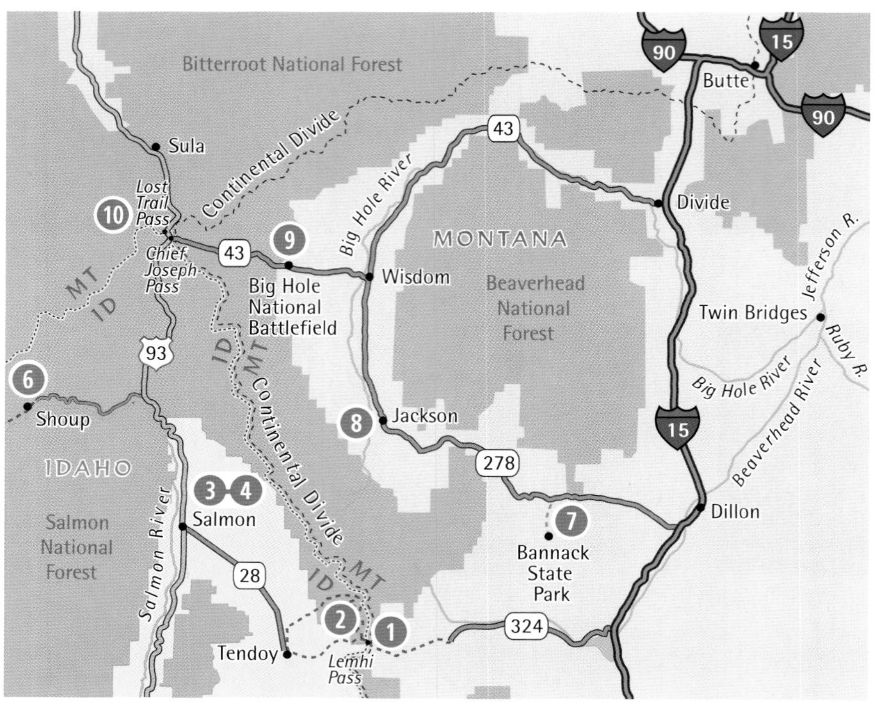

Lemhi Pass across the Continental Divide is closed much of the year. Locals take either Route 278 or Route 43 to cross the Continental Divide at Chief Joseph Pass on Route 43. Lost Trail Pass is at the junction of US-93 and Route 43 at the Montana-Idaho state line. It is one mile beyond Chief Joseph Pass.

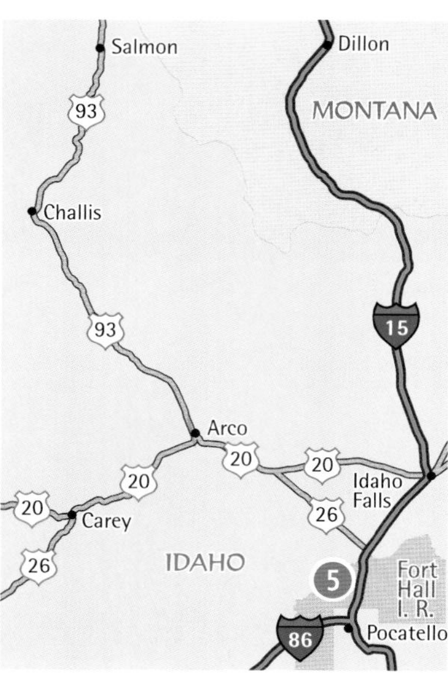

Sacajawea's tribe, the Lemhi-Shoshone, live on the Fort Hall Reservation, located about 210 miles south of Salmon on US Highways 93 and 26; or 180 miles south of Dillon on Interstate 15.

1 LEMHI PASS

From I-15 Exit 62 at Dillon go south on I-15 for 18 miles. Turn right (west) onto Route 324. Go 19.7 miles. Turn right (west) onto Lemhi Pass Road. Go 14.4 miles to the Pass. Lemhi Pass Road is a gravel, narrow, single-lane mountain road. The last four miles are usually closed due to snow from late November to early June. The road is not good when it is wet. Cell phone service is limited.

If continuing on to Idaho, the Back Country Byway is the route down to Highway 28.

2 BACK COUNTRY BYWAY TENDOY ID

From Tendoy go east on Tendoy Ln 0.2 mile. Turn north on Old Hwy 28. Go 3.3 miles. Turn east on Warm Springs Rd. Go 14.5 miles to the Continental Divide. Go south on Warm Springs Rd 9.3 miles to Lemhi Pass. Go west 11.1 miles to Old Hwy 28. Go north 0.3 mile to Tendoy Ln. The Byway is single lane, gravel, with occasional pullouts for passing. Snow usually closes the road from November until June.

Have good tires, properly inflated, and carry a spare tire in good working order. Tire punctures are frequent on the Byway. Be prepared for emergencies and bad weather (lightening storms, rain, sleet and snow).

Agency Creek Road (on the south) is steep, narrow and winding; and is not suitable for motor homes or vehicles towing trailers. It is the shortest route, about 12 miles to the highway from Lemhi Pass. Warm Springs Wood Road (on the north) is about 26 miles to the highway from Lemhi Pass.

3 SACAJAWEA INTERPRETIVE CENTER SALMON ID

From the junction of US 93 and Route 28 go one mile east to the Interpretive Center.

4 SALMON-LEMHI COUNTY MUSEUM—SALMON ID

210 Main Street.
From the junction of US 93 and Route 28 go 0.5 mile west to the Salmon-Lemhi County Museum.

5 SHOSHONE-BANNOCK TRIBAL MUSEUM FORT HALL RESERVATION

I-15 Exit 80.

6 CLARK'S RECONNAISSANCE SALMON RIVER SHOUP ID

From Salmon go north 20 miles to North Fork. Turn west on Salmon River Rd. Go 6 miles to the Moose Creek sign. Continue 12 miles to Shoup. Go one mile further to the Pine Creek Bridge. The sign is at Pine Creek Rapids.

7 BANNACK GHOST TOWN

From I-15 Exit 59 go west 20 miles on Route 278. Turn south for four miles on a good quality gravel road to Bannack State Park.

8 JACKSON HOT SPRINGS JACKSON MT

From I-15 Exit 59 go west 43 miles on Route 278 to Jackson.

9 BIG HOLE NATIONAL BATTLEFIELD

From I-15 Exit 59 (Dillon) go west on Rte 278 for 43 miles, At Wisdom go west on Rte 43 for 9.6 miles to the Battlefield.
From I-15 Exit 102 (Divide) go west 51 miles on Rte 43 to Wisdom. Continue west 9.6 miles on Rte 43 to the Battlefield.

10 LOST TRAIL PASS VISITOR CENTER

From I-15 Exit 102 (Divide) go west 51 miles on Rte 43 to Wisdom. Continue west 26.1 miles on Rte 43 to the Visitor Center at Lost Trail Pass at the junction of US-93 and Route 43.
From Sula go south on Camp Creek Rd 1.4 miles to US 93. Go south 11.5 miles to Lost Trail Pass and the Visitor Center.

Lost Trail Pass

The Lewis and Clark Expedition got lost in the area on September 1-4, 1805, but Lost Trail Pass was named for a party of surveyors who got lost here in 1871.

On Sept. 3, 1805 the expedition was forced to climb hills so steep that several horses fell and were injured. Rain, sleet and snow further added to their miseries. But on September 4th, they came down into a valley where 400 Flathead (Salish) Indians were camping. This meeting at Ross's Hole is depicted in a famous painting by Charles Russell, which hangs in the Montana State Capitol in Helena.

Big Hole Nat'l Battlefield
Montana Travel

Bannack Ghost Town
Travel Montana

Salmon River
Idaho Travel Council

Sacajawea Center
Idaho Travel Council

Across the Divide to Salmon

1 LEMHI PASS—CONTINENTAL DIVIDE NATIONAL HISTORIC LANDMARK

Lemhi Pass at 7,323 feet was the highest point reached by the Corps of Discovery; it is in the Beaverhead Mountains of the Bitterroot Mountain range at the Continental Divide and the state boundary line of Montana and Idaho.

When Lewis's advance party crossed over Lemhi Pass on August 12, 1805 they were no longer in the Louisiana Purchase; they were entering an area inhabited by Indians who had lived there thousands of years; and which was claimed by the US, Britain, Russia and Spain. Lewis was dismayed to see "immence ranges of high mountains still to the West" instead of the river route to the ocean he hoped to find. The next day the four men encountered Shoshone Indians, who invited them back to their camp and fed them salmon—tangible proof that the ocean lay somewhere to the west.

■ (208) 756-5400 Bureau Land Management, Salmon ID or (406) 683-3900 Beaverhead-Deer Lodge National Forest, Dillon MT

■ For a virtual tour of Lemhi Pass, visit www.fs.fed.us/r1/b-d/lewis-clark

2 LEWIS AND CLARK NATIONAL BACK COUNTRY BYWAY—TENDOY ID

The 39 mile byway is a single lane gravel road loop route from Tendoy; it takes about half a day to drive it. It can be safely driven in a car with good tires. The road climbs 3000 feet, and grades can exceed 5%; use lower gears and good sense. Have plenty of gas. Bring water. The byway has Lewis and Clark interpretive signs; a wildflower trail at the Sacajawea Memorial (in Montana at the Pass), and spectacular scenery.

State Route 28 from Salmon to Tendoy, a distance of 20 miles, also has interpretive signage and is near the location of the historic Shoshone campsite.

■ The National Back Country Byway is jointly managed by the Salmon-Challis National Forest (208) 756-5100 and the Bureau of Land Management at Salmon (208)756-5400. www.fs.fed.us/r4/sc/recreation/lewis-clark

3 SACAJAWEA INTERPRETIVE, CULTURAL AND EDUCATIONAL CENTER—SALMON

The Sacajawea Center is located in a 71 acre park with an outdoor amphitheater; interpretive exhibits and trails. The Center has exhibits and provides an interesting variety of old time arts and crafts classes for both kids and adults during summer months on many days. Overnight camping at the primitive campgrounds is also available. The annual Sacajawea Heritage Days are held in mid August.

■ Open last wkd May-1st wkd Sept. daily, 9-6. May and Oct, wkds only, 9-5. Admission: $4 per person; 6 and under free. $12 family rate.

■ School of Discovery classes are included with price of admission. Classes start at 10 AM. Wednesday is kids day; adults may also participate. Reservations needed.

■ Park is open year round during daylight hours. (208) 756-1188 www.sacajaweacenter.org

4 SALMON-LEMHI COUNTY MUSEUM SALMON, IDAHO

The museum features Lewis and Clark information. It also has a large collection of Lemhi Shoshone artifacts, including headdresses and peace pipes; and a large Asian and Chinese artifacts collection. An exhibit on Elmer Keith, a notorious sharp shooter, includes his 5 gallon hat, pistol and boots.

■ Open Apr 15-Oct, Mon-Sat, 9-5. Admission: $2; under 16 free. (208) 756-3342 www.sacjaweahome.com

5 SHOSHONE-BANNOCK TRIBAL ENTERPRISES—FORT HALL RESERVATION

Sacajawea's tribe. the Lemhi Shoshone, live together with the Bannock tribe on the Fort Hall Reservation. Sho-Ban Tribal Enterprises include a tribal museum, arts and crafts store, Oregon Trail Restaurant, high stakes bingo, grocery store and truck stop. Their top-rated Indian Festival is held the 2nd week in August.

■ Museum open daily, April-Oct, 10-6; Nov-Mar, 10-5. Admission: $2 adults, 50¢ children. (208) 237-9791 www.sho-ban.com

6 CLARK'S RECONNAISSANCE ROUTE SALMON RIVER—SHOUP, IDAHO

The Indians told him it couldn't be done, but William Clark had to see the Salmon River for himself to discover it was impossible to navigate: "roling, foaming and beating against innumerable rocks" through deep canyons. 90% of Clark's reconnaissance route can be seen from a car on US-93 and the local Salmon River Road. Local outfitters offer white water rafting trips and fishing on the "River of No Return."

■ Salmon Chamber of Commerce
(208) 756-3214 www.salmonchamber.com

7 BANNACK STATE PARK GHOST TOWN BANNACK, MONTANA

After gold was discovered on Grasshopper Creek in 1862, Bannack became the first Territorial Capital of Montana in 1864. Virginia City became the capital when gold was discovered there in 1865. Bannack's population once numbered 3000. Now it is a ghost town of over 60 buildings, and a popular tourist destination.

■ Open year round: May-first part of Oct, from 8 AM to 9 PM. Off season, 8-5. Visitor Center open daily during the summer, 10-6.
(406) 834-3413 www.bannack.org

8 JACKSON HOT SPRINGS JACKSON, MONTANA

Clark's party was returning over the mountains en route to the Yellowstone, guided by Sacajawea, who knew the area well. They stopped at the Boiling Springs, which were too hot for a man to put his hand in for 3 seconds.—meat boiled in 25 minutes. Clark named the "butifull vally" the "hot spring vally." Today Jackson Hot Springs Lodge is open year round for swimming, skiing and other recreation. Lodge and cabin accomodations. Dining. Travelers are welcome to use the hot springs for a $5 fee.

■ (406) 834-3151 www.jacksonhotsprings.com

9 BIG HOLE NATIONAL BATTLEFIELD AND NEZ PERCE NAT'L HISTORICAL PARK WISDOM, MONTANA

The Big Hole Battlefield in the 1877 Nez Perce War is one of 38 different sites in five states which make up the Nez Perce National Historical Park. The War of 1877 was fought for five months, when about 750 Nez Perce under the leadership of Chief Joseph fled Idaho rather than move onto a reservation. The Visitor Center has a small museum. A visit of at least 4 hours is recommended; daily ranger talks in the summer, introductory film and battlefield walking trails. Big Hole Battlefield Reenactments are held in early August.

■ Open daily, May-Sept, 9-6; Oct-April, 9-5. Admission: May-Sept, $3 individual. No food service. (406) 689-3155 www.nps.gov/biho

10 LOST TRAIL PASS VISITOR CENTER HIGHWAY 93, ID/MT STATE BORDER

The Visitor Information Center has an interpretive ranger and volunteers during the season.

■ (406) 363-7100 www.fs.fed.us/r1/bitterroot
(406) 363-2400 www.bvchamber.com

8

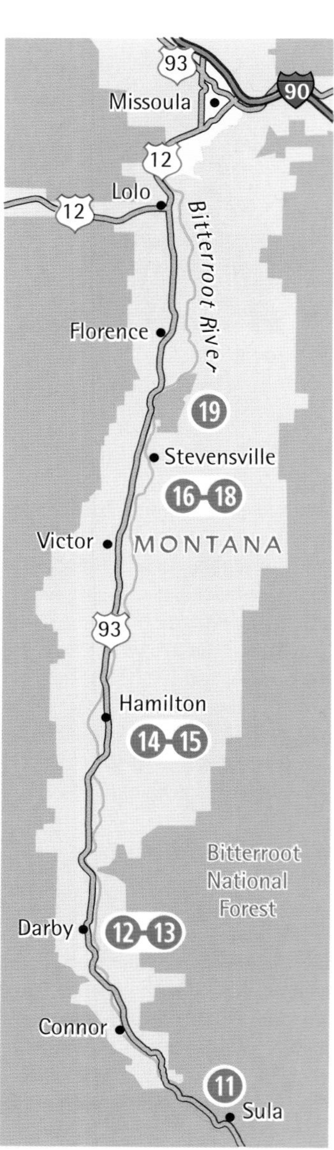

Bitterroot Valley

8

11 ROSS' HOLE
SULA RANGER STATION
SULA MT

From Salmon go north on US 93 for 58 miles.

12 DARBY HISTORICAL VISITOR CENTER
DARBY MT

712 N Main Street.
The Visitor Center is across from the Darby Grade School and adjacent to the Darby Ranger Station on US 93.

13 DARBY PIONEER MUSEUM
DARBY MT

US 93, Council Park.
The Museum is on Main Street (US 93) in the business section of town. It is behind the public library and the city hall bordering Council Park. The museum is marked with a sign clearly visible from the street.

14 RAVALLI COUNTY MUSEUM
HAMILTON MT

205 Bedford Street.
The Ravalli County Museum is in the old Ravalli County Courthouse at South 3rd Street and Bedford Street.

15 BITTER ROOT BREWING
HAMILTON MT

101 Marcus Street.
The Brewery is one and one half blocks east of First Street (US 93). It is east of the railroad tracks; behind the Safeway Store.

16 HISTORIC ST MARY'S MISSION
STEVENSVILLE MT

From US 93 turn right (southeast) onto Stevensville Road. Go 1.3 miles. Bear south onto Eastside Highway (Main Street). Go 0.3 mile. Turn right (west) onto 4th Street. Go 0.2 mile to the Mission at the end of 4th Street.

17 FORT OWEN STATE PARK
STEVENSVILLE MT

From US 93 turn right (southeast) onto Stevensville Road (State Route 203). Go 0.9 miles. Turn left (north) onto Fort Owen Ranch Road. Go 0.2 mile to Fort Owen.

18 STEVENSVILLE MUSEUM
STEVENSVILLE MT

517 Main Street.
From US 93 turn right (southeast) onto Stevensville Road. Go 1.3 miles. Bear south onto Eastside Highway (Main Street). Go 0.5 mile past South Avenue to the Stevensville Museum.

19 LEE METCALF NATIONAL WILDLIFE REFUGE
STEVENSVILLE MT

4567 Wildfowl Lane.
From US 93 turn right (southeast) onto Stevensville Road. Go 1.3 miles. Turn left (east) onto Eastside Highway. Go 0.2 mile. From this intersection the Refuge Visitor Center is 2.3 miles up Wildfowl Lane. Turn left (north). Go 1.4 miles. Turn left (west). Go 0.3 mile. Turn right (north) Go 0.7 mile. Turn right (east) Go 0.2 mile. Turn left (north). Go 0.7 mile. Turn right (east). Go 0.4 mile to the Visitor Center.

Bitterroot Names

The bitterroot is the Montana state flower

Bitterroot Flower

Lewis collected two kinds of bitterroot flowers in 1806; one at Traveler's Rest and the other near the Clearwater River. Their scientific names are Lewisia rediviva and Lewisia triphylla, honoring their discoverer. The flowers bloom in spring across the western United States, in colors ranging from white to deep pink.

Bitterroot River

The Bitterroot River flows north along Highway 93 from Connor to join the Clark Fork River at Missoula. The explorers named the Bitterroot River the Clark River, and the Salmon River, the Lewis River. Neither name survived, but the name of the Clark Fork River has lasted.

Bitterroot Valley

The Bitterroot Valley, lying between the Bitterroot Mountains on the west, and the Sapphire Mountains on the east, is one of Montana's prime agricultural areas. The valley has been inhabited for over 12,000 years. It is the ancestral home of the Flathead Indians, also known as the Bitterroot Salish. The Nez Perce and other Indians also hunted and gathered plants here. The Salish name for this valley is "Waters of the Red Osier Dogwood."

Bitterroot Mountain Range

Modern travelers cross over the Bitterroot Mountains at Lost Trail Pass on US-93, and at Chief Joseph Pass on Hwy 43. The Bitterroot Range extends for 300 miles from the area of these passes northwest to the Lake Pend Oreille area, defining the Montana/Idaho border.

Bitterroot National Forest

The Bitterroot National Forest covers 1.6 million acres. Almost half of the forest is designated as wilderness area, the largest wilderness area in the continental United States.

On August 22, 1805 Lewis tried some of the bitter roots, when they were offered to him by the Shosone. He found boiling made the bulbs soft, but the bitter taste made him "naucious." He gave them to the Indians "who had eat them heartily."

Highly Recommended

The Salish People and the Lewis and Clark Expedition

by Salish-Pend d'Oreille Culture Committee and Elders Cultural Advisory Council Confederated Salish and Kootenai Tribes

University of Nebraska Press, 2005.

(photo: Ravalli County Museum)

Fort Owen State Park

Stevensville Museum
Travel Montana

St Mary's Mission

Bitterroot Valley, Highway 93

11 ROSS' HOLE AND SULA RANGER STATION—SULA MT

See the place where the Corps of Discovery met the Flathead (Salish) Indians, who fed them, gave them blankets, and fresh horses in trade; it is the subject of Charlie Russell's famous painting at the Montana State Capitol. The area, called Ross' Hole, is north of the Sula Ranger Station. The ranger station has parking, rest rooms and interpretive panels. It also provides information on nearby Lewis and Clark sites.

■ Open year round, hours are 8:30-4:30.
(406) 821-3201 www.fs.fed.us/r1/bitterroot

12 DARBY HISTORICAL VISITOR CENTER DARBY, MONTANA

The old Alta Ranger Station, built in 1937-39, has been restored and serves as a museum and visitor center. It was the first USDA Forest Service Ranger Station. Historic forest service items are on display. Brochures, gift shop, and weather/road reports.

■ Open May-Nov, Mon-Sat, 9-5; Sun, 1-5. The Darby Ranger Station, located next door, is open year round. (406) 821-3913
www.fs.fed.us/r1/bitterroot

13 DARBY PIONEER MUSEUM—DARBY, MT

The museum is housed in a hand hewn log cabin that dates back to 1886. It was moved to Darby's City Park on US-93, where it serves as a museum honoring Darby's pioneer families, with exhibits of old artifacts and photos.

■ Open June-Aug, Mon-Fri, 1-5.
(406) 821-4503 www.visitmt.com

14 RAVALLI COUNTY MUSEUM HAMILTON, MONTANA

The museum is housed in the old 1900 courthouse. It is considered one of the finest small museums in the Northwest. It has a Lewis and Clark Discovery Room; a Native American collection; and many other exhibits including both tick and tack exhibits (Rocky Mountain Spotted Fever Laboratory Museum and Horse Tack).

■ Weekly Chautauqua Sunday Series program at 2 PM on historical/cultural subjects.

■ Mid May to mid-Oct, Saturdays, 9-12:30, Bitterroot Valley Farmer's Market with live music in front of the museum.

■ Open all year, Mon, Thurs, Fri, Sat, 10-4; and Sunday, 1-4. (406) 363-3338
www.cybernet1.com/rcmuseum

15 BITTER ROOT BREWING—HAMILTON

Lewis ate a bitter root. Here you can drink a Bitter Root. The Bitter Root Brewing Company's tasting room offers both handcrafted ales and a variety of sodas. The Brewer's Grill is located inside the tasting room; it also has a wireless highspeed internet connection for customers.

■ Brewery open Mon-Fri, 3-8; Sat, 12-8; Sun, 2-6. Restaurant is closed on Sunday.
(406) 363-7468 www.bitterrootbrewing.com

16 HISTORIC ST MARY'S MISSION STEVENSVILLE

The first permanent white settlement in Montana began with the establishment of St. Mary's Mission by Father De Smet in 1841. The church building dates back to 1866. A restored version of Chief Victor's cabin, the son of the Salish chief, and Father Ravalli's house and pharmacy are included the mission complex. The Visitor Center has a gift shop, library and large museum.

■ Open daily, April-Dec, 10-5. Tours are offered April-Oct, 10:15 AM-4 PM. Tours: $3 adults, $1 students. (406) 777-5734
www.stmarysmission.org

17 FORT OWEN STATE PARK STEVENSVILLE, MONTANA

Major John Owen establishing a trading center here in 1850, supplying Oregon Trail immigrants and Indians. He served as Flathead Indian Agent from 1856-62. Fort Owen, built of adobe and logs, was the site of many Montana "firsts." Period furnishing and a small museum.

■ Open year round, daylight hours. Free.
(406) 542-5500 www.fwp.mt.gov

18 STEVENSVILLE MUSEUM

The museum features the history of the Mission, Fort Owen, the settlement of the Bitterroot Valley, its timber and mining industries, Salish Indians, Lewis and Clark, and town history.

■ Open last wkd May-1st wkd Sept. Thurs, Fri, Sat, 11-4 and Sun, 1-4. Free admission.
(406) 777-1007 www.visitmt.com

19 LEE METCALF NAT'L WILDLIFE REFUGE STEVENSVILLE

There are 2½ miles of walking trails along the Bitterroot River at this migratory bird refuge. Also an auto tour route on Wildfowl Lane.

■ Open year round, daylight hours.
(406) 777-5552 http://leemetcalf.fws.gov

1801-1873

Father Pierre Jean De Smet

Known as the "Great Black Robe" Father De Smet is one of the major historical figures in the early American West.

The Salish (Flathead) and Nez Perce became acquainted with Christianity and Catholic missionaries through the influence of Iroquois Indians, who were brought to the Bitterroot Valley by the Hudson's Bay Company to trap beaver. Some of the Iroquois men married Salish women and were adopted into the tribe. Between 1831-1839, the Nez Perce and Salish tribes sent four delegations to St Louis requesting a "Black Robe" to come and live with them. In 1839 they met the young Belgian Jesuit, Pierre Jean De Smet, at his mission for Pottawattamie Indians in Council Bluffs, Iowa, who agreed to go back with them.

William Clark's last official act as Superintendent of Indian Affairs was to sign the passport for Father De Smet allowing him to serve in Indian Country. Father De Smet was a great traveler and diplomat. He did not remain long at St. Mary's; instead he established missions at Fort Vancouver and elsewhere. He made 19 trips across the Atlantic during his lifetime, and traveled widely in the American West.

Father De Smet is buried in Calvary Cemetery in St. Louis near the memorial to the Nez Perce Indian Warriors.

(See Region 4:21 and Region 5:36)

8

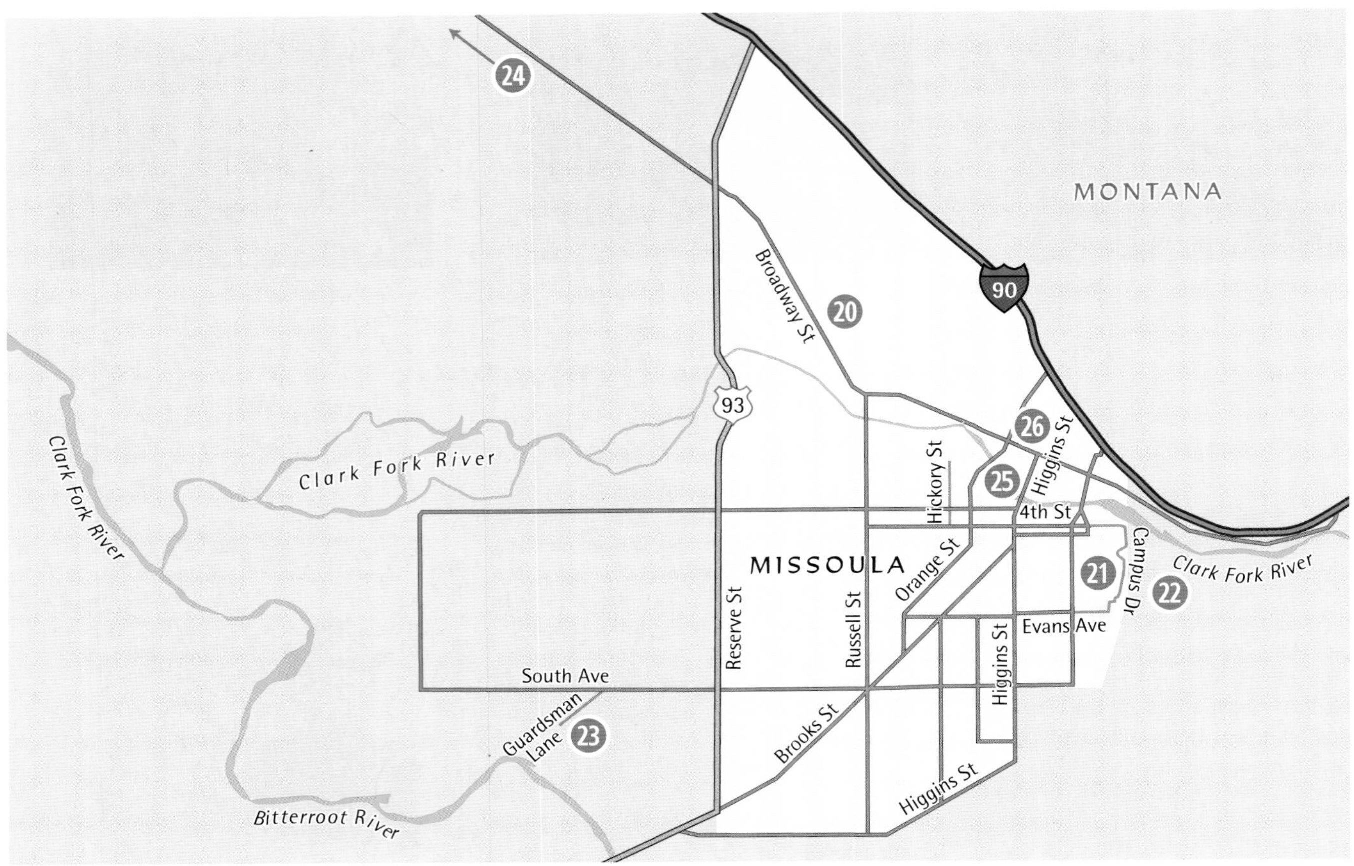

Missoula

Caras Park Missoula Carousel

> **Glacial Lake Missoula & Ice Age Floods**
>
> 15,000 years ago Glacial Lake Missoula extended 200 miles from the Idaho border to the Clearwater River junction with the Blackfoot River near the Continental Divide. Lake Missoula, the size of Lake Ontario and Lake Erie combined, and 2000 feet deep, was caused by an ice dam at Pend Oreille, Idaho, damming up the Clark Fork River. When the ice dam melted, the immense force of the water from Lake Missoula created gravel mountains, deep gouges in the landscape, and the Columbia River Gorge, on its way to the ocean. This process happened repeatedly over a period of 2500 years, causing the unusual landscape features seen today. It is estimated that Lake Missoula would have emptied in as little as 48 hours.

20 ROCKY MOUNTAIN ELK FOUNDATION MISSOULA MONTANA

2291 West Broadway Street.
From I-90 Exit 104 go southwest on Orange Street for 0.5 mile. Turn right (west) onto Broadway Street. Go 1.6 miles to the Elk Foundation.

21 UNIVERSITY OF MONTANA BOOKSTORE MISSOULA MONTANA

University Center, 5 Campus Drive.
From I-90 Exit 105 go southwest on Van Buren Street 0.3 mile. Turn left (east) onto Campus Drive. Go 0.2 mile to the Bookstore.

22 MOUNT SENTINEL "M" TRAIL MISSOULA MONTANA

From I-90 Exit 105 go southwest on Van Buren Street 0.3 mile. Park and walk across the University campus to the foot of Mount Sentinel (about 1/3 mile).

23 FORT MISSOULA HISTORICAL MUSEUM MISSOULA MONTANA

Building 322, Fort Missoula.
From I-90 Exit 105 go southwest on Van Buren Street 0.1 mile. Turn right (west) onto Broadway Street. Go 0.6 mile. Turn left (south) onto Higgins Avenue. Go 0.7 mile. Turn right (southwest) onto Brooks Street. Go 1.4 miles. Turn right (west) onto South Avenue. Go 1.9 miles. Entrance to the Museum is from South Avenue opposite Big Sky High School.

24 SMOKE JUMPER VISITOR CENTER-MISSOULA

Aerial Fire Depot.
From I-90 Exit 101 go 0.5 mile south on Airway Blvd. Turn northwest (right) onto US-93 (Broadway). Go 1 mile to Visitor Center. The Center is located 0.5 mile northwest of the Missoula Airport.

25 CARAS PARK MISSOULA MONTANA

Caras Park.
From I-90 Exit 104 go southwest on Orange Street 0.6 mile. Turn left (east) onto Front St. Go 0.1 mile.

26 PAXSON MURALS AT THE MISSOULA COUNTY COURTHOUSE AND THE MISSOULA ART MUSEUM

Missoula County Courthouse.
200 West Broadway.
From I-90 Exit 104 go southwest on Orange Street for 0.5 mile. Turn left (east) onto Broadway Street. Go 0.1 mile to the Courthouse.
Missoula Art Museum.
335 North Pattee.
From I-90 Exit 105 go southwest on Van Buren Street 0.1 mile. Turn right (west) onto Broadway Street. Go 0.5 mile. Turn right (north) onto Pattee Street. Go 1/2 block.

Elk Country Visitor Center
Randi Mysse

Hiking the "M" Trail on Mount Sentinel
Janet Sproull

Fort Missoula Museum
Travel Montana

Missoula at the Crossroads

 ELK COUNTRY VISITOR CENTER
ROCKY MOUNTAIN ELK FOUNDATION
MISSOULA

If you want to see what the animals look like that the Lewis and Clark Expedition encountered, this is the place to visit. The Elk Country Visitor Center has an extensive collection of life-size mounts, including grizzly bear, mountain goat, bighorn sheep, wolf, lynx and more; and displays of world-record elk. It also has an art gallery of paintings, prints and bronzes by well known wildlife artists, and a large gift shop. The Elk Country Visitor Center serves as a center for the international conservation efforts of the Elk Foundation, which has more than 150,000 hunter-conservationist members. The foundation has protected and enhanced more than 4.3 million acres of wildlife habitat in North America.

■ Open daily, last wkd May-1st wkd Sept, 8-6. Closed Sundays during rest of year. Call to confirm hours of operation.
(800) CALL-ELK (225-5355) www.rmef.org

 UNIVERSITY OF MONTANA
BOOKSTORE AND WEBSITE—MISSOULA

The University of Montana is a national leader in providing information about the Lewis and Clark Expedition. Its award-winning website, on line since 1998, is the premiere information source for all matters regarding the expedition. The producer and principal writer is retired professor Dr. Joseph Mussulman, who calls it a "hyperhistory in progress."

The campus bookstore located in the University Center has a wide selection of Lewis and Clark merchandise and handles website orders. Your support is appreciated.

■ Open 8-6, Mon-Fri, and 10-6, Sat.
(888) 333-1995 www.lewis-clark.org

 MOUNT SENTINEL "M" TRAIL
MISSOULA

Mount Sentinel dominates the skyline of Missoula. A giant concrete "M" is located near the top (for Missoula, Montana). The "M" trail is less than a mile long, but can be quite a hike: eleven switchbacks zigzag 620 feet up the hill. The elevation is from 3200 ft to 3820 ft to reach the "M." Most hikers are happy to get this far, but you can continue on up to the top of the mountain (5,158 ft), for a spectacular view of this valley crossroads. The trail is closed in winter, as wild elk herds like to hike Mount Sentinel themselves.

■ Open from March 15. (800) 338-5072
(406) 543-6623 www.missoulacvb.org
www.missoulian.com

 FORT MISSOULA HISTORICAL MUSEUM
AND ROCKY MOUNTAIN MUSEUM OF
MILITARY HISTORY—MISSOULA MT

Fort Missoula (1877-1947) has 13 historic structures. The historical museum and military history museum are both located at the Fort. Other historic sites include a fire lookout and guard cabin; a WWII Internment Barracks; an 1879 cemetery; a homestead cabin and barn, and other early structures. There is also an old logging train and equipment.

■ Historical Museum: Open last wkd May-1st wkd Sept, Mon-Sat, 10-5; Sun, 12-5. From Sept-May, Tues-Sun, 12-5. Admission: $3 adults, $1 students, $2 seniors, $10 families; ages 6 and under, free. (406) 728-3476
www.fortmissoulamuseum.org

■ Military History Museum: Open last wkd May-1st wkd Sept, Tues-Sun, 12-6:30.
(406) 549-5346 www.visitmt.com

 SMOKE JUMPER VISITOR CENTER
MISSOULA

Smoke jumpers are tough. If the Corps of Discovery were around today, they might become smoke jumpers fighting forest fires. The Visitor Center is located on the largest active smoke jumper base in the US. The Center has a replica of a 1930's look out tower, and the National Smokejumper Memorial and fire fighter exhibits. Tours of the working facilities are offered.

■ Open last wkd May-1st wkd Sept, Mon-Fri, 8:30-5. From Sept-May, 7:30-4.

■ Tours are available at 10, 11, 2, 3, and 4 during summer season. Appointments are recommended during summer and accepted during off season. (406) 329-4934
www.visitmt.com

㉕ LEWIS AND CLARK RIVERFRONT
OVERLOOK AND MISSOULA
CAROUSEL AT CARAS PARK

The Clark Fork Riverfront is a favorite place for Missoulans to go for a walk, or jog, or bike. Lewis and Clark markers may be found at a riverfront overlook in Caras Park, the home of the Missoula Carousel. The Carousel horses were hand carved by local volunteers, and represent over 100,000 hours of volunteer labor from 1991-95. The Carousel gift shop has local arts and crafts items, carousel collectibles, and souvenirs. In Missoula it is customary for adults to ride the carousel.

■ Open daily. June-August, 11-7; Sept-May, 11-5:30. Token Rides: $1, ages 19-55; 50¢ under 19 and over 55.
406) 549-8382 www.carousel.com

 MISSOULA ART MUSEUM AND
PAXSON MURALS AT MISSOULA
COUNTY COURTHOUSE

The museum has about 25 exhibitions annually and features a Contemporary Native American Art Collection. It also features the work of local and regional artists, including Dale Chihuly. The museum, accredited by the American Association of Museums, is housed in a Carnegie building which was recently renovated with a new addition. "Lewis and Clark Back to the Earth" by Dwight Billedeaux and "Dancing on the Lewis and Clark Trail" by Ramon Murillo are part of this outstanding and lively art museum's collection. It has published dozens of artists catalogues which are available for sale online.

COURTHOUSE MURALS

The museum manages the Missoula County Art Collection, the work of frontier artist Edgar S. Paxson (1852-1919), who was one of the first painters of Lewis and Clark scenes. Paxson, who lived in Deer Lodge, Butte, and Missoula, Montana was a friend of Charles Russell, Salish Chief Charlo, and Buffalo Bill Cody. He lived an authentic frontier life as a scout, stagecoach guard, and telegraph line rider, and served in the state militia and US Army. The Missoula Art Museum and the Buffalo Bill Historical Center in Cody, Wyoming are two museums showing the work of this talented artist. Most of his paintings remain in private collections.

The Missoula County Courthouse has eight Paxson murals including several scenes from Lewis and Clark at the south foyer entrance.

■ Museum is open Tues, Weds, Fri, 10-5; Thurs, 10-7; and Sat, 10-3. (406) 728-0447
www.artmissoula.org

■ Missoula County Courhouse
Open Mon-Fri, 8-5.

8

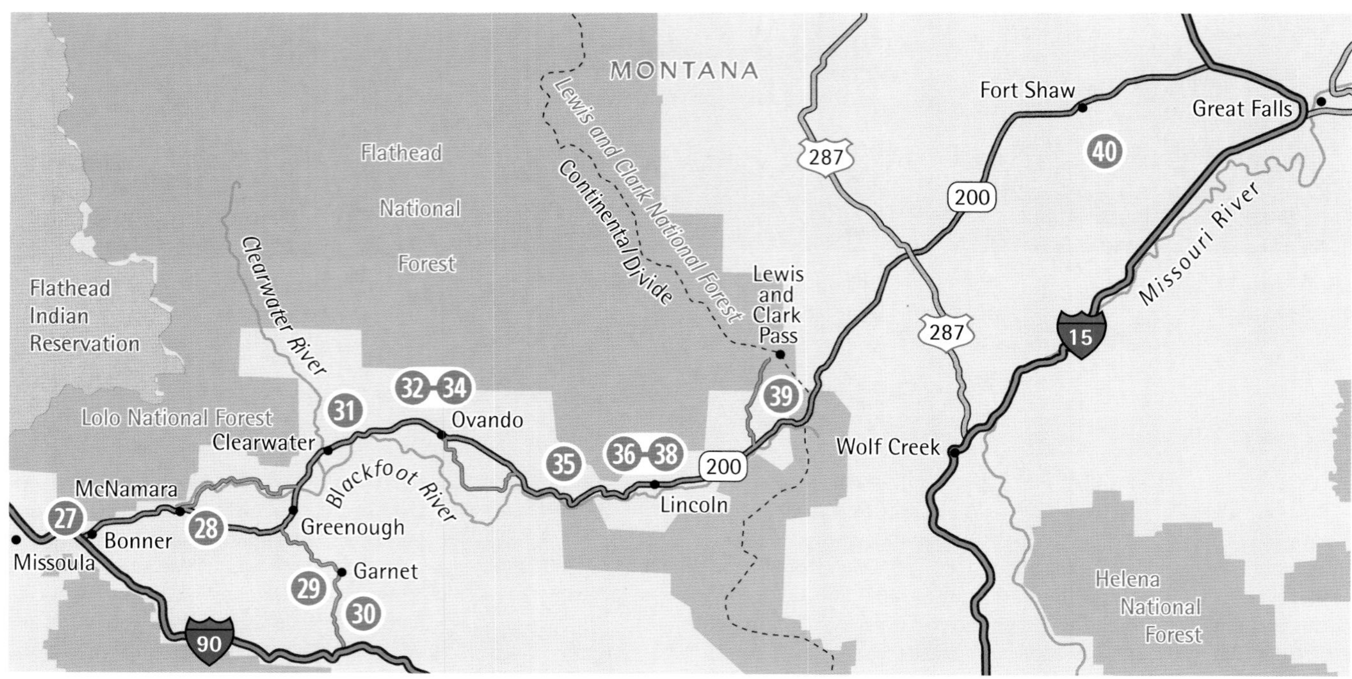

Montana Highway 200 from Missoula to Great Falls: Lewis' return route on the Indian Road to the Buffalo across the Continental Divide

Square Butte/Fort Mountain
Don Peterson

Hay Stack Butte/Shishequaw Mountain
Don Peterson

Lewis and Clark Pass Behind Three Peaks
Don Peterson

8

27 BLACKFOOT GATEWAY KIOSK
BONNER MONTANA

From I-90 Exit109 go east on Rte 200 to milepost 1. The kiosk is on the east side before entering Bonner.

28 BLACKFOOT RIVER RECREATION CORRIDOR

From milepost 11 on Rte 200 go northwest on Belmont-McNamara Rd for 0.7 mile. Road changes name to Johnsrud Park Rd and heads east. Go 5.4 miles. Turn east onto Ninemile Prairie Rd. Wind east 10.2 miles. Turn northeast back onto Rte 200 at Milepost 27. Caution: Narrow gravel road with washboards. Not suitable for large RVs or tour buses.

29 GARNET GHOST TOWN
GARNET MONTANA

From Route 200, between mileposts 22 and 23, turn south onto Garnet Range Road. Go 11 miles to the Ghost Town over a gravel road.

30 BACK COUNTRY BYWAY
GARNET TO I-90

From Garnet go south 0.1 mile on Centennial Rd. Continue south on Bear Gulch Rd. for 9.1 miles. Turn right (west) onto Frontage Rd. Go 6 miles to I-90 Exit 138. The byway is over gravel roads.

31 BLACKFOOT CLEARWATER KIOSK
CLEARWATER MONTANA

At Route 200 milepost 32. At Rest Area across from junction with Route 83.

32 MONTURE/SEAMAN CREEK
OVANDO MONTANA

At Route 200 milepost 40.

33 BAR BRAND MUSEUM
OVANDO MONTANA

From Rte 200, between mileposts 44 and 45, go south to the Town Square in the center of town..

34 PRAIRIE OF THE KNOBS SCENIC ROUTE

From Rte 200, between mileposts 44 and 45, go south on Ovando-Helmville Rd for 4.8 miles. Turn east onto Browns Lake Rd. Go 7.9 miles. Turn east onto local road. Go one mile back to Rte 200.

35 PONDEROSA PINE GROVE

At Route 200 milepost 59.

36 UPPER BLACKFOOT MUSEUM
LINCOLN MONTANA

1 Lincoln Gulch Road.
At Rte 200 milepost 69. Museum is in the Hi-Country Trading Post.

37 UPPER BLACKFOOT KIOSK
LINCOLN MONTANA

Hooper Park Pavilion.
At Route 200, milepost 72. The Pavilion is between 9th Avenue and Sucker Creek Road.

38 LANDERS FORK ROCK CAIRNS
LINCOLN MONTANA

From Route 200, between mileposts 77 and 78, Turn north on Copper Creek Road. Go 1.5 miles to the Rock Cairns.

39 ALICE CREEK ROAD TO LEWIS AND CLARK PASS

From Route 200 milepost 72 turn north onto Alice Creek Road. Go 10.5 miles to the end of the road. Hike 1.7 miles to the Pass.

40 FORT MOUNTAIN (SQUARE BUTTE)
FORT SHAW MONTANA

From Rte 200 at Fort Shaw turn south on Gilbert Ave/Birdtail Creek Rd. for 2 miles. Go east on Dr. Russel Rd for 1 mile. Go south on Knapstad Rd for 0.3 mile. Go east on Leistiko Rd for 3 miles. Go south on Sun River Cascade Rd for 3.8 miles. Go south, then west, then north on Muddy Creek Rd (gravel) for 4.1 miles.

Blackfoot Gateway Kiosk

Garnet Ghost Town
Travel Montana

Monture Creek/ Seaman Creek
Don Peterson

Blackfoot River Corridor, Highway 200

27 BLACKFOOT GATEWAY KIOSK BONNER

This is the entrance to the prehistoric Indian "Road to the Buffalo" that Lewis and nine companions followed on their Return Route in July,1806. Lewis wrote its name as "Cokahlarishkit." The old Indian road is now Route 200; it follows the path of the Blackfoot River from its confluence with the Clark Fork River up to it origin at the Continental Divide, and then the road goes over the mountain to the plains.

The Blackfoot Challenge is a coalition group which has published a guide "Journey Through the Blackfoot, Lewis' Return Trail" which may also be viewed on their website. Destinations 29-39 are taken from the guide, which contains many more sites.

■ (406) 442-4002
www.blackfootchallenge.org

BLACKFOOT RIVER RECREATION CORRIDOR—BONNER

The Blackfoot River is one of the great trout fishing and boat float rivers of Montana. The lower thirty miles has been developed as a recreation corridor for fishing, camping and floating. A narrow gravel road provides a 16 mile scenic detour from Highway 200. The corridor has Lewis Return Route and other signs; numerous river access points; and 4 campgrounds.

■ www.bigskyfishing.com
www.blackfootriver.com (river trips and guides)

29 GARNET GHOST TOWN

Garnet is Montana's best preserved ghost town, located in the Garnet Mountain Range. It was a late developing mining town, settled by families. Gold, silver and copper were once mined here. The town has a visitor center, and is a popular international tourist attraction.

■ Open year round, if you go by snowmobile or skis. Self guided tours. From late May-Sept a park ranger leads tours daily from 10-4.
(406) 329-3914 www.garnetghosttown.org

BACK COUNTRY BYWAY GARNET TO I-90

There are 8 stops along the 26 mile byway from Garnet to the interstate. It is passable for car travel during the summer. In the winter it provides access to 116 miles of groomed ski and snowmobile trails, open from January-April.

■ (406) 329-3914 www.garnetghosttown.org

31 BLACKFOOT-CLEARWATER KIOSK CLEARWATER

A kiosk with Lewis and Clark exhibits is located at a highway rest area near the junction of the Blackfoot and Clearwater Rivers.

■ www.blackfootchallenge.org

MONTURE/SEAMAN CREEK OVANDO

Generations of school children learned Lewis' Newfoundland dog was named "Scannon." Historian Donald Jackson, editor of the ***Letters of the Lewis and Clark Expedition,*** realized looking at the name "Seaman's Creek" on William Clark's map that earlier scholars had misread the handwriting in the journals, and the dog's name must have been "Seaman." (See ***We Proceeded On,*** Vol 11:3, Aug, 1985) Newfoundland dogs were commonly used on board boats, as their large size, heavy coats, and webbed feet made them ideally suited for water rescue.

The creek Lewis named for Seaman on July 5, 1806 has since been renamed Monture Creek for a half breed scout and interpreter, a friend of early settlers. The old Indian road is nearby.

■ www.blackfootlctrail.homestead.com

33 BRAND BAR MUSEUM—OVANDO

Ovando, population 50, claims more scenery per capita than any other town. It also has inns, ranch bed and breakfasts, and restaurants. The Brand Bar Museum used to be a saloon called the "Bucket of Blood." The museum is always open, just ask for the key at the Blackfoot Inn. A Lewis and Clark marker is on the Ovando Town Square near the museum and inn.

■ Blackfoot Inn (406) 793-5566
www.ovando.net

PRAIRIE OF THE KNOBS SCENIC ROUTE OVANDO

This prairie of glacial "knobs," left over from Lake Missoula days, is one of the few remaining untouched areas of prairie grasslands in North America. As fast as Lewis was traveling through Blackfeet Indian country, he still collected a dozen plants along the Blackfoot River.

■ www.blackfootlctrail.homestead.com

PONDEROSA PINE GROVE

Look for a large stand of pine trees after crossing the bridge over Arrastra Creek. It is likely Lewis' party saw these centuries old pines. They still bear scars from the Indian practice of peeling back the outer bark to harvest the sweet inner layer to use as a medicine, and sweet treat.

■ www.blackfootlctrail.homestead.com

UPPER BLACKFOOT MUSEUM AND HI-COUNTRY TRADING POST—LINCOLN

The trading post is home to the Upper Blackfoot Valley Historical Society; it has antiques and artifacts, and exhibits on Lewis and Clark and the Upper Blackfoot area. The post is the retail outlet for "Hi-Country Snack Foods," nationally known for its jerkies and fudge.

■ (800) 433-3916 www.hicountry.com

37 UPPER BLACKFOOT KIOSK—LINCOLN

The third Lewis and Clark kiosk continues the story of Lewis' Route through the valley.

■ www.blackfootchallenge.org

LANDERS FORK ROCK CAIRNS LINCOLN

Rock cairns were trail markers and places of spiritual significance. They have existed for hundreds of years. Respect their significance by not disturbing them. Access is provided by a private land owner and the state of Montana.

■ www.blackfootchallenge.org

ALICE CREEK ROAD TO LEWIS AND CLARK PASS

This is the wildest part of the entire Lewis and Clark Trail. Be warned and be cautious. Lewis' party reached the pass on July 7th. Do not leave the road until mile 7.4 when you can stop to read interpretive signs in Helena National Forest. There are interpretive displays at the end of Alice Creek Road. From there it is a 1.5 mile hike up to Lewis and Clark Pass (elevation 6408 feet) in the Flathead Mountain Range. Bring water and extra jackets for the windy Divide. Make noise as you walk to keep grizzly bears away, and travel with a group if at all possible.

■ (406) 362-4265 www.fs.fed.us/r1/helena

FORT MOUNTAIN/SQUARE BUTTE SIMMS

When Lewis saw the landmark "Fort Mountain" from Lewis and Clark Pass he knew he was about to reenter the Sun River Valley.

■ www.lewis-clark.org

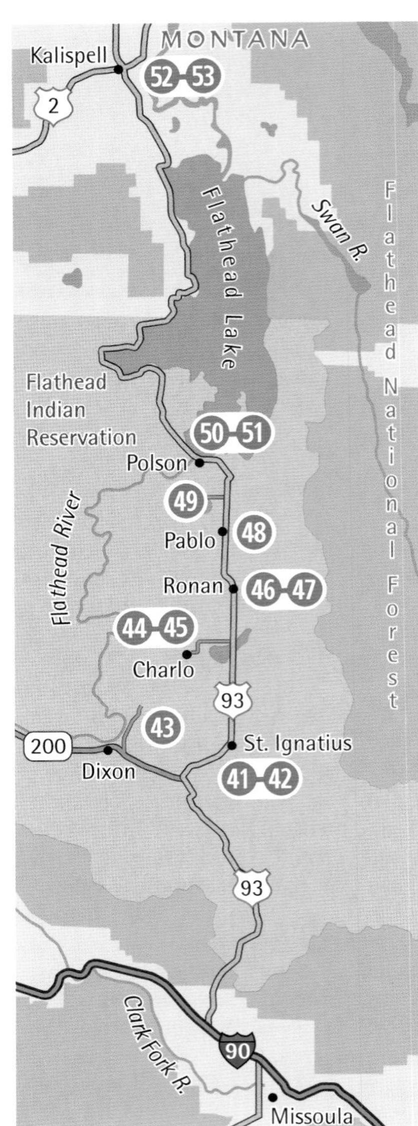

The Flathead Valley

National Bison Range
Jean-Michel Huctin

An estimated 60 million buffalo roamed North America before the arrival of Europeans. Returning from the Pacific, on August 29, 1806 William Clark climbed a high hill near the White River in South Dakota and saw "near 20,000" feeding on the plain.

The systematic extermination of buffalo began in the 1860's, after the building of the trans-continental railroad. By 1883 the great herds were gone. The largest remaining wild herd was in Yellowstone, which was established as the first National Park in 1872. The 3,500 free roaming buffalo in today's Yellowstone are still the largest remaining wild herd.

In 1872, a Pend d'Oreille Indian living with the Flatheads established a herd of 13 tame buffalo. These buffalo became the nucleus of many public and private herds. By actual count, only 1,024 buffalo were alive in North America in 1900. The National Bison Range was established on the reservation in 1908.

The Confederated Salish and Kootenai Tribes and the US Fish and Wildlife Services share in the joint management of the herd of about 350-500 buffalo. There are an estimated 350,000 buffalo alive today, of which 90% are in private herds. Native American owned buffalo are estimated to number 7,000.

8

41 ST IGNATIUS MISSION
ST IGNATIUS MONTANA

In St Ignatius 2 blocks from US 93. Signs on the highway. The Mission can be seen from the highway.

42 FLATHEAD INDIAN MUSEUM AND TRADING POST
ST IGNATIUS MONTANA

1 Museum Lane.
Located at the heart of the Flathead Indian Reservation on US 93 in St Ignatius.

43 NATIONAL BISON RANGE
MOISE MONTANA

132 Bison Range Road.
From Rte 200 and Rte 212 go north on Rte 212 for 4.7 miles. Go east on Bison Range Rd 0.5 mile to the Visitor Center.

44 NINEPIPES AND PABLO NAT'L WILDLIFE REFUGES
CHARLO AND PABLO MONTANA

Ninepipes Refuge: 6 miles south of Ronan on the west side of US 93.
Pablo Refuge: 2 miles north of Pablo and 0.7 mile west of US 93.

45 NINEPIPES MUSEUM
CHARLO MONTANA

10962 US Highway 93.
Six miles south of Ronan on US 93 at Eagle Pass Trail.

46 RONAN VISITOR INFORMATION CENTER
RONAN MONTANA

201 Main Street SW.
From US 93 go west two blocks on Main St to the Visitor Center.

47 GARDEN OF THE ROCKIES MUSEUM
RONAN MONTANA

400 W. Round Butte Road.
From US 93 go west four blocks on Round Butte Road to the Garden of the Rockies Museum.

48 THE PEOPLE'S CENTER
PABLO MONTANA

53253 US Highway 93.
At the intersection of Old US 93 and US Highway 93.

49 KWA TAQ NUK RESORT
POLSON MONTANA

303 US Highway 93 East.
8.2 miles north of Pablo on US 93.

50 MIRACLE OF AMERICA MUSEUM AND PIONEER VILLAGE
POLSON MONTANA

58176 US Highway 93.
On US 93 0.8 mile south of Route 35 (S Shore Road).

51 POLSON-FLATHEAD HISTORICAL MUSEUM
POLSON MONTANA

708 Main Street.
From US 93 go south on Main Street for five blocks to the Flathead Historical Museum.

52 HOCKADAY MUSEUM OF ART
KALISPELL MONTANA

302 2nd Avenue East.
From the intersection of US 93 and US 2 go south Main Street (US 2) for 1/2 mile. Turn left onto Third Street and continue east for two Blocks to 2nd Ave.

53 MUSEUM AT CENTRAL SCHOOL
KALISPELL MONTANA

124 2nd Avenue East.
From the intersection of US 93 and US 2 go south Main Street (US 2) for 0.3 mile. Turn left onto First Street and continue east for two blocks. Turn right and go south 1/2 block to the Museum.

National Bison Range
Travel Montana

St Ignatius Mission
Travel Montana

The People's Center
The People's Center

Mission Valley, Highway 93

41 ST IGNATIUS MISSION—ST IGNATIUS

The Mission Mountains and Mission Valley derive their names from St Ignatius Mission, founded by two Jesuit Fathers, Adrian Hoecken and Pierre-Jean De Smet, in 1854. Their log cabin home is now a small museum. Another log cabin, a convent for the Sisters of Providence, built in 1864, is also a museum. The 1890's church is decorated with 61 beautiful frescoe paintings. It is open for tourists; and regular weekly masses are still held here.

■ Open daily summer 9-8 winter 9-5.
(406) 745-2768 www.visitmt.com
Search for St. Ignatius Mission

42 FLATHEAD INDIAN MUSEUM AND TRADING POST—ST IGNATIUS

The museum has an extensive collection of art, crafts and artifacts from the Flathead and Kootenai tribes; and some from other tribes. It has a gift shop and store.

■ Open daily May-Sept 9-9 Oct-Apr 9-6. (406) 745-2951. www.visitmt.com
Search for Flathead Indian Museum

43 NATIONAL BISON RANGE-MOISE

The 18,500 acre refuge has 350-500 buffalo. Much of it is in native prairie. Forests, wetlands and streams encourage a wide variety of wildlife; with over 200 species of birds.

■ Open all year during daylight hours. Entry fee $5 mid-May through Oct. (406) 644-2211 www.visitmt.com Search for Bison Range

44 NINEPIPES AND PABLO NATIONAL WILDLIFE REFUGES—CHARLO AND PABLO

Over 800 glacial potholes and a reservoir create a wetlands environment on this 1,770 acre bird refuge. The refuge is an important breeding ground for many species of birds. The reservoir is used for irrigation and flood control.

■ Open all year. No entry fee. (406) 644-2211 www.visitmt.com Search for Ninepipes

45 NINEPIPES MUSEUM OF EARLY MONTANA—CHARLO

The museum was established in 1998 to memorialize the history of the Reservation and early Montana. Exhibits include: weaponry (clubs, bows and arrows, antique Indian guns); spurs and saddlery; a "grizzly set"; a large collection of beadwork; and life size dioramas of wild animals and an Indian Camp. Outdoor exhibits of wagons, buggies and an old cabin. The museum has a Gallery of Art of the Old West, and a Hall of Photographs. There is a Nature Trail with interpretive signage.

■ Open daily last wkd May-1st wkd Sept 8-6. 1st wkd Sept-last wkd May Wed-Sun 11-5. Admission: $4 adult, $3 student, $1 ages 6-12. (406) 644-2928 www.ninepipes.org

46 RONAN VISITOR'S CENTER

An old building from the 1870's, the Sloan Stage Stop, is a now a visitor information center staffed by community volunteers during summer months.

■ Open May 12-5 Jun-Aug 10-7 Sept 12-5 (406) 676-8300 www.visitmt.com Search for Ronan Chamber of Commerce

47 GARDEN OF THE ROCKIES MUSEUM RONAN

The Garden of the Rockies Museum is housed in the first church in Ronan. Many old buildings have been restored by community volunteers, "remembering the way it was."

■ Open last wkd May-Ist wkd Sept Mon-Fri 11-4. Free admission. (406) 676-5210 or (406) 676-8450 www.visitmt.com Search for Ronan

48 THE PEOPLE'S CENTER AND NATIVE ED-VENTURE TOURS —PABLO

This unique cultural center honors the Salish, Kootenai and Pend d'Oreille peoples. Guided tour/audio cassette tour of the center's exhibits. Gift shop features traditional arts and crafts.

Native Ed-Venture Tours include:
Reservation tours
Pow wow tours/Tipi camping
Hiking, camping and fishing (with permits)
Activities on site (Native games, arts, crafts)
Make your own souvenirs
Step On tours

■ Native Ed-Venture prices are $20 hour/per person; for each additional adult, $5/hour; and children under 12 free (with adult). Transportation may increase the cost.
Contact Mary Jane Charlo at (406) 883-5344 or e-mail tours@peoplescenter.org

■ Open Apr-Sept 9-6 Oct-Mar 9-5. Admission: $3 adult, $2 senior, $2 student. (800) 883-5344 (406) 675-0160 or (406) 883-5344 www.peoplescenter.org

49 KWA TAQ NUK RESORT AND CASINO POLSON

The Best Western Resort, owned by the tribe, is located in the town of Polson on the south end of Flathead Lake. Kwa Taq Nuk offers a 50 passenger riverboat cruise on Flathead Lake with a guided tour of Wild Horse Island, home to many species of wild life. Its restaurant, Jocko's Steakhouse and Lounge, is open daily at 7 AM; there is a 24 hour casino.

■ (800) 882-6363 (406) 883-3636 www.kwataqnuk.com

50 MIRACLE OF AMERICA MUSEUM AND PIONEER VILLAGE—POLSON

Western Montana's largest museum with over 100,000 items and an outdoor village. Live History Days on the third weekend in July.

■ Open last wkd May-1st wkd Sept 8-8 1st wkd Sept-last wkd May Mon-Sat 8-5 Sun 1:30-5. Admission: $4 adult over 12, $1 ages 3-12. (406) 883-6804 www.cyberport.net/museum

51 POLSON-FLATHEAD HISTORICAL MUSEUM—POLSON

The museum has a chuck wagon, stage coach, vintage farm equipment, boat display, and exhibits on the history of the Flathead Lake area.

■ Open last wkd May-1st wkd Sept Mom-Sat 9-5 Sun 12-4 Admission: $2.50 adult, $2 senior, free under 13. (406) 883-3049 or (406) 883-2386. www.visitmt.com Search for Polson

52 HOCKADAY MUSEUM OF ART KALISPELL

Montana art, with an emphasis on the art of Glacier National Park, located in a Carnegie Library building. Rotating exhibits of national and emerging artists. Gift shop.

■ Open Jun-Aug Mon-Sat 10-6 Sun 12-4 Sept-May Tues-Sat 10-5. Admission: $5 adult, $4 senior, $2 student, $1 ages 6-18.
(406) 755-2023 www.hockadaymuseum.org

53 MUSEUM AT CENTRAL SCHOOL KALISPELL

Museum of the Northwest Montana Historical Society, located in an1894 school building with community activities and a gift shop.

■ Open Jun-Sept Mon-Sat 10-5. Admission: $5 adult, $4 senior.
(406) 756-8381 www.yourmuseum.org

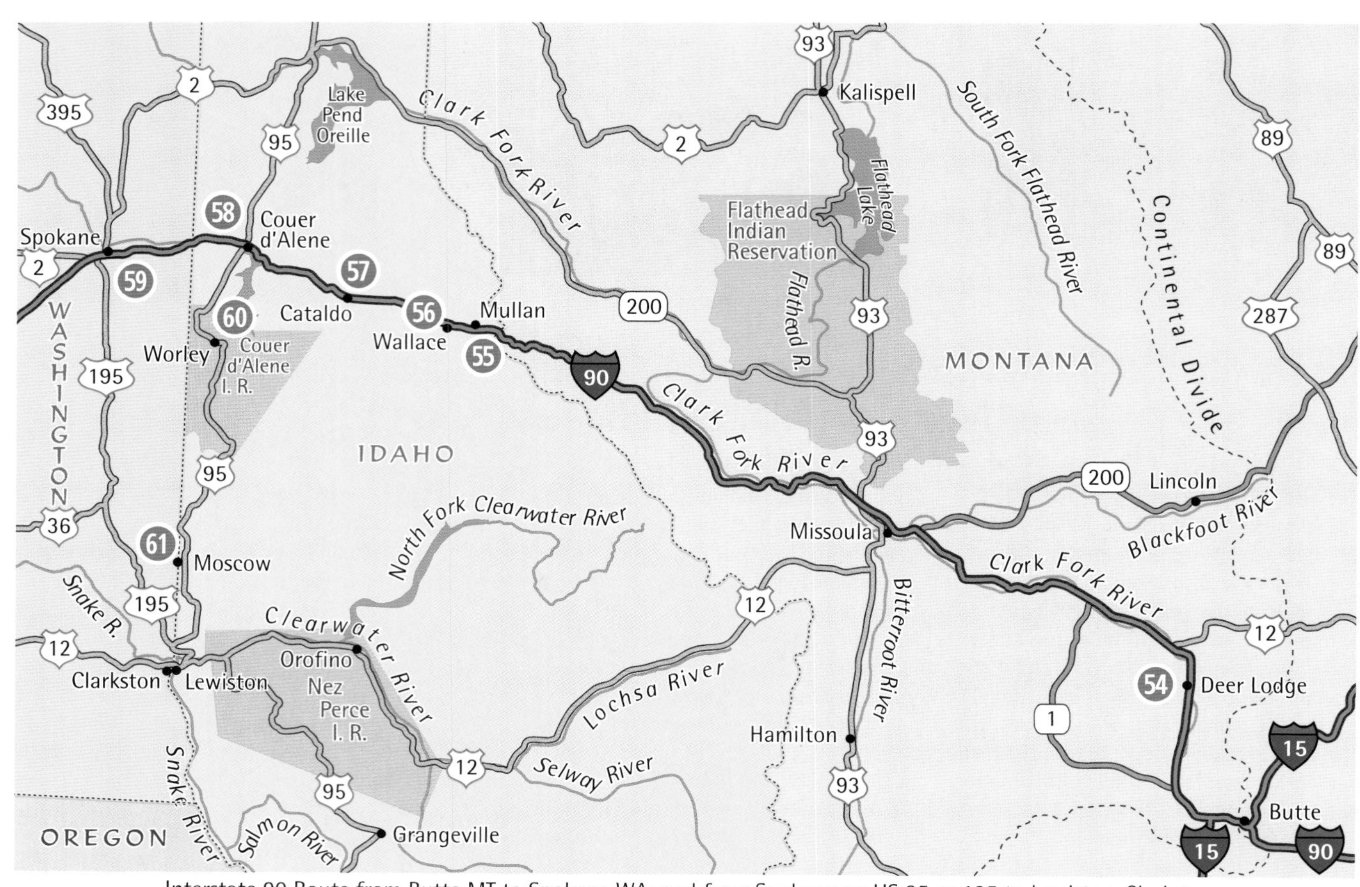

Interstate 90 Route from Butte MT to Spokane WA; and from Spokane on US 95 or 195 to Lewiston-Clarkston

8

54 GRANT-KOHRS RANCH
DEER LODGE, MONTANA

266 Warren Lane.
From I-90 Exit 184 go west on Sam Beck Road 0.6 mile to the Ranch.

55 JOHN MULLAN MUSEUM
MULLAN, IDAHO

229 Earle Street.
From I-90 Exit 69 go one block north on Atlas Road. Turn west on River Street. Go 0.7 mile. Turn north on 3rd Street. Go two blocks.. Turn west on Earle Street.

56 WALLACE HISTORIC DIST.
WALLACE, IDAHO

At I-90 Exit 61.

57 OLD MISSION STATE PARK
CATALDO, IDAHO

At I-90 Exit 39.

58 MUSEUM OF NORTHERN IDAHO
COEUR D'ALENE IDAHO

115 Northwest Boulevard.
From I-90 Exit 15 go west 1.7 miles on Sherman Avenue (name changes to Northwest Boulevard).

59 NORTHWEST MUSEUM OF ART AND CULTURE
SPOKANE, WASHINGTON

2316 West First Avenue.
From I-90 Exit 280 A go north on Walnut Street for two blocks. Turn west on Second Avenue. Go four blocks. Go north on Cannon Street for two blocks. Turn west on First Avenue. Go past Hemlock Street to the Museum.

60 COEUR D'ALENE CASINO, RESORT AND HOTEL
WORLEY, IDAHO

From I-90 Exit 12 in Coeur d'Alene go south on US 95 for 28 miles to the Casino at 1st Street.

61 APPALOOSA MUSEUM
MOSCOW, IDAHO

2720 West Pullman Road.
From US Highway 95 (Main Street) go west on Third Street for 0.3 mile. Keep straight onto West Pullman Road. Go 1.4 miles to the Appaloosa Museum. The museum is located on Hwy 8/ Moscow-Pullman Hwy, just at the state line (next door to Applebee's).

Was the Clark Fork the Key to the All-Water Northwest Passage?

The original mission of the Corps of Volunteers for Northwestern Discovery was to find an all water route to the Pacific Ocean, the long sought "Northwest Passage." Although they didn't use it, there was an all water route—the Clark Fork River to the Pend Oreille River to the Columbia River to the Pacific Ocean.

Why didn't the captains take the Clark Fork route? First of all, because there was "no sammon" in the Bitterroot River. If salmon couldn't get up the Clark Fork River to the Bitterroot, they reasoned they might not be able to get down it, due to waterfalls.

Secondly, they heard the Clark Fork route would take months longer than going across the Bitterroots Mountains on the Lolo Trail to the Clearwater River.

The explorers misnamed the Clark Fork. It is the principal of the three rivers which meet at Missoula. Both the Bitterroot (which they called the Clark River) and the Blackfoot are tributaries of the Clark Fork River, which originates near Butte, Montana.

Interstate 90 follows the path of the Clark Fork from Butte through the mountains to Missoula. The river leaves the interstate 70 miles west of Missoula, and swings northwest to Lake Pend Oreille.

Pend Oreille (ponderay) is the French name for the Kalispel Indians, who wore dangling pendant earrings. The Pend Oreille River goes east and then north, where it joins the Columbia River 43 miles north of the Canadian border at Balfour, British Columbia. Both the Clark Fork and the Pend Oreille are considered tributaries of the Columbia River, the second largest river in the United States.

John Mullan Marker

Mullan Museum
Idaho Tourism

Wallace Historic District
Idaho Tourism

Coeur d'Alene Casino
Idaho Tourism

Apaloosa Horses
Idaho Tourism

Appaloosa Museum
Idaho Tourism

Old Cataldo Mission
Idaho Tourism

I-90 & Highway 95 to Lewiston

54 GRANT-KOHRS RANCH NATIONAL HISTORIC SITE— DEER LODGE, MT

The ranch was once the headquarters of a ten million acre cattle empire in the 1800's, grazing cattle in four states and Canada. It has been carefully preserved. The ranch now covers 1500 acres, and is managed by the National Park Service and the US Department of Agriculture. Cattle still graze and draft horses still work the land. Living history activities in the summer.

■ Open daily May 28-Sept 1 8-5:30 Sept 2-May 27 9-4:30. Free admission. (406) 846-2070 www.nps.gov/grko

55 JOHN MULLAN MUSEUM MULLAN, IDAHO

John Mullan led military and civilian work crews in building the 624 mile Mullan Road from Fort Walla Walla, Washington to Fort Benton, Montana in 1859-60. Its route across the Rockies is followed by I-90 today. One Mullan Road marker is located 13 miles east of Coeur d'Alene at 4th of July Pass.

■ Open Jun-Aug Mon-Fri 10-4. Free admission. (208) 744-1461 www.visitidaho.org

56 WALLACE HISTORIC DISTRICT WALLACE, IDAHO

Wallace is known as the "Silver Capital of the World." Over one billion ounces of silver have been extracted from its mines since 1884. The Sierra Silver Mine Tour, the Northern Pacific Railroad Museum, the Wallace District Mining Museum, and the Oasis Bordello Museum are popular tourist attractions. Every building in downtown Wallace is listed on the National Register of Historic Places. There are many jewelry and antiques stores. Wallace is also known for its skiing, winter sports, and mountain and motor biking.

■ (208) 753-7151 www.wallace-id.com

57 OLD MISSION STATE PARK CATALDO, IDAHO

Father De Smet built the original Cataldo Mission in 1842 which was destroyed by flooding. A new site was chosen on a hill near the Coeur d'Alene River, and the mission was rebuilt in 1848-53. Cataldo Mission is Idaho's oldest standing building.

It was designed by Father Anthony Ravalli, who also designed the mission at Stevensville, Washington. The church was built by members of the Coeur d'Alene Indian tribe, using the "wattle and daub" technique. The interior was decorated by Father Ravalli, who was also an artist, sculptor and physician. He used newspaper, fabric and tin to create this beautiful mission with a dome. The only tools he had were a broad axe, auger, ropes and pulleys, a pen knife, and improvised whip saw.

A new Visitor Center is being built to display the world-class "Sacred Encounters" exhibit which was purchased by the Coeur d'Alene tribe after the exhibit toured the country in 1994-97. A paperback, "Sacred Encounters: Father De Smet and the Indians of the Rocky Mountain West" is still available.

■ Open daily 9-5 (208) 682-3814 www.idahoparks.org

58 MUSEUM OF NORTHERN IDAHO COEUR D'ALENE

Museum exhibits feature regional history: sawmills, logging, agriculture, steamboats, railroads, the Coeur d'Alene tribe and the Cataldo Mission. The museum admission also includes entrance to the Fort Sherman Museum, located on the North Idaho College Campus. Gift shop with local history books and silver jewelry.

■ Open Apr-Oct Tues-Sat 11-5. Admission: $2 adult, $1 ages 6-16. (208) 664-3448 www.visitidaho.org www.museum.ni.org

59 NORTHWEST MUSEUM OF ART AND CULTURE—SPOKANE, WASHINGTON

The museum collaborates with four Northern Plateau tribes and has one of the pre-eminent collections of Plateau materials. It specializes in regional history, historic regional art, fine arts and American Indian and other cultures. Most visitors spend over two hours in museum. There is a museum store. Cafe MAC is popular with locals and tourists alike.

The Campbell House Museum is included with museum admission. It has an award winning public history program: the Campbell family, a maid, politician and detective, enact a drama for guided tours.

■ Open Tues-Sun 11-5. Admission: $7 adult, $5 senior, $5 student, free under age 6. (509) 456-3931 www.northwestmuseum.org

60 COEUR D'ALENE CASINO RESORT HOTEL—WORLEY, IDAHO

200 room resort hotel, 24-hour indoor pool, award-winning, reasonably priced, restaurants and lounge. One of the "top ten best new" golf courses (***Golf Digest***); video arcade; and conference center. Voted most popular casino in the Inland Northwest.

■ (800) 523-2464 (hotel reservations) www.cdaccasino.com

61 APPALOOSA MUSEUM AND HERITAGE CENTER—MOSCOW, IDAHO

The spotted horse, the Appaloosa, is the horse of the Nez Perce Indians. The museum has exhibits and a live Appaloosa outdoor exhibit.

■ Open Mon-Fri 10-5 Sat 10-4.
Free admission.
(208) 882-5578 www.appaloosamuseum.org

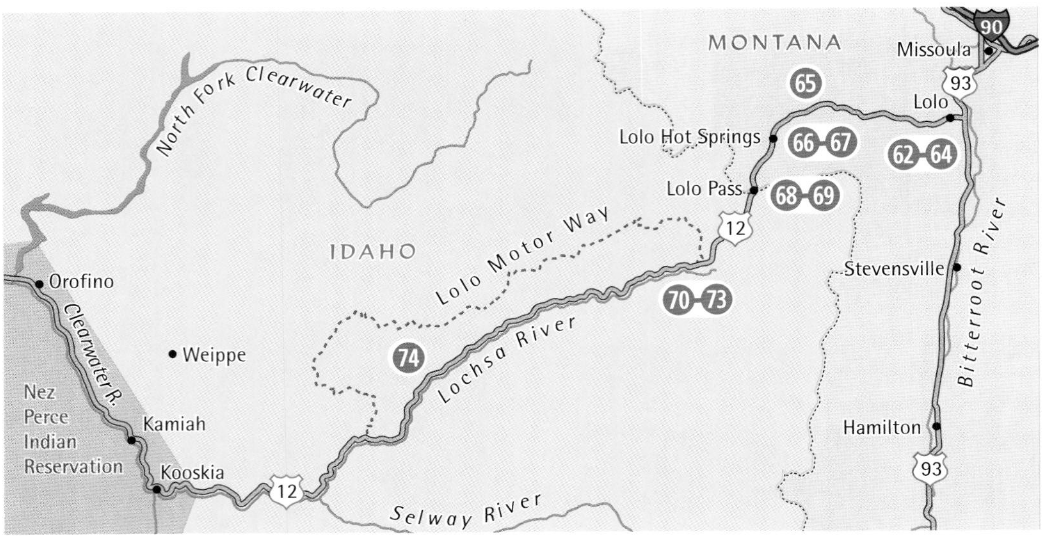

The Lolo Pass Trail on Highway 12 through the Bitterroot Mountains

Lolo Hot Springs

Lewis and Clark Trail Crossing

■ US Highway 12 is a paved, two lane, winding road with a speed limit of 50 miles per hour ■ It takes 3½ to 4 hours to travel non-stop from Lolo MT to Kooskia ID (132 miles) ■ Daylight hours are in short supply in mountain valleys ■ Two time zones: MST in Montana; PST in Idaho (one hour earlier) ■ Cell phones don't work in mountain valleys ■ Kooskia to Orofino is 32 miles ■ Orofino to Lewiston is 45 miles ■ If you want to stop and enjoy the attractions on the Lolo Trail and west of the mountains, make arrangements to spend the night en route and/or book a room in Kooskia, Kamiah or Orofino. www.kooskia.com wwwkamiahchamber.com www.orofino.com

8

62 TRAVELERS REST
LOLO, MONTANA

6550 Mormon Creek Road.
From I-15 Exit 105 go southwest on Van Buren Street 0.1 mile. Turn west on Broadway Street. Go 0.6 mile. Turn south on US 12 (Higgins Avenue). Go 10.9 miles. Keep straight onto US 93. Go 0.6 mile. Turn west on Mormon Creek Road. Go 1/4 mile to Travellers Rest.

63 HOLT HERITAGE MUSEUM
LOLO, MONTANA

6800 Lewis and Clark Highway.
From I-15 Exit 105 go southwest on Van Buren Street 0.1 mile. Turn west on Broadway Street. Go 0.6 mile. Turn south on US 12 (Higgins Avenue). Go 10.9 miles. Turn west on Lolo Creek Road (US 12). Go 0.2 mile to the Museum.

64 FORT FIZZLE
HIGHWAY 12, MONTANA

From I-15 Exit 105 go southwest on Van Buren Street 0.1 mile. Turn west on Broadway Street. Go 0.6 mile. Turn south on US 12 (Higgins Avenue). Go 10.9 miles. Turn west on Lolo Creek Road (US 12). Go 3.7 miles to Fort Fizzle.

65 HOWARD CREEK TRAIL
HIGHWAY 12, MONTANA

From the junction of US 93 and US 12 at Lolo go west 18.5 miles on US 12 to Howard Creek.

66 LOLO HOT SPRINGS
HIGHWAY 12, MONTANA

From the junction of US 93 and US 12 at Lolo go west 25.2 miles on US 12 to Lolo Hot Springs.

67 LOLO TRAIL CENTER
HIGHWAY 12, MONTANA

From the junction of US 93 and US 12 at Lolo go west 26 miles on US 12 to the Lolo Trail Center.

68 LOLO PASS VISITOR CENTER
HIGHWAY 12, MONTANA

From the junction of US 93 and US 12 at Lolo go west 32.4 miles on US 12 to Lolo Pass Visitor Center.

69 PACKER MEADOWS AND GLADE CREEK–LOLO PASS

From the junction of US 93 and US 12 at Lolo go west 32.4 miles on US 12 to Lolo Pass Visitor Center. Go east past the Visitor Center on Forest Service Road 373. Continue on Forest Service Road 373 past the intersection with Forest Service Road 5670 to the intersection with Forest Sevice Road 5954. Distance from the Visitor Center about 1/2 mile. Park and walk along Forest Service Road 373 to Packer Meadows.

70 DE VOTO MEMORIAL GROVE
HIGHWAY 12, IDAHO

From the junction of US 93 and US 12 at Lolo go west 41.7 miles on US 12 to De Voto Memorial Grove.

71 POWELL RANGER STATION
HIGHWAY 12, IDAHO

From the junction of US 93 and US 12 at Lolo go west 44.8 miles on US 12. Turn south on Forest Service Road 102. Go 0.9 mile to the Powell Ranger Stattion.

72 LOLO MOTORWAY
FOREST ROAD 500

The motorway is single-lane extending 76 miles. From the east it is reached by Parachute Hill Rd; 44.6 miles from Lolo on US 12. From the west end of the Lolo motorway return to US 12 via Dead Man Rd, Middle Butte Rd, and Van Camp Rd.

73 WENDOVER CROSSING WHITEHOUSE POND
HIGHWAY 12, IDAHO

From the junction of US 93 and US 12 at Lolo go west 47.7 miles on US 12 to Whitehouse Pond.

74 LOCHSA HISTORICAL RANGER STATION
HIGHWAY 12, IDAHO

From the junction of US 93 and US 12 at Lolo go west 86.3 miles on US 12 to the Historic Station.

De Voto Grove and Lochsa River

Lolo Motorway
Idaho Tourism

Lochsa River, Highway 12

Just Beyond Lolo Hot Springs
Janet Sproull

Lolo Pass Trail, Highway 12

TRAVELERS REST STATE PARK NATIONAL HISTORIC LANDMARK LOLO, MONTANA

Missoula is at the crossroads of five mountain valleys. Traveler's Rest has been a campground forever, along Lolo Creek near the Bitterroot River. The expedition camped here coming and going, on Sept 9-11, 1805 and June 30-July 3, 1806. Visitor Center and book store.

■ Open daily, last wkd May-1st wkd Sept 8-8 Off season: Mon-Fri 8-4 Sat-Sun 12-4. Entry fee $2 per person.
(406) 273-4253 www.travelersrest.org

HOLT HERITAGE MUSEUM—LOLO, MT

The museum is dedicated to "Cowboys and Indians—Rodeos and Pow Wows."

■ Open Jul-Sept daily 11-4.
Tours by appointment $4. (406) 273-6743.
www.holtheritagemuseum.com

FORT FIZZLE HISTORIC SITE HIGHWAY 12, MONTANA

Fort Fizzle was a wooden barricade erected by Missoula volunteers to stop the advance of Chief Joseph and about 700 members of the non-treaty bands of Nez Perce (including William Clark's Nez Perce son) on July 26-28,1877. After a council with the military, the Nez Perce avoided capture by going around "Fort Fizzle."

■ Open all year. No entry fee. (406) 329-3814
www.visitmt.com Search for Fort Fizzle
www.lewis-clark.org
Search for William Clark's Nez Perce son

HOWARD CREEK HISTORIC LOLO TRAIL HIGHWAY 12, MONTANA

Part of the trail network of ancient footpaths through the Bitterroot Mountains. There is a 0.4 mile steep and rocky loop trail. Wear appropriate footwear; be extra careful if wet or icy.

■ Open all year. No entry fee. (406) 329-3814
www.visitmt.com Search for Howard Creek

66 LOLO HOT SPRINGS HIGHWAY 12, MONTANA

These are the springs that they enjoyed on their return journey on June 29, 1806. Lewis commented that the springs were about the temperature of the warmest baths in Virginia, and that he could stay in them for only 19 minutes with difficulty. The men and Indians amused themselves at the bath; but the Indians went back and forth between the baths and the icy waters of the creek, ending with the baths.

■ Open daily. Both indoor bathing (103°-105°) and outdoor swimming (80°). May-Sept, 10-10. Oct-Apr, Sun-Thurs, 10-8, Fri-Sat, 10-10. Springs use fee: $7 adults, $6 senior, $5 ages under 13.
(800) 273-2290 (406) 273-2290
www.lolohotsprings.com

LOLO TRAIL CENTER HIGHWAY 12, MONTANA

Located near Lolo Hot Springs, the Trail Center has 30 guest lodge/motel rooms. There are no telephones or televisions in rooms. Cell phones don't work here; phone service at office and pay phone. Thermal soaking. The Trail Center has a museum building with Lewis and Clark and Indian exhibits; gift shop and book store. Full service restaurant next door.

■ Open daily, year round. No entry fee.
(406) 273-2201 www.lolotrailctr.com

LOLO PASS VISITOR CENTER HIGHWAY 12, MT/ID STATE BORDER

The Visitor Center is located at the state line. It has exhibits and tourist information. Packer Meadows and Glade Creek road access is through here. Skiing/snowmobiling are weekend activities in winter months. Montana is on Mountain Standard Time; the Idaho Panhandle is on Pacific Standard Time (one hour later).

■ Open last wkd May-Oct daily 8-4:30 PST
Nov-Mar, Fri-Mon 8-4:30. (208) 942-1234
www.fs.us/r1/clearwater

PACKER MEADOWS AND GLADE CREEK LOLO PASS

Packer Meadows is an ancient campground. If you want to hike part of the expedition's trail there is a 7.5 mile trail from Packer Meadow to Lolo Hot Springs. The expedition camped at Glade Creek on September 13, 1805. There are-interpretive signs and walking paths.

■ www.lolo.k12.mt.us

DE VOTO MEMORIAL CEDAR GROVE HIGHWAY 12, IDAHO

Bernard De Voto (1895-1955) was an early editor of the Lewis and Clark Journals; a conservationist, author and historian. This peaceful grove is a very pleasant stop.

■ (406) 727-8733 www.fs.fed.us/r1

71 POWELL RANGER STATION, FOREST SERVICE CAMPGROUNDS, LOCHSA LODGE AND RESTAURANT HIGHWAY 12, IDAHO

Powell Ranger Station has five Forest Service campgrounds in its immediate vicinity. The Powell Campground has RV facilities (reservations: (208) 942-3113). Lochsa Lodge is a resort with a gas station, convenience store and restaurant across from the campground; it has cabins/rustic cabins. Restaurant open 365 days/year.

■ Open Mon-Fri 7:30-4. No entry fee.
(208) 942-3113 www.visitidaho.org
Search for Powell Ranger Station
■ Lochsa Lodge (208) 942-3405
www.lochsalodge.com

LOLO MOTORWAY NATIONAL HISTORIC LANDMARK

This is the route the expedition took on top of the mountain ridges; enduring perhaps the most difficult conditions of their entire journey. (September 11-22,1805). Their return journey was much easier (June 15-21, 1806).

Lolo Motorway/Forest Service Road 500/the Lewis and Clark Lolo Trail, goes for 76 miles along the mountain tops. (See above photo.) A single lane road, motorists need to be able to back up a quarter of a mile, with steep drop-offs. Vehicles going up hill have the right of way. Vehicles going down hill must back up. Drive a high clearance vehicle with good tires, bring a spare tire, food and water, maps, binoculars. Clearwater National Forest has a list of guides/outfitters for the Lolo Trail.

■ (208) 942-4274 Kooskia office
www.fs.fed.us/r1/clearwater (Lewis and Clark)

WENDOVER CROSSING AND WHITEHOUSE POND—HWY 12, IDAHO

Campground along the Lochsa River near a pond named for Sergeant Joseph Whitehouse. Interpretive signage.

■(208) 926-6413 www.lewisandclarkidaho.com

LOCHSA HISTORICAL RANGER STATION HIGHWAY 12, IDAHO

Eight ranger station buildings from 1926-34 are a memorial to the Forest Service and its management of National Forests. Interpreters are on duty to answer questions.

■ Open daily last wkd may-1st wkd Sept 9-5
(208) 926-4275 www.lewisandclarkidaho.com

8

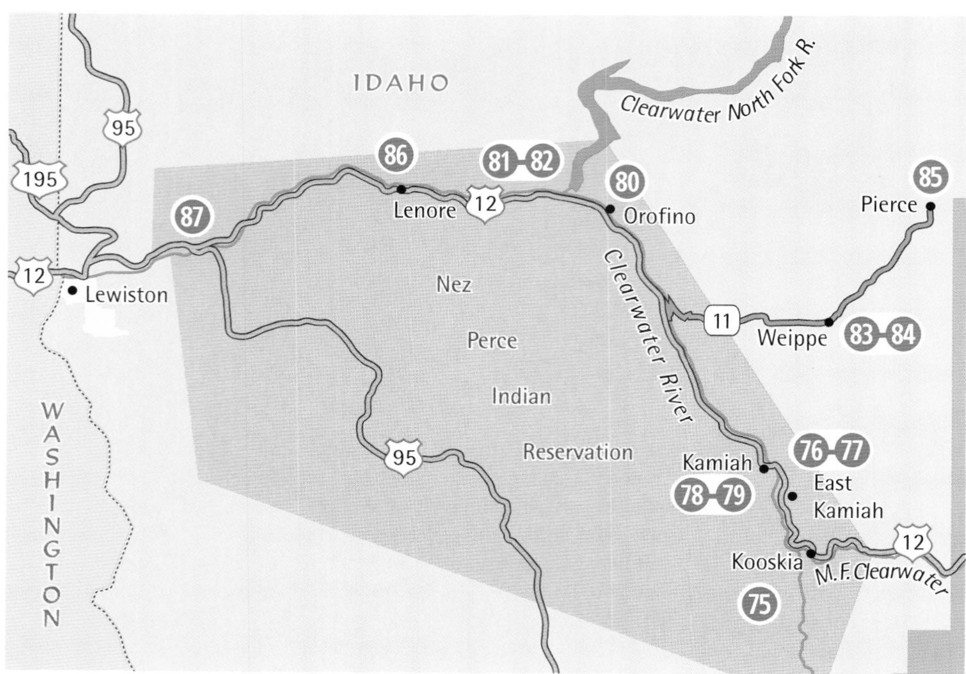

Highway 12 on the Nez Perce Reservation

Cover Photo, near Lenore
Mike McElhatton

Clearwater River near Orofino

8

75 KOOSKIA KIOSK/MURALS
KOOSKIA, IDAHO

From the intersection of of US 12 and Route 13 go west 1/8 mile on US 12 to the Kiosks.

76 FIRST INDIAN PRESBYTERIAN CHURCH
EAST KAMIAH, IDAHO

On US 12 2.7 miles south of Kamiah.

77 HEART OF THE MONSTER
EAST KAMIAH, IDAHO

On US 12 1.5 miles south of Kamiah.

78 LEWIS AND CLARK LONG CAMP HISTORIC MARKER
KAMIAH, IDAHO

Riverfront Park south of Hwy 12 bridge at Kamiah.

79 KAMIAH WELCOME CENTER AND LEWIS AND CLARK EXHIBIT HALL
KAMIAH, IDAHO

518 Main Street.
From the US 12 bridge across the Clearwater River go southwest on Third Street. Turn south on Main Street. Go two blocks to the Lewis and Clark Exhibit Hall.

80 CLEARWATER MUSEUM
OROFINO, IDAHO

315 College Avenue.
From the US 12 bridge cross the Clearwater River on Route 7. Turn south on Michigan Avenue. Turn left on College Avenue. Go 1/4 mile to the Museum.

81 LEWIS AND CLARK CANOE CAMP
OROFINO, IDAHO

On US 12, 4 miles west of Orofino.

82 DWORSHAK DAM AND FISH HATCHERY
OROFINO, IDAHO

From the US 12 bridge cross the Clearwater River on Route 7. Turn northwest on Riverside Avenue. Keep straight onto Ahsahka Road. Go to the Fish Hatchery. Turn east onto Northfork Drive to go to the Dam Visitor Center.

83 WEIPPE DISCOVERY CENTER
WEIPPE, IDAHO

204 Wood Street.
From US Highway 12 turn east on State Route 11. Go 17 miles to Weippe. Continue east on Pierce Street for 0.3 mile. Turn south on Wood Street. Go 0.1 mile to the Discovery Center.

84 WEIPPE PRAIRIE
WEIPPE, IDAHO

Weippe Prairie is about nine miles by twenty miles running from northwest to southeast with the town of Weippe in its center. Weippe is (11 miles east of US 12) 17 miles by road over Route 11. Historical Marker #261 at milepost 17.2 on Route 11 in Weippe.

85 BRADBURY LOGGING MUSEUM
PIERCE, IDAHO

103 South Main Street.
From US Highway 12 turn east on State Route 11. Go 29 miles to Pierce. In Pierce, Rte 11 is Main St. Continue 0.5 mile to the Museum.

86 LENORE REST AREA (BIG EDDY)
LENORE, IDAHO

North side of US Highway 12 about 25 miles east of Lewiston.

87 COYOTE'S FISHNET, ANT AND YELLOWJACKET,
SPALDING, IDAHO

Coyote's Fishnet is on US 95 milepost 306.8; 7 miles east of Lweiston.
Ant and Yellowjacket is on US 12 milepost 10.7; 9 miles east of Lewiston.
Both sites are near Nez Perce National Historical Park.

Long Camp
Idaho Tourism

Weippe Prairie

Heart of the Monster
Mike McElhatton

Clearwater Museum
Idaho Tourism

Nez Perce Country, Highway 12

(Pronounced "Nezz-Purse")

75 KOOSKIA KIOSK AND MURALS KOOSKIA, IDAHO

(Pronounced "Koos-kee"). Named after the Nez Perce word for the Clearwater River, The Kooskia Kiosk is located near the junction of Highways 12 and 13 and the Kooskia bridge. The mural on Main Street depicts the area as it might have appeared in 1806. The "Wild and Scenic" Middle Fork of the Clearwater River divides here into the South fork of the Clearwater River and the main Clearwater River.

■ (208) 926-4362 www.kooskia.com

76 FIRST INDIAN PRESBYTERIAN CHURCH EAST KAMIAH, IDAHO

The Nez Perce's first church, founded in 1871, sits on the north side of the highway. It is the oldest continually used church in Idaho.

■ (208) 935-2672 www.kamiahchamber.com

77 HEART OF THE MONSTER NEZ PERCE NAT'L HISTORICAL PARK EAST KAMIAH, IDAHO

(Pronounced "Kam-mee-eye) Kamiah was the winter home of the Nez Perce for thousands of years. "Heart of the Monster" is the story of Coyote and the origin of the "Nee-mee-poo" or Nez Perce people. There are two audio station interpretive sites at the park, and short trails.

■ Open all year. No entry fee. (208) 843-2261 www.visitidaho.org

78 LEWIS AND CLARK LONG CAMP NEZ PERCE NAT'L HISTORICAL PARK KAMIAH, IDAHO

The campsite is commemorated in Kamiah's Riverfront Park south of the Hwy 12 bridge. The camp was called "Camp Choppunish" after the captain's name for the Nez Perce, or "Long Camp" for the reason that they stayed here from May 14-June 10, 1806. The original campsite was located across the river from Kamiah on the site of the present day lumber mill.

Travelers today may also relax in Kamiah and stay awhile. The tribe has a small casino near the park, the It'Se-Ye-Ye Casino, with a full kitchen and grill.

■ Open all year. No entry fee. (208) 935-2290 www.visitidaho.org www.crcasino.com

79 KAMIAH WELCOME CENTER AND LEWIS AND CLARK EXHIBIT HALL KAMIAH

Local area history is displayed in the Exhibit Hall near the Welcome Center. Kamiah holds an annual Nez Perce Root Festival and Pow Wow on the third weekend in May; and Chief Lookingglass Days on the third weekend in August. The public is invited to attend.

■ Open Mon-Fri 10-4 Sat 9-1. Free admission. (208) 935-2290 or (208) 935-2342 www.kamiahchamber.com

80 CLEARWATER MUSEUM—OROFINO, ID

The museum has exhibits on the missionaries; the 1860 gold rush; mining and logging industries; pioneer homesteads; Dworshak Dam; over 4500 historical photographs; and Nez Perce history and artifacts.

■ Open Jun-Sept Tues-Sat 12:30-5:30 Oct-May Tues-Sat 1:30-4:30. Free admission. (208) 476-5033 clearwatermuseum.org

81 LEWIS AND CLARK CANOE CAMP NEZ PERCE NAT'L HISTORICAL PARK OROFINO, IDAHO

The expedition camped here along the banks of the Clearwater River 4 miles west of Orofino from Sept. 26- Oct. 7, 1805 to make five dugout canoes that would carry them to the Pacific Ocean. They branded 38 horses and left them in the care of the Nez Perce to be retrieved on the return journey. The Canoe Camp site has interpretive signage, restrooms and a 0.5 mile walking trail.

■ Open year round. No entry fee. (208) 843-2261 www.nps.gov/nepe

82 DWORSHAK DAM AND NATIONAL FISH HATCHERY—OROFINO, IDAHO

Dworshak Dam is 717 feet tall; it is the highest straight-axis, concrete gravity dam in North America. It's 54 mile long reservoir lake has many campground areas, boating and fishing. The National Fish Hatchery produces steelhead trout and spring chinook salmon.

■ Visitor Center open last wkd May-1st wkd Sept daily 8:30-4:30 Sept-May Mon-Fri 8:30-4:30. (208) 476-1255. Hatchery open daily 7:30-4:00. (208) 476-4591 www.nww.usace.army.mil

83 WEIPPE DISCOVERY CENTER AND PUBLIC LIBRARY—WEIPPE, IDAHO

(Pronounced "Wee-ipe") The Visitor and Interpretive Center is also a library/technology/small business center. It has free internet access, tourist information and souvenirs. There is a wonderful series of Lewis and Clark Murals and a living landscape garden.

■ Open daily May-Aug 11-5 with various extended hours. Sept-Apr Mon-Fri 11-5 Sat 9-12. Free admission. (208) 435-4406 (208) 435-4058. www.weippe.com

84 WEIPPE PRAIRIE NEZ PERCE NAT'L HISTORICAL PARK

Weippe Prairie was a camas field at 3,100 feet elevation in the mountains. The Nez Perce lived here in summer and fall harvesting the tasty root bulb. This is where the expedition met the Nez Perce for the first time on Sept. 20, 1805.

■ Open all year. No entry fee. (208) 843-2261 www.nps.gov/nepe

85 J. HOWARD BRADBURY LOGGING MUSEUM—PIERCE, IDAHO

The Idaho Gold Rush started in Pierce in 1860. Western White Pine has proved to be "green gold" for the area. The museum has logging and mining equipment and historic photographs.

■ Open Jun-Oct Fri-Sat 12-4. Nov-May Sat 12-4. Free admission. (208) 464-2677 www.pierceweippechamber.com

86 BIG EDDY, LENORE REST AREA LENORE, IDAHO

This site is called "Big Eddy" because of a large eddy (backwater swirl) in the Clearwater River. Archeology digs due to highway construction have shown that Lenore was continuously inhabited by the Nez Perce for over 8,000 years.

■ (208) 843-2261 www.nps.gov/nepe

87 COYOTE AND BEAR, ANT AND YELLOW JACKET, NEZ PERCE NAT'L HIST. PARK SPALDING, IDAHO

Two traditional Nez Perce story sites along Highway 12. See the next pages for information about the Nez Perce Museum and the Spalding Visitor located here at the junction of US-95 and US-12 Highways.

■ (208) 843-2261 www.nps.gov/nepe

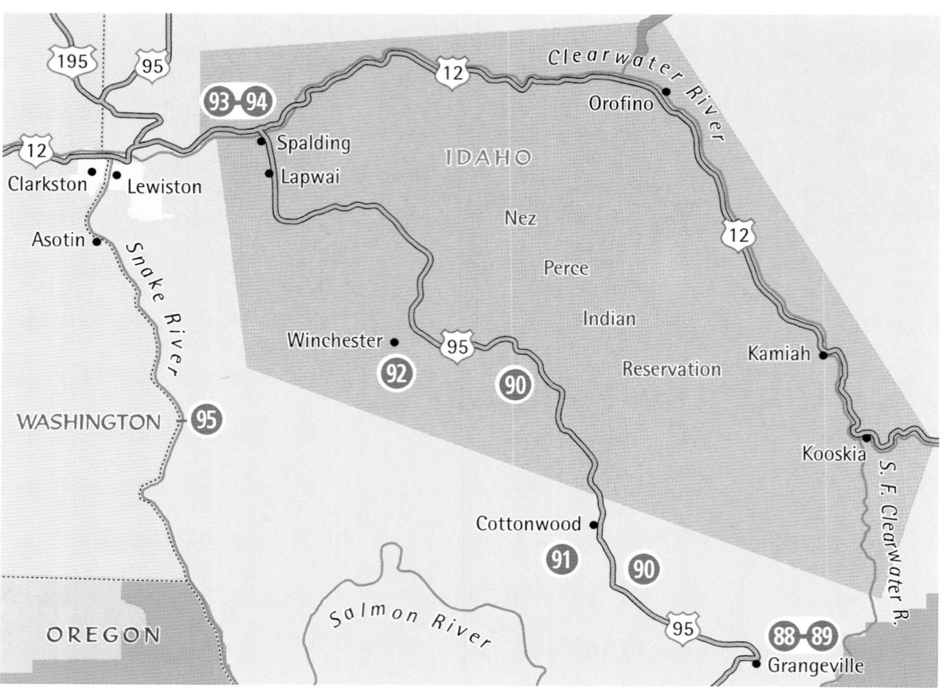

Highway 95, Nez Perce Indian Reservation

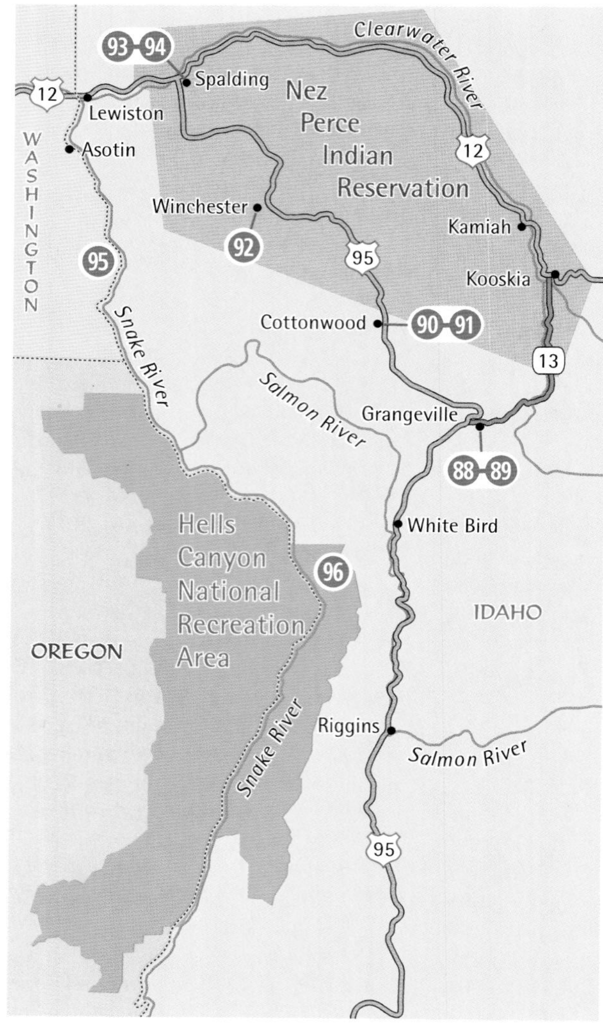

Hells Canyon

88 GRANGEVILLE VISITORS CENTER/MAMMOTH EXH. GRANGEVILLE IDAHO

US Highway 95 at Pine Street.

89 BICENTENNIAL HISTORICAL MUSEUM GRANGEVILLE IDAHO

305 North College Street.

From US 95 go east on Main Street 0.4 miles. Turn north on College Street. Go 0.1 mile to the Museum.

90 ORDWAY MARKERS COTTONWOOD, IDAHO

Lewis and Clark Marker #488.

At US 95 milepost 252.9; 4.5 miles south of Cottonwood.

Lewis and Clark Marker #489.

At US 95 milepost 268.6: 11.3 miles north of Cottonwood.

91 HISTORICAL MUSEUM AT ST GERTRUDE COTTONWOOD IDAHO

From US 95 go northwest on Main Street. Go 0.4 mile. Turn west on Front Street. Go 0.8 mile. Keep straight onto Keuterville Road. Go west, then south for a total of 1.7 miles to the Historical Museum.

92 WOLF EDUCATION RESEARCH CENTER WINCHESTER IDAHO

From US 95 turn west onto US 95 Bus.. Go 2.1 miles to Winchester Lake State Park. Approaching the Lake campground, instead of entering the campground, continue on the dirt road. Watch for the signs for the Wolf Education and Research Center.

93 NEZ PERCE VISITOR CENTER AND MUSEUM SPALDING IDAHO

39063 Highway 95.

From the junction of US 12 and US 95 go east on US 95 1.1 miles to the Nez Perce Visitor Center.

94 SPALDING MISSION SITE SPALDING IDAHO

From the junction of US 12 and US 95 go east on US 95 2.1 miles. Turn northeast on Thunderhill Road. Go northeast 0.1 mile, then east 0.3 mile. Turn east on Spalding Mill Road (403 Road). Go 0.1 mile to Spalding MissionParking.

95 BUFFALO EDDY PETROGLYPHS ASOTIN WASHINGTON

From the east side of Asotin near the Snake River go south on Snake River Road for 15 miles to a place on the river where there are huge jumbles of rocks jutting into the river on both sides. There is a large pullout for parking above a white sand beach. Look downriver for a trail that goes 300 yards to the petroglyphs on the rocks.

96 HELLS CANYON NATIONAL RECREATION AREA WHITE BIRD IDAHO

2535 Riverside Drive.

Pittsburg Landing. From US 95 near White Bird go southwest on River Road (Old Highway 95). Go two miles over the Salmon River Bridge. Go south on Deer Creek Road for 10 miles. Go south on National Forest Road 493 for 9 miles. Continue south on local road 1.2 miles to the Visitor Center at Pittsburg Landing.

Nez Perce Visitor Center and Museum
Mike McElhatton

www.digitalartsphotography.com

Big Horn Sheep, Hell's Canyon
Mike McElhatton

Buffalo Eddy Petroglyphs
Mike McElhatton

Jet Boat, Hell's Canyon
Mike McElhatton

Nez Perce Country, Highway 95

88 GRANGEVILLE VISITORS CENTER AND MAMMOTH REPLICA EXHIBIT

The Visitor Center is staffed by local retirees. It has tourism information, and hand-crafted art (wood carving, rawhide braiding, leather art and silver engraving). There is an actual mammoth bone on exhibit; and a life size replica of a mammoth skeleton. Grangeville Border Days, the oldest rodeo in Idaho, happens over the 4th of July weekend.

■ Open summer Mon-Fri 9-5 winter Mon, Wed, Fri 10-2. Free admission. (208) 983-0460 www.grangeville.com

89 BICENTENNIAL HISTORICAL MUSEUM GRANGEVILLE, IDAHO

The museum has an exceptional collection of Nez Perce artifacts; a complete mining exhibit; and pioneer life displays.

■ Open Jun-Sept Wed, Fri 1-5 or by appointment. Free admission. (208) 983-2104. www.grangeville.com

90 ORDWAY MARKERS, HIGHWAY 95 COTTONWOOD, IDAHO

Sergeant John Ordway and two others were sent in search salmon on May 27, 1806. The Nez Perce told them Indians could be found fishing on the Snake River. Two historical markers tell the story of their journey.

■ www.lewisandclarkidaho.org

91 HISTORICAL MUSEUM AT ST GERTRUDE—COTTONWOOD, IDAHO

The blue flowers of the camas prairie near Cottonwood are a beautiful sight in June.Lewis said camas flowers looked like "lakes of fine clear water." The historical museum was founded by a Benedictine Sister; it is one of the oldest and largest museums in north central Idaho, run by the Sisters of the Monastery of St Gertude. Area history includes the Nez Perce, Basque sheep herders, Chinese miners, Lewis and Clark, and others. There are also artifacts from Europe, dating back to the Middle Ages.

■ Open May-Sept Tues-Sat 9:30-4:30 Sun 1:30-4:30, Apr-Oct Tues-Sat 9:30-4:30, Admission: $4 adult, $1 student ages 7-17. (208) 962-7123 www.historicalmuseumatstgertrude.com

92 WOLF CENTER—WINCHESTER, IDAHO

1/3 mile round trip to see the wolf enclosure self- guided tour. An interpreter will lead you on daily 1½ hour tours (about 1/2 mile round trip) at 7:30 AM or 7 PM (except Sunday PM and Monday AM). Call ahead to reserve a space.

■ Open for self-guided tours and general visitation last wkd May-1st wkd Sept daily 9-5, May wkds 9-4. Sept wkds 9-4. Guided tours last wkd May-1st wkd Sept. May wkds by appointment. Sept wkds by appointment. Guided tours outside of listed hours by appointment. Tour fees: self-guided $5 adult, $2 ages 6-13; guided tours $10 adult, $3 ages 6-13. (208) 924-6960 www.wolfcenter.org

93 NEZ PERCE VISITOR CENTER AND MUSEUM—SPALDING, IDAHO

The Nez Perce National Historical Park has 38 sites in Idaho, Oregon, Washington and Montana. There is an auto tour booklet available which follows the trail of the Nez Perce during the summer of 1877, tracing the flight of Chief Joseph and the non-treaty bands to escape capture by the United States Army, ending in the Nez Perce defeat at the Battle of Bear Paw Mountains in Montana.

The Visitor Center and Museum have world-class exhibits on the Nez Perce people. A 27 minute film is available upon request. During summer months rangers give daily programs.

The tribe has an excellent website. Check out the FAQ for history/cultural information.

■ Open last wkd May-1st wkd Sept daily 8-5 winter months daily 8-4:30. Free admission. (208) 843-7001 www.nps.gov/nepe

■ www.nezperce.org

94 SPALDING MISSION SITE SPALDING, IDAHO

In 1831 four Nez Perces traveled to St Louis seeking "the book of Heaven and the teachers." The American Board of Commissioners of Foreign Missions sent out two missionary couples, Marcus and Narcissa Whitman and Henry and Eliza Spalding. In 1836, the women became the first white women to travel across the Rocky Mountains. Thousands would follow within a few short years on the Oregon Trail.

The Whitmans settled in Walla Walla, Washington. The Spaldings established a mission at Lapwai, where the Nez Perce have lived for over 11,000 years. The mission site is now part of the Nez Perce National Historical Park. Henry Spalding baptized over 900 Indians, including the father of Chief Joseph. As many as 2,000 Indians attended his Sunday services.

The site has interpretive signage, and several old buildings located in the area surrounding the Visitor Center.

■ Open last wkd May-1st wkd Sept daily 8-5 winter months daily 8-4:30. Free admission. (208) 843-7001 www.nps.gov/nepe

95 BUFFALO EDDY PETROGLYPHS ASOTIN, WA

This rock art dates from 4,500 years ago. The website warns to wear life jackets if you are going to climb to view the rock art, as the eddies in the water are strong. If you visit the site from the Idaho side, you do not need to go into the water. Follow a 300 yard trail from the parking area to the rocks. You have to find the art yourself on the rocks which jut out from the banks of the Snake River. Do not climb on the rocks when not necessary. Vandalism is a federal offense.

■ www.spokaneoutdoors.com
Search for Indian Rock Art

96 HELLS CANYON

Hells Canyon is North America's deepest river gorge. The gorge is over 8,000 feet deep. Over 1500 archaeological sites have been identified in the Canyon, including villages and shelters that date back 8,000 years.

Only about 12% of Hells Canyon National Recreation Area is accessible by car. Pittsburgh Landing has the only paved public road providing year round acess. There is a recreational hiking trail at Pittsburgh Landing, with some loop trails. The Snake River is designated as a "wild" river for 31.5 miles between Hells Canyon Dam and Pittsburgh Landing.

Jet boat and rafting trips depart from Hells Canyon State Park in Lewiston (see next pages).

■ (509) 758-0616 www.fs.fed.us/hellscanyon

8

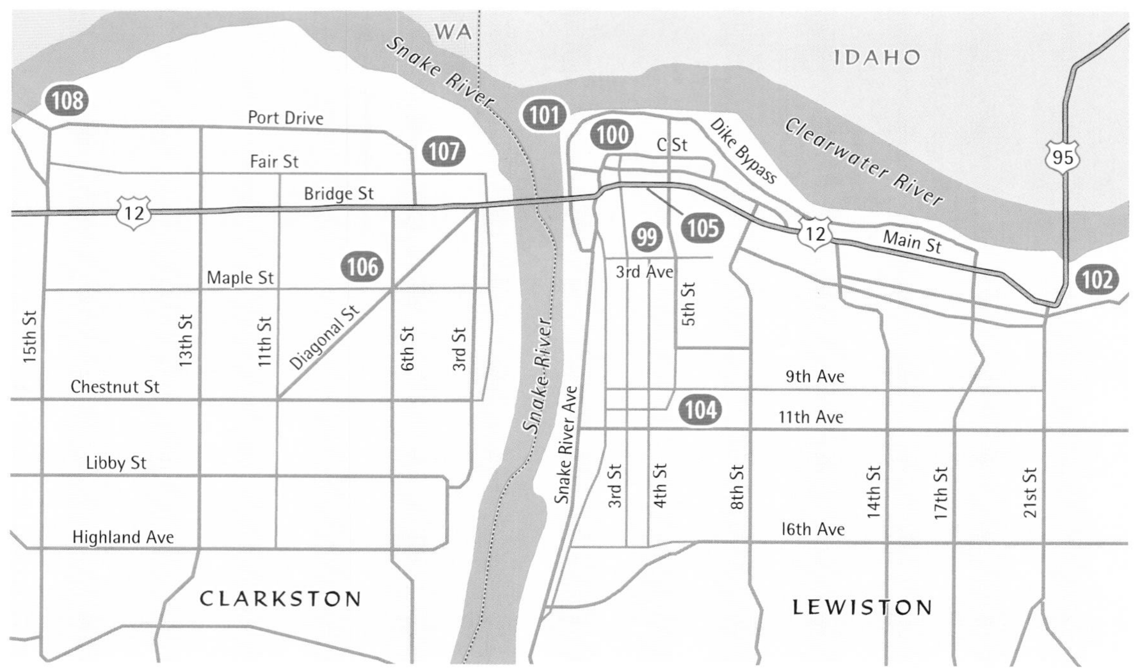

Lewiston and Clarkston at the Confluence of the Snake and Clearwater Rivers

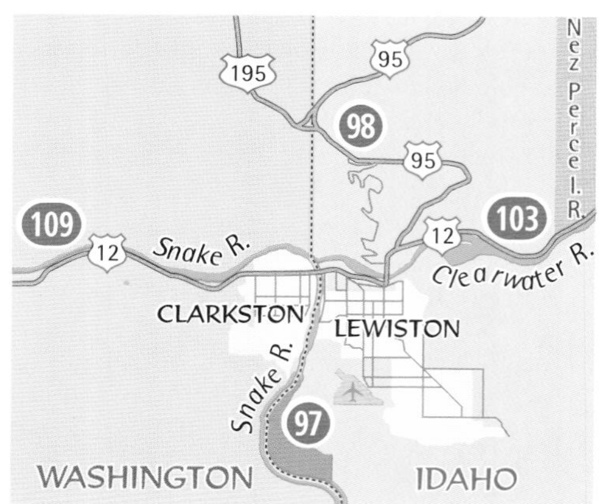

Lewiston and Clarkston Area

8

97 LEWIS AND CLARK DISCOVERY CENTER HELLS GATE STATE PARK

5100 Hells Gate Road.

From the intersection of US 12 Main St) and Snake River Ave. Go south on Snake River Ave for 3.35 miles. Turn west onto local road. Go 0.65 mile to Discovery Center.

98 THREE STATES SCENIC OVERLOOK AND SPIRAL HIGHWAY LEWISTON IDAHO

From the junction of US 95 and US 12 in Lewiston go north on US 95 for 6 miles to north end of the Spiral Highway and access road to the overlook.

To access the Spiral Road from the valley, turn left at the second exit north of the Clearwater Bridge.

99 NEZ PERCE COUNTY MUSEUM LEWISTON. ID

306 Third Street.

From US 12 (Main St) go south 0.3 mile to 3rd Ave. Go west two blocks to the Museum.

100 LEWIS AND CLARK CENTER AT CONFLUENCE LEWISTON IDAHO

From US 12 (Main St) go to 5th St. Turn north. Go to D St. Turn west. Go past 1st St; go over RR tracks. Turn north to parking.

101 CLEARWATER AND SNAKE RIVER NATIONAL TRAIL

25 mile levee trail system can be accessed from destinations #97 and #100 above; and from Asotin and Clarkston Washington.

102 CLEARWATER BRIDGE SCULPTURES LEWISTON IDAHO

Both ends of the US 12 bridge over the Clearwater River.

South end near the 21st St interchange.

North end at the US 95/US12 junction.

103 CLEARWATER RIVER CASINO LEWISTON IDAHO

17818 Nez Perce Road.

From the US 12/US 95 junction go east 4.4 miles to Nez Perce Rd (North and South Highway 95/12).

104 CENTENNIAL MALL SCULPTURES LEWIS-CLARK COLLEGE LEWISTON IDAHO

500 8th Avenue.

From Main St (US 12) go south on 5th St for 0.6 mile to 8th Ave.

105 LEWIS-CLARK CENTER FOR ART AND HISTORY LEWISTON IDAHO

415 Main Street.

From 5th St and Main (US 12) go west to the Center.

106 LEWIS AND CLARK DISCOVERY CENTER CLARKSTON WASHINGTON

721 6th Street.

From Bridge Street (US 12) go south 0.3 mile (past Maple Street) to the Discovery Center.

107 LEWIS AND CLARK GARDEN CLARKSTON WASHINGTON

From Bridge Street (US 12) go north 0.3 mile on 5th Street to the Lewis and Clark Garden along the Snake River.

108 LEWIS AND CLARK RIVERFRONT TIMELINE CLARKSTON WASHINGTON

1515 Port Drive.

From Bridge Street (US 12) go north 0.2 mile on 15th Street to Port Drive. Go east 0.2 mile to the Timeline on the pier.

109 CHIEF TIMOTHY PARK SILCOTT WASHINGTON

From Clarkston go west 8 miles on US 12 to Silcott. Turn north on Silcott Road. Go over bridge to Timothy Hay Park on island in the Snake River.

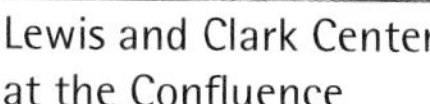

Lewis and Clark Center at the Confluence

Spiral Highway

Hells Gate State Park Lewis and Clark Discovery Center Mike McElhatton

Lewis and Clark at Clearwater Bridge
Betty Kluenser
Discovery Expedition of St Charles

Lewiston and Clarkston

97 LEWIS AND CLARK DISCOVERY CENTER, HELLS GATE STATE PARK LEWISTON, IDAHO

The Discovery Center has a two acre Lewis and Clark interpretive plaza along the banks of the Snake River; educational displays; and a beautiful moving stream with sculptures by Rip Caswell. There is an original 32 minute Lewis and Clark film; and a gift shop and book store.

Jet boat tours depart regularly from Hells Canyon; other boating experiences are also available. Use links on the park website or ask at the office. Reservations are advised for RV and tent campgrounds and camper cabins.

■ Open daily, 9-5. Admission: $4 vehicle entrance fee (866) 634-3246 (208) 799-5015 www.idahoparks.org

■ Campgound reservations (866) 634-3246 www.parksandrecreation.idaho.gov

98 THREE STATES SCENIC OVERLOOK AND SPIRAL HIGHWAY—LEWISTON, ID

Goats and motorbikes may be hazards on this road, the "Old Lewiston Grade" or Spiral Highway. The view is from the Three State Scenic Overlook (2,750 feet above the valley), which provides a great view of the confluence of the Clearwater and Snake Rivers and the towns of Lewiston and Clarkston. I-95 also goes to the Scenic Overlook.

■ (208) 843-2261 www.hellscanyonvisitor.com

99 NEZ PERCE COUNTY MUSEUM LEWISTON. ID

Exhibits feature: the Nez Perce and Lewis and Clark; and Lewiston history. Media Center and gift shop.

■ Open Mar-Dec 10-4. Donation.
(208) 743-2535 www.npchistsoc.org

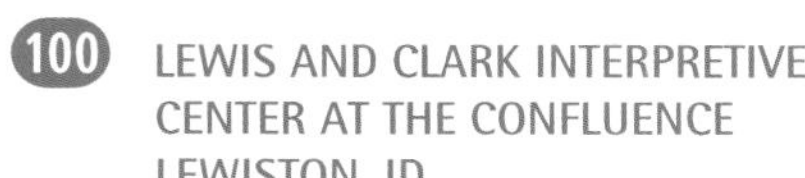

100 LEWIS AND CLARK INTERPRETIVE CENTER AT THE CONFLUENCE LEWISTON, ID

The confluence of the Snake and Clearwater Rivers may be viewed from this lovely open air interpretive center near a network of riverfront trails on the levee. The Tsenicum statue by Nancy Dreher depicts Mother Earth. Reached by a footpath overpass.

■ Open daily all year. No fee.
www.lctoday.net/sports_recreation.htm

101 CLEARWATER AND SNAKE RIVER NATIONAL TRAIL—LEWISTON, IDAHO

The 25 mile trail connects Lewiston with Hells Gate State Park. The trail is built on an extended levee system and is wheelchair accessible.

■ (208) 743-3531
www.lctoday.net/recreation.htm

102 CLEARWATER BRIDGE SCULPTURES LEWISTON, ID

Lewiston has extensively landscaped and placed 20 Lewis and Clark sculptures on both sides of the Memorial Bridge over the Clearwater River. Five groups of sculptures represent Lewis and Clark meeting the Nez Perce, made out of Core-10 steel, protected by rust. Three sculptures are bronze works.

■ (208) 743-3531
www.lctoday.net/cultural/sculptures.htm

103 CLEARWATER RIVER CASINO LEWISTON

The Clearwater Casino, owned by the Nez Perce tribe, has the Aht' Wy Plaza with RV and tent camping. Heated swimming pool. Rest rooms, showers, coin operated laundry. Riverside Grill offers $1.99 ham and egg breakfast all day; and $6.99 dinner specials.

The tribe also has a smaller casino at Kamiah, the It'Se-Ye-Ye Casino with a full service kitchen and grill.

■ Casino and Riverside Grill open every day 24 hrs. (208) 746-0723 www.crcasino.com

104 CENTENNIAL MALL SCULPTURES LEWIS-CLARK STATE COLLEGE—LEWISTON

The college has a Lewis and Clark and Nez Perce sculpture group on the Centennial Mall that is one of the nicest outdoor exhibits on the Trail.

■ (208) 792-5272 www.lcsc.edu

105 LEWIS-CLARK CENTER FOR ART AND HISTORY—LEWISTON, ID

The Center has a Chinese temple, the Beuk Aie Temple Museum, representing the area's Chinese heritage. The art gallery is the second largest in Idaho. Many cultural events are held here. Sales and rental art gallery.

■ Gallery open Mon-Fri 11-4. Free admission.
(208) 792-2243 www.artsandhistory.org

106 LEWIS AND CLARK DISCOVERY CENTER—CLARKSTON, WA

The historical artifacts that used to be displayed at Chief Timothy Park relating to the Alpowai village of the Nez Perce (once located at the park) are displayed here. Lewis and Clark items for sale. Visitor information.

■ Open May-Sep Mon-Sat 10-3. Free admission. (509) 758-3126 www.lcoday.net/tourism/tourist _information.htm

107 LEWIS AND CLARK GARDEN CLARKSTON, WA

Plants of the region made known to science by Lewis and Clark are on display in Granite Lake Park on the riverfront.

■ (509) 758-7712
www.hellscanyonvisitor.com

108 LEWIS AND CLARK RIVERFRONT TIMELINE—CLARKSTON, WA

The beautiful sidewalk etchings showing the adventures of the Lewis and Clark Expedition are located at the Hells Canyon Resort Marina, adjacent to the Rooster's Landing Waterfront Restaurant in Clarkston. Rooster's Landing opens at 11 AM.

■ (509) 751-0155 www.roosterslanding.com

109 CHIEF TIMOTHY PARK SILCOTT, WA

The park is located on an island in the Snake River, eight miles west of Clarkston on Hwy 12. Archaeology digs have established the area as being occupied for 6,000 years. The island will become the site of the second Maya Lynn Confluence Project (www.confluenceproject.org)

The park was the home of the Alpowai band of the Nez Perce. Chief Timothy as a little boy saw the Lewis and Clark Expedition, when it camped near here on October 11, 1805 and May 4, 1806. Chief Timothy was one of the first Christian Nez Perce. His band fought on the side of the US Army during the Indian Wars of the 1850's. The chief and his people continued to live here through the late 1800's.

RV and tent campground and boating managed by the NW Land Management.

■ (509) 758-8613 $5 day use fee.
(877) 444-6777 campground reservations
www.nwww.usace.army.mil/corpsoutdoors

8

Region Eight: References

BIOGRAPHY

ANDREW HENRY: MINE AND MOUNTAIN MAJOR
by Margaret Hawkes Lindsley. Jelm Mountain Publications (1990)

THE BEAVER MEN: SPEARHEADS OF EMPIRE
by Mari Sandoz. University of Nebraska Press (1978)

BEHOLD THE SHINING MOUNTAINS
by Gary H. Wiles and Delores M. Brown. Photosensitive (1966)

BILL SUBLETTE: MOUNTAIN MAN
by John E. Sunder. University of Oklahoma Press (1959)

BROKEN HAND: THE LIFE OF THOMAS FITZPATRICK MOUNTAIN MAN, GUIDE, AND INDIAN AGENT
by Leroy R. Hafen. University of Nebraska Press (1981)

EDWARD WARREN
by William Drummond Stewart. Mountain Press Publishing Company (1986)

ENCYCLOPEDIA OF FRONTIER BIOGRAPHY: IN THREE VOLUMES
by Dan L. Thrapp. University of Nebraska Press (1991)

THE EXPLORATIONS OF WILLIAM H. ASHLEY AND JEDEDIAH SMITH 1822-1829 / WITH THE ORIGINAL JOURNALS
edited by Harrison Clifford Dale. University of Nebraska Press (1991)

FORTY YEARS A FUR TRADER ON THE UPPER MISSOURI: THE PERSONAL NARRATIVE OF CHARLES LARPENTEUR, 1833-1872
by Charles Larpenteur. University of Nebraska Press (1989)

JEDEDIAH SMITH AND THE OPENING OF THE WEST
by Dale L. Morgan. University of Nebraska Press (1964)

JESSIE BENTON FREMONT: A WOMAN WHO MADE HISTORY
by Catherine Coffin Phillips. University of Nebraska Press (1995)

JIM BRDGER
by J. Cecil Alter. University of Okalahoma Press (1962)

JOE MEEK: THE MERRY MOUNTAIN MAN
by Stanley Vestal. University of Nebraska Press (1963)

JOURNAL OF A MOUNTAIN MAN
by James Clyman. Mountain Press Publishing Company (1984)

BIOGRAPHY

JOURNAL OF A TRAPPER: WITH A BIOGRAPHY OF OSBOURNE RUSSELL, AND MAPS OF HIS TRAVELS WHILE A TRAPPER IN THE ROCKY MOUNTAINS
by Aubrey L Haines. University of Nebraska Press (1965)

THE LIFE AND ADVENTURES OF JAMES P. BECKWORTH: MOUNTAINEER, SCOUT, PIONEER AND CHIEF OF THE CROW NATION
written from his own dictation by T. D. Bonner. Ross & Haines, Inc. (1965)

LIFE IN THE FAR WEST
by George Frederick Ruxton, edited by Leroy R. Hafen. University of Oklahoma Press (1951)

LIFE IN THE ROCKY MOUNTAINS: A DIARY OF WANDERINGS ON THE SOURCES OF THE RIVERS MISSOURI, COLUMBIA, AND COLORADO 1830-1835; WITH A BIOGRAPHY OF FERRIS
diary by Warren Angus Ferris, biography by Paul C. Phillips. The Old West Publishing Company (1983)

NARRATIVE OF THE ADVENTURES OF ZENAS LEONARD: WRITTEN BY HIMSELF
edited by Milo Milton Quaife. University of Nebraska Press (1978)

THE PERSONAL NARRATIVE OF JAMES O. PATTIE
by James O. Pattie. University of Nebraska Press (1831/1984)

THE ROCKY MOUNTAIN JOURNALS OF WILLIAM MARSHALL ANDERSON: THE WEST IN 1834
edited by Dale L. Morgan. University of Nebraska Press (1967)

ROCKY MOUNTAIN LIFE: OR STARTLING SCENES AND PERILOUS ADVENTURES IN THE FAR WEST, DURING AN EXPEDITION OF THREE YEARS
by Rufus B. Sage. University of Nebraska Press (1858/1982)

WILLIAM H. ASHLEY: ENTERPRISE AND POLITICS IN THE TRANS-MISSISSIPPI WEST
by Richard M. Clokey. University of Oklahoma Press (1990)

HISTORY

ACROSS THE SNOWY RANGES: THE LEWIS AND CLARK EXPEDITION IN IDAHO AND WESTERN MONTANA
by James R. Fazio. Woodland Press (2001)

THE AMERICAN FUR TRADE OF THE FAR WEST (TWO VOLUMES)
by Hiram Martin Chittenden. University of Nebraska Press (1902/1986)

HISTORY

DO THEM NO HARM: LEWIS AND CLARK AMONG THE NEZ PERCE
by Zoa L. Swayne. Claxton Press (2003)

FIREARMS, TRAPS, & TOOLS OF THE MOUNTAIN MEN
by Carl P. Russell. University of New Mexico Press (1996)

GIVE YOUR HEART TO THE HAWKS: A TRIBUTE TO THE MOUNTAIN MEN
by Winfred Blevins. Tamarack Books, Inc. (1995)

THE GREAT GATES: THE STORY OF THE ROCKY MOUNTAIN PASSES
by Marshall Sprague. Little, Brown and Company (1964)

LEWIS & CLARK IN THE BITTERROOT
by Jeanne O'Neill, Jean Clary, Patricia B. Hastings, Diann Ladd, Katie White, Riga Winthrop. Stoneydale Press Publishing Company (1998)

A MAJORITY OF SCOUNDRELS: AN INFORMAL HISTORY OF THE ROCKY MOUNTAIN FUR COMPANY
by Don Berry. Comstock Editions, Inc. (1961)

ROCKY MOUNTAIN RENDEZVOUS: A HISTORY OF THE FUR TRADE RENDEZVOUS 1825-1840
by Fred R. Gowans. Brigham University Press (1975)

MISCELLANEOUS

EXPLORING THE FUR TRADE ROUTES OF NORTH AMERICA: DISCOVER THE HIGHWAYS THAT OPENED A CONTINENT
by Barbara Huck et al. Heartland (2002)

IDAHO
by John Gottberg. Compass American Guides (2001)

MOON HANDBOOKS: IDAHO
by Don Root. Avalon Travel (2001)

NATIONAL PARKS OF THE ROCKY MOUNTAINS AND THE GREAT PLAINS. THE SIERRA CLUB GUIDES
by Conger Beasley Jr., C. W. Bucholtz, Paul Schullery, and Stephen Trimble. Stewart, Tabori & Chang, Inc. (1984)

THE NORTHERN ROCKIES: IDAHO, MONTANA, WYOMING. THE SMITHSONIAN GUIDES TO NORTH AMERICA
by Jeremy Schmidt and Thomas Schmidt. Smithsonian Books (1995)

RIVER OF NO RETURN
by Johnny Carrey and Cort Conley. Backeddy Books (1978)

REGION NINE
WASHINGTON AND OREGON

- Dayton to Pendleton
- Tri-Cities and Yakama Indian Reservation
- Columbia River Gorge: The Dalles Area
- Historic Columbia River Highway Area
- Portland, Mt Hood and Warm Springs Indian Reservation
- Vancouver to Skamokawa
- Cape Disappointment and Long Beach
- Astoria to Tillamook Bay

1. Clatsop Burial Boat, Astoria Column, Astoria OR 2. Beacon Rock, Stevenson WA 3. Cathlapotle Plank House, Ridgefield WA 4. Cape Disappointment, Ilwaco WA 5. Patit Creek Campsite Sculptures, Dayton WA 6. Multnomah Falls, Multnomah Falls OR 7. Fort Clatsop Visitor Center, Astoria OR 8. Journey's End, Pacific Ocean 9. Dugouts, Knapptown WA

Credits: (1) Catherine Jett; (2) Lyn Topinka; (3) Ridgefield National Wildlife Refuge; (4) (6) (8) (9) Betty Kluesner, Discovery Expedition of St Charles; (5) Dayton Washington Visitor Center

9

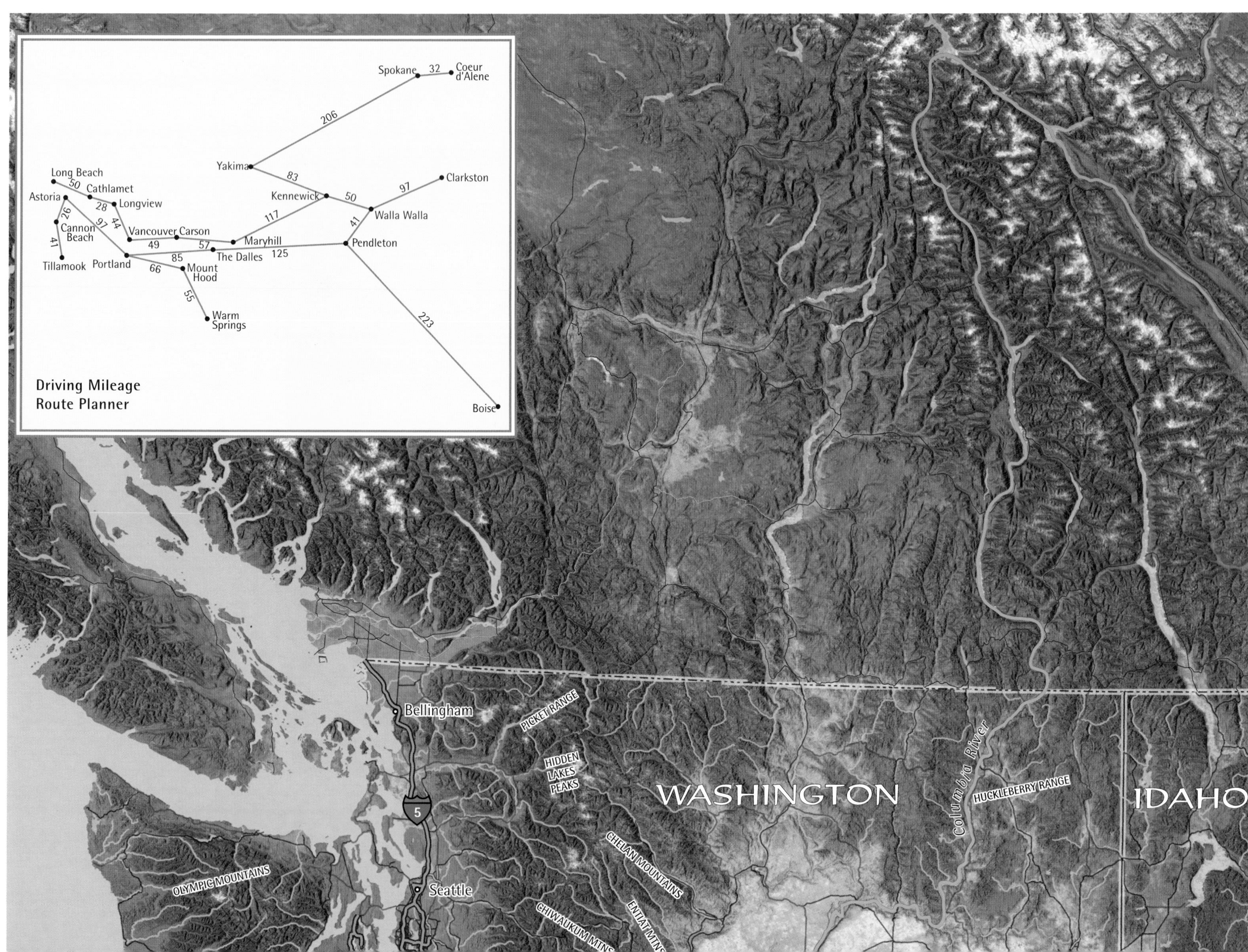
Driving Mileage Route Planner
Spokane
32
Coeur d'Alene
206
Yakima
83
Kennewick
50
Walla Walla
97
Clarkston
41
Pendleton
125
223
Boise
117
Maryhill
Long Beach
50
Cathlamet
28
Longview
44
Astoria
26
Cannon Beach
41
Tillamook
97
Vancouver
Carson
49
57
The Dalles
Portland
85
66
Mount Hood
55
Warm Springs
Bellingham
PICKET RANGE
HIDDEN LAKES PEAKS
WASHINGTON
Columbia River
HUCKLEBERRY RANGE
IDAHO
5
OLYMPIC MOUNTAINS
Seattle
CHELAN MOUNTAINS
CHIWAUKUM MTNS
ENTIAT MTNS

9

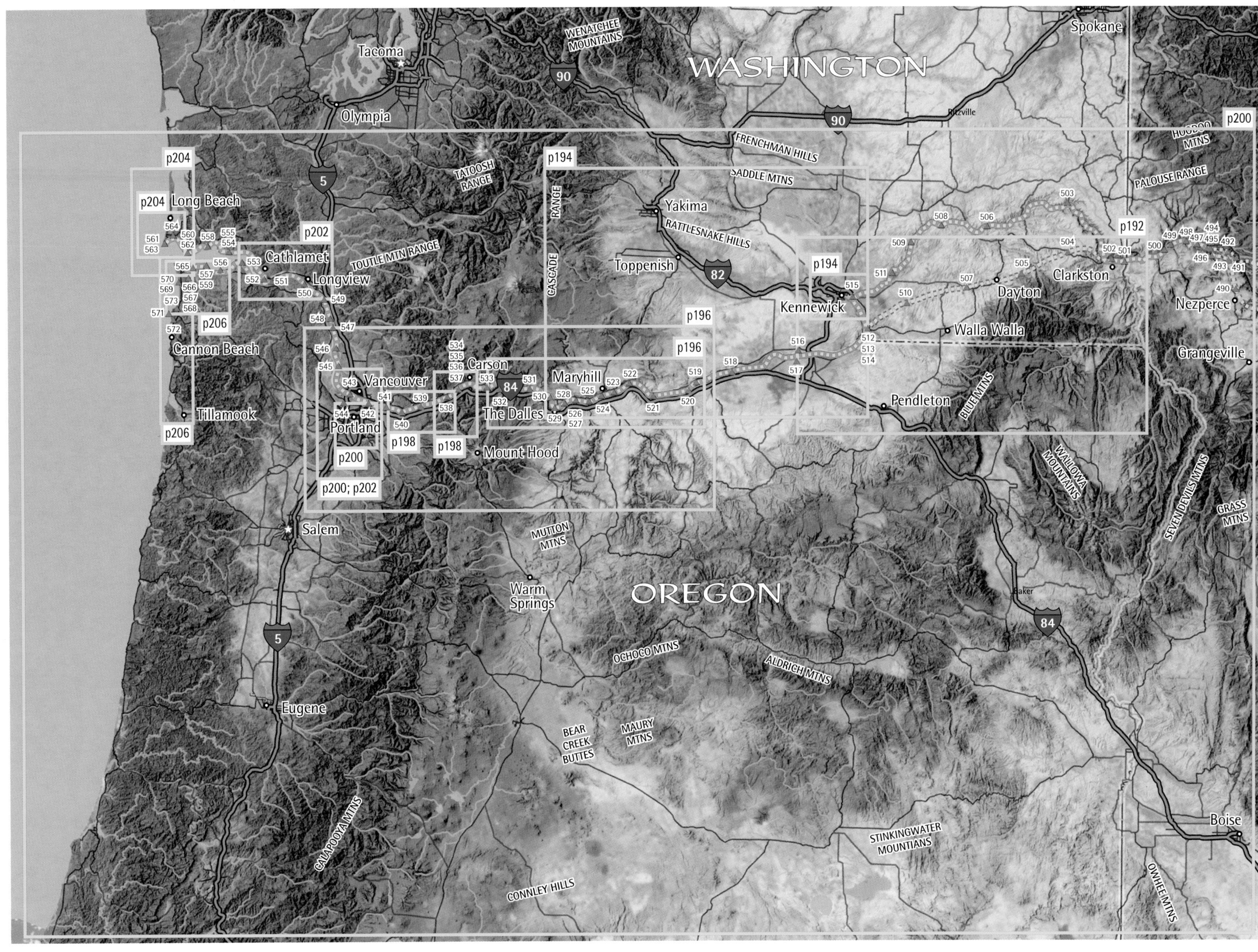

WASHINGTON
OREGON
Spokane
Ritzville
Tacoma
Olympia
Yakima
Toppenish
Kennewick
Walla Walla
Dayton
Clarkston
Nezperce
Grangeville
Pendleton
Baker
Boise
Long Beach
Cathlamet
Longview
Cannon Beach
Tillamook
Vancouver
Portland
Carson
Maryhill
The Dalles
Mount Hood
Salem
Eugene
Warm Springs
WENATCHEE MOUNTAINS
FRENCHMAN HILLS
SADDLE MTNS
RATTLESNAKE HILLS
CASCADE RANGE
TATOOSH RANGE
TOUTLE MTN RANGE
PALOUSE RANGE
BLUE MTNS
WALLOWA MOUNTAINS
SEVEN DEVILS MTNS
GRASS MTNS
MUTTON MTNS
OCHOCO MTNS
ALDRICH MTNS
BEAR CREEK BUTTES
MAURY MTNS
STINKINGWATER MOUNTIANS
OWHEE MTNS
CONNLEY HILLS
CALAPOOYA MTNS
90
82
84
5
p192
p194
p196
p198
p200
p200; p202
p202
p204
p206

Patit Creek Sculptures on the "Forgotten Trail"
Dayton, Washington Visitor Center

View of the Columbia River near Cape Disappointment
Betty Kluesner, Discovery Expedition of St Charles

Beacon Rock
Lynn Topinka

Vista House at Crown Point
Lyn Topinka

Sandy River, Troutdale
Lyn Topinka

Memaloose Island Burial Grounds
Memaloose State Park and Rest Area

America 200 Years Ago

The Pacific Northwest

REACHING THE COLUMBIA RIVER

Jefferson's letter of instructions to Lewis stated that his mission was to explore the Missouri River to its source; investigate its principal streams; and determine the most direct and practical river routes to the Pacific Ocean for the purpose of commerce. Once out in the West, he was to decide which rivers he would explore, but Jefferson anticipated he would go to the mouth of the Columbia River.

9

The United States had already established a claim to the Pacific Northwest: an American ship captain, Robert Gray, had visited the river in 1792, naming it for his ship the ***Columbia.*** In the years to come, the Pacific Northwest would be claimed by three countries, the United States, Great Britain and Spain; and the United States would almost go to war over it. Spain relinquished its claims in 1819. After that, "Oregon Country" was jointly occupied by the United States and Great Britain until a treaty finally established the border between Canada and the United States in 1846.

DID THE EXPEDITION SUCCEED?

In achieving their first goal—to find the source waters of the Missouri—they took the long way around to the Lolo Trail using Lemhi Pass. It took them fifty seven days to go from their camp at Great Falls to their Travelers' Rest camp at the start of the Lolo Trail (July 15-Sept 9, 1805). On the way back, Lewis used the route the Indians recommended; he followed the Blackfoot River through the mountains and made the trip in only seven days (July 3-10, 1806). The two captains split up on the return journey, to explore the Marias River and the Yellowstone River, two of the Missouri's principal streams.

In addition to discovering the geography of the region, the "most practical" route to the ocean depended upon establishing good relationships with Indian tribes along the way: they formed alliances with three tribes, the Shoshone, Salish and Nez Perce, who had not dealt with white men before. Their enemies, the Blackfeet and Atsina (Gros Ventre) of Canada and northern Montana, were already in alliances with British-Canadian fur traders.

If the expedition had not established these relationships, and not spent the winter of 1805-06 at Fort Clatsop, the geography of the United States might look a lot different today.

INDIANS OF THE COLUMBIA RIVER

Two old Nez Perce chiefs, Tetokarsky and Twisted Hair, accompanied them on their way west. They interpreted for them and introduced them to other tribes, upstream of Celilo Falls, who spoke the Shahaptian language. From there to the ocean, tribes spoke the Chinookian language. The chiefs guided them on the Clearwater and Snake Rivers and for part of the way on the Columbia River, until they announced they were at war with the Indians below Celilo Falls and would proceed no further.

At the Falls, the Corps saw the first houses made of wood they had seen since leaving the Illinois Country. The area of Celilo Falls (which is now submerged under The Dalles Dam) was the center of the great Indian trading market. Indians came from all over the West to trade with each other. Items of trade included dried salmon from the Columbia River, dried buffalo and other meat jerkies from the east, dried roots and berries, skin clothing, buffalo robes, and bear grass for making cooking baskets and hats. In later years, beads and European metal goods played a big role in the trading. The market was also a social event with horse trading, horse races, dancing, and gambling.

The trading season had mostly ended by the time the expedition arrived at The Dalles in late October of 1805. Indians along the Columbia River were in contact with sailing ships at the Pacific Ocean through coastal tribes who played a middleman role. On January 14th, 1806 after traveling the length of the river, Lewis estimated they prepared about 30,000 pounds of dried salmon each year for trading purposes.

As the Corps moved down the river, they were seldom out of sight of Indian dwellings. During winter months families lived together along the river. In other seasons, they traveled to dig roots, hunt, and harvest berries at the proper times. Around half the population had died in smallpox epidemics in the thirty

Seaman at Skamokawa Bay
Betty Kluesner, Discovery Expedition of St Charles

Multnomah Falls
Lyn Topinka

See Lyn Topinka's photos at www.englishriverwebsite.com

Fort Clatsop Visitor Center

See Discover Expedition of St Charles at www.lewisandclark.net

Cathlomet Plank House
Ridgefield National Wildlife Refuge

Cape Disappointment Walking Trail

years before the Corps' arrival. The disease was first brought by European ships in about 1775. Another epidemic had occurred in 1801. This might explain some of their poor behavior towards the expedition.

The Corps found many of them to be persistent thieves and sharp traders, and developed an unfavorable opinion of coastal Indians. On balance, they were impressed by many aspects of their lives and skills; but kept their distance and never socialized with them to the extent that they had with the Indians at Fort Mandan.

THE COLUMBIA RIVER ESTUARY

On October 31st, they saw a "remarkable high detached rock" (in fact it is the second largest rock in the world, an 840 foot monolith), which they named Beacon Rock. For the first time they observed the effects of tidal flow on the Columbia River. Ocean tides, going in and out, caused the river to rise and fall as much as 18 inches in a day. They had entered the tidal estuary of the Columbia River, where fresh and salt water mix together.

From November 1-3 they were portaging (carrying their goods) around the Great Rapids, or Cascades of the Columbia. On November 3rd, they passed the Sandy River, which was still discharging great volumes of volcanic ash and mud flow from an eruption of Mt Hood in the the rather recent past. Next they passed the big sand bar between present day Portland, Oregon and Vancouver, Washington. This sand bar had created another channel of the Columbia, the Willamette River heading south. They followed the north bend of the Columbia River.

On November 7th, Clark wrote, "Great joy in camp we are in *View* of the *Ocian."* They were near Pillar Rock in what is now the Lewis and Clark National Wildlife Refuge at Skamokawa. They were piloted through the tidal waters by an "Indian dressed in a Salors dress" with a flat head. All the Indian nations west of the Rockies, flattened the heads of their infants with a board press so that their foreheads sloped upwards to a point on top of the head, which was considered an attractive feature.

DISMAL NITCH AND STATION CAMP

As they approached the ocean, high winds and tidal waters caused immense waves, and carried along drifting trees, "maney of them 200 feet long and 4 feet through." They sought refuge in a "dismal nitch" in the cliffs on a bed of drift logs that had been caught against the rocks, where they stayed from Nov 10th-12th.

It was "truly disagreeable" Clark wrote; they were cold, wet, and miserable as their clothing rotted away in the rain. To their amazement, Indians came by in canoes, riding the high waves, to trade fish with them for small goods. Clark wrote that the Indians crossed the five miles of the harbor "through the highest Sees I ever Saw a Small Vestle ride....Certain it is they are the best canoe navigators I ever Saw."

By November 15th, they had managed to get themselves around the point of land near today's Astoria Bridge, and set up camp on a sandy beach in "full view of the Ocian." They considered Station Camp near Chinook Point to be the official end of their journey. Clark calculated they had come 4,142 miles in the seventeen months since leaving Wood River Camp at the mouth of the Missouri.

On November 18th, Clark took eleven men on an exploring trip, crossing over Cape Disappointment to reach the waters of the Pacific, and then heading north on the Long Beach pennisula. On November 24th, the entire company voted (even Sacagawea and York) on the matter of where to establish their winter camp. The majority favored going across the river. The next day they set out for the Clatsop lands south of present day Astoria, Oregon.

FORT CLATSOP

They began building Fort Clatsop on Dec. 7th and left it on March 23rd, anxious to start for home. They experienced only 12 days without rain and 6 days of sunshine. They passed the time making moccasins and clothing from leather skins. Near Seaside, Oregon they boiled sea water in kettles to make about 20 gallons of salt; it was used as a preservative to keep meat from spoiling. On January 6th they visited the remains of a whale on the beach. Sacagawea had complained that she had traveled a long way with them and wanted to see "the great waters" and "the monstrous fish" so Clark agreed to take her and Charbonneau along with about a dozen others to see the skeleton.

The captains wrote up their reports and observations about Indians, plants and animals. Clark made lists, tables, illustrations and maps. Lewis wrote long descriptive essays, praised by James Ronda, author of ***Lewis and Clark Among the Indians*** as representing a "substantial achievement in ethnography." The captains summed up their stay at Fort Clatsop with the words: "we have lived quite as comfortably as we had any reason to expect we should."

THE FORGOTTEN TRAIL

On their return journey, the expedition visited the Walla Walla Indian Village from April 27th-30th, at the Walla Walla River, where Chief Yelleppit gave them an "eligant white horse" and two canoes, and advised them to take an 80 mile shortcut along a good road following the Walla Walla and Touchet Rivers. This is called the "Forgotten Trail of Lewis and Clark."

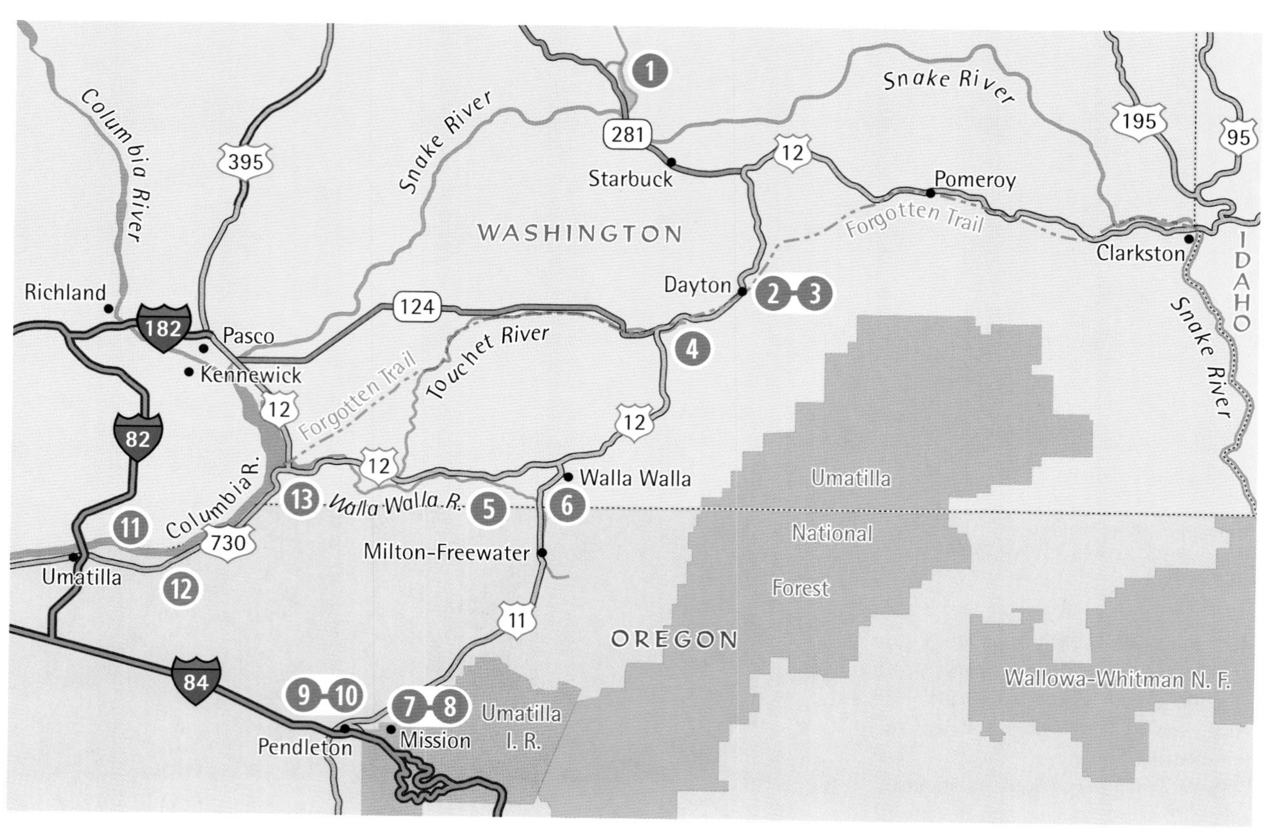

Clarkston, Washington to Pendleton, Oregon and The Forgotten Trail of Lewis and Clark in 1806

1 PALOUSE FALLS STATE PARK STARBUCK WASHINGTON

From US 12 go west, then north-west on Route 261 for 20.6 miles. Turn east on Palouse Falls Road. Go 2.3 miles to the State Park.

2 PATIT CREEK CAMPSITE SCULPTURES DAYTON WASHINGTON

From US 12 in Dayton go about two miles east on Patit Road to the replica encampment.

3 PALUS ARTIFACT MUSEUM DAYTON WASHINGTON

305 East Main Street.
On US 12 (Main Street). At Third and Main Street.

4 LEWIS AND CLARK STATE PARK DAYTON WASHINGTON

From Dayton go west about 5.4 miles on US 12 to Lewis and Clark Trail State Park.

5 FORT WALLA WALLA MUSEUM COMPLEX WALLA WALLA WASHINGTON

755 Myra Road.
From US 12 in Walla Walla go south one block on 13th Avenue. Turn east on Pine Street. Go east 0.3 mile. Turn south on 8th Avenue. Road changes name to 9th Avenue. Go 1.4 miles. Turn southeast onto Route 125. Go one mile. Turn northwest on Myra road. Go 0.3 mile to the Fort.

6 WHITMAN MISSION WALLA WALLA WASHINGTON

328 Whitman Mission Road.
From the junction of US 12 and Route 125 in Walla Walla go west for 4.9 miles. Turn south on Last Chance road. Go 0.8 mile. Turn west on Whitman Mission Road. Go 0.7 mile to the Mission.

7 TAMASTSLIKT INSTITUTE PENDLETON, OREGON

72789 Highway 331.
From I-84 Exit 216 turn north on County Road 334. Go 0.7 mile. Turn east on Tamastslikt Road. Go 1.3 miles to the Institute.

8 WILD HORSE RESORT AND CASINO PENDLETON OREGON

72777 Highway 331.
From I-84 Exit 216 turn north on County Road 334. Go 0.7 mile. Turn east on Tamastslikt Road. Go 0.3 miles to the Resort and Casino.

9 PENDLETON WOOLEN MILLS TOUR PENDLETON OREGON

1307 SE Court Place.
From I-84 Exit 213 go northwest on US 30 (Pendleton Highway) for 1.8 miles. Turn north on 15th Street. Go one block. Turn west on Court Place. Go two blocks to the Woolen Mill.

10 PENDLETON ROUNDUP HALL OF FAME PENDLETON OREGON

1205 SW Court Avenue.
From I-84 Exit 213 go northwest on US 30 (Pendleton Highway) for 1.8 miles. Turn north on 15th Street. Go one block. Turn west on Court Place (road chanes name to Court Avenue). Go 1.3 miles to the Hall of Fame.

11 McNARY DAM OVERLOOK UMATILLA OR

From I-84 Exit 1 go east on US 395/ US 730. Go 0.7 mile. Keep straight onto Columbia River Highway 2. Go 2 miles. Turn north onto County Road 1279 (Port Road). Go 0.9 mile. Go north onto McNary Beach Road. Go 0.4 mile to the Overlook.

12 HAT ROCK STATE PARK UMATILLA OREGON

From I-84 Exit 1 go east on US 395/ US 730. Go 0.7 mile. Keep straight onto Columbia River Highway 2. Go 5.4 miles. Turn north onto Hat Rock State Park Road. Go 2.0 miles. Turn left onto Beach Shore Drive. Go 1/8 mile to Hat Rock.

13 MARIE DORION HISTORICAL PARK UMATILLA OREGON

From the junction of US 12 and US 730 in Washington State go west on US 730 for 0.7 mile. Turn north on local road. Go 0.4 mile to Park.

Patit Creek Campsite Sculptures
Dayton, Washington Visitor Center

Whitman Mission

Tamaslikt Institute

Hat Rock State Park

Dayton to Pendleton

1 PALOUSE FALLS STATE PARK STARBUCK, WASHINGTON

Palouse Falls is a 105 acre camping park, with one of the state's most beautiful waterfalls. The falls are the only remaining major falls created by the Lake Missoula glacial floods 15,000 years ago. The 10,000 year old "Marmes Man" was found near Palouse Falls. The park has an observation shelter and historical displays.

■ Open summer, 6:30 AM to dusk; winter, 8 AM to dusk. Day visits, $5 vehicle fee. For camping info, call (360) 902-8844, Mon-Fri, 8-5.
www.parks.wa.gov

2 PATIT CREEK CAMPSITE SCULPTURES DAYTON, WA

Over 80 life sized steel scultures have been installed along Patit Creek representing the Lewis and Clark encampment of May 2, 1806. There are 37 human figures, 27 horse figures and one dog, with various other paraphenalia. Lewis and Clark traveled through Dayton on their way back on what is called the "Forgotten Trail."

■ Dayton Visitor Center, 166 E Main St,
(800) 882-6299 www.historicdayton.com
www.forgottentrail.com

3 PALUS ARTIFACT MUSEUM DAYTON, WASHINGTON

The museum displays a collection of local area artifacts from the Palus Tribe, and has a beautiful collection of native plants. The tribe spent their winters near Palouse Falls, and their summers in the Dayton area. The Palus are part of the 12 Confederated Tribes of the Colville Reservation in northern Washington. Lewis and Clark called them the "So-yen-now."

■ Open Fridays and Saturdays, 1-4, and by appointment. Call (509) 382-4820 or e-mail ethorn@velocitus.net for more information.
www.historicdayton.com

4 LEWIS AND CLARK STATE PARK DAYTON, WA

This rare, old-growth forest along the Touchet River has a mini-rain forest climate, caused by periodic flooding. Long leaf Ponderosa pine, (which Lewis and Clark noted), and cottonwoods are here. A 37 acre camping park.

■ Open summer, 6:30 AM to dusk; winter, 8 AM to dusk. Day visits, $5 vehicle fee. For camping info, call (360) 902-8844, Mon-Fri, 8-5.
www.parks.wa.gov

5 FORT WALLA WALLA MUSEUM COMPLEX—WALLA WALLA, WA

Lewis and Clark in Wallah Wallah Country, Fort Walla Walla, Pioneer Settlement, and horse era agriculture are portrayed in the 17 buildings and 5 exhibit halls, with living history weekends.

■ Open daily, Apr 1-Oct 31, 10-5. Museum is closed Nov 1-March 31. Admission: $7 adults, $6 seniors and students, $3 ages 6-12.
(509) 525-7798 www.fortwallamuseum.org

6 WHITMAN MISSION NATIONAL HISTORIC SITE—WALLA WALLA, WA

Slide program and exhibits tell the story of the Whitmans, and their mission among the Cayuse Indians (1836-47), the massacre at the Mission, and the Oregon Trail. Outside, visitors can visit the mass grave where the Whitmans are buried, the Memorial Monument, and explore the original mission grounds.

■ Open daily. Summer, 8-6, rest of the year, 8-4:30. Admission: $3 adult, under age 17 free. Maximum $5 fee per family.
(509) 522-6357 www.nps.gov/whmi

7 TAMASTSLIKT INSTITUTE PENDLETON,OR

("Tah-mahst-slick-t") The Museum of the Confederated Tribes of the Umatilla Indian Reservation, has unique galleries, interactive displays and living culture weekends from Memorial Day until November. Native American food at the Kinship Cafe and a museum store with Native American arts and crafts.

■ Open Mon-Sat, 9-5. Admission: $6 adults; $4 seniors, children, students; $12, families up to 5 people; under 5 free.
(541) 966-9748 www.tamastslikt.com

8 WILD HORSE RESORT CASINO PENDLETON, OREGON

Next door to the Tamastslikt Institute, 18 holes golf course, Wildhorse Restaurant, Hot Rock Cafe, lodging and meeting facilities. The Resort Casino is owned and operated by the Confederated Tribes of the Umatilla Reservation.

■ Open 24 hours, 7 days a week.
(800) 654-9453 www.wildhorseresort.com

9 PENDLETON WOOLEN MILLS TOUR

The Washougal Mill Store offers tours of the mill, showing the dyeing, spinning, and weaving of their famous Indian blankets. The Mill store has wearing apparel, blankets and fabrics.

■ Free tours, Mon-Fri, 9, 10, 11, 1:30. The Mill is closed for 2 weeks ixxn December and August.
(800) 568-2480 or (360) 835-1118
www.pendletonmillstore.com

10 PENDLETON ROUNDUP HALL OF FAME

The Pendleton Round-Up Rodeo started in 1909, and is held every year in mid September. It includes the Happy Canyon Night Show Indian Pageant by the Confederated Tribes, concerts, parades, Native American arts and crafts, and many other activities. The Hall of Fame under the Rodeo Grandstands has exhibits and artifacts.

■ Round-Up Hall of Fame is open during summer months, Mon-Sat, 10-4, and by appointment. (800) 457-6336 (541) 276-2553
www.pendletonroundup.com

11 McNARY DAM OVERLOOK AND PACIFIC SALMON CENTER—UMATILLA

Lewis and Clark interpretive markers at the McNary Dam Overlook, where Clark saw Mt. Adams in the distance. The Salmon Recovery Program is located at the Pacific Salmon Visitor Center at the Dam. Fish viewing windows. and wildlife nature trails.

■ Open year round, 9-5.
(541) 922-4388 www.umatilla.org

12 HAT ROCK STATE PARK—UMATILLA, OR

Hat Rock is located on the south shore of Lake Wallula behind McNary Dam on the Columbia River. Lewis and Clark named Hat Rock on Oct. 19, 1805. Boating, fishing, water sports.

■ Park is free, open year round.
(541) 922-2268 www.oregonstateparks.org

13 MARIE DORION HISTORICAL PARK UMATILLA, OREGON

The Historical Park is located where the Walla Walla and Columbia Rivers meet. Marie Dorion was the Iowa Indian wife of Pierre Dorion, Jr. After Sacagawea she was the second woman to come west overland. She traveled with the Hunt-Astorian Expedition in 1811-12, pregnant and with two toddlers, and was the first settler in the Walla Walla Valley. A 46 acre day use and camping park is named in her memory.

■ www.englishriverwebsite.com
(541) 922-4825 www.umatilla.org

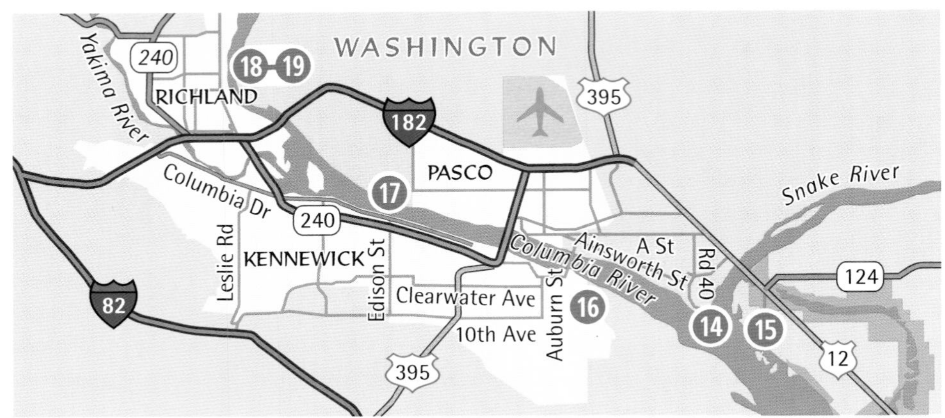

The Tri-Cities: Richland, Kennewick and Pasco

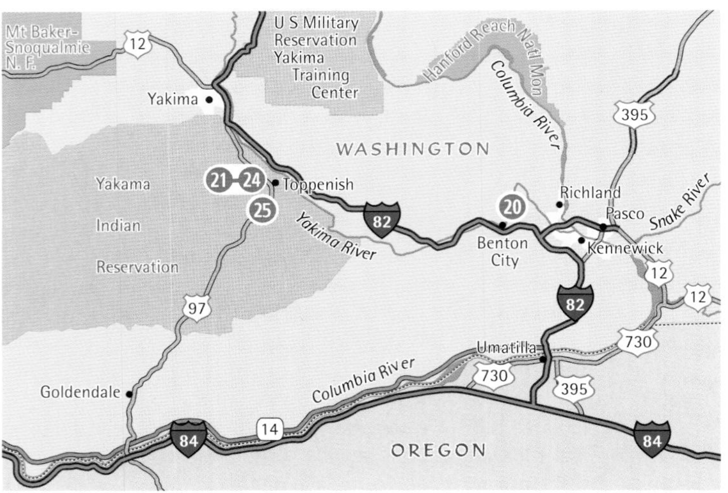

Yakama Indian Reservation

14 SACAJAWEA STATE PARK
PASCO WASHINGTON

2503 Sacajawea Road.
From I-182 (US 12) Exit 14A take US 12 southeast. Go 3.1 miles. Turn southwest onto Sacajawea Park Road. Go southwest; then southeast for 2.0 miles to Sacajawea State Park.

15 MCNARY WILDLIFE CENTER AND REFUGE
BURBANK WASHINGTON

600 East Maple.
From I-182 (US 12) Exit 14A take US 12 southeast. Go 4.0 miles. Turn south on 5th Street. Go 0.6 mile. Turn east on Maple. Go 1/4 mile.

16 EAST BENTON COUNTY HISTORICAL MUSEUM
KENNEWICK WASHINGTON

205 Keewaydin Drive.
From I-182 Exit 12A go 2.5 miles south on US 395 to the US 240 Exit. Go 1 mile east on Columbia Dr. Go 0.2 mile south on Benton St. Go east one block on Kennewick Ave. Go 0.4 mile south on Auburn St. to the Museum.

17 LEWIS AND CLARK INTERPRETIVE OVERLOOK
KENNEWICK WASHINGTON

Coulmbia Center Boulevard and Columbia Park Trail.
From I-182 Exit 5 go southest 2.6 miles on Route 240 to the Columbia Center Boulevard Exit. Go north 0.4 mile to the Overlook.

18 CREHST MUSEUM
RICHLAND WASHINGTON

95 Lee Boulevard.
From I-182 Exit 5 go 1.1 miles northwest on George Washington Way. Turn east on Lee Boulevard. Go one block. Turn south on Amon Park Road.

19 COLUMBIA RIVER JOURNEYS JETBOAT TOURS
RICHLAND WASHINGTON

From I-182 Exit 5 go 1.4 miles northwest, then north on George Washington Way. Turn east one block on Newton St. Turn north on Amon Park Road. Go 0.2 mile to the dock.

20 COLUMBIA VALLEY WINERIES
BENTON CITY WASHINGTON

Sunset Road.
From I-82 Exit 96 go 0.2 mile east on Kennedy Road. Turn north onto State Route 224. Go 1.2 miles. Turn north onto Sunset Road. Seven wineries are located along the 2.4 mile length of Sunset Road.

21 YAKAMA NATION CULTURAL HERITAGE CENTER
TOPPENISH WASHINGTON

From I-82 Exit 52 go 2 miles south on Toppenish-Zilah Rd. Turn west on Toppenish Ave. Go 0.9 mile. Bear west onto 1st Ave. Go 0.7 mile. Name changes to Fort Rd. Go 0.2 mile. Go 0.5 mile northwest on US 97. Go south on Buster Rd.

22 YAKAMA NATION CASINO
TOPPENISH WASHINGTON

From I-82 Exit 52 go 2 miles south on Toppenish-Zilah Rd. Turn west on Toppenish Ave. Go 0.9 mile. Bear west onto 1st Ave. Go 0.7 mile. Name changes to Fort Rd. Go 1.1 mile to the Casino.

23 TOPPENISH MURALS
TOPPENISH WASHINGTON

From I-82 Exit 52 go 0.9 mile south on Toppenish-Zilah Rd. Turn west onto Fraley Rd. GO 1.3 miles. Turn south Route 22 (Evergreen Hwy/ Buena Way). Go 0.3 mile. Turn east onto Jordan Way. Go two blocks. Turn south onto Nation Street.

24 AMERICAN HOP MUSEUM
TOPPENISH WASHINGTON

22 South B Street.
From I-82 Exit 52 go 2 miles south on Toppenish-Zilah Rd. Turn west on Toppenish Ave. Go 0.6 mile. Turn south onto B Street.

25 TOPPENISH NATIONAL WILDLIFE REFUGE
TOPPENISH WASHINGTON

From Toppenish go 4.7 miles south on US 97 (Evergreen Highway). Turn west on Pumphouse Road (BIA 96 Road). Go one mile to the Wildlife Refuge.

Wanapum Tule Mat House
McNary Wildlife Center

Sacajawea Interpretive Center
Washington State Parks

Lewis and Clark Interpretive Overlook
Tri-Cities Visitor and Convention Bureau

Tri-Cities and Yakama Indian Reservation

14 SACAJAWEA STATE PARK AND INTERPRETIVE CENTER –PASCO, WA

Located at the confluence of the Snake and Columbia Rivers in the homelands of the Confederated Tribes of the Umatille Reservation, the park will be the second site where a Maya Lin sculpture is placed. It was a major salmon fishery when the expedition camped here from Oct. 16-18, 1805.

The Interpretive Center has an outstanding collection of stone and bone tools in the Jay Perry Room of Indian Artifacts.

■ Park is day use only. Open summer 6:30 AM to dusk. Closed from Nov 1-March 25. Hours at Interpretive Center:
(509) 545-2361
www.parks.wa.gov www.confluenceproject.org

15 MCNARY NATIONAL WILDLIFE CENTER AND REFUGE–BURBANK, WA

The 15,000 acre refuge opposite Sacajawea State Park is an important resting and feeding stop for up to 100,000 migrating waterfowl in the Pacific Fly-way. More than 212 species are regularly sighted here. The center is staffed by knowledgeable "birders" who conduct workshops and nature walks. It has 70 life-like mounted birds and animals, and a Wanapum Tule Mat Lodge.

■ Open daily. (509) 547-4942 (refuge)
(509) 543-8322 (center)
www.nwr.mcnary.wa.us

16 EAST BENTON COUNTY HISTORICAL MUSEUM–KENNEWICK, WA

Called the "best small museum building in the state," with a beautiful petrified wood floor and natural lighting. Its displays feature the story of the 10,000 year old "Kennewick Man" and a Kennewick Man bust; Indian artifacts; transportation on the Columbia River; local agricultural crops; and photographs.

■ Open Tues-Sat, 12-4. Admission: $2 adults, 50 cents, children and students.
(509) 582-7704 www.owt.com/ebchm

17 LEWIS AND CLARK INTERPRETIVE OVERLOOK–KENNEWICK , WA

A 10 by 16 foot Lewis and Clark Trail map is part of the concrete plaza at the Columbia River overlook. The Sacagawea Heritage Riverfront Trail is nearby.

■ (509) 735-8486 www.visittri-cities.com

18 CREHST MUSEUM–RICHLAND, WA

The Columbia River Exhibition of History, Science and Technology is a Museum and Science Center with state of the art interactive exhibits, featuring the unique history and geology of the area. The "Boomers on Wheels" exhibit tells the story of the world's largest trailer park with 51,000 residents, who were part of the top secret Manhattan Atom Bomb Project. The Hanford Nuclear Reactor Plant, which was built in Richland in 1943, was closed in 1994. Other museum exhibits include "Lewis and Clark–Scientists in Buckskin."

■ Open daily. Mon-Sat, 10-5, and Sun, 12-5. Admission: $3.50 adults, $2.75 seniors, and $2.50 ages 7-16. (877) 789-9935
www.crehst.org

19 COLUMBIA RIVER JOURNEYS JETBOAT TOURS–RICHLAND, WA

Narrated jet boat tours of the Hanford Reach National Monument, the last free flowing stretch of the Columbia River, and an unspoiled natural wildlife area, where the Hanford nuclear facility was located.

■ Schedule: May Sept, departs at 8 AM and returns at about 12:30. Oct 1-15, boat departs at 1 PM and returns at about 5:30. Fares: $54, adults, $39 ages 4-11. Trips dependent upon minimum number of passengers, water and weather conditions. (509) 946-3651
www.columbiariverjourneys.com

20 COLUMBIA VALLEY WINERIES BENTON CITY, WA

Visit the wineries and scenic vineyards of the Columbia River Valley: 1/3 of Washington state's wineries and 90% of its vineyards are within 90 miles of the Tri-Cities. Columbia Valley wineries win more awards, proportional to production, than any other region in the world. The vineyards lie in the same latitude as the Burgundy and Bordeaux regions of France.

■ (866) 360-6611 or (509) 628-8082
www.columbiavalleywine.com

21 YAKAMA NATION CULTURAL HERITAGE CENTER–TOPPENISH, WA

The Cultural Heritage Center features the history and art of the Plateau People, the Yakama Indians. The Center provides a special special cultural experience. It has the Heritage Inn Restaurant for fine dining, a banquet and convention facility, the Heritage movie theater, a public library and a gift shop.

■ Open daily, 8-5. Restaurant is open Thurs-Sat, 8 AM-9 PM; Sun, 8-5; Mon-Weds, 8-3.
(509) 865-2800 www.yakamamuseum.com

22 YAKAMA NATION LEGENDS CASINO AND RV PARK–TOPPENISH, WA

There is year round entertainment at the casino; and an annual pow wow, rodeo and stick game tournament on the 3rd wkd in August. The Casino has an all-you-can-eat buffet with an award winning salad bar, a deli, and an espresso snack bar.

The RV Park is next door to the Yakama Cultural Heritage Center, with 125 large RV sites, and tipis available for overnight stays. Activities include a lap swimming pool; jogging track; and other recreational sports.

■ Casino is open daily. Fri-Sat, 9 AM-5 AM, Sun-Thurs, 9 AM-4 AM. (877) 7COME11
(509) 865-5322 www.legendscasino.com
■ For RV Park info, call (800) 874-3087 or (509) 865-2000 www.yakamanation.com

23 TOPPENISH CITY OF MURALS

"Where the West Still Lives in a City of Murals and Museums." The 68 award-winning murals depict Toppenish area history. Some are small, some as long as 200 feet. A new one is added on the first Saturday in June each year.

■ Visitors Info Center, 5A So Toppenish Ave, self guided tour brochure. (800) 569-3982
(509) 865-3262 www.toppenish.net

24 AMERICAN HOP MUSEUM–TOPPENISH

Most of the hops grown in the United States are grown in the Yakima Valley. The nation's only hop museum chronicles the story of the obscure perennial vine used in making of beer. The hop industry began on Manhattan Island in 1607 with the first colonists–making it the first Manhattan Project.

■ Open May-Sept, Weds-Sun, 11-4. Admission: $3 adults, $2 students, $7 families.
(509) 865-4677 www.americanhopmuseum.org

25 TOPPENISH NAT'L WILDLIFE REFUGE

The refuge has a managed wetlands which attracts thousands of waterfowl in the agriculturally intensive Yakima Valley.
(509) 865-2405
www.fws.gov/midcolumbiariver

9

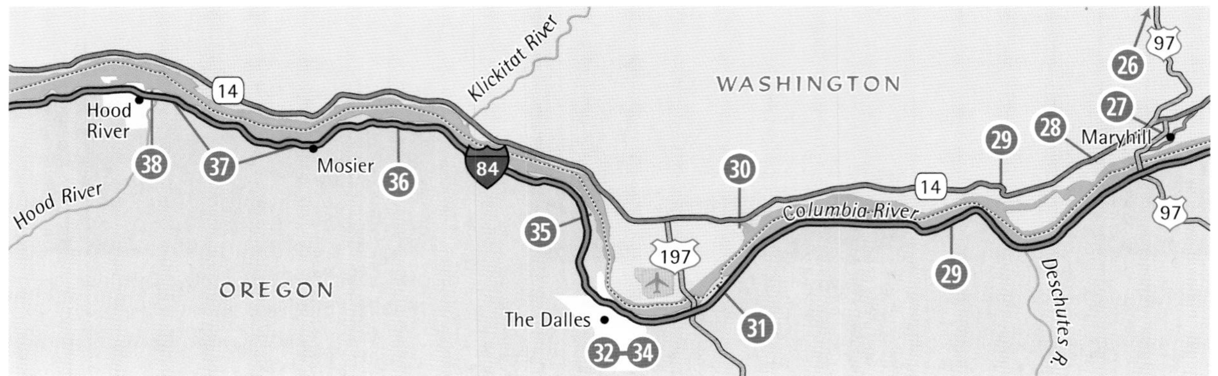

The Dalles Area of the Columbia River Gorge

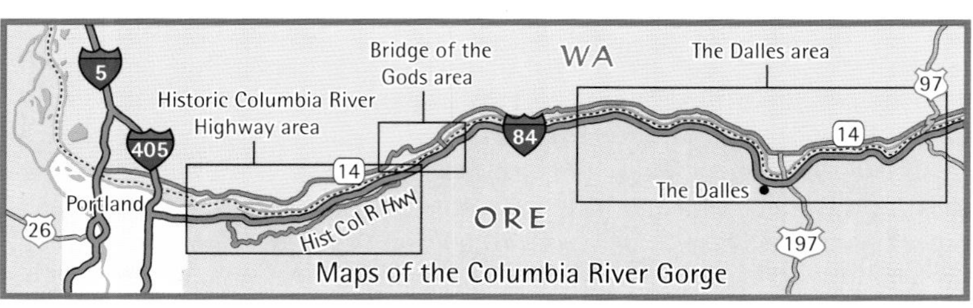

Maps of the Columbia River Gorge

26 GOLDENDALE OBSERVATORY GOLDENDALE WASHINGTON
1602 Observatory Drive.
From I-84 Exit 104 go 13.1 miles north on US 97. Go west one mile on Rte 142. Turn north on Columbus Ave. Go 0.6 mile. Road changes name to Observatory Dr. Go 0.8 mile to the Observatory.

27 MARYHILL MUSEUM OF ART LEWIS AND CLARK OVERLOOK MARYHILL WASHINGTON
35 Maryhill Museum Drive.
From I-84 Exit 104 go one mile north on US 97. Keep straight onto Maryhill Hwy. Go 0.8 mile. Go north 0.2 mile on Stonehenge Dr. Go west on Tsubota Rd.

28 STONEHENGE MEMORIAL AND THE LOOPS ROAD TRAIL MARYHILL WASHINGTON
Stonehenge Memorial.
From I-84 Exit 104 go one mile north on US 97. Keep straight onto Maryhill Hwy. Go 0.8 mile. Go north 0.7 mile on Stonehenge Dr.
Loops Road.
From Stonehenge continue 0.9 mile on Stonehenge Dr. Bear right onto Rte 14 (US 97). Go 0.2 mile to the south end of Loops Road which goes 2.5 miles north.

29 CELILO FALLS OVERLOOK AT WISHRAM, WA AND CELILO PARK AT THE DALLES
From I-84 Exit 97 go 4.6 miles west on Fulton Canyon Rd, Turn north onto Celilo Park Rd. Go 0.3 miles.

30 COLUMBIA HILLS STATE PARK HORSETHIEF LAKE WA
From I-84 Exit 87 go 3.3 miles north on US 197 (Dalles California Hwy). Turn east onto Rte 14. Go 1.6 miles. Bear east onto Horsethief Lake State Park Rd. Go 1.1 miles to the Park.

31 THE DALLES DAM VISITOR CENTER THE DALLES OREGON
From I-84 Exit 88 go 0.5 mile west on local road to the Visitor Center.

32 ROCK FORT AND THE RIVER FRONT TRAIL THE DALLES OREGON
From I-84 Exit 84 go west 0.5 mile on 2ns St. Turn north on Webber St. Go 0.2 mile. Turn east onto 1st St. Go 0.7 mile to the Rock Fort.

33 THE DALLES MURALS THE DALLES OREGON
From I-84 Exit 84 go east 0.5 mile on 2nd St to Liberty St. The murals are on 2nd and 3rd Streets over 9 blocks from Liberty St east to Taylor Street.

34 FORT DALLES MUSEUM THE DALLES, OREGON
From I-84 Exit 84 go 0.2 mile south on Mount Hood St. Go 0.2 mile east on 6th St. Go 0.5 mile south on Trevitt St. Go one block east on 15th Street.

35 COLUMBIA GORGE DISCOVERY CENTER THE DALLES OREGON
5000 Discovery Drive.
From I-84 Exit 82 go 1.5 miles north on US 30. Turn right on Discovery Dr. Go 0.4 mile to the Center.

36 MEMALOOSE STATE PARK AND REST AREA
At milepost 73 on I-84 West.

37 HISTORIC COLUMBIA RIVER HIGHWAY STATE TRAIL MOSIER OREGON
From I-84 Exit 64 follow the signs to the west Trailhead.

38 HOOD RIVER COUNTY MUSEUM HOOD RIVER OREGON
300 East Port Marina Drive.
From I-84 Exit 64 turn north on Hood River Bridge Rd.; then west on Port Marina Drive for 0.4 mile.

THE DALLES

Native Americans have lived in the area of Celilo Falls for over 10,000 years. It was a major salmon fishery until the construction of The Dalles Dam. The Dalles is a French word for the smooth basalt large rocks that constricted the Columbia River channel and created the falls.

Tribes came from all over to barter for dried salmon which the locals made by pounding the salmon and then wrapping it in woven grass baskets lined with salmon skins. William Clark counted 107 of these packages, weighing an estimated 10,000 pounds. Much of it went down river to be traded for goods carried on sailing ships. Natives had been dealing with white traders for over a generation.

Expedition Daredevils

The Indians gathered on the tops of high rocks to watch the expedition attempt to pass through the "short narrows," a 45 yard wide channel ten miles above Celilo Falls. Clark described "the horrid appearance of this agitated gut Swelling, boiling and whorling in every direction." He added "however, we passed Safe to the astonishment of all the Inds." (10/24/1805)

Rock Fort at The Dalles

They camped at Rock Fort, an ancient Indian rock fortification, where they remained for three days taking celestial observations (10/25-27/1805; and 4/15-18/1806 returning).

Dr. Ken Karsmizki of the Columbia Gorge Discovery Center is conducting an archaeological investigation at Fort Rock.

Maryhill Museum of Art

Maryhill Exhibit

Memaloose Island

The Discovery Center at The Dalles

Columbia River Gorge: The Dalles Area

26 GOLDENDALE OBSERVATORY STATE PARK

A unique observatory and library facility created by amateurs and adopted by the state of Washington. Year round free public viewing through a 24.5 inch Cassegrain reflecting telescope on a hilltop north of Goldendale.

■ Open April-Sept, Weds-Sun, from 2-5 PM and from 8-12 PM. Solar viewing and telescope displays in afternoon; celestial viewing in PM. Arrive by 8 PM to hear interpretive program.
(509) 773-3141 www.parks.wa.gov
www.community.gorge.net/friendsofgosp

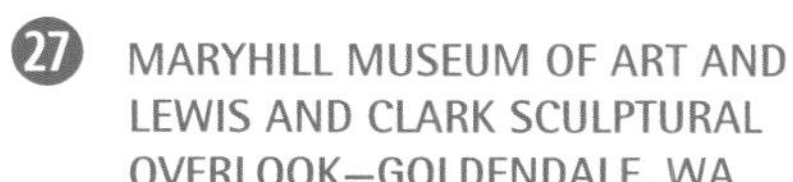

27 MARYHILL MUSEUM OF ART AND LEWIS AND CLARK SCULPTURAL OVERLOOK—GOLDENDALE, WA

More than 10,000 visitors from all over the world come to visit Maryhill per month. It includes the region's finest collection of Pacific Northwest Indian basketry and other goods; original Auguste Rodin sculptures; paintings; international chess sets; Russian icons; Faberge artifacts; Folies Bergere posters; and Queen Marie of Roumania regalia and gilded furniture.

The Lewis and Clark Sculptural Overlook is next door to the museum. Osage orange trees from the Midwest have been planted here. The sculpture bust of Sam Hill, next to the museum's front entrance, was created by Alonzo Lewis, a family descendant of Meriwether Lewis.

■ Open Mar 15-Nov 15, 9-5. Cafe, gift shop and picnic grounds. Admission: $7 adults, $6 seniors, $2 ages 6-16. Sculpture grounds, parking and picnic area are free.
(509) 773-3733 www.maryhillmuseum.org

28 STONEHENGE MEMORIAL AND THE LOOPS ROAD TRAIL—GOLDENDALE

A replica of England's Stonehenge Monument, built by Sam Hill, is a memorial to America's war dead. The 1913 Loops Road, an experiment in road design, was the first paved highway in the Pacific Northwest. It was completely refurbished in 1998: its 3.6 mile trail is open only to pedestrians and bicyclists. Sam Hill envisioned and promoted the Columbia River Highway (1913-22), which became the nation's first scenic highway. (See pages 198-199).

Maryhill State Park is located nearby, with camping and boating facilities.

■ $5 vehicle entry fee for state park.
(888)226-7688 www.parks.wa.gov

29 CELILO FALLS OVERLOOK, WISHRAM, WA AND CELILO PARK AT THE DALLES, OR

Maya Lin's project for Celilo Falls is under consideration by Native American tribes.

■ www.confluenceproject.org
www.englishriverwebsite.com

30 COLUMBIA HILLS STATE PARK PETROGLYPHS, WA

Approximately 30 petroglyphs may be seen on the self-guided Petroglyph Walk in the Horsethief Lake District of Columbia Hills State Park. The "She Who Watches" pictograph/petroglyph may only be seen on ranger-guided tours.

■ Open daily, 9-5. $5 vehicle entry permit. Ranger tours, April-Oct, Fri-Sat. Tours begin promptly at 10 AM, and take about 1½ hours. Wear comfortable shoes. Reservations are required: call 3-4 weeks in advance. (509) 767-1159 www.parks.wa.gov

31 THE DALLES DAM VISITOR CENTER THE DALLES, OREGON

The Dalles Dam Visitor Center at Seufert Park is operated by the Corps of Engineers.

■ Open mid May-late Sept, Weds-Sun, 9-5. Contact The Dalles Chamber for more info.
(541) 296-4547 www.thedalleschamber.com

32 ROCK FORT AND RIVERFRONT TRAIL THE DALLES, OREGON

The Rock Fort is one of the most important campsites on the Lewis and Clark Trail. The 9½ mile Riverfront Trail, a pedestrian/bike path with interpretive signs, goes from the Columbia Gorge Discovery Center to The Dalles Dam, and provides access to Rock Fort.
(541) 296-9533 www.thedalleschamber.com

33 THE DALLES MURALS

Downtown murals portraying Lewis and Clark, the Oregon Trail, and Native Americans.

■ Walking tour brochures of the murals and other historic attractions may be obtained at The Dalles Chamber office, 404 W 2nd St.
(800) 574-1325 www.thedalleschamber.com

34 FORT DALLES MUSEUM—THE DALLES

Located in the Fort's 1856 Surgeon's Quarters, the museum has a new exhibit featuring Lewis and Clark and their modes of transportation.

■ Open daily, mid May-Labor Day, 10-5. Admission: $3 adults, students free.
(541) 296-4547 www.wascochs.org

35 COLUMBIA GORGE DISCOVERY CENTER AND WASCO COUNTY HISTORICAL MUSEUM—THE DALLES, OREGON

The official interpretive center for the Columbia River Gorge National Scenic Area, with 26,000 feet of exhibition space; featuring interactive exhibits on the volcanoes and glacial floods that shaped the area. The 50 acres surrounding the center is being restored to native plants. Lewis and Clark archaeologist and historian Dr. Ken Karzmiski is Executive Director of the Center.

■ Open daily, 9-5. Admission: $6.50 adults, $5.50 seniors, $3 ages 6-16.
(541) 296-8600 www.gorgediscovery.org

36 MEMALOOSE STATE PARK AND REST AREA—MOSIER, OREGON

The rest area and state park provide a view of Memaloose Island, where the Chinook Indians placed their dead in vaults. Lewis and Clark visited the island on April 15, 1806, and called it "Sepulchre Rock."

■ RV and tent campgrounds; open mid March-Oct. Wind surfing, living history, nature programs. (800) 551-6949 or (541) 478-3008
www.oregonstateparks.org

37 HISTORIC COLUMBIA RIVER HIGHWAY STATE TRAIL—MOSIER, OREGON

Part of the Historic Highway, America's first scenic highway, has been converted to a bike and pedestrian trail. Trailheads at Mosier (east) and Hood River (west). The trail consists of two disconnected, abandoned roadways, 5 miles long, that pass through the Twin Tunnels. Spectacular geology and plant life.

■ A self service machine at each end dispenses $3 parking fee permits. Visitor info center at Hood River. (800) 551-6949
www.oregonstateparks.org

38 HOOD RIVER COUNTY MUSEUM HOOD RIVER, OREGON

The museum and Columbia Gorge Windsurfing Association have collaborated on documenting the history of windsurfing (1978-present). The Gorge is the sailboarding capitol of the mainland US. Other exhibits include Native American, fruit and logging industries, Finnish, Japanese and Hispanic cultures.

■ Open April-Aug, Mon-Sat, 10-4;Sun 12-4. Sept-Oct, daily, 12-4. Free admission.
(541) 386-6772 www.hoodriver.org

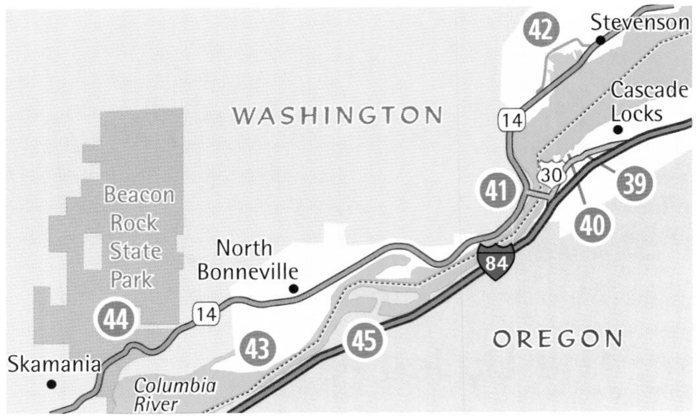

Bridge of Gods near Cascade Locks

Bridge of the Gods

39 CASCADE LOCKS MUSEUM CASCADE LOCKS OREGON

1 NW Portage Road.
From I-84 Exit 47 go 0.7 mile west on US 30 (Wa-Na-Pa St). Turn north on Lakeside Dr; then immediately west on Portage Road.

40 STERNWHEELER CASCADE LOCKS OREGON

From I-84 Exit 44 go 0.6 mile east on US 30 (Wa-Na-Pa St). Wind north and east 0.3 mile on local road to the Sternwheeler dock.

43 FORT CASCADES NORTH BONNEVILLE WA

From Washington State Route 14 milepost 37 turn south onto the Dam Access road. At the stop sign, turn west. Immediately turn south into the parking lot .

44 BEACON ROCK STATE PARK STEVENSON WASHINGTON

From Washington State Route 14 milepost 35 turn north into Beacon Rock State Park.

46 MULTNOMAH FALLS LODGE MULTNOMAH FALLS OR

From I-84 Exit 31 go 0.2 mile south on East Crown Point Connector. Go west on Historic Columbia River Highway to the Lodge.

47 CROWN POINT VISTA HOUSE CORBETT OREGON

From I-84 Exit 18 go 12.6 miles east on the Historic Columbia River Highway to Crown Point.

50 THE BARN MUSEUM TROUTDALE OREGON

726 Columbia River Highway.
From I-84 Exit 18 go 0.2 mile south on Crown Point Highway. Turn west onto East Columbia River Highway. Go 0.2 mile. Turn north on East Columbia River Highway. Go 0.1 mile to The Barn Museum.

Multnomah Falls
Lyn Topinka

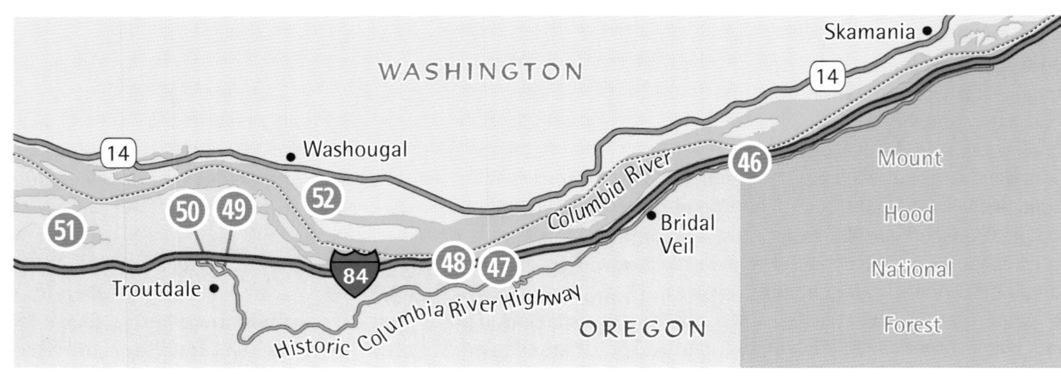

Historic Columbia River Highway: Troutdale to Multnomah Falls

9

41 BRIDGE OF THE GODS CASCADE LOCKS OREGON

The Bridge of the Gods joins US 30 in Oregon and Washington Route 14. From I-84 Exit 44 go 0.6 mile east on US 30 (Wa-Na-Pa St). to the south end of the Bridge.

42 COLUMBIA GORGE INTERPRETIVE CENTER STEVENSON WASHINGTON

990 SW Rock Creek Drive.
From I-84 Exit 44 go 0.6 mile east on US 30 (Wa-Na-Pa St). Cross the Bridge of the Gods. Go 1.5 miles east on Rte 14. Turn north onto Rock Creek Dr. Go 0.3 mile.

45 BONNEVILLE DAM VISITOR CENTERS/FISH HATCHERY OREGON AND WASHINGTON

Bradford Island Visitor Center, OR.
From I-84 East take Exit 40. At the flag intersection bear right. Go about one mile on park roads.
Bonneville Fish Hatchery, OR.
From I-84 East take Exit 40. At the flag intersection bear left to the Fish Hatchery.
Washington Shore Visitor Complex, WA.
From Washington State Route 14 milepost 40 go south to Hatchery.

48 CHANTICLEER POINT CORBETT OREGON

From I-84 Exit 18 go 8.3 miles east on the Historic Columbia River Highway. Turn north on local road. Go 0.2 mile to Chanticleer Point.

49 LEWIS AND CLARK STATE RECREATION SITE TROUTDALE OREGON

From I-84 Exit 18 go 0.2 mile south on Crown Point Highway to the Lewis and Clark Recreation Site.

51 NICHAQWLI MONUMENT AT BLUE LAKE FAIRVIEW OREGON

From I-84 Exit 16 go 0.1 mile north on 238th Dr. Go 0.7 mile west on Sandy Blvd. Go 0.8 mile north on 223rd Ave. Go one mile west on Blue Lake Road.

52 CAPTAIN WM CLARK PARK AT COTTONWOOD BEACH WASHOUGAL WASHINGTON

From State Route14 go 0.5 mile south on 32nd Street to the trailhead at Cottonwood Beach.

Vista House at Crown Point
Lyn Topinka

Columbia Gorge Interpretive Center
Lyn Topinka

Beacon Rock
Lyn Topinka www.englishriverwebsite.com

Historic Columbia River Highway Area

39 CASCADE LOCKS HISTORICAL MUSEUM
CASCADE LOCKS, OREGON

Exhibits feature history of Bridge of the Gods, the old portage around Cascade Falls, and the construction of the unique water powered locks and canal in 1878-98. Home of the first steam locomotive in Oregon Territory.

■ Open daily, May-Sept, noon-5.
(541) 374-8535 www.gorgeexplorer.com

40 COLUMBIA GORGE STERNWHEELER
CASCADE LOCKS, OREGON

The sternwheeler departs from Marine Park at the Cascade Locks. The triple deck paddle wheeler provides a chance to see the breathtaking vistas of the Columbia Gorge as the expedition experienced them.

■ Daily, June-Sept: Narrated excursions, 12-2 PM, and 3-5 PM. Fares: $20 adults, $15 seniors, $10 children. Weekends: Sunset Dinner Cruises: Fri, 7-9 and Sat, 6:30-8:30. $45 adults, $20 children. Champagne Brunch Cruises, noon-2, $35 adults, $20 children. Inquire for Bonneville Locks Dinner Cruises, Friday Night Dance Cruises, and limited schedule from Oct-May.
(800) 643-1354 (541) 374-8427
www.sternwheeler.com

41 BRIDGE OF THE GODS
CASCADE LOCKS, OREGON

The original bridge and dam were formed by a landslide which created the Cascade Falls about 1000 years ago; Indians called it the "Great Cross Over." Now the Cascade Falls are under water at Bonneville Dam. Beautiful murals on the supports underneath the 1926 bridge depict the Indian legends and Lewis and Clark.

■ www.inthegorge.com

42 COLUMBIA GORGE INTERPRETIVE
CENTER—STEVENSON, WASHINGTON

The Interpretive Center has a dramatic film showing the cataclysmic creation of the Gorge; a 37 foot replica of a 1800's fishwheel; an exhibit on Native American dip netting; a restored saw mill steam engine; the world's largest Rosary collection; Lewis and Clark and Oregon Trail exhibits, and many other displays. Its architecture and exhibit design are award winning.

■ Open daily, 10-5. Admission: $6 adults, $5 seniors and students, $4 ages 6-12.
(800) 991-2338 or (509) 427-8211
www.columbiagorge.org

43 FORT CASCADES NAT'L HISTORIC SITE
NORTH BONNEVILLE, WASHINGTON

Located on Hamilton Island, the site commemorates four different forts that once guarded the Cascade Rapids. 1½ mile interpretive trail. Lewis and Clark called it "Strawberry Island."

■ Photographer Lyn Topinka has an extensive website devoted to Lewis and Clark sites in the Columbia Gorge: www.englishriverwebsite.com

44 BEACON ROCK STATE PARK
STEVENSON, WASHINGTON

The 840 foot basalt monolith is second only in size to the Rock of Gilbraltar. Lewis and Clark named it Beacon Rock on Nov. 2, 1805; they saw their first tidal flow here. Henry Biddle, an heir of Nicholas Biddle, the editor of the Lewis and Clark journals, bought Beacon Rock and built a trail with 53 switchbacks to the top.

■ Open Apr-mid Oct for camping. Rock climbing permitted. Hours, 8 AM-10 PM summer, and 8 AM-5 PM winter day-use. $5 vehicle entry fee permit. A first-come, first-served park.
(509) 427-8265 www.parks.wa.gov

45 BONNEVILLE DAM VISITOR CENTERS
OREGON AND WASHINGTON

One of the largest public viewing facilities in the Corps of Engineers. The two facilities on either side of the river are comparable; however, the fish hatchery is on the Oregon side.

■ Open daily, 9-5. Guided tours available. Call ahead to confirm public accessibility due to security measures. (541) 374-8820 (OR)
(509) 427-4281 (WA) www.nwp.usace.army.mil

46 MULTNOMAH FALLS LODGE
MULTNOMAH FALLS, OREGON

Multnomah Falls is the second highest waterfalls in the United States (625 ft). The1925 stone lodge is one of the most visited tourist sites in the nation. Enjoy Northwest cuisine with a view of the falls at the lodge restaurant.

■ Open daily, 8-9. Forest Service Visitor Information Center, 8-5. (503) 695-2372
www.multnomahfallslodge.com

47 VISTA HOUSE AT CROWN POINT
STATE PARK, CORBETT, OR

Vista House at Crown Point is a National Historic Landmark. The recently restored German Art Nouveau style building was built in 1916-18, on top of the 733 foot bluff. It has exhibits, a gift shop with regional arts and crafts, and an espresso cafe.

■ Open daily, 9-6. (503) 695-2230
www.vistahouse.com

48 PORTLAND WOMEN'S FORUM
STATE PARK—TROUTDALE, OREGON

The beautiful scenic views of the Columbia Gorge at Chanticleer Point (Portland Women's Forum) are a favorite of photographers. The Vista House photo was taken from here.

■ www.oregonstateparks. org

49 LEWIS AND CLARK STATE RECREATION
SITE—TROUTDALE, OREGON

Near the mouth of the Big Sandy River, the park is one of the entrances to the Historic Columbia River Highway on the Crown Point Highway. The Sandy River delta will have a Maya Lin bird viewing site. One of the most popular swimming spots on the Big Sandy, and a public boat launch are adjacent. The Corp visited the Big Sandy on Nov 3, 1805 and found it to be quicksand; dumping sand into the Columbia much like the Platte River did at the Missouri.

■ (800) 551-6949 www.oregonstateparks.org
www.confluenceproject.org

50 BARN MUSEUM—TROUTDALE, OREGON

Native American art and artifacts; display of Lewis and Clark weapons and tools, and panels portraying Chinook life and Corps of Discovery. Native plant displays. Replica of Jefferson's office at Monticello.

■ Open June-Sept, Tues-Sun, 1-4. Oct-May, Sat-Sun, 1-4. Hours may vary. Call to confirm.
(503) 661-2164 www.troutdalehistory.org

51 NICHAQWLI MONUMENT
AT BLUE LAKE—FAIRVIEW, OREGON

("Nee-chalk-lee") The monument at Blue Lake Regional Park on the Columbia riverfront commemorates the Upper Chinookan people who lived here near the mouth of the Big Sandy.

52 CAPTAIN WILLIAM CLARK PARK
WASHOUGAL, WASHINGTON

The park is located at Cottonwood Beach, where the expedition camped for six days, March 31-April 5, 1806 to hunt and to explore the Willamette River. The park honors Captain Clark with a bronze bust.

■ www.ci.vancouver.wa.us/parks

9

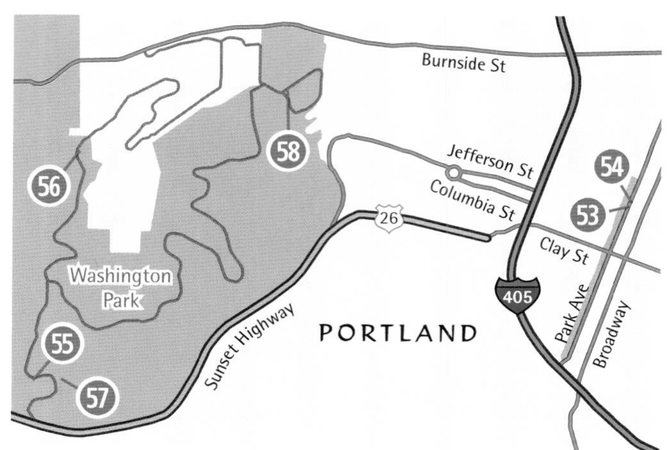

Downtown Portland and Washington Park

Mt Hood, Warm Springs Indian Reservation, Charbonneau's Grave

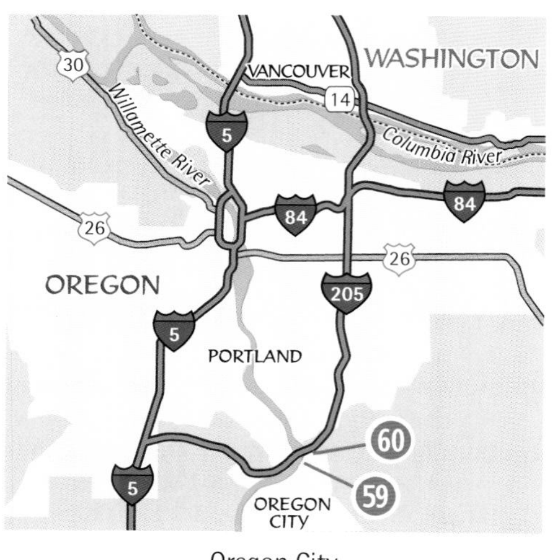

Oregon City

53 OREGON HISTORICAL SOCIETY
PORTLAND OREGON

1200 SW park Avenue.
From I-405 Exit 1C go 0.3 mile north on SW 8th Avenue. Go two blocks west on Clay St. Turn north onto SW Park Avenue. Go three blocks to the History Center.

54 PORTLAND ART MUSEUM
PORTLAND OREGON

1219 SW Park Avenue.
From I-405 Exit 1C go 0.3 mile north on SW 8th Avenue. Go two blocks west on Clay St. Turn north onto SW Park Avenue. Go three blocks. Pass Madison St.

55 FORESTRY DISCOVERY CENTER
WASHINGTON PARK
PORTLAND OREGON

4033 SW Canyon Road.
From I-405 take Exit 1D to Hwy 26 West. Go 1.5 miles to Exit 72 (Zoo-Forestry Center).

56 HOYT ARBORETUM
WASHINGTON PARK
PORTLAND OREGON

4000 Fairview Boulevard.
From I-405 take Exit 1D to Hwy 26 West. Go 1.5 miles to Exit 72 (Zoo-Forestry Center). Go past the Zoo parking lot, the Forestry Center, and up Knight's Blvd to Fairview Blvd. Go right 0.1 mile to the Arboretum Visitor Center.

57 OREGON ZOO
WASHINGTON PARK
PORTLAND OREGON

4001 SW Canyon Road.
From I-405 take Exit 1D to Hwy 26 West. Go 1.5 miles to Exit 72 (Zoo-Forestry Center). Go to the Zoo parking lot.

58 LEWIS AND CLARK CIRCLE
WASHINGTON PARK
PORTLAND OREGON

From I-405 take Exit 1D to Hwy 26 West. Go 1.5 miles to Exit 72 (Zoo-Forestry Center). Go past the Zoo parking lot. Turn right on Kingston Drive. Go 1.5 miles. Turn right onto Sherwood Blvd. Go 0.7 mile to Lewis and Clark Circle.

59 McLOUGHLIN HOUSE
OREGON CITY OREGON

713 Center Street.
From I-205 Exit 9 go 0.4 mile southwest on McLoughlin Blvd. Turn southeast on 10th St. Turn southwest on Singer Hill Rd. Go southeast on 7th St.

60 END OF THE OREGON TRAIL INTERPRETIVE CENTER
OREGON CITY OREGON

1726 Washington Street.
From I-205 Exit 9 go 0.2 mile southwest on McLoughlin Blvd. Turn southeast on 14th St. Go 0.3 mile northeast on Washington St.

61 TIMBERLINE LODGE
MT HOOD OREGON

From I-205 Exit 12 go 11.5 miles east on Route 212. Turn southeast onto US 26 (Mount Hood Highway). Go 33.5 miles. Turn north onto Timberline Highway. Go 1.5 miles to the Timberline Lodge.

62 MUSEUM AT WARM SPRINGS
WARM SPRINGS OREGON

2189 US Highway 26.
From I-205 Exit 19 to the Museum at Warm Springs is 96 miles southeast over US Highway 26.

63 KAH-NEE-TA HIGH DESERT RESORT AND CASINO
WARM SPRINGS OREGON

From I-205 Exit 19 to the Museum at Warm Springs is 96 miles southeast over US Highway 26.

64 CHARBONNEAU'S GRAVE
JORDAN VALLEY OREGON

From Portland, OR go east and south on I-84 for 380 miles. Turn south on US 95. Go 93 miles. Go 5 miles west on Danner Loop Rd. Go 1.6 miles north on Danner Road to the gravesite.

Oregon Historical Society in Portland

View of Mount Hood Timberline Lodge

Museum at Warm Springs
Confederated Tribes of Warm Springs

Portland, Mt Hood and Warm Springs Indian Reservation

53 OREGON HISTORICAL SOCIETY PORTLAND

The award winning exhibit "Oregon My Oregon" covers an entire floor. The OHS owns Meriwether Lewis's branding iron, which he bartered away on April 20, 1806. Check out the Oregon History Project on the website's education link.

■ Open daily 9-9. Admission: $10 adults, $8 seniors/students.

(503) 222-1741 www.ohs.org

54 PORTLAND ART MUSEUM

The Portland Art Museum is the oldest (1892) art museum in the Pacific Northwest. The newly renovated Mark Building is home for the Center for Modern and Contemporary Art and headquarters for the NW Film Center. The historic Belluschi Building has Native American and Pre-Columbian art, in addition to European, American, and African art and sculpture.

■ Open Tues-Sat, 10-5, and Sun, 12-5. Admission: $15 adults; $13 seniors and students (ages 19+); and $6 ages 5-18.

(503) 226-2811 www.pam.org

55 FORESTRY DISCOVERY CENTER WASHINGTON PARK—PORTLAND

The Discovery Center has an "Indoor Forest" where trees are displayed in a deep woods environment. An on site wood worker is creating a marquetry mural. Films, and kids play area. Visitors may watch woodworking operations from a glass enclosed skyway at the Koetter Woodworking manufacturing plant next door.

■ Open Mon-Fri, 9-2. Admission: $5.50 adults, $4.50 seniors, $3 ages 6-12.

(812) 923-1590 www.forestcenter.com

56 HOYT ARBORETUM WASHINGTON PARK—PORTLAND

The Arboretum is a favorite place for Portland residents to walk, covering 185 ridge tops acres, with 12 miles of trails. Over 1,100 species of trees and shrubs are represented, labeled with both common and scientific names. Most of the trees are arranged in family groups.

■ Visitor Center has maps and trail guides. Free guided tours, first Sat each month, Apr-Oct. There are two miles of hard surfaced trails. The Visitor Center is open Mon-Fri 9-4 and Sat 9-3. Grounds open daily from 6 AM to 10 PM.

(503) 865-8733 www.hoytarboretum.org

57 OREGON ZOO AND WASHINGTON PARK AND ZOO RAILWAY—PORTLAND

The Oregon Zoo highlights animals and their habitats. There are twelve major exhibits of different geographical areas in the world; and a large botanical garden. The Washington Park and Zoo Railway does a one mile loop around the zoo during a train ride that includes the Forest Arboretum, Japanese Garden, and International Rose Test Garden. The Cascade Grill Restaurant is located at the zoo.

■ Open daily. Apr 15-Sept 15, 9-6. Sept 16-Apr 14, 9-4. Admission: $9.50 adults, $8 seniors, $6.50 ages 3-11. Parking $1 per car. Train riders must pay zoo admissions. Fares: $2.50 adults, $2 senior, $2 ages 3-11.

(503) 226-1561 www.oregonzoo.com

58 LEWIS AND CLARK CIRCLE WASHINGTON PARK—PORTLAND

There are two monuments at the circle: the granite shaft Lewis and Clark Memorial (1908) and the Sacajawea Statue (1906). Susan B. Anthony, women's voting rights leader, and Eva Emory Dye, whose 1902 book, *The Conquest*, immortalized Sacajawea, were present at the statue dedication. Eva Dye and her husband were responsible for the erection of the statue and for rescuing the McLoughlin House.

59 McLOUGHLIN HOUSE—OREGON CITY

Dr. John McLoughlin, a physician, served as Chief Factor at the British Fort Vancouver from 1825-1845. When he retired, he became an American citizen and Mayor of Oregon City. He is considered the "Father of Oregon" and his home is a National Historic Site.

■ Open Feb-mid Dec, Weds-Sat, 10-4 and Sun, 1-4. Free admission.

(800) 832-3599 or (360) 696-7655 x10
www.nps.gov/mcho

60 END OF THE OREGON TRAIL INTERPRETIVE CENTER—OREGON CITY

Visitors spend an average of two hours in the center. A 30 minute film, regularly scheduled daily history talks, and hands on activities and exhibits tell the story of the Oregon Trail.

■ Open daily, Mon-Sat, 11-4 and Sun 12-4. Admission: $7 adults/seniors, $5 ages 5-17.

(503) 657-9336
www.endoftheoregontrail.org

61 TIMBERLINE LODGE NATIONAL HISTORIC LANDMARK—MT HOOD, OR

Midway up to the summit of Mt Hood is a masterpiece of mountain lodges, Timberline Lodge. It was built entirely by hand, inside and out, by craftsmen in 1936-37. Foot passengers may ride the "Magic Mile Sky Ride' ski lift, which provides a safe and comfortable ride. Be sure to bring cold weather gear, even in summer, and wear sturdy walking shoes. Telescope viewing at 7000 feet. Many other recreational activities at the lodge and nearby, at all seasons.

■ Open daily. General Info, (503) 622-7979.

■ Magic Mile Sky Rides are daily, weather permitting. Closed 2 weeks in early Sept for maintenance. $12 adults, $8 ages 7-12.

(503) 622-0717 or (503) 622-0717
www.skitimberlodge.com

62 MUSEUM AT WARM SPRINGS WARM SPRINGS, OREGON

This world class museum houses the single, largest collection of Indian artifacts under one roof. Owned and operated by the Warm Springs, Wasco and Paiute Native American Tribes. Tribal members present living culture demonstrations on summer weekends. Large selection of locally made items at the Museum Gift shop.

■ Open daily, 9-5. Admission $6 adults, $5 seniors, $4.50 tribal/student ID, $3 ages 3-12.

(541) 553-3331 www.warmsprings.com

63 KAH-NEE-TA HIGH DESERT RESORT AND CASINO, WARM SPRINGS. OR

The Confederated Tribes Casino and Resort has natural hot springs, kayaking on the Warm Springs River, horseback riding, biking, golf, volleyball, tennis, swimming pool. The Resort has a lodge, convention center and restaurants. The Juniper Room offers elegant dining.

■ Open daily. (800) 554-4SUN (4786)
www.warmsprings.com

64 JEAN BAPTISTE CHARBONNEAU GRAVESITE—JORDAN VALLEY, OR

Pompey, the baby who accompanied the Lewis and Clark Expedition, led an adventurous and interesting life. Born February 11, 1805, he died of pneumonia on May 16, 1866 while en route to gold fields in Montana. He is buried in the remote Jordan Valley of eastern Oregon.
www.nps.gov/jeff

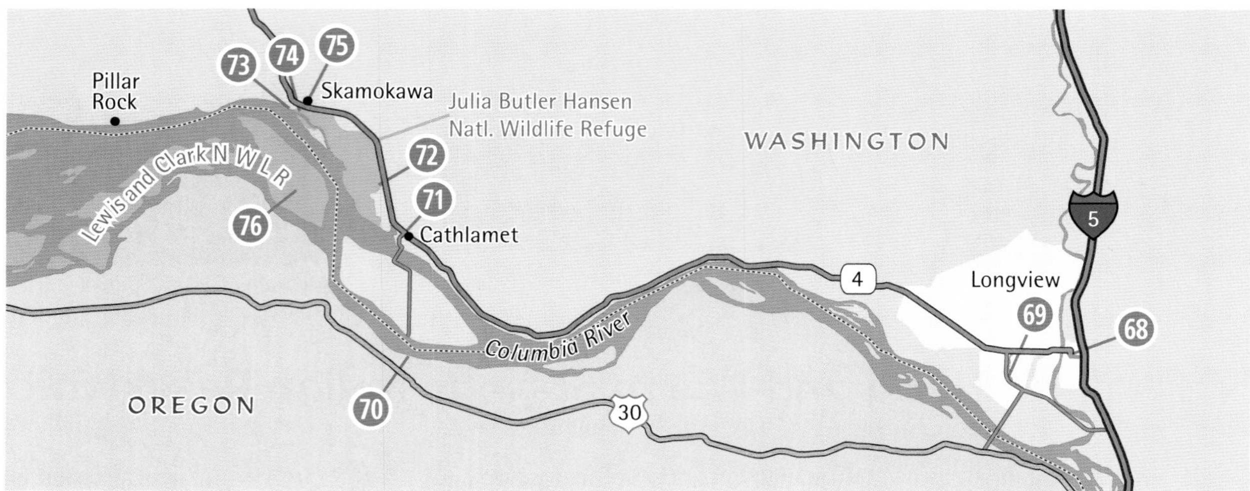

On November 7, 1805, they camped near Pillar Rock. Clark wrote "Great joy in camp, we are in View of the Ocian." They were actually seeing the Columbia River estuary. (An estuary is where the tide of an ocean meets the current of a river.)

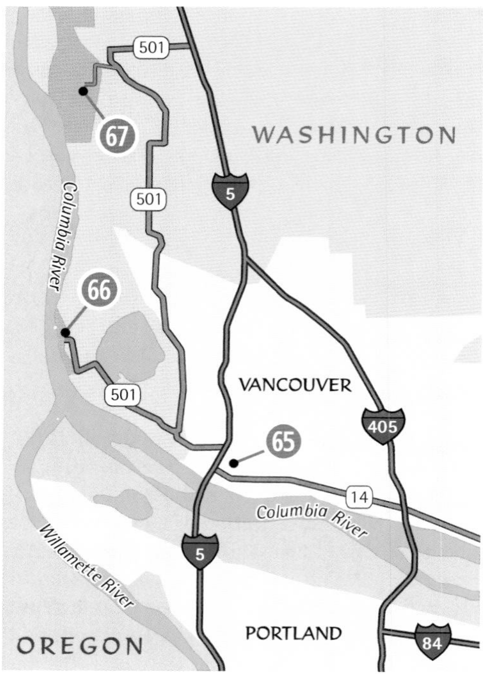

Vancouver and the confluence area of the Columbia and Willamette Rivers.

9

65 FORT VANCOUVER VISITOR CENTER
VANCOUVER WA

612 East Reserve Street.
From I-5 Exit 1C/D go 0.6 mile east on Mill Plain Blvd. Turn south on East Reserve Street. Go 0.2 mile to the Visitor Center.

66 FRENCHMAN'S BAR STATE PARK
CLARK COUNTY WA

From I-5 Exit 1C/D go 1.6 miles west on Route 501 (Mill Plain Blvd). Continue west 5.1 miles on Route 501 (Lower River Road) to Frenchman's Bar State Park.

67 CATHLAPOTLE PLANK HOUSE
RIDGEFIELD NATIONAL WILDLIFE REFUGE
RIDGEFIELD WA

From I-5 Exit 14 go 3.2 miles west and then south on Route 501. Turn onto South Refuge Road. Go southwest then west for 0.6 mile. Road changes name to East West Road. Go 0.5 mile. Turn south onto Ridgefield Wildlife Road. Go 0.8 mile to the Plankhouse.

68 COWLITZ COUNTY HISTORICAL MUSEUM
KELSO WA

405 Allen Street.
From I-5 Exit 39 go 0.3 mile west on Allen Street to the Cowlitz County Historical Museum.

69 LAKE SACAJAWEA
LONGVIEW WA

From I-5 Exit 36 go 3.3 miles northwest on Route 432 to the Lake.

70 WAHKIAKUM COUNTY CAR FERRY
WESTPORT OR

From the Oregon side.
From US 30 go north 0.4 mile on Westport Road to the Ferry Dock.
From the Washington side.
From Ocean Beach Highway (State Route 4) in Cathlamet go 4 miles south on State Route 409 through the town; over the bridge; across Puget Island to the Ferry dock at the end of the road.

71 WAHKIAKUM COUNTY HISTORICAL MUSEUM
CATHLAMET WA

65 River Street.
From Ocean Beach Highway (State Route 4) turn south onto Una Avenue. Go 0.2 mile Turn southwest onto Division Street. Go 100 yards. Turn south onto River Street. Go 100 yards to the Historical Museum.

72 JULIA BUTLER HANSEN NAT'L WILDLIFE REFUGE
SKAMOKAWA WA

From I-5 take Exit 40 at Longview. Go west 27 miles on State Route 4 (Ocean Beach Highway). One mile past Cathlamet turn west onto Steamboat Slough Road. The Refuge Headquarters is about 1/4 mile to the right.

73 SKAMOKAWA VISTA PARK
SKAMOKAWA WA

In Skamokawa, going west on State Route 4, cross the bridge over the mouth of the Skamokawa Creek. Turn toward the Columbia River. Continue to Vista Park.

74 SKAMOKAWA CENTER
SKAMOKAWA WA

From State Route 4, going west into Skamokawa; before crossing the bridge over Skamokawa Creek; turn south onto Steamboat Slough Road. Skamokawa Center is immediately on your right.

75 RIVER LIFE INTERPRETIVE CENTER
SKAMOKAWA WA

From State Route 4, going west into Skamokawa; after passing Steamboat Slough Road, and before crossing the bridge over Skamokawa Creek; turn right into the driveway of the River Life Interpretive Center which is atop a steep knoll.

76 LEWIS AND CLARK NAT'L WILDLIFE REFUGE
SKAMOKAWA WA

The islands that make up the Wildlife Refuge are accessible only by boat. Launch facilities are at John Day Point, OR; Aldrich Point, OR; and Skamokawa, WA.

Fort Vancouver
Lyn Topinka

Cathloptle Plank House
Ridgefield Nat'l Wildlife Refuge

Skamokawa Center
Betty Kluesner, DESC

Vancouver to Skamokawa

65 FORT VANCOUVER VISITOR CENTER VANCOUVER, WASHINGTON

Fort Vancouver National Historic Reserve will be the site of a Confluence Project; uniting historic Fort Vancouver with the riverfront by means of a 40 foot wide land bridge across State Route 14 designed by Architect Johnpaul Jones. Maya Lin will provide the landscaping and artwork once the bridge is completed. Fort Vancouver was headquarters for the British Hudson Bay Co (1825-49); its Chief Factor Dr. John McLoughlin helped many pioneers on the Oregon Trail. Fort Vancouver has nine reconstructed buildings. Officers Row, Pearson Air Museum, Vancouver Barracks, and the Center for Columbia River History make up the rest of the reserve attractions.

■ Open daily, Apr-Oct, 9-5 and Nov-Mar, 9-4. Admission good for 7 days: $5 family fee, $3 individual. (360) 696-7655 x 17
www.vancouverhistoricreserve.org
www.confluenceproject.org

66 FRENCHMAN'S BAR STATE PARK CLARK COUNTY, WASHINGTON

This site is an important part of the Confluence Project's mission to restore land to its natural state. Almost directly across from the confluence of the Columbia and Willamette rivers, it is next to a large tract of natural wetlands. Preserving it will protect a migratory bird flyway and nest grounds for many species, including blue herons and bald eagles.

■ Open daily late May-early Sept. Wkds only in early May and late Sept,. Hours are from 7 AM to dusk. Parking fees: $4 RV's, $2 cars, vans, $1 motorcycles. Free to pedestrians and bicyclists. (360) 693-0123 www.parks.wa.gov
www.confluenceproject.org

67 CATHLAPOTLE PLANK HOUSE AND RIDGEFIELD NAT'L WILDLIFE REFUGE RIDGEFIELD, WA

Over 3500 hours of volunteer labor went into building this replica of a Chinook cedar plank house. The refuge includes the site of the one of the largest Chinook villages encountered by Lewis and Clark; ten years of archaeological research have been conducted here. Plans are to build a Chinook heritage center and museum. The refuge is headquarters for five refuges in southwestern Washington. It has 5,150 acres. There is a 2 mile hiking trail, and a 4.2 mile auto tour route on gravel roads.

■ Ridgefield Refuge's automatic gate is open from 6 AM-7 PM. Free admission.
(503) 625-4377 www.plankhouse.org
www.fws.gov/ridgefieldrefuges

68 COWLITZ COUNTY HISTORICAL MUSEUM—KELSO, WASHINGTON

The museum director spent six weeks biking the Lewis and Clark Trail from St Louis to Astoria, a 3282 mile journey, in 2005. The museum has an extensive photo collection, Native American artifacts, decoys, and local history exhibits.

■ Open Tues-Sat, 9-5 and Sun 1-5. Donations. (360) 577-3119 www.cowlitz.wa.us/museum

69 LAKE SACAJAWEA—LONGVIEW, WA

Take the Lewis and Clark Bridge across the Columbia from Kelso to Longview's downtown Lake Sacajawea. The lake has a 1.64 mile walk that displays a scale model of the solar system; 3½ miles of walking trails with an arboretum; fishing; kayaking and canoeing; and an island Japanese garden. Longview began as a planned city built by a lumber mill in 1922-23. Before that, in 1849, it was a town called Monticello.

■ (360) 423-8400
www.kelsolongviewchamber.com

70 WAHKIAKUM COUNTY CAR FERRY WESTPORT, OREGON TO PUGET ISLAND

The Wahkiakum County car ferry is the last remaining car ferry on the Lower Columbia.

■ Ferry schedule: daily. From Westport, Oregon, every quarter past the hour, 5:15 AM-10:15 PM. From Puget Island, every hour on the hour, 5 AM-10 PM. Rates: $3 cars/pickups, $2 motorcycles, $1 bicycles, 50 cents pedestrians. Large trucks/RV's depends on length.
(360) 795-3301 www.cwcog.org/ferry

71 WAHKIAKUM COUNTY HISTORICAL MUSEUM—CATHLAMET, WASHINGTON

Cathlamet is the second oldest town in Washington (1846). The county museum features Northwest Indian tribes artifacts; guns; logging, agricultural and commercial fishery equipment.

■ Open May-Oct, Tues-Sun, 11-4. Nov-April, Thurs-Sun, 1-4. $1 adult, 50¢ kids. Donations are appreciated. (360) 795-3954
www.cwcog.org/museums

72 JULIA BUTLER HANSEN NATIONAL WILDLIFE REFUGE—SKAMOKAWA, WA

The refuge protects and manages endangered white tailed deer. It contains over 5,600 acres of forested tidal swamps, sloughs, marshes, pastureland and woodlots on both sides of the Columbia River. Many other animals benefit from the habitat, including a herd of Roosevelt elk. Wildlife viewing site off Route 4.

■ Open daily, dawn to dusk. Refuge office open Mon-Fri, 7:30-4. (360) 795-3915
www.pacific.fws.gov/refuges

73 SKAMOKAWA VISTA PARK SKAMOKAWA, WASHINGTON

Lewis and Clark Trail kiosk and markers. Great views of the Columbia River and river beach for walking. Full service campground for RV's and tents. Day use facilities, small boat launch.

■ (306) 795-8605 daytime
www.cwcog.org/tourism

74 SKAMOKAWA CENTER—SKAMOKAWA

The premiere location for the best kayaking and canoeing on the Lower Columbia. Located between two great National Wildlife Refuges. Columbia River tours; canoe and kayak rental; bed and breakfast; and local fine dining cafe.

,■ (888) 920-2777 (360) 795-8300
www.skamokawakayak.com

RIVER LIFE INTERPRETIVE CENTER SKAMOKAWA, WASHINGTON

The Center is housed in a historic 1894 schoolhouse, overlooking Skamokawa Creek and the Columbia River. It depicts early life in the region, when the river was the means of livelihood and travel. Bookshop.

■ Open Thurs-Sun, 12-4. Donations are appreciated. (360) 795-3007
www.riverlifeinterpretivecenter.org

LEWIS AND CLARK NAT'L WILDLIFE REFUGE—SKAMOKAWA, WASHINGTON

The 35,000 acre refuge is a wintering area for tundra swans, geese and ducks; home for shorebirds and bald eagles; and provides vital food resources for young salmon. Large numbers of wildlife from Oct-April, including seals and sea lions. Tidal waters make boating difficult.

■ (360) 795-3915
www.fws.gov/pacific/willapa/LewisClarkNWR

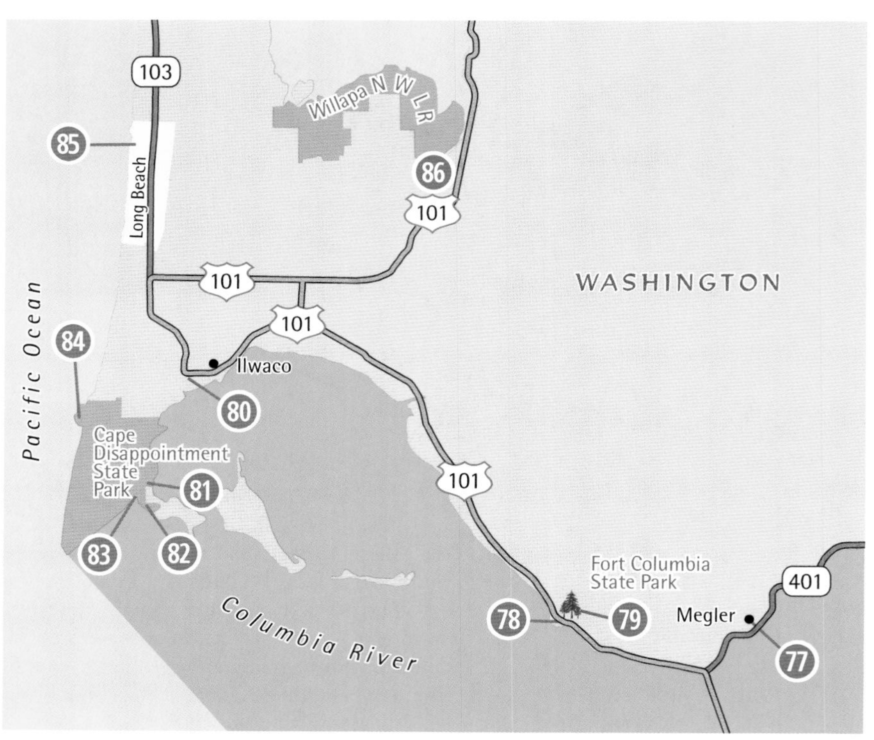

Lewis and Clark National and State Historical Parks in Washington State

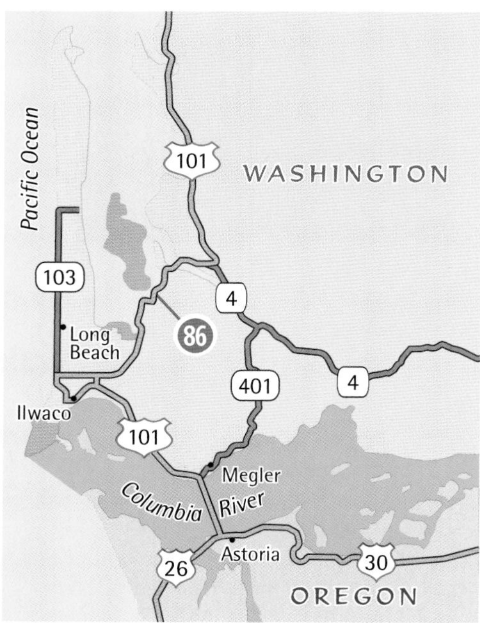

Long Beach and Willapa Bay

LEWIS AND CLARK NATIONAL AND STATE HISTORICAL PARKS (LCNSHP)

America's newest National Park (LCNSHP) is a joint venture between the National Park Service and the States of Oregon and Washington. The Fort Clatsop Visitor Information Center is the general contact. (503) 861-2471 x 214 www.nps.gov/lewi

▸ If going near the water, be aware of tides and carry tide tables. Be prepared for windy and wet weather.

77 CLARK'S DISMAL NITCH MEGLER REST AREA MEGLER WA

From the Washington side of the Columbia River (Skamokawa area) go west 26.5 miles on Route 4. Turn south onto Route 401. Go 6.7 miles to the Megler Rest Area.

From the Oregon side of the Columbia River; (Astoria) cross the river on the US 101 Bridge. Turn east on Route 401. Go 0.9 mile to the Megler Rest Area.

78 STATION CAMP McGOWAN WA

From Astoria OR: cross the river on the US 101 Bridge. Turn west on US 101. Go 2.5 miles to the Station Camp Park Area.

79 FORT COLUMBIA STATE PARK McGOWAN, WA

From Astoria OR: cross the river on the US 101 Bridge. Turn west on US 101. Go 2.3 miles to Fort Columbia State Park.

80 ILWACO HERITAGE MUSEUM—ILWACO WA

115 SE Lake Street.

From Astoria OR: cross the river on the US 101 Bridge. Turn west on US 101. Go 11 miles to Ilwaco. Go south one block on 1st Avenue to the Museum.

81 INTERPRETIVE CENTER CAPE DISAPPOINTMENT ILWACO WA

From US 101 in Ilwaco go west one block on Spruce St. Turn south on 2nd Ave. Road changes name to Robert Gray Drive. Go 1.7 miles. Turn south on Fort Canby Rd. Go 0.6 mile. Turn west onto Fort Canby State Park Rd. Go 0.4 mile.

82 JEFFERSON MEMORIAL CAPE DISAPPOINTMENT ILWACO WA

From US 101 in Ilwaco go west one block on Spruce St. Turn south on 2nd Ave. Road changes name to Robert Gray Drive. Go 1.7 miles. Turn south on Fort Canby Rd. Go 0.6 mile. Turn west onto Fort Canby State Park Rd. Go 0.2 mile.

83 MAYA LIN CONFLUENCE PROJECT CAPE DISAPPOINTMENT ILWACO WA

From US 101 in Ilwaco go west one block on Spruce St. Turn south on 2nd Ave. Road changes name to Robert Gray Drive. Go 1.7 miles. Turn south on Fort Canby Rd. Go 0.6 mile. Turn southwest onto Fort Canby State Park Rd. Go 0.3 mile.

84 NORTH HEAD LIGHTHOUSE CAPE DISAPPOINTMENT ILWACO WA

From US 101 in Ilwaco go west one block on Spruce St. Road changes name to North Head Road. Go 1.4 miles. Continue west and then south on Robert Gray Drive. Go 1.4 miles. Turn west onto North Lighthouse Road. Go 0.7 mile to the Lighthouse.

85 DISCOVERY TRAIL LONG BEACH WA

17th St S to 16th St N.

From Ilwaco take US 101 1.8 miles north to Long Beach. Continue north 0.6 mile on Route 103.

86 WILLAPA NATIONAL WILDLIFE REFUGE ILWACO WA

From Ilwaco take US 101 north and east 11.4 miles to Willapa National Wildlife Refuge.

MAYA LIN'S CONFLUENCE PROJECT
www.confluenceproject.org

Cape Disappointment State Park (LCNSHP) is the first Confluence Project by artist Maya Lin. The Vietnam Veterans Memorial in Washington DC reflects her vision of integrating sculpture with landscape. Other planned sites are:

Frenchman's Bar State Park
Confluence of the Columbia and Willamette Rivers
Clark County, WA

Vancouver National Historic Reserve *Vancouver, WA*

Lewis and Clark State Recreation Area
Sandy River Delta Troutdale, OR

Celilo Falls Park
The Dalles OR

Sacajawea State Park
Confluence of the Snake and Columbia Rivers, Pasco WA

Chief Timothy Park
Snake River, Clarkston WA

Ocean in View
Betty Kluesner, DESC

Lewis and Clark Interpretive Center
Lyn Topinka

Seagulls
Betty Kluesner
Discovery Expedition of St Charles

Clark's Tree Sculpture, Discovery Trail
Long Beach Pennisula Visitors Bureau

Cape Disappointment and Long Beach, Washington

77 CLARK'S DISMAL NITCH (LCNSHP) MEGLER SAFETY REST AREA

The Dismal Nitch area is near the Megler Safety Rest Area, just east of the Astoria Bridge. This is where the Corps of Discovery spent a miserable time (Nov 10-14, 1805) camping on a mass of drift logs in continuous rain. Their dugout canoes and skills were not up for the challenge of the winter storms and dangerous tides at the mouth of the Columbia, but the Indians came by in their canoes to sell them fish. Clark wrote "Certain it is they are the best canoe navigators I ever Saw."

■ Rest area is open daily. www.nps.gov/lewi

78 STATION CAMP (LCNSHP) McGOWAN, WA

The expedition made it around "Point Distress" and set up camp at Chinook Point on the Columbia River. The one acre park is very near the original campsite of Nov. 15-24th. On Nov. 24th the captains consulted everyone, including Sacagawea and York, and recorded their opinions as to where they should make winter camp. It was decided to cross the river and examine the south side of the mouth of the Columbia. They took the long way around, going back to the calmer waters near Pillar Rock and the islands of the Lewis and Clark National Wildlife Refuge before crossing over to the Oregon side.

■ www.nps.gov/lewis

79 FORT COLUMBIA STATE PARK (LCNSHP) McGOWAN, WA

Fort Columbia defended the Columbia harbor from 1896 to 1947 through three wars. During the time of Lewis and Clark it was the home of Chief Comcomly's Chinook Village. The park's Interpretive Center has exhibits on fort history and Chinook Tribal history. A Commander's House Museum and other historic buildings are also on the site. Vacations houses are available for rent year round. No camping facilities.

■ Interpretive Center and House Museum open daily from May 26-Sept. 30th from 10-5.
Park hours, summer 6:30 AM-9:30 PM; winter 8 AM-5 PM. Vehicle entrance fee, $5.
(888) 226-7688 www.parks.wa.gov

 80 ILWACO HERITAGE MUSEUM ILWACO, WA

The museum is directly on the site of an ancient Chinook trail that the Corps of Discovery followed to the ocean. The museum has four thematic galleries: Nature Provides, Land of the Canoe People, Fur Trade and Explorers, and the Columbia River Estuary Industry, with a working model of the estuary system. A large bookstore and gift shop.

■ Open daily, Mon-Sat, 10-4 and Sun, 12-4. Admission: $5 adults, $4 seniors, $2.50 ages 12-17, $1 ages 6-11. (360) 642-3446
www.ilwacoheritagemuseum.org

81 LEWIS AND CLARK INTERPRETIVE CENTER—CAPE DISAPPOINTMENT STATE PARK (LCNSHP)—ILWACO, WA

The Center stands high on a cliff overlooking the ocean; it was built on top of the old Fort Canby's coastal defense bunkers. Its Lewis and Clark exhibits include a display of Patrick Gass's prized possessions: the razor box carved by Sacagawea as a gift for him; the flask and hatchet he carried on the expedition; an 1812 edition of his published journal, the family bible, his personal account book and other books. Maritime exhibits include the giant old 1841 fresnel lens from the Cape Disappointment lighthouse. The Center also has short films, a gift shop, and a glassed-in observation deck with fabulous views of the Pacific Ocean.

■ State Park open dawn to dusk. Vehicle entrance fee of $5. RV and tent campgrounds.
(360) 642-3078 www.parks.wa.gov

■ Interpretive Center open daily, 10-5. Admission: $3 adults, $1 ages 7-17.
(360) 642-3029 www.nps.gov/lewi

82 JEFFERSON MEMORIAL PROJECT SITE CAPE DISAPPOINTMENT S P (LCNSHP)

The National Park Service has a proposal to build a Thomas Jefferson National Memorial at Cape Disappointment State Park on a 20 acre site overlooking the Pacific Ocean.

■ (506) 861-2471 x 214 www.nps.gov/lewi

83 CONFLUENCE PROJECT ARTWORK BY MAYA LIN AND HIKING TRAILS AT CAPE DISAPPOINTMENT STATE PARK

Two of Maya Lin's confluence artworks are located between the Interpretive Center and the old Cape Disappointment Lighthouse. The third artwork is located at Wakiki Beach. There are six hiking trails with trail markers.

■ Open daily, dawn to dusk. $5 vehicle fee.
(360) 642-3078 www.confluenceproject.org

84 NORTH HEAD LIGHTHOUSE TOUR CAPE DISAPPOINTMENT STATE PARK

The 1856 Cape Disappointment Lighthouse is the oldest operating lighthouse on the West Coast; it guides sailors into the mouth of the Columbia. The 1898 North Head Lighthouse guides sailors approaching from the north. This area is called "the graveyard of the Pacific," as many ships and lives have been lost here. The North Head has winds up to 120 miles per hour; it is a popular whale watching site during late December, early January and March through May. The Cape Disapointment Lighthouse is not open for tours.

■ Northhead Lighthouse open daily, last wkd in May to 1st wkd in Sept, 10 AM-6 PM. Tours every 15 minutes. Admission: $1, and vehicle fee of $5. (360) 642-3078 www.nps.gov/lewi

85 DISCOVERY TRAIL—LONG BEACH, WA

Ilwaco is the gateway for the 8.2 mile Discovery Trail that traces the path of William Clark and his party of 11 men who explored the coastline north to Long Beach on November 18, 1805. Attractions include the Beard's Hollow wetlands bridge at Ilwaco; the McKenzie Head Bas Relief at Cape Disappointment; and the Gray Whale Skeleton, the Basalt Monolith, and Clark's Tree along the beach. There is a boardwalk at Long Beach near the Discovery Trail.

■ (800) 451-2542 www.funbeach.com

86 WILLAPA NAT'L WILDLIFE REFUGE SALMON TRAIL, ILWACO, WA

Willapa Bay has salt marshes, tidal flats, old growth forest, coastal dunes. A Salmon Art Interpretive Trail boardwalk is near a stream where salmon spawn (Oct 15-Nov 15).

■ Open 7:30 AM-4:30 PM Mon-Fri.
(360) 484-3482 www.fws.gov/willapa

87 ASTORIA COLUMN
ASTORIA OR

From Maritime Drive (US 30) go 0.5 mile south on 15th St. Turn east on Madison Ave. Go one block. Turn south on 16th St.. Go one block. Turn east on Coxcomb Dr. Go 0.6 mile. Turn south onto Astoria Park Rd. Go 0.1 mile.

88 COLUMBIA RIVER MARITIME MUSEUM
ASTORIA OR

1792 Marine Drive.
On Marine Drive (US 30) between 17th and 18th Streets.

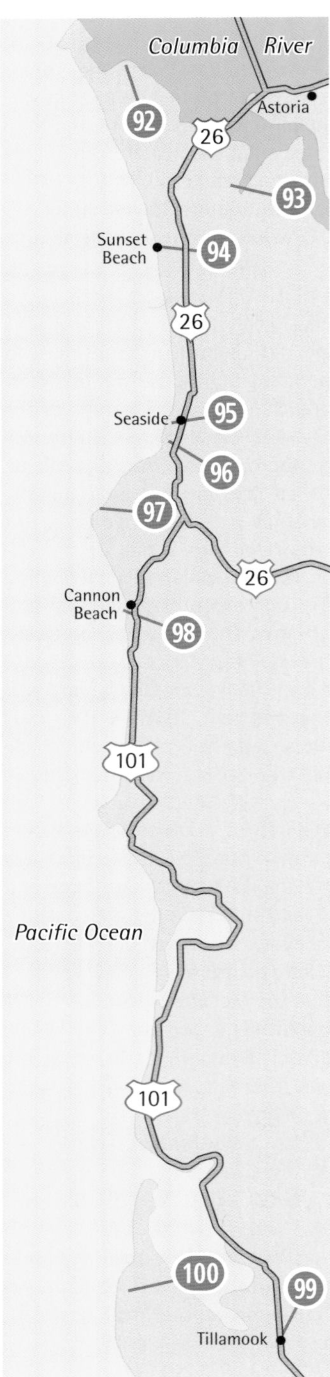

Oregon Coast

89 HERITAGE MUSEUM
ASTORIA OREGON

1618 Exchange Street.
From Marine Drive (US30) go two blocks south on 16th St. Turn east onto Exchange St.

90 FORT ASTORIA PARK
ASTORIA OR

15th and Exchange Streets
From Marine Drive (US 30) go three blocks south on 15th Street.

91 ASTORIA WATERFRONT AND TROLLEY

The Riverfront Trolley runs along the riverfront from the Port of Astoria at the west end of town to 36th Street.

92 FORT STEVENS STATE PARK
WARRENTON OREGON

From Astoria take the US 101 bridge 2.7 miles southwest across Youngs Bay to Marlin Ave. Go north 0.4 mile to E Harbor St. Go west one mile. Turn north on Fort Stevens Hwy. Go 2.2 miles. Turn northwest onto Rte 104. Go 1.2 miles. Go north 0.6 miles to the Fort Stevens Museum.

93 FORT CLATSOP NATIONAL HISTORIC PARK
ASTORIA, OREGON

From Astoria take the US 101 bridge 2.7 miles southwest across Youngs Bay to Marlin Ave. Go south 0.3 mile. Turn east onto US 101A. Go 2 miles south and then east. Turn south onto Fort Clatsop Rd. Go 0.8 mile to Fort Clatsop.

94 FORT TO SEA TRAIL
ASTORIA OR

East trailhead is at Fort Clatsop Visitor Center. Driving directions; destination 93 above.
West trailhead is at Sunset Beach Recreation Site. From US 101 go 1 mile west on Sunset Beach Lane.

95 SEASIDE AQUARIUM
SEASIDE OR

200 N Prom.
From US 26 (Roosevelt Dr) go 0.4 mile west on Broadway St. Turn north onto N Prom. Go 3 blocks.

96 SALT WORKS
SEASIDE, OREGON

From US 26 (Roosevelt Dr) go 0.4 mile west on Avenue G. Turn south on Beach Drive. Go 0.4 mile to Lewis and Clark Way. Park and walk west to the Salt Works.

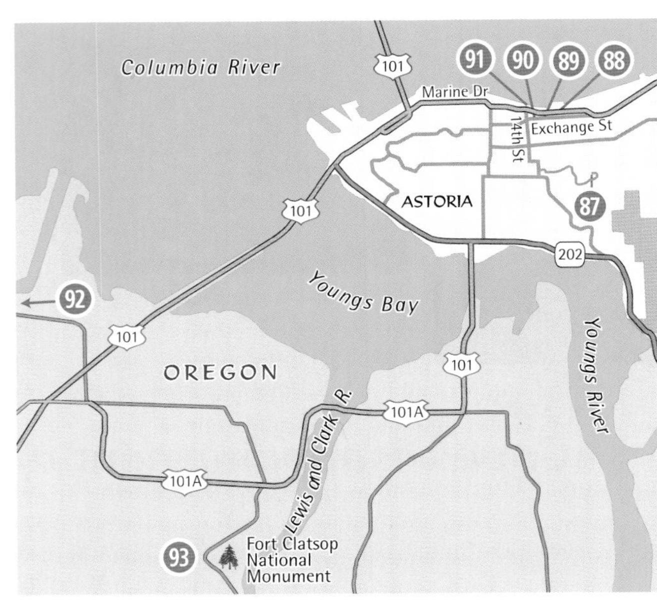

Astoria and Fort Clatsop

97 ECOLA STATE PARK
CANNON BEACH OR

From US 101 take the north exit for Cannon Beach. Go 0.3 mile southwest on Beach Loop. Go 0.1 mile northwest on 5th St. Go 1.5 miles north on Ecola Park road.

98 HAYSTACK ROCK
CANNON BEACH OR

From US 101 go west 0.2 mile on Sunset Boulevard. Turn south on Hemlock St. Go 0.3 mile. Walk 0.2 mile to the shore.

99 TILLAMOOK COUNTY PIONEER MUSEUM
TILLAMOOK OR

2106 Second Street.
From US 101 (Main Ave) go one block east on 2nd Avenue.

100 CAPE MEARES LIGHTHOUSE AND WILDLIFE REFUGE
TILLAMOOK OR

From US 101 (Main Ave) go 1.7 miles west on Netarts Hwy. Turn west onto Bayocean Road. Go 5.3 miles. Go 2.1 miles south on Cape Meares Loop to the Lighthouse.

JOHN JACOB ASTOR'S VISION FOR A GLOBAL EMPIRE

John Jacob Astor, German born, was New York's wealthiest fur merchant. He dreamed of establishing a chain of trading posts across the country, supplying furs to China. In 1810-11 he sent one expedition by sea, and another by land, to the mouth of the Columbia River.

The ship's crew established a trading post at Astoria in April, 1811; the overland expedition reached Astoria in January, 1812. The War of 1812 between Great Britain and the United States had begun. The Astorians, many of whom were British-Canadians, sold Fort Astoria to the British North West Fur Company in October, 1813; much to the dismay of a British war ship which arrived in December to claim the prize. Renamed Fort George, it became one of the biggest and best trading posts in the West, until it was resold to the Hudson Bay Company in 1821. The period of joint occupancy of Oregon Country lasted from 1818 until 1846, when the boundary line between the United States and Canada was settled.

Ranald MacDonald

Ranald MacDonald, the son of a Fort George factor and his wife, a daughter of Chief Comcomly, became the first westerner in two centuries to gain access to Japan. In 1848, at age 24, he became the first teacher of English in Japan; thus helping to achieve the trade agreement reached with Japan in 1854 by Commodore Perry.

Astoria Column
Lyn Topinka

Columbia River Maritime Museum
Lyn Topinka

Fort Clatsop Visitor Center

Ocean Beach near Saltworks

Astoria to Tillamook Bay, Oregon

87 ASTORIA COLUMN—ASTORIA, OREGON

The Astoria Column was built in 1926 to commemorate Astoria's history as the first American settlement west of the Rockies. There are 164 steps leading to the viewing platform overlooking the coastal waters.

■ (503) 325-2963 www.oregoncoast.com

88 COLUMBIA RIVER MARITIME MUSEUM ASTORIA, OREGON

Riverboats —a tugboat, Coast Guard rescue craft, WWII Navy Destroyer, and a floating lighthouse; world class maritime exhibits; and an award winning film inspire respect for the dangers of the sea, and those who go to sea. More than 200 major shipwrecks have occurred here at "the graveyard of the Pacific."

■ Open daily, 9:30-5. Admission: $8 adults, $7 seniors, $4 ages 6-17; $24 family rate. (503) 325-2323 www.crmm.org

89 HERITAGE MUSEUM ASTORIA, OREGON

The Old City Hall has exhibits on: Chinook and Clatsop basketry; Fort Astoria; logging and fishing industries; vice and virtue; and the many diverse ethnic groups who settled here. The society also owns the Captain George Flavel House, a Victorian mansion.

■ Open daily May-Sept, 10-5; open Tues-Sat, Oct-April, 11-4. Admission: $3 adults, $2 seniors, $1 ages 6-17. (503) 325-2203 www.clatsophistoricalsociety.org

90 FORT ASTORIA PARK—ASTORIA, OR

The founding of Astoria dates to 1811 when Americans established the Astoria Trading Post. The site of the original trading post and fort is a city park with a marvelous combination of murals and recreated stockade and fencing.

■ (503) 325-6311 www.astoriavisualarts.org

91 ASTORIA WATERFRONT AND TROLLEY

Waterfront viewing places are 6th St deck, 14th St ferry dock and 17th St Coast Guard dock. The1913 trolley car runs along the riverfront on a track, serving tourists and locals alike; The Old #300 ride usually include a narrated tour. During heavy rains the car stays in its barn. Check the website for its schedule.

■ Daily during the season; weekends off season; Fare: $1, or $2 if you want to get on and off. (503) 325-8790 trolley barn www.old300.org

92 FORT STEVENS STATE PARK (LCNSHP) WARRENTON, OREGON

Fort Stevenson was the primary defense installation of the three forts defending the harbor. Today the 3700 acre park is Oregon's largest campground with 530 campsites. The museum features Civil War history. During the summer there are guided walking tours and truck tours of the fort. An old shipwreck can be seen here. The fort is also the site of an old Clatsop Village, for which interpretation is being planned.

■ Open year-round. (503) 861-2000, museum; (503) 861-1671, information; (800) 452-5687, campground, RV, and yurt reservations. www.nps.gov/lewi www.oldoregon.com

93 FORT CLATSOP (LCNSHP) ASTORIA, OREGON

This is where the Corps of Discovery spent the winter of 1805-06. The replica of Fort Clatsop built in 1955 burned to the ground in 2005. It is being rebuilt in a more authentic manner in 2006. The Visitor Center has films, exhibits, gift shop and bookstore. The 1½ mile Netul Landing walking trail along the Lewis and Clark River gives visitors a chance to explore the Fort Clatsop area. Netul Landing (LCNSHP) is the non-motorized boat launch for one end of the Lower Columbia River Water Trail; the other end is Bonneville Dam. It also serves as a parking area and bus shuttle stop during peak season.

■ Open daily, mid-June through 1st wkd in Sept, 9-6; Sept-June, 9-5. Admission: peak season, $5 ages 17 and older; $2.50 16 and younger. Off season: $3 and free. (503) 861-2471 x 214 www.nps.gov/lewi

94 FORT TO SEA TRAIL (LCNSHP) ASTORIA, OREGON

The Fort to Sea Trail is 6½ miles from Fort Clatsop to Sunset Beach and the ocean. Parts of the trail may be walked at either end. There is a public bus route and taxi transport between the two trailheads. (503) 861-2471 x 214 www.forttosea.org www.nps.gov/lewis

95 SEASIDE AQUARIUM—SEASIDE, OR

The family-owned aquarium has been in operation since 1937. The performing seals are 3rd and 4th generation offspring of the aquarium's original seals. Staff members enjoy answering questions about the many sea creatures on exhibit.

■ Open daily, 9-5. From June-late August, open 9-6, Sun-Thurs, and 9-8 on Fri-Sat. Admission: $7, ages 14 and older, $3.50 ages 6-13. (503) 738-6211 www.seasideaquarium.com

96 SALT WORKS (LCNSHP) SEASIDE, OREGON

The salt-making party boiled 1,400 gallons of sea water to make 20 gallons of salt, which was used both to flavor food and preserve meat. On the 3rd wkds of July and August, re-enactors make salt at Seaside. A reconstructed saltworks stone oven is located in a residential neighborhood near the ocean at Seaside.

■ 503) 861-2471 x 214 www.nps.gov/lewi

97 ECOLA STATE PARK (LCNSHP) CANNON BEACH

Sacagawea and her family accompanied Clark and his party to see the dead whale at Ecola Beach on Jan 7-8, 1806. Ecola State Park has beautiful vistas; a hiking trail up Tillamook Head, and primitive cabins. The highest point on Tillamook Head is now called "Clark's Mountain." Clark said "it was grandest and most pleasing prospects which my eyes ever surveyed."

■ (503) 861-2471 x 214 www.nps.gov/lewi

98 HAYSTACK ROCK—CANNON BEACH, OR

Haystack Rock is one of the Oregon Coast's most popular attractions; its tidal pools are home to many intertidal animals. Interpretive programs during morning low tides in the summer.

■ (503) 436-2623 www.cannonbeach.org

99 TILLAMOOK COUNTY PIONEER MUSEUM—TILLAMOOK, OR

The museum has well known natural history collection and one of the best pioneer history exhibits in the state. The museum owns Kilchis Point, just north of Tillamook, the site of the old Tillamook Indian Village.

■ Open Tues-Sat, 9-5; Sun, 11-5. Admission: $3 general, $2.50 seniors. (503) 842-4553 www.tcpm.org

100 CAPE MEARES LIGHTHOUSE AND WILDLIFE REFUGE—TILLAMOOK, OR

A State Scenic Viewpoint at the Cape Meares Lighthouse provides views of sea bird and sea lion colonies; whale migration in season.

■ Lighthouse is open by appt. (call at least 3 weeks ahead). (503) 842-2244 www.capemeareslighthouse.org

Region Nine: References

BIOGRAPHY

ACROSS THE GREAT DIVIDE: ROBERT STUART AND THE DISCOVERY OF THE OREGON TRAIL
by Laton McCartney. Free Press (2003)

ADVENTURES OF THE FIRST SETTLERS ON THE OREGON OR COLUMBIA RIVER: 1810-1813
by Alexander Ross. Oregon State University Press (2000)

THE DISCOVERY OF THE OREGON TRAIL: ROBERT STUART'S NARRATIVES OF HIS OVERLAND TRIP EASTWARD FROM ASTORIA IN 1812-13
edited by Philip Ashton Rollins. University of Nebraska Press (1995)

JOHN JACOB ASTOR: AMERICA'S FIRST MULTIMILLIONAIRE
by Axel Madsen. John Wiley & Sons, Inc. (2001)

MADAME DORION
by Jerome Peltier, edited by Edward J. Kowrach. Ye Galleon Press (1980)

MARCUS AND NARCISSA WHITMAN AND THE OPENING OF OLD OREGON (TWO VOLUMES)
by Clifford M. Drury. Northwest Interptretive Association (1994)

NARRATIVE OF A JOURNEY ACROSS THE ROCKY MOUNTAINS TO THE COLUMBIA RIVER
by John Kirk Townsend. University of Nebraska Press (1978)

THE NORTHWEST COAST: OR, THREE YEARS' RESIDENCE IN WASHINGTON TERRITORY
by James G. Swan. University of Washington Press (1988)

SAM HILL: THE PRINCE OF CASTLE NOWHERE
by John E. Tully. Maryhill Museum of Art (1991)

SWAN AMONG THE INDIANS: LIFE OF JAMES G. SWAN, 1818-1900. BASED UPON SWAN'S HITHERTO UNPUBLISHED DIARIES AND JOURNALS
by Lucile McDonald. Binfords & Mort, Publishers (1972)

HISTORY

ANCIENT ENCOUNTERS: KENNEWICK MAN AND THE FIRST AMERICANS
by James C. Chatters. Simon and Schuster (2001)

ASTORIA
by Washington Irving. Binsfort & Mort (1967)

ASTORIA AND EMPIRE
by James P. Ronda. University of Nebraska Press (1990)

THE CHINOOK INDIANS: TRADERS OF THE LOWER COLUMBIA RIVER
by Robert H. Ruby and John A. Brown. University of Oklahoma Press (1976)

THE FIST IN THE WILDERNESS
by David Lavender. Doubleday & Company, Inc. (1964)

FUR TRADERS FROM NEW ENGLAND: THE BOSTON MEN IN THE NORTH PACIFIC, 1797-1800: THE NARRATIVES OF WILLIAM DANE PHELPS, WILLIAM STURGIS, AND JAMES GILCHRIST SWAN
edited by Briton C. Busch and Barry M. Gough. The Arthur H. Clark Company (1996)

THE HISTORICAL WALLA WALLA VALLEY
by Chester Collins Maxey. The Walla Walla Valley Historical Society (1934/2000)

INDIANS OF THE PACIFIC NORTHWEST: A HISTORY
by Robert H. Ruby and John A Brown. University of Oklahoma Press (1981)

LAND OF GIANTS: THE DRIVE TO THE PACIFIC NORTHWEST 1750-1950
by David Lavender.University of Nebraska Press (1979)

THE NEZ PERCE INDIANS AND THE OPENING OF THE NORTHWEST
by Alvin M. Josephy, Jr. The University of Nebraska Press (1979)

NCH'I-WANA "THE BIG RIVER": MID-COLUMBIA INDIANS AND THEIR LAND
by Eugene S. Hunn. University of Washington Press (1990)

OCIAN IN VIEW! O! THE JOY: LEWIS AND CLARK IN WASHINGTON STATE
by Robert C. Carriker. Washington State Historical Society (2005)

PLATEAU REGION: CAYUSE, WALLA WALLA AND UMATILLA PEOPLE
by Mary Null Boule. Merryant Publisher, Inc. (1999)

THE SALISH PEOPLE AND THE LEWIS AND CLARK EXPEDITION
by Salish-Pend d'Orielle Culture Committee and Elders Cultural Council, Confederated Salish and Kootenai Tribes. University of Nebraska Press (2005)

THE SANDAL & THE CAVE: THE INDIANS OF OREGON
by Luther S. Cressman. Oregon State University Press (2005)

MISCELLANEOUS

CATACLYSMS ON THE COLUMBIA: A LAYMAN'S GUIDE TO THE FEATURES PRODUCED BY THE CATASTROPHIC BRETZ FLOODS IN THE PACIFIC NORTHWEST
by John Eliot Allen, Marjorie Burns, and Samuel C, Sargent. Timber Press (1986)

THE COLUMBIA GORGE: A UNIQUE AMERICAN TREASURE
by Michael S. Spranger. Washington State University (1985)

COLUMBIA RIVER GORGE: MOON HANDBOOKS
by Stuart Warren and Brian Litt. Avalon Travel (2002)

COLUMBIA RIVER GORGE HISTORY (2 VOLUMES)
by Jim Attwell. Tahlkie Books (1974)

THE COLUMBIA RIVER: A HISTORICAL TRAVEL GUIDE
by JoAnn Roe. Fulcrum Publishing (1992)

FLOOD BASALTS AND GLACIER FLOODS: ROADSIDE GEOLOGY OF PARTS OF WALLA WALLA, FRANKLIN, AND COLUMBIA COUNTIES, WASHINGTON
by Robert J. Carson and Kevin R. Pogue. Washington State Department of Natural Resources (1996)

GLACIAL LAKE MISSOULA AND ITS HUMONGOUS FLOODS
by David Alt. Mountain Press Publishing Company (2001)

IN SEARCH OF ANCIENT OREGON: A GEOLOGICAL AND NATURAL HISTORY
by Ellen Morris Bishop. Timber Press (2003)

KONAPEE'S EDEN: HISTROIC AND SCENIC HANDBOOK: THE COLUMBIA RIVER GORGE
by Oral Bullard. TMS Book Service (1985)

THE LEWIS AND CLARK COLUMBIA RIVER WATER TRAIL: A GUIDE FOR PADDLERS, HIKERS, AND OTHER EXPLORERS
by Keith G. Hay. Timber Press (2004)

THE LEWIS & CLARK EXPEDITION: A TRAVELER'S COMPANION FOR OREGON AND WASHINGTON
by Stuart and Kathy Watson. East Oregonian Publishing Company (200)

OREGON: MOON HANDBOOKS
by Stuart Warren and Ted Long Ishikawa. Avalon Travel (2001)

ROLL ON, COLUMBIA: THE "KING OF ROADS" STILL WEARS ITS CROWN
by David J. Sell. American Road. Volume III: Number 3; Autumn 2005

REGION TEN
NEW ORLEANS AND THE NATCHEZ TRACE

- New Orleans
- Baton Rouge and Natchez
- Natchez Trace: Natchez to Nashville
- Nashville, Memphis and New Madrid

1. Cabildo Louisiana State Museum, New Orleans 2. Meriwether Lewis Portrait by Charles Willson Peale 3. Old Natchez Trace 4. Meriwether Lewis Gravesite, Natchez Trace 5. The Hermitage, Home of President Andrew Jackson, Nashville 6. New Orleans Street Scene 7. Jackson Square, New Orleans 8. New Madrid Riverfront 9. Natchez Trace Parkway 10. Grand Village of the Natchez Indians, Natchez

Credits: (2) Independence National Historical Park; The Hermitage Foundation.

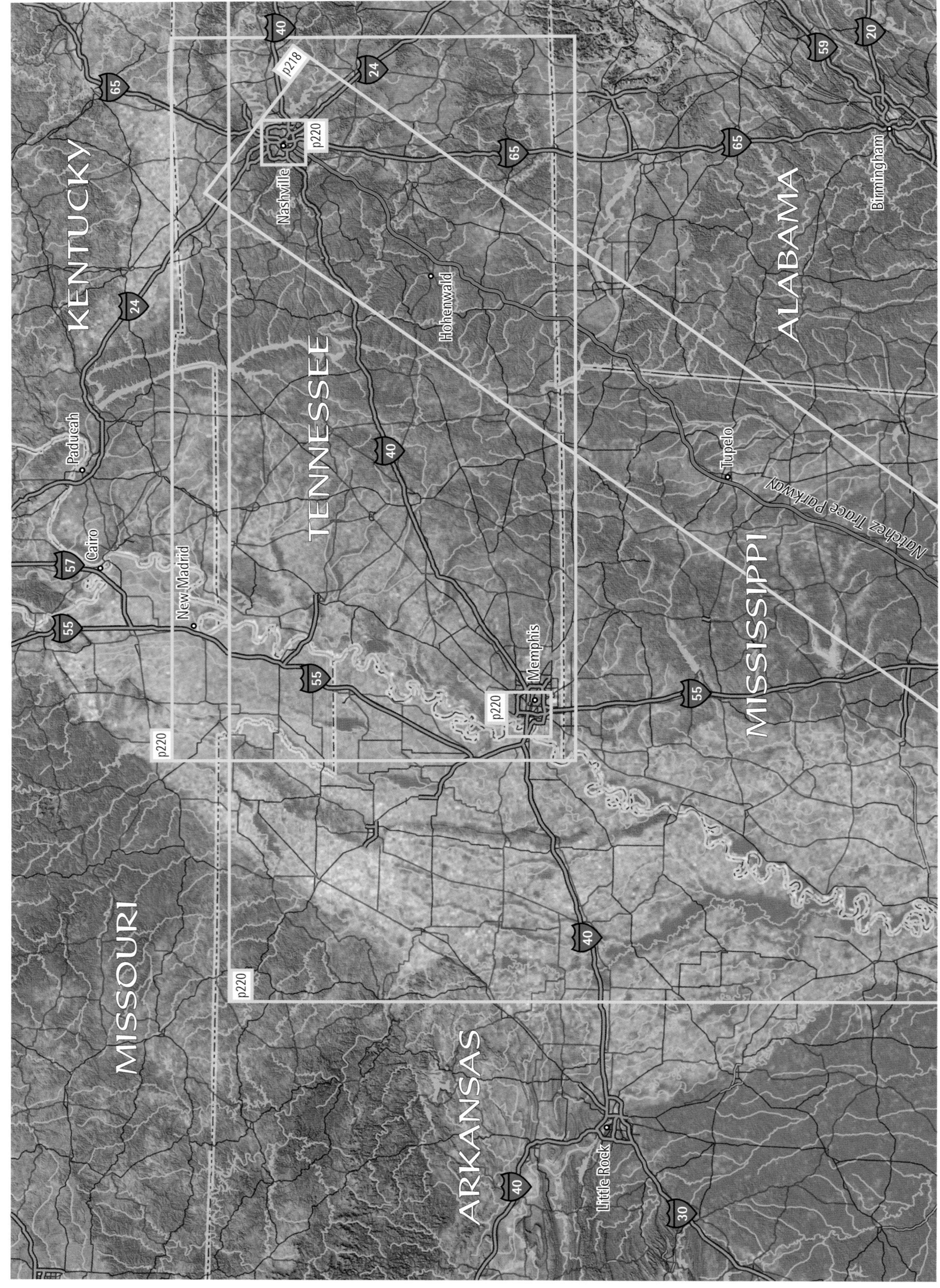

KENTUCKY
MISSOURI
TENNESSEE
ARKANSAS
MISSISSIPPI
ALABAMA
Paducah
Cairo
New Madrid
Nashville
Hohenwald
Memphis
Tupelo
Birmingham
Little Rock
Natchez Trace Parkway
p218
p220
p220
p220
p220
p220
65
24
40
59
20
65
65
24
40
57
55
55
55
40
40
30

10

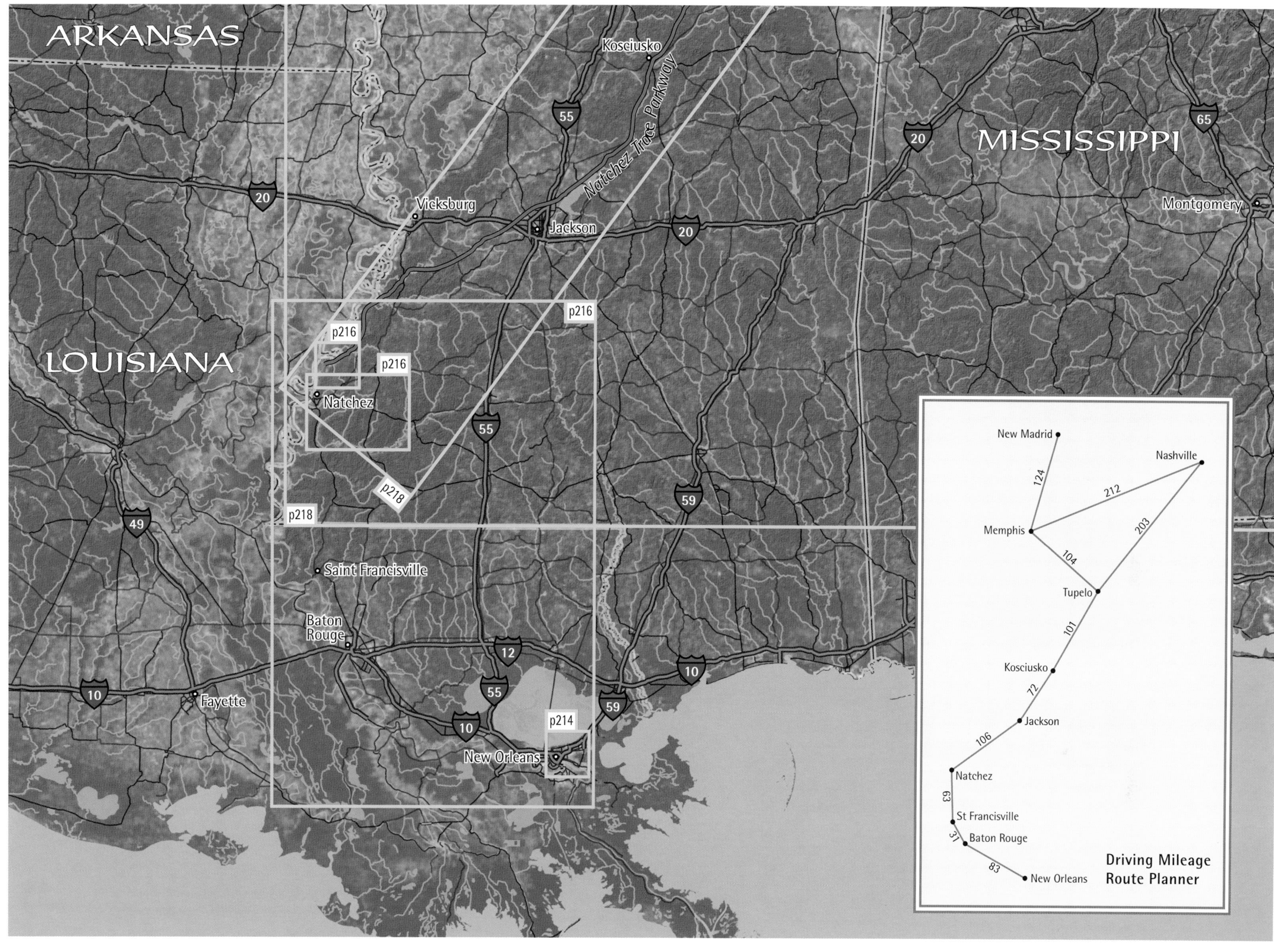
ARKANSAS
LOUISIANA
MISSISSIPPI
Kosciusko
Natchez Trace Parkway
Vicksburg
Jackson
Montgomery
Natchez
Saint Francisville
Baton Rouge
Fayette
New Orleans
p216
p216
p216
p218
p218
p214
55
20
20
20
65
55
59
49
12
10
55
10
59
10
Driving Mileage Route Planner
New Madrid
Nashville
Memphis
Tupelo
Kosciusko
Jackson
Natchez
St Francisville
Baton Rouge
New Orleans
124
212
203
104
101
72
106
63
31
83

10

The Cabildo in New Orleans where the Louisiana Purchase was signed in 1803.

The Hermitage, President Andrew Jackson's home in Nashville, Tennessee.

New Madrid was the site of an American colony settled under Spanish rule in 1789. It was also the epicenter of some of America's biggest earthquakes in 1811-12.

America 200 Years Ago

New Orleans and the Death of Meriwether Lewis

FRENCH LOUISIANA

The city of New Orleans is situated at the mouth of the Mississippi River where it enters the waters of the Gulf of Mexico. The Gulf is a major body of water surrounded by land on nearly all sides, connecting both to the Atlantic Ocean and the Caribbean Sea. Thus, the location of New Orleans at the mouth of the Mississippi River is one of the most strategic locations on the continent.

The area was settled in 1699 by French Canadians. The town itself was laid out in 1718-1721, on a crescent-shaped bend of the Mississippi, giving New Orleans its oldest name, the "Crescent City." Over the next decades the French established three small centers of population on the river: New Orleans, Natchez, and Kaskaskia. The population of "New France" consisted of about 5,000 whites; and 3,000 slaves brought from Africa to the New World against their will. At that time, when all work was performed by human and animal labor, many people in the world lived in conditions of slavery or feudal servitude.

France, England and Spain were the great super powers of their age, fighting to control areas for commercial development far removed from their own countries. In North America Great Britain established thirteen colonies east of the Allegheny Mountains; France established colonies in Canada and on the Mississippi River; and Spain established colonies in Mexico and the Pacific Coast.

The "French and Indian War" (1754-63) is the name by which the British and French war for control of the North American Continent is known to students of American history. It was one of a series of wars between Britain and France. They employed colonial militias and Native American allies, as well as their own armies and navies. The young George Washington, as a colonel in the Virginia militia, is credited with starting the French and Indian War (see Fort Necessity National Battlefield, pages 20-21).

When Britain and its American colonies won the war, the entire French empire in the New World was demolished. France ceded New Orleans and western Louisiana (its land west of the Mississippi) to its ally Spain in 1762 in order to prevent Britain from getting it. Louisiana would serve as a buffer state for Spain, protecting its silver mines in Mexico from British and American expansion efforts.

At the Treaty of Paris in 1763, Britain gained all the land east from the Mississippi to the Allegheny Mountains; but forbade its American colonists to settle in the area. It couldn't provide defense against Indian attacks. Britain also obtained Florida from Spain, in exchange for Cuba and the Phillipines which it had captured during the war.

SPANISH LOUISIANA

French Louisiana no longer existed, except for the fact that most of the European population in these areas were the same French-speaking people who had lived there for years. In 1769, the first Spanish Governor of Louisiana arrived in New Orleans: his name was Alexandro O'Reilly, an Irishman in the service of Spain. Governor O'Reilly established the "Illustrious Cabildo," or Spanish governing body in the new "Casa Capitular," or Council House, which opened in 1770. It is now the Cabildo Museum.

Spain governed New Orleans and Louisiana until 1803, although, in fact, it had returned Louisiana to France in 1800. The secret deal included the stipulation that Louisiana could not be resold to a third party; which, of course, is just what happened when Napoleon sold it to the United States in 1803.

THE EARLY AMERICAN REPUBLIC

When the American War for Independence began in 1775 it was against this background of competing English, French and Spanish interests. American settlers had moved into the area west of the Allegheny Mountains and established settlements along the Ohio River. In 1779 George Rogers Clark became the hero of the western frontier by capturing the British fort at Vincennes. When the war ended in 1783, Britain ceded all of its land claims up to the Mississippi River because of Clark's victories. However, despite their treaty promises, the British continued to arm their Indian allies and didn't relinquish their forts in the Ohio Valley until the end of the Indian Wars in 1796. The relationship between Britain and its former

Meriwether Lewis (1774-1809)

The Old Natchez Trace

The Broken Column Monument at Meriwether Lewis' Gravesite

Interpretive Center near the Monument

colonies continued to deteriorate until "America's Second War for Independence," the War of 1812, broke out. The war ended in a stalemate in December of 1814, when a peace treaty was arranged at Ghent, Belgium. Two weeks later—not aware of the proceedings at Ghent—General Andrew Jackson won an enormous victory at the Battle of New Orleans with the help of the Lafitte brothers and the Barratarian pirates under their command.

THE LOUISIANA PURCHASE

France reacquired Louisiana from Spain in 1800 with the promise not to sell it to a third party. However, President Jefferson was alarmed at the prospect of France controlling the port of New Orleans. He wrote, "There is on the globe one single spot the possessor of which is our natural and habitual enemy. It is New Orleans, through which the produce of three eighths of our territory must pass to market." Jefferson had even written, "The day that France takes possession of New Orleans. . . .we must marry ourselves to the British fleet and nation."

Jefferson dispatched envoys to Paris in 1802 with an offer to buy New Orleans. He sent James Monroe in January, 1803 with the authority to increase the American offer. Napoleon Bonaparte was ready to make a deal. He had sent troops to Haiti to put down a ten year slave rebellion led by Toussaint L' Overture in which 50,000 French troops had died, most from a yellow fever epidemic. He offered to sell not only New Orleans but all of Louisiana to the United States. The United States acquired 828,000 square miles of land for a cost of fifteen million dollars, or about 3¢ an acre, more than doubling the nation's size.

Meriwether Lewis served as Jefferson's private secretary during this time, and lived in the East Room of the White House. Together they made plans for Lewis, an army captain on leave, to lead a military expedition into the Pacific Northwest, which would pass through Louisiana. But as events unfolded, it turned out that the "Corps of Volunteers for Northwestern Discovery" would be exploring the newly-acquired Louisiana Purchase. On the 27th anniversary of the Declaration of Independence news of the purchase was announced in the Washington newspapers. Captain Lewis set off on his journey to the Pacific the next day, July 5, 1803.

From November 30 to December 20, 1803 the flag of France flew over New Orleans for the last time. It was first of two ceremonies commemorating the sale of Louisiana. The documents were signed in the Cabildo. The second ceremony, attended by Meriwether Lewis and William Clark, was held in St. Louis on March 9-10, 1804. The flag of Spain was lowered, and the flag of France was flown, before the flag of the United States was raised over Louisiana.

INTRIGUE ON THE FRONTIER

For many years the frontier lands between the Alleghenies and the Mississippi were filled with intrigue, border warfare, land speculation, and political maneuvering. The original 13 states were not eager to absorb these frontier communities into the Union. Communication was difficult, distances were great, and transportation of goods was not practical except by way of the Mississippi River. Many believed there would be a second, western, United States located in the Mississippi River Valley.

France, Britain and Spain all played roles in shifting alliances and plots that never quite worked out. Native Americans fought hard to keep their lands. The most famous intriguer was James Wilkinson, Commanding General of the United States Army, and first Governor of Louisiana Territory. General Wilkinson survived three courts martial and one congressional inquiry during the course of his career. It was widely believed at the time that he was in the pay of Spain; this was proven when Spanish records were examined in the 20th century.

Wilkinson and President Jefferson's former Vice-President, Aaron Burr, were involved in a plot to invade Mexico during the years of the Lewis and Clark Expedition. Wilkinson betrayed Burr, who was then arrested and charged with treason. He was acquitted in a courtroom trial in Richmond, Virginia in 1807. Wilkinson was not charged. Meriwether Lewis attended the trial as an observer for President Jefferson.

ST LOUIS

In the Spring of 1808, Lewis arrived in St Louis to succeed Wilkinson as Governor of Louisiana. William Clark was already there, serving as Superintendent of Indian Affairs; a post he would hold until his death in 1838. One of Governor Lewis' main responsibilities was to accomplish the safe return of Sheheke, or "Big White," the Mandan Chief, to his village on the Knife River. Big White and his entourage had accompanied them to Washington to meet President Jefferson in 1806. An 1807 expedition to return him, led by Nathaniel Pryor, was attacked by the Arikara and three members of the expedition were killed. George Shannon lost his leg, which had to be amputated.

In the summer of 1809, a large expedition led by Pierre Chouteau succeeded. However, Lewis had overspent the authorized amount; the War Department refused to reimburse him. Jefferson was no longer President. James Madison was now President. Lewis decided to go to Washington to protest the bills. Clark, going by another route, planned to join him there.

THE DEATH OF MERIWETHER LEWIS

Lewis started for Washington by way of the Mississippi River, intending to go by boat from the Gulf Coast. At Fort Pickering in Memphis, he changed his mind and decided to take an overland route. Lewis died on October 11, 1809 at Grinders Stand near the Natchez Trace. He died of gun shot wounds. Some believe they were self inflicted, some believe it was murder. It has been said he was suicidally depressed. It has been said he was in the grips of malarial delusions. Undoubtedly he was sick with malarial fevers during his journey. There was no federal government investigation. Jefferson, though he said it was a suicide, also said of his friend, that Meriwether Lewis was

> "of courage undaunted, possessing a firmness and perserverance of purpose which nothing but impossibilities could divert from its direction."

Jackson Square

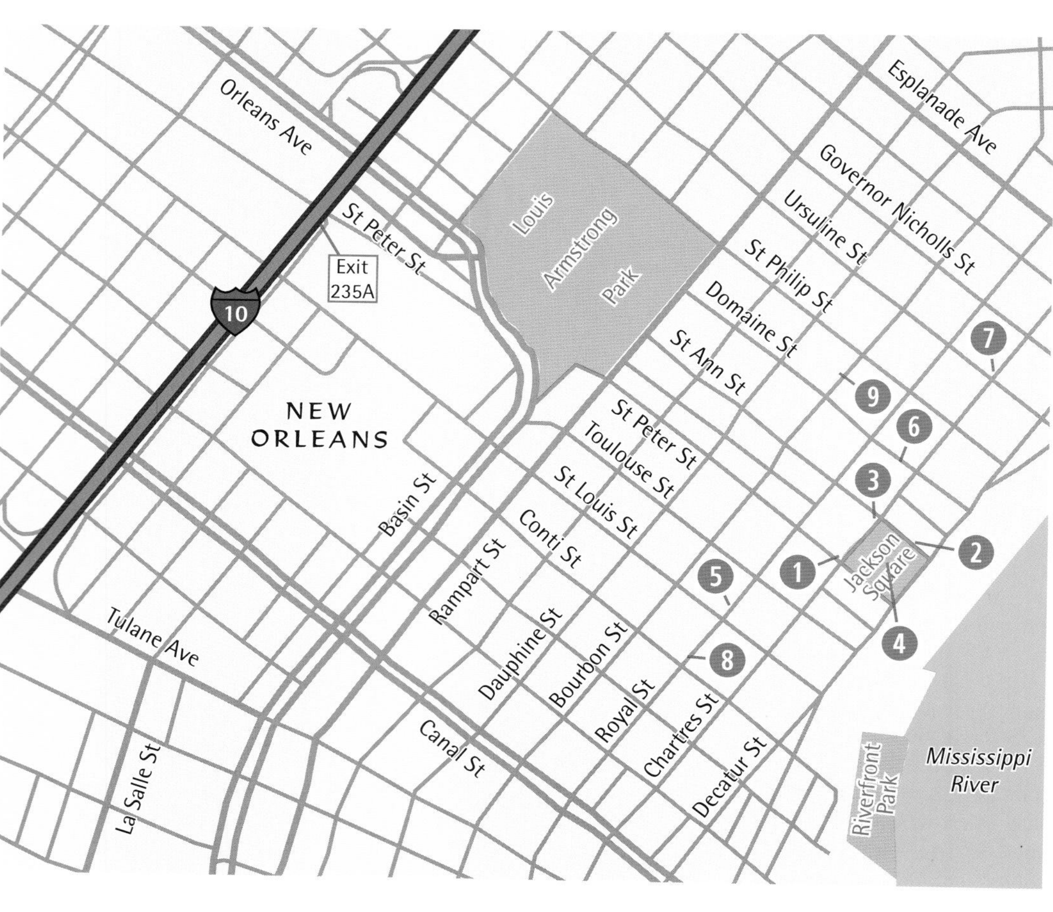

New Orleans

1 THE CABILDO

701 Chartres Street.

From I-10 Exit 235A go southeast 0.2 mile onto St Peter St. Merge onto Orleans Ave. Go 0.1 mile. Merge southwest onto Basin St. Go 0.1 mile. Turn southeast onto Conti St. Go 0.5 mile. Turn northeast onto Chartres St. Go three blocks to the Cabildo. The Arsenal is adjacent to the Cabildo at 600 St Peter St.

2 FRIENDS OF THE CABILDO 2 HOUR WALKING TOUR

Starts at 1850 House, 523 St. Ann. From I-10 Exit 235A merge north onto Claiborne Ave. Go 0.1 mile. Turn southeast onto Esplanade Ave. Go 0.8 mile. Turn southwest onto Decatur St. Go 0.4 mile. Turn northwest to 1850 House.

3 THE PRESBYTERE

751 Chartres.

From I-10 Exit 235A merge north onto Claiborne Ave. Go 0.1 mile. Turn southeast onto Esplanade Ave. Go 0.4 mile. Turn southwest onto Rampart St. Go 0.4 mile. Turn southeast onto St. Ann St. Go 0.3 mile. Turn southwest on Chartres Street.

4 JACKSON SQUARE

Jackson Square is bounded by Decatur Street (open to auto traffic); and by St Peter Street, Chartres Street, and Ann Street (which form a pedestrian mall closed to auto traffic).

From I-10 Exit 235A go southeast 0.2 mile onto St Peter St. Merge onto Orleans Ave. Go 0.1 mile. Merge southwest onto Basin St. Go 0.1 mile. Turn southeast onto Conti St. Go 0.5 mile. Turn northeast onto Decatur St.

5 HISTORIC NEW ORLEANS COLLECTION

533 Royal Street.

From I-10 Exit 235A go southeast 0.2 mile onto St Peter St. Merge onto Orleans Ave. Go 0.1 mile. Merge southwest onto Basin St. Go 0.1 mile. Turn southeast onto Conti St. Go 1/16 mile. Turn northeast onto Rampart St. Go two blocks. Turn southeast onto Toulouse St. Go 4 blocks. Turn southwest onto Royal Street.

6 MADAME JOHN'S LEGACY

623 Dumaine Street.

From I-10 Exit 235A merge north onto Claiborne Ave. Go 0.1 mile. Turn southeast onto Esplanade Ave. Go 0.8 mile. Turn southwest onto Decatur St. Go 0.3 mile. Turn northwest onto Dumaine St. Go 1.5 blocks to Madame John's Legacy.

7 OLD URSULINE CONVENT

1112 Chartres Street.

From I-10 Exit 235A merge north onto Claiborne Ave. Go 0.1 mile. Turn southeast onto Esplanade Ave. Go 0.8 mile. Turn southwest onto Decatur St. Go three blocks. Turn northwest onto Chartres Street. Go one block to the Convent.

8 JEAN LAFITTE HISTORICAL PARK AND PRESERVE

419 Decatur Street.

From I-10 Exit 235A go southeast 0.2 mile onto St Peter St. Merge onto Orleans Ave. Go 0.1 mile. Merge southwest onto Basin St. Go 0.1 mile. Turn southeast onto Conti St. Go 0.5 mile. Turn northeast onto Decatur Street. The Visitor Center is on the left side of the street.

9 LAFITTE'S BLACKSMITH SHOP BAR

941 Bourbon Street.

From I-10 Exit 235A go southeast 0.2 mile onto St Peter St. Merge onto Orleans Ave. Go 0.1 mile. Merge southwest onto Basin St. Go 0.1 mile. Turn southeast onto Conti St. Go 0.3 mile. Turn northeast onto Bourbon Street. Go 0.4 mile to Lafitte's.

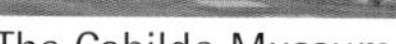
The Cabildo Museum

The Presbytere Museum

Lafitte's Blacksmith Bar

New Orleans Street Scene

New Orleans

1 THE CABILDO/ARSENAL NATIONAL HISTORIC LANDMARK LOUISIANA STATE MUSEUM

Located on Jackson Square, the Cabildo is one of the most historic buildings in the United States. It was built in 1799 to house the governing body of Spanish Louisiana; the Louisiana Purchase was signed here on December 20, 1803. The Cabildo became a State Museum in 1911, showcasing Louisiana's rich history and traditions. One of its most famous artifacts is Napoleon's death mask. The nearby Arsenal, a National Historic Landmark, was built in 1839.

■ Open Tues-Sun, 10-4. Admission for both museums: $6 adults, $5 students and seniors, ages 12 and under, free.
(800) 568-6868 or (504) 568-6968
www.lsm.crt.state.la.us
www.neworleansmuseums.com

2 FRIENDS OF THE CABILDO TWO HOUR WALKING TOUR

No reservations are needed for this walking tour of historic Vieux Carre, one of the oldest communities in the United States. It starts at the 1850 Museum House Store on Jackson Square.

■ Tours are offered on a limited basis due to Hurricane Katrina. Currently, Fridays, Saturdays and every other Sunday at 10 and 1:30.
Tickets: $12 adults, $10 seniors and students. Ages 12 and under free. Call for information.
(504) 523-3939 www.friendsofthecabildo.org

3 THE PRESBYTERE NATIONAL HISTORIC LANDMARK LOUISIANA STATE MUSEUM

The Presbytere, originally an ecclesiastical resident for Capuchin monks, is the home of the Mardi Gras Museum and gift shop. It is located on Jackson Square, flanking the St Louis Cathedral with the Cabildo Museum. The Mardi Gras has been celebrated in New Orleans since 1699. The museum houses exhibits of floats, costumes, and other memorabilia.

■ The Presbytere is currently closed due to Hurricane Katrina. However it suffered no damage and will reopen with renewed tourism. Admission prices are the same as for the Cabildo.
(800) 568-6868 ir (504) 568-6968
www.lsm.crt.state.la.us
www.neworleansmuseums.com

4 JACKSON SQUARE/CAFE DU MONDE

The heart of Old New Orleans, Jackson Square is the old Place d'Armes of French and Spanish times, the most historic spot in Louisiana. Here the church, the government, and the military were headquartered together on the riverfront. Today it is known as Jackson Square for its monument to Andrew Jackson, who won the Battle of New Orleans in 1815, the final battle of the War of 1812 with Great Britain. An open air artist's colony displays paintings; artists do portrait sketches. Across the way is Cafe du Monde, open 24 hours a day, offering New Orleans famous coffee and beignets, the sugared French doughnuts.

■ (800) 772-2927 www.cafedumonde.com

5 HISTORIC NEW ORLEANS COLLECTION

The museum complex in the French Quarter was the first to reopen after Hurricane Katrina. Seven buildings are included in the Historic New Orleans Collection on Royal Street. The Williams Research Center is located a few blocks away. The house museums have galleries featuring the history and artifacts of New Orleans, and a gift shop.

■ Open Tues-Sat, 10-4:30. Tours of the history galleries and the Williams residence are at 10 and 11 AM; 2 and 3 PM at a cost of $5 per person. The Williams Research Center at 410 Chartres St is open Tues-Sat, 9:30-4:30.
(504) 523-4662 www.hnoc.org

6 MADAME JOHN'S LEGACY NATIONAL HISTORIC LANDMARK LOUISIANA STATE MUSEUM

Another New Orleans treasure that survived the hurricane, Madame John's Legacy will reopen when tourism resumes. The 1789 house is a rare survivor of the fire of 1795, which destroyed much of early New Orleans. It is a fine example of Louisiana Creole style architecture, once prevalent in Canada, Illinois Country and the French West Indies. The name comes from a 1874 short story, " 'Tite Poulette," by George Washington Cable, in which the heroine, a beautiful Quadroon, owned the house. It was an early study in black-white racial issues.

■ (800) 568-6968 or (504) 568-6968
www.lsm.crt.state.la.us
www.neworleansmuseums.com

7 OLD URSULINE CONVENT NATIONAL HISTORIC LANDMARK

The Old Ursuline Convent is the oldest building in the Mississippi Valley, and the only one to survive from French colonial times. Built in 1745, the convent was operated by the Ursuline nuns for the education of girls. Six buildings are included in the site, dedicated to the memory of pioneer Archbishop Antoine Blanc. The buildings and the herb and old rose gardens have been completely restored.

■ Guided tours of the convent and St Mary's Church are conducted Tues-Fri, at 10,11,1,2,3. Sat and Sun, 11:15, 1 and 2. Admission: $5 adults, $4 seniors, $2 students and ages 8 and under, free. (504) 529-2001
www.neworleansmuseums.com

8 JEAN LAFITTE NATIONAL HISTORICAL PARK AND PRESERVE

Jean Lafitte was a legendary local pirate who helped win the Battle of New Orleans. The Park and Preserve consists of six sites; the Chalmette National Battlefield and National Cemetery site is closed due to hurricane damage. The Visitor Center in the French Quarter has exhibits on the history of New Orleans and the Mississippi Delta. The next nearest site is the Barataria Preserve 17 miles south of New Orleans; 20,000 acres of forest, baldcypress swamp, and marshland, with walking trails. Other sites in the region have bayou boat tours.

■ French Quarter Visitor Center open daily, from 9-5. (504) 589-2133 www.nps.gov/jela

■ Barataria Preserve has daily ranger-led walks at 10 AM. Ranger-led canoe treks, Mar-May, Saturdays at 9:30 AM (reservations required).
(504) 589-2330 www.nps.gov/jela

9 LAFITTE'S BLACKSMITH SHOP BAR NATIONAL HISTORIC LANDMARK

Is this the only National Historic Landmark that's a working bar? A very old building of uncertain age, it has been associated with the story of the pirate Lafitte Brothers. The earliest records of transfer of ownership date back to 1772. This popular neighborhood piano bar is located on the non-trendy end of Bourbon Street. Currently closed due to Hurricane Katrina, it's bound to reopen.

■ www.atneworleans.com

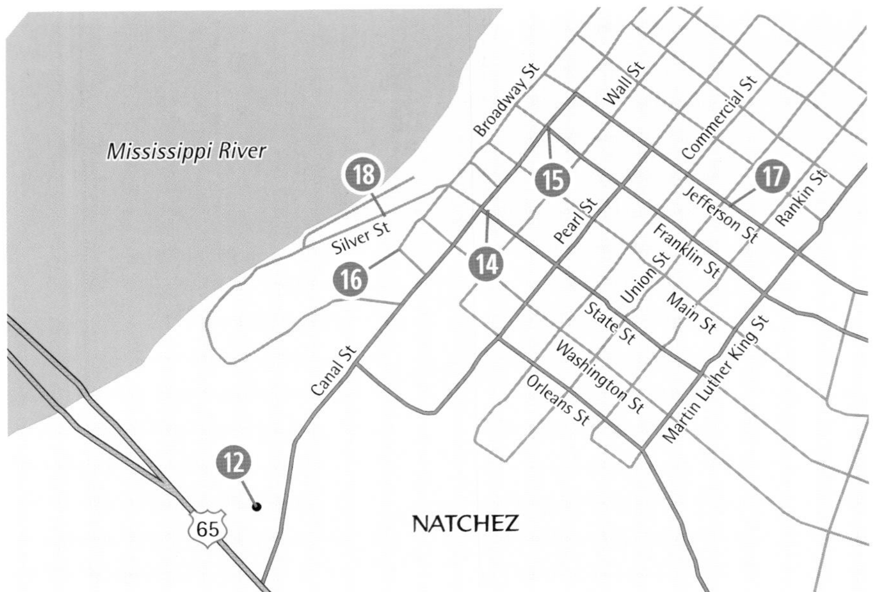

Natchez Visitor Reception Center

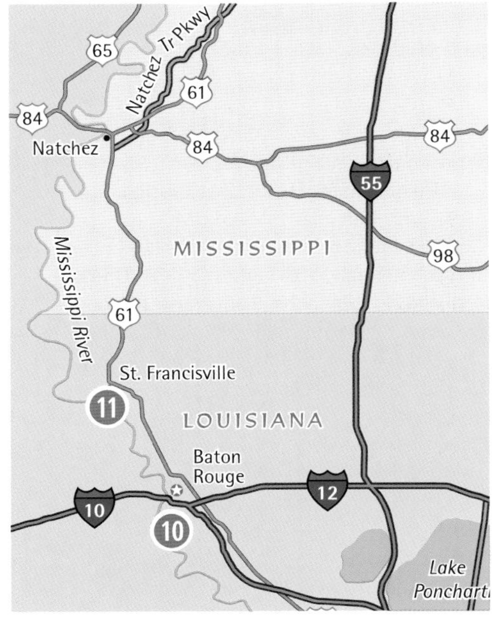

New Orleans to Natchez

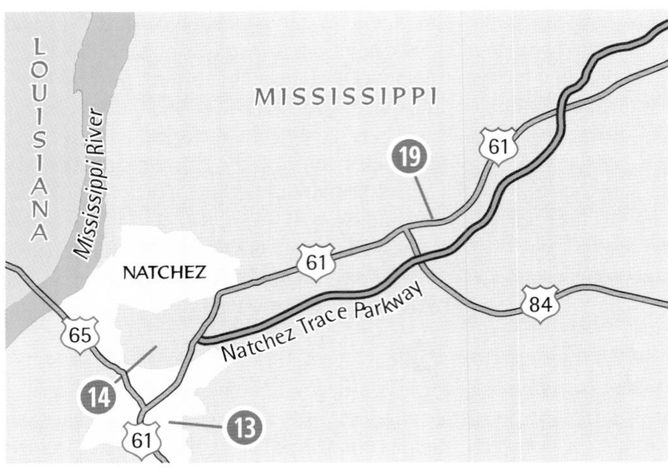

Natchez Trace Parkway

10 MAGNOLIA MOUND PLANTATION BATON ROUGE LA

2161 Nicholson Drive.
From I-10 East take Exit 155A. Turn south onto Nicholson Drive. Go 0.7 mile to the Plantation.

11 AUDUBON STATE HISTORIC SITE ST FRANCISVILLE LA

11788 Highway 965.
From I-10 East take Exit 155B to I-110. Go 8.5 miles. Take Exit 8A to US 61. Go 18.5 miles. Turn northeast onto State Route 966. Go 0.6 mile. Turn north onto Audubon Lane. Go 2.2 miles. Turn west onto State Route 965. Go 0.2 mile to the Audubon Site.

12 NATCHEZ VISITOR RECEPTION CENTER NATCHEZ MS

640 South Canal Street.
From US 65 (US 84) go 0.3 mile northeast on Canal Street to the Visitor Center.

13 GRAND VILLAGE OF THE NATCHEZ INDIANS NATCHEZ MS

400 Jefferson Davis Boulevard.
From US 61 about 3.5 miles south of Natchez turn west onto Jefferson Davis Boulevard. Go 0.3 mile to the entrance gate of the Grand Village.

14 NATCHEZ NATIONAL HISTORICAL PARK NATCHEZ MS

William Johnson House.
State St and Canal St in Natchez.
From US 65 go 0.7 mile northeast on Canal St.
Melrose Estate.
From the US 65 bridge over the Mississippi River go south 2.6 miles. Turn northeast onto US 61. Go 0.5 miles. Turn north onto Melrose Montebello Parkway. Go 0.9 mile to Ratcliff Place.

15 ELLICOTT HILL NATCHEZ MS

211 Canal Street.
From US 65 go 0.9 mile northeast on Canal St.

16 ROSALIE MANSION NATCHEZ MS

100 Orleans Street.
From US 65 go 0.6 mile northeast on Canal St.

17 KING'S TAVERN NATCHEZ MS

619 Jefferson Street.
From US 65 go 0.8 mile northeast on Canal St. Turn right (southeast) on Jefferson St. Go four blocks to King's Tavern.

18 UNDER-THE-HILL SALOON NATCHEZ MS

25 Silver Street.
From US 65 go 0.9 mile northeast on Canal St. Turn northwest onto State St. Go one block. Turn west onto Silver St. Go 0.1 mile to the Under-the-Hill Saloon.

19 HISTORIC JEFFERSON COLLEGE WASHINGTON MS

16 Old North Street.
From the US 65 bridge over the Mississippi River go south 2.6 miles. Turn northeast onto US 61. Go 6.6 miles. Turn north onto Jefferson College St. Go 0.1 mile to Historic Jefferson College.

Historic Jefferson College

Grand Village of the Natchez Indians

Rosalie Mansion
Natchez Convention and Visitors Bureau

Ellicott House

Baton Rouge and Natchez

10 MAGNOLIA MOUND PLANTATION HOUSE—BATON ROUGE, LA

One of the earliest buildings in Baton Rouge, the house museum is an example of the early French Creole style of architecture. Built c. 1786-91, and enlarged in 1802-05, the house and its surrounding buildings and gardens have been authentically restored with outstanding collections. The plantation hosts numerous community workshops, festivals and lectures.

■ Open daily, Mon-Sat, 10-4; Sun, 1-4. Tours are conducted from 10 AM until 3 PM. Admission: $8 adults, $6 seniors and students, $3, ages 5-17. (Free to LA residents from 1-4.)
(225) 343-4955 www.brec.org

11 AUDUBON STATE HISTORIC SITE ST FRANCISVILLE LA

The painter John James Audubon briefly stayed at Oakley Plantation in 1821. He was hired to tutor and teach drawing to the daughter of the plantation owner. Built c. 1806, the plantation is located in a forest setting of magnolia and poplar trees, where Audubon once sketched birds. The Visitor Center has an orientation video, guided tours, and a nature walk trail.

US-61 between Baton Rouge and St Francisville is the Louisiana Scenic Bayou Byway route, with five state historic sites located nearby representing the era of "English Louisiana" cotton plantations along the Mississippi River.

■ All are open daily, 9-5. Admission to the Audubon State Historic Site is $2, ages 13-61. Otherwise, free. (888) 677-1400
(225) 342-8111 www.LaStateParks.com

12 NATCHEZ VISITOR RECEPTION CENTER NATCHEZ, MS

The Visitor Reception Center serves as an orientation and information center for the city of Natchez, the state of Mississippi, the National Park Service, and Natchez Pilgrimage Tours. There is a skyramp walk overlooking the Mississippi River; interactive exhibits; a large bookstore and gift shop; and a film, "The Natchez Story." Bus tours of the historic district depart from the center. Tourists may also drive themselves to several historic homes open daily.

Annual Pilgrimage tours of Natchez' historic homes and gardens have been held since 1931. Spring tours are mid March-mid April; fall tours are the first two weeks in October. Natchez has over 300 antebellum (pre-Civil war) homes. It is two years older than New Orleans, having been established in 1716 when Fort Rosalie was built by the French.

■ Open daily. From Mar-Oct: Mon-Sat, 8:30-6, and Sun, 9-4. From Nov-Feb: Mon-Sat, 8:30-5, and Sun, 9-4. Free admission. Orientation film ticket: $2, adult, $1.50 seniors, $1 youth.

■ A 50 minute, deluxe, narrated riding tour of the Historic City of Natchez departs from the center daily at 10, 11, 1,2, 3, 4. Cost is $15 adult and $7.50 ages 12 and under.
(800) 647-6724 or (601) 446-6345
www.visitnatchez.com

13 GRAND VILLAGE OF THE NATCHEZ INDIANS, NAT'L HISTORIC LANDMARK NATCHEZ, MS

The Grand Village site was once inhabited by the Natchez Indians, who lived in the area from c. 700 AD to 1730. They first entered the historical record in 1682, when they were encountered by the La Salle Expedition. French accounts provide a rare glimpse of a ceremonial mound-building culture, whose ruler was called the "Great Sun." The 128 acre site has three ceremonial mounds; both the Great Sun Mound and Temple Mound were excavated by archaeologists and then rebuilt. There is a an accredited museum; reconstructed house; nature trail; and a visitor center with a gift shop featuring Native American crafts.

■ Open daily. Mon-Sat, 9-5, and Sun, 1:30-5. Free admission. (601) 446-6502
www.mdah.state.mus.us
www.cr.nps.gov/NR/travel/mounds

14 NATCHEZ NATIONAL HISTORICAL PARK NATCHEZ, MS

The National Park Service preserves three important sites in Natchez: the Melrose estate, an 1845 Greek Revival mansion with many original furnishings and outbuildings; the William Johnson House, the 1841 home of a free African-American barber, businessman and slave holder; and Fort Rosalie, the site of the first European fort, located on the grounds of the Rosalie Mansion. The William Johnson House has a visitor center and bookstore, where his diary, *William Johnson's Natchez,* may be purchased.

■ Melrose is open daily, 8:30-5. Guided tours every hour from 9-4. Admission: $8 adult, $4 seniors, $4 ages 6-17. (601) 446-5790

■ William Johnson House is open Thurs-Sun, 9-4:30. Free admission (601) 445-5345
www.nps.gov/natc

15 ELLICOTT HILL—NAT'L HISTORIC LANDMARK—NATCHEZ, MS

Meriwether Lewis was trained in the use of surveying equipment by Andrew Ellicott, who lived in Lancaster, Pennsylvania in 1803. In 1797 he lived in Natchez. Following orders from President George Washington, he raised the flag of the United States for the first time at this house on the hill, establishing the boundary line between the United States and Spanish Louisiana. The house is currently undergoing restoration and is not open for tours.
(800) 647-6724 or (601) 446-6345
www.visitnatchez.com

16 ROSALIE MANSION—NATIONAL HISTORIC LANDMARK—NATCHEZ, MS

Tours of the c.1820-22 mansion and its gardens are available daily every hour from 9-4:30.

■ House and garden tour tickets are $8 adults and $4 children. Garden tour tickets are $3.
(601) 445-4555 www.rosaliemansion.com

17 KING'S TAVERN—NATCHEZ, MS

Located in historic downtown Natchez, this popular restaurant was built in 1769, The oldest building in Natchez, it has ghosts as well as steaks and seafood. Full service bar and Wi-Fi hot spot. Take out is available.

■ Reservations are not required, but are suggested. Open nightly. (601) 446-8845
http://myweb.cableone.net/kingstavern

18 UNDER-THE-HILL SALOON—NATCHEZ

The saloon is a popular destination for tourists from all around the world. Under-the-Hill was once a notorious entertainment and vice district on the Mississippi River. The building was built in the late 1700's or early 1800's, and has seen many uses; it is located directly on the riverfront. Sometimes piano or jazz music. Mark Twain guest house available above the bar.

■ (601) 446-8023
www.underthehillsaloon.com

19 HISTORIC JEFFERSON COLLEGE WASHINGTON, MS

The first educational institution in Mississippi Territory, incorporated in 1802, the college is the site where Aaron Burr was arraigned for treason under an oak tree in February, 1806; the local grand jury dismissed the charges.

■ Open daily. Buildings, Mon-Sat, 9-5 and Sun, 1-5. Grounds open sunup-sundown.
(601) 442-2901 www.mdah.state.ms

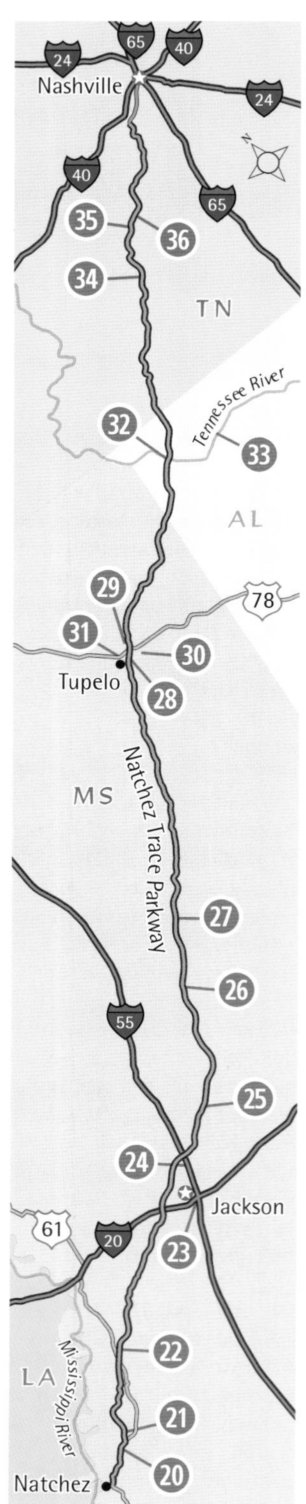

Natchez Trace Parkway

20 EMERALD MOUND
(10.3 MILEPOST)
From milepost 10.3 on Natchez Trace Parkway turn north onto State Route 553. Go 1/8 mile. Bear northwest on Emerald Mound Road. Go 0.8 mile to the mound.

21 MOUNT LOCUST
(15.5 MILEPOST)
From milepost 15.3 on Natchez Trace turn west on local road to Mount Locust.

22 SUNKEN TRACE
(41.5 MILEPOST)
At milepost 41.5 on Natchez Trace.

23 MISSISSIPPI MUSEUM NATURAL SCIENCE–JACKSON
2148 Riverside Drive.
From I-55 Exit 96B go east 1/4 mile on Lakeland Dr. Turn south on Riverside Park Circle. Go 0.7 mile. Turn east, then south. Go 0.4 mile to the Museum.

24 MISSISSIPPI CRAFTS CENTER
(102.4 MP)
At milepost 102.4 on Natchez Trace Parkway.

25 CYPRESS SWAMP WALKING TRAIL
(122 MILEPOST)
At milepost 122 on Natchez Trace Parkway.

26 KOSCIUSKO MUSEUM AND VISITOR CENTER
(159.7 MP)
At milepost 159.7 on Natchez Trace Parkway.

27 FRENCH CAMP
(180.7 MILEPOST)
At milepost 180.7 on Natchez Trace Parkway.

28 CHICKASAW VILLAGE SITE
(261.8 MILEPOST)
At milepost 261.8 on Natchez Trace Parkway.

29 NATCHEZ TRACE PARKWAY VISITOR CENTER
TUPELO MS
(266 MILEPOST)
300 West Main Street.
At milepost 266 on Natchez Trace Parkway turn east onto Rte 178 (McCullough Blvd). Go 1.7 miles. Take Exit for US 45. Go southeast 1.3 miles. Take Jefferson St Exit. Go west onto US 278 (Main St). Go 0.7 mile to the Visitor Center.

NATCHEZ TRACE PARKWAY AND TRAIL

The Natchez Trace Parkway, a National Scenic Byway, extends 444 miles. The Natchez Trace National Scenic Trail has 63 miles of hiking trails and campsites in four areas along the Parkway.

- National Park Service Visitor Center, Tupelo (800) 305-7417 or (662) 680-4025 www.nps.gov/natr (Parkway) www.nps.gov/natt (Trail) www.byways.org (biking)
- Tourist info: (866) 872-2356 www.scenictrace. com
- In case of emergency call (800) 300-PARK (7275)

Natchez Trace Locator Map

30 ELVIS PRESLEY BIRTHPLACE HOME AND MUSEUM
TUPELO MS
306 Elvis Presley Drive.
At milepost 266 on Natchez Trace Parkway turn east onto Rte 178 (McCullough Blvd). Go 1.7 miles. Take Exit for US 45. Go southeast 1.3 miles. Take Jefferson St Exit. Go east onto US 278 (Main St). Go 0.8 mile. Turn north onto Elvis Presley Dr. Go 0.2 mile to the Birthplace.

31 TUPELO BUFFALO PARK AND ZOO
TUPELO MS
2272 North Coley Road.
At milepost 266 on Natchez Trace Parkway turn west onto Rte 178 (McCullough Blvd). Go 2.7 miles to the Buffalo Park at Coley Road.

32 COLBERT FERRY
(327.3 MILEPOST)
CHEROKEE AL
From milepost 327.3 on Natchez Trace Parkway, just east of the Tennessee River, turn south onto County Road 2. Go 0.1 mile. Turn northeast onto County Road 186. Go 0.1 mile to the Ferry.

33 FLORENCE MOUND AND MUSEUM
FLORENCE AL
1028 South Court St.
From milepost 327.3 on Natchez Trace Parkway, just east of the Tennessee River, turn south onto County Road 2. Go south, then east for 11 miles. Road changes name to County Road 2. Continue east for 3.5 miles.. Go south then east on Rte 20 for 2.2 miles. Turn south on Court St. Go 0.2 mile to the Mound.

34 MERIWETHER LEWIS GRAVESITE
(385.9 MILEPOST)
At milepost 385.9 on Natchez Trace Parkway.

35 OLD TRACE
(403.7 MP)
At milepost 403.7 on Natchez Trace Parkway.

36 GORDON HOUSE AND FERRY
(407.7 MILEPOST)
From milepost 407.7 turn west on Old State Route 50 (Webster Road). Go 0.3 miles to the House at Duck River.

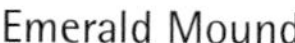
Emerald Mound

Kosciusko Visitor Center

Natchez Trace Parkway

Natchez Trace: Natchez to Nashville

20 EMERALD MOUND (10.3 MILEPOST) NATIONAL HISTORIC LANDMARK

Emerald Mound, covering 8 acres, is one of the largest mounds in North America. The ceremonial temple mound was used by the Natchez Indians between 1250-1600 AD, before they moved to the Grand Village site in Natchez. The mound measures 770 x 435 ft x 35 ft high. A trail leads to the top.

■ Open daily. Free. www.mdah.state.ms.us www.cr.nps.gov/NR/travel/mounds

21 MOUNT LOCUST (15.5 MILEPOST)

Mount Locust is one of the oldest buildings in Mississippi, built c. 1780; restored to its period as a 1820's frontier home and traveler's inn, or "stand." More than 50 stands once operated on the Trace. Boatmen would take cargo down the Mississippi on flatboats, and travel back north on the Trace, mostly by walking. Mount Locust's slave burial ground is nearby.

■ Open daily dawn to dusk. No fees.

22 SUNKEN TRACE (41.5 MILEPOST)

You can walk on the Sunken Trace, a portion of the trail that has been worn 20 feet deep in the soft loess soil, from countless numbers of travelers and horses passing through.

23 MISSISSIPPI MUSEUM OF NATURAL SCIENCE–JACKSON MS

Life-size dioramas, an aquarium, greenhouse, and other exhibits showcase the many different habitats found in Mississippi. Over 2.5 miles of walking trails through a 300 acre natural area.

■ Open daily. Mon-Fri, 8-5; Sat 9-5, Sun 1-5. Admission: $5 adults, $4 seniors, $3 ages 3-18. (601) 354-7303 www.mdwfp.com

24 MISSISSIPPI CRAFTS CENTER (102.4 MP)

Located in a dog trot cabin, the Crafts Center features work of the highest quality, including Choctaw Indian cane baskets, and other crafts both traditional and modern from the Craftsmen's Guild of Mississippi.

■ Open daily, 9-5. Free. (601) 856-7546 www.mscraftsmensguild.org

25 CYPRESS SWAMP WALKING TRAIL (122 MILEPOST)

A favorite with visitors; the boardwalk trail through the water tupelo, bald cypress swamp is a 20 minutes walk.

26 KOSCIUSKO MUSEUM AND VISITOR CENTER (159.7 MILEPOST)

Oprah Winfrey was born in Kosciusko, named for the Polish General who volunteered his services during the American Revolution. There is an Oprah Winfrey Heritage Trail, and an annual Natchez Trace Festival on the last Saturday in April. The town is one of the oldest on the Trace, and is known for its historic painted homes.

■ (662) 289-2981 www.kosckiuskotourism.com

27 FRENCH CAMP (180.7 MILEPOST)

The Natchez Trace Historic Village is located here at the French Camp Academy boarding school for young people. Homemade bread, soup and sandwiches and desserts are served at the Council House Cafe. French Camp has the only Bed and Breakfast on the Trace.

■ Cafe open Mon-Sat, 10:30-2:30. Take out orders welcome. Call (662) 547-9860. www.frenchcamp.org

28 CHICKASAW VILLAGE SITE (261.8 MP)

Exhibits and a nature trail at the Chickasaw village site. The Chickasaw Council House (milepost 251.1) is the site of Pontotoc, capital of the Chickasaw Nation in the 1820's. The tribe, located in Oklahoma, has recently partnered with the Archaeological Conservancy to preserve another old village site on the Trace. www.chickasaw.net

29 NATCHEZ TRACE PARKWAY VISITOR CENTER–TUPELO, MS (270 MILEPOST)

National Park Service headquarters for the Natchez Trace Parkway and Trail. A 12 minute film about the Natchez Trace is available upon request. Bookstore and gift shop. Visitor information.

■ Open daily 9-5. (800) 305-7417 or (662) 680-4025 www.nps.gov/natr

30 ELVIS PRESLEY BIRTHPLACE HOME AND MUSEUM–TUPELO, MS

The birthplace home of Elvis Presley still stands near a museum dedicated to his memory.

■ Open Mon-Sat, May-Sept, 9-5:30; Oct-Apr. 9-5. Sundays 1-5 year round. Admission: House, $2.50, adult, $1.50 child. Museum, $6 adult, $3 child. Combined admission, $7/$3.50 (662) 841-1245 www.elvispresleybirthplace.com

31 TUPELO BUFFALO PARK AND ZOO

The Buffalo Park and Zoo has over 100 buffalo, including a white buffalo named "Tukota," in honor of the Sioux who consider a white buffalo to be sacred. Annual Native American Pow Wow in mid September.

■ Open daily. Call for hours. Admission: $10 adults, $8 seniors, $8 ages 1-12; $25 family. $2 Bison bus or trolley rides. (662) 844-8709 or (866) 27BISON www.tupelobuffalopark.com

32 COLBERT FERRY (327.3 MILEPOST)

George Colbert, a mixed-blood Chief of the Chickasaw, operated a ferry across the Tennessee River in the early 1800's. It is now a ranger station and bike-only campground with restrooms, picnic area, boat launch.

33 FLORENCE MOUND AND MUSEUM FLORENCE, ALABAMA

The Tennessee River Valley's largest temple mound, "Wawmanona" dates to c. 500 AD. The museum has an extensive collection of prehistoric Indian artifacts, dating back 10,000 years. Annual festival in September.

■ Open Tues-Sat, 10-4. Admission $2. adults, 50¢ students. (206) 760-6427 www.flo-tour.org

34 MERIWETHER LEWIS GRAVESITE MONUMENT (385.9 MP)

The monument and an interpretive center mark the lonely spot where Meriwether Lewis died under mysterious circumstances on October 11, 1809. He was 35 years old. See "America 200 Years Ago," pages 214-215.

35 OLD TRACE (403.7 MILEPOST)

This portion of the original Trace is a 2000 foot section that the modern visitor may walk on. Over 8000 years old, the trace is an ancient Indian and game trail to salt licks in Tennessee.

36 GORDON HOUSE AND FERRY (407.7 MILEPOST)

The Gordon House was the first brick home in the area when it was built in 1818. John and Dorothea Gordon operated a ferry across the Duck River for many years, starting in 1801. John Gordon was awarded 640 acres of land for his military service in Indian campaigns. www.gordonhouse.50megs.com

Nashville

Memphis Monorail
Mud Island River Park

Memphis

Spanish Explorers Exhibit, Mississippi River Museum
Mud Island River Park

Nashville to Memphis

10

37 THE HERMITAGE
NASHVILLE TN

4580 Rachel's Lane.

From I-40 Exit 221 go 0.3 mile north on Old Hickory Boulevard (State Route 45). Turn right (east) onto Rachel's Lane. Turn left (north) onto local road. Go 0.1 mile to the Hermitage.

TENNESSEE STATE
MUSEUM
NASHVILLE TN

506 Deaderick Street.

From I-40 West Exit 209A or from I-40 East Exit 209B; go east on Church Street for 0.7 mile. Turn left (north) onto 5th Avenue. Go three blocks. The museum is on the left between Union and Deaderick Streets.

MISSISSIPPI RIVER
MUSEUM
MEMPHIS TN

125 North Front Street.

From I-40 West Exit 1A turn right (west) onto Winchester Avenue. Go 0.2 mile. Turn left (south) onto North Front Street. Go 0.3 mile to the Mississippi River Museum.

MUD ISLAND RIVER PARK
MEMPHIS TN

Mud Island Drive.

From I-40 West Exit 1A turn right (west) onto Winchester Avenue. Go one block. Turn right (north) onto Main Street. Go 0.3 mile. Turn left (west) onto Auction Avenue. Turn left (south) onto Island Drive.

METAL MUSEUM
MEMPHIS TN

375 Metal Museum Drive.

From I-55 Exit 12C go south on Metal Museum Drive for 0.2 mile. Turn right (west) on Metal Museum Drive. Go 0.2 mile to the Metal Museum.

NEW MADRID
HISTORICAL MUSEUM
NEW MADRID MO

1 Main Street.

From I-55 Exit 44 turn right (east) onto I-55 Bus (US61/US62). Go 1.9 miles northeast. Turn left (east) onto Mill Street. Go 1.1 miles. Turn right (south) onto Main Street. Go two blocks to the Museum.

MISSISSIPPI RIVER
SCENIC OVERLOOK
NEW MADRID MO

From I-55 Exit 44 turn right (east) onto I-55 Bus (US61/US62). Go 1.9 miles northeast. Turn left (east) onto Mill Street. Go 1.1 miles. Turn right (south) onto Main Street. Go three blocks to Levee Road. The Scenic Overlook is reached by a boardwalk extending 60 yards south to the river bank.

The Hermitage
The Hermitage Foundation

Mississippi River Walk
Mud Island River Park

New Madrid Museum

Nashville, Memphis & New Madrid

 37 THE HERMITAGE. HOME OF PRESIDENT ANDREW JACKSON, NATIONAL HISTORIC LANDMARK—NASHVILLE TN

Andrew Jackson, a frontier lawyer and land speculator, was the first American president to come from an ordinary background. The original cabins where he and his wife Rachel lived are still located here. Known as "Old Hickory" he won fame as a General in the War of 1812 when he defeated the British at the Battle of New Orleans. In 1828 Jackson became the first President to be elected from a state west of the Appalachian Mountains; he served two terms as the 7th President of the United States.

The mansion has been restored to its 1837 appearance. 44 slaves worked on the 1,000 acre cotton plantation. Seasonal tours of the grounds included in the admission price are: Hermitage Garden and the Jacksons' tomb; Workyard and Farm; and Archaeological Sites. Inquire as to the daily schedule. Horse drawn wagon tours, which take half an hour, are available from April to October. The Andrew Jackson Visitor Center has an orientation film, exhibits, and a bookstore. The center's Cafe Monell serves southern style food.

■ Open daily, 9-5 except Christmas, Thanksgiving and third week in January. Grounds open until 6. Admission: $12 adults, $11 seniors, $11 ages 13-18, $5 ages 6-12; children 5 and under free; $34 family pass.

■ Wagon tours: $6 per person; children ages 5 and under are free.

(615) 889-2941 x 220 (ticket office)
www.thehermitage.com

 38 TENNESSEE STATE MUSEUM NASHVILLE TN

The Tennessee State Museum is one of the largest state museums in the country. It has one of the country's best Civil War collections. Its Prehistoric and Native American exhibits are extensive.Other exhibits cover the Age of Jackson; and the Frontier, Antebellum and Reconstruction Periods. The Military Museum located across the street features the Spanish-American War to the end of WWII.

■ Open Tues-Sat, 10-5. Sun, 1-5. Closed Mon. (Military Museum is also closed on Sun.) Free.

(615) 741-2692 www.tnmuseum.org

 39 MISSISSIPPI RIVER MUSEUM MEMPHIS, TENNESSEE

Eighteen galleries tell the story of life on the Lower Mississippi: exploration and settlement; transportation on the Mississippi; riverfolk/theater of disasters; river engineering; civil war; delta music; river room; and changing exhibits.

■ Open early April-Oct. 31st. Closed Mondays. Hours: Apr-May, 10-5; last wkd in May to 1st wkd in Sept, 10-6; early Sept-Oct, 10-5. Last admission is one hour prior to closing. Museum admission includes roundtrip monorail ride and guided river walk tour: $8 adults, $6 seniors, $5 ages 5-12. Roundtrip monorail ride is $2.

(800) 507-6507 or (901) 576-7241
www.mississippirivermuseum.org

 40 MUD ISLAND RIVER PARK MEMPHIS, TENNESSEE

The Swiss-made monorail travels 1/3 of a mile across the harbor, at a speed of about 7 mph, providing great views of Memphis, the river, and Mud Island River Park. The monorail ride and a guided River Walk Tour are included in the price of admission to the museum.

The extraordinary River Walk is a five block long representation of the lower Mississippi River from Cairo, Illinois to New Orleans, Louisiana. Each 30 inches represents one mile on the river, for a total of 1,000 miles. Along the way, exhibits interpret the river's history and geography. The walk ends at the "Gulf of Mexico" a one acre enclosure, where visitors can float around in pedal boats, or paddle Canoes and kayaks in the calm waters of the harbor; bikes may also be rented at Mud Island.

■ General admission to the park is free. Pedal boats: $1 per ½ hour per person. Canoe rental, $20/hour; kayak rental $15/hour and up; bike rental, $10/2 hours.

(800) 507-6507 or (901) 576-7241
www.mississippirivermuseum.org

 41 METAL MUSEUM—MEMPHIS, TN

The only museum in America devoted to fine metalwork. The Metal Museum's permanent collection has more than 3000 objects. There are picnic tables at the River Bluff Pavillion overlooking the river. The bluff is the site of Fort Pickering (1803-10) where Meriwether Lewis spent some of the last days of his life. Ancient Indian mounds are in nearby DeSoto Park.

The Metal Museum is located on a high bluff just south of Interstate 55. State highway 78/178 follows the general route of the old Chickasaw Trace which Lewis' party took on their fateful journey down to the Natchez Trace near Tupelo, Mississippi.

■ Open Tues-Sat, 10-5; Sun, 12-5. Closed Mondays, Easter, Thanksgiving, last week of Dec. Admission: $4 adults, $3 seniors, $2 students, $2 ages 5-12; $10 family.

 42 NEW MADRID HISTORICAL MUSEUM NEW MADRID, MISSOURI

The great New Madrid Earthquakes of 1811-12 centered in this tiny town near the junction of the Ohio and Mississippi Rivers. Some of the quakes are thought to have reached a magnitude of 8.0 on the Richter scale. The Mississippi River ran backwards for a while, and the quake was felt all over the eastern United States. New Madrid's motto is "It's Our Fault!" There is a seismograph in the museum which gives evidence of continuing activity along the New Madrid fault.

American settlement began in 1789 when Revolutionary War veteran George Morgan established a colony under Spanish rule, and named it New Madrid. Located in a former saloon, the museum has Native American and prehistoric artifacts, Civil War, and other exhibits.

■ Open daily. Mon-Sat, 9-4. Sun, 12-4. Last wkd in May to 1st wkd in Sept, hours extend to 5 PM. Admission: $2.50 adults, $2 seniors, $1.50 ages 6-12.

(573) 748-5944 www.new-madrid.mo.us

 43 MISSISSIPPI RIVER SCENIC OVERLOOK NEW MADRID, MISSOURI

Only three minutes from the Interstate, the Mississippi River Observation Deck offers a grand view of eight miles of the river at the New Madrid Bend. Meriwether Lewis spent two days in New Madrid en route to Memphis in 1809.

■ Open daily.

www.new-madrid.mo.us

Region Ten: References

BIOGRAPHY

ANDREW JACKSON: VOLUME ONE; THE COURSE OF AMERICAN EMPIRE 1767-1821
by Robert V. Remini. The Johns Hopkins University Press (1998)

THE HERMITAGE: HOME OF ANDREW JACKSON
by Charles Phillips. Ladies' Hermitage Ass'n (1997)

JACKSON'S WAY: ANDREW JACKSON AND THE PEOPLE OF THE WESTERN WATERS
by John Buchanan. John Wiley & Sons, Inc. (2001)

THE JEFFERSON CONSPIRACIES: A PRESIDENT'S ROLE IN THE ASSASSINATION OF MERIWETHER LEWIS
by David Leon Chandler. Wm. Morrow and Co. (1994)

THE JOURNEY OF CORONADO: PEDRO DE CASTENADA, ET AL.
edited by George Parker Winship. Dover Publ. (1990)

LAFITTE THE PIRATE
by Lyle Saxon. Pelican Publishing Company (1999)

THE MYSTERIOUS DEATH OF MERIWETHER LEWIS
by Ron Burns. St. Martin's Press (1993)

MERIWETHER LEWIS: A BIOGRAPHY
by Richard Dillon. Coward-McCann, Inc. (1965)

THE OUTLAW YEARS: THE HISTORY OF THE LAND PIRATES OF THE NATCHEZ TRACE
by Robert M. Coates. Univ. of Nebraska Press (1986)

THE PASSIONS OF ANDREW JACKSON
by Andrew Burstein. Alfred A. Knopf (2003)

PEDRO VIAL AND THE ROADS TO SANTA FE
by Noel M. Loomis and Abraham P. Nasitir. University of Oklahoma Press (1967)

THE PIRATES LAFITTE: THE TREACHEROUS WORLD OF THE CORSAIRS OF THE GULF
by William C. Davis. Harcourt, Inc. (2005)

SUICIDE OR MURDER? THE STRANGE DEATH OF GOVERNOR MERIWETHER LEWIS
by Vardis Fisher. Swallow Press and Ohio University Press (1993)

WILLIAM JOHNSON'S NATCHEZ: THE ANTE-BELLUM DIARY OF A FREE NEGRO
edited by William Ransom Hogan and Edwin Adams Davis. Louisiana State University Press (1993)

HISTORY

THE AMERICAN UNION AND THE PROBLEM OF NEIGHBORHOOD: THE UNITED STATES AND THE COLLAPSE OF THE SPANISH EMPIRE 1783-1829
by James E. Lewis Jr. University of North Carolina Press (1998)

AMERICA'S FIRST WORLD WAR: THE FRENCH AND INDIAN WAR, 1754-1763
by Timothy J. Todish. Purple Mountain Press (2002)

THE BATTLE OF NEW ORLEANS: ANDREW JACKSON AND AMERICA'S FIRST MILITARY VICTORY
by Robert V. Remini. Penguin Books (2001)

BORDERLAND IN RETREAT: FROM SPANISH LOUISIANA TO THE FAR SOUTHWEST
by Abraham P. Nasitir. University of New Mexico Press (1976)

THE CABILDO ON JACKSON SQUARE: THE COLONIAL PERIOD 1723-1803. THE AMERICAN PERIOD 1803 TO THE PRESENT
by Samuel Wilson, Jr. and Leonard V. Huber. Pelican Publishing Company (1998)

THE CAUSES OF THE WAR OF 1812: NATIONAL HONOR OR NATIONAL INTEREST
edited by Bradford Perkins. Krieger Publ. Co. (1983)

THE DEVIL'S BACKBONE: THE STORY OF THE NATCHEZ TRACE
by Jonathan Daniels. Mc-Graw-Hill Book Co. (1962)

FATHER LOUIS HENNEPIN'S DESCRIPTION OF LOUISIANA: BY CANOE TO THE UPPER MISSISSIPPI IN 1680
by Louis Hennepin. Univ. of Minnesota Press (1938)

THE FORT OF NATCHEZ AND THE COLONIAL ORIGINS OF MISSISSIPPI
by Jack D. Elliott. Jr. Eastern National (1998)

FLOOD TIDE OF EMPIRE: SPAIN AND THE PACIFIC NORTHWEST 1543-1819
by Warren L. Cook. Yale University Press (1973)

THE FRENCH AND INDIAN 1754-1763: THE IMPERIAL STRUGGLE FOR NORTH AMERICA
by Seymour I. Schwartz. Castle Books (1994)

FRONTIERS IN CONFLICT: THE OLD SOUTHWEST, 1795-1830
by Thomas D. Clark and John D. W. Guice, University of New Mexico Press (1989)

JEFFERSON & SOUTHWESTERN EXPLORATION: THE FREEMAN & CUSTIS ACCOUNTS OF THE RED RIVER EXPEDITION OF 1806
edited by Dan L. Flores. Univ. of Oklahoma Press (1984)

JEFFERSON'S WESTERN EXPLORATIONS: DISCOVERIES MADE IN EXPLORING THE MISSOURI, RED RIVER AND WASHITA BY CAPTAINS LEWIS AND CLARK, DOCTOR SIBLEY, AND WILLIAM DUNBAR, AND COMPILED BY THOMAS JEFFERSON; THE NATCHEZ EXPEDITION, 1806
edited by Doug Erickson, Jeremy Skinner, and Paul Merchant. Arthur H. Clark Company (2004)

HISTORY

THE LOUISIANA PURCHASE
by Carl J. Richard. Center for Louisiana Studies (1995)

THE NATCHEZ INDIANS
by Jim Barnett, Mississippi Department of Archives and History (1998)

NATCHEZ TRACE: TWO CENTURIES OF TRAVEL
by R. C. Gildart. Amer. & World Geographic Publ. (1996)

MISSISSIPPI VALLEY BEGINNINGS: AN OUTLINE OF THE EARLY HISTORY OF THE EARLIER WEST
by Henry E. Chambers. C. P. Putnam's Sons (1922)

THE OPENING OF THE MISSISSIPPI: A STRUGGLE FOR SUPREMACY IN THE AMERICAN INTERIOR
by Frederic Austin Ogg. Greenwood Press Publ. (1969)

THE SPANISH FRONTIER IN NORTH AMERICA
by David J. Weber. Yale University Press (1922)

SPANISH WAR VESSELS ON THE MISSISSIPPI 1792-1796
by Abraham P. Nasitir. Yale University Press (1968)

TRAVEL, TRADE, AND TRAVAIL: SLAVERY ON THE OLD NATCHEZ TRACE
by Kelly Obernuefemann and Lynell Thomas. Eastern National (2001)

THE WAR OF 1812
by Henry Adams. Cooper Square Press (1999)

THE WAR OF 1812
by Carl Benn. Osprey Publishing (2002)

THE WAR OF 1812
by John K. Mahon. Da Capo Press, Inc. (1991)

A WILDERNESS SO IMMENSE: THE LOUISIANA PURCHASE AND THE DESTINY OF AMERICA
by Jon Kukla. Alfred A. Knopf (2003)

MISCELLANEOUS

BICYCLING THE NATCHEZ TRACE: A GUIDE TO THE NATCHEZ TRACE PARKWAY AND NEARBY SCENIC ROUTES
by Glen Wanner. Pennywell Press (2002)

GUIDE TO THE NATCHEZ TRACE PARKWAY
by F. Lynne Bachelder. Menasha Ridge Press (2005)

OLD NEW ORLEANS: WALKING TOURS OF THE FRENCH QUARTER
by Stanley Clisby Arthur. Pelican Publishing Co. (1995)

Headwaters Region

This map of the Three Forks of the Missouri River is one of the most complex and interesting map areas on the trail. Forty campsites are in the headwaters area.

The Jefferson, Madison and Gallatin Rivers are highlighted with blue lines. The expedition followed the Jefferson fork, and then the Beaverhead fork of the Jefferson River, to the modern town of Dillon, where they proceeded by land to Lemhi Pass. Their route by water is shown by yellow dots. Red triangles mark campsites. Their route on land is shown by the yellow and red dashed line. From Dillon to the Clark Canyon Reservoir, the site of Camp Fortunate, they followed the route of Interstate 15. Clark's return party in 1806 followed the route of Interstate 90 in the Bozeman area.

Campsites Table: A Geographic Key to Following the Story

How were the locations of the historic campsites determined?

The locations represent the "best guesses" of trail experts who consulted the journals, studied historic and modern maps, and walked and flew over the area. In creating the table we relied primarily on information supplied by Bob Bergantino, the leading trail map expert. His campsite placements are in general agreement with the work of Martin Plamandon II, author of the three volume set, *Lewis and Clark Trail Maps.* We also consulted Gary Moulton's footnotes found throughout the journals.

Have all the campsites been found?

573 historic campsite locations along the Trail are identified. All of the campsites for parties led by Lewis and/or Clark are in the table. But sometimes, when the expedition split up into smaller parties under other leaders, their acounts do not contain enough geographic information (or the records don't exist) to identify the locations.The exact location of most campsites is an ongoing puzzle for which there will never be complete answers. New findings will continue to appear as local people become more involved in doing research.

The table as a geographic key

The unique feature of this table is that it is organized around the geographic locations of the campsites. All of the campsites used by the expedition's parties while going out, returning, and making side trips are grouped together for a given area.

The campsite numbers run from east to west, starting at the White House and ending at the Pacific Ocean. The numbering system does not indicate the direction in which the party was traveling. This information is in the table.

How do you find the Lewis and Clark stories that go with a particular place?

If you know the names of counties you are interested in, or notice familiar town names in the table, you can locate campsites by searching the columns which list counties and nearest town locations in a region. If you are interested in a general area, go to the regional map and find the campsite numbers, and then use these numbers to search the table.

When you locate the campsite listing, you will find the dates they camped there, and the page and volume numbers for all the journal entries. Since there were six journal writers, and 27 locations were used two or more times, the journal references are complex.

The Journals are on the internet at http://lewisandclarkjournals.unl.edu

The University of Nebraska Press has published the complete Lewis and Clark Journals online. An especially nice feature of the website is that writings by all the journal keepers are grouped together by date, allowing for easy comparison of information. The footnotes, which contain so much valuable and interesting information, are also included. The entries can be printed out. You will need to know the dates the campsite was occupied, because page and volume numbers are not used in the online version. The website offers additional features, including multimedia extras and supplementary text by other writers.

The Trail on the Regional Maps

This is the first time that the Lewis and Clark Trail can be understood in both large and small geographical detail. Our maps are large enough to show both individual campsites, and a broad area surrounding them. The expedition's campsites stretch in a narrow corridor across many states. Our regional maps cross state lines and show where the corridor runs.

There are ten double page regional maps in the book. Nine of the ten maps (Regions 1-9) have campsites. Region 10, from New Orleans to Nashville, has no campsites. This final section concerns the Louisiana Purchase and Meriwether Lewis's death on the Natchez Trace Trail.

Mountains and rivers on the maps

The maps are based on satellite images photographed from space; they show mountains, rivers, forests, other vegetation, or lack of vegetation. Modern highways and towns, campsite locations, and page-referenced local map boxes, are superimposed on the satellite images. The terrain features are vital to understanding the story of the Lewis and Clark Expedition. How can you understand the path of a trail across the mountains if you can't see the mountains on the map? Or follow a river journey?

Montana, the fourth largest state in the nation, has the most number of campsites, 166, or 29% of the trail total. The Yellowstone River which originates in Yellowstone National Park runs northward along US-89 through the mountains, and then heads east along I-90 from Livingston. It is the largest tributary of the Missouri River.

How to Use the Campsite Table

(1) Campsite Number Column

Each campsite location has been given a number, 1 through 572. Letters follow the numbers when the site was used more than once. The 572 locations were used 620 times. 48 were repeat visits.

Campsite numbers are found in the topological maps for Regions 1 through 9. On the maps each campsite is marked by a small red triangle and an accompanying number. These numbers correspond to the numbers in the table.

(2) Group Leader Column

When the entire expedition traveled as a single party, Lewis and Clark are the designated leaders. On many occasions the Corps of Discovery split into smaller parties. Usually there were two groups, one led by Lewis and the other led by Clark. Sometimes small parties were led by one of the Sergeants or others.

(3) Symbol Column

Quick Visual Reference

Shapes indicate the group leader

Meriwether Lewis	■■■
William Clark	●●●
John Ordway	▲
Other	★

Colors indicate direction of the journey

out	■
return	■
side trip	■

(4) Journey Column

The direction of travel is indicated

out	outbound to Pacific Coast
return	return to the East
side trip	local exploration

(5) Date Column

Date or dates the campsite was occupied.

(6) County Column

County the campsite is located in. However, in order to avoid map clutter, counties are not shown on the regional maps.

(7) State Column

State the campsite is located in.

(8) Location Column

The approximate location for each campsite is given. The exact point at which the expedition camped is unknown except for a very few spots. Decades of scholarly research by Bob Bergantino, Martin Plamandon, and others have resulted in "best guesses," that generally are in close agreement with one another to within a few hundred feet. However these exact estimates have not been made public. Plamondon's trail maps do not have "x marks the spot" locations.

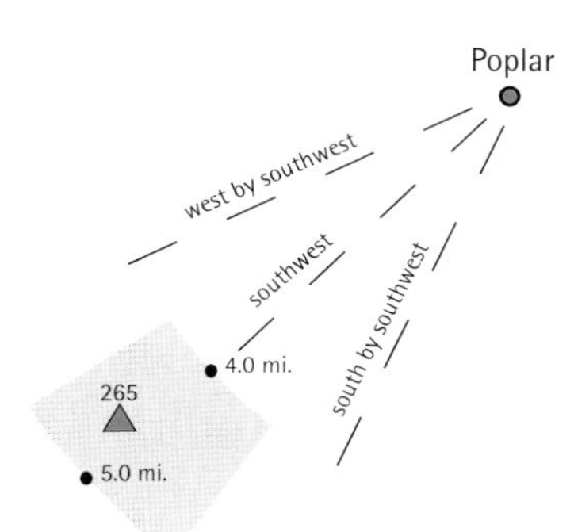

Approximate location of a campsite

Locations in the table are specified to within a half mile. This is intentional. Almost all the campsites are inaccessible to the public—either because they are on private land, or because they are under lakes created by modern dams. In the past, landowners have been troubled by trespassers wishing to explore the encampment sites. Out of respect for their privacy rights, we have decided to give only approximate positions.

How approximate? The extent of approximation is shown in the above example. Campsite #265 is listed as 4.5 miles SW of Poplar, MT. Does this mean #265 is 4.5 miles southwest of Poplar? Not necessarily. The distance is given to the nearest half mile. Therefore the site is between 4.0 and 5.0 miles from Poplar. Also the direction SW is not exact. It only means #265 is closer to southwest than any other compass direction. The neighboring compass directions are west by southwest and south by southwest. This increases inexactness by about another mile. Putting both together; distance is uncertain by about a mile and direction is indefinite by about a mile as illustrated in the gray area. In short, Campsite #286 is somewhere in the gray area.

Trail Reference Points

The reference points for the location of campsites are usually the nearest sizeable towns found in standard maps and atlases. For the parts of the expedition journey that are along rivers (all but a few hundred miles) reference locales are on the same side of the river as the campsite because bridges across the rivers are often far distant from them. In unpopulated areas of Montana and Idaho, road junctions may be the reference sites. In some cases the confluence of large rivers are the reference points because of their historic and geographic significance.

For the journey between Letart Falls, Ohio and Fort Massac, Illinois, Lewis made no journal entries. So campsite positions have been estimated on a prorated daily travel basis, (total distance divided by number of travel days).

(9) Journals Column

The journal citations in the table bring to life the geography of the trail in the words of Lewis, Clark, and other members of the Corps of Discovery. Perhaps equally remarkable as the physical rigors of the journey is that by the flickering light of the campfire, they recorded the days events, characterized and mapped the geography, entered navigational astronomic measurements, described new species of plants and animals, and recounted the ways of the native peoples.

Over the years many versions of the Lewis and Clark journals have been published. The most authoritative is the 13 volume edition published by University of Nebraska Press, *The Journals of the Lewis and Clark Expedition*, edited by Professor Gary Moulton. The last column of the table lists the volumes and pages of the Moulton edition related to each campsite occupancy; some 1,891 reference citations are listed in all.

The Journal Keepers

In addition to the journals kept by Captains Lewis and Clark, the journals of four other members of the expedition are published in the Moulton edition. The journal keepers are: Sergeants Charles Floyd, Patrick Gass and John Ordway; and Private Joseph Whitehouse. Other writers are known to have kept journals, but their journals are lost.

Each of the published journals has a unique contribution to make to the story of the expedition. The University of Nebraska Press has made all of them available online. The history of the actual journals is a matter of some uncertainty. There are no journal entries written by Meriwether Lewis for months at a time. It is likely that one or more of his journals were lost en route. Anytime there is a gap in the records it is a matter of speculation whether a journal was lost or never written.

Clark wrote entries for all but ten of the expedition's 863 days. Entries written by Lewis cover 441 days. Clark made almost all of the expedition's maps. Lewis recorded much of the scientific data. After Lewis's death in 1809, Clark asked Nicholas Biddle of Philadelphia to edit the journals, which were published in 1814. The scientific data was first published in 1893.

Sergeant Floyd's journal is the shortest, due to his untimely death from a ruptured appendix on August 20, 1804 near present day Sioux City, Iowa. Floyd, the only man to die on the expedition, was replaced by Sergeant Patrick Gass, whose journal was the first to be published in 1807. Sergeant John Ordway's journals have entries for every one of the 863 days. Private John Whitehouse's journal begins at the departure from St. Charles and goes through to the Columbia River; a paraphrased copy of a lost journal covers a few more months.

The Lewis and Clark Journals edited by Gary Moulton will remain an enduring landmark in American book publication.

There are four versions available through the University of Nebraska Press. The definitive paperback edition lacks Volume 1, the large atlas, shown in the photo. The abridged one volume edition is available both in paperback for $15 and hardcover for $29.95. The journals and other materials are available online in the complete definitive edition, without the atlas.

Paperback Edition
The Definitive Journals of Lewis and Clark

Gary E. Moulton, Editor and Thomas W. Dunlay, Assistant Editor, The Nebraska Edition, University of Nebraska Press, 2002-2004. (The volume numbers correspond to the hardcover edition.)

From the Ohio to the Vermillion (Vol 2)
August 30,1803–August 24, 1804
612 pages $24.95 ISBN: 0-8032-8009-2

Up the Missouri to Fort Mandan (Vol 3)
August 25, 1804–April 6, 1805
544 pages $24.95 ISBN: 0-8032-8010-6

From Fort Mandan to Three Forks (Vol 4)
April 7–July 27, 1805
464 pages $24.95 ISBN: 0-8032-8011-4

Through the Rockies to the Cascades (Vol 5)
July 28–November 1, 1805
415 pages $24.95 ISBN: 0-8032-8012-2

Down the Columbia to Fort Clatsop (Vol 6)
November 2, 1805–March 22, 1806
531 pages $24.95 ISBN: 0-8032-8013-0

From the Pacific to the Rockies (Vol 7)
March 23–June 9, 1806
383 pages, $24.95 ISBN: 0-8032-8014-9

Over the Rockies to St. Louis (Vol 8)
June 10–September 26, 1806
456 pages $24.95 ISBN: 0-8032-8015-7

The Journals of John Ordway (Vol 9)
May 14, 1804–September 23, 1806
and Charles Floyd, May 14–August 18, 1804
419 pages $24.95 ISBN: 0-8032-8021-1

The Journal of Patrick Gass (Vol 10)
May 14, 1804–September 23, 1806
300 pages $24.95 ISBN: 0-8032-8022-X

The Journals of Joseph Whitehouse (Vol 11)
May 14, 1804–April 2, 1806
459 pages $24.95 ISBN: 0-8032-8023-8

Herbarium of the Lewis and Clark Expedition (Vol 12)
356 pages $29.95 ISBN: 0-8032-8032-7

Comprehensive Index (Vol 13)
174 pages $24.95 ISBN: 0-8032-8033-5

The Lewis & Clark Journals

One Volume Abridgement
The Lewis and Clark Journals:
An American Epic of Discovery

by Meriwether Lewis, William Clark and Members of the Corps of Discovery
Abridgement of The Nebraska Edition
Edited and introduction by Gary E. Moulton, Univ of Nebraska Press, 2003

Hardcover 413 pages $29.95
ISBN: 0-8032-2950-X

Paperback 497 pages $15.00
ISBN: 0-8032-8039-4

Hard Cover Edition
Journals of the Lewis and Clark Expedition

Atlas of the Lewis and Clark Expedition
14" x 20 " hardcover edition 186 pages
$200.00 ISBN: 0-8032-2861-9 (Vol 1)
The other volumes in the series are $95 each.

Online Edition
Lewis and Clark Journals and related materials

http://lewisandclarkjournals.unl.edu

Other Books & Resources

Letters of the Lewis and Clark Expedition with Related Documents 1783–1854
Edited by Donald Jackson, University of Illinois Press, boxed two volume set, 2nd edition, 1979.
806 pages $100.00 ISBN: 0-2520-0697-6
Absolutely essential addition to any library which contains the complete journals edition.

Original Journals of the Lewis and Clark Expedition, 8 volume set
Edited by Reuben Thwaites, with illustrations by Karl Bodmer. Digital Scanning, 2001, 3070 pages. $219.95
ISBN: 1-5821-8651-0
Reprinted from the 1903-04 classic edition based on the original journals published in 1814, with extensive footnotes. Includes an Atlas and CD-ROM version of the Atlas.
www.digitalscanning.com

Explorations Into the World of Lewis and Clark: 194 Essays from the Pages of We Proceeded On
Edited by Robert Saindon, Digital Scanning, 2003.
Vol 1 paperback ISBN 1582187614
Vol 2 paperback ISBN 1582187630
Vol 3 paperback ISBN 1582187657
Paperback, $24.95; Hardcover, $44.95
Best of the essays from the quarterly journal of the Lewis and Clark Trail Heritage Foundation. These essays are great reading material for anyone interested in learning more about the trail and the people who have been the "keepers of the story and stewards of the trail."

Map posters by Bob Bergantino. Montana Campsites and Portage Route maps are $15-17. Available at the Portage Cache Store, Lewis and Clark National Historic Trail Interpretive Center, Great Falls, MT. (406) 453-6248.

Lewis and Clark Trail Maps: A Cartographic Reconstruction, 3 volumes
by Martin Plamondon II, Washington State Univerity Press, 2000-2004. Available in three versions, hardcover, spiral bound and paperback. Prices ranging from $75 to $45 each.
Vol 1: Wood River to Fort Mandan Maps
191 pages ISBN 0-87422-232-X
Vol 2: Fort Mandan to Columbia River Maps
222 pages ISBN: 0-87422-242-7
Vol 3: Columbia to Pacific, Marias and Yellowstone Explorations Maps 237 pages
ISBN 0-87422-265-6
Martin Plamondon used William Clark's maps and notes to show old river beds on modern maps. Campsites are shown, with quotations from the journals. The black and white maps are detailed close ups with elevation lines.

Atlas of Lewis and Clark in Missouri
by James D. Harlan and James M. Denny
University of Missouri Press, Book and Map Edition, 2003 138 pages $59.95
ISBN: 0826214738
Combines early 19th century survey maps with modern cartography to trace the route of Lewis and Clark in Missouri. Campsites are shown.

Chasing Lewis and Clark Across America:
A 21st Century Aviation Adventure
by Ron Lowery and Mary Walker
Windsock Media, 2004
$45.00, ISBN: 0-9749207-1-1
Very interesting landscape photos from the air. DVD behind the scenes is available for $15.00
www.windsockmedia.com

Lewis and Clark Across Missouri
http://lewisclark.geog.missouri.edu

National Geographic Lewis and Clark Journey
www.nationalgeographic.com/
lewisandclark/journey

Lewis and Clark Expedition Campsites

campsite #	group leader (Lewis ■, Clark ■, Ordway ●, Other ▲ ★)		journey (out - black, return - red, side trip - blue)	date	county	state	location	Journals of the Lewis and Clark Expedition U of Nebr Press (Volumes 2-8 Lewis and Clark; Volume 9 Ordway; Floyd; Volume 10 Gass; Volume 11 Whitehouse)
REGION ONE (#1-11)							**East of the Alleghenies**	**Map pages 3-4**
1a	Lewis	■	out	Mar 14 03	Washington	DC	White House	**2**: 3-5
1b	Lewis	■	out	Jun 17 03	Washington	DC	White House	**2**: 3-5
1c	Lewis	■	return	Dec 28 06	Washington	DC	White House	**10**: xv
2	Lewis	■	out	Apr 19 03	Lancaster	PA	Lancaster, Andrew Ellicott House	**2**: 5
3	Lewis	■	out	May 10 03	Philadelphia	PA	Philadelphia PA arsenal, Patterson	**2**: 11
4	Lewis	■	out	Jul 5 03	Frederick	MD	Frederick MD	**2**: 6
5a	Lewis	■	out	Mar 15 03	Jefferson	WV	Harpers Ferry, Armory	**4**: 370, **6**: 441, **7**: 169
5b	Lewis	■	out	Apr 17 03	Jefferson	WV	Harpers Ferry, Armory	**4**: 370, **6**: 441, **7**: 169
5c	Lewis	■	out	Jul 8 03	Jefferson	WV	Harpers Ferry, Armory	**4**: 370, **6**: 441, **7**: 169
6	Lewis	■	out	Jul 9 03	Jefferson	WV	7 mi SW of Harpers Ferry	**2**: 6
7	Lewis	■	out	Jul 10 03	Hampshire	WV	32 mi NW of Charles Town	**2**: 6
8	Lewis	■	out	Jul 11 03	Mineral	WV	19 mi NW of Forks of Cacapon	**2**: 6
9	Lewis	■	out	Jul 12 03	Somerset	PA	37 mi NW of Fort Ashby	**2**: 6
10	Lewis	■	out	Jul 13 03	Fayette	PA	32 mi NW of Somerfield	**2**: 6
11	Lewis	■	out	July 14 03	Allegheny	PA	17 mi N of Brownsville	**2**: 6
REGION TWO (#12-47)							**Pittsburgh to Cincinnati**	**Map pages 24-25**
12a	Lewis	■	out	Jul 15 03	Allegheny	PA	Pittsburgh, 13 mi N of Elizabeth	**2**: 6
12b	Lewis	■	out	Aug 15 03	Allegheny	PA	Pittsburgh, 0.5 mile NE of Fort Pitt Museum	**2**: 6
13	Lewis	■	out	Aug 31 03	Allegheny	PA	Neville Island, 8 miles WNW of Pittsburgh	**2**: 59, 65-66
14	Lewis	■	out	Sep 1 03	Allegheny	PA	opposite Sewickley	**2**: 67-68
15	Lewis	■	out	Sep 2 03	Beaver	PA	2.5 miles N of Aliquippa	**2**: 68-69
16	Lewis	■	out	Sep 3 03	Beaver	PA	3 miles WSW of Monaca	**2**: 70
17	Lewis	■	out	Sep 4 03	Hancock	OH	1 mile ENE of East Liverpool	**2**: 70-72
18	Lewis	■	out	Sep 5 03	Jefferson	OH	2 miles WSW of Toronto	**2**: 72
19	Lewis	■	out	Sep 6 03	Jefferson	OH	4.5 miles SSE of Steubenville	**2**: 72-73
20	Lewis	■	out	Sep 7-8 03	Belmont	WV	Wheeling	**2**: 73-76
21	Lewis	■	out	Sep 9 03	Marshall	WV	1 mile SSE of McMechen	**2**: 76
22	Lewis	■	out	Sep 10 03	Marshall	WV	0.5 mile SW of Kent	**2**: 76-79

Lewis and Clark Expedition Campsites

campsite #	group leader (Lewis ■, Clark ●, Ordway ▲, Other ★)		journey (out - black, return - red, side trip - blue)	date	county	state	location	Journals of the Lewis and Clark Expedition U of Nebr Press (Volumes 2-8 Lewis and Clark; Volume 9 Ordway; Floyd; Volume 10 Gass; Volume 11 Whitehouse)
REGION TWO (#12-47)							**Pittsburgh to Cincinnati**	**Map pages 24-25**
23	Lewis	■	out	Sep 11 03	Washington	OH	New Matamoras	**2**: 79-80
24	Lewis	■	out	Sep 12 03	Pleasants	WV	4 miles WSW of Belmont	**2**: 80
25	Lewis	■	out	Sep 13 03	Washington	OH	Marietta at confluence of Muskingham River	**2**: 80-81
26	Lewis	■	out	Sep 14 03	Washington	OH	Belpre	**2**: 81-82
27	Lewis	■	out	Sep 15 03	Wood	WV	0.5 mile WNW of Belleville	**2**: 82-83
28	Lewis	■	out	Sep 16 03	Jackson	WV	1 mile NW of Ravenswood	**2**: 83
29	Lewis	■	out	Sep 17 03	Meigs	OH	2.5 miles ESE of Saxon	**2**: 83-84
30	Lewis	■	out	Sep 18 03	Mason	WV	1.5 miles ENE of New Haven	**2**: 84-85
31	Lewis	■	out	Sep 19 03	Gallia	OH	estimated, 2 miles N of Cheshire	**2**: 59, 85
32	Lewis	■	out	Sep 20 03	Mason	WV	estimated, Apple Grove	**2**: 59, 85
33	Lewis	■	out	Sep 21 03	Cabell	WV	estimated 4 mi S of Lesage WV	**2**: 59, 85
34	Lewis	■	out	Sep 22 03	Lawrence	OH	estimated, 0.5 mile WSW of Coal Grove	**2**: 59, 85
35	Lewis	■	out	Sep 23 03	Greenup	KY	estimated, 2 miles NNW of Oliver Station	**2**: 59, 85
36	Lewis	■	out	Sep 24 03	Scioto	OH	estimated, 2 miles WSW of Sugar Grove	**2**: 59, 85
37	Lewis	■	out	Sep 25 03	Adams	OH	estimated, 12.5 miles ESE Manchester	**2**: 59, 85
38	Lewis	■	out	Sep 26 03	Brown	OH	estimated, 3 miles ESE of Aberdeen SE	**2**: 59, 85
39	Lewis	■	out	Sep 27 03	Bracken	KY	estimated, 1.5 miles W of Augusta	**2**: 59, 85
40	Lewis	■	out	Sep 28 03	Clermont	OH	estimated, 2.5 miles SSE of Richmond	**2**: 59, 85
41	Lewis	■	out	Sep 29-Oct 5 03	Hamilton	OH	Cincinnati	**2**: 59, 85
42	Lewis	■	out	Oct 6 03	Dearborn	IN	estimated, Aurora	**2**: 59, 85
43	Lewis	■	out	Oct 7 03	Switzerland	IN	estimated, 2 mi W of Big Bone Lick State Park, KY	**2**: 59, 85
44	Lewis	■	out	Oct 8 03	Carroll	KY	estimated, Carrollton	**2**: 59, 85
45	Lewis	■	out	Oct 9 03	Jefferson	IN	estimated, Madison	**2**: 59, 85
46	Lewis	■	out	Oct 10 03	Oldham	KY	estimated, 8 miles NW of La Grange	**2**: 59, 85
47	Lewis/Clark	■●	out	Oct 11-25 03	Clark	IN	Clarksville	**2**: 59, 85
REGION THREE (#48-82)							**Louisville to Wood River Camp**	**Map pages 46-47**
48	Lewis/Clark	■●	out	Oct 26 03	Jefferson	KY	estimated, Louisville	**2**: 59, 85
49	Lewis/Clark	■●	out	Oct 27 03	Meade	KY	estimated, Brandenburg	**2**: 59, 85

CAMP SITES TABLE

Lewis and Clark Expedition Campsites

campsite #	group leader (Lewis ■ Clark ● Ordway ● Other ★)		journey (out - black, return - red, side trip - blue)	date	county	state	location	Journals of the Lewis and Clark Expedition, U of Nebr Press: Volumes 2-8 Lewis and Clark	Volume 9 Ordway; Floyd	Volume 10 Gass	Volume 11 Whitehouse
REGION THREE (#48-82)							**Louisville to Wood River Camp**				**Map pages 46-47**
50	Lewis/Clark	■●	out	Oct 28 03	Crawford	IN	estimated, 2.5 miles SW of Leavenworth	**2**: 59, 85			
51	Lewis/Clark	■●	out	Oct 29 03	Meade	KY	estimated, 2 miles W of Alton	**2**: 59, 85			
52	Lewis/Clark	■●	out	Oct 30 03	Breckenridge	KY	estimated, 3.5 miles WSW of Stephensport	**2**: 59, 85			
53	Lewis/Clark	■●	out	Oct 31 03	Perry	IN	estimated, Tell City	**2**: 59, 85			
54	Lewis/Clark	■●	out	Nov 1 03	Daviess	IN	estimated, 10 miles NNE of Owensboro	**2**: 59, 85			
55	Lewis/Clark	■●	out	Nov 2 03	Daviess	KY	estimated, 10 mi NW of Owensboro	**2**: 59, 85			
56	Lewis/Clark	■●	out	Nov 3 03	Vandenburgh	IN	estimated., Angel Mounds Historic Site	**2**: 59, 85			
57	Lewis/Clark	■●	out	Nov 4 03	Vandenburgh	IN	estimated, Evansville	**2**: 59, 85			
58	Lewis/Clark	■●	out	Nov 5 03	Posey	IN	estimated., 0.5 mile W of West Franklin	**2**: 59, 85			
59	Lewis/Clark	■●	out	Nov 6 03	Union	KY	estimated., 4 miles NNE of Uniontown	**2**: 59, 85			
60	Lewis/Clark	■●	out	Nov 7 03	Union	KY	estimated., 4.5 miles WSW of Sturgis	**2**: 59, 85			
61	Lewis/Clark	■●	out	Nov 8 03	Pope	IL	estimate.d, Golconda	**2**: 59, 85			
62	Lewis/Clark	■●	out	Nov 9 03	Livingston	KY	estimate.d, Smithland	**2**: 59, 85			
63	Lewis/Clark	■●	out	Nov 11-12 03	Massac	IL	Fort Massac State Park, Metropolis	**2**: 59, 85			
64	Lewis/Clark	■●	out	Nov 13 03	Massac	IL	Joppa	**2**: 59, 85			
65	Lewis/Clark	■●	out	Nov 14-19 03	Alexander	IL	junction Ohio and Mississippi Rivers	**2**: 86-94			
66	Lewis/Clark	■●	out	Nov 20 03	Alexander	MO	5.5 miles NNW of Alfalfa Center	**2**: 95-97			
67	Lewis/Clark	■●	out	Nov 21 03	Scott	MO	island; 3 miles ESE of Lusk	**2**: 97-101			
68	Lewis/Clark	■●	out	Nov 22 03	Alexander	IL	1 mile S of Thebes	**2**: 101-105			
69	Lewis/Clark	■●	out	Nov 23 03	Cape Girardeau	MO	Cape Girardeau	**2**: 105-110			
70	Lewis/Clark	■●	out	Nov 24 03	Cape Girardeau	MO	Trail of Tears State Park	**2**: 110-111			
71	Lewis/Clark	■●	out	Nov 25 03	Perry	MO	3.5 miles E of Altenburg; opposite Grand Tower IL	**2**: 111-114			
72	Lewis/Clark	■●	out	Nov 26 03	Perry	MO	2 miles NW of Seventysix	**2**: 114-116			
73	Lewis/Clark	■●	out	Nov 27 03	Perry	MO	4 miles SE of Kaskaskia	**2**: 116-117			
74	Lewis/Clark	■●	out	Nov 28 03	Randolph	IL	2.5 miles N of Kaskaskia	**2**: 117-119			
75	Lewis	■	out	Nov 29-Dec 5 03	Randolph	Il	Fort Kaskaskia	**2**: 118-122			
76	Clark	●	out	Dec 4 03	Monroe	IL	island; 2 miles WSW of Kidd	**2**: 123-124			
77	Clark	●	out	Dec 5 03	Monroe	IL	1 mi SW of Harrisonville	**2**: 124-126			
78	Clark	●	out	Dec 6 03	St. Louis	MO	12 miles NE of Wickes	**2**: 126-127			

Lewis and Clark Expedition Campsites

campsite #	group leader (Lewis ■ Clark ● Ordway ▲ Other ★)		journey (out - black, return - red, side trip - blue)	date	county	state	location	Journals of the Lewis and Clark Expedition U of Nebr Press (Volumes 2-8 Lewis and Clark; Volume 9 Ordway, Floyd; Volume 10 Gass; Volume 11 Whitehouse)
REGION THREE (#48-82)							**Louisville to Wood River Camp**	**Map pages 46-47**
79	Lewis/Clark	■●	out	Dec 7-9 03	St. Clair	IL	Cahokia	**2**: 127-128
80	Lewis/Clark	■●	return	Sep 23 06	St Louis City	MO	St Louis	**8**: 370-371, **9**: 366, **10**: 280
81	Clark	●	out	Dec 10 03	St. Clair	IL	1.5 miles WSW of East St. Louis	**2**: 128-129
82	Clark	●	out	Dec 11 03	Madison	IL	island 4 miles W of Granite City	**2**: 129-130
REGION FOUR (#83-139)							**St Louis to Kansas City**	**Map pages 66-67**
83	Clark	●	out	Dec 12 03-May 13 04	St Charles	MO	5 miles E of West Alton	**2**: 130-214
84	Lewis/Clark	■●	return	Sep 22 06	St. Louis	MO	3 miles N of Spanish Lake	**8**: 369-370, **9**: 366
85	Clark	●	out	May 14 04	St Charles	MO	2 miles SSE of West Alton	**2**: 215-217, 227-229, **9**: 3, **10**: 1-8, **11**: 1-8
86	Clark	●	out	May 15 04	St Charles	MO	4 miles S of Portage des Sioux	**2**: 229-232, **9**: 6, **10**: 8, **11**: 9
87a	Clark	●	out	May 16-20 04	St Charles	MO	St Charles	**2**: 233-244, **9**: 6, **10**: 8, **11**: 9-10
87b	Lewis/Clark	■●	return	Sep 21 06	St Charles	MO	St Charles	**8**: 368-369, **9**: 365
88	Lewis/Clark	■●	out	May 21 04	St. Louis	MO	island; 4 miles SSW of St Charles	**2**: 244-245, **9**: 6, **10**: 8, **11**: 11
89	Lewis/Clark	■●	out	May 22 04	St Charles	MO	10 miles W of Chesterfield	**2**: 245-246, **9**: 7, **10**: 8, **11**: 11
90	Lewis/Clark	■●	out	May 23 04	St Charles	MO	7 miles NNE of Gray Summit	**2**: 246-249, **9**: 7, **10**: 9, **11**: 12
91	Lewis/Clark	■●	out	May 24 04	St Charles	MO	4 miles SW of Augusta	**2**: 249-251, **9**: 7, **10**: 9, **11**: 12-13
92a	Lewis/Clark	■●	out	May 25 04	Warren	MO	I miles S of Marthasville	**2**: 251-253, **9**: 7, **10**: 9, **11**: 13
92b	Lewis/Clark	■●	return	Sep 20 06	Warren	MO	1 mile S of Marthasville	**8**: 366-368, **9**: 365
93	Lewis/Clark	■●	out	May 26 04	Warren	MO	12 miles SW of Warrenton	**2**: 254-259, **9**: 7, **10**: 9, **11**: 13-14
94	Lewis/Clark	■●	out	May 27-28 04	Gasconade	MO	6 miles WSW of Hermann	**2**: 259-261, **9**: 7, **10**: 9-10, **11**: 14-15
95	Lewis/Clark	■●	out	May 29 04	Gasconade	MO	7.5 miles ENE of Chamois	**2**: 261-264, **9**: 8, **10**: 10, **11**: 15
96	Lewis/Clark	■●	out	May 30-31 04	Callaway	MO	I mile E of Mokane	**2**: 264-267, **9**: 8-9, **10**: 10-11, **11**: 15-16
97a	Lewis/Clark	■●	out	Jun 1-2 04	Cole	MO	8 miles E of Jefferson City	**2**: 267-272, **9**: 9, **10**: 11, **11**: 16-17
97b	Lewis/Clark	■●	return	Sep 19 06	Cole	MO	8 miles E of Jefferson City	**8**: 365-366, **9**: 364-365, **10**: 280
98	Lewis/Clark	■●	out	Jun 3 04	Cole	MO	4.5 miles ESE of Jefferson City	**2**: 272-275, **9**; 9, **10**: 12, **11**: 17
99	Lewis/Clark	■●	out	Jun 4 04	Boone	MO	2 miles SW of Hartsburg	**2**: 275-277, **9**: 9-10, **10**: 12, **11**: 18
100	Lewis/Clark	■●	out	Jun 5 04	Boone	MO	9 miles NW of Ashland	**2**: 277-281, **9**: 10, **10**: 12, **11**: 18
101	Lewis/Clark	■●	out	Jun 6 04	Cooper	MO	2 miles N of Wooldridge	**2**: 281-283, **9**: 10-11, **10**: 12, **11**: 19
102	Lewis/Clark	■●	out	Jun 7 04	Howard	MO	6 miles WSW of Franklin	**2**: 283-285, **9**: 11, **10**: 12, **11**: 19-20

Lewis and Clark Expedition Campsites

campsite #	group leader (Lewis ■■ Clark ●● Ordway ● Other ▲★)	journey (out - black, return - red, side trip - blue)	date	county	state	location	Journals of the Lewis and Clark Expedition U of Nebr Press (Volumes 2-8 Lewis and Clark; Volume 9 Ordway; Floyd; Volume 10 Gass; Volume 11 Whitehouse)
REGION FOUR (#83-139)						**St Louis to Kansas City**	**Map pages 66-67**
103	Lewis/Clark ■●	return	Sep 18 06	Howard	MO	6 miles WNW of Boonville	**8**: 365, **9**: 364, **10**: 280
104	Lewis/Clark ■●	out	Jun 8 04	Cooper	MO	7.5 miles W of Franklin	**2**: 285-288, **9**: 11, **10**: 12-13, **11**: 20-21
105	Lewis/Clark ■●	out	Jun 9 04	Saline	MO	7 miles SE of Gilliam	**2**: 288-291, **9**: 12, **10**: 13, **11**: 21
106	Lewis/Clark ■●	out	Jun 10-11 04	Chariton	MO	11 miles S of Keytesville	**2**: 291-294, **9**: 12, **10**: 13, **11**: 21-22
107	Lewis/Clark ■●	out	Jun 12 04	Chariton	MO	6 miles SW of Dalton	**2**: 294-295, **9**: 12-13, **10**: 13-14, **11**: 22-23
108	Lewis/Clark ■●	out	Jun 13 04	Carroll	MO	1.5 miles W of Brunswick	**2**: 295-300, **9**: 13, **10**: 14, **11**: 23-24
109	Lewis/Clark ■●	return	Sep 17 06	Saline	MO	4.5 miles NNE of Miami	**8**: 362-365, **9**: 363-364, **10**: 279-280
110	Lewis/Clark ■●	out	Jun 14 04	Carroll	MO	1.5 miles SE of De Witt	**2**: 300-301, **9**: 13, **10**: 14, **11**: 24
111	Lewis/Clark ■●	out	Jun 15 04	Carroll	MO	4 miles NNE of Malta Bend	**2**: 301-304, **9**: 14, **10**: 14, **11**: 24-25
112	Lewis/Clark ■●	out	Jun 16 04	Lafayette	MO	1 mile SE of Waverly	**2**: 304-305, **9**: 14, **10**: 14, **11**: 25
113	Lewis/Clark ■●	out	Jun 17-18 04	Carroll	MO	4.5 miles S of Bowdry	**2**: 305-308, **9**: 14, **10**: 15, **11**: 25-26
114	Lewis/Clark ■●	return	Sep 16 06	Lafayette	MO	5.5 miles SSE of Norborne	**8**: 362, **9**: 363, **10**: 279
115	Lewis/Clark ■●	out	Jun 19 04	Ray	MO	5.5 miles SSE of Hardin	**2**: 308-310, **9**: 14-15, **10**: 15, **11**: 26
116	Lewis/Clark ■●	out	Jun 20 04	Lafayette	MO	5 miles S of Henrietta	**2**: 310-312, **9**: 15, **10**: 15, **11**: 27
117	Lewis/Clark ■●	out	Jun 21 04	Lafayette	MO	1 mile SE of Camden	**2**: 312-315, **9**: 15, **10**: 16, **11**: 27-28
118	Lewis/Clark ■●	out	Jun 22 04	Jackson	MO	3 miles NE of Buckner	**2**: 315-317, **9**: 16, **10**: 16, **11**: 28
119	Lewis/Clark ■●	out	Jun 23 04	Jackson	MO	3 miles WSW of Orrick	**2**: 317-318, **9**: 16, **10**: 16, **11**: 28-29
120	Lewis/Clark ■●	return	Sep 15 06	Jackson	MO	5 miles NW of Sibley	**8**: 361, **9**: 363, **10**: 279
121	Lewis/Clark ■●	out	Jun 24 04	Clay	MO	6 miles SE of Liberty	**2**: 318-321, **9**: 16, **10**: 16, **11**: 29-30
122	Lewis/Clark ■●	out	Jun 25 04	Clay	MO	2 miles SE of Birmingham	**2**: 321-323, **9**: 17, **10**: 17, **11**: 30
123	Lewis/Clark ■●	out	Jun 26-28 04	Clay	MO	confluence of Missouri and Kansas Rivers	**2**: 323-328, **9**: 17-18, **10**: 17, **11**: 31-32
124	Lewis/Clark ■●	out	Jun 29 04	Platte	MO	3 miles SW of Houston Lake	**2**: 328-333, **9**: 18, **10**: 17, **11**: 32
125	Lewis/Clark ■●	out	Jun 30 04	Wyandotte	KS	7 miles SE of Lansing	**2**: 333-336, **9**: 18-19, **10**: 17, **11**: 33
126	Lewis/Clark ■●	return	Sep 14 06	Platte	MO	4 miles WNW of Farley	**8**: 360, **9**: 362, **10**: 278-279
127	Lewis/Clark ■●	out	Jul 1 04	Platte	MO	7 miles SW of Platte City	**2**: 336-340, **9**: 19, **10**: 18, **11**: 33
128	Lewis/Clark ■●	out	Jul 2 04	Leavenworth	KS	8 miles NNW of Leavenworth	**2**: 340-343, **9**: 19, **10**: 18, **11**: 33-34
129	Lewis/Clark ■●	out	Jul 3 04	Platte	MO	3.5 miles SE of Lewis and Clark Village	**2**: 343-345, **9**: 19-20, **10**: 18, **11**: 34
130	Lewis/Clark ■●	out	Jul 4 04	Atchison	KS	4 miles NE of Atchison	**2**: 345-349, **9**: 20, **10**: 18, **11**: 34-35
131	Lewis/Clark ■●	out	Jul 5 04	Platte	MO	1 mile NNE of Iatan	2: 350-352, 9: 20-21, 10: 18-19, 11: 35

Lewis and Clark Expedition Campsites

campsite #	group leader (Lewis ■ Clark ● Ordway ● Other ▲ ★)		journey (out - black, return - red, side trip - blue)	date	county	state	location	Journals of the Lewis and Clark Expedition U of Nebr Press (Volumes 2-8 Lewis and Clark, Volume 9 Ordway; Floyd, Volume 10 Gass, Volume 11 Whitehouse)
REGION FOUR (#48-82)							**St Louis to Kansas City**	**Map pages 66-67**
132	Lewis/Clark	■●	return	Sep 13 06	Buchanan	MO	9.5 miles SW of St. Joseph	**8**: 358-360, **9**: 362, **10**: 278, **9**: 362, **10**: 278
133	Lewis/Clark	■●	out	Jul 6 04	Doniphan	MO	1.5 miles SW of Wathena	**2**: 352-354, **9**: 21, **10**: 19, **11**: 35-36
134	Lewis/Clark	■●	return	Sep 12 06	Doniphan	KS	1 mile E of Elwood	**8**: 357-358, **9**: 361-362, **10**: 278, **9**: 361-362
135	Lewis/Clark	■●	out	Jul 7 04	Doniphan	KS	10 miles E of Troy	**2**: 355-357, **9**: 21-22, **10**: 19, **11**: 36
136	Lewis/Clark	■●	return	Sep 11 06	Doniphan	KS	11 miles E of Troy	**8**: 356-357, **9**: 360, **10**: 278, **9**: 360-361
137	Lewis/Clark	■●	out	Jul 8 04	Holt	MO	2 miles WSW of Nodaway	**2**: 357-361, **9**: 22, **10**: 19, **11**: 36-37
138	Lewis/Clark	■●	out	Jul 9 04	Holt	KS	5.5 miles SSW of Oregon	**2**: 361-364, **9**: 22-23, **10**: 19, **11**: 37
139	Lewis/Clark	■●	out	Jul 10 04	Holt	MO	5.5 miles SSE of Fortescue	**2**: 364-366, **9**: 23, **10**: 19, **11**: 37-38
REGION FIVE (#140-187)							**Nebraska and Iowa**	**Map pages 88-89**
140	Lewis/Clark	■●	out	Jul 11-12 04	Holt	MO	3 miles WSW of Fortescue	**2**: 366-374, **9**: 23-24, **10**: 20, **11**: 38-39
141	Lewis/Clark	■●	return	Sep 10 06	Holt	MO	on Big Lake; 4 miles SW of Bigelow	**8**: 355-356, **9**: 360, **10**: 277
142	Lewis/Clark	■●	out	Jul 13 04	Holt	MO	5 miles WNW of Craig	**2**: 374-376, **9**: 24, **10**: 20, **11**: 39
143	Lewis/Clark	■●	out	Jul 14 04	Nemaha	NE	1.5 miles NE of Indian Cave State Park	**2**: 376-379, **9**: 24-25, **10**: 20, **11**: 39
144	Lewis/Clark	■●	out	Jul 15 04	Nemaha	NE	3.5 miles SSE of Brownsville	**2**: 379-382, **9**: 25-26, **10**: 20-21, **11**: 40
145a	Lewis/Clark	■●	out	Jul 16-17 04	Atchison	MO	3.5 miles NNW of Watson	**2**: 383-391, **9**: 26-27, **10**: 21, **11**: 40
145b	Lewis/Clark	■●	return	Sep 9 06	Atchison	MO	3.5 miles NNW of Watson	**8**: 354-355, **9**: 360, **10**: 277
146	Lewis/Clark	■●	out	Jul 18 04	Fremont	IA	6 miles NNW of Hamburg	**2**: 391-394, **9**: 27, **10**: 21, **11**: 41
147	Lewis/Clark	■●	out	Jul 19 04	Fremont	IA	3.5 miles SW of Percival	**2**: 394-397, **9**: 27-28, **10**: 21-22, **11**: 41-42
148	Lewis/Clark	■●	out	Jul 20 04	Cass	NE	4.5 miles ENE of Union	**2**: 397-400, **9**: 28, **10**: 22, **11**: 42
149	Lewis/Clark	■●	out	Jul 21 04	Sarpy	NE	2.5 mi NNE of Missouri and Platte River confluence	**2**: 400-404, **9**: 28-29, **10**: 22, **11**: 42-43
150a	Lewis/Clark	■●	out	Jul 22-26 04	Pottawattamie	IA	9 miles NNW of Mineola	**2**: 404-421, **9**: 29-30, **10**: 22-23, **11**: 43-45
150b	Lewis/Clark	■●	return	Sep 8 06	Pottawattamie	IA	9 miles NNW of Mineola	**8**: 353-354, **9**: 360, **10**: 277,
151	Lewis/Clark	■●	out	Jul 27 04	Douglas	NE	Eppley Airfield	**2**: 421-423, **9**: 30, **10**: 23, **11**: 45-46
152	Lewis/Clark	■●	out	Jul 28 04	Pottawattamie	NE	4.5 WSW of Crescent	**2**: 423-426, **9**: 30-31, **10**: 23, **11**: 46-47
153	Lewis/Clark	■●	out	Jul 29 04	Pottawattamie	IA	6 miles NW of Honey Creek	**2**: 426-428, **9**: 31, **10**: 23-24, **11**: 47
154	Lewis/Clark	■●	out	Jul 30-Aug 2 04	Washington	NE	Fort Atkinson; 1.5 miles SE of Fort Calhoun	**2**: 428-438, **9**: 31-33, **10**: 24-25, **11**: 48-50
155	Lewis/Clark	■●	out	Aug 3 04	Washington	IA	Desoto National Wildlife Refuge	**2**: 438-444, **9**: 33-34, **10**: 25, **11**: 50-51

Lewis and Clark Expedition Campsites

campsite #	group leader (Lewis ■■ Clark ●● Ordway ▲ Other ★)		journey (out - black, return - red, side trip - blue)	date	county	state	location	Journals of the Lewis and Clark Expedition U of Nebr Press (Volumes 2-8 Lewis and Clark; Volume 9 Ordway; Floyd; Volume 10 Gass; Volume 11 Whitehouse)
REGION FIVE (#140-187)							**Nebraska and Iowa**	**Map pages 88-89**
156	Lewis/Clark	■●	out	Aug 4 04	Harrison	IA	7 miles W of Missouri Valley	**2**: 444-447, **9**: 34, **10**: 25, **11**: 51
157	Lewis/Clark	■●	return	Sept 7 06	Harrison	IA	9 miles W of Missouri Valley	**8**: 352-353, **9**: 359-360, **10**: 276-277
158	Lewis/Clark	■●	out	Aug 5 04	Harrison	IA	2.5 miles W of Modale	**2**: 447-452, **9**: 34-35, **10**: 25-26, **11**: 52
159	Lewis/Clark	■●	out	Aug 6 04	Harrison	IA	1 mile NW of Mondamin	**2**: 452-455, **9**: 35, **10**: 26, **11**: 52
160	Lewis/Clark	■●	return	Sep 6 06	Harrison	IA	4 miles NW of Mondamin	**8**: 351-352, **9**: 359, **10**: 276
161	Lewis/Clark	■●	out	Aug 7 04	Burt	NE	5 miles ESE Tekamah	**2**: 455-458, **9**: 35-36, **10**: 26, **11**: 52
162	Lewis/Clark	■●	out	Aug 8 04	Monona	IA	9 miles NW of Little Sioux	**2**: 458-463, **9**: 36, **10**: 26-27, **11**: 52-53
163	Lewis/Clark	■●	return	Sept 5 06	Monona	IA	2 miles SW of Onawa	**8**: 350-351, **9**: 359, **10**: 276
164	Lewis/Clark	■●	out	Aug 9 04	Monona	IA	2.5 miles NW of Onawa	**2**: 463-465, **9**: 36-37, **10**: 27, **11**: 53
165	Lewis/Clark	■●	out	Aug 10 04	Monona	IA	6 miles WSW of Whiting	**2**: 465-467, **9**: 37, **10**: 27, **11**: 53-54
166	Lewis/Clark	■●	out	Aug 11 04	Monona	IA	7 miles S of Sloan	**2**: 467-471, **9**: 37, **10**: 27, **11**: 54
167	Lewis/Clark	■●	out	Aug 12 04	Woodbury	IA	4 miles W of Sloan	**2**: 471-475, **9**: 38, **10**: 27-28, **11**: 54-55
168a	Lewis/Clark	■●	out	Aug 13-19 04	Dakota	NE	5 miles E of Homer	**2**: 475-491, **9**: 38-41, **10**: 28-29, **11**: 55-58
168b	Lewis/Clark	■●	return	Sep 4 06	Dakota	NE	5 miles E of Homer	**8**: 348-350, **9**, 358-359, **10**: 275-276
169	Lewis/Clark	■●	out	Aug 20 04	Woodbury	IA	Sioux City	**2**: 494-496, **9**: 41, **10**: 29, **11**: 58-59
170a	Lewis/Clark	■●	out	Aug 21 04	Union	SD	4 miles W of North Sioux City	**2**: 496-499, **9**: 41-42, **10**: 29, **11**: 59
170b	Lewis/Clark	■●	return	Sep 3 06	Union	SD	4 miles W of North Sioux City	**8**: 346-348, **9**: 358, **10**: 275
171	Lewis/Clark	■●	out	Aug 22 04	Union	SD	3.5 miles WSW of Elk Point	**2**: 499-502, **9**: 42, **10**: 30, **11**: 59-60
172	Lewis/Clark	■●	out	Aug 23 04	Clay	SD	2 miles S of Burbank	**2**: 502-503, **9**: 42-43, **10**: 30, **11**: 60
173	Lewis/Clark	■●	out	Aug 24 04	Clay	SD	3.5 miles South of Vermillion	**2**: 503-506, **9**: 43-44, **10**: 30, **11**: 61
174	Lewis/Clark	■●	out	Aug 25 04	Clay	SD	3 miles SW of Vermillion	**3**: 7-13, **9**: 44-45, **10**: 31, **11**: 61-62
175	Lewis/Clark	■●	out	Aug 26 04	Clay	SD	5 miles SW of Meckling	**3**: 13-15, **9**: 45, **10**: 31, **11**: 62
176	Lewis/Clark	■●	return	Sep 2 06	Yankton	SD	4.5 miles WSW of Gayville	**8**: 344-345, **9**: 357-358, **10**: 275
177	Lewis/Clark	■●	out	Aug 27 04	Yankton	SD	4 miles E of Yankton	**3**: 16-19, **9**: 45, **10**: 31-32, **11**: 63
178	Lewis/Clark	■●	out	Aug 28-31 04	Yankton	SD	Gavins Point Dam; 4 miles WSW Yankton	**3**: 19-37, **9**: 46-51, **10**: 32-33, **11**: 63-67
179	Lewis/Clark	■●	return	Sep 1 06	Yankton	SD	Gavins Point Dam; 4 miles WSW Yankton	**8**: 337-344, **9**: 357, **10**: 274-275
180	Lewis/Clark	■●	out	Sep 1 04	Knox	NE	12 miles NW of Crofton	**3**: 37-40, **9**: 51-52, **10**: 33, **11**: 67
181	Lewis/Clark	■●	out	Sep 2 04	Bon Homme	SD	8 miles SW of Tabor	**3**: 40-44, **9**: 52-53, **10**: 33-34, **11**: 67-68
182	Lewis/Clark	■●	out	Sep 3 04	Bon Homme	SD	4.5 miles SSW of Springfield	**3**: 44-46, **9**: 53, **10**: 34-35, **11**: 68-69

Lewis and Clark Expedition Campsites

campsite #	group leader (Lewis ■ Clark ● Ordway ▲ Other ★)		journey (out - black, return - red, side trip - blue)	date	county	state	location	Journals of the Lewis and Clark Expedition U of Nebr Press (Volumes 2-8 Lewis and Clark; Volume 9 Ordway; Floyd; Volume 10 Gass; Volume 11 Whitehouse)
REGION FIVE (#140-187)							**Nebraska and Iowa**	**Map pages 88-89**
183	Lewis/Clark	■●	out	Sep 4 04	Bon Homme	SD	10 miles SW of Springfield	**3**: 46-48, **9**: 53-54, **10**: 35, **11**: 69
184	Lewis/Clark	■●	return	Aug 31 06	Knox	NE	4 miles NNW of Verdel	**8**: 332-334, **9**: 356-357, **10**: 274
185	Lewis/Clark	■●	out	Sep 5 04	Knox	NE	5 miles NE of Monowi	**3**: 48-51, **9**: 54, **10**: 35-36, **11**: 69-70
186	Lewis/Clark	■●	out	Sep 6 04	Boyd	NE	7.5 miles NE of Lynch	**3**: 51-53, **9**: 55, **10**: 36, **11**: 70
187	Lewis/Clark	■●	out	Sep 7 04	Boyd	NE	7 miles N of Lynch	**3**: 53-54, **9**: 55, **10**: 36, **11**: 70-71
REGION SIX (#188-278)							**South and North Dakota**	**Map pages 106-107**
188	Lewis/Clark	■●	out	Sep 8 04	Charles Mix	SD	8 miles W of Pickstown	**3**: 54-57, **9**: 55-56, **10**: 37, **11**: 71
189	Lewis/Clark	■●	out	Sep 9 04	Gregory	SD	Whetstone Bay Recreation Area	**3**: 57-61, **9**: 56-57, **10**: 37, **11**: 71-72
190	Lewis/Clark	■●	out	Sep10 04	Charles Mix	SD	12 miles WSW of Platte	**3**: 61-64, **9**: 57, **10**: 37-38, **11**: 72
191	Lewis/Clark	■●	return	Aug 30 06	Charles Mix	SD	13 miles W of Platte	**8**: 329-332, **9**: 355-356, **10**: 274
192	Lewis/Clark	■●	out	Sep 11 04	Charles Mix	SD	12 miles SW of Eagle	**3**: 64-66, **9**: 57-58, **10**: 38, **11**: 72-73
193	Lewis/Clark	■●	out	Sep 12 04	Gregory	SD	7 miles SE of Iona	**3**: 66-68, **9**: 58, **10**: 38-39, **11**: 73-74
194	Lewis/Clark	■●	return	Aug 29 06	Brule	SD	7 miles NE of Iona	**8**: 327-329, **9**: 355, **10**: 273-274
195	Lewis/Clark	■●	out	Sep 13 04	Brule	SD	7 miles WNW Ola	**3**: 68-69, **9**: 58-59, **10**: 39, **11**: 74
196	Lewis/Clark	■●	out	Sep 14 04	Lyman	SD	12 miles NE of Hamill	**3**: 69-74, **9**: 59, **10**: 39, **11**: 74-75
197	Lewis/Clark	■●	out	Sep 15 04	Brule	SD	2 miles SSW of Oacoma	**3**: 74-76, **9**: 59-60, **10**: 39-40, **11**: 75-76
198a	Lewis/Clark	■●	out	Sep 16-17 04	Lyman	SD	1 mile SSE of Oacoma	**3**: 76-86, **9**: 60-61, **10**: 40, **11**: 76-77
198b	Lewis/Clark	■●	return	Aug 28 06	Lyman	SD	1 mile SSE of Oacoma	**8**: 326-327, **9**: 355, **10**: 273
199	Lewis/Clark	■●	out	Sep 18 04	Lyman	SD	larboard, 4 miles N Chamberlin	**3**: 86-88, **9**: 61, **10**: 40-41, **11**: 77
200	Lewis/Clark	■●	out	Sep 19 04	Lyman	SD	4 miles ESE Lower Brule	**3**: 88-91, **9**: 62, **10**: 41, **11**: 77-78
201	Lewis/Clark	■●	return	Aug 27 06	Lyman	SD	2 miles NE of Lower Brule	**8**: 325-326, **9**: 354, **10**: 272-273
202	Lewis/Clark	■●	out	Sep 20 04	Hughes	SD	West Bend Recreation Area	**3**: 92-96, **9**: 62-63, **10**: 41-42, **11**: 78-80
203	Lewis/Clark	■●	out	Sep 20 04	Lyman	SD	1.5 miles E of West Bend Recreation Area	**3**: 92-96, **9**: 62-63, **10**: 41-42, **11**: 78-80
204	Lewis/Clark	■●	out	Sep 21 04	Hughes	SD	1 mile E of Joe Creek Recreation Area	**3**: 96-99, **9**: 63, **10**: 42, **11**: 80
205	Lewis/Clark	■●	return	Aug 26 06	Lyman	SD	1.5 miles SE of Joe Creek Recreation Area	**8**: 323-325, **9**: 354, **10**: 272
206	Lewis/Clark	■●	out	Sep 22 04	Hughes	SD	3 miles SSE of De Grey Recreation Area	**3**: 99-103, **9**: 63-64, **10**: 42-43, **11**: 80-82
207	Lewis/Clark	■●	out	Sep 23 04	Stanley	SD	1 mile SW of Alto	**3**: 104-107, **9**: 64-65, **10**: 43, **11**: 82
209	Lewis/Clark	■●	out	Sep 26-27 04	Stanley	SD	3 miles N of Fort Pierre	**3**: 115-123, **9**: 68-71, **10**: 45-47, **11**: 86-89

CAMP SITES TABLE

CAMP SITES TABLE

Lewis and Clark Expedition Campsites

campsite #	group leader (Lewis ■, Clark ●, Ordway ▲, Other ★)	journey (out - black, return - red, side trip - blue)		date	county	state	location	Journals of the Lewis and Clark Expedition U of Nebr Press (Volumes 2-8 Lewis and Clark; Volume 9 Ordway; Floyd; Volume 10 Gass; Volume 11 Whitehouse)
REGION SIX (#188-278)						South and North Dakota		Map pages 106-107
210	Lewis/Clark	■●	out	Sep 28 04	Hughes	SD	2 miles SE of Oahe Mission Recreation Area	**3**: 123-125, **9**: 71-72, **10**: 47-48, **11**: 89-91
211	Lewis/Clark	■●	return	Aug 25 06	Hughes	SD	2 miles SW of Oahe Mission Recreation Area	**8**: 322-323, **9**: 353-354, **10**: 271-272
212	Lewis/Clark	■●	out	Sep 29 04	Hughes	SD	1.5 miles WSW of Spring Creek Recreation Area	**3**: 125-128, **9**: 72-73, **10**: 48, **11**: 91-92
213	Lewis/Clark	■●	out	Sep 30 04	Stanley	SD	8 miles ENE of Mission Ridge	**3**: 129-132, **9**: 73-74, **10**: 49, **11**: 92-93
214	Lewis/Clark	■●	out	Oct 1 04	Dewey	SD	22.5 miles SSE of Ridgeview	**3**: 132-138, **9**: 74-75, **10**: 49, **11**: 93
215	Lewis/Clark	■●	return	Aug 24 06	Sully	SD	23.5 miles WNW of Onida	**8**: 213-322, **9**: 353, **10**: 271
216	Lewis/Clark	■●	out	Oct 2 04	Sully	SD	17.5 miles W of Agar	**3**: 138-140, **9**: 75, **10**: 49-50, **11**: 93-94
217	Lewis/Clark	■●	out	Oct 3 04	Potter	SD	17.5 miles NW of Agar	**3**: 140-142, **9**: 75, **10**: 50, **11**: 94
218	Lewis/Clark	■●	out	Oct 4 04	Dewey	SD	21 miles ESE of Ridgeview	**3**: 142-144, **9**: 76, **10**: 50, **11**: 95
219	Lewis/Clark	■●	return	Aug 23 06	Dewey	SD	18.5 miles WNW of Gettysburg	**8**: 320-321, **9**: 353, **10**: 271
220	Lewis/Clark	■●	out	Oct 5 04	Dewey	SD	19 miles NW of Gettysburg	**3**: 144-146, **9**: 76, **10**: 51, **11**: 95-96
221	Lewis/Clark	■●	out	Oct 6 04	Walworth	SD	15.5 miles W of Lowry	**3**: 146-148, **9**: 76-77, **10**: 51, **11**: 96
222	Lewis/Clark	■●	return	Aug 22 06	Walworth	SD	5 miles WSW of Glenham	**8**: 317-320, **9**: 353, **10**: 270-271
223	Lewis/Clark	■●	out	Oct 7 04	Walworth	SD	1 mile SW of Mobridge	**3**: 148-150, **9**: 77, **10**: 51-52, **11**: 96-97
224	Lewis/Clark	■●	out	Oct 8-10 04	Campbell	SD	5.5 miles N of Mobridge	**3**: 150-158, **9**: 77-79, **10**: 52-53, **11**: 97-98
225	Lewis/Clark	■●	return	Aug 21 06	Corson	SD	6 miles ESE of Wakpala	**8**: 311-317, **9**: 352-352, **10**: 269-270
226	Lewis/Clark	■●	out	Oct 11 04	Corson	SD	6 miles E of Wakpala	**3**: 158-160, **9**: 82-83, **10**: 53-54, **11**: 98-99
227	Lewis/Clark	■●	out	Oct 12 04	Campbell	SD	11 miles W of Mound City	**3**: 160-167, **9**: 83-84, **10**: 54, **11**: 99
228	Lewis/Clark	■●	return	Aug 20 06	Corson	SD	21 miles E of McLaughlin	**8**: 310-311, **10**: 269
229	Lewis/Clark	■●	out	Oct 13 04	Campbell	SD	7 miles NNW Pollock	**3**: 167-172, **9**: 84, **10**: 54-55, **11**: 99-100
230	Lewis/Clark	■●	out	Oct 14 04	Emmons	ND	21 miles SSW of Strasburg	**3**: 172-173, **9**: 84, **10**: 55, **11**: 100
231	Lewis/Clark	■●	out	Oct 15 04	Emmons	ND	22 miles W of Strasburg	**3**: 173-175, **9**: 84-85, **10**: 55-56, **11**: 100-101
232	Lewis/Clark	■●	out	Oct 16 04	Sioux	ND	16.5 miles W of Linton	**3**: 175-179, **9**: 85-86, **10**: 56, **11**: 101
233	Lewis/Clark	■●	out	Oct 17 04	Sioux	ND	1 mile E of Cannonball	**3**: 179-181, **9**: 86, **10**: 56, **11**: 101
234	Lewis/Clark	■●	out	Oct 18 04	Emmons	ND	13.5 miles NW of Hazelton	**3**: 181-184, **9**: 86-87, **10**: 56-57, **11**: 101-102
235	Lewis/Clark	■●	out	Oct 19 04	Burleigh	ND	20.5 miles W of Moffit	**3**: 184-186, **9**: 87-88, **10**: 47, **11**: 102
236	Lewis/Clark	■●	return	Aug 19 06	Burleigh	ND	7 miles SSW of Lincoln	**8**: 309-310, **9**: 351, **10**: 269
237	Lewis/Clark	■●	return	Aug 18 06	Morton	ND	4.5 miles SSE of Mandan	**8**: 307-309, **9**: 351, **10**: 268-269

Lewis and Clark Expedition Campsites

campsite #	group leader (Lewis ■ Clark ● Ordway ● Other ★)		journey (out - black, return - red, side trip - blue)	date	county	state	location	Journals of the Lewis and Clark Expedition U of Nebr Press (Volumes 2-8 Lewis and Clark, Volume 9 Ordway; Floyd, Volume 10 Gass, Volume 11 Whitehouse)
REGION SIX (#188-278)							**South and North Dakota**	**Map pages 106-107**
238	Lewis/Clark	■●	out	Oct 20 04	Morton	ND	3.5 miles SE of Mandan	**3**: 186-189, **9**: 88, **10**: 57, **11**: 102-103
239	Lewis/Clark	■●	out	Oct 21 04	Burleigh	ND	3 miles NW of Bismarck	**3**: 189-191, **9**: 88, **10**: 58, **11**: 103
240	Lewis/Clark	■●	out	Oct 22 04	Burleigh	ND	13 miles NNW of Bismarck	**3**: 191-193, **9**: 88-89, **10**: 58, **11**: 103
241	Lewis/Clark	■●	out	Oct 23 04	Mclean	ND	9.5 miles WNW of Wilton	**3**: 193-194, **9**: 89, **10**: 58, **11**: 103-104
242	Lewis/Clark	■●	out	Oct 24 04	Mclean	ND	2.5 miles SE of Washburn	**3**: 194-196, **9**: 89, **10**: 58-59, **11**: 104
243	Lewis/Clark	■●	return	Aug 17 06	Oliver	ND	3.5 miles ENE of Hensler	**8**: 305-307, **9**: 351, **10**: 268
244	Lewis/Clark	■●	out	Oct 25 04	Mclean	ND	14.5 miles S of Underwood	**3**: 196-199, **9**: 90, **10**: 59, **11**: 104
245	Lewis/Clark	■●	out	Nov 2 04-Apr 6 05	Mclean	ND	13.5 miles SSW of Underwood	**3**: 225-332, **9**: 93-125, **10**: 61-86, **11**: 107-131
246	Lewis/Clark	■●	out	Oct 26 04	Mercer	ND	4 miles NW of Fort Clark	**3**: 199-202, **9**: 90, **10**: 59, **11**: 104-105
247	Lewis/Clark	■●	out	Apr 7 05	Mclean	ND	13.5 miles SW of Underwood	**4**: 7-13, **9**: 126-127, **10**: 77, **11**: 132-133
248	Lewis/Clark	■●	out	Oct 27-Nov 1 04	Mclean	ND	13.5 miles WSW of Underwood	**3**: 203-225, **9**: 90-92, **10**: 60-61, **11**: 105-107
249	Lewis/Clark	■●	out	Apr 8 05	Mclean	ND	12 miles WSW of Riverdale	**4**: 13-14, **9**: 127, **10**: 77-78, **11**: 133-134
250	Lewis/Clark	■●	return	Aug 13-16 06	Mclean	ND	5 miles NNE of Pick City	**8**: 297-305, **9**: 349-351, **10**: 267-268
251	Lewis/Clark	■●	out	Apr 9 05	Mclean	ND	11 miles SW of Garrison	**4**: 14-19, **9**: 128, **10**: 78, **11**: 134
252	Lewis/Clark	■●	out	Apr 10 05	Mclean	ND	15.5 miles S of Roseglen	**4**: 19-21, **9**: 128-129, **10**: 78, **11**: 134
253	Lewis/Clark	■●	out	Apr 11 05	Mclean	ND	19.5 miles SW of Roseglen	**4**: 21-24, **9**: 129, **10**: 78, **11**: 134
254	Lewis/Clark	■●	out	Apr 12 05	Dunn	ND	18 miles NNE of Halliday	**4**: 24-29, **9**: 129-130, **10**: 79, **11**: 134-135
255	Lewis/Clark	■●	out	Apr 13 05	Mclean	ND	14.5 miles SSE of New Town	**4**: 29-34, **9**: 130, **10**: 79, **11**: 135
256	Lewis/Clark	■●	return	Aug 12 06	Mountrail	ND	14.5 miles SSE of New Town	**8**: 289-292, **9**: 348-349, **10**: 266
257	Lewis/Clark	■●	out	Apr 14 05	Mountrail	ND	12 miles SW of New Town	**4**: 34-41, **9**: 131, **10**: 79-80, **11**: 135
258	Clark	●	return	Aug 11 06	Mountrail	ND	4 niles NW of New Town	**9**: 288-289
259	Lewis/Clark	■●	out	Apr 15 05	Mckenzie	ND	10.5 miles NE of Hawkeye	**4**: 41-45, **9**: 131-132, **10**: 80, **11**: 135
260	Lewis	■	return	Aug 11 06	Mckenzie	ND	10 miles NNE of Hawkeye	**8**: 154-157, **9**: 347-348, **10**: 265
261	Clark	●	return	Aug 9-10 06	Williams	ND	18 miles SSW of White Earth	**8**: 286-288
262	Lewis/Clark	■●	out	Apr 16 05	Mckenzie	ND	14.5 miles NNW of Keene	**4**: 45-47, **9**: 132, **10**: 80, **11**: 135-136
263	Clark	●	return	Aug 7-8 06	Mckenzie	ND	12 miles S of Wheelock	**8**: 283-286
264	Lewis/Clark	■●	out	Apr 17 05	Williams	ND	16 miles SSE of Epping	**4**: 47-50, **9**: 132-133, **10**: 80-81, **11**: 136
265	Lewis/Clark	■●	out	Apr18-19 05	Williams	ND	14.5 miles SSE of Spring Brook	**4**: 51-54, **9**: 133-143, **10**: 81, **11**: 136

CAMP SITES TABLE

Lewis and Clark Expedition Campsites

campsite #	group leader (Lewis ■ Clark ● Ordway ● Other ▲ ★)		journey (out - black, return - red, side trip - blue)	date	county	state	location	Journals of the Lewis and Clark Expedition U of Nebr Press (Volumes 2-8 Lewis and Clark; Volume 9 Ordway; Floyd; Volume 10 Gass; Volume 11 Whitehouse)
REGION SIX (#188-278)							**South and North Dakota**	**Map pages 106-107**
266	Lewis/Clark	■●	out	Apr 20 05	Williams	ND	14 miles N of Arnegard	**4**: 54-57, **9**: 134, **10**: 81, **11**: 136-137
267	Clark	●	return	Aug 6 06	Williams	ND	4 miles SE of Williston	**8**: 282-283
268	Lewis/Clark	■●	out	Apr 21 05	Williams	ND	2.5 miles SSE of Williston	**4**: 57-59, **9**: 135, **10**: 81-82, **11**: 137
269	Lewis	■	return	Aug 10 06	Mckenzie	ND	3 miles S of Williston	**8**: 153-154, **9**: 347, **10**: 264
270	Lewis	■	return	Aug 8-9 06	Williams	ND	5.5 miles ENE of Trenton	**8**: 152-153. **9**: 347, **10**: 264
271	Lewis/Clark	■●	out	Apr 22 05	Williams	ND	4 miles E of Trenton	**4**: 59-63, **9**: 135-136, **10**: 82, **11**: 137
272	Clark	●	return	Aug 5 06	Williams	ND	1.5 miles E of Trenton	**8**: 281-282
273	Lewis/Clark	■●	out	Apr 23-24 05	Williams	ND	5 miles SE of Marley	**4**: 63-66, **9**: 136, **10**: 82, **11**: 137-138
274	Lewis	■	return	Aug 7 06	Mckenzie	ND	4 miles SSE of Marley	**8**: 149-152, **9**: 346, **10**: 263
275	Lewis/Clark	■●	out	Apr 25 05	Williams	ND	3 miles E of Buford	**4**: 66-69, **9**: 137, **10**: 82-83, **11**: 138
276	Clark	●	return	Aug 4 06	Williams	ND	2.5 miles ESE of Buford	**8**: 280-281
277	Lewis/Clark	■●	out	Apr 26 05	Mckenzie	ND	confluence of Yellowstone and Missouri Rivers	**4**: 69-76, **9**: 137-138, **10**: 83, **11**: 139
278	Clark	●	return	Aug 2 06	Mckenzie	ND	2.5 miles SW of Cartwright	**8**: 272-275
REGION SEVEN (#279-424)							**Montana to the Rockies**	**Map pages 130-131**
279	Lewis/Clark	■●	out	Apr 27 05	Richland	MT	1.5 miles ENE of Nohly	**4**: 76-80, **9**: 138, **10**: 83, **11**: 139-140
280	Lewis/Clark	■●	out	Apr 28 05	Roosevelt	MT	9 miles SW of Bainville	**4**: 81-84, **9**: 139, **10**: 84, **11**: 140
281	Lewis/Clark	■●	out	Apr 29 05	Roosevelt	MT	5 miles W of Culbertson	**4**: 84-88, **9**: 139-140, **10**: 84, **11**: 140-141
282	Lewis/Clark	■●	out	Apr 30 05	Richland	MT	2 miles SE of Brockton	**4**: 88-96, **9**: 140-141, **10**: 84, **11**: 141
283	Lewis	■	return	Aug 6 06	Richland	MT	3 miles S of Brockton	**8**: 149, **9**: 346, **10**: 263
284	Lewis/Clark	■●	out	May 1 05	Roosevelt	MT	2 miles ESE of Sprole	**4**: 96-100, **9**: 141, **10**: 85, **11**: 141-142
285	Lewis/Clark	■●	out	May 2 05	Richland	MT	4 miles SE of Sprole	**4**: 100-102, **9**: 141-142, **10**: 85, **11**: 142-143
286	Lewis/Clark	■●	out	May 3 05	Mccone	MT	4.5 miles SW of Poplar	**4**: 102-107, **9**: 142, **10**: 85, **11**: 143-145
287	Lewis/Clark	■●	out	May 4 05	Roosevelt	MT	5 miles ESE of Macon	**4**: 108-111, **9**: 142, **10**: 85-86, **11**: 145
288	Lewis/Clark	■●	out	May 5 05	Mccone	MT	2 miles SE of Wolf Point	**4**: 111-116, **9**: 143, **10**: 86, **11**: 145-147
289	Lewis	■	return	Aug 5 06	Mccone	MT	5 miles SW of Wolf Point	**8**: 148-149, **9**: 345-346, **10**: 262-263
290	Lewis/Clark	■●	out	May 6 05	Mccone	MT	4.5 miles SW of Oswego	**4**: 117-121, **9**: 143-144, **10**: 86, **11**: 147-148
291	Lewis/Clark	■●	out	May 7 05	Valley	MT	5 miles SW of Frazer	**4**: 121-124, **9**: 144, **10**: 86, **11**: 148-149
292	Lewis	■	return	Aug 4 06	Mccone	MT	4 miles S of Kintyre	**8**: 147-148, **9**: 345, **10**: 262

Lewis and Clark Expedition Campsites

campsite #	group leader (Lewis ■ Clark ● Ordway ● Other ▲ ★)	journey (out - black, return - red, side trip - blue)	date	county	state	location	Journals of the Lewis and Clark Expedition U of Nebr Press (Volumes 2-8 Lewis and Clark; Volume 9 Ordway; Floyd; Volume 10 Gass; Volume 11 Whitehouse)
REGION SEVEN (#279-424)						**Montana to the Rockies**	**Map pages 130-131**
293	Lewis/Clark	■●	out	May 8 05	Valley	MT	5.5 miles S of Nashua	**4**: 124-130, **9**: 144-145, **10**: 86-87, **11**: 149-150
294	Lewis/Clark	■●	out	May 9 05	Valley	MT	2.5 miles S of Wheeler	**4**: 130-136, **9**: 145, **10**: 87, **11**: 150-151
295	Lewis/Clark	■●	out	May 10 05	Valley	MT	5.5 miles S of Wheeler	**4**: 136-139, **9**: 145-146, **10**: 87, **11**: 151-152
296	Lewis/Clark	■●	out	May 11 05	Garfield	MT	3.5 miles E of The Pines Recreation Area	**4**: 139-145, **9**: 146, **10**: 87, **11**: 152-154
297	Lewis/Clark	■●	out	May 12 05	Garfield	MT	21 miles SW of Fort Peck Dam	**4**: 145-149, **9**: 146-147, **10**: 88, **11**: 154
298	Lewis	■	return	Aug 3 06	Valley	MT	7 miles SW of The Pines Recreation Area	**8**: 146-147, **9**: 344-345, **10**: 262
299	Lewis/Clark	■●	out	May 13 05	Garfield	MT	8 miles NNE of Hell Creek State Park	**4**: 149-150, **9**: 147, **10**: 88, **11**: 154-155
300	Lewis/Clark	■●	out	May 14-15 05	Valley	MT	10 miles S of Murray Place	**4**: 150-156, **9**: 147-148, **10**: 88-89, **11**: 155-158
301	Lewis/Clark	■●	out	May 16 05	Valley	MT	3.5 miles ESE of Bone Trail Recreation Area	**4**: 156-158, **9**: 148-149, **10**: 89, **11**: 158-159
302	Lewis/Clark	■●	out	May 17 05	Phillips	MT	10 miles E of Fourchette Recreation Area	**4**: 158-163, **9**: 149, **10**: 89, **11**: 159-160
303	Lewis/Clark	■●	out	May 18 05	Phillips	MT	2.5 miles WSW of Devils Creek Recreation Area	**4**: 163-166, **9**: 149-150, **10**: 89-90, **11**: 160-161
304	Lewis	■	return	Aug 1-2 06	Garfield	MT	9 miles NNE of mouth of Musselshell River	**8**: 144-146, **9**: 344-345, **10**: 261-262
305	Lewis/Clark	■●	out	May 19 05	Garfield	MT	4.5 miles NNE of mouth of Musselshell River	**4**: 166-169, **9**: 150-151, **10**: 90, **11**: 161-162
306	Lewis/Clark	■●	out	May 20 05	Garfield	MT	mouth of Musselshell River	**4**: 170-175, **9**: 151-152, **10**: 90, **11**: 162-163
307	Lewis/Clark	■●	out	May 21 05	Phillips	MT	9 miles NE of Woods Place	**4**: 176-179, **9**: 152, **10**: 90, **11**: 163-164
308	Lewis/Clark	■●	out	May 22 05	Petroleum	MT	6 miles NNW of Woods Place	**4**: 179-182, **9**: 152-153, **10**: 90-91, **11**: 165-165
309	Lewis	■	return	Jul 31 06	Fergus	MT	19 miles N of Valentine	**8**: 141-144, **9**: 344, **10**: 261
310	Lewis/Clark	■●	out	May 23 05	Fergus	MT	15.5 miles SSE of DY Junction	**4**: 183-187, **9**: 153-154, **10**: 91, **11**: 165-166
311	Lewis/Clark	■●	out	May 24 05	Phillips	MT	11 miles SSW of DY Junction	**4**: 187-192, **9**: 154, **10**: 91, **11**: 166-167
312	Lewis/Clark	■●	out	May 25 05	Fergus	MT	14 miles WSW of DY Junction	**4**: 193-200, **9**: 154-155, **10**: 92, **11**: 167-169
313	Lewis	■	return	Jul 30 06	Fergus	MT	19 miles SW of Landusky	**8**: 141, **9**: 343-344, **10**: 260
314	Lewis/Clark	■●	out	May 26 05	Fergus	MT	18.5 miles NNE of Winifred	**4**: 200-207, **9**: 155-156, **10**: 92-93, **11**: 169-170
315	Lewis/Clark	■●	out	May 27 05	Fergus	MT	13 miles N of Winifred	**4**: 207-210, **9**: 156, **10**: 94-95, **11**: 171-175
316	Lewis/Clark	■●	out	May 28 05	Choteau	MT	9 miles SE of Iliad	**4**: 210-214, **9**: 156-157, **10**: 95, **11**: 175-176
317	Lewis/Clark	■●	out	May 29 05	Choteau	MT	6.5 miles SW of Iliad	**4**: 215-221, **9**: 157-158, **10**: 95-96, **11**: 177-179
318	Lewis	■	return	Jul 29 06	Choteau	MT	6.5 miles SW of Iliad	**8**: 139-140, **9**: 343, **10**: 260
319	Lewis/Clark	■●	out	May 30 05	Choteau	MT	7 miles WSW of Iliad	**4**: 221-224, **9**: 158-159, **10**: 96, **11**: 179-180
320	Lewis/Clark	■●	out	May 31 05	Choteau	MT	13 miles W of Eagleton	**4**: 224-238, **9**: 159-160, **10**: 96, **11**: 180-181

Lewis and Clark Expedition Campsites

campsite #	group leader (Lewis ■, Clark ●, Ordway ▲, Other ★)	journey (out - black, return - red, side trip - blue)	date	county	state	location	Journals of the Lewis and Clark Expedition U of Nebr Press (Volumes 2-8 Lewis and Clark, Volume 9 Ordway; Floyd, Volume 10 Gass, Volume 11 Whitehouse)
REGION SEVEN (#279-424)						**Montana to the Rockies**	**Map pages 130-131**
321	Lewis/Clark	■●	out	Jun 1 05	Choteau	MT	0.5 mile WSW of Virgelle	**4**: 238-241, **9**: 160-161, **10**: 96-97, **11**: 181-182
322	Lewis	■	return	Jul 28 06	Choteau	MT	22 miles NNW of Montague	**8**: 137-139, **9**: 341-343, **10**: 259-260
323	Lewis/Clark	■●	out	Jun 2 05	Choteau	MT	17 miles N of Montague	**4**: 241-245, **9**: 161, **10**: 97, **11**: 182-184
324a	other	★	out	Jun 3-5 05	Choteau	MT	mouth of Marias River	**4**: 245-260, **9**: 161-163, **10**: 97-98, **11**: 184-188
324b	Clark	●	out	Jun 6 -7 05	Choteau	MT	mouth of Marias River	**4**: 260-262, **9**: 163-164, **10**: 99-100, **11**: 188-190
324c	Lewis/Clark	■●	out	Jun 8-10 05	Choteau	MT	mouth of Marias River	**4**: 265-277, **9**: 164-165, **10**: 100-101, **11**: 190-193
324d	Clark	●	out	Jun 11 05	Choteau	MT	mouth of Marias River	**4**: 277-279, **9**: 166, **10**: 101, **11**: 193-194
325	Lewis	■	side trip	Jun 4 05	Chouteau	MT	15 miles NNW of Loma	**4**: 256-257, **9**: 162, **10**: 98, **11**: 186-187
326	Lewis	■	side trip	Jun 5 05	Liberty	MT	17.5 miles SSW of Chester	**4**: 257-260
327	Lewis	■	side trip	Jun 6 05	Chouteau	MT	26 miles SSW of Joplin	**4**: 260-261, **9**: 164, **10**: 99, **11**: 189-190
328	Lewis	■	side trip	Jun 7 05	Chouteau	MT	9 miles NW of Loma	**4**: 262-263, **9**: 164, **10**: 100, **11**: 189-190
329	Clark	●	side trip	Jun 4 05	Chouteau	MT	3 miles SE of Carter	**4**: 256-257, **9**: 162, **10**: 98-99, **11**: 186-187
330	Clark	●	side trip	Jun 5 05	Chouteau	MT	3 miles WNW of Fort Benton	**4**: 259-260, **10**: 99, **11**: 188-189
331	Lewis	■	out	Jun 11 05	Choteau	MT	5 miles NE of Fort Benton	**4**: 277-279, **9**: 166, **10**: 101, **11**: 193
332	Clark	●	out	Jun 12 05	Choteau	MT	5.5 miles ENE Fort Benton	**4**: 280-282, **9**: 166, **10**: 101, **11**: 194-195
333	Clark	●	out	Jun 13 05	Choteau	MT	5.5 miles SW of Fort Benton	**4**: 287-289, **9**: 167, **10**: 101-102, **11**: 195-196
334	Clark	●	out	Jun 14 05	Choteau	MT	3.5 miles S of Carter	**4**: 294-296, **9**: 167, **10**: 102, **11**: 196-198
335	Lewis	■	out	Jun12 05	Choteau	MT	3.5 miles E of Floweree	**4**: 279-281
336	Clark	●	out	Jun 15 05	Cascade	MT	4.5 miles SE of Portage	**4**: 297-299, **9**: 167-168, **10**: 102, **11**: 198
337a	Clark	●	out	Jun 16 05	Choteau	MT	4.5 miles N of Salem	**4**: 301-302, **9**: 168-169, **10**: 102-103, **11**: 199-201
337b	Clark	●	out	Jun 20-21 05	Choteau	MT	4.5 miles N of Salem	**4**: 318-321, 324-325, **9**: 170-172, **11**: 205-207
337c	Clark	●	out	Jun 23-27 05	Choteau	MT	4.5 miles N of Salem	**4**: 328-333, 335, 337, **9**: 172-175, **11**: 209-213
337d	Lewis	■	out	Jun 16-21 05	Choteau	MT	4.5 miles N of Salem	**4**: 299-318, 323-324, **10**: 102-104, **11**: 199-207
337e	Ordway	▲	return	Jul 25 -26 06	Choteau	MT	4.5 miles N of Salem	**9**: 340-341, **10**: 257-258
338	Ordway	▲	return	Jul 23-24 06	Cascade	MT	3 miles NW of Salem	**9**: 339-340, **10**: 256-257
339	Lewis	■	return	Jul 16 06	Cascade	MT	2.5 miles SSE of Sheffels	**8**: 111-112
340	Lewis	■	side trip	Jul 17 06	Choteau	MT	32 miles E of Dutton	**8**: 112-115
341	Lewis	■	side trip	Jul 18 06	Liberty	MT	5 miles ESE of Marias	**8**: 115-116

Lewis and Clark Expedition Campsites

campsite #	group leader (Lewis ■ Clark ● Ordway ▲ Other ★)	journey (out - black, return - red, side trip - blue)	date	county	state	location	Journals of the Lewis and Clark Expedition, U of Nebr Press (Volumes 2-8 Lewis and Clark; Volume 9 Ordway; Floyd; Volume 10 Gass; Volume 11 Whitehouse)
REGION SEVEN (#279-424)						**Montana to the Rockies**	**Map pages 130-131**
342	Lewis	■	side trip	Jul 19 06	Liberty	MT	5.5 miles NNE of Marias	**8**: 116-118
343	Lewis	■	side trip	Jul 20 06	Toole	MT	6 miles SSW of Shelby	**8**: 118-120,
344	Lewis	■	side trip	Jul 21 06	Glacier	MT	2 miles SSW of Cut Bank	**8**: 120-122,
345	Lewis	■	side trip	Jul 22-25 06	Glacier	MT	11.5 miles NE of Browning	**8**: 122-127,
346	Lewis	■	side trip	Jul 26 06	Pondera	MT	25 miles ESE of Browning	**8**: 127-133,
347	Lewis	■	side trip	Jul 27 06	Choteau	MT	5 miles NW of Carter	**8**: 133-137,
348	Lewis	■	out	Jun 13-15 05	Cascade	MT	2.5 miles SSE of Sheffels	**4**: 283-297, **10**: 102, **11**: 196-198
349	Clark	●	out	Jun 17 05	Cascade	MT	2.5 miles WSW of Cooper	**4**: 304-305, **10**: 103, **11**: 201
350	Clark	●	out	Jun 28-30 05	Cascade	MT	10.5 miles ENE of Great Falls	**4**: 338-349, **9**: 176-178, **11**: 214-215
351	Lewis	■	out	Jun 23 05	Cascade	MT	14.5 miles E of Sun River	**4**: 326-328, **10**: 105, **11**: 209
352a	Clark	●	out	Jun 18-19 05	Cascade	MT	3.5 miles S of Great Falls	**4**: 307-317, **10**: 104,
352b	Clark	●	out	Jun 22 05	Cascade	MT	3.5 miles S of Great Falls	**4**: 326, **10**: 104-105, **11**: 207-208
352c	Lewis	■	out	Jun 24-Jul 12 05	Cascade	MT	3.5 miles S of Great Falls	**4**: 329-381, **10**: 105-111, **11**: 210-224
352d	Clark	●	out	Jul 1-9 05	Cascade	MT	3.5 miles S of Great Falls	**4**: 350-371, **9**: 178-181, **11**: 214-222
352e	Lewis	■	return	Jul 13-15 06	Cascade	MT	3.5 miles S of Great Falls	**8**: 107-111, **10**: 253-254
352f	Ordway	▲	return	Jul 19-20 06	Cascade	MT	3.5 miles S of Great Falls	**9**: 337-339, **10**: 255-256
353a	Clark	●	out	Jul 10-12 05	Cascade	MT	11.5 miles WNW of Sand Coulee	**4**: 373-377, **9**: 182-183, **11**: 222-224
353b	Lewis/Clark	■●	out	Jul 13-14 05	Cascade	MT	11.5 miles WNW of Sand Coulee	**4**: 378-381, **9**: 183, **10**: 111, **11**: 225-226
354	Lewis/Clark	■●	out	Jul 15 05	Cascade	MT	3.5 miles NE of Riverdale	**4**: 382-386, **9**: 184, **10**: 112, **11**: 227-228
355	Clark	●	out	Jul 16 05	Cascade	MT	3.5 miles SSW of Cascade	**4**: 387-391, **9**: 184-185, **10**: 112-113
356	Lewis	■	out	Jul 16 05	Cascade	MT	2 miles SSW of Hardy	**4**: 386-387, **10**: 112-113, **11**: 228-229
357	Lewis/Clark	■●	out	Jul 17 05	Cascade	MT	5.5 miles NE of Craig	**4**: 391-397, **9**: 185, **10**: 113, **11**: 229-230
358	Lewis	■	out	Jul 18 05	Lewis and Clark	MT	2 miles SE of town of Holter Dam	**4**: 397-400, **9**: 185-186, **10**: 114, **11**: 231
359	Clark	●	out	Jul 18 05	Lewis and Clark	MT	7 miles SSE of Wolf Creek	**4**: 401-402, **10**: 114, **11**: 230-232
360	Lewis	■	out	Jul 19 05	Lewis and Clark	MT	16 miles E of Canyon Creek	**4**: 402-405, **9**: 186, **10**: 114, **11**: 232-233
361	Lewis	■	out	Jul 20 05	Lewis and Clark	MT	14 miles NE of Helena	**4**: 406-409, **9**: 187, **10**: 115, **11**: 233-235
362	Clark	●	out	Jul 19 05	Lewis and Clark	MT	11.5 miles ENE of Helena	**4**: 405-406, **9**: 186
363	Lewis	■	out	Jul 21 05	Lewis and Clark	MT	11.5 miles E of East Helena	**4**: 411-414, **9**: 187, **10**: 115-116, **11**: 235-236

Lewis and Clark Expedition Campsites

campsite #	group leader (Lewis ■ Clark ● Ordway ● Other ★)	journey (out - black, return - red, side trip - blue)	date	county	state	location	Journals of the Lewis and Clark Expedition U of Nebr Press (Volumes 2-8 Lewis and Clark; Volume 9 Ordway; Floyd; Volume 10 Gass; Volume 11 Whitehouse)
REGION SEVEN (#279-424)						**Montana to the Rockies**	**Map pages 130-131**
364	Clark	●	out	Jul 21 05	Broadwater	MT	17.5 miles ESE of East Helena	**4**: 414-415
365	Clark	●	out	Jul 20 05	Broadwater	MT	5 miles ENE of Winston	**4**: 409-411, **9**:187, **11**: 234-235
366	Lewis/Clark	■ ●	out	Jul 22 05	Broadwater	MT	5.5 mles E of Winston	**4**: 415-419, **9**: 187-188, **10**: 116, **11**: 236-237
367	Lewis	■	out	Jul 23 05	Broadwater	MT	1.5 miles ENE of Bedford	**4**: 419-421, **9**: 188-189, **10**: 116-117, **11**: 237-238
368	Lewis	■	out	Jul 24 05	Broadwater	MT	6 miles SSE of Townsend	**4**: 422-425, **9**: 189, **10**: 117, **11**: 239
369	Clark	●	out	Jul 23 05	Broadwater	MT	3 miles NNW of Toston	**4**: 418-419, **10**: 116-117, **11**: 237-238
370	Lewis	■	out	Jul 25 05	Broadwater	MT	1 mile S of Brewer	**4**: 426-428, **9**: 189, **10**: 117, **11**: 239-241
371	Clark	●	out	Jul 24 05	Broadwater	MT	1 mile SW of Clarkston	**4**: 425, **9**: 189, **11**: 239
372	Lewis	■	out	Jul 26 05	Gallatin	MT	1.5 miles E of Eustis	**4**: 429-432, **9**: 189-190, **10**: 117-118, **11**: 241-242
373	Lewis/Clark	■ ●	out	Jul 27-29 05	Broadwater	MT	3.5 miles NE of Three Forks	**4**: 433-439, **5**: 7-14, **9**: 190-191, **10**: 118-119, **11**: 242-246
374	Clark	●	out	Jul 30 05	Gallatin	MT	3.5 miles SSW of Three Forks Junction	**5**: 16-17, **9**: 191-192, **10**: 119, **11**: 246-247
375	Lewis	■	out	Jul 30 05	Gallatin	MT	1 mile NNW of Willow Creek	**5**: 14-16, **10**: 119, **11**: 246-247
376	Clark	●	out	Jul 25 05	Jefferson	MT	4 miles ENE of Sappington	**4**: 428-429, **9**: 189, **11**: 239-241
377	Clark	●	out	Jul 26 05	Gallatin	MT	1 mile S of Willow Creek	**4**: 432-433, **9**: 189-190, **11**: 241-242
378	Clark	●	out	Jul 12 06	Gallatin	MT	1 mile NE of Sappington	**8**: 177-178, **9**: 335
379	Lewis/Clark	■ ●	out	Jul 31 05	Gallatin	MT	5 miles ENE of Summit Valley	**5**: 17-24, **9**: 192-193, **10**: 119-120, **11**: 247-249
380	Clark	●	out	Aug 1 05	Jefferson	MT	1.5 miles NW of La Hood Park	**5**: 29-30, **9**: 193-194, **11**: 249-251
381	Lewis	■	out	Aug 1 05	Jefferson	MT	2 miles SSE of Sunlight	**5**: 25-29, **9**: 193-194, **10**: 120, **11**: 249-251
382	Clark	●	out	Aug 2 05	Madison	MT	3.5 miles SE of Whitehall	**5**: 34-35, **9**: 194, **11**: 251-252
383	Clark	●	out	Aug 3 05	Madison	MT	4 miles S of Piedmont	**5**: 38-40, **9**: 194-195, **10**: 121, **11**: 252-253
384	Lewis	■	out	Aug 2 05	Madison	MT	6 miles SSE of Vendome	**5**: 30-34, **10**: 120-121
385	Clark	●	out	Aug 4 05	Madison	MT	0.5 miles SSE of Silver Star	**5**: 43-44, **9**: 195-196, **10**: 121, **11**: 254-255
386a	Lewis/Clark	■ ●	out	Aug 6 05	Madison	MT	confluence of Jefferson and Bighole Rivers	**5**: 52-55, **9**: 197, **10**: 122, **11**: 256-258
386b	Clark	●	return	Jul 11 06	Madison	MT	confluence of Jefferson and Bighole Rivers	**8**: 176-177, **9**: 334-335
387	Clark	●	out	Aug 5 05	Madison	MT	1 mile NW of Twin Bridges	**5**: 47-52, **9**: 196-197, **11**: 255-256
388	Lewis/Clark	■ ●	out	Aug 7 05	Madison	MT	1 mile SSE of Twin Bridges	**5**: 55-58, **9**: 197-198, **10:** 122, **11**: 258-259
389	Lewis	■	out	Aug 5 05	Madison	MT	8 miles WNW of Sheridan	**5**: 44-47, **10**: 121-122,
390	Lewis	■	out	Aug 4 05	Madison	MT	10 miles E of Glen	**5**: 40-43, **10**: 121, **10**: 121, **11**: 254-255

Lewis and Clark Expedition Campsites

campsite #	group leader	Lewis ■ Clark ● Ordway ● Other ▲ ★	journey: out - black, return - red, side trip - blue	date	county	state	location	Journals of the Lewis and Clark Expedition U of Nebr Press: Volumes 2-8 Lewis and Clark; Volume 9 Ordway; Floyd; Volume 10 Gass; Volume 11 Whitehouse
REGION SEVEN (#279-424)							**Montana to the Rockies**	**Map pages 130-131**
391	Lewis/Clark	■ ●	out	Aug 8 05	Madison	MT	10 miles ENE of Sodak Mill	**5**: 58-61, **9**: 198-199, **10**: 122-123, **11**: 259-261
392	Clark	●	out	Aug 9 05	Madison	MT	9 miles ESE of Sodak Mill	**5**: 62-63, **9**: 199, **10**: 123-124, **11**: 261-262
393	Clark	●	out	Aug 10 05	Beaverhead	MT	2.5 miles W of Beaverhead State Park	**5**: 66-67, **9**: 199-200, **10**: 124, **11**: 263-264
394	Lewis	■	out	Aug 3 05	Madison	MT	6 miles E of Beaverhead State Park	**5**: 35-38, **10**: 121
395	Clark	●	return	Jul 10 06	Beaverhead	MT	8.5 miles ESE of Apex	**8**: 174-175, **9**: 334
396	Clark	●	out	Aug 11 05	Beaverhead	MT	5 miles E of Bond	**5**: 72-73, **9**: 200-201, **10**: 124, **11**: 264-265
397	Lewis	■	out	Aug 9 05	Beaverhead	MT	4 miles NE of Dillon	**5**: 61-62, **10**: 123, **11**: 261-262
398	Clark	●	out	Aug 12 05	Beaverhead	MT	2.5 miles NNE of Dillon	**5**: 75-76, **9**: 201, **10**: 124-125, **11**: 265-266
399	Clark	●	out	Aug 13 05	Beaverhead	MT	10 miles SE of Argenta	**5**: 84-87, **9**: 201-202, **10**: 125, **11**: 266-267
400	Clark	●	out	Aug 14 05	Beaverhead	MT	0.5 miles NE of Barretts	**5**: 93-95, **9**: 202, **10**: 125, **11**: 267-269
401	Clark	●	out	Aug 15 05	Beaverhead	MT	1 mile SSW of Dalys	**5**: 99-102, **9**: 202-203, **10**: 125-126, **11**: 269-270
402	Lewis	■	return	Jul 6 06	Lewis and Clark	MT	1.5 miles W of Lincoln	**8**: 93-95, **9**: 331-332, **10**: 249-250
403	Lewis	■	return	Jul 7 06	Lewis and Clark	MT	8 miles SW of Milford Colony	**8**: 95-96, **9**: 332, **10**: 250-251
404	Lewis	■	return	Jul 8 06	Lewis and Clark	MT	1.5 milese ENE of Riebeling	**8**: 96-98, **9**: 332-333, **10**: 251
405	Lewis	■	return	Jul 9 06	Teton	MT	0.5 mile NNE of Simms	**8**: 98-99, **9**: 333-334, **10**: 251
406	Lewis	■	return	Jul 10 06	Cascade	MT	1 mile SW of Manchester	**8**: 99-100, **9**: 334, **10**: 252
407	Lewis	■	return	Jul 11 06	Cascade	MT	9 miles ENE of Ulm	**8**: 104-106, **9**: 334-335, **10**: 252
408	Lewis	■	return	Jul 12 06	Cascade	MT	3 miles S of Great Falls	**8**: 106-107, **9**: 335, **10**: 252-253
409	Clark	●	return	Aug 1 06	Dawson	MT	9.5 miles SSW Savage	**8**: 267-272,
410	Clark	●	return	Jul 31 06	Dawson	MT	7 miles SSW of Glendive	**8**: 257-267,
411	Clark	●	return	Jul 30 06	Prairie	MT	6.5 miles WSW of Terry	**8**: 252-257,
412	Clark	●	return	Jul 29 06	Custer	MT	1.5 miles NNE of Miles City	**8**: 248-252,
413	Clark	●	return	Jul 28 06	Rosebud	MT	1 mile ENE of Hathaway	**8**: 243-248,
414	Clark	●	return	Jul 27 06	Rosebud	MT	8 miles WNW of Forsyth	**8**: 235-243,
415	Clark	●	return	Jul 26 06	Treasure	MT	4.5 miles ENE of Custer	**8**: 229-235,
416	Clark	●	return	Jul 25 06	Yellowstone	MT	I mile NE of town of Pompeys Pillar	**8**: 223-229,
417	Clark	●	return	Jul 24 06	Yellowstone	MT	6 miles ESE of Billings	**8**: 217-223,
418	Clark	●	return	Jul 19-23 06	Stillwater	MT	1.5 miles S of Park City	**8**: 204-212,

CAMP SITES TABLE

Lewis and Clark Expedition Campsites

campsite #	group leader (Lewis ■ Clark ● Ordway ▲ Other ★)		journey (out - black, return - red, side trip - blue)	date	county	state	location	Journals of the Lewis and Clark Expedition U of Nebr Press (Volumes 2-8 Lewis and Clark; Volume 9 Ordway; Floyd; Volume 10 Gass; Volume 11 Whitehouse)
REGION SEVEN (#279-424)							**Montana to the Rockies**	**Map pages 130-131**
419	Clark	●	return	Jul 18 06	Stillwater	MT	2.5 miles WSW of Columbus	**8**: 198-204,
420	Clark	●	return	Jul 17 06	Sweetgrass	MT	0.5 mile W of Reed Point	**8**: 193-198,
421	Clark	●	return	Jul 16 06	Sweetgrass	MT	3.5 miles WSW of Big Timber	**8**: 189-193,
422	Clark	●	return	Jul 15 06	Park	MT	9 miles ENE of Livingston	**8**: 183-189,
423	Clark	●	return	Jul 14 06	Gallatin	MT	4.5 miles ESE of Bozeman	**8**: 180-183,
424	Clark	●	return	Jul 13 06	Gallatin	MT	1 mile ENE of Logan	**8**: 179-181,
REGION EIGHT (#425-500)							**Western Montana and Idaho**	**Map pages 160-161**
425	Clark	●	out	Aug 16 05	Beaverhead	MT	1 mile NE of Clark Canyon Dam	**5**: 107-108, **9**: 203-204, **10**: 126
426a	Lewis	■	out	Aug 17-23 05	Beaverhead	MT	0.5 mile SW of junction; SR 324 and I-15	**5**: 109-138, 141-155, **9**: 204-209, **10**: 126-132
426b	Clark	●	out	Aug 17 05	Beaverhead	MT	0.5 mile SW of junction; SR 324 and I-15	**5**: 114-115, **9**: 204-206, **10**: 126-127
426c	Clark	●	return	Jul 8-9 06	Beaverhead	MT	0.5 mile SW of junction; SR 324 and I-15	**8**: 171-174, **9**: 333-334
427	Lewis	■	out	Aug 16 05	Beaverhead	MT	0.5 miles SSW of Clark Canyon Dam	**5**: 102-107, **10**: 126
428	Lewis	■	out	Aug 10 05	Beaverhead	MT	14 miles NE of Chinatown	**5**: 63-66, **10**: 124
429	Lewis	■	out	Aug 24 05	Beaverhead	MT	13 miles NE of Chinatown	**5**: 158-162,
430	Lewis	■	out	Aug 11 05	Beaverhead	MT	8 miles WNW of Grant	**5**: 68-72
431	Clark	●	out	Aug 18 05	Beaverhead	MT	8 miles W of Grant	**5**: 118-119, **9**: 206, **10**: 127
432	Lewis	■	out	Aug 15 05	Beaverhead	MT	7 miles E of Lemhi Pass	**5**: 95-99
433	Lewis	■	out	Aug 25 05	Beaverhead	MT	7 miles E of Lemhi Pass	**5**: 164-168, **9**: 210
434	Lewis	■	out	Aug 12 05	Lemhi	ID	10.5 miles NE of Lemhi	**5**: 73-75, **10**: 124-125
435	Clark	●	out	Aug 19 05	Lemhi	ID	4 miles NE of Tendoy	**5**: 124-125, **10**: 127-128
436a	Lewis	■	out	Aug 26-28 05	Lemhi	ID	3 miles N of Tendoy	**5**: 170-173, **9**: 211-213, **10**: 133-134
436b	Lewis/Clark	■●	out	Aug 29 05	Lemhi	ID	3 miles N of Tendoy	**5**: 177-178, **9**: 213-214, **10**: 134
437	Lewis	■	out	Aug 13-14 05	Lemhi	ID	5 miles SSE of Baker	**5**: 76-84, 87-93, **10**: 125
438	Clark	●	out	Aug 20 05	Lemhi	ID	0.5 miles ESE of Baker	**5**: 130-132, **10**: 128-129
439	Lewis/Clark	■●	out	Aug 30 05	Lemhi	ID	6 miles SE of Salmon	**5**: 178-179, **9**: 214-215, **10**: 134
440	Clark	●	out	Aug 26-28 05	Lemhi	ID	5 miles SE of Salmon	**5**: 173-177, **9**: 211-213, **10**: 133-134
441a	Clark	●	out	Aug 21 05	Lemhi	ID	4.5 miles N of Carmen	**5**: 135-141, **10**: 129-130
441b	Clark	●	out	Aug 25 05	Lemhi	ID	4.5 miles N of Carmen	**5**: 167-170, **10**: 132-133

Lewis and Clark Expedition Campsites

campsite #	group leader (Lewis ■ Clark ● Ordway ▲ Other ★)		journey (out - black, return - red, side trip - blue)	date	county	state	location	Journals of the Lewis and Clark Expedition U of Nebr Press (Volumes 2-8 Lewis and Clark; Volume 9 Ordway; Floyd; Volume 10 Gass; Volume 11 Whitehouse)
REGION EIGHT (#425-500)							**Western Montana and Idaho**	**Map pages 160-161**
442	Clark	●	return	Jul 7 06	Beaverhead	MT	5.5 miles SE of Jackson	**8**: 169-171, **9**: 332
443	Clark	●	out	Aug 24 05	Lemhi	ID	10.5 miles E of Shoup	**5**: 162-164, **10**: 132
444	Clark	●	out	Aug 23 05	Lemhi	ID	10 miles W of North Fork	**5**: 152-157, **10**: 131-132
445	Clark	●	out	Aug 22 05	Lemhi	ID	1 mile W of North Fork	**5**: 145-148, **10**: 130-131
446	Lewis/Clark	■●	out	Sep 1 05	Lemhi	ID	4 miles N of North Fork	**5**: 182-183, **9**: 215-216, **10**: 135
447	Lewis/Clark	■●	out	Sep 2 05	Lemhi	ID	3.5 miles NW of Gibbonsville	**5**: 183-185, **9**: 216-217, **10**:135-136
448	Clark	●	return	Jul 6 06	Beaverhead	MT	8.5 miles WSW of Wisdom	**8**: 166-169, **9**: 331-332
449	Lewis/Clark	■●	out	Sep 2 05	Lemhi	ID	3.5 miles NW of Gibbonsville	**5**: 183-185, **9**: 216-217, **10**:135-136
450	Lewis/Clark	■●	out	Sep 3 05	Ravalli	MT	2.5 miles WNW of Lost Trail Pass	**5**: 185-187, **9**: 217, **10**: 136-137
451	Clark	●	return	Jul 5 06	Ravalli	MT	2.5 miles SSE of Sula	**8**: 164-166, **9**: 332
452	Lewis/Clark	■●	out	Sep 4-5 05	Ravalli	MT	0.5 mile SSE of Sula	**5**: 187-189, **9**: 217-219, **10**: 137-138
453	Lewis/Clark	■●	out	Sep 6 05	Ravalli	MT	5 miles SE of Conner	**5**: 189-190, **9**: 219-220, **10**: 138
454	Clark	●	return	Jul 4 06	Ravalli	MT	0.5 mile w of Conner	**8**: 163-164, **9**: 330-331
455	Lewis/Clark	■●	out	Sep 7 05	Ravalli	MT	6.5 miles S of Hamilton	**5**: 190, **9**: 220, **10**: 139
456	Clark	●	return	Jul 3 06	Ravalli	MT	9 miles S of Victor	**8**: 161-162, **9**: 330
457	Lewis/Clark	■●	out	Sep 8 05	Ravalli	MT	2.5 miles S of Stevensville	**5**: 190-191, **9**: 220-221, **10**: 139
458a	Lewis/Clark	■●	out	Sep 9-10 05	Missoula	MT	0.5 miles SSE of Lolo	**5**: 191-198, **9**: 221-222, **10**: 139-140
458b	Lewis/Clark	■●	return	Jun 30-Jul 2 06	Missoula	MT	0.5 miles SSE of Lolo	**8**: 65-81, **9**: 329-330, **10**: 246-247
459	Lewis	■	return	Jul 3 06	Missoula	MT	4 miles NW of Missoula	**8**: 82-87, **10**: 247-248
460	Lewis	■	return	Jul 4 06	Missoula	MT	12.5 miles ENE of Missoula	**8**: 87-90, **10**: 249-249
461	Lewis	■	return	Jul 5 06	Powell	MT	4 miles W of Ovando	**8**: 90-93, **10**: 249
462	Lewis/Clark	■●	out	Sep 11 05	Missoula	MT	1.5 miles ESE of jct; Elk Meadows Rd and US 12	**5**: 198-201, **9**: 222. **10**: 140
463	Lewis/Clark	■●	out	Sep 12 05	Missoula	MT	0.1 mile SE of jct; Spring Gulch Rd and US 12	**5**: 201-202, **9**: 222, **10**: 141
464	Lewis/Clark	■●	return	Jun 29 06	Missoula	MT	0.5 mile SE of Lolo Hot Springs	**8**: 61-65, **9**: 328-329, **10**: 145-246
465	Lewis/Clark	■●	out	Sep 13 05	Idaho	ID	1 mile S of Lolo Pass Interpretive Center	**5**: 202-204, **9**: 223, **10**: 141
466	Lewis/Clark	■●	out	Sep 14 05	Idaho	ID	one-tenth mile WSW of Powell Ranger Station	**5**: 204-206, **9**: 223-224, **10**: 142
467	Lewis/Clark	■●	return	Jun 28 06	Idaho	ID	one-eighth mile W of Powell Junction	**8**: 59-61, **9**: 327-328, **10**: 245
468	Lewis/Clark	■●	out	Sep 15 05	Idaho	ID	1.5 miles SE of Cayuse Junction	**5**: 206-207, **9**: 224, **10**: 142-143

Lewis and Clark Expedition Campsites

campsite #	group leader (Lewis ■ Clark ● Ordway ▲ Other ★)		journey (out - black, return - red, side trip - blue)	date	county	state	location	Journals of the Lewis and Clark Expedition U of Nebr Press (Volumes 2-8 Lewis and Clark; Volume 9 Ordway; Floyd; Volume 10 Gass; Volume 11 Whitehouse)
REGION EIGHT (#425-500)							**Western Montana and Idaho**	**Map pages 160-161**
469	Lewis/Clark	■●	return	Jun 27 06	Idaho	ID	3 miles NE of junction; Doe Creek Rd and Lolo Trail	**8**: 55-59, **9**: 327, **10**: 245
470	Lewis/Clark	■●	out	Sep 16 05	Idaho	ID	3 miles ENE of jct; Road 588 and Lolo Trail	**5**: 207-210, **9**: 224-225, **10**: 143
471	Lewis/Clark	■●	out	Sep 17 05	Idaho	ID	2 miles WSW of jct; Gravey Creek Rd and Lolo Trail	**5**: 210-211, **9**: 225, **10**: 143
472	Lewis/Clark	■●	return	Jun 26 06	Idaho	ID	2 miles WNW of junction; FR 561 and Lolo Trail	**8**: 52-55, **9**: 327, **10**: 244-245
473	Lewis	■	out	Sep 18 05	Idaho	ID	2 miles ENE of jct; Liz Butte Rd and Lolo Trail	**5**: 211-213, **9**: 225-226, **10**: 143-144
474	Clark	●	out	Sep 18 05	Idaho	ID	4 miles NW of junction; Fish Creek Road and US 12	**5**: 213-215, **9**: 225-226
475	Lewis/Clark	■●	return	Jun 17 06	Idaho	ID	5.5 miles SSE of jct; Weites Butte Rd and Lolo Trail	**8**: 31-33, **9**: 323-324, **10**: 240-241
476	Lewis/Clark	■●	return	Jun 25 06	Idaho	ID	3.5 miles S of jct; Weites Butte Rd and Lolo Trail	**8**: 50-52, **9**: 327, **10**: 244
477	Lewis	■	out	Sep 19 05	Idaho	ID	4 miles ESE of junction; FR 104 and Lolo Trail	**5**: 215-216, **9**: 226, **10**: 144-145
478	Lewis/Clark	■●	return	Jun 16 06	Idaho	ID	6 miles NE of jct; Friday Creek Rd and Lolo Trail	**8**: 27-31, **9**: 323, **10**: 240
479	Lewis	■	out	Sep 20 05	Idaho	ID	2.5 miles ENE of jct; FR 481 and Middle Butte Rd	**5**: 217-219, **9**: 227, **10**: 145
480	Lewis/Clark	■●	return	Jun 15 06	Idaho	ID	0.5 mile SSW of junction; FR 124 and FR 500	**8**: 25-27, **9**: 322-323, **10**: 239-240
481a	Lewis/Clark	■●	return	Jun 18-20 06	Clearwater	ID	one-fourth mile SW of jct; FR 124 and FR 500	**8**: 34-43, **9**: 324-325, **10**: 241-242
481b	Lewis/Clark	■●	return	Jun 24 06	Clearwater	ID	one-fourth mile SW of jct; FR 124 and FR 500	**8**: 48-50, **9**: 326-327, **10**: 243-244
482	Lewis	■	out	Sep 21 05	Idaho	ID	0.5 miles ENE of jct; FR 124 and Dora Creek Road	**5**: 225-226, **9**: 227, **10**: 146
483	Clark	●	out	Sep 19 05	Idaho	ID	1 mile ENE of jct; FR 124 and Dora Creek Road	**5**: 216-217
484a	Lewis/Clark	■●	out	Sep 22 05	Clearwater	ID	3 miles SE of Weippe	**5**: 228-231, **9**: 228, **10**: 146-147
484b	Lewis/Clark	■●	return	Jun 10-14 06	Clearwater	ID	3 miles SE of Weippe	**8**: 7-24, **9**: 321-322, **10**: 237-239
484c	Lewis/Clark	■●	return	Jun 21-23 06	Clearwater	ID	3 miles SE of Weippe	**8**: 43-48, **9**: 325-326, **10**: 242-243
485	Clark	●	out	Sep 20 05	Clearwater	ID	9.5 miles W of Musselshell	**5**: 219-225, **9**: 227, **10**: 144-145
486	Lewis/Clark	■●	out	Sep 23 05	Clearwater	ID	0.5 miles SSW of Weippe	**5**: 231-232, **9**: 228-229, **10**: 147
487	Lewis/Clark	■●	return	May 13 06	Ravalli	ID	2.5 miles NNE of East Kamiah	**7**: 252-255, **9**: 309, **10**: 227
488	Lewis/Clark	■●	return	May 14-Jun 9 06	Idaho	ID	1 mile N of Kamiah	**7**: 255-350, **9**: 310-321, **10**: 227-237
489	Lewis/Clark	■●	return	May 10-12 06	Lewis	ID	7.5 miles ESE of Nezperce	**7**: 237-251, **9**: 308-309, **10**: 224-227
490	Lewis/Clark	■●	return	May 9 06	Lewis	ID	4.5 miles WSW of Greer	**7**: 233-237, **9**: 307-308, **10**: 224
491	Clark	●	out	Sep 21 05	Clearwater	ID	1 mile S of Orofino	**5**: 226-228
492	Lewis/Clark	■●	out	Sep 24 05	Clearwater	ID	1.5 miles ESE of Riverside	**5**: 232-233, **9**: 229, **10**: 147-148
493	Lewis/Clark	■●	return	May 8 06	Clearwater	ID	11.5 WSW of Cooper	**7**: 226-233, **9**: 307, **10**: 223-224
494	Lewis/Clark	■●	out	Sep 25-31 05	Clearwater	ID	0.5 mile WSW of Ahsahka	**5**: 233-243, **9**: 229-231, **10**: 148-150

Lewis and Clark Expedition Campsites

campsite #	group leader (Lewis ■ Clark ■ Ordway ● Other ▲ ★)	journey	out - black, return - red, side trip - blue	date	county	state	location	Journals of the Lewis and Clark Expedition U of Nebr Press: Volumes 2-8 Lewis and Clark, Volume 9 Ordway; Floyd, Volume 10 Gass, Volume 11 Whitehouse
REGION EIGHT (#425-500)							**Western Montana and Idaho**	**Map pages 160-161**
495	Lewis/Clark	■●	out	Oct 1-6 05	Clearwater	ID	0.5 mile W of Ahsahka	**5**: 243-248, **9**: 232-234, **10**: 150-151
496	Lewis/Clark	■●	return	May 7 06	Nez Perce	ID	0.5 mile SSE of Peck	**7**: 220-225, **9**: 306-307, **10**: 223
497	Lewis/Clark	■●	out	Oct 7 06	Nez Perce	ID	3 miles W of Big George	**5**: 248-251, **9**: 234, **10**: 151
498	Lewis/Clark	■●	return	May 6 06	Nez Perce	ID	5 miles SW of Leland	**7**: 215-220, **9**: 306, **10**: 222-223
499	Lewis/Clark	■●	return	May 5 06	Nez Perce	ID	8 miles SSW of Juliaetta	**7**: 209-215, **9**: 305-306, **10**: 222
500	Lewis/Clark	■●	out	Oct 8-9 05	Nez Perce	ID	4 miles NNE of Lapwai	**5**: 251-253, **9**: 234-236, **10**: 151-152
REGION NINE (#501-573)							**Washington and Oregon**	**Map pages 186-187**
501	Lewis/Clark	■●	out	Oct 10 05	Whitman	WA	2.5 miles WNW of North Lewiston, ID	**5**: 255-260, **9**: 236, **10**: 152, **11**: 345-347
502	Lewis/Clark	■●	return	May 4 06	Whitman	WA	3.5 miles E of Moses	**7**: 205-209, **9**: 304-305, **10**: 221-222
503	Lewis/Clark	■●	out	Oct 11 05	Whitman	WA	one-sixth mile SW of Almota	**5**: 261-264, **9**: 237, **10**: 153, **11**: 348-349
504	Lewis/Clark	■●	return	May 3 06	Garfield	WA	5.5 miles E of Pomeroy	**7**: 202-205, **9**: 303-304, **10**: 220-221
505	Lewis/Clark	■●	return	May 2 06	Columbia	WA	6 miles E of Dayton	**7**: 199-202, **9**: 303, **10**: 220
506	Lewis/Clark	■●	out	Oct 12 05	Whitman	WA	0.5 mile SW of Riparia	**5**: 264-266, **9**: 237, **10**: 154, **11**: 349-350
507	Lewis/Clark	■●	return	May 1 06	Walla Walla	WA	3.5 miles WNW of Waitsburg	**7**: 195-198, **9**: 301-302, **10**: 218-219
508	Lewis/Clark	■●	out	Oct 13 05	Franklin	WA	8 miles W of Perry	**5**: 266-269, **9**: 238, **10**: 154, **11**: 351-352
509	Lewis/Clark	■●	out	Oct 14 05	Walla Walla	WA	0.5 mile SW of Scott	**5**: 269-273, **9**: 238-239, **10**: 155, **11**: 352-354
510	Lewis/Clark	■●	return	Apr 30 06	Walla Walla	WA	11 Miles N of Touchet	**7**: 187-195, **9**: 300-301, **10**: 218
511	Lewis/Clark	■●	out	Oct 15 05	Franklin	WA	2.5 miles SSW of Redd	**5**: 274-276, **9**: 239, **10**: 155, **11**: 354
512	Lewis/Clark	■●	return	Apr 29 06	Walla Walla	WA	1.5 miles SW of Wallula	**7**: 181-187, **9**: 300, **10**: 217-218
513	Lewis/Clark	■●	return	Apr 27-28 06	Benton	WA	0.5 mile NE of Yellepit	**7**: 173-181, **9**: 298-300, **10**: 216-217
514	Lewis/Clark	■●	out	Oct 18 05	Walla Walla	WA	1 mile WSW of Port Kelley	**5**: 291-301, **9**: 240-241, **10**: 157-158 **11**: 358-360
515	Lewis/Clark	■●	out	Oct 16-17 05	Franklin	WA	3.5 miles E of Kennewick	**5**: 276-291, **9**: 239-240, **10**: 155-157, **11**: 354-358
516	Lewis/Clark	■●	return	Apr 26 06	Benton	WA	2.5 miles WSW of Plymouth	**7**: 169-173, **9**: 298, **10**: 216
517	Lewis/Clark	■●	out	Oct 19 05	Umatilla	OR	3 miles WSW of Umatilla	**5**: 301-308, **9**: 241, **10**: 158, **11**: 360-361
518	Lewis/Clark	■●	return	Apr 25 06	Klickitat	WA	7 miles WSW of Whitcomb	**7**: 165-169, **9**: 297, **10**: 215-216
519	Lewis/Clark	■●	out	Oct 20 05	Klickitat	WA	9.5 miles SW of McCredie	**5**: 309-313, **9**: 242, **10**: 159, **11**: 361-362
520	Lewis/Clark	■●	return	Apr 24 06	Klickitat	WA	0.5 mile SE of Roosevelt	**7**: 162-165, **9**: 296-297, **10**: 215
521	Lewis/Clark	■●	return	Apr 23 06	Klickitat	WA	1.5 miles W of Bates	**7**: 159-162, **9**: 296, **10**: 214-215

CAMP SITES TABLE

Lewis and Clark Expedition Campsites

campsite #	group leader (Lewis ■, Clark ●, Ordway ▲, Other ★)		journey (out - black, return - red, side trip - blue)	date	county	state	location	Journals of the Lewis and Clark Expedition U of Nebr Press (Volumes 2-8 Lewis and Clark, Volume 9 Ordway; Floyd, Volume 10 Gass, Volume 11 Whitehouse)
REGION NINE (#501-573)							**Washington and Oregon**	**Map pages 186-187**
522	Lewis/Clark	■●	return	Apr 22 06	Klickitat	WA	5 miles SW of Towai	**7**: 155-159, **9**: 295-296, **10**: 214
523	Lewis/Clark	■●	out	Oct 21 05	Kilckitat	WA	5 miles ENE of Maryhill	**5**: 314-320, **9**: 242, **10**: 159, **11**: 362-364
524	Lewis/Clark	■●	return	Apr 21 06	Klickitat	WA	1.5 miles E of Wishram	**7**: 151-155, **9**: 295, **10**: 213-214
525	Lewis/Clark	■●	out	Oct 22-23 05	Klickitat	WA	1.5 miles WSW of Wishram Heights	**5**: 320-328, **9**: 243-244, **10**: 160-161 **11**: 364-368
526	Lewis/Clark	■●	out	Oct 24 05	Klickitat	WA	4 miles NE of Dallesport	**5**: 328-336, **9**: 244, **10**: 161-162, **11**: 368-370
527	Lewis/Clark	■●	return	Apr 19-20 06	Kilickitat	WA	3 miles E of Smithville	**7**: 142-151, **9**: 294-295, **10**: 212-213
528	Lewis/Clark	■●	return	Apr 18 06	Klickitat	WA	3.5 miles SE of Murdock	**7**: 136-142, **9**: 294, **10**: 212
529a	Lewis/Clark	■●	out	Oct 25-27 05	Wasco	OR	Fort Rock, The Dalles	**5**: 336-346, **9**: 244-246, **10**: 162-163, **11**: 370-374
529b	Lewis/Clark	■●	return	Apr 15-17 06	Wasco	OR	Fort Rock, The Dalles	**7**: 123-135, **9**: 292-294, **10**: 211-212
530	Lewis/Clark	■●	out	Oct 28 05	Wasco	OR	2.5 miles NE of Chenoweth	**5**: 346-348, **9**: 246, **10**: 163, **11**: 374-375
531	Lewis/Clark	■●	return	Apr 14 06	Klickitat	WA	3.5 miles WNW of Lyle	**7**: 118-123, **9**: 291-292, **10**: 210-211
532	Lewis/Clark	■●	out	Oct 29 05	Skamania	WA	5.5 miles WSW of Hood River	**5**: 348-354, **9**: 246-247, **10**: 163-164, **11**: 375-377
533	Lewis/Clark	■●	return	Apr 13 06	Skamania	OR	3.5 miles WSW of Cook	**7**: 115-117, **9**: 291, **10**: 210
534	Lewis/Clark	■●	return	Apr 12 06	Skamania	WA	2.5 miles SW of Reid	**7**: 111-115, **9**: 290-291. **10**: 290-291
535	Lewis/Clark	■●	out	Oct 30-31 05	Skamania	WA	2 miles SSW of Stevenson	**5**: 354-366, **9**: 247-248, **10**: 164, **11**: 377-379
536	Lewis/Clark	■●	out	Nov 1 05	Skamania	WA	2.5 miles NE of Bonneville Dam	**5**: 366-381, **9**: 248, **10**: 165, **11**: 379-380
537	Lewis/Clark	■●	return	Apr 10-11 06	Skamania	WA	3 miles ENE of North Bonneville	**7**: 101-111, **9**: 289-290, **10**: 208-209
538	Lewis/Clark	■●	return	Apr 9 06	Multnomah	OR	0.5 mile NW of Bonneville	**7**: 96-101, **9**: 288-289, **10**: 208
539	Lewis/Clark	■●	return	Apr 6-8 06	Multnomah	OR	1 mile NE of Bridal Veil	**7**: 78-96, **9**: 287-288, **10**: 206-208
540	Lewis/Clark	■●	out	Nov 2 05	Multnomah	OR	1.5 miles NE of Corbett	**6**: 7-10, **9**: 248, **10**: 165, **11**: 380-382
541a	Lewis/Clark	■●	return	Mar 31-Apr 1 06	Clark	WA	0.5 mile SSE of Washougal	**7**: 38-53, **9**: 283-284, **10**: 204, **11**: 437-438
541b	Lewis	■	return	Apr 2 06	Clark	WA	0.5 mile SSE of Washougal	**7**: 53-55, **9**: 284-285, **10**: 204-205
541c	Lewis/Clark	■●	return	Apr 3-5 06	Clark	WA	0.5 mile SSE of Washougal	**7**: 62-78, **9**: 285-287, **10**: 205-206
542	Lewis/Clark	■●	out	Nov 3 05	Multnomah	OR	7.5 miles NW of Gresham	**6**: 10-14, **9**: 249, **10**: 165-166, **11**: 382-384
543	Lewis/Clark	■●	return	Mar 30 06	Clark	WA	2 miles SW of Vancouver	**7**: 32-38, **9**: 283, **10**: 203-204, **11**: 436-437
544	Clark	●	return	Apr 2 06	Multnomah	OR	2 miles SE of Cathedral Park	**7**: 55-62, **9**: 285, **11**: 438-440
545	Lewis/Clark	■●	out	Nov 4 05	Clark	WA	6 miles NW of Salmon Creek	**6**: 14-21, **9**: 249-250, **10**: 166-167, **11**: 384-387
546	Lewis/Clark	■●	return	Mar 29 06	Clark	WA	1 mile NW of Ridgefield	**7**: 26-32, **9**: 282-283, **10**: 203, **11**: 436

Lewis and Clark Expedition Campsites

campsite #	group leader (Lewis ■, Clark ●, Ordway ●, Other ▲ ★)	journey	out - black, return - red, side trip - blue	date	county	state	location	Journals of the Lewis and Clark Expedition U of Nebr Press (Volumes 2-8 Lewis and Clark; Volume 9 Ordway, Floyd; Volume 10 Gass; Volume 11 Whitehouse)
REGION NINE (#501-573)							**Washington and Oregon**	**Map pages 186-187**
547	Lewis/Clark	■ ●	return	Mar 28 06	Columbia	OR	4 miles N of Deer Island	**7**: 22-26, **9**: 282, **10**: 202-203, **11**: 435
548	Lewis/Clark	■ ●	return	Mar 27 06	Columbia	OR	1 mile S of Goble	**7**: 18-22, **9**: 281-282, **10**: 202, **11**: 434-435
549	Lewis/Clark	■ ●	out	Nov 5 05	Columbia	OR	0.5 mile ESE of Lindbergh	**6**: 21-25, **9**: 250, **10**: 167, **11**: 387-388
550	Lewis/Clark	■ ●	return	Mar 26 06	Columbia	OR	5 miles NW of Ranier	**7**: 15-17, **9**: 281, **10**: 202, **11**: 434
551	Lewis/Clark	■ ●	return	Mar 25 06	Columbia	OR	2.5 NNW of Clatskanie	**7**: 11-15, **9**: 281, **10**: 201-202, **11**: 433-434
552	Lewis/Clark	■ ●	out	Nov 6 05	Wahkiakum	WA	6 miles SE of Cathlamet	**6**: 25-30, **9**: 251, **10**: 167-168, **11**: 388-389
553	Lewis/Clark	■ ●	return	Mar 24 06	Clatsop	OR	2 miles NE of Brownsmead	**7**: 9-11, **9**: 280-281, **10**: 201, **11**: 433
554	Lewis/Clark	■ ●	out	Nov 7 05	Wahkiakum	WA	6.5 miles W of Skamokawa	**6**: 30-35, **9**: 251, **10**: 168, **11**: 389-390
555	Lewis/Clark	■ ●	out	Nov 25 05	Wahkiakum	WA	1 mile W of Dahlia	**6**: 86-87, **9**: 256, **10**: 177-178, **11**: 398-399
556	Lewis/Clark	■ ●	out	Nov 26 05	Clatsop	OR	0.5 mile WNW of Svensen	**6**: 87-90, **9**: 257, **10**: 178, **11**: 399
557	Lewis/Clark	■ ●	out	Mar 23 06	Clatsop	OR	1 mile NNW of Fern Hill	**7**: 7-9, **9**: 279-280, **10**: 200-201, **11**: 200-201
558	Lewis/Clark	■ ●	out	Nov 8-9 05	Pacific	WA	3 miles E of Knappton	**6**: 35-38, **9**: 251-252, **10**: 168-169, **11**: 390-391
559a	Lewis/Clark	■ ●	out	Nov 27-28 05	Clatsop	OR	0.5 mile NNE of Tongue Point Village	**6**: 90-92, **9**: 257, **10**: 178, **11**: 399-400
559b	Clark	●	out	Nov 29-Dec 4 05	Clatsop	OR	0.5 mile NNE of Tongue Point Village	**6**: 93-101, 103-108, **9**: 257-258, **10**: 178-180, **11**:400-401
559c	Lewis/Clark	■ ●	out	Dec 6 05	Clatsop	OR	0.5 mile NNE of Tongue Point Village	**6**: 109, **9**: 258, **10**: 180, **11**: 402
559d	Lewis/Clark	■ ●	out	Dec 6 05	Clatsop	OR	0.5 mile NNE of Tongue Point Village	**6**: 109, **9**: 258, **10**: 180, **11**: 401-402
560a	Lewis/Clark	■ ●	out	Nov 10-13 05	Pacific	WA	one-fourth mile SSW of Megler	**6**: 38-46, **9**: 252-253, **10**: 169-170, **11**: 391-393
560b	Clark	●	out	Nov 14 05	Pacific	WA	one-fourth mile SSW of Megler	**6**: 46-48, **9**: 253, **10**: 170-171, **11**: 393
561	Lewis	■	out	Nov 14-16 05	Pacific	WA	Fort Canby	**6**: 46-48, 50
562a	Clark	●	out	Nov 15-16 05	Pacific	WA	one-fourth mile WSW of McGowan	**6**: 48-61, **9**: 253-254, **10**: 171-172, **11**: 393-394
562b	Lewis/Clark	■ ●	out	Nov.17, 20-24 05	Pacific	WA	one-fourth mile WSW of McGowan	**6**: 60-62, 71-86, **9**: 254-256, **10**: 172, 175-177, **11**: 394-398
562c	Lewis	■	out	Nov 18-19 05	Pacific	WA	one-fourth mile WSW of McGowan	**6**: 62, **9**: 254-255, **10**: 175, **11**: 395-396
563	Clark	●	out	Nov 18 05	Pacific	WA	0.5 miles WSW of Fort Canby	**6**: 62-68, **9**: 254-255, **10**: 175, **11**: 395
564	Clark	●	out	Nov 19 05	Pacific	WA	1 mile NE of Ilwaco	**6**: 68-71
565	Lewis	■	out	Nov 29-Dec 4 05	Clatsop	OR	1.5 miles SW of Astoria	**6**: 92-96, 101-105, **9**: 257, **10**: 178-179, **11**: 400, 401
566	Lewis/Clark	■ ●	out	Dec 7 05	Clatsop	OR	2.5 miles ENE of Clatsop Station	**6**: 109-115, **9**: 258-259, **10**: 180-181, **11**: 402-403
567a	Lewis	■	out	Dec 8-9 05	Clatsop	OR	one-eighth mile ENE of Ft Clatsop Natl Memorial	**9**: 259, **10**: 181, **11**: 403
567b	Lewis/Clark	■ ●	out	Dec 10-14, 16-31 05	Clatsop	OR	one-eighth mile ENE of Ft Clatsop Natl Memorial	**6**: 120-151, **9**: 260-263, **10**: 181-185, **11**: 403-409
567c	Lewis	■	out	Dec 15 05	Clatsop	OR	one-eighth mile ENE of Ft Clatsop Natl Memorial	**10**: 183

CAMP SITES TABLE

Lewis and Clark Expedition Campsites

campsite #	group leader (Lewis ■ Clark ● Ordway ▲ Other ★)		journey (out - black, return - red, side trip - blue)	date	county	state	location	Journals of the Lewis and Clark Expedition U of Nebr Press (Volumes 2-8 Lewis and Clark; Volume 9 Ordway; Floyd; Volume 10 Gass; Volume 11 Whitehouse)
REGION NINE (#501-573)							**Washington and Oregon**	**Map pages 186-187**
567d	Lewis/Clark	■ ●	out	Jan 1-5 06	Clatsop	OR	one-eighth mile ENE of Ft Clatsop Natl Memorial	**6**: 151-168, **9**: 263-265, **10**: 185-187, **11**: 409-410
567e	Lewis	■	out	Jan 6-9 06	Clatsop	OR	one-eighth mile ENE of Ft Clatsop Natl Memorial	**6**: 168-169, 174-175, 179, **9**: 265, **11**: 410-411
567f	Lewis/Clark	■ ●	out	Jan 10-Mar 22 06	Clatsop	OR	one-eighth mile ENE of Ft Clatsop Natl Memorial	**6**: 192-444, **9**: 265-279, **10**: 188-200, **11**: 411-430
568	Clark	●	out	Dec 15 05	Clatsop	OR	2.5 miles E of Glenwood	**6**: 125-126, **9**: 261, **10**: 183, **11**: 405
569	Clark	●	out	Dec 8-9 05	Clatsop	OR	1 mile NNW of Dellmoor	**6**: 116-120, **9**: 259, **10**: 181, **11**: 403
570	Clark	●	side trip	Jan 6 06	Clatsop	OR	Sunset Beach	**6**: 169-173, **9**: 265 **11**: 410-411
571	Clark	●	side trip	Jan 7 06	Clatsop	OR	3 miles W of Cannon Beach Junction	**6**: 175-179, **10**: 187
572	Clark	●	side trip	Jan 8 06	Clatsop	OR	1 mile N of Cannon Beach	**6**: 180-186
573	Clark	●	side trip	Jan 9 06	Clatsop	OR	1.5 miles SSW of Seaside	**6**: 188-192, **10**: 187

☑ Check List of Destinations

Region One: East of the Alleghenies

Region Two: Pittsburgh to Cincinnati

Region Two: Pittsburgh to Cincinnati, Cont.

47 ☐ Int'l Museum of the Horse and KY Horse Park, Lexington
48 ☐ Ashland, Henry Clay Estate, Lexington
49 ☐ Kentucky History Center, Frankfort
50 ☐ Kentucky Military History Museum, Frankfort
51 ☐ Kentucky Old State Capitol, Frankfort
52 ☐ Liberty Hall Historic Home, Frankfort
53 ☐ Buffalo Trace Distillery, Frankfort

54 ☐ Fort Boonesborough State Park, Richmond
55 ☐ Shaker Village of Pleasant Hill, Harrodsburg
56 ☐ Old Fort Harrod State Park, Harrodsburg
57 ☐ Constitution Square State Historic Site, Danville
58 ☐ William Whitley House State Historic Site, Stanford
59 ☐ Levi Jackson Wilderness Road State Park, London
60 ☐ Cumberland Falls State Resort Park, Corbin
61 ☐ Dr Thomas Walker State Historic Site, Barbourville

Region Three: Louisville to Wood River Camp

1a ☐ Louisville Waterfront Park
1b ☐ York Statue
1c ☐ Belle of Louisville Steamboat
2 ☐ Frazier Historical Arms Museum
3 ☐ Filson Historical Society Museum
4 ☐ Speed Art Museum
5 ☐ Kentucky Derby Museum
6 ☐ Mulberry Hill
7 ☐ Cave Hill Cemetery
8 ☐ Locust Grove
9 ☐ Farmington Historic Home

10 ☐ Southern Indiana Visitor Center
11 ☐ Falls of the Ohio Interpretive Center
12 ☐ Clark's Cabin at Clark's Point
13 ☐ Howard Steamboat Museum

14 ☐ John Shields Marker, West Point
15 ☐ Squire Boone Caverns, Mauckport
16 ☐ Corydon State Capitol
17 ☐ Lincoln Boyhood National Memorial, Lincoln City
18 ☐ Audubon Museum and State Park, Henderson
19 ☐ Angel Mounds State Historic Site, Evansville
20 ☐ Land Between the Lakes, Golden Pond
21 ☐ Flood Wall Murals, Paducah
22 ☐ Quilt Museum, Paducah
23 ☐ Fort Massac State Park, Metropolis
24 ☐ Superman Museum, Metropolis

25 ☐ Historic New Harmony
26 ☐ George Rogers Clark National Historical Park, Vincennes
27 ☐ The Old Cathedral, Library and Museum, Vincennes
28 ☐ The Old French House and Indian Museum, Vincennes
29 ☐ Grouseland, Home of Wm Henry Harrison, Vincennes
30 ☐ Log Cabin, Visitors Center, Vincennes
31 ☐ Sugarloaf Mounds, Vincennes
32 ☐ George Rogers Clark US 50 Route

33 ☐ Confluence of Ohio and Mississippi Rivers, Cairo
34 ☐ U. S. Customs House Museum, Cairo
35 ☐ Tywappity Bottoms and River Ridge Winery, Commerce
36 ☐ The Red House, Cape Girardeau
37 ☐ Cape Rock Park
38 ☐ Cape Girardeau Murals
39 ☐ Southeast Missouri Regional Museum
40 ☐ Trail of Tears State Park
41 ☐ Tower Rock & Tower Rock Winery

42 ☐ Kaskaskia Bell State Historic Site, Kaskaskia
43 ☐ Great River Road Interpretive Center, Ste Genevieve
44 ☐ Bolduc House Museum, Ste Genevieve
45 ☐ Bolduc La Meilleur House, Ste Genevieve
46 ☐ Felix Valle State Historic Site, Ste Genevieve
47 ☐ La Maison Guibourd-Valle, Ste Genevieve
48 ☐ Ste Genevieve Museum
49 ☐ Ste Genevieve-Modoc Ferry
50 ☐ Pierre Menard Home State Historic Site, Ellis Grove
51 ☐ Fort Kaskaskia State Historic Site, Ellis Grove
52 ☐ Fort de Chartres III, Prairie du Rocher

53 ☐ Martin Boismenue House, Cahokia
54 ☐ Cahokia Courthouse
55 ☐ Jarrot Mansion, Cahokia
56 ☐ Holy Family Church, Cahokia
57 ☐ Jefferson Barracks, St Louis County
58 ☐ Mastodon State Historic Site and Museum, Imperial
59 ☐ Cahokia Mounds World Heritage Site, Collinsville

60 ☐ Lewis and Clark Interpretive Center, Hartford
61 ☐ Lewis and Clark Memorial Tower, Hartford
62 ☐ Meeting of Great Rivers Scenic Byway, Hartford
63 ☐ Wood River Museum and Visitor Center
64 ☐ Nat'l Great Rivers Museum #1 Lock & Dam, East Alton
65 ☐ Bald Eagle and Pelican Migration, Alton
66 ☐ Sacagawea Statue, Lewis & Clark College, Godfrey
67 ☐ Clark Bridge, Alton
68 ☐ Confluence Point State Park, West Alton
69 ☐ Columbia Bottom Conservation Area, St Louis County
70 ☐ Fort Belle Fontaine, St Louis County

Region Four: St Louis to Kansas City

1 ☐ Gateway Arch
2 ☐ Museum of Westward Expansion
3 ☐ Old Cathedral Museum
4 ☐ Old Courthouse Museum
5 ☐ William Clark House and Museum Site
6 ☐ Laclede's Landing
7 ☐ Gateway Arch Riverboat Cruises
8 ☐ Campbell House Museum

9 ☐ Missouri Botanical Gardens
10 ☐ St Louis University Museum of Art
11 ☐ Missouri History Museum
12 ☐ St Louis Zoo
13 ☐ St Louis Science Center
14 ☐ St Louis Art Museum
15 ☐ Forest Park Tree Walk
16 ☐ St Louis Walk of Fame - Jewel Box
17 ☐ Faust County Park Historic Village
18 ☐ Thornhill Estate of Frederick Bates
19 ☐ Butterfly House, Faust County Park
20 ☐ William Clark Grave, Belle Fontaine Cemetery
21 ☐ Nez Perce Warriors Memorial, Calvary Cem.
22 ☐ General Daniel Bissell House

CHECK LIST

Region Five: Nebraska and Iowa

☑ Check List of Destinations

ONAWA TO SIOUX CITY, CONT. 100-101

53 ☐ Winnavegas Casino, Inn and Restaurant, Sloan
54 ☐ John G Neihardt Center, Bancroft
55 ☐ Blackbird Hill Scenic Overlook, Macy
56 ☐ Winnebago Cultural Center and Museum, Winnebago
57 ☐ AllNative Store, Winnebago
58 ☐ Tonwantonga Village Site, Homer
59 ☐ Sergeant Floyd Monument, Sioux City
60 ☐ Lewis and Clark Murals and AllNative Store, Sioux City
61 ☐ Sgt Floyd Riverboat Museum/Welcome Center, Sioux City
62 ☐ Lewis and Clark Interpretive Center. Sioux City
63 ☐ Sioux City Public Museum

NORTHEASTERN NEBRASKA 102-103

64 ☐ Ponca State Park Missouri River Visitor Center, Ponca
65 ☐ Shannon Trail, Crofton
66 ☐ Corps of Discovery Welcome Center, Crofton
67 ☐ Ponca Tribal Museum, Niobrara
68 ☐ Santee Tribal Museum, Niobrara
69 ☐ Ohiya Casino and Restaurant, Niobrara
70 ☐ Chief Standing Bear Memorial Bridge, Niobrara
71 ☐ Niobrara State Park
72 ☐ Kreycik Riverview Elk & Buffalo Ranch, Niobrara
73 ☐ Old Baldy, Lynch
74 ☐ Ashfall Fossil Beds State Historical Park, Royal

Region Six: South and North Dakota

SIOUX CITY TO CHAMBERLAIN 110-111

1 ☐ Adams Homestead and Nature Preserve, North Sioux City
2 ☐ Elk Point Heritage Park, Elk Point
3 ☐ W H Over Museum, Vermillion
4 ☐ National Music Museum, Vermillion
5 ☐ Spirit Mound Historic Prairie, Vermillion
6 ☐ Pierre Dorian Grave and Marker, Yankton
7 ☐ Dakota Territorial Museum, Yankton
8 ☐ Gavins Point Dam and Powerplant, Yankton
9 ☐ Gavins Point Nat'l Fish Hatchery and Aquarium, Yankton
10 ☐ Lewis and Clark Visitor Center, Yankton
11 ☐ Missouri National Recreational River, Yankton
12 ☐ Lewis and Clark Recreation Area and Lake, Yankton
13 ☐ Fort Randall Dam/Lake Francis Case Visitor Center, Pickston
14 ☐ Fort Randall Military Post, Chapel and Cemetery, Pickston
15a ☐ Fort Randall Casino, Hotel and Restaurant, Pickston
15b ☐ Yankton Sioux Reservation Tours, Pickston

CHAMBERLAIN TO PIERRE NATIVE AMERICAN SCENIC BYWAY ...112-113

16 ☐ Lewis and Clark Information Center I-90 Rest Area
17 ☐ Akta Lakota Museum and Cultural Center, Chamberlain
18 ☐ South Dakota Hall of Fame Museum, Chamberlain
19 ☐ Sioux Crossing of the Three Rivers, Hwy 50, Crow Creek Res.
20 ☐ Big Bend Dam/Lake Sharpe Recreation Area, Fort Thompson
21a ☐ Lode Star Casino, Motel and Restaurant, Fort Thompson
21b ☐ Crow Creek Sioux Reservation Tours, Fort Thompson
22a ☐ Golden Buffalo Casino, Motel, Restaurant, Lower Brule
22b ☐ Lower Brule Sioux Reservation Tours
23 ☐ Lower Brule Sioux Buffalo Interpretive Center

FORT PIERRE AND PIERRE 114-115

24 ☐ Fort Pierre National Grasslands
25 ☐ Lilly Park, Fort Pierre
26 ☐ Verendrye Monument Nat'l Historic Landmark, Fort Pierre
27 ☐ South Dakota Discovery Center and Aquarium, Pierre
28 ☐ South Dakota State Capitol and Capitol Lake, Pierre
29 ☐ South Dakota Cultural Heritage Center and Museum, Pierre
30 ☐ Pierre Native Plant Arboretum and Nature Area
31 ☐ La Framboise Island, Pierre
32 ☐ Farm Island State Park and Visitor Center, Pierre
33 ☐ Medicine Knoll Overlook, Pierre
34 ☐ Fort Pierre Chouteau National Historic Landmark, Fort Pierre
35 ☐ Scotty Philip the "Buffalo King" Cemetery, Fort Pierre
36 ☐ Oahe Dam/Oahe Lake Visitor Center, Pierre
37 ☐ Triple U Buffalo Ranch "Dances With Wolves" film location

PIERRE TO BISMARCK 116-117

38 ☐ Arikara Lodge Whitlock Recreation Area, Gettysburg
39 ☐ Dakota Sunset Museum, Gettysburg
40a ☐ H V Johnston Lakota Cultural Center, Eagle Butte
40b ☐ Cheyenne River Sioux Reservation Tours, Eagle Butte
41 ☐ Timber Lake and Area Museum, Timber Lake
42 ☐ Grand River Casino and Bay Resort, Mobridge
43 ☐ Sitting Bull and Sacagawea Monuments, Mobridge
44 ☐ Klein Museum and Historical Monuments, Mobridge
45 ☐ Indian Prayer Rocks at City Park, Mobridge
46 ☐ Oscar Howe Murals at City Auditorium, Mobridge
47 ☐ Fort Manuel, Kenel
48a ☐ Prairie Knight Casino and Resort, Fort Yates
48b ☐ Standing Rock Reservation Tours, Fort Yates
49 ☐ Sitting Bull Burial State Historic Site, Fort Yates

SIOUX CITY TO BISMARCK INTERSTATE ROUTE 118-119

50 ☐ Delbridge Museum of Natural History and Zoo, Sioux Falls
51a ☐ Pipestone National Monument, Pipestone
51b ☐ Song of Hiawatha Pageant, Pipestone
52 ☐ Royal River Casino Bingo and Motel, Flandreau
53 ☐ Corn Palace, Mitchell
54 ☐ Dakota Discovery Museum
55 ☐ Mitchell Prehistoric Indian Village
56 ☐ Dakota Sioux Casino and Hotel, Waterton
57 ☐ Dakota Sioux Magic Casino and Hotel, Hankinson
58 ☐ Heritage Hjemkomst Interpretive Center, Moorhead
59 ☐ Bonanzaville USA, West Fargo
60 ☐ National Buffalo Museum/Frontier Village, Jamestown

BISMARCK AND MANDAN 120-121

61 ☐ On-A-Slant Indian Village, Mandan
62 ☐ Five Nations Arts, Mandan
63 ☐ Chief Looking's Village River Overlook, Bismarck
64 ☐ Lewis and Clark Riverboat and Keelboat Park, Bismarck
65 ☐ Captain Meriwethers Restaurant, Bismarck
66 ☐ North Dakota State Capitol, Bismarck
67 ☐ North Dakota Heritage Center/Sakakawea Statue, Bismarck
68 ☐ Double Ditch Indian Village State Historic Site, Bismarck

FORT MANDAN AND THE KNIFE RIVER VILLAGES 122-123

69 ☐ No Dakota Lewis and Clark Interpretive Center, Washburn
70 ☐ Cross Ranch State Park. Washburn
71 ☐ Fort Mandan, Washburn
72 ☐ Fort Clark Trading Post State Historic Site, Stanton
73 ☐ Knife River Villages National Historic Site, Stanton
74 ☐ Lake Sakakawea State Park, Pick City
75 ☐ Garrison Dam/Lake Sakakawea, Pick City
76 ☐ Garrison Dam National Fish Hatchery, Pick City
77 ☐ Audubon National Wildlife Refuge Complex, Cole Harbor
78 ☐ Paul Broste Rock Museum, Parshall

NEW TOWN AND CONFLUENCE...................... 124-125

79 ☐ Crow Flies High Butte Historic Site
80 ☐ Reunion Point Bay
81 ☐ 4 Bears Casino and Lodge and Jetboat Tours
82a ☐ Three Tribes Museum
82b ☐ Fort Berthold Reservation Tours
83 ☐ Lewis and Clark State Park
84 ☐ Missouri Yellowstone Confluence Int Center, Williston
85 ☐ Fort Buford State Historic Site, Williston
86 ☐ Fort Union Trading Post National Historic Site, Williston

Region Seven: Montana to the Rockies

Region Eight: Western Montana and Idaho

ACROSS THE DIVIDE TO SALMON, IDAHO 166-167

1 ☐ Lemhi Pass National Historic Landmark
2 ☐ Lewis and Clark Backcountry Byway, Tendoy
3 ☐ Sacajawea Interpretive, Educ and Cultural Center, Salmon
4 ☐ Salmon-Lemhi County Museum, Salmon
5 ☐ Shoshone-Bannock Tribal Museum, Fort Hall
6 ☐ Clark's Reconnaissance on the Salmon River, Shoup
7 ☐ Bannack Ghost Town, Jackson
8 ☐ Hot Springs and Lewis and Clark Marker, Jackson
9 ☐ Big Hole National Battlefield, Wisdom
10 ☐ Lost Trail Pass Visitor Center, Highway 93

BITTERROOT VALLEY, HIGHWAY 93 168-

11 ☐ Ross's Hole/Sula Ranger Station
12 ☐ Darby Historical Visitor Center
13 ☐ Darby Pioneer Museum
14 ☐ Ravalli County Museum
15 ☐ Bitter Root Brewing
16 ☐ Historic St Mary's Mission
17 ☐ Fort Owen State Park
18 ☐ Stevensville Museum
19 ☐ Lee Metcalf National Wildlife Refuge

MISSOULA AT THE CROSSROADS 170-171

20 ☐ Rocky Mountain Elk Foundation
21 ☐ University of Montana Bookstore
22 ☐ Mount Sentinel "M" Trail
23 ☐ Fort Missoula Historical Museum
24 ☐ Montana Natural History Center
25 ☐ Lewis and Clark Riverfront Overlook at Caras Park
26 ☐ Missoula Art Museum

BLACKFOOT RIVER CORRIDOR, HIGHWAY 200 172-173

27 ☐ Blackfoot Gateway Kiosk, Bonner
28 ☐ Blackfoot River Recreation Corridor, Bonner
29 ☐ Garnet Ghost Town
30 ☐ Back Country Byway, Garnet
31 ☐ Blackfoot-Clearwater River Junction Kiosk, Clearwater
32 ☐ Monture Creek (Seaman Creek), Ovando
33 ☐ Historic Ovando and Museum
34 ☐ Prairie of the Knobs Scenic Route, Ovando
35 ☐ L and C Bicentennial Ponderosa Pine Grove, Lincoln
36 ☐ Upper Blackfoot Museum/Hi Country Trading Post, Lincoln
37 ☐ Upper Blackfoot Kiosk, Lincoln
38 ☐ Lander's Fork Rock Cairns, Lincoln
39 ☐ Alice Creek Trail to Lewis and Clark Pass, Lincoln
40 ☐ Fort Mountain (Square Butte), Simms

FLATHEAD VALLEY, HIGHWAY 93 174-175

41 ☐ St Ignatius Mission
42 ☐ Flathead Indian Museum and Trading Post, St Ignatius
43 ☐ National Bison Range, Moiese
44 ☐ Ninepipes and Pablo Nat'l Wildlife Refuges, Charlo and Pablo
45 ☐ Ninepipes Museum of Early Montana, Charlo
46 ☐ Ronan Visitor's Center, Ronan
47 ☐ Garden of the Rockies Museum, Ronan
48a ☐ Peoples Center, Pablo
48b ☐ Native Ed-Venture, Pablo
49 ☐ Best Western KwaTaq Nuk Resort and Casino, Polson
50 ☐ Miracle of America Museum and Pioneer Village, Polson
51 ☐ Polson-Flathead Museum, Polson
52 ☐ Hockaday Museum of Art, Kalispell
53 ☐ Museum at Central School, Kalispell

I- 90 AND US-95 ROUTE TO LEWISTON, IDAHO 176-177

54 ☐ Grant Kohrs Ranch National Historic Site, Deer Lodge
55 ☐ John Mullan Museum, Mullan
56 ☐ Wallace Historic District, Wallace
57 ☐ Old Mission State Park, Cataldo
58 ☐ Museum of Northern Idaho, Coer d'Alene
59 ☐ Northwest Museum of Art and Culture, Spokane
60 ☐ Coeur d'Alene Casino Resort Hotel, Worley
61 ☐ Appaloosa Museum and Heritage Center, Moscow

LOLO TRAIL ON HIGHWAY 12 178-179

62 ☐ Traveler's Rest State Park and Nat'l Hist Landmark, Lolo
63 ☐ Holt Heritage Museum, Lolo
64 ☐ Fort Fizzle Historic Site, Lolo
65 ☐ Howard Creek Historic Lolo Trail
66 ☐ Lolo Hot Springs Campsite
67 ☐ Lolo Trail Center and Mountain Lodging
68 ☐ Lolo Pass Visitor Information Center
69 ☐ Packer Meadows and Glade Creek Campsite
70 ☐ De Voto Memorial Cedar Grove
71 ☐ Powell Ranger Station
72 ☐ Lolo Motorway
73 ☐ Wendover Crossing and Whitehouse Pond
74 ☐ Lochsa Historical Ranger Station

NEZ PERCE COUNTRY, HIGHWAY 12

75 ☐ Kooskia Kiosk and Downtown Murals
76 ☐ First Indian Presbyterian Church, Kamiah
77 ☐ Heart of the Monster Nez Perce Historical Park, Kamiah
78 ☐ Lewis and Clark Long Camp Marker, Kamiah
79 ☐ Kamiah Welcome Center/Lewis and Clark Exhibit Hall, Kamiah
80 ☐ Clearwater Historical Museum, Orofino
81 ☐ Lewis and Clark Canoe Camp, Orofino
82 ☐ Dworshak Dam and Fish Hatchery, Orofino
83 ☐ Weippe Discovery Center, Weippe
84 ☐ Weippe Prairie
85 ☐ Bradbury Logging Museum, Pierce
86 ☐ Lenore (Big Eddy) Rest Area, Lenore
87 ☐ Nez Perce Legend Sites, Spalding

NEZ PERCE COUNTRY, HIGHWAY 95 182-183

88 ☐ Grangeville Visitors Center and Mammoth Replica Exhibit
89 ☐ Bicentennial Historical Museum
90 ☐ Ordway Markers
91 ☐ Historical Museum at St Gertrude
92 ☐ Wolf Research and Education Center
93 ☐ Nez Perce NHP Visitor Center and Museum, Spalding
94 ☐ Nez Perce NHP Spalding Mission Site, Spalding
95 ☐ Buffalo Eddy Petroglyphs
96 ☐ Hells Canyon National Recreation Area

LEWISTON-CLARKSTON AREA 184-185

97 ☐ Lewis and Clark Discovery Center, Hells Gate State Park
98 ☐ Three State Scenic Overlook and Spiral Highway
99 ☐ Nez Perce County Museum
100 ☐ Lewis and Clark Interpretive Center at Confluence
101 ☐ Clearwater and Snake River National Trail
102 ☐ Clearwater Bridge Sculptures at Hwys 12 and 95
103 ☐ Clearwater River Casino
104 ☐ Centennial Mall Sculptures, Lewis-Clark State College
105 ☐ Lewis-Clark Center for Arts and History
106 ☐ Lewis and Clark Discovery Center
107 ☐ Lewis and Clark Garden
108 ☐ Lewis and Clark Riverfront Timeline
109 ☐ Maya Lin Confluence Sculpture Project, Chief Timothy Park

Region Nine: Washington and Oregon

CLARKSTON TO PENDLETON 192-193

1 ☐ Palouse Falls State Park, Starbuck
2 ☐ Patit Creek Campsite Sculptures, Dayton
3 ☐ Palus Artifact Museum, Dayton
4 ☐ Lewis and Clark Trail State Park, Dayton
5 ☐ Fort Walla Walla Museum, Walla Walla

6 ☐ Whitman Mission National Historic Site, Walla Walla
7 ☐ Tamastslikt Institute, Pendleton
8 ☐ Wild Horse Resort Casino, Pendleton
9 ☐ Pendleton Woolen Mills Tour
10 ☐ Pendleton Round Up Hall of Fame
11 ☐ McNary Dam Overlook & Salmon Recovery Center, Umatilla
12 ☐ Hat Rock State Park, Umatilla
13 ☐ Marie Dorion Historical Park, Milton-Freewater

TRI-CITIES AND YAKAMA INDIAN RESERVATION 194–195

14 ☐ Sacajawea State Park, Pasco
15 ☐ McNary Wildlife Center and Wildlife Refuge, Burbank
16 ☐ East Benton County Historical Museum, Kennewick
17 ☐ Lewis and Clark Interpretive Overlook, Kennewick
18 ☐ CREHST Museum, Richland
19 ☐ Columbia River Jetboat Journeys, Richland
20 ☐ Columbia Valley Wineries, Benton City
21 ☐ Yakama Nation Cultural Center and Museum, Toppenish
22 ☐ Yakama Nation Casino and RV Park, Toppenish
23 ☐ Toppenish City of Murals
24 ☐ American Hop Museum, Toppenish
25 ☐ Toppenish National Wildlife Refuge

COLUMBIA RIVER GORGE: THE DALLES AREA 196–197

26 ☐ Goldendale Observatory, Goldendale
27a ☐ Maryhill Museum of Art, Goldendale
27b ☐ Lewis and Clark Interpretive Overlook, Goldendale
28 ☐ Stonehenge Memorial, Goldendale
29a ☐ Celilo Falls Overlook, Wishram, Washington
29b ☐ Celilo Park, The Dalles, Oregon
30 ☐ Columbia Hills State Park Petroglyphs, Smithville
31 ☐ The Dalles Dam Visitor Center, The Dalles
32 ☐ Rock Fort and Riverfront Trail, The Dalles
33 ☐ The Dalles Murals
34 ☐ Fort Dalles Museum, The Dalles
35 ☐ Columbia Gorge Discovery Center, The Dalles
36 ☐ Memaloose State Park and Rest Area, Mosier
37 ☐ Historic Columbia River Hwy State Trail, Mosier
38 ☐ Hood River County Historical Museum, Hood River

HISTORIC COLUMBIA RIVER HIGHWAY AREA 198–199

39 ☐ Cascade Locks Historical Museum, Cascade Locks
40 ☐ Columbia Gorge Sternwheeler, Cascade Locks
41 ☐ Bridge of the Gods, Cascade Locks
42 ☐ Columbia Gorge Interpretive Center, Stevenson
43 ☐ Fort Cascades National Historic Site, North Bonneville
44 ☐ Beacon Rock State Park, Stevenson
45 ☐ Bonneville Dam Visitor Center, Bonneville
46 ☐ Multnomah Falls Lodge, Multnomah Falls
47 ☐ Vista House and Crown Point Nat'l H Landmk, Corbett
48 ☐ Chanticleer Pt/Portland Womans Forum SP, Troutdale
49 ☐ Lewis and Clark State Recreation Site, Troutdale
50 ☐ Troutdale Historical Society Barn Museum
51 ☐ Nichaqwli Monument at Blue Lake Park, Fairview
52 ☐ Capt Wm Clark Park at Cottonwood Beach, Washougal

PORTLAND, MT HOOD AND WARM SPRINGS RESERVATION 200–201

53 ☐ Oregon Historical Society, Portland
54 ☐ Portland Art Museum
55 ☐ Forestry Discovery Center, Portland
56 ☐ Hoyt Arboretum, Portland
57 ☐ Oregon Zoo, Portland
58 ☐ Lewis and Clark Memorial, Sacajawea Statue, Portland
59 ☐ McLoughlin House Nat'l Historic Site, Oregon City
60 ☐ End of Oregon Trail Interpretive Center, Oregon City
61 ☐ Timberline Lodge Nat'l Historic Landmark, Mt Hood
62 ☐ Museum at Warm Springs, Warm Springs
63 ☐ Kah-Nee-Ta High Desert Resort and Casino, Warm Springs
64 ☐ Jean Baptiste Charbonneau Gravesite, Jordan Valley

VANCOUVER TO SKAMOKAWA 202–203

65 ☐ Fort Vancouver Visitor Center, Vancouver
66 ☐ Frenchman's Bar State Park, Vancouver
67 ☐ Cathlapotle Plank House, Ridgefield
68 ☐ Cowlitz County Historical Museum, Longview
69 ☐ Lake Sacajawea, Longview
70 ☐ Wahkiakum County Car Ferry, Westport
71 ☐ Wahkiakum County Historical Museum, Cathlamet
72 ☐ Julia Butler Hansen Nat'l Wildlife Refuge, Skamokawa
73 ☐ Skamokawa Vista Park
74 ☐ Skamokawa Center
75 ☐ River Life Interpretive Center, Skamokawa
76 ☐ Lewis and Clark National Wildlife Refuge, Skamokawa

CAPE DISAPPOINTMENT TO LONG BEACH 204–205

77 ☐ Clark's Dismal Nitch, Megler
78 ☐ Station Camp, McGowan
79 ☐ Fort Columbia State Park, McGowan
80 ☐ Ilwaco Heritage Museum, Ilwaco
81 ☐ Lewis and Clark Interpretive Center, Ilwaco
82 ☐ Jefferson Memorial Project, Ilwaco
83 ☐ Maya Lin Confluence Project and Trails, Ilwaco
84 ☐ North Head LIghthouse Tour, Ilwaco
85 ☐ Discovery Trail, Long Beack
86 ☐ Willapa National Wildlife Refuge Salmon Trial, Ilwaco

ASTORIA TO TILLAMOOK BAY 206–207

87 ☐ Astoria Column, Astoria
88 ☐ Columbia River Maritime Museum, Astoria
89 ☐ Heritage Museum, Astoria
90 ☐ Fort Astoria Park, Astoria
91 ☐ Astoria Riverfront and Trolley
92 ☐ Fort Stevens State Park, Warrenton
93 ☐ Fort Clatsop National Historical Park, Astoria
94 ☐ Fort to Sea Trail and Sunset Beach, Astoria
95 ☐ Seaside Aquarium, Seaside
96 ☐ Salt Works, Seaside
97 ☐ Ecola State Park and Tillamook Head, Cannon Beach
98 ☐ Haystack Rock, Cannon Beach
99 ☐ Tillamook County Pioneer Museum, Tillamook
100 ☐ Cape Meares Lighthouse and Wildlife Refuge, Tillamook

Region Ten: New Orleans and Natchez Trace

NEW ORLEANS 214–215

1 ☐ The Cabildo
2 ☐ Friends of the Cabildo Walking Tour
3 ☐ The Presbytere
4 ☐ Jackson Square
5 ☐ Historic New Orleans Collection
6 ☐ Madame John's Legacy
7 ☐ Old Ursuline Convent
8 ☐ Jean Lafitte Historical Park and Preserve
9 ☐ Lafitte's Blacksmith Shop Bar

BATON ROUGE AND NATCHEZ 216–217

10 ☐ Magnolia Mound Plantation, Baton Rouge
11 ☐ Audubon State Historic Site, St Francisville
12 ☐ Natchez Visitor Reception Center, Natchez
13 ☐ Grand Village of the Natchez Indians, Natchez
14 ☐ Natchez National Historical Park
15 ☐ Ellicott Hill, Natchez
16 ☐ Rosalie Mansion, Natchez
17 ☐ Kings Tavern, Natchez
18 ☐ Under-the-Hill Saloon, Natchez
19 ☐ Historic Jefferson College, Washington

NATCHEZ TRACE 218–219

20 ☐ Emerald Mound (10.3 Milepost)

Region Ten: New Orleans and Natchez Trace, cont.

21 ☐ Mount Locust (15.5 Mile Post)
22 ☐ Sunken Trace (41.5 Mile Post)
23 ☐ Mississippi Museum of Natural Science, Jackson
24 ☐ Mississippi Crafts Center (102.4 Milepost)
25 ☐ Cypress Swamp Walking Trail (122 Mp)
26 ☐ Kosciusko Museum and Visitor Center (159.7), Kosciusko
27 ☐ French Camp (180.7 Milepost), French Camp
28 ☐ Chickasaw Village (261.8)
29 ☐ Natchez Trace Parkway Visitor Center (270), Tupelo
30 ☐ Elvis Presley Birthplace Home and Museum, Tupelo
31 ☐ Tupelo Buffalo Park and Zoo
32 ☐ Colbert Ferry (327.3 Milepost)
33 ☐ Florence Indian Mound and Museum, Florence
34 ☐ Meriwether Lewis Gravesite (385.9 Milepost)
35 ☐ Old Trace (403.7 Milepost)
36 ☐ Gordon House and Ferry (407.7 Milepost)

NASHVILLE, MEMPHIS, NEW MADRID 220–221

37 ☐ The Hermitage, Nashville
38 ☐ Tennessee State Museum, Nashville
39 ☐ Mississippi River Museum, Memphis
40 ☐ Mud Island River Park, Memphis
41 ☐ Metal Museum, Memphis
42 ☐ New Madrid Historical Museum, New Madrid
43 ☐ Mississippi River Scenic Overlook, New Madrid

Notes

Index

A

B

I

Y

Z

General References

ACTS OF DISCOVERY: VISIONS OF AMERICA IN THE LEWIS AND CLARK JOURNALS
by Albert Furtwangler. University of Illinois Press (1999)

ALONG THE TRAIL WITH LEWIS AND CLARK
by Barbara Fifer and Vicky Soderberg. Montana Magazine (2001)

ART OF THE LEWIS AND CLARK TRAIL: ART BY CHARLES M. RUSSELL, ROBERT BATEMAN, JOHN F, CLYMER, KARL BODMER, MICHAEL HAYNES AND MORE
by Jeff Evenson. Whisper'n Waters, Inc. (2003)

ARTS OF DIPLOMACY: LEWIS AND CLARK'S INDIAN COLLECTION
by Castle McLaughlin. University of Washington Press (2003)

CHASING LEWIS AND CLARK ACROSS AMERICA: A 21ST CENTURY AVIATION ADVENTURE
by Ron Lowery and Mary Walker. Windsock Media (2004)

THE CONQUEST: THE TRUE STORY OF LEWIS AND CLARK
by Eva Emery Dye. A. C. McClurg & Company (1902)

A CURRENT ADVENTURE: IN THE WAKE OF LEWIS AND CLARK
by Chris Bechtold. Arnica Publishing (2003)

DISCOVERING LEWIS AND CLARK FROM THE AIR
by Joseph A. Mussulman. Mountain Press Publishing Company (2004)

ENCYCLOPEDIA OF THE LEWIS & CLARK EXPEDITION
by Elin Woodger and Brandon Toropov. Checkmark Books (2004)

EXPLORATIONS INTO THE WORLD OF LEWIS AND CLARK: ESSAYS FROM THE PAGES OF "WE PROCEEDED ON" (3 VOLUMES)
edited by Robert A. Saindon. Digital Scanning, Inc. (2003)

EXPLORING WITH LEWIS AND CLARK: THE 1804 JOURNAL OF CHARLES FLOYD
edited by James L. Holmberg. University of Oklahoma Press (2005)

THE FATE OF THE CORPS: WHAT BECAME OF THE LEWIS AND CLARK EXPLORERS AFTER THE EXPEDITION
by Larry E. Morris. Yale University Press (2004)

A HISTORY OF THE LEWIS AND CLARK JOURNALS
by Paul Russell Cutright. University of Oklahoma Press (1976)

THE HISTORY OF THE LEWIS AND CLARK EXPEDITION: BY MERIWETHER LEWIS AND WILLIAM CLARK (IN 3 VOLUMES)
edited by Elliott Coues. Dover Publications, Inc. (1979)

JOINED BY A JOURNEY: THE LIVES OF THE LEWIS AND CLARK CORPS OF DISCOVERY
by Mike Crosby. Bureau of Land Management (2005)

KARL BODMER'S AMERICA
by Karl Bodmer, David C. Hunt, and Marsha V. Gallagher. University of Nebraska Press (1984)

LETTERS OF THE LEWIS AND CLARK EXPEDITION, WITH RELATED DOCUMENTS, 1783-1854
edited by Donald Jackson. Univ. of Illinois Press (1962)

LEWIS AND CLARK - ACROSS THE DIVIDE
by Carolyn Gilman. Smithsonian Books (2003)

LEWIS AND CLARK AMONG THE INDIANS
by James P. Ronda. University of Nebraska Press (1988)

THE LEWIS AND CLARK COMPANION: AN ENCYCLOPEDIC GUIDE TO THE VOYAGE OF DISCOVERY
by Stephenie Ambrose Tubbs and Clay Straus Jenkinson. Henry Holt and Company (2003)

LEWIS AND CLARK FOR DUMMIES
by Sammye J. Meadows and Jana Sawyer Prewitt. Wiley Publishing, Inc. (2003)

LEWIS AND CLARK AND THE IMAGE OF THE AMERICAN NOERTHWEST
by John Logan Allen. Dover Publications Inc. (1975)

LEWIS AND CLARK: THE JOURNEY OF THE CORPS OF DISCOVERY: AN ILLUSTRATED HISTORY
by Dayton Duncan. Alfred A. Knopf (1998)

LEWIS AND CLARK: PARTNERS IN DISCOVERY
by John Bakeless. William Morrow & Co. (1947)

LEWIS AND CLARK: PIONEERING NATURALISTS
by Paul Russell Cutright. Univ. of Nebraska Press (1989)

LEWIS AND CLARK: TAILOR MADE, TRAIL WORN: ARMY LIFE, CLOTHING AND WEAPONS OF THE CORPS OF DISCOVERY
by Robert J. Moore, Jr. and Michael Haynes. Farcountry Press (2003)

LEWIS AND CLARK TRAIL MAPS: A CARTOGRAPHIC RECONSTRUCTION (3 VOLUMES)
by Martin Plamondon II. Washington State University Press (2000, 2001, 2004)

LEWIS AND CLARK: VOYAGE OF DISCOVERY
by Stephen E. Ambrose. National Geographic (2002)

LEWIS AND CLARK'S GREEN WORLD: THE EXPEDITION AND ITS PLANTS
by A. Scott Earle and James L. Reveal. Farcountry Press (2003)

LEWIS AND CLARK'S TRANSCONTINENTAL EXPLORATION 1804-1806
by Roy E. Appleman. Jefferson National Parks Association (2000)

MR. JEFFERSONS'S LOST CAUSE: LAND, FARMERS, SLAVERY, AND THE LOUISIANA PURCHASE
by Roger G. Kennedy. Oxford University Press (2003)

NATIONAL GEOGRAPHIC GUIDE TO THE LEWIS AND CLARK TRAIL
by Thomas Schmidt. National Geographic ((2002)

THE MEN OF THE LEWIS AND CLARK EXPEDITION: A BIOGRAPHICAL ROSTER OF THE FIFTY-ONE MEMBERS
by Charles G. Clarke. Arthur H. Clark Company (2001)

THE NATURAL HISTORY OF THE LEWIS AND CLARK EXPEDITION
edited by Raymon Darwin Burroughs. Michigan State University Press (1995)

ON THE RIVER WITH LEWIS AND CLARK
by Verne Huser. Texas A&M University Press (2004)

ONLY ONE MAN DIED: THE MEDICAL ASPECTS OF THE LEWIS AND CLARK EXPEDITION
by E. G. Chuinard. Ye Galleon Press (1979)

OR PERISH IN THE ATTEMPT: WILDERNESS MEDICINE IN THE LEWIS AND CLARK EXPEDITION
by David J. Peck. Farcountry Press (2002)

PASSAGE OF DISCOVERY: THE AMERICAN RIVERS GUIDE TO THE MISSOURI RIVER OF LEWIS AND CLARK
by Daniel Botkin. Berkeley Publishing Group (1999)

THE SAGA OF LEWIS AND CLARK INTO THE UNCHARTED WEST
by Thomas Schmidt and Jeremy Schmidt. DK Publishing, Inc. (1999)

SCENES OF VISIONARY ENCHANMENT: REFLECTIONS ON LEWIS AND CLARK
by Dayton Duncan. University of Nebraska Press (2004)

SEDUCED BY THE WEST: JEFFERSON'S AMERICA AND THE LURE OF THE LAND BEYOND THE MISSISSIPPI
by Laurie Winn Carlson. Ivan R. Dee (2003)

TRAVELING THE LEWIS AND CLARK TRAIL
by Julie Fanselow. Falcon Publishing, Inc. (2000)

UNDAUNTED COURAGE: MERIWETHER LEWIS, THOMAS JEFFERSON, AND THE OPENING OF THE AMERICAN WEST
by Stephen E. Ambrose. Simon & Schuster (1997)

VENEREAL DISEASE AND THE LEWIS AND CLARK EXPEDITION
by Thomas P. Lowry. University of Nebraska Press (2004)

VOYAGES OF DISCOVERY: ESSAYS ON THE LEWIS AND CLARK EXPEDITION
edited by James P. Ronda. Montana Historical Society Press (1998)